Dēmokratia

Dēmokratia

A CONVERSATION ON DEMOCRACIES,
ANCIENT AND MODERN

*Josiah Ober and
Charles Hedrick, Editors*

PRINCETON UNIVERSITY PRESS
PRINCETON, NEW JERSEY

Library of Congress Cataloging-in-Publication Data

Dēmokratia : a conversation on democracies, ancient and modern /
[edited by] Josiah Ober and Charles Hedrick.
p.   cm.
Includes bibliographical references and index.
ISBN 0-691-01109-5 (alk. paper). — ISBN 0-691-01108-7 (pbk. : alk. paper)
1. Democracy—Greece—Athens—History.   2. Democracy.   I. Ober,
Josiah, 1953–   .   II. Hedrick, Charles W., 1956–   .
JC75.D36D47   1996
320.438′5—dc20   96-33717

This book has been composed in Adobe Times Roman.

Princeton University Press books are printed on acid-free paper,
and meet the guidelines for permanence and durability of the
Committee on Production Guidelines for Book Longevity of the
Council on Library Resources

Printed in the United States of America by Princeton Academic Press

1 3 5 7 9 10 8 6 4 2
1 3 5 7 9 10 8 6 4 2
(Pbk.)

To our graduate mentors,
Chester G. Starr and Martin Ostwald

preeminent students and teachers of Greek democracy

CONTENTS

PART TWO: *Civil Ritual and the Education of Citizens*

ACKNOWLEDGMENTS

THE CONVERSATION represented in this book has developed over several years, and many people apart from the editors and contributors have had a part in shaping it. Planning for a conference on "Democracy Ancient and Modern" began in 1989, under the auspices of the American School of Classical Studies at Athens, whose Trustees and staff deserve much credit for the success of the undertaking. Above all we thank Catherine Vanderpool, the Associate Director of the "Democracy 2500" project, who played a central administrative role throughout; the Chairman of the School's Board of Trustees, Hunter Lewis, who supported the project in every way; and the Chairwoman Emerita, Doreen Spitzer, whose leadership got the project off the ground.

In the spring of 1993, the conference opened at the National Archives Building in Washington, D.C. The Archives public programs staff, under the direction of Edith James, helped to make the opening session a success. Georgetown University provided its splendid facilities for all other sessions. We owe special thanks to the Georgetown Classics department and its chairs, Joseph O'Connor and Victoria Pedrick. Major funding for the conference was provided by a grant from the National Endowment for the Humanities. Other funds were provided by our home institutions, the University of California at Santa Cruz and Princeton University.

In moving from conference to book, we received invaluable editorial assistance from Ryan Balot and from the staff of Princeton University Press. We owe much to the wise advice and toleration of our wives, Adrienne Mayor and Charmaine Curtis. We owe the impulse to undertake the comparative investigation of ancient and modern political thought and practice to our graduate advisors, to whom this volume is dedicated.

Princeton, New Jersey, and Santa Cruz, California
September 1995

ABBREVIATIONS

Authors

Aen. Tact.	Aeneas Tacticus
Aesch.	Aeschylus
Aeschin.	Aeschines
Alc.	Alcaeus
Alcm.	Alcmaeon
Anac.	Anacreon
Andoc.	Andocides
Ant.	Antiphon
Apollod.	Apollodorus
Ar.	Aristophanes
Archil.	Archilochus
Arist.	Aristotle
Bacchyl.	Bacchylides
Call.	Callinus
Dem.	Demosthenes
Democr.	Democritus
Din.	Dinarchus
Dio Chrys.	Dio Chrysostom
Diod.	Diodorus Siculus
Diog. Laert.	Diogenes Laertius
Dion. Hal.	Dionysius of Halicarnassus
Epich.	Epicharmus
Eur.	Euripides
Harp.	Harpocration
Hdt.	Herodotus
Hes.	Hesiod
Hipp.	Hippocrates
Hsch.	Hesychius
Isoc.	Isocrates
Lyc.	Lycurgus
Lys.	Lysias
Mimn.	Mimnermus
Paus.	Pausanias
Phoc.	Phocylides
Plaut.	Plautus
Plut.	Plutarch

Poll.	Pollux
Polyb.	Polybius
Semon.	Semonides
Simon.	Simonides
Soph.	Sophocles
Stes.	Stesichorus
Stob.	Stobaeus
Theog.	Theognis
Theophr.	Theophrastus
Thuc.	Thucydides
Tyrt.	Tyrtaeus
Val. Fl.	Valerius Flaccus
Veg.	Vegetius
Xen.	Xenophon
Xenoph.	Xenophanes

WORKS

Ach.	(Ar.)	*Acharnians*
Ag.	(Aesch.)	*Agamemnon*
ag. Alc.	(Ps. Andoc.)	*Against Alcibiades*
ag. Dem.	(Din.)	*Against Demosthenes*
Alc.	(Plato, Plut.)	*Alcibiades*
Andr.	(Eur.)	*Andromache*
Ant.	(Soph.)	*Antigone*
Anth. Pal.		*Palatine Anthology*
Ant. Rom.	(Dion. Hal.)	*Roman Antiquities*
Ap.	(Plato)	*Apology*
Arist.	(Plut.)	*Aristides*
Ath. Pol.	(Arist., Ps. Xen.)	*Constitution of Athens*
Av.	(Ar.)	*Birds*
Bibl.	(Apollod.)	*Bibliotheca*
Char.	(Theophr.)	*Characters*
Def.	(Plato)	*Definitions*
Dith.	(Bacchl.)	*Dithyramb*
Eccl.	(Ar.)	*Ecclesiazusae*
Ep.		*Letters*
Eq.	(Ar.)	*Knights*
Eth. Eud.	(Arist.)	*Eudemian Ethics*
Eth. Nic.	(Arist.)	*Nicomachean Ethics*
Eum.	(Aesch.)	*Eumenides*
Flor.	(Stob.)	*Anthology*
Gorg.	(Plato)	*Gorgias*

Hec.	(Eur.)	*Hecuba*
Hell.	(Xen.)	*Hellenica*
Heracl.	(Eur.)	*Heraclidae*
Hipp.	(Eur.)	*Hippolytus;* (Xen.) *Cavalry Commander*
HN	(Pliny)	*Natural History*
Hymn. Hom.		*Homeric Hymn*
IA	(Eur.)	*Iphigeneia at Aulis*
In Ctes.	(Aeschin.)	*Against Ctesiphon*
Isthm.	(Pindar)	*Isthmean* odes
Leoc.	(Lyc.)	*Against Leocrates*
Lyc.	(Plut.)	*Lycurgus*
Lys.	(Ar.)	*Lysistrata*
Lys.	(Dion. Hal.)	*On Lysias*
Med.	(Eur.)	*Medea*
Mem.	(Xen.)	*Memorabilia*
Men.	(Plaut.)	*Menaechmi*
Menex.	(Plato)	*Menexenus*
Milt.	(Nepos)	*Miltiades*
Mor.	(Plut.)	*Moralia*
Nem.	(Pindar)	*Nemean* odes
Nub.	(Ar.)	*Clouds*
Oec.	(Ps. Arist., Xen.)	*Oeconomica, Oeconomicus*
Ol.	(Pindar)	*Olympian* odes
Onom.	(Poll.)	*Onomasticon*
Op.	(Hes.)	*Works and Days*
Or.	(Eur.)	*Orestes*
Paneg.	(Isoc.)	*Panegyricus*
Pax	(Ar.)	*Peace*
Per.	(Plut.)	*Pericles*
Pers.	(Aesch.)	*Persians*
Phdr.	(Plato)	*Phaedrus*
Phlb.	(Plato)	*Philebus*
Phoen.	(Eur.)	*Phoenician Women*
Pol.	(Arist.)	*Politics*
Prot.	(Plato)	*Protagoras*
PV	(Aesch.)	*Prometheus Bound*
Pyth.	(Pindar)	*Pythian* odes
Ran.	(Ar.)	*Frogs*
Rep.	(Plato)	*Republic*
Rh.	(Arist.)	*Rhetoric*
Rom. Ant.	(Dion. Hal.)	*Roman Antiquities*
Rust.	(Varro)	*De Re Rustica*
Sept.	(Aesch.)	*Seven against Thebes*

Supp.	(Aesch., Eur.)	*Suppliants*
Symp.	(Plato)	*Symposium*
Th.	(Hes.)	*Theogony*
Them.	(Plut.)	*Themistocles*
Tht.	(Plato)	*Theaetetus*
Trach.	(Soph.)	*Trachiniae*
Vect.	(Xen.)	*Ways and Means*
Vesp.	(Ar.)	*Wasps*
Vita Aesch.		*Life of Aeschylus*

MISCELLANEOUS

ap.	*apud,* "quoted/cited in"
c.	circa
ch(s).	chapter(s)
dith.	dithyramb
esp.	especially
fr(s).	fragment(s)
Ps.	(before the name of a classical author) Pseudo
rev.	revised

REFERENCE WORKS

CGF	*Comicorum Graecorum Fragmenta.* G. Kaibel, ed. Berlin, 1899.
DK	*Die Fragmente der Vorsokratiker.* Hermann Diels and Walther Kranz, eds., 12th ed. Berlin: Weidmann, 1966–67.
FGrHist	*Die Fragmente der griechischen Historiker.* Felix Jacoby, ed. Berlin: Weidmann, 1923– and Leiden: Brill, 1954–.
HCT	Gomme, A. W. (with Antony Andrewes and Kenneth J. Dover). *A Historical Commentary on Thucydides.* 5 vols. Oxford: Clarendon Press, 1945–81.
IG	*Inscriptiones Graecae.* Berlin, 1873–.
LSJ	*A Greek-English Lexicon,* compiled by Henry George Liddell and Robert Scott, revised and augmented throughout by Sir Henry Stuart Jones, 9th ed., with supplement. Oxford: Oxford University Press, 1968.
P. Oxy.	Oxyrhynchus papyrus
RE	*Paulys Real Encyclopädie der klassischen Altertumswissenschaft,* rev. begun by Georg Wissowa. . . . Stuttgart, later Munich: J. B. Metzler, succeeded by Alfred Druckenmuller, 1894–1980.

SIG *Sylloge Inscriptionum Graecarum.* 3d ed. W. Dittenberger, ed.
    Leipzig, 1915–24.
TLG *Thesaurus Linguae Graecae.* CD ROM. Irvine: University of
    California, 1985–.

CONTRIBUTORS

BENJAMIN R. BARBER is the Walt Whitman Professor of Political Science and the Director of the Whitman Center for the Culture and Politics of Democracy at Rutgers University. His many books include *Strong Democracy* (1984), *The Conquest of Politics* (1988), *An Aristocracy of Everyone* (1992), and *Jihad versus McWorld* (1995).

ALAN BOEGEHOLD is Professor of Classics at Brown University and Chairman of the Managing Committee of the American School of Classical Studies at Athens. He is author of *The Athenian Agora XXVIII: The Lawcourts at Athens. Sites, Buildings, Equipment, Procedure, and Testimonia* (1995) and coeditor of *Athenian Identity and Civic Ideology* (1994). In addition to his expertise in Athenian law, he writes on Greek history, art, and literature.

PAUL CARTLEDGE is Reader in Greek History at Cambridge University and Fellow of Clare College. His books include *Agesilaos and the Crisis of Sparta* (1987) and *The Greeks, A Portrait of Self and Others* (1993); he has also coedited a number of books, including *Nomos: Essays in Athenian Law, Politics and Society* (1990). His current research focuses on ancient Greek political thought.

SUSAN GUETTEL COLE is Associate Professor of Classics and History at the State University of New York at Buffalo. Her publications include *Theoi Megaloi: The Cult of the Great Gods at Samothrace* (1984) and articles on a variety of subjects, including Greek sanctions against sexual assault, literacy of Greek women, and rites of maturation.

W. ROBERT CONNOR is the Director of the National Humanities Center, a private center for advanced study, and Professor of Classics at Duke University. He has published on many aspects of Greek history and literature. His best known books are *The New Politicians of Fifth-Century Athens* (1971) and *Thucydides* (1984).

CAROL DOUGHERTY is Associate Professor of Classics at Wellesley College. She is the author of *The Poetics of Colonization: From City to Text in Archaic Greece* (1992) and articles on Greek literature, and also coeditor of *Cultural Poetics in Archaic Greece: Cult, Performance, Politics* (1993).

J. PETER EUBEN is Professor of Politics at the University of California at Santa Cruz. He is the author of *The Tragedy of Political Theory: The Road Not Taken* (1990) and *Corrupting Youth: Political Education, Democratic Culture, and Political Theory* (forthcoming), and coeditor of *Athenian Political Thought and the Reconstruction of American Democracy* (1994).

MOGENS HERMAN HANSEN is Reader in Greek History in the Department of Greek and Latin, University of Copenhagen and director of the Copenhagen Polis Center. He has published a great many articles and books on various aspects of Athenian democracy, including his magisterial *The Athenian Democracy in the Age of Demosthenes: Structure, Principles, Ideology* (1991).

VICTOR DAVIS HANSON is Professor of Classics in the Department of Foreign Languages at the California State University at Fresno. His books include *Warfare and Agriculture in Classical Greece* (1983), *The Western Way of War: Infantry Battle in Classical Greece* (1989), *The Other Greeks: The Family Farm and the Agrarian Roots of Western Civilization* (1995), and *Fields without Dreams: Defending the Agrarian Idea* (1996).

CHARLES HEDRICK is Associate Professor and chair of the History Board at the University of California at Santa Cruz. His research focuses on the intersection between literary theory and Greek and Roman history and epigraphy. He is author of *The Decrees of the Demotionidai* (1990) and coeditor of the exhibition catalogue *The Birth of Democracy* (1993).

CARNES LORD, a political scientist specializing in classical political philosophy, is John M. Olin Professor of Civilization and Statecraft at the Fletcher School of Law and Diplomacy of Tufts University. He is the author of *Education and Culture in the Political Thought of Aristotle* (1982), coeditor of *Essays on the Foundations of Aristotelian Political Science* (1991), and translator of Aristotle's *Politics*.

PHILIP BROOK MANVILLE is a partner and, at the time of writing, was Director of Information and Technology at McKinsey and Company, New York, where he is now Director of Knowledge Management. Formerly a professor of classics and ancient history, he is the author of an influential book, *The Origins of Citizenship in Classical Athens* (1990), articles on Greek history, and publications in the field of information management and organizational learning.

IAN MORRIS is Professor of Classics and History at Stanford University. He is the author of *Burial and Ancient Society: The Rise of the Greek City-State* (1987) and *Death-Ritual and Social Structure in Classical Antiquity* (1992) and editor of *Classical Greece: Ancient Histories and Modern Archaeologies* (1994). He has excavated in Greece and Britain and is publishing the Iron Age remains from Lerna. His current project is the history of equality in early Greece.

JOSIAH OBER is the Magie Professor of Ancient History and chair of the Department of Classics at Princeton University. His publications include *Fortress Attica* (1985), *Mass and Elite in Democratic Athens: Rhetoric, Ideology, and the Power of the People* (1989), and *The Athenian Revolution: Essays on Ancient Greek Democracy and Political Theory* (1996).

MARTIN OSTWALD, a member of the American Academy of Arts and Sciences and the American Philosophical Society, is Professor Emeritus of Classics at Swarthmore College and the University of Pennsylvania. He has served as editor of the *Cambridge Ancient History*; his books include *Nomos and the Beginnings of the Athenian Democracy* (1969) and *From Popular Sovereignty to the Sovereignty of Law* (1986).

KURT A. RAAFLAUB is Professor of Classics and History at Brown University and Co-Director of the Center for Hellenic Studies in Washington, D.C. His research explores the relationship between political thought and practice in both ancient Greece and Rome. His publications include *Die Entdeckung der Freiheit* (1985) and *Politisches Denken und Krise der Polis: Athen im Verfassungskonflikt des späten 5. Jh v. Chr.* (1992).

JENNIFER TOLBERT ROBERTS is Professor of Classics at the City University of New York. Her work focuses on social and political values; her publications include *Accountability in Athenian Government* (1982) and *Athens on Trial: The Anti-Democratic Tradition in Western Thought* (1994). She is currently exploring images of antiquity in the American media.

BARRY S. STRAUSS is Professor of History and Classics at Cornell University and director of Cornell's Peace Studies Program. His research centers on the intersection of politics, war, and social relations from antiquity to the present. His books include *Athens after the Peloponnesian War* (1986) and *Fathers and Sons in Athens: Ideology and Society in the Era of the Peloponnesian War* (1993); he is coeditor of *Hegemonic Rivalry from Thucydides to the Nuclear Age* (1991).

ROBERT W. WALLACE is Associate Professor of Classics at Northwestern University. His research ranges from political history to the history and theory of ancient Greek music. He is the author of *The Areopagos Council, to 307 B.C.* (1989) and articles on ancient Greek history and culture, and coeditor of *Harmonia Mundi: Music and Philosophy in the Ancient World* (1991).

SHELDON S. WOLIN, Professor Emeritus of political theory at Princeton University, has been Eastman Professor at Oxford University and Clark Professor at the University of California at Los Angeles. His major publications include the classic *Politics and Vision: Continuity and Innovation in Western Political Thought* (1961), *The Berkeley Revolution and Beyond* (with John Schaar, 1970), and *The Presence of the Past* (1989).

ELLEN MEIKSINS WOOD is Professor of Politics at York University, Ontario. Her books include *Class Ideology and Ancient Political Theory* (with Neal Wood, 1978), *Peasant-Citizen and Slave: The Foundations of Athenian Democracy* (1988), *The Pristine Culture of Capitalism: A Historical Essay on Old Regimes and Modern States* (1992), and *Democracy against Capitalism: Renewing Historical Materialism* (1995).

Dēmokratia

―――――――――――――

DEMOCRACIES ANCIENT AND MODERN

JOSIAH OBER AND CHARLES HEDRICK

THE CHOICE of the term *conversation* for the subtitle of this book is a statement of the editors' intentions as well as a description of the book's contents. In spring of 1993 the American School of Classical Studies at Athens, with major funding from the National Endowment for the Humanities, sponsored a scholarly conference at Georgetown University in Washington, D.C., on the topic "Democracy Ancient and Modern." Greek historians and political theorists from North America and Europe presented papers in six sessions devoted to the themes of Origins of Democracy, Freedom, Equality, Law, Citizenship, and Education. The goal of the conference was to further the project—most clearly and memorably articulated by Moses I. Finley in his seminal *Democracy Ancient and Modern*—of applying insights gained from political and social theory to problems in Greek history, and in turn using the historical Greek experience of democracy as a resource for building normative political theory. Each of the essays presented here began either as a "theme paper" or as a "response paper" presented at that conference. The papers were extensively revised in light of the very lively conference discussions (formal and informal) and again on the basis of drafts circulated subsequently among participants. This ongoing process of cross-fertilization has rendered obsolete both the subdivision of papers into six distinct topics and the distinction between "theme" and "response" papers. Hence we have regrouped the papers around two broad themes—liberty, equality, and law; and civic ritual and the education of the citizens. These categories are themselves highly permeable; there is much to do with civic ritual and education in several of the liberty/equality/law papers and vice versa.

The essays presented here are united by the conviction that an interdisciplinary study of classical history and political theory is worth undertaking because the political experience of classical Athens is not only interesting in itself but also an important tool for rethinking contemporary political dilemmas. The authors share a sensitivity for the complexity of classical democracy, and they recognize *dēmokratia* as encompassing much more than simply a set of governmental institutions. Moreover, they tend to be united in their focus on the contradictions embraced by political systems, ancient and modern, rather than on the formal, rational coherence of those systems. The essays constituting this volume spend relatively little time praising classical (or modern) democracy for its consistency. Rather, they seek to reveal and explain within the values or ideologies and the practices that variously created, informed, sustained, and threatened classical democratic life significant tensions and contradictions: between that which was radically progressive in Athenian governmental practices and thinking and that which was fundamentally conservative; between ideals of equality among citizens and the freedom of the individual citizen; between the role of democracy in establishing behavioral norms and in stimulating criticisms of those norms; between leadership elites and their unruly mass audiences; between middling and lower-class citizens; between the body of native, adult, male citizens and those systematically denied citizenship: women, children, slaves, foreigners; between the social and political effects of democracy within and outside the citizen body; between democracy as defined in terms of revolutionary transgression and democracy as productive of a high degree of political stability.

If general agreement about the importance and complexity of the subject of "democracies ancient and modern" and the utility of historical/theoretical interaction in coming to a better understanding of that subject unifies this collection of essays, it is also marked by a broad range of opinion on the moral worth and normative value of classical democracy. While none of these essays engages in simple polis nostalgia, some of the authors clearly feel that at least some aspects of classical democratic citizenship are truly admirable and worthy of emulation; others argue that the classical notion of citizenship was defined primarily by its rigorous exclusions and that, as a result, classical democracy is so deeply flawed as to be useful to modern democrats only as a negative example. There is a similar range of opinion on the question of how different ancient *dēmokratia* was from modern democracy and on the interpretive issue of whether similarities or differences are of greater moment. The contributors disagree (inter alia) about the historical origins of democracy, about the relative importance of freedom and equality, about the status of law, about the social consequences of political changes, about the relationship between institutions and ideologies. Nor does inclusion in this volume indicate that a contributor agrees with the editors on all substantive or interpretive points; a quick perusal of the footnotes will show that our own published positions on various issues are frequently and directly challenged in these pages. The authors are, moreover, diverse in their analytic approaches and their sources of theoretical or methodological inspiration; the latter range from the Anti-Federalists, to Hannah Arendt, Pierre Bourdieu, Primo Levi, Robert Dahl, Michel Foucault, Leo Strauss, Jean-Jacques Rousseau, and Peter Drucker, among many others. And yet despite the differences of opinion and approach, the vigorous series of debates that began (or, in some cases, were continued) at the conference, have, we believe, produced a good deal more light than heat within the community of the contributors.

It is our active encouragement of the reader to join that conversational community, to negotiate among the interwoven substantive, methodological, and ideological debates, that distinguishes this collection of essays. The authors have engaged deeply with classical texts and theory, but moreover they have engaged with the substance and premises of one another's approaches and arguments. The frequency of cross-referencing among the essays leads the reader into an ongoing conversation that cuts across topics and across academic disciplines. It also invites him/her to continue the conversation. The reader will, we hope, end up convinced of the value of learning more about the history of classical democracy. We express this hope in the conviction that the more one learns of that history, the more important it becomes as a resource for moral, ethical, and political reflection. The comprehensive bibliography at the end of the book, listing all works cited in the essays, allows the interested reader to follow a wide variety of paths into the increasingly rich and varied field of comparative democratic studies.

We are in particular need of historically grounded political reflection today. With Marxism (at least as a workable system of government) so thoroughly discredited, liberal democracy has lost its historical interlocutor. This has led some pundits to claim that history itself—conceived as the dialectic between totalitarian forms of socialism and liberal, capitalist democracy—has come to an end. And yet history stubbornly keeps happening. The simplistic notion that the collapse of communist regimes in Europe meant that capitalism "won" and so liberal democracy would quickly be implemented throughout the world has been rudely dashed by subsequent events in Asia, Europe, and Africa. Meanwhile, traditional individual-centered liberalism seems to many people increasingly inadequate as a theory and as a basis for contemporary social/political practice. Communitarianism has recently emerged as the main challenge to the still-dominant liberal consensus among political theorists, but communitarians have had a hard time enunciating a clear vision of what a communitarian politics might actually entail. The ancient polis (and especially Aristotle's description of it in the *Politics*) is an important source of communitarian inspiration, but many communitarian writers seem to know relatively little about the history of ancient democracy or about classical texts other than Aristotle. Thus a fuller and more complex articulation of how the democratic polis really worked and how it might be related to contemporary forms of democracy can claim a central place in the ongoing discussion of what sort of politics we (whoever we imagine ourselves to be) might hope for and work toward.

This collection comes at a significant point in the history of the interpretation of classical Greek democracy. After three years of conferences and other events more or less closely linked to the twenty-five hundredth anniversary of the Athenian revolution and Cleisthenic reforms of 508–507 B.C., after the publication of a spate of books and articles devoted to various aspects of the history of ancient democracy, and with classical democracy now securely reestablished as a field within both political theory and classical studies, it is fitting to ponder where the study of participatory politics stands and where it might be going. It would be absurd to claim that any collection of essays can be a genuinely comprehensive survey of a single field, much less of two areas as internally diverse as Greek history and democratic theory. Yet we hope that, as a group, these essays sketch at least some of the main lines of the best contemporary English-speaking discussion on the subject of ancient and modern democracy. But we reiterate that this volume is not meant as a capstone to a completed edifice, but as an invitation to engagement in an ongoing conversation and as a stimulus to further investigation. It does not claim to speak with a single voice, but to point out the current state of a particularly exciting set of debates.

Finally, this is a conversation in which many varieties of expertise are wanted. It can, however, be carried on in a language that is accessible to a wide range of interlocutors. Each essay presented here is written by an expert in Greek history or political theory, but all have been written with a broad and non-specialized audience in mind. The volume assumes neither a knowledge of ancient Greek nor of the current status of debates within political philosophy. Translations are by the chapter authors, unless otherwise indicated. We have not attempted to impose utter consistency of style and usage on the authors, nor, given their various backgrounds, do we think such homogeneity is desirable. We have not attempted to settle the age-old problem of whether to anglicize Greek kappa with English *c* or *k;* in general, names that have a traditional English spelling (e.g., Socrates) retain it, while those that do not (e.g., Kos) may be transliterated with *K.* Some (particularly ancient historians) have preferred to render Greek case endings faithfully with English characters (e.g., *nomothetai*); others have chosen to anglicize these (e.g., *nomothetes*). We presume that the inconsistencies we have allowed to linger will nevertheless be intelligible. Abbreviations of classical authors and texts, as listed on pp. xi–xv, follow the standard format of the *Oxford Classical Dictionary,* second edition.

Summary of Chapters

Where does Greek democracy come from in the first place? Ian Morris attempts to transcend what he regards as analytically impoverished functionalist re-descriptions of ancient political development to explain the origin of democracy in an ideological conflict encompassing most of the Greek-speaking world. Employing both literary evidence (archaic poetry) and archaeological materials (especially patterns of burials and votive offerings), he argues that in many parts of Greece a conflict between elitist and "middling" sensibilities emerged by the late eighth century B.C. By 500 B.C. the middling ideology had won out virtually everywhere in the Greek world. Democratic institutions and ideology, as manifested most clearly in the extensive oratorical and epigraphic sources from fourth-century Athens, are therefore regarded by Morris as regional manifestations of a much more widespread phenomenon. Moreover, the fifth-century democracy retained the mark of its origins in the middling ideology: the Athenians remained scornful and suspicious of both the very rich and the very poor among them. Morris invokes Robert Dahl's "Strong Principle of Equality" to explain and to criticize the ideological content of the Greek practice of equalizing shares in the community among adult native males. For Morris, as for several other contributors, classical democracy was a version of essentialism—an "equality among shareholders" predicated on the exclusion from shareholding and oppression of women and unfree populations. And so, for Morris, democratic equality was bought at too great a price.

The issue of shareholding in the community is also central to Martin Ostwald, who takes on what has long been recognized as a key issue in the ancient/modern debate—modern rights versus ancient duties. With special reference to Aristotle and the U.S. Constitution, Ostwald defends the proposition that the Greek concept of citizenship is indeed a foundation for modern political culture—not because modern citizenship is like that of the Greeks, but because the central place that Greece happens to hold in our American multicultural heritage helps us to see what is distinctive, indeed historically peculiar, about how modern democracies have construed citizenship. The modern citizen gains her civic identity through her assumption of inalienable individual rights (defined as inviolability); the ancient citizen through belonging to (not necessarily by active and ongoing participation in) a community "that was yours and whose you were"—a community in which he was an equal shareholder by virtue of his status as free man. Thus ancient citizens were equal because they were free. Ostwald demonstrates, by reference to the Fourteenth Amendment to the U.S. Constitution, that by contrast the modern citizen is free because he is equal: he enjoys freedom by virtue of his status of equality in respect to rights.

Like Ostwald, Sheldon Wolin finds both Aristotle and the Declaration of Independence important for understanding freedom, equality, and "the political animal." But, using language borrowed from Hannah Arendt and Spinoza, Wolin rejects the Aristotelian idea that the democratic ideal is realized within an institutional form; rather democracy is most fully realized in agonistic action that breaks with constitutional forms. For Wolin, what is distinctive about classical democracy is the spectacle of the demos ("the people") as collective historical actor and agent: *dēmokratia* is "the demos enabling itself to emerge." And thus (contrast Morris) Athenian democracy is not merely the extension of something old, but the creation of something very new. The focus on demotic self-realization leads Wolin to reject both historical narratives that derive democracy from changes in military organization (contrast Raaflaub, Hanson, Strauss) and the idea that post-Periclean democracy failed due to inadequate leadership. Classical democracy, in Wolin's view, entails a will to power: Plato's dialogues provide ample evidence of the violent, aggressive "cultural challenge of democracy." The boundary-defying energy of the demos creates the Athenian Empire and thereby transcends the political structures of the polis. Yet this very transcendence provided a resource for counterrevolutionary aristocrats like Alcibiades to claim that the polis to which their loyalty is owed is not defined by its form of government. The democratic challenge led other aristocrats (like Aristotle) to attempt to intellectualize the political, and indeed it is the overtly political (rather than economic or social) nature of ancient democracy that distinguishes it from "electoral democracy"—its bland, institutionalized modern counterpart.

Mogens H. Hansen swims against the tide of recent scholarship to claim that there is much more similarity than difference between ancient and modern liberal notions of freedom. In both systems, there is considerable overlap between the concepts of freedom and equality, and yet in both systems "freedom is trumps." Both systems recognized a variety of types of freedom, but in both systems specifically democratic freedom can be resolved into two basic freedoms: the positive freedom to participate in politics and (contrast Ostwald) the negative freedom from interference. The concept of negative freedom in turn required the elaboration of a private sphere that was conceptually distinct from the public realm. It is his insistence that Athenian democracy recognized both negative liberty and a clearly articulated private sphere that is Hansen's most controversial point: he buttresses his argument by showing that the democratic constitution protected rights of privacy, property, and free speech. Yet Hansen refuses to extrapolate a genealogy for modern liberalism from these conclusions: the similarity between ancient and modern ideas of freedom must be explained as similar responses to similar circumstances.

Robert Wallace pursues the issue of negative and positive freedoms through an investigation of the role of law in protecting the individual and the community. Athenian law ensured personal freedoms by granting the individual citizen certain protections (e.g., against execution without trial) and by refusing to rule on matters that had no bearing on the safety of the community (drinking, prostitution, gambling). Wallace acknowledges that in principle the demos could restrict personal freedoms at will, but he emphasizes that in practice, the Athenian demos only employed its coercive powers against citizens in the face of a manifest danger to the community. While, because of the dangers faced by a Greek polis, the Athenian threshold of sensitivity to perceived threat was higher than that typical of modern democracies, it was still remarkably low given the Greek context. The only documented cases of legal action against intellectuals are the trial for impiety of Socrates and the ostracism of Damon. Wallace explains both of these incidents in terms of a contextually defensible fear on the part of the Athenian demos that the activities of the two men constituted a genuine threat to the community. In sum, the claims of both democrats and their critics to the effect that Athens was defined by a powerful ideology of freedom are borne out by the historical record. And so, despite the absence of a general guarantee of freedom (contrast Hansen), the Athenian's enjoyment of both specific protections and freedom from interference in private life meant that "his personal freedoms were greater than those of contemporary Americans."

In a paper that originated as a formal response to Hansen, Ellen M. Wood reasserts the differences between ancient and modern understandings of freedom, but (contrast Wolin) she focuses on the social consequences of democracy rather than on narrowly political issues. The difference between active ancient and passive modern citizenship is elucidated by comparing Plato on *isēgoria* (literally, "equality in respect to speech") with Alexander Hamilton on freedom of speech. Hamilton's position ends in evacuating the social content of democracy; by contrast, as Plato makes clear, the Greek term *dēmos* (as it was used in democratic Athens) explicitly included the poor, the "necessary" people, and so citizenship remained socially consequential. Hamilton's evocation of The People as a narrowly political concept ultimately gave license to the rule of the wealthy elite and so modern (unlike Athenian) citizenship leaves property relations fundamentally undisturbed. Wood suggests that the *Federalist Papers* show that modern democracy was actually constructed in self-conscious contradiction to the Athenian experience of popular rule and thereby contributed to the ideological process of giving democracy a genealogy that traced itself to Rome by way of the Magna Carta rather than to Athens by way of the Chartists. For Wood, Athenian democracy cannot be understood as merely an extension of traditional privileges (contrast Raaflaub, Strauss) but the ancient conception of freedom was indeed developed in a context in which privilege was a relevant category. In Wood's view, modern democracy, with its focus on "checks and balances," borrows its conception of freedom from an era in which privilege was still the main issue and applies it to conditions in which privilege per se is no longer the real problem. In this process, modern democracy obscures the inequalities of capitalist wealth distribution.

Kurt Raaflaub, like Morris, recognizes the need to search out the foundations of the general Greek notion of equality in the early polis, but he regards the origins of specifically democratic equality (as found in Aristotle) to be a product of distinctively Athenian fifth-century conditions. While *iso*-root terminology ("equality" language) can be dated to the mid-sixth century, the equality offered by Cleisthenes' reforms was strictly limited to the hoplite class; Cleisthenes' achievement was not democracy but rather a "hoplite republic," and it is in hoplite warfare that one must seek the origins of general Greek ideas of equality (compare Hanson, contrast Wolin). Citizens with the social status of thetes (i.e., laborers with little or no land) were not, in Raaflaub's view, full citizens until the late 460s; their political integration, established by the Ephialtic reforms, was a product of their newly essential military service as rowers in the fleet, first during the Persian Wars and then in the service of the Empire (compare Strauss). Democracy was thus a uniquely Athenian invention and a product of (rather than, with Wolin, a source of) the Empire. Yet Raaflaub concludes that even with the institutional changes (e.g., jury pay) that cemented their political gains, thetes remained unequal within the polis in various symbolic ways. The thetes were unable to develop or to support a value system alternative to the hoplite republic ideal (contrast Strauss) and they remained social unequals. Thus their political identity as participatory citizens was centrally important to them; without the institutional support provided by citizenship, thetes would quickly have descended to the level of inferiors.

Insisting that concepts can only be understood in their discursive context, Paul Cartledge concentrates on the differences between ancient and modern understandings of equality. He explores the dialectic between democratic ideology and practice by looking at some of the ways that the concepts of equality of political status, of well-faring, and of opportunity were used in Greek political arguments. Equality of status (*isokratia*) was regarded as desirable by oligarchs as equality of public speech *(isēgoria)* was by democrats; neither favored equal economic shares (*isomoiria*). While logically equality may imply sameness, in practice the goal was not identity but similitude. Yet in response to aristocrats who developed the notion of things being dealt with "on a fair and equal basis," democrats asserted that citizens must actually be "similars and equals" (*homoioi kai isoi*). Athenian men had become political equals by the 460s, even if they retained elections for certain offices in recognition that not all were of equal capacity. By contrast, the Spartans were only "similars" in terms of their uniform lifestyle: Spartans were not equal in voting, did not employ the lottery, and were beset by the overlapping hierarchies typical of a hypermilitarized society. In Athens there was considerably more space between a man's civic and military occupations (contrast Raaflaub, Strauss). Cartledge concludes by citing Primo Levi in order to underline the depth of the moral content of the concept of equality in the modern world and the horrors that attend its practical disappearance.

Beginning with Aristotle's discussion of arithmetical versus geometrical equalities, Jennifer Roberts shows that the Athenians rejected the "geometrical" argument that individuals must be equal in order to have equal shares in the polity, in favor of a generalized equality before the law of free males. The intended result was that the aristocracy of birth would be replaced by a natural and constantly revised aristocracy of merit; but this system meant that economic equalities remained. Most postclassical commentators tended to ignore economic inequality and to consistently characterize Athens as uniformly egalitarian. The "flux" of Roberts' title refers to the wide range of opinions held by modern writers on the meaning of the Athenian demos as a community of equals. Critics often regarded Athenian equality as an evil: elitists saw it as suppressing the aspiration of great men; feminists (and protofeminists like Mahaffy), as allowing the oppression of women; Marxists, as leading to the uniform oppression of slaves. Apologists for slavery, on the other hand, praised Athenian citizen equality. Recent feminist theory, which concentrates on gender difference, has gone further, suggesting that the very concepts of free and equal may be unsuitable to the problems feminists should be asking. Citing Carole Pateman, Roberts argues that the Athenian polis built an equal community only by cheating, "leaving some parts out of the kit"—notably women and slaves. She argues that the exclusion of these out-groups was psychologically and economically essential to Athenian democracy (compare Morris) and reiterates the degree of economic inequality which pertained even within the in-group. It is, she suggests, the failure to keep both sorts of inequality in mind that has led to the skewed portrait of an egalitarian Athens by moralists of various political stripes.

By presenting a series of historical vignettes, Alan Boegehold argues that the Athenians' very conservative attitude toward law allowed them to maintain a radically democratic government. He demonstrates that Athenian laws were meant to be permanent by showing that Athenians regarded claims to the effect that "to destroy a law has no effect on the polis" as evil. Athenian legal conservatism was demonstrated by the use of entrenchment clauses and by the *graphē paranomōn* procedure—whereby he who successfully passed a decree in the Assembly could be indicted for having passed a measure that contravened the law. This background elucidates Socrates' response to Crito in Plato's dialogue: Socrates was true to conservative Athenian legal ideals (compare Euben, contrast Barber) when he chose to protect the law at the cost of his own unjust death and rejected the chance to practice an "educational resistance" by fleeing Athens. Boegehold concludes by offering a solution to a well-known problem: when, in the *Apology,* Socrates states that in obedience to the god he could not obey an order to desist from public inquiry into the truth, he did not risk contradicting by practice his claim to have obeyed the law in all cases. The conservative procedures of Athenian law made no allowance for jurors setting conditions other than those proposed by the litigants: since neither the prosecutor nor defendant had proposed a gag order, Socrates knew perfectly well that it was not an option he would have to face.

W. R. Connor introduces the general issue of civic ritual by emphasizing the need to focus on democracy as a cultural process rather than as a political event (contrast Wolin). He dismisses the notion that the form of Athenian democracy might be useful for modern democrats, but suggests that the substructure of Athenian civil society may offer salutary examples of how voluntary associations—groups based on kinship, village, and religious ritual—mediate between individual and society. The quasi-democratic internal procedures of these same associations, and their concern for justice, may also help to explain the role of preexisting culture in the rise of political democracy. Yet why does democracy arise in Athens specifically? Connor answers by suggesting that Cleisthenes added a vital active ingredient to a general Greek set of habits of group equality and shared decision-making: the "Dionysian social imaginary." The carnivalesque inversions typical of Dionysiac celebration undermined established hierarchies and offered a vision of an alternate community, open to all, where speech was free. The old political reality suffered in comparison, and so the Dionysiac sense of liberation, was eventually transferred from the sacred space of ritual to the political space of governance. The City Dionysia, which Connor suggests was originally established by Cleisthenes as a "freedom festival," remained a pointed reminder of how the practices of civil society might be translated to the public realm and of possible alternatives to the forms of domination and exclusion which persisted within Athenian democratic politics.

Like Connor, Susan G. Cole directs our attention toward the polis as a community constituted by groups defined by metaphors of kinship. The Athenian state was, metaphorically, "one family"; Athenians marked their belonging to this family through rituals that both drew the community together and marked distinctions of gender and status within it. Its great number of participant-citizens meant that democratic Athens had a particularly strong need for expressions of unity among free men; Cole focuses on the ritual of oath-sacrifice as a salient example. The animal sacrifice performed by the oath-taker at key political moments (i.e., by a magistrate at his formal scrutiny [*euthuna*] upon leaving public office) was marked by high expense and by the unusually close relationship between (adult, male, uncastrated) victim and sacrificer. The sacrifice and oath ceremony were performed in the local community of the deme (village or neighborhood). The oath itself threatened the transgressor with the destruction of self, family, and paternity—and thereby linked the family to politics and the polis. Other forms of oath established, variously, equality among men and hierarchical distinctions between them. The limit on the power of men to challenge another to take an oath reinforced gender-based hierarchies. Cole concludes by noting that the oath ritual was not an archaic survival, "but part of the living discourse by which citizens made agreements" and through which they objectified women and minors.

The political problem of foundation and Euripides' tragedy *Ion* are Carol Dougherty's starting points for an exploration of how Athenian self-identity accounted for democracy and empire by laying claim to authochthonous and Ionian origins. Drawing on Pierre Bourdieu's concept of "the synoptic view," she shows how the overlapping and inconsistent elements that structured "what it meant to be Athenian" are revealed by the reappearance of Ionian identity long after Cleisthenes' suppression of the four Ionian tribes. In the fifth century "being Ionian" was very useful as an Athenian justification for empire. But Ionia's aristocratic associations required the addition of an Athenian identity based on the democratic myth of autochthony, which emphasized the "sameness" of all Athenians (compare Cartledge). The *Ion* brings these contradictory identities together through a "synoptic illusion" enhanced by the play's setting in Delphi—the site of Apollo's authorization for many Greek colonization projects. Creusa, mother of the eponymous Ion, is (as the only child of the earth-born kings of Attica) a symbol of autochthony, yet her barrenness signals the insufficiency of a narrowly autochthonous identity: Athens needed a father.

Thus Creusa must be reunited with her lost son. Ion, product of Apollo's rape of Creusa (rape is a common theme in colonial narratives), is peculiarly suited to father the Athenians (who thereby gain their autochthonous nature) and to colonize (and thereby vindicate Athenian imperial control over) the territory of Ionia. The illusion of resolution is made possible by the fusion of the dramatic space of Delphi with the civic space of the theater of Dionysos. Dougherty's essay may thus be read as an example of how Connor's "Dionysiac imaginary" could have worked in practice.

Through his attempt to reconstruct Aristotle's theory of education, Carnes Lord asks whether moral and ethical education should conform to the political and ideological requirements of democratic society. Aristotle's answer seems at first to be that it should conform and so his position appears close to that of modern communitarians. Yet Aristotle rejected the ideal of the fully homogeneous community; Lord argues that he also transcended civic education to offer a theory of a truly liberal education designed not only to produce good citizens and free men, but also to train statesmen and to support a life of cultured leisure. Because Aristotle did not regard the polis as simply natural, education was central to Aristotle's notion of how a polis should be formed and sustained. Aristotle's educational theory had elements in common with contemporary Greek notions of *paideia* (cultural/moral education) and aimed at producing a sort of aristocracy, but it was self-consciously critical not only of democratic notions of public life as intrinsically educational, but also of traditional aristocratic ideas of education (compare Morris). Lord concludes that Aristotle taught aristocrats how they might live noble lives within democratic regimes by focusing on serious yet nonpolitical uses of leisure. But, Lord argues, Aristotle also hoped to train a more restricted elite how to employ rhetoric in articulating moral principles and thus how to shape attitudes and guide public policy. This sort of guidance by an elite trained in the exercise of prudence, Lord suggests, is in the best genuine interests of democracy, whether ancient or modern.

Victor Hanson approaches the issue of democratic education by tracing the process by which the large class of "middling" hoplites, a class that he believes dominated the "normative" Greek polis as a broad-based oligarchy or timocracy, came to embrace democracy at Athens. The glue that bound Hansen's normative polis was the triad farmer/hoplite/voting citizen; the slave-owning *mesos* (man of the middle) who fulfilled each of these functions was a member of a self-conscious class. Hanson argues that the *mesoi* were fundamentally anti-aristocratic and their timocratic ideology was the forerunner to democracy (compare Morris). Yet by the same token, democracy could not flourish without coopting the *mesoi*. The radical economic and social changes that accompanied the formation of the fifth-century empire undermined the exclusive claims to full citizenship of the hoplite landowner, but in practice "convolution" rather than conflict characterized relations between hoplites and thetes. This was possible because the hoplites remained essential to the democratic imperial polis: under the empire, they fought more often than before, but the battles they fought, as marines, were less lethal than the traditional pitched battle. Moreover, middling farmers benefited from the growing urban market for their produce and from the cash economy. Because hoplite-farmers now shared the defense of the polis with the lower-class rowers of the fleet (compare Strauss), they felt solidarity with them and so were unwilling to support antidemocratic revolutionaries. In return, democratic imagery sought to reconstitute, not to destroy, the "hoplite mirage"; and thus Athens functioned as a big tent that symbolically raised thetes to hoplite status (contrast Raaflaub). Democracy allowed hoplites to retain their sense of political preference even as it destroyed their agrarian exclusivity and replaced it with an exclusivity based on the distinction between citizens and metics or slaves (compare Roberts).

Barry Strauss takes up the other side of the social-military equation, arguing that training in the cooperative discipline of rowing a trireme was a key factor in the civic education of the Athenian thetes. Rowing a trireme taught the thete the payoffs of cooperative action and bound him to his fellows through a shared experience of patriotic service, danger, and effort. Trireme service, Strauss suggests, created its own "social imaginary" (compare Connor) whereby the slogans of freedom *(eleutheria)*, equality *(isonomia)*, and *dēmokratia* were instantiated as "living realities"; consequently the thetes became a disciplined community and thus a social and political force to be reckoned with. Moreover, thetes may even have realized a degree of solidarity with the metics and slaves who also served as rowers. This could help to explain the valiant (if generally ill-rewarded) efforts of noncitizens to reestablish democracy in 404–403. Due to the self-confidence of the thetes, Athenian political culture remained only partially aristocratic in temper (compare Wolin, contrast Raaflaub); indeed Strauss suggests that the Athenian seaman may have cared rather less about the depictions of cavalrymen on the Parthenon frieze than he did for "the iconography of the emblem painted on the stem of the trireme on which he served."

Peter Euben continues the discussion of democratic education and its critics by arguing that Plato's Socrates—even in the dialogue the *Gorgias*—is not best read as an antidemocrat. Because of its polyphonic character, its willingness to put ideas at risk, and its determination to use language for contestation of received truths rather than for domination by the establishment of a truth regime, Platonic dialectic offers important resources for democratic readings—even as it exposes the misuse of rhetorical techniques by Pericles and other Athenian political leaders. For Euben, democracy demands the ability to see things from another's perspective, and this is what dialectic (unlike Gorgias' version of rhetoric) seeks to do. Euben's Socrates does not attempt to control the interpretations of his listeners; rather, he draws attention to the incomplete nature of his own arguments and democratically urges each Athenian to achieve self-mastery and to remain suspicious of claims to mastery in the apparently seamless arguments offered by corrupt, sophist-trained political orators. Hence, even in the *Republic* Plato's use of the dialogical form means that he can offer no final political *technē* (science or craft) or a fixed vision of truth. And thus, rather than regarding Plato as the source of final answers (as do some supporters of "the Western canon") or as the demonic progenitor of logocentrism (per some anticanonists), we can read his dialogues both contextually and theoretically, and they offer resources for a wide array of political projects.

In a direct engagement with Euben's essay, Benjamin Barber distinguishes between democracy as discursive conversation and democracy as action in the face of uncertainty. Barber argues that Plato's Socrates regards democracy as necessarily (rather than contingently) corrupt and so incapable of amelioration, because Socrates rightly, in Barber's view, defines democracy as majority rule rather than dialogical deliberation. Barber disputes Euben's claim that Socrates is a genuine dialectician, arguing that the dialogues are "monophony masquerading as polyphony." Plato's Socrates always wins his debates, he knows where he is headed in debate, and he seeks to establish an uncontestable truth. This is incompatible with Barber's conception of democracy, which recognizes the need to make decisions in the face of ineradicable ignorance and conflict among citizens over ends and means. Barber regards democracy not as a cognitive system, but as a pragmatic, "antifoundational" system of conduct: It is not a way of knowing, but of doing politics. Among democracy's central attributes is its revolutionary spirit (compare Wolin); by contrast, Barber suggests, Plato's Socrates is neither revolutionary nor irreverent. Yet if democracy is not just discourse, democratic rule is only legitimate as long as it remains reflexively subject to democratic deliberation and to the decisions that result from such deliberation. Barber concludes by moving the discussion away from Athens (compare Morris), citing Rousseau to claim that because the Athenians think aright, while the Spartans act rightly, democracy was in a sense "made in Athens but enacted and practiced in Sparta" (contrast Cartledge).

Finally, Brook Manville sums up the discussion of democratic citizenship by developing eleven postulates regarding Athenian beliefs about citizenship. Most of these are very different from the standard modern understandings of the meaning of state citizenship, and yet Manville argues that the classical democratic notion of citizenship has a close analog in the relationship of members to various sorts of modern and "postmodern" organizations other than the state. Elaborating on an organizational theory proposed by management consultant Peter Drucker and drawing on his own experience as a manager and partner in a major corporation, Manville suggests that the "new organization" (notably, he does not refer exclusively to the business corporation but also to various not-for-profit organizations) is currently undergoing a radical transformation in the way that knowledge is valued, gathered, processed, and distributed. In the less hierarchical, "flatter," postmodern organization, knowledge itself becomes the primary product. Moreover, the intraorganizational distribution of knowledge and the decision-making based on that knowledge are best predicated on democratic practices and on an ideology of citizenship strikingly reminiscent of those pertaining in classical Athens. Manville argues that far-sighted systems planners must give up their notions of centralized control and pyramidal command structure and turn to Aristotle and Athens if they wish to accommodate themselves and their organizations to the world of the future.

Manville's provocative paper generated a great deal of debate at the conference—not everyone relished the prospect of becoming a citizen of the "new organization,"—or a noncitizen stranded outside it. It moves us from scholarly research into Greek democracy and theoretical discussion about the meanings and values that may be extrapolated from ancient texts and practices to the world in which most of us live much of our lives: the world of organized work. If Manville is right, the structures of democratic polis citizenship may be in the process of being reinvented, albeit in an economic rather than political environment. And so, if ancient Greek democracy is not modern, perhaps it may be postmodern after all. As editors, we trust that those who find this prospect attractive or horrifying, impossible or inevitable, will find in these pages some of the materials and the guidance they need to explore it and to test it—against a body of evidence, through a set of sustained arguments, and in a productive engagement with their own experiences, ideas, and intuitions.

PART ONE

Liberty, Equality, and Law

THE STRONG PRINCIPLE OF EQUALITY AND THE ARCHAIC ORIGINS OF GREEK DEMOCRACY

Ian Morris

I. Introduction

Origins are out of fashion.[1] For most of this century, social scientists have held it as self-evident that synchronic analysis is prior to diachronic, and in the last few years many Greek historians have come to share this view, treating democracy as a static, functioning system.[2] This approach has good antecedents, most notably Aristotle's treatment of the eighty years or so from 403 to his own time as "the current constitution" (*Ath. Pol.* 42.1). But critics have always stressed that functionalism does not so much *explain* a situation as *redescribe* it in technical language—a view that Aristotle appears to have shared, prefacing his account of fourth-century institutions with a long narrative describing Athenian development since the seventh century, and beginning the *Politics* (1252a1–1253a40) with a model of the origins of the polis.

Any society can be said to function, but to understand why people live within one social system rather than another, we have to look to historical factors.[3] When the social system in question is as unusual as that of city-state democracy, we cannot be content with showing how different institutions intersected to maintain the system, no matter how skillfully the analysis may be done. But the most influential recent treatments of Athenian democracy—including most of the papers in this book—have little to say about the Archaic social order that made democracy possible.[4]

This leaves us unable to explain why Athenians chose to organize their society in this particular way, rather than in some equally functional but quite different way. In this paper I sketch the history of what I see as some of the necessary conditions for the emergence of Greek democracy. I argue four points:

1. There was a massive social change all across central Greece in the eighth century B.C., which produced a conception of the state as a community of "middling" citizens.

2. Not everyone liked this. Those who did not argued that authority lay outside these middling communities, in an inter-polis aristocracy that had privileged links to the gods, the heroes, and the East.

3. Much of the social history of the archaic period is best understood as a conflict between these two conceptions of social order.
4. At the end of the sixth century, the elitist ideology suffered major reverses. It became very difficult to claim a level of political skill denied to other citizens, and once this had happened, citizen democracy became a plausible system of government.

I suggest that we treat the origins of democracy as a process that is equally cultural and political. Mogens Hansen has recently argued that "it is the political institutions that shaped the 'democratic man' and the 'democratic life', not vice versa,"[5] but I take issue with this interpretation, arguing that a longer historical perspective shows that democratic institutions were merely one response to the emergence of broader egalitarian attitudes and ideologies. I structure my analysis around Robert Dahl's useful discussion of what he calls "the Strong Principle of Equality." Dahl suggests that "it is obvious . . . that the emergence and persistence of a democratic government among a group of people depends in some way on their *beliefs*. . . . Among a group whose members believe that they are all about equally well qualified to participate in the decisions of the group, the chances are relatively high that they will govern themselves through some sort of democratic process." This Strong Principle of Equality actually rests on two propositions:

All members are sufficiently well qualified, taken all around, to participate in making the collective decisions binding on the association that significantly affect their good or interests. In any case, none are so definitely better qualified than the others that they should be entrusted with making the collective and binding decisions.[6]

The first of these propositions corresponds to what Dahl calls the Principle of Equal Consideration of Interests.[7] This affords to each citizen equal respect and an equal right to be heard, but reserves the possibility that some citizens may be able to decide what is in everyone's best interests and are thus qualified to make the decisions for all. I suggest that something like the Principle of Equal Consideration appeared in the eighth century, and something like the Strong Principle of Equality in the late sixth. As I imply in my title, I see the origins of democracy as a long process, spanning the whole archaic period, and a broad one, involving the whole Greek world.

The Strong Principle of Equality is not synonymous with democracy as an institutional order. But when enough people hold views of this kind, it becomes possible—and perhaps logical—to respond to the collapse of an oligarchy (whether through internal dissension or outside force) by developing new conceptions of majority rule, instead of simply finding a different group of guardians. This is what happened at Athens in 507.

A Strong Principle of Equality within a bounded citizen group crystallized over much of Greece between c. 525 and 490. As Dahl implies, in such a context the establishment of democracy is not so surprising. The remarkable thing is that such an ideology could gain the upper hand in the first place, and explaining this ought to be one of the central questions in archaic Greek history. In this paper I propose at least a partial explanation, arguing that the Strong Principle of Equality was a late-sixth-century phenomenon, which can only be explained in the light of its eighth-century roots. The core ideas were already present, and important, by 700 B.C. What I offer here is a kind of social history of ideologies spanning three centuries; I pursue the longer-term history of these ideologies and their connections with broader cultural and economic processes in more detail elsewhere.[8]

I concentrate in this paper on the literary evidence from Archaic Greece. I argue that the source problems of the poetry of the period c. 700–525 are such that we must adopt a synchronic approach (section IV). Only archaeology can reveal detailed regional and chronological variations; archaic literature is too traditional to sustain a narrative history. But what we lose in detail we gain in understanding social dynamics. Historians have read this poetry too literally, systematically mistaking the elitist ideology for an objective account of social relations, characterizing the archaic poleis as "zero-sum" agonal societies dominated by aristocratic feuding over honor.[9] I dispute this. I suggest that the elitist position was a "dominant ideology" only in the sense that sociologists use that expression: it reinforced solidarity *within* a would-be elite, persuading its members of the justness of their claims, but had less influence on other groups.[10] It was not a "false consciousness," duping people into accepting aristocratic authority. On the contrary it was oppositional, working best outside the civic space, in the world of interstate aristocratic ties and closed symposia; and it was contested on all points by a rival "middling" philosophy.

I begin, though, at the end of this part of the story, with the "middling" ideology of fourth-century Athens. Such a teleological approach is perhaps an inevitable result of pursuing what Foucault castigated as the "chimera of origins." We could construct other narratives, with other beginning and end points; but if we are to understand ancient democracy, rather than redescribing it, we cannot do without such points. Chartier rightly concludes that "history stripped of all temptation to teleology would risk becoming an endless inventory of disconnected facts abandoned to their teeming incoherence for want of a hypothesis to propose a possible order among them."[11] I begin in the fourth century, then, for two reasons. First, this is where our sources are strongest; and second, I argue that this conception of equality goes back as far as we can follow the literary sources, all over the central regions of Greece.

II. ATHENIAN CITIZEN EQUALITY

Fourth-century Athenian sources present the polis as a community of *metrioi* or *mesoi,* words that, following Walt Whitman's usage, I will translate as "mid-

dling men."[12] Like Whitman's middling man, the Athenian *metrios* was an ideological category that benefited from the vagueness of its definition. It allowed
all Athenian citizens to think of themselves as members of a community of restrained, sensible men, characterized by "same-mindedness" (*homonoia*) and
tied together by *philia,* which literally means "friendship" but carries a sense
like Sahlins's category of "balanced reciprocity." The *metrios* was said to be
content with "a little" money and was contrasted with both the rich and the poor.
Yet even a wealthy liturgist could be called *metrios* if he lived properly. He was
defined through everyday actions—providing well for his family and community, having a strong sense of shame, and above all keeping his appetites under
control. Neither *mesoi* nor *metrioi* meant an economic "middle class," or a hoplite *Mittelschicht,* although membership in the phalanx was an important part
of their self-imagination.[13]

The spatial metaphor of the citizens as the midpoint of a universe of excluded
outsiders seems to have been a fundamental cosmological principle.[14] Citizens
were supposed to idealize the polis as a community under threat from marginal
groups who lacked the virtues of *metrioi*. A man judged to stand at any extreme
lacked control. In Winkler's words, he was "socially deviant in his entire being,
whose deviance was principally observable in behavior that flagrantly violated
or contravened the dominant social definition of masculinity . . . the *kinaidos,*
mentioned only with laughter or indignation, is the unreal, but dreaded, anti-
type behind every man's back." Anyone defined as rich, especially if young,
was seen as prone to hubris, "the serious assault on the honour of another, which
is likely to cause shame, and lead to anger and attempts at revenge." Aristotle
(*Rh.* 1378b28–29) explains that "they think that in this they show their superiority," and after an exhaustive study, Fisher concludes that hubris was "constantly seen as a major crime, endangering the cohesion of the community as
well as the essential self-esteem and identity of the individual."[15]

Poverty, on the other hand, forced a man to do undignified things, making
him vulnerable to exploitation. Halperin suggests that in popular thought the
poor, "deprived of their autonomy, assertiveness, and freedom of action—of
their masculine dignity, in short—were in danger of being assimilated not only
to slaves but to prostitutes, and so ultimately to women: they were at risk of
being effeminized by poverty." Even if relatively few citizens actually fulfilled
the ideal, when Athenians called themselves *metrioi* they imagined one another
as self-sufficient farmers on their own land, heads of households, married with
children, responsible, and self-controlled. The phalanx provided a useful
metaphor for the solidarity and interdependence of the citizens. By general
agreement—a willing suspension of disbelief—they thought of each other as
metrioi and *philoi:* "rich" and "poor" became categories of exclusion. The philosophy of the *metrios* was a useful democratic fiction, a powerful structuring
principle that guided behavior. A full share in the community, and therefore in
its politics, flowed directly from the fact of being born a free male: as Halperin

bluntly puts it, "The symbolic language of democracy proclaimed on behalf of each citizen, 'I, too, have a phallus.'"[16]

Athenian citizen society was egalitarian, but in a historically specific sense. Equality in one sphere of life inevitably means inequalities in others. Modern liberal societies privilege equality of opportunity, the belief that everyone has an equal right to compete for life's rewards, but sanction inequalities of outcome. Critics would help the underprivileged by restricting the equal freedoms of the successful, through policies such as affirmative action or banning private education and health care. Champions of the various models of equality accuse one another of treating people unfairly. Similarly, in fourth-century Athens supporters of "geometric" equality could claim that the democratic "arithmetic" equality was unfair: by giving all men equal voting power, it treated them unequally in terms of competence and virtue.[17]

Depending on political choices, different "spaces" for equality appear obvious or natural. Sen observes that "critiques of egalitarianism tend to take the form of being—instead—egalitarian in some *other* space." Conflicts cluster around attempts to impose such choices on others.[18] In most situations some group of people impose their view that a particular quality—wealth, birth, strength, education, beauty, or whatever—is *the* dominant good. Claiming to monopolize it, they try to convert their monopoly over one good into monopolies over others. Thus, in a plutocracy, equal rights to make money and dispose of it freely allow the rich to create inequalities in other spheres, such as politics, subsistence, or health. There will be pockets of nonconvertibility—it may not be possible, say, to buy divine grace or beauty—but the holders of the dominant good will struggle to breach these citadels of resistance.

Walzer observes that "since dominance is always incomplete and monopoly imperfect, the rule of every ruling class is unstable. It is continually challenged by other groups in the name of alternative patterns of conversion." The social order is constructed, not given. Thus, against the interests of plutocrats, a nobility might hold that certain goods—say, land, high office, dignity, and royal favor—cannot be bought. If they are successful in advancing their claims, plutocracy might gradually give way to aristocracy, with genealogical distance becoming the standard for judging equality, and wealth following in its train—"all good things come to those who have the one best thing."[19]

In Athens the one best thing was male citizen birth. Other goods, even money, could only be converted into citizenship under extraordinary circumstances. The exclusion of women and the near impossibility of naturalization were not unfortunate quirks in an otherwise admirable system. The strong principle of equality was essentialist—in Bourdieu's neat formulation: "Regarding existence as an emanation of essence, [essentialists] set no intrinsic value on [their] deeds and misdeeds. . . . They prize them only insofar as they clearly manifest, in the nuances of their manner, that their one inspiration is the perpetuating and celebrating of the essence by virtue of which they are accomplished".[20] Everyone who was born an Athenian man was a *metrios,* deserving equal respect and an equal share in the polis, unless he forfeited it. What mattered was that Athens was a group of *metrioi.* Every *metrios* had a share in the community, and no one else had any share at all.

But as always dominance was imperfect and contested, and compromises had to be reached with other visions of equality. Athenians did not insist on wealth, land, or influence strictly following equal dignity; not because they valued only equality of political opportunity, as Hansen argues, but because opposition from the rich made it difficult. Further, they did not need equality of resources to guarantee the basal dimension, what Kerferd calls "equality of attitude and respect between citizens." Some archaic states did cancel debts, redistribute land, control inheritance, or even massacre the rich, but after 500 this only happened when states were destabilized through war.[21]

III. THE EIGHTH-CENTURY REVOLUTION

The strong principle of equality was not peculiar to fourth-century Athens, but neither was it a timeless "Greek" *Zeitgeist.* Such beliefs were probably not important in the world of the Mycenaean palaces, and I see them beginning to take the forms we see in classical Greece in an eighth-century upheaval visible in the archaeological record.[22]

Most evidence from the Greek Dark Age (c. 1100–750) is from graves, and I have argued that in central Greece funerals drew a line within each community, between an elite group and lower, dependent groups. Most children were excluded from elite rituals. Elite funerals produced distinctive remains, which are well known to excavators, while the less formal funerals of the lower orders are only detected under favorable circumstances. The evidence for sacrifice has a similar pattern. In Dark Age central Greece, the major rites may have taken place in chiefs' houses, effectively excluding most people and defining a subgroup of full members of the community. Whitley argues that forms of rationing similarly limited other forms of symbolic behavior. All these classes of evidence, as well as house remains, suggest an elite ideology of homogeneity: rituals aggressively denied differences within the elite.[23]

There were huge changes in the eighth century. A new funerary system emerged, incorporating the whole adult and child population, often in the same cemeteries. The first signs appear at Corinth around 775, and at Argos, Athens, Megara, and many other sites by 750. Intramural burial largely ended (at Corinth by 750, elsewhere by 700), and cemeteries and settlements were now often walled. The most spectacular change was in sacrificial space. Around 750 areas for worship began to be walled, and by 700 nearly all communities had one or more substantial temples, while a few sanctuaries won Panhellenic importance. Most poleis adopted a "bipolar" religious structure, with a major sanctuary in the town and another near a frontier. The Dark Age rituals in chiefs' houses died out.[24]

At first the quantity and quality of grave goods increased, presumably as some people went on differentiating status within the new ritual terrain. Spending peaked at Corinth by 750, at Athens by 725, and at Argos by 700. At most sites this phase lasted only about a generation, and a shift toward large, poor, and homogeneous citizen cemeteries followed. Around 750 the new sanctuaries began to receive huge numbers of votives, at first mainly pottery, but by 700 in many cases expensive metal items too. Snodgrass links this to the fall in grave goods: by 700 it was rarely acceptable to lavish wealth on funerals, but such offerings could be made at sanctuaries.[25] In the fourth century Aristotle (*Eth. Nic.* 1122b19–1123a4; cf. Xen., *Oec.* 2.5–7) defined spending money on sacrifices as "magnificence" (*megaloprepeia*), and concluded that "the magnificent man spends not for himself but for the common good" (*ta koina*). Historians of the eighth century often see the shift from grave goods to votives in these terms, as a victory for the community over individual families within it. However, Aristotle also observed that *megaloprepeia* must be in proportion to a man's resources, and that the poor man (*penēs*) cannot be magnificent, since if he spends lavishly he is simply foolish (*ēlithios*). Spending on the gods was ambiguous, creating both a sense of community and a hierarchical structure of honor within it. I return to this in section VI.

These changes were contested, and the archaeological record reveals varied outcomes. On Crete, despite the early appearance of "civic" forms such as agoras, temples, and lawcodes, sacrifice retained local peculiarities, and grave goods escalated until about 625; then virtually all finds except inscriptions disappear until the fourth century. In Thessaly some elements of the general pattern apply in the eighth century, but rich warrior burials continue in the seventh.[26] Athens is the most interesting case: here the eighth-century shifts are very clear, but then around 700 they were reversed. Distinct elite burials returned, while rich votives, monumental temples, and religious bipolarity are absent in the seventh century. This seems to have been a self-conscious attempt to restore the lost order of the Dark Age, and Athens remained unique in ritual terms well into the sixth century.[27]

IV. SOURCE PROBLEMS

Generalizations must, then, be qualified by region and period, but this is not easy to do with the written sources. Nagy argues that much of what comes down to us under the names of specific poets was in fact formed by broader processes: "The pan-Hellenic tradition of oral poetry appropriates the poet, potentially transforming even historical figures into generic ones who merely represent the traditional functions of their poetry."[28] He suggests that prior to the eighth century there was enormous regional variety in Greek oral poetry, but that by 700 some bards were traveling widely. Discrepancies between local traditions became more apparent to them, and they tried to produce poems that were relevant to all areas of Greece but specific to none, developing fixed ideas about the heroic past. It became useful for them to imagine performance as the reconstitution of a fixed text by a noncomposing rhapsode. Local mythology was marginalized in opposition to *alēthea,* "unforgotten things," known by authoritative bards. As traditions coalesced, rhapsodes retrojected into the distant past Ur-poets—first Homer, then Hesiod, Archilochus, and a range of other personas in a series of bids for Panhellenic status. This does not necessarily mean that these poets were not real people; only that they were already submerged within the genre in archaic times. Only at the end of the sixth century, Nagy suggests, did individual poets emerge as "authors."[29]

Something like this clearly happened with "Theognis." Some verses should date before 625, and others after 490; and many are also attributed to other poets. "Theognis" was a poetic persona, into which anyone could step to compose in this genre, just as "Anacreon" continued to be into the Middle Ages.[30] Ancient disputes over the poets' cities of origin might represent competing retrojections.

The problem is most acute with Archilochus. His characters' names have long aroused suspicion, and Miralles and Pòrtulas suggest that the poems resemble the worldwide "trickster" genre, in which a cunning Brer Rabbit figure with insatiable hungers for food and sex outwits opponents and unmasks their hypocrisy—he is "the outcast able to cause someone else's casting out, the figure that has been excluded but has the power to exclude." Some of his characters also appear in a third-century B.C. inscription, but this only adds to the problem. The text was set up by one Mnesiepes, a name meaning "he who remembers the words."[31] However we interpret him, we are dealing here with a long-term process like those that Hobsbawm and Ranger have called the invention of tradition, or perhaps better still, as Herzfeld puts it, the *negotiation* of tradition, in which actors recast one another's notions in a competitive process of literary construction.[32]

We have to recognize the continuities between certain groups of archaic poets, and the constraining powers of genre. I see three implications for historians. First, we can only approach the main body of texts synchronically. Tracing an intellectual evolution by stringing the poems together in their supposed chronological order is unwise. It finds change by ignoring continuity and explains all differences diachronically. Literary critics then step into the persona of Mnesiepes, becoming an active part of the invention of tradition.

Second, we cannot reconstruct specific events. Archilochus and Alcaeus may well have been real people, singing about other real people, but when performing they adopted poetic personas. They sang through conventional *topoi;* it was perhaps impossible for them to think constructively in any other terms.

When Alcaeus called Pittacus "fatty" and "base born," we cannot assume that these charges were true, or even that the poet expected anyone to find them credible. A man singing Alcaeus took the part of the betrayed one, trying to recreate an ideal, homogeneous world by casting out the traditional enemy, just as Archilochus cast out Neoboule the "fickle one," Hipponax cast out Boupalos the "big-dick," and Demosthenes was to cast out Aeschines with accusations of servile origin. If we take anything from these stories at face value, we may be seriously misled.[33]

These are negative arguments, but the third implication is positive. The *topoi* within which events were constructed had immense cultural importance. In sections V and VI, I develop the arguments of Mazzarino and Kurke that we should divide archaic poetry into two broad traditions, which I call "elitist" and "middling." These partly correspond to formal distinctions, with lyric poetry dominating the former and elegy and iambus the latter, but the boundaries are not rigid. Hexameter was used in both traditions, with Homer in some regards standing at the head of the elitist tradition, and Hesiod of the middling; but in neither case is this a clear-cut relationship.[34]

For all the antagonism between the traditions (section VI), they were not rigidly separated. They should be seen as ideal types, representing the ends of a spectrum of social attitudes. Phocylides, for example, is more "middling" than Theognis, whose complex attitudes were sometimes hostile to ordinary citizens. Further, like any artists, individual poets (or traditions) were not consistent, occupying a single point on this spectrum; they rather occupied a range of positions. Thus Alcman gives us some strikingly elitist statements in his *partheneia* but in fr. 17 apparently adopts a middling, iambic persona, calling himself the eater of everything (*pamphagos*) who rejoices in common foods (*ta koina*) just like the people (*ho damos*).[35] Similarly, the same literary *topos* could be reworked in strikingly different ways within each tradition, as when Alcaeus reused Hesiod's image of the lustiness of women and the weakness of men in the dog days of summer.[36]

Both traditions were "elite" in the sense that most poems were produced by and for elites of birth, wealth, and education. The hostility between the extant traditions was primarily a conflict within the highest social circles over what constituted legitimate culture. Bourdieu suggests that such struggles are common to all elites, and that very often some people will claim to monopolize a high culture that is beyond the reach of the masses, while others assert their power by deliberately transgressing, conferring high status on values and objects excluded from the privileged aesthetics. The popular aesthetic is normally not simply a failure to grasp elitist tastes, but also a conscious refusal of them, among ordinary people and among the elite. I suggest in section VI that those aristocrats who adopted the middling position deliberately assimilated themselves to the dominant civic values within archaic poleis. They were not surrendering their claims to be elite: a wealthy symposiast insisting on the excellence of *to meson* represented a situation very different from that of a poor farmer pronouncing the same words.[37] However, they claimed leadership as special members of the polis, not as a wholly distinct aristocratic community of the kind created by the elitist tradition. There is no reason to think that middling aristocrats struggled across the seventh and sixth centuries to create democracy. But the unintended consequence of their beliefs was that when the elitist ideology collapsed after 525, the general acceptance of middling values made democracy a real possibility; and when a ruling elite fell apart in disorder, as at Athens in 507, democratic institutions were one obvious response.

V. The Middling Tradition

The core features of the middling ideology go back at least to Hesiod's *Works and Days* (c. 700 B.C.). Like the fourth-century *metrios,* Hesiod's good man was married with children, ideally owning land, two oxen, a slave woman, a hired laborer, and dependents of some kind, who received rations. He strongly endorsed the essentialist argument that the ideal community is male: women were a late addition sent to curse men. Good men knew that the gods filled the barns of those who ordered their works with due measure (*Op.* 306: *erga metria kosmein*). Hard work was the key to the gods' favor, and the only alternative was begging.[38]

Hesiod never used words such as *astoi* or *politai* for "citizens." His community consisted of neighbors (*geitones*). Possibly no concept of citizenship had yet emerged, but this may be too literal an approach. *Geitones* had a long history as a poetic *topos,* lasting into the fourth century. Hesiod advised Perses that neighbors were more important than kin, and his neighbors interacted much like fourth-century citizens. They lived in a certain tension with one another: a man had to respect his equals but also be sensitive to slights, balancing healthy rivalry and even dealings. He had to be tough but welcoming, because either too much or too little trust would ruin him.[39]

The good man's attitude toward "the poor" was also like that of the fourth-century *metrios.* They should not be mocked, but neither should they be trusted, for their empty bellies degraded them and forced them to lie.[40] The relationship with the rich was more complex. In the *Works and Days,* Hesiod said the "lords" (*basilēes*) were "gift-devouring judges" who relied on violence, not right: "The fools know neither how much greater the half is than the whole, nor what advantage there is in mallow and asphodel" (40–41)—that is, that a fair share was better than unjustly seizing everything, and that peasant foods were better than luxury. But in the *Theogony* Hesiod praised the *basilēes* to whom the Muses gave honey-sweet tongues for settling quarrels. The whole people treated them like gods when they walked through their assemblies. There is no contradiction here. The *Theogony* sets out the ideal, and the *Works and Days* shows it under attack from the unjustness endemic in the Age of Iron. When the nobles show proper respect, the city flourishes; when they do not, Shame flees to Olympus, and Zeus makes the whole community pay. Hubris—another central fourth-century concern—then destroys the city.[41]

In both poems the *basilēes* have a divine right to settle disputes, manifested in their eloquence and respect for gods and men. This is strikingly different from what we see in the fourth century, but we should hesitate before concluding that Boeotian villages around 700 really were ruled by *basilēes*. Hesiod's account parallels Homer's in *Od.* 8.166–77, and both probably drew on a tradition of advice-poetry.[42] Indeed, Ascra (and all the people in it) were probably as much a *topos* as the Thebes of tragedy: Ascra was the place where Zeus' will, personified by the good *basilēes*, was undermined by hubris.[43] Detienne suggests that in Hesiod *alēthea* was not an abstract "truth" but a form of "magico-religious" speech, available only to kings, poets, and seers, who monopolized contact with an invisible realm and drew wisdom, justice, and prophecy from it. In the *Works and Days*, Hesiod judged the *alēthea* of the *basilēes* by their behavior. It did not live up to expectations, showing that they were masters not of *alēthea* but of *apatē*.[44]

Like the *basilēes*, Hesiod appeals to outside sources of authority, casting himself as an "exterior insider" whose origin and position on the edge of the community give him privileged insights. As Nagy observes, in Ascra "the function of the *basileus* 'king' as the authority who tells what is and what is not *themis* 'divine law' by way of his *dikē* 'judgment' is taken over by the poem itself."[45] We see a similar idea of the poet absorbing external sources of legality in elegy, through identifying with semilegendary middling lawgivers who went to Crete or Delphi to legitimate laws, which they then brought back within the community, writing them down and putting them increasingly under civic control.[46] By 500 B.C. the citizen body itself took authority for the laws. Ostwald argues that the sixth-century Athenian word for "law," *thesmos*, implied "something imposed by an external agency, conceived as standing apart and on a higher plane than the ordinary," while the fifth-century word, *nomos*, implied something "motivated less by the authority of the agent who imposed it than by the fact that it is regarded and accepted as valid by those who live under it."[47]

Hesiodic society has parallels in other literatures, and its mythology overlaps with Near Eastern wisdom texts. The roughly contemporary Egyptian *Instructions of Amenemopet* agrees that unrighteous profits are fleeting (9.16–10.13), but Hesiod's egalitarianism is unique. Even in the superficially similar Middle Kingdom *Protests of the Eloquent Peasant*, the good steward Rensi only believes the peasant Khun-Atep after beatings that in Ascra would have been hubristic (B.185–190).[48] I suggest that Hesiod's egalitarianism was a peculiarly Greek product of the eighth-century transformation. Similarly, Nagy notes that while Greek hexameter poetry shares much with other Indo-European traditions, it also has important differences, which he also links to eighth-century changes in the archaeological record.[49]

The core of Hesiod's ideal persona recurs in elegy, despite a major change in audience. Hesiod's song was open to all, but he also knew of songs limited to those who understand (*phroneousi*). He called these *ainos* (*Op.* 202), which meant "praise" but was also the root of *ainigma,* denoting coded speech. Most elegy and iambus was *ainos* poetry, intended for a small group of "the wise" (*sophoi*). Theognis called his verses "*ainigmata* hidden by me for the good men" (681). But although they were produced by and for aristocrats, "elegiac poetics in general amount to a formal expression of the ideology of the polis, in that the notion of social order is envisaged as the equitable distribution of communal property among equals."[50] In this poetry some members of the aristocracy came to terms with the polis of middling citizens while acquiring a useful weapon in intra-elite struggles. Poets and audiences could still see themselves as *sophoi* who guided the polis with special wisdom and piety, but elegists presented their own symposia as a force for moderation, not elitism. "The wise" might claim to know what was good for ordinary citizens better than the citizens did themselves, but they did so within a Principle of Equal Consideration of Interests.[51]

To be in the middle was best. Solon called himself a shield held over rich and poor, a wolf at bay among hounds, one who made laws alike (*homoios*) for good and bad, and a boundary stone at the midpoint (*en metaichmiō*) between them (frs. 4c; 36.26–27, 18–20; 37.9–10).[52] Phocylides said simply, "*mesos* in the polis I would be" (fr. 12), and Theognis, "the middle is best in everything" (335). Restraint and moderation were the keys, expressed first as *aidōs,* and later as *sōphrosunē.* The middling man needed moderate wealth (as in Hesiod, *man* was the operative word: women were reviled ferociously). Phocylides, again like Hesiod, saw a fertile farm as the source of plenty, and Theognis wished only "to be rich without evil cares, unharmed, with no misfortune" (1153–54). As in Hesiod and in the fourth century, the middle was defined against the poor as well as the rich. Men were constrained (*biatai:* Solon 13.41) by poverty, and its victim "cannot say or do anything, and his tongue is tied" (Theog. 177–78). All men despised the poor, and the hungry belly was to blame for their lack of dignity and self-control. For Solon, "luxury in belly, sides, and feet" was equal (*ison*) to silver, gold, land, and horses (21.1–4).[53]

If moderate wealth was the precondition for the ideal of middling life from the seventh to the fourth century, the ogre of greed was just as consistently its enemy. Men pursued wealth through any means, setting no limits. Wealth and hubris were inseparable. For Solon "excess breeds hubris when great wealth follows men who do not have a complete mind" (6.3–4). Hubris then destroyed the polis: "The *astoi* themselves, obsessed by greed, are prepared to ruin this great city" (4.5–6). He would check this by setting up *eunomia,* a "well-ordered world" that "makes all things wise and perfect among men" (4.39). This presumably refers to Solon's own reforms of 594, but it also continues the Hesiodic tradition of creating the ideal order by asserting it poetically, merging the lawgiver and poet.[54]

To a great extent the middle was constructed in opposition to the bogeyman of the hubristic aristocrat, defined—as in the fourth century—through his decadence and lack of control. To understand this dimension, we must now turn to the elitist tradition.

VI. THE ELITIST TRADITION AND THE CONFLICT OF VALUES

In an earlier paper I argued that the *Iliad* and *Odyssey* were written down in the upheavals of the eighth century, as attempts to fix against alternative constructions an elitist view of the heroic age as a time when the community depended for its very survival on mighty individuals. The poems show us eighth-century assumptions about what a heroic age would be like, and, not surprisingly, they share some elements with the "middling" tradition. Fisher shows that hubris is the main offense of both Agamemnon in the *Iliad* and the suitors in the *Odyssey,* and that its overtones are "entirely compatible with those found in our study of *hybris* in classical Athens." There is, however, a crucial difference: the victim of hubris in each case is no middling citizen but a mighty hero, and hubris is avenged not by communal action but by individual *biē* (force) or *mētis* (cunning). Similarly, it is only partly true that Homer criticizes heroic excess in favor of polis institutions, or that the Thersites episode (*Il.* 2.270–78) undermines elitism. The main thrust of both poems was the dependence of the community on the individual hero.[55]

The heroic past assumed immense importance in the eighth century, and the variety of cults at Bronze Age tombs attests debates over its meaning. The story that Helen never went to Troy (which certainly goes back to Stesichorus, and probably to Hesiod) also suggests the scale of variations, but the Panhellenization of Homer over the next two centuries effectively silenced most alternatives.[56]

Hesiod knew there could be lying poetry and saw poets and *basilēes* as competing in truth, but Homer was more aggressive, claiming to be merely the audience's point of contact with the total knowledge of the Muses. Ford notes that "by neglecting the possibility that two mortal poets might differ in their versions of a given story, [Homer] encourages us to regard the story as the enunciation of earlier deeds in their timeless structure." Homer thus naturalized a specific vision of the heroic age.[57]

Elitist sympotic poetry took for granted this appropriation of the heroic age, and the heroic warrior became a potent symbol. Some historians use references to heroic-style warfare to date the "hoplite reform,"[58] but it makes more sense to see these passages as synecdochical: the part stands for the whole, and the hero evokes a package of heroic values, loyalties, and dependencies. The

"heroic" war scenes are associated with those poets who express elitist sentiments. For example, only one martial fragment (14) survives from Mimnermus,
and it describes in epic tones a hero rushing forward to rout the Lydian cavalry.
Alcaeus fr. 140 uses epic language for arms and armor hanging on a wall while
his companions share a peaceful feast. But then the pace changes: we move to
a jumbled heap of weapons on the floor, described with nonepic words such as
spathē (sword), and to the seamy facts of the fragmented fellowship and civil
war on Lesbos. The hero's weapons stand for the perfect aristocratic community, now disordered.[59]

But on the whole the world of "contemporary" nobles was a far cry from the
brutal heroic age. It was a place of delicacy, elaborate manners, sweet perfumes,
and wealth. Sappho's simple statement "I love luxury" (*habrosunē:* fr. 58.25)
was the direct opposite of Phocylides' "*mesos* in the polis I would be." Luxury
was not just a way to make life pleasant—it collapsed the distances between the
aristocracy and the gods, the heroes, and the great rulers of Lydia. Even as the
middling poets brought the external grounding of law under communal control,
the elitists emphasized their own similarities to these three outside sources of
legitimacy. They described the gods as dressed in gold and living in a golden
house, pouring drinks from golden vessels, and coming to worshipers who
made offerings in similar golden cups. Gentili observes that Sappho merged divine and mortal luxury in personalized epiphanies of Aphrodite, claiming to
have "*privileged* religious experiences bringing closer communion with the
god." Luxury bridged the gulf between mortals and gods. Sappho and her
friends dwelled in a realm more like the heroic age than the seventh century.
The gods moved among them, and Sappho identified as strongly with Aphrodite
as Odysseus did with Athena. Lavish display made the aristocracy something
more than human.[60]

Giving a golden cup or a bronze tripod to the gods was an act of *megaloprepeia* which benefited the whole community, but, as in Aristotle's account, it
was open to varying interpretations. It was more than the "increasing competition for status via the conspicuous consumption of wealth" stressed by Morgan;[61] to those steeped in the elitist culture, it gave the dedicator a direct experience of the gods which was denied to ordinary mortals. These lavish
dedications became common shortly before 700, and I would suggest that they,
and the themes in Sappho, were reactions to the eighth-century social transformation. Assertions of elite power were generally banished from the explicit
arena of funerals, but, like aristocracies in all ages, Greek nobles were adapt-
able. They shifted one of their primary arenas of self-definition to a more ambiguous context. At Athens, where I have suggested that a powerful elite re-
gained control and rejected the middling ideology, rich seventh-century votives
are scarce. Athenian nobles apparently did not need these new-fangled ideas
and tried to recreate the simpler, ancestral rites of the Dark Age. Seventh-

century Corinth and Argos, on the other hand, combined strikingly homogeneous cemeteries with fabulously wealthy rural sanctuaries of Hera.

In these dedications the worlds of nobles, gods, heroes, and Easterners intersected, most strikingly in bronze tripod-cauldrons. Catling argues that no tripods were made in Dark Age Greece, but Bronze Age Cypriot heirlooms continued to circulate; Matthäus thinks that local tripods were being made in Crete and the islands by the tenth century, in close imitation of Cypriot models. Either way, by the eighth century tripods were intimately linked with both the past and the East and were established as *the* gift of heroes. Examples dating from before c. 750 were made from almost pure copper, but in the second half of the century a new series appeared, imitating both the designs and the high tin content of Eastern (probably north Syrian) tripods. The tripod simultaneously heroized and Orientalized: all sources of external power flowed together in the act of giving a tripod to the gods. By about 650, fewer Greek-made Orientalizing tripods were being dedicated, and more hoplite arms and armor. Coming as it did at about the same time as the emergence of the phalanx as a poetic metaphor for citizen solidarity, this might represent an alternative, "middling" kind of gift to the gods; but it was paralleled by an increase in dedications of imported Oriental tripods.[62]

True aristocrats were comfortable using the East, moving within their own version of the culture of Gyges. Aristeas, significantly said to have been an ecstatic devotee of Apollo, supposedly traveled all over Asia in the seventh century, seeing mythical beasts everywhere. Elite religion adapted Eastern rites, and Carter suggests that Alcman's *partheneia* borrowed Phoenician elements.[63] The dependence on the East was just as true of the symposium, the primary context for the performance of lyric monody, as of the sanctuary. Drinking groups had probably been an important way for chiefs to gather and reward followers since at least 900, as suggested by the heavily worn krater from Koukounaries on Paros, the consistent use of ceramic kraters and amphoras to mark prestigious burials, and the burial of complete Attic drinking sets in Knossian tombs.[64] But around 700, symposia had their own Orientalizing revolution, adapting special rooms and furniture from the East. Reclining on couches of Near Eastern type and using vessels with Lydian prototypes, aristocrats sang about Lydian dress, women, and military might, judging Greek life against these standards. The new symbols justified their users' claims to superiority—they virtually mixed with the gods themselves, just like the ancient heroes, on whom society had depended for its very existence; and they felt like the kings of the East, whose power vastly exceeded that of the Greeks.[65]

The Orientalizing movement was a class phenomenon. As in many other contexts, decisions to adopt or to resist artistic innovation from overseas were political. Would-be aristocrats who felt marginalized and unfairly excluded from power welcomed new and disruptive ideas, looking outward to the past, the

East, and the divine for justification. Those who believed in middling values resisted these novelties.[66]

The outcomes of these struggles varied enormously. At Athens Eastern imports and Orientalizing styles were welcomed enthusiastically in the last quarter of the eighth century but after 700 were used much more carefully by the elite. In Argos Eastern metalwork was given to Hera in large quantities,[67] but otherwise the East had a minimal impact on material culture. Only a handful of local Orientalizing potsherds are known. Corinthian aristocrats used expensive Eastern and Orientalizing objects in similar ways, but the makers of Protocorinthian pottery, probably in use across the social scale and in all contexts, debased the Eastern styles, effectively vulgarizing them. The Cretans, on the other hand, had (in Burkert's words) "been 'orientalizing' all the time." Phoenicians had been coming to Kommos since the tenth century, and there may have been a community of Levantine craftsmen at Knossos by 850. A vigorous Orientalizing pottery style, Protogeometric B, flourished in the late ninth century alongside a Middle Geometric style. The East must have meant entirely different things in Crete than in the central Aegean.[68]

In eastern Greece a handful of sanctuaries received spectacular Oriental votives in the seventh century, but few lavish Archaic burials are known, and indeed few burials of any kind before about 550.[69] Most elitist poets were placed in eastern Greece—Sappho and Alcaeus on Lesbos, Mimnermus in Colophon, Anacreon in Teos. Even Alcman of Sparta was linked with Sardis, and Ibycus of Rhegion spent much of his career on Samos. But there is no way to know whether elitist poetry really was a product of the fringes of Asia, or whether it was located there because the East was so important for it. Oriental power was more threatening for east Greeks than for mainlanders, but Nagy is surely right that these poets achieved canonical status by being generalized across Greece in a series of Panhellenic "promotions." Regardless of their ultimate origins, "eastern" poets appealed to symposiasts on the mainland and in the islands.

The elitist version of sympotic culture directly opposed the middling ideology. Murray suggests that "the *symposion* became in many respects a place apart from the normal rules of society, with its own strict code of honour in the *pistis* [trust] there created, and its own willingness to establish conventions fundamentally opposed to those within the *polis* as a whole."[70] The primary assets were beauty, eroticism, love of wine, arcane mythical knowledge, and athletic skills. The games perhaps owed as much to the East as did the symposium, and both merged with ritual friendship to form a coherent culture beyond polis morality. No rules barred ordinary citizens from entering the games, but the expense of training effectively achieved this. Stories of goat- and cowherds winning at Olympia have a mythical air, and in any case, the scale of rewards made victory an avenue of rapid promotion into elite circles. Serious competitors constituted in their own eyes an interstate elite, and it is from their literature, rather than from that of the majority of citizens, that Burckhardt created his image of

Greece as an agonal society. Ordinary citizens enjoyed the spectacle of elite conflicts and honored the victors, much as fourth-century Athenian jurymen watched the struggles of wealthy litigants; but for the participants, athletic victory renewed the household's glory. The presence of a victor in one's family, like the correct use of luxury, identified a true aristocrat, someone who stood close to the gods and heroes.[71]

The middling poets resisted all these beliefs. The phalanx became the standard image for citizen solidarity and remained so until the fourth century. Archilochus mocked the heroic model by describing in lofty language how he abandoned his "blameless armament" (*entos amōmēton*) to a Thracian tribesman—but Archilochus didn't care and found the whole episode amusing (fr. 5). He preferred a short, bowlegged man with his feet on the ground to a tall, elegant, heroic officer (fr. 114). In Tyrtaeus and Callinus, the phalanx is a metaphor for the ideal citizen group. Begging is the only alternative to hard work in Hesiod (*Op.* 397–400), and to standing your ground in the ranks in Tyrtaeus (fr. 10.1–14). These are not transparent accounts of tactical changes: they are part of a series of exchanges between the two poetic traditions, what Rose calls "matters of discursive conflict."[72]

Xenophanes questioned the epic gods. Far from being companions of the elite, the gods of middling poets kept the ends of life hidden from all men.[73] But the harshest attacks were on the East. For Phocylides "an orderly polis on a rock is better than silly Nineveh" (fr. 5), and Xenophanes told how Colophon "learned useless luxuries from the Lydians while they were still free from hateful tyranny" (fr. 3.1–2). In fr. 19 Archilochus had Charon the carpenter say, "I don't care for Gyges the Golden's things, and I've never envied him. I'm not jealous of the works of gods either, and I don't lust after a magnificent tyranny. These are beyond my gaze." Aristotle describes Charon's comments as *agroikia,* "rustic" or "boorish." Fränkel suggested that "the carpenter was a stock example of the industrious man," and perhaps the audience was supposed to react to Charon as a solid, worthy citizen.[74] What he rejected was a virtual checklist of elitism—the desire to be like the king of Lydia, to rival the gods, and (at least in the eyes of critics) to be a tyrant. But perhaps the most effective attack on elite pretensions came from Hipponax, who abused the delicacy, eroticism, and Orientalism that Sappho and others saw as sources of social power. The dung-covered hero of fr. 92 found himself in a toilet with a woman who performed an obscure act on his anus while beating his genitals with a fig branch. The fragment ends with a cloud of dung beetles whirring out of the filth. The woman was *Ludizousa,* "speaking in a Lydian fashion"; perhaps the whole episode was so down-market that it did not even involve a real Lydian. This is classic iambic abuse, making it hard to take the *habrosunē* ideology seriously, and that was surely the point.[75]

There was no way to transcend the polis in the middling tradition. Not even athletic victory brought a man closer to the gods and heroes. The differences between the two poetic traditions came down to a single point: the elitists legitimated their special role from sources outside the polis; the middling poets rejected such claims. The former blurred distinctions between male and female, present and past, mortal and divine, Greek and Lydian, to reinforce a distinction between aristocrat and commoner; the latter did the opposite. Each was probably guilty of disgusting and polluting behavior in the eyes of the other. Elitist poetry was the oppositional literature of an *immanent elite,* an imagined community evoked in the interstices of the polis world—at interstate games, in the arrival of a *xenos* from a different city, or behind the closed doors of the symposium.[76]

It was opposed on all counts by beliefs that made the polis the center of the world, but that we can only see through the poetry of aristocrats who accepted it. The voices of ordinary citizens like Archilochus' Charon might express the middling ideology even more vigorously. But even as it is, we see a spectrum of opinions among the upper classes. The middle was malleable, just as "equality" and "freedom" would be in classical times. For instance, Solon and Theognis agreed that the combination of hubristic rich and desperate poor led to tyranny, but in Theognis this verged on antagonism toward the *dēmos.* "Drive the empty-headed vulgar herd with kicks," he said; "jab them with sharp goads and put a galling yoke on their neck; you will not find, among all the men the sun looks down upon, a people that loves a master more than this one" (847–50).[77]

This flexibility allowed some upper-class Greeks to accept the community of middling citizens as the source of legitimate authority, while still monopolizing political decision-making as the subcommunity of the wise. The middle was put into action in different ways in different poleis and at different times, even if the convention-bound, Panhellenic poetry does not allow us to document this.

VII. The Emergence of Democracy

The middling tradition goes back to the eighth century, over a wide area of Greece.[78] It contained some of the key elements of the Strong Principle of Equality, but democratic institutions only emerged in the late sixth century. Herodotus mentions several experiments with popular rule around the time of Cleisthenes' reforms. About a generation earlier, Demonax of Mantineia came to Cyrene in a dynastic crisis. He divided the citizens into new tribes, set aside some land and offices for the kings, and "gave all the other things which the kings had formerly held into the midst of the people" (*es meson tōi dēmōi*: 4.161). It is hard to know exactly what Herodotus meant, or if the story is true, but he used similar language in three more passages. In 522, he says, Maiandrios wished to lay aside his tyranny over Samos. He set up a shrine of Zeus as God of Freedom and offered *isonomia,* "equality before the law," to the people (3.142). In the best-known but least plausible tale, Herodotus claims that in the very next year, the Persian noble Otanes proposed that the whole empire should be a democracy (3.80). All these plans fell through, but Herodotus mentions in passing that in 499 certain rich men were thrown out of Naxos by the *dēmos* (5.30), and that at some time around 500 Cadmus, tyrant of Cos, inspired by his sense of justice (*dikaiosynē*), "gave his rule into the midst of the Koans" (*es meson Kōoisi:* 7.164), and moved to Sicily. He probably felt comfortable there: in 491, the Syracusan demos expelled their notables and set up their own democracy (7.155). Herodotus knew that not everyone believed his story about Otanes, so he bolstered it by emphasizing that in 492 the Persians had set up democracies all through Ionia (6.43).[79]

All these stories have well-known problems, and none can be pressed too hard,[80] but their chronological clustering is nevertheless striking. They suggest a broad trend toward granting political powers to the *dēmos* between 525 and 490. At Athens democracy was established in a violent rejection of all authority external to the polis itself, as Hippias' base in the club of tyrants and Isagoras' in Sparta were denied in favor of Cleisthenes' total commitment to the citizenry.[81] Changes in poetry and archaeology suggest that this was part of a widespread development in the last decades of the sixth century, and that with the collapse of the elitist ideology democracy became a possibility.

Around 520, aristocrats started commissioning odes in honor of returning athletic victors, to be performed by a chorus in the home city.[82] This poetry brought the victor's glory back to the community. It was an old idea: Crotty observes that in Homer "it is only by rejoining his fellows that the warrior can receive their acknowledgement and honor." The heroes had worried about what "someone" (*tis*) from the people might say, but the new epinician odes go much further, offering to incorporate everyone in the polis into a single song. The praise of other nobles was now not enough, even for such diehards as the dynasts of Thessaly. There was a crisis of praising.[83]

A group of professional poets emerged, arguing that ordinary citizens' praise was shapeless and therefore futile. It was easily misdirected, being no better than gossip. The poets' technical virtuosity, verging on incomprehensibility, marked their words as standing outside ordinary speech. They presented themselves as a neutral group, mediating between mass and elite, turning aside ordinary men's envy of those who were more successful. Pindar could describe himself at one moment as the guest-friend of Sogenes of Aegina (*Nem.* 7.61–65), and at another as an ordinary citizen (*Pyth.* 2.13), identifying with each group as the need arose.[84]

Epinician poets embraced the image of the middling citizen. Pindar agreed that the "middle rank" (*ta mesa*) had the most enduring prosperity (*Pyth.* 11.52–53), heaping praise on those who pursued the *metron.* For Bacchylides, whoever had his health and lived off his own estate rivaled "the first men" (*Ode* 1.165–68).[85] But they did not simply continue the middling tradition. They envisaged an elite distinguished from ordinary citizens by more than just greater wisdom and moderation. Pindar baldly asserted that "the piloting of poleis is passed from father to son, in the hands of the nobles" (*Pyth.* 10.71–72). Pindar divided the world into gods, extraordinary men, and ordinary men. For him, as Most puts it, "the gods are superior in that they always possess felicity, the extraordinary men in that they have, at least on one occasion and if only briefly, attained felicity." But this was not the bold elite of Sappho and Alcman. Those who won in the games attained special links with the gods and heroes (Heracles had set up and won the first Olympics), but their victories were mainly *megaloprepeia.* The elite's spending and efforts were not just for themselves or their class but were "in the common interest" (Pindar, *Pyth.* 9.93), obliging all citizens to repay it with *charis,* "gratitude," which the poet converted into praise.[86]

Like the men in Xenophanes' ideal symposia, Pindar's extraordinary men were wise enough to be pious. But Pindar also believed that in return for piety the gods granted them favor, which translated into wealth, to be spent on the games. Their wealth then became "a conspicuous star, truest light for a man" (Pindar, *Ol.* 2.55–56), illuminating the whole city. The only alternative to this public spending was to hoard wealth in the darkness, hiding the family's fame. Pindar's universe simply had no room for the Sapphic manipulation of luxury.[87]

Pindar described the nobleman with his golden cups in similar terms to the gods on Olympus, but the poets agreed that an unbridgeable gulf separated mortals from the divine. "One is the race of men, one is the race of gods," explains Pindar, "and from one mother do we both draw our breath; but a wholly sundered power has divided us, so that the one is nothing, while for the other, brazen Heaven remains secure for ever" (*Nem.* 6.1–4).[88] Aristocrats were cut off from the East just as brutally. Persia had crushed Lydia in 546, and the epinician Lydia was little more than a source of music. Luxury continued to be associated with the East, but by the time of Aeschylus' *Persians* in 472 this was entirely negative: luxury, softness, and hubris explained the Persian defeats in 490–479. It was much harder to draw on the East as a source of legitimacy after this, but the meager evidence does not allow us to say whether these changes were already underway before 500.[89]

Shorn of external sources of authority, aristocrats had to fall back on themselves and their poleis. The only alternative was to retreat to the mystery cults that flourished at this time, but as Detienne points out, "the priests and the initiates lived on the [social] margins of the city, and aspired only to a completely interior transformation." And even when transformed, the priest claimed only an inner superiority over ordinary men, rather than domination, as the archaic elitists had done.[90] For those who wished to stay in the mainstream, essentialist definitions of the aristocrat no longer held good. For Simonides there could be no "all-blameless man . . . built four-square, without blame, in hand, foot, and mind" (fr. 542.24, 2–3). The best a man could hope for was to avoid doing anything disgraceful, and to be mindful of civic justice (542.27–29, 34–35). Not without cause does Gentili speak of "Simonides' deconsecration of aristocratic values," or Detienne of his demotion of *alēthea* in favor of *doxa*. Virtue became a relative matter, defined from the point of view of the polis. Simonides summed his view up in an elegiac fragment: "It is the polis that teaches the man" (fr. 15 West).[91]

The major exception perhaps proves the rule. In *Ode* 3.17–66, Bacchylides says that Hieron, tyrant of Syracuse, gave more gold to Apollo than anyone except Croesus of Lydia, and that both men had special divine favor. Burnett points out that the peculiarity of Hieron's triumph—"the victor did not drive his own team or even train his own horses, but simply paid the bills"—made the praise of his wealth most appropriate, but there is more to it.[92] Gelon had begun the Syracusan generosity to Delphi and Olympia. Herodotus (7.158–62) says that Gelon had been willing to help against Persia in 480, but only if he were made commander. His dedications perhaps continued his claims to hegemony, representing Himera as equivalent to Salamis and Plataea in preserving the freedom of the Greeks. Hieron went further, blending ritual and architecture to justify an expansionist kingship unlike anything in old Greece.[93] Likening Hieron to Croesus, as an ambitious ruler on the edge of the Greek world, with a special relationship to Apollo because of his gifts to Olympia and Delphi, fitted very well with the tyrant's program. But Bacchylides immediately undermined this message. Croesus stood for wealth and piety, but also for lack of moderation. Apollo had not saved Lydia, and Croesus despaired of the gods' *charis*, unwilling to wait any longer (3.38). Bacchylides' Apollo points out that nothing can be foreseen. Men should be cheerful, because pious deeds (*hosia*)—apparently, *any* pious deeds—bring the highest gains. "I sing clearly for the wise," explains Bacchylides (3.85). This is *ainos* poetry, giving the audience of the wise a story that ought to be chilling for a tyrant: the gods respect piety, regardless of wealth, and there is no guarantee that they will preserve the domain of any king if he forgets proper measure. McGlew concludes that "epinician seems to question, even as it proclaims, the happiness of the poet's tyrant-patron."[94]

The emergence of Athenian tragedy around 500 was part of this Panhellenic trend. The tragedians' confrontations between heroic individuals and civic-minded choruses parallel developments in non-Athenian epinician, although the tragedians found different resolutions; and the list of awards for the best tragedy is dominated by citizens of other states down to the 470s.[95] But the Panhellenic scale of changes is clearest in archaeology. Spending on aristocratic display, particularly burials, had increased slowly in many places in the sixth century, but everywhere this declined abruptly c. 500. Until about 425 burials were normally very simple, with few grave goods and no monuments. Fifth-century houses tended to be larger than those of the sixth century, but, so far as we can tell from excavation, there were hardly any differences in size and decoration between the houses at any site before the end of the fifth century. The literary sources also say that aristocrats gave up expensive clothes, fancy hair-styles, and jewelry. So little precious plate is known that some archaeologists suggest none was made during the fifth century. By 500, aristocratic efforts to differentiate themselves from other citizens in their rituals were declining. Votive offerings also declined, and the few spectacular offerings, like the temples themselves, were now normally made by the state.[96]

Dahl's Principle of Equal Consideration requires that all members of a group should agree that they are about equally well qualified to participate in making its decisions. The middling ideology was such a belief and had been important since the eighth century; but at the end of the sixth century, all viable alternatives collapsed. No doubt many nobles, whether in Thebes, Aegina, or Athens, continued to believe that they were special beings, but they increasingly conceded that they needed to be judged not just by their peers, but also by the citizens of their home communities. Many of them must also have continued to believe that aristocratic government should guide the people, just as praise and blame should be channeled through professional poets. The collapse of faith in external sources of legitimation and the establishment of the Strong Principle of Equality did not automatically produce democracy, but it made democracy a possibility. Aristocrats had to make their way within a community of men who were, after all, about equally well qualified to participate in the decisions of the group.

VIII. CONCLUSION

In this paper I have tried to trace, within the archaic period, a set of ideological shifts that made Greek democracy a possibility. I have argued that the eighth century was in many ways the crucial moment. In this obscure period the polis was established as a community of *mesoi,* founded on something like what Dahl calls the Principle of Equal Consideration of Interests. *To meson* was not a class but an ideological construct, allowing *all* citizens to locate themselves in the middle. Like any construct, it was open to reinterpretation: I have suggested that Theognis appropriated it for the upper class more than he assimilated a "moderate" elite to the mass of citizens the way that Hesiod, Xenophanes, Solon, or Phocylides did. Nevertheless, I believe that it is wrong to imagine a slow evolution across the archaic period from royal to aristocratic to hoplite to thetic power. From the earliest sources, "the middle" includes all citizens: in Walzer's terms the "one good thing" was citizen birth. To call a man rich or poor, to deny his middling status, was to cast him out of the ideal polis.

But some aristocrats happily cast themselves out, forming alternative fellowships outside (and in their view above) the polis. They wanted to be a privileged supra-polis elite, dining and loving with the gods, heroes, and Lydians. The only problem was that many of their fellow citizens refused to recognize their superiority, preferring instead to mock them, and on occasion to kill them. But by 500 B.C. the elitist ideology was in disarray: powerless in the face of growing citizen confidence, aristocrats everywhere conceded the second proposition in Dahl's Strong Principle of Equality, that no external source of authority made them so much better qualified than other citizens that they alone should automatically be entrusted with making the collective and binding decisions.

But it required more to make a democracy. Many *poleis* entrusted themselves to the guardianship of oligarchies throughout the classical period. On the whole, it seems that democracy was only tried out when a military crisis raised the stakes and made it impossible for the guardians to claim to represent the middle. In the seventh century, the obvious response had been to find a new, better set of guardians; by the end of the sixth, it could seem sensible to do away with guardians altogether, and to find some method for the citizens to make their decisions directly.

There were many ways to do this. Democracy cannot be defined solely by a decision-making assembly. It was also possible to allow smaller bodies, such as a *boulē* (council) or a tribal assembly, to make some decisions.[97] Democracy is not something that a community either has or does not have: it consists of bundles of attitudes and institutions, and we should perhaps range the poleis along an imaginary spectrum. Some constitutions allowed citizens to make more of the binding decisions than did others, and the roles of elected representatives and other officeholders varied. Different states extended democracy into different spaces and allowed different kinds of assemblies to make the decisions. Each city-state moved around on this spectrum according to the outcome of local struggles, such as those in Athens in 510–507, 462, and 411–399.

Perhaps the best reason to seek the origins of Greek democracy is to understand its limitations. It took to an extreme the idea of a community of middling men but remained, in Dahl's terms, a guardianship of citizens over women, children, aliens, and slaves; in Held's, a "democracy of patriarchs"; and in Walzer's, "not communal freedom but oppression . . . Indeed, the rule of citizens over non-citizens, members over strangers, is probably the most common form of tyranny in human history."[98] But recognizing this does not require us to reject the significance of the Greek experience. Finley rightly stressed that "moral condemnation, no matter how well-founded, is no substitute for historical or social analysis. 'Rule by the few' or 'rule by the many' was a meaningful choice, the freedom and rights that the factions claimed for themselves were worth fighting for, despite the fact that even 'the many' were a minority of the whole population."[99] These archaic origins are important, not because Greek democracy ushered in a utopia or because it began an historical trajectory leading directly to us, but because it was *different*. Wealth justified dominance over a mass of subjects in many ancient states, but the Greeks—perhaps for the first time in history—substituted for it birth within a broad male citizen body, creating new inclusions and possibilities, and new exclusions and oppressions. The consequence of this was the Strong Principle of Equality; the consequence of that, Greek democracy.

Acknowledgements

I wrote most of this paper in spring 1993, when I had the honor of being a Visiting Fellow at the Institute for Research in the Humanities at the University of Wisconsin-Madison. I would like to thank the Director and Fellows of the Institute and the University of Chicago for their generous support, and the members of the Institute and the Classics Department at Madison for their company and stimulation. Special thanks go to Charles Hedrick and Josh Ober for inviting me to the Democracy Ancient and Modern conference; the process of writing my original paper and thinking about the questions raised at the conference led me to rethink my research project, and the final version of this paper sums up ideas I am exploring in more detail in a new book, *Darkness and Heroes*. Joseph Bryant, Paul Cartledge, Carol Dougherty, Kenneth Dover, Brien Garnand, Leslie Kurke, Hilary Mackie, Lisa Maurizio, Greg Nagy, Martin Ostwald, Kurt Raaflaub, Anthony Snodgrass, Hans van Wees, and James Whitley have all read and provided valuable comments on earlier drafts of this paper, but none of them, of course, is responsible for what I have done with their advice.

Notes

1. Unless otherwise indicated, I cite the fragments of the early Greek poets from the following editions (full documentation is in the Bibliography of this volume):
Aeschylus fragments: Smyth, *Aeschylus* II.
Alcaeus, Sappho: Lobel and Page, *Poetarum Lesbiorum Fragmenta.*
Alcman, Anacreon, Simonides, Stesichorus: Page, *Poetae Melici Graeci.*
Archilochus, Callinus, Hipponax, Mimnermus, Semonides, Simonides (elegiac fragments), Solon, Tyrtaeus: West, *Iambi et Elegi Graeci.*
Bacchylides: Snell and Maehler, *Bacchylidis, Carmina cum Fragmentis.*
Hesiod fragments: Merkelbach and West, *Fragmenta Hesiodea.*
Pindar fragments: Maehler, *Pindari, Carmina cum Fragmentis.*
Xenophanes: Diels and Kranz, *Die Fragmente der Vorsokratiker.*

2. Ober, *Mass and Elite,* 36–38; Hansen, *Athenian Democracy,* 19–22; and Bleicken, *Athenische Demokratie,* 9, justify differing versions of this approach.

3. Particularly Giddens, *Central Problems.*

4. Most books review developments from Solon to Cleisthenes (e.g., Meier, *Discovery,* 29–52; Bleicken, *Athenische Demokratie,* 13–169; Ober, *Mass and Elite,* 55–75; Hansen, *Athenian Democracy,* 27–36), but very few make historical explanation of archaic social dynamics a key issue in their undertandings of democracy (Manville, *Origins,* is a notable exception).

5. Hansen, *Athenian Democracy,* 320; cf. 71–72, 319.

6. Dahl, *Democracy,* 30–31, 98.

7. Ibid., 55, 85–86, 167.

8. Morris, *Darkness and Heroes.*

9. Stein-Hölkeskamp, *Adelskultur,* 86–138, is an important recent exception, providing a more nuanced account of aristocratic ideology in Theognis.

10. Abercrombie et al., *Dominant Ideology Thesis; Dominant Ideologies.*

11. Foucault, *Language,* 139–64; Chartier, *Cultural Origins,* 7.

12. Whitman, *Democratic Vistas,* 343.

13. For these features see Aesch. 1.42; 3.11, 218; Dem. 21.183; 29.24; 54.15, 17; Din. 2.8; Hyp. 4.21; Isoc. 7.40; Lys. fr. 73; see Ober, *Mass and Elite,* 257–59, 297–99. *Philia:* Arist. *Eth. Nic.* 1157b35, 1158b11–1159a5, 1171b32–1172a8, with Sahlins, *Economics,* 193–230. On the varied senses of "middle class," see Giddens, *Class Structure,* 30–32, 42–45, 61–64, 177–97. In favor of a hoplite middle class, see Spahn, *Mittelschicht,* 70–83, 174–78; Meier, *Discovery,* 29–52; on the hoplite as a model, Loraux, *Invention,* 34, 37, 98, 151; and on hoplite values, Hanson, *Western Way of War,* passim. Hanson, this volume, offers a sophisticated combination of these models.

14. Hedrick, "Zero degree," 292–93.

15. Quotations from Winkler, *Constraints,* 45–46; Fisher, *Hybris,* 1, 493.

16. Quotations from Halperin, *Homosexuality,* 99, 103. Cf. Loraux, *Children,* 16–17. Suspension of disbelief: Ober, *Mass and Elite,* 152–55. Shares: Ostwald, this volume.

17. Rae, *Equalities,* 55–59; Mulhall and Swift, *Liberals,* 59–63; Harvey, "Two Kinds."

18. Sen, *Inequality,* 15; cf. Nagel, *Equality,* 63–74; Cartledge, this volume.

19. Walzer, *Spheres,* 11.

20. Bourdieu, *Distinction,* 24. Cf. Thuc. 2.42.3; Plato *Men.* 234C; Dion. Hal. *Rom. Ant.* 5.17.5–6. Loraux, *Invention,* 99–103, 153, 171, sees this essentialism as evidence for the subversion of democratic values by aristocratic, but cf. Ober, *Mass and Elite,* 262, 290.

21. Hansen, *Athenian Democracy,* 83–85; Kerferd, "Equality," 14. Link, *Landverteilung,* discusses *stasis* and redistribution in archaic Greece; Gehrke, *Stasis,* in classical Greece.

22. In this section I summarize very briefly the arguments of Morris, *Darkness and Heroes,* chs. 5–8.

23. Morris, *Burial; Darkness and Heroes,* chs. 5–7; Whitley, *Style and Society,* 116–62, 181–83, 191–94.

24. Sanctuaries: Coldstream, *Geometric Greece,* 317–40, de Polignac, *Naissance;* and recent finds in Mazarakis-Ainian, *Rulers' Dwellings;* and Hägg et al., *Cult Practice.*

25. Snodgrass, *Archaic Greece,* 52–63, 99–100; "Economics."

26. Whitley, "Diversity;" Morris, *Darkness and Heroes,* ch. 5.

27. Morris, *Burial,* 205–10; *Darkness and Heroes,* ch. 8.

28. Nagy, *Mythology,* 48n.40.

29. Nagy, *Pindar's Homer,* 52–115, 174–98, 418–37; "Questions," 38–41. Nagy emphasizes broad evolutionary forces rather than individual rhapsodes, as I do here.

30. Chronology: Theog. 773–82, 891–94, 1103–4. Attributions, Theog. 145–48, 153–54, 227–32, 315–18, 719–28, 793–96, 1003–6, 1017–22, 1253–54. See Nagy, "Theognis," 51, but cf. West, *Studies,* 40–61. Anacreon: Rosenmeyer, *Imitation.*

31. Quotation: Miralles and Pòrtulas, *Archilochus,* 22. The names have often been discussed. See, e.g., West, *Studies,* 25–29; Burnett, *Archaic Poets,* 15–32; Nagy, *Achaeans,* 243–52; *Pindar's Homer,* 430–32.

32. Hobsbawm and Ranger, *Invention of Tradition;* Herzfeld, *Place in History,* 205.

33. Pittacus: Alc. frs. 67.4, 75.12, 106.3, 129.21, 348.1, cf. Diog. Laert. 1.81; Kurke, "Crisis," 69–75, 83–92. On the historicity of these charges, see, e.g., Page, *Sappho and Alcaeus,* 169–79; Kirkwood, *Monody,* 67–76. Compromises: Dover, "Archilochus," 199–212; Rosen, "Hipponax." Demosthenes: Ober, *Mass and Elite,* 268–79.

34. Mazzarino, *Occidente,* 191–246; Kurke, "Politics." On forms see West, *Metre,* 29–56. The choral/monodic distinction makes little difference to cultural assumptions (Davies, "Monody"). Choral context: Burnett, *Bacchylides,* 5–14. Monodic: Kirkwood, *Monody,* 1–19.

35. Cf. frs. 95, 96, 98. His "biography" is similarly ambivalent: the *Anth. Pal.* (7.18, 19, 709) calls him Lydian as well as Spartan, but the *Suda* says he was descended from slaves.

36. Alc. fr. 347; Hes., *Op.* 582–96. See Burnett, *Three Archaic Poets,* 132–34; Petropulos, *Heat and Lust.*

37. Bourdieu, *Distinction,* 40, 47–50, 88, 92–93.

38. Family: 376–80, 695–705. Bulls: 436–37. Slave: 405–6 (unless *ktētēn* is interpolated: West, *Works and Days,* 260). Laborer: 602–3. *Dmōes:* 470, 502, 559–60, 573, 597, 607–8. Women: *Op.* 58–92, 519–25, 695–705, 753–55; *Th.* 570–612. Work: *Op.* 303–14, 381–82. Begging: *Op.* 397–400. Cf. Ober, *Mass and Elite,* 220–21.

39. *Op.* 23–24, 343–45, 349–51, 370–72, 706–14. Neighbors: Alc. fr. 123; Theog. 302; Anac. fr. 354; Pindar *Nem.* 7.87–89. Fourth century: Cohen, *Law,* 85–90.

40. *Op.* 717–18; *Th.* 26–28, with Svenbro, *Parole,* 50–59; Nagy, *Mythology,* 274–75.

41. *Basilēes: Op.* 38–39, 202–12, 263–64; *Th.* 79–93. Respect, Shame, and hubris: *Op.* 174–201, 213–18, 225–64, with Fisher, *Hybris,* 185–200, 213–16.

42. Martin, "Hesiod, Odysseus"; Kurke, "Sixth *Pythian*," 104–07.

43. Griffith, "Personality"; Lamberton, *Hesiod,* 1–37; Nagy, *Mythology,* 36–82; Martin, "Metanastic Poetics," 12–16. Cf. Zeitlin, "Thebes," and Dougherty, this volume, on Delphi.

44. Detienne, *Maîtres,* 34–50, 68–78, emphasizing *Th.* 27–28.

45. Nagy, *Mythology,* 67. Exterior insider: Martin, "Metanastic Poetics," 14.

46. Szegedy-Maszak, "Legends"; Nagy, "Theognis," 31–32.

47. Ostwald, *Nomos,* 55. Arch. fr. 232 has a tantalizing reference to someone "learning the Cretan *nomoi,*" apparently said in mockery.

48. Parallels: West, *Theogony,* 40–48; *Works and Days,* 3–15; Walcot, *Near East;* Millett, "Hesiod," 93–106. The Ptolemaic *Instructions of 'Onqsheshonquy* has still more striking parallels with the *Op.,* and Walcot, "Instructions," suggests that it imitated Hesiod. However, it is in any case more hierarchical than the *Op.* (e.g., 7.12–15; 8.11; 17.17, 25; 18.7–8, 12). The Egyptian texts are translated by Pritchard, *Texts,* 407–10, 421–25, and Lichtheim, *Literature* I, 169–84; II, 146–63; III, 159–84.

49. Nagy, *Mythology,* 9–17.

50. Ibid., 270. Audience: Walsh, *Varieties,* 22–36; Nagy, "Theognis," 22–27.

51. See Xenoph. fr. 1, and Archil. fr. 124b; Xenoph. fr. 22; Theog. 469–98, 503–10, 837–44; Phoc. fr. 11; cf. Anac. fr. 356.

52. Loraux, "Solon au milieu," makes a series of excellent points about the theme of the middle in Solon's poetry.

53. Cf. Solon, fr. 5, 24.1–4; Theog. 219–20, 331–32, 401–6, 543–46, 693–94, 719–28 (= Solon fr. 24); North, *Sophrosyne,* 12–18. Moderate wealth: Phoc. fr. 7. Women: Phoc. fr. 3; Theog. 457–60; Semon. frs. 6, 7, with Loraux, *Children,* 72–110. Constraints of poverty: Theog. 173–82, 383–98, 649–52, 1062. All despise the poor: Theog. 267–70, 621–22, 699–718, 927–30; cf. Alc. fr. 360. Belly: Archil. fr. 124b; Hipp. fr. 128, with West, *Studies,* 148.

54. No limits on wealth: Solon fr. 13.71–76 = Theog. 227–32; unrighteous gain, Solon frs. 4.5–6; 13.7–11; Theog. 145–48, 465–66, 753–56. On hubris, cf. Theog. 603–4, 731–52, 833–36, 1103–04; and Archil. fr. 45, "hanging their heads they spewed up their hubris." Even if this refers to the suicide of the Lycambids (contra, West, *Studies,* 125), it is also a general comment on destructive hubris. See Fisher, *Hybris,* 201–16.

55. Morris, "Use and Abuse," 115–29. As Nagy observes ("Questions," 52), this is not inconsistent with an evolutionary model. Quotation from Fisher, *Hybris,* 176. For the other views cited, see Donlan, *Aristocratic Ideal,* 20–23; Rose, *Sons of the Gods,* 43–140; Thalmann, "Thersites"; Thornton, *Homer's Iliad,* 144–47.

56. Antonaccio, *Archaeology of Ancestors,* presents the evidence in detail, and the extensive modern literature. I set out my own views in Morris, "Tomb Cult" and develop them further in *Darkness and Heroes,* ch. 6. Helen: Hes. fr. 358; Stes. fr. 192, with Sisti, "Palinodie," 307–8; cf. Hdt. 2.112–20. Lord, *Singer,* 194, believed that there was such variety that a version of the *Iliad* existed in which the embassy in book 9 was successful.

57. Hes. *Op.* 26, 654–59; *Th.* 22–35, with Walsh, *Varieties,* 26–33. Ford, *Homer,* 92.

58. The issues remain controversial; Snodgrass, "Hoplite Reform," and van Wees, "Homeric Way of War," are the most recent discussions.

59. See Burnett, *Archaic Poets,* 123–26. Page (*Sappho and Alcaeus,* 222) makes the important point that the terminology used for these heroic arms is very like that which Herodotus (1.34) uses for Lydian armor, suggesting the kind of heroic-oriental link that I discuss below.

60. Quotation from Gentili, *Poetry,* 83–84. Delicacy: Sappho frs. 2.14; 30.4–5; 44.8–10; 46; 81; 92; 94.12–22; 98; 192; Alcm. frs. 1.64–68; 3.77; 56.3; 91; 117; Alc. fr. 130B.17–20; Anac. frs. 388.10–12; 481; Kurke, "Politics," 93–99. Divine luxury: Sappho frs. 1.7–8; 2; 33; 54; 96.27–28; 103.6, 13; 123; 127. Sappho and Aphrodite: Nagy, *Mythology,* 223–62. Burnett, *Archaic Poets,* 243–76 and 161, suggests that Alcaeus "stands in an almost priestly relation" to Zeus, Hera, and Dionysus in fr. 129. Sappho explicitly associates luxury with the heroic age in fr. 44.5–10.

61. C. Morgan, *Athletes,* 45.

62. Catling, "Workshop and Heirloom"; Matthäus, "Heirloom or Tradition?" Tin content: Filippakis et al., "Bronzes." Imports: Snodgrass, *Archaic Greece,* 105–6; Kilian-Dirlmeier, "Weihungen"; Muscarella, "Cauldrons."

63. Bolton, *Aristeas,* 134–41, 179–81. Hdt. 4.13–16 fully believed these stories. Religious borrowings: Burkert, *Revolution;* Carter, "Masks," 91, with de Polignac, "Influence," 114–17.

64. Murray, "Symposion." Koukounaries: Schilardi, "Paro," 247; Grave markers: Boardman, "Differentiation"; Catling and Lemos, *Lefkandi* II.1, 25–26. Knossos: Coldstream, "Gift Exchange," 204–6.

65. Lydian luxury: Sappho frs. 16. 17–20; 39; 96.7–8; 98a.10–11; 132.3; Alcm. frs. 1.64–65; 13c; 16. Cf. Alc. frs. 49.5; 69.1–6; Anac. fr. 481; eleg. 3; Alcm. fr. 13d. Symposia: Fehr, *Gelage;* Dentzer, *Banquet;* Boardman, "Furniture."

66. Cf. Curtin, *Trade;* Appadurai, "Introduction."

67. Kyrieleis, "Babylonische Bronzen," argues that in fact most of the Oriental imports in Greek sanctuaries were given by Eastern kings, while Strøm, "Evidence from the Sanctuaries," suggests that the priests organized trade with the Near East to guarantee themselves Eastern ritual paraphernalia. Neither theory accounts very well for either the imported finds or the imitations; I assume here that most of the objects were dedicated by users of the sanctuaries, primarily Greeks (Morris, *Darkness and Heroes,* ch. 6). Borell, *Schalen,* 93–96, and Markoe, *Bowls,* 121–22, have important comments on Eastern influences.

68. Burkert, *Orientalizing,* 16. Phoenicians: Shaw, "Phoenicians"; Negbi, "Presence," 607–9. Immigrants: Boardman, *Greeks Overseas,* 56–62. Protogeometric B: Coldstream, *Geometric Greece,* 68–70, 99–102. Differences from mainland: Markoe, *Bowls,* 82–83, 110–17; Morris, *Darkness and Heroes,* chs. 5–7.

69. Simon, "Votive Offerings," 4–165, 410–21; Philipp, "Archaische Gräber."

70. Murray, "Sympotic History," 7.

71. Boutros, *Phoenician Sport.* Interstate elite: Herman, *Friendship,* 118–65. Young, *Olympic Myth,* 107–70, argues that not all athletes were aristocrats, but also emphasizes the scale of rewards (pp. 115–33). Training: Poliakoff, *Combat Sports,* 11–19. Agonal society: Burckhardt, *Greek Culture,* 53–56, with Poliakoff, *Combat Sports,* 104–15. Athenian juries: Ober, *Mass and Elite,* 144. Renewing household: Kurke, *Traffic,* 15–62.

72. Rose, *Sons of the Gods,* 160. Phalanx: Call. fr. 1; Tyrt. frs. 10; 12; Theog. 1003–6.

73. Xenoph. frs. 10–16; 2. See also Arch. frs. 16; 130; Semon. fr. 1; Solon frs. 13.65–47; 16; Theog. 133–42, 155–60, 557–60, 585–90 (=Solon fr. 13.65–74), 1075–78; Xenoph. frs. 18; 34.

74. Fränkel, *Poetry,* 138.

75. See also frs. 32; 38; 42; 72.7; 79; 125.

76. Against athletes, in favor of more useful types: Tyrt. fr. 12.1–12; Xenoph. fr. 2; Solon, in Diod. 9.2.5. On aristocrats as outsiders, see Herman, *Ritualised Friendship;* Stein-Hölkeskamp, *Adelskultur,* 233; generally, Anderson, *Imagined Communities.*

77. Classical equality, freedom: Raaflaub, *Entdeckung,* 313–27; this volume. Rich, poor, and tyranny: Solon frs. 4.7–8, 23; 9.3–4; 33; 36.20–25; Theog. 39–52. On the *dēmos* see Donlan, "Changes," and on tyranny, McGlew, *Tyranny,* 87–123. Alcaeus and Solon both feared tyrants, but Pittacus had more in common with Solon than with Solon's tyrant: e.g., Simon. fr. 542.13; Diog. Laert. 1.77, 79; Arist. *Pol.* 1285a37–39; Strabo 13.2.3; Diod. 9.12.3. These are poor sources for a "historical" Pittacus but illustrate the negotiation of long-term traditions opposing luxury.

78. Indeed, as I argue in *Darkness and Heroes,* in certain ways it can be said to go back to the late eleventh century.

79. For further sources see Zimmermann, "Ansätze," with Ostwald, *Nomos,* 161–67. Sartoris, "Verfassung," and Berger, *Revolution,* 15–56, present the western evidence.

80. Hölkeskamp, "Demonax" is the most recent sceptical discussion, with references to others.

81. Ober, "Revolution."

82. The performance context is disputed. See K. Morgan, "Pindar."

83. Crotty, *Song and Action,* 109–10; de Jong, "Voice."

84. Professionalism: Nagy, *Pindar's Homer,* 188–90; Kurke, *Traffic,* 240–50; K. Morgan, "Pindar." Defining praise: Carson, "*Protagoras,*" 119–24. The power of gossip was an old theme, going back to the middling poets (e.g., Hes. *Op.* 701, 719–21; Archil. frs. 13, 14; Mimn. frs. 6 [=Theog. 793–800], 7, 15, 16; Phoc. fr. 6; Theog. 367–70), and continuing into the fourth century (Cohen, *Law,* 90–95; Hunter, *Policing Athens,* 96–119). Citizens' views: Pindar, *Ol.* 5.16; 7.89–90; 13.2–3; *Pyth.* 2.81–82; 4.295–97; 11.28–30; *Nem.* 7.65–67; 8.38–39; 11.17; *Isthm.* 1.50–51; 2.37–38; 3.1–3; fr. 109. Technique: Most, *Measures,* 23–24. Envy: Pindar *Ol.* 2.95; 11.7–8; *Pyth.* 2.89–92; 7.18–19; *Nem.* 8.21–23; *Isthm.* 2.43; Bacchyl. *Ode* 13.199–203, although cf. *Pyth.* 1.85. Kurke, *Traffic,* 86–90, 135–47, points out that by referring to *xeinoi* (e.g., *Ol.* 7.89–90; 13.3; *Pyth.* 3.69–71; *Isthm.* 1.50–51; 6.66–72) Pindar assures the victors of the existence of an elite community as well as incorporating them into the citizen community; and that when relating to a victor, even other aristocrats were "ordinary" men who might fall prey to *phthonos.* Cf. Goldhill, *Poet's Voice,* 130–32, 138–42.

85. Middle: Pindar, *Nem.* 11.47–48; *Isthm.* 6.66–72; *Paean* 1.2–5; 4.32–53. The belly theme appears at Pindar, *Isthm.* 1.49, and poverty at Pindar fr. 109; Bacchyl., *Ode* 1.168–71. Living justly, and in proportion: Pindar, *Pyth.* 2.86–88; 3.107–08; 5.14; 10.67–68; *Nem.* 7.87–89; cf. *Ol.* 7.90–92; *Pyth.* 4.284–285; 8.8–20; 11.54–56; *Nem.* 7.65–67; *Isthm.* 3.1–3; fr. 180.3; Bacchyl. *Ode* 13.44–45, against hubris.

86. Most, *Measures,* 75. Links with gods and heroes: Pindar *Ol.* 7.20–24; 10.16–19, 43–77, 102–5; *Pyth.* 4.253; 9.39–42; 10.1–3, 49–53; *Isthm.* 5.26–27; 6.19, with Nagy, *Pindar's Homer,* 116–56; Rose, *Sons of the Gods,* 160–62. *Megaloprepeia:* Kurke, *Traffic,* 163–224. Poem as recompense: Most, *Measures,* 72; Kurke, *Traffic,* 102, 116. Victory in the common interest: Pindar *Ol.* 5.4; 7.93–94; 9.19–22; *Nem.* 2.8; Bacchyl. *Ode* 6.15–16; 13.77–83. *Charis:* MacLachlan, *Age of Grace,* 87–123, again adapting a middling theme (ibid., 73–86), which continued into fourth-century Athens (Ober, *Mass and Elite,* 226–33).

87. Wise spending: Pindar *Ol.* 2.53–56; 5.23–24; *Pyth.* 2.56; 5.1–2, 14; 6.47. Hoarding: Pindar *Ol.,* 2.55–56; *Nem.* 1.31–33; *Isthm.* 1.67–68; 4.29; Bacchyl., *Ode* 3.13–14; Kurke, *Traffic,* 225–29; Most, *Measures,* 90–91.

88. Divine wealth: Pindar *Ol.* 6.39–40, 104–5; 8.51; 9.32–33. 13.65–66; *Pyth.* 1.1–2; 3.9–10, 89–90, 93–95; 4.53–54, 178; 5.9, 104; 9.6, 9, 56, 59, 109; *Nem.* 5.2–4; 6.37–38; 7.77–79; *Isthm.* 1.1; 2.1–2, 26; 4.60; 6.75; 8.6–7; *Paean* 6.1; frs. 29.1, 3; 30.1–2, 6; 75.14; 139.1, 9; 195; Bacchyl., *Ode* 9.1, 100; 11.4, 37–38, 49; 13.194–95; *Dith.* 3.34–36; 5.22; fr. 15.12; Simon. fr. 577b. Heroic wealth: Pindar *Ol.* 7.64; *Pyth.* 4.232; 10.40; *Nem.* 8.27; *Isthm.* 6.19; fr. 166.3; Bacchyl. *Dith.* 1.4. No achievement without the gods' help: Pindar *Ol.* 8.67; *Pyth.* 8.76–78; 12.29–30; *Nem.* 10.29–30; *Isthm.* 3.4–6; 5.52–53; Bacchyl. *Dith.* 3.117–118; fr. 24; Simon. fr. 526. Cannot equal the gods: Pindar *Ol.* 5.23–24; *Pyth.* 2.49–53, 88–89; 3.59–62; 10–21.29; *Nem.* 7.55–56; 11.13–16; *Isthm.* 3.17–18; 5.14–16; Bacchyl. *Ode* 5.94–96.

89. Lydia: Pindar *Ol.* 5.19; 14.17–18; *Nem.* 4.45; 8.15; fr. 125 Maehler; Bacchyl. fr. 14. Pindar *Nem.* 8.16–18 may be an exception, with Pindar offering Ajax a Lydian *mitra* (headband) decked with song, which is then linked with a mythical priest of Aphrodite. We can only speculate on what Aeschylus intended in fr. 29 (Smyth). Recent scholarship on the East as a mirror in which "Greekness" was constructed has perhaps exaggerated the role of the Persian Wars; in her excellent treatment, Hall (*Inventing the Bar-*

barian, 17–19) does not do justice to the archaic material, and Miller ("Parasol") shows that even after 479 a few Athenians continued to look to the East for legitimacy.

90. Detienne, *Maîtres,* 125, 137.

91. Gentili, *Poetry,* 63–71; Detienne, *Maîtres,* 105–19; Carson, "*Protagoras;*" Crotty, *Song and Action,* 33–40.

92. Burnett, *Bacchylides,* 66. See Carson, "Burners," 116–19, on 3.87.

93. Krumeich, "Dreifüsse;" Dougherty, *Poetics,* 83–102.

94. The uncertainty of life had been a popular middling theme (Archil. frs. 16, 130; Semon. fr. 1; Solon frs. 13.65–74 [=Theog. 585–90]; 16; Theog. 133–42, 155–60, 557–60, 1075–78) and was also used in Pindar *Ol.* 7.24–26; 12.10–12; *Pyth.* 3.103–6; 8.92–97; 10.63; 11.42–46; *Isthm.* 3.17–18; 4.5–6; Simon. fr. 521. McGlew, *Tyranny,* 49, although his overall argument (35–51) is rather different from mine.

95. Vernant and Vidal-Naquet, *Myth and Tragedy,* 23–48.

96. Morris, *Death-Ritual,* 118–29, 145, 151–53. Housing: Hoepfner and Schwandner, *Haus und Stadt,* 1–26, 256–67; Hoepfner, "Architekturforschung." Votives: Snodgrass, "Economics."

97. See Ruzé, "*Plethos*"; "Tribus"; Sealey, *Republic,* 91–98; Dahl, *Democracy,* 135–52.

98. Dahl, *Democracy,* 96, 97; Held, *Models,* 23; Walzer, *Spheres,* 62.

99. Finley, *Politics,* 9.

SHARES AND RIGHTS: "CITIZENSHIP" GREEK STYLE AND AMERICAN STYLE

MARTIN OSTWALD

THE CELEBRATION of the anniversaries of three revolutionary events that have shaped the social and political outlook of our world affords a welcome excuse to take a close look at some of the assumptions on which our social and political system is based. Two of these events mark the triumph over an internal tyrannical regime: the reforms of Cleisthenes of about 508 B.C., which laid the groundwork for Athenian democracy, and the *Déclaration des droits de l'homme et du citoyen,* adopted by the French Assembly in 1789. The American Declaration of Independence of 1776, followed in 1789 by the Constitution of the United States and two years later by the Bill of Rights, constitutes the liberation from an oppressive external colonial rule. What can these three events teach us in an age that is trying to find multicultural values beyond those of the Western world? I believe that the multiculturalism we seek is best approached through exploring the multiculturalism that is already part of our tradition, and I propose to deal with one of its features in this paper.

Citizenship, as the late Charles Norris Cochrane observed, is one of the two fundamental concepts that Hellenism bequeathed to Western civilization.[1] But concepts of citizenship also differentiate basic American attitudes so fundamentally from those of the ancient Greeks that a comparison of the two will, I hope, lead to a deeper understanding of the foundations on which our own social and political culture rests as well as of the structure we have erected on those foundations.

My primary purpose here is not to explore certain formal or legal requirements of citizenship in ancient Greece and the United States, respectively, and then compare one with the other. I propose, rather, to treat citizenship as reflecting different sets of social values, which can be dubbed "individualistic" on the American side and "communal" on the Greek. I hope to show that what Americans tend to see in terms of the "rights" of the individual, the Greeks tended to see in the more comprehensive context of sharing in and being part of a community on which the individual depends for his or her sense of identity.

There are pitfalls along the way: while my aim is to compare basic assumptions underlying views of citizenship in two different cultures, citizenship itself is not an unchanging unitary concept, frozen within each of the two cultures that concern us here; on the Greek side there is the difficulty of trying to derive one general notion of "citizenship" from the multiplicity of Greek city-states over the many centuries of their development; on the American side, there are problems of growth and shifts of meaning of what constitutes a "citizen" even within the short span of American history: to be a "citizen" did not mean the same in 1775 as it meant in 1777; it did not mean the same before as after Reconstruction, or before and after the Civil Rights legislation of the 1960s.[2] And yet I believe that within each culture certain basic values did not change: on the Greek side, Aristotle, one of the greatest social theorists of all time, managed to distill in his *Politics* social and political beliefs and principles that can be accepted as characterizing all Greek states at most stages in their development, and that will, therefore, give us a valid insight into a general Greek view of citizenship. There is no comparable theoretical work on the American side; but an examination of great public documents such as the Declaration of Independence and the Fourteenth Amendment reveals a striking consistency in the delineation of what characterizes a person as a citizen, that is, as a person acknowledged by the community as its member. This makes it possible to recognize salient differences among the many similarities between Greek and American political culture. We are helped by the fact that "equality" and "freedom" (or "liberty")[3] are key words in defining the society and the individual who is part of it in both Aristotle's *Politics* and in the American documents; if this indicates a close relation of modern political principles with those of the ancients, an examination of the differences between Greek and American *equality* and Greek and American *freedom* will reveal to us two dissimilar kinds of social perspective that are equally part of the foundations of Western culture.

The Declaration of Independence does not speak of citizenship, but it lays the groundwork for it in proclaiming as a self-evident truth "that all Men are created equal, that they are endowed by their Creator with certain unalienable Rights, that among these are Life, Liberty, and the Pursuit of Happiness" and "that to secure these Rights, Governments are instituted among Men." What is revolutionary about this is, first, that it applies ideas generated by the English Enlightenment[4] to give moral impetus and support to the political measures that brought about the American Revolution. Second, in doing so it justifies the institution of government on the grounds that government secures and guarantees as rights for each individual certain gifts granted equally to every Man[5] by whoever created him or her—be it God or nature or none of the above. With the benefit of hindsight, we know that some crucial terms in the Declaration were left for later generations to define, or rather refine, in a principled way,[6] especially as it became necessary to translate its general moral principles into legal principles: the question whether slaves and women are to be included among "all Men"; the question of what is meant by *happiness* and what are the parameters within which an individual is free to pursue it, and so forth. Important though these later developments are, they are less germane to the issue under consideration than the more fundamental article of faith here enunciated, namely that the individual, insignificant though he or she may be, has the right to assert his/her share of life, liberty, and the pursuit of happiness even against the powers of the state, and that the state, in its turn, is powerless to deprive him/her of these rights. We shall look in vain for any Greek text before or after Aristotle for a similar recognition of individual rights.

The Declaration of Independence predicates these rights as self-evident truths applicable to all, that is, even those over whom our Founding Fathers had no political authority. It does not speak of "citizens," because the regulation of citizenship was in 1776 a matter for each state to decide. In other words, it is a statement of general principles that, at the time, were moral but not legal, because they could not be enforced by a court of law.

It is the Fourteenth Amendment to the Constitution, ratified on July 28, 1868, as part and parcel of the Reconstruction, that legally confirmed the end of a process that had transformed a moral into a legal principle and at the same time made the regulation of citizenship a federal matter. Its first section reads, "All persons born or naturalized in the United States, and subject to the jurisdiction thereof, are citizens of the United States, nor shall any State deprive any person of life, liberty, or property, without due process of law, nor deny to any person within its jurisdiction the equal protection of the laws."

Unlike the Declaration of Independence, the Fourteenth Amendment claims applicability not to all men, but to "all persons [now explicitly gender-free] born or naturalized in the United States, and subject to the jurisdiction thereof," and it calls these persons "citizens" both of the United States and of the several states in which they reside. In enjoining the several states from making or enforcing "any law which shall abridge the privileges and immunities of citizens of the United States," the framers of the Fourteenth Amendment not only clearly established federal citizenship as a legal right but also reserved to the federal government the eminent protection of this right: the federal judiciary guarantees that this right shall not be abridged by a particular state. That the federal judiciary did not always conscientiously implement this injunction is immaterial to the present point; what matters is that it establishes certain legal rights to protect the individuals who are recognized as members of the community, the citizens. The moral "rights" affirmed by the Declaration of Independence are translated into legal language as "privileges and immunities" guaranteeing "life, liberty, and property" to the citizen.[7]

In the same spirit, the "equality" with which the Declaration of Independence distributed "unalienable Rights" is now reflected in the equal protection of the laws. The federal government extends this protection—not to "all Men," over whom no single government can claim jurisdiction—but to all citizens over whom it has jurisdiction and for whom it can legislate. Thus the "equality," predicated of "all Men" as a birthright ("are created"), which had still been denied to slaves as late as the Dred Scott case of 1857, came closer to realization.

Nevertheless, women had to wait until the Nineteenth Amendment was passed in 1920 before they were recognized as full citizens.

In differentiating a "human being" from a "citizen," the Fourteenth Amendment gave an answer to a problem harder to deal with in terms of Aristotelian principles: if man is "by nature"—a reasonable facsimile of the faceless "Creator" of the Declaration of Independence—a "social and political being," a *zōion politikon*,[8] it becomes tricky to make precise distinctions between the two. The repercussions of this difficulty can be seen in Aristotle's treatment of kingship in Book 3 of the *Politics:* absolute kingship (*pambasileia*) is said to be viewed by some as not being a "constitution" (*politeia*) at all , "because it is not in accordance with nature that one person should have authority over all citizens, wherever a state consists of equals."[9]

The question of who these "equals" (*homoioi*) are, is unequivocally answered in one sense: they are the "free" (*eleutheroi*).[10] This not only denies equality to slaves but excludes from the political community also a number of free persons, such as resident aliens and foreign visitors (Arist. *Pol.* 3.1, 1275a7–14), to whom the United States extends at least some equality in the form of equal protection of the law, trial by jury, etc. At the same time, the "freedom" on which this "equality" rests has only a limited application to women, children, and, surprisingly enough, to old men: while Aristotle concedes that women "constitute half of the free population," children are "incomplete citizens" (*politai ateleis,* 3.5, 1278a4–6), who "by reason of their age have not yet been registered" and only "develop into partners of the political community."[11] Old men are not citizens in an unqualified sense, because they are "superannuated."[12] Complete equality as citizens, then, is extended in the Greek sense only to free males who are still in their prime. Citizenship has, accordingly, a much narrower compass than it has in the United States. The Fourteenth Amendment recognizes no disabilities of women and children. But that such disabilities actually existed is shown by the fact that the Twenty-Sixth Amendment, ratified on July 1, 1971, extended the franchise to eighteen year olds. This implies a partial disability of the young until the end of their seventeenth year. The Nineteenth Amendment, ratified August 26, 1920, likewise implies an earlier disability of women in that it gave them the suffrage for the first time in the United States.

We might here note another aspect of the narrow confines of citizenship in Aristotle: whereas the Fourteenth Amendment explicitly puts born and naturalized citizens on the same level,[13] Aristotle dismisses the problem of naturalization as marginal (*Pol.* 3.1, 1275a2–6), though he concedes a minimal share in the community also to free noncitizens.[14] Birth, when accepted by the relevant social institutions as legitimate, was the universal criterion for citizenship among the Greeks;[15] naturalization was rare, exceptional, and usually honorific.[16]

The difference between American and Aristotelian "equality" goes considerably further. The high value attached to equality in both cultures does not mean that either the Americans or the Greeks claim that all men are "equal" in all respects. The equality the Declaration of Independence attributes to all men as a birthright is "unalienable," because no human power can remove it—the Greeks would say that it exists "by nature." It entitles all "equally" to enjoy life, liberty, and the pursuit of happiness. But we are far from "equal" in the way we each exercise that equality: what I do with my life is different from what you do with yours, my "liberty" or right to privacy is likely to result in different activities from the way you use yours, and we are not equal in the way we severally pursue happiness. Equality of rights also constitutes practical limits on each individual's freedom of action. In saying that no citizen shall be deprived of life, liberty, and property without due process of law, the Fourteenth Amendment establishes legal limits on what we are naturally equally entitled to do: the statement that no person shall be denied the "equal" protection of the laws means that the same laws protect all citizens equally.

The differences between this approach to "equality" and the corresponding Greek view of *isotēs* or *to ison* are more glaring than their similarities. Equality derived from the enjoyment of freedom by all citizens makes its only appearance in Aristotle in his criticism of democrats for mistakenly believing that equal enjoyment of freedom makes them equal in every respect.[17] Note that no rights are involved: although Aristotle shares with the Declaration of Independence the belief that all men are "by nature" equal,[18] the conclusion he draws from that is radically different: since natural equality makes the rule of one man unjust, "all men should have a share in ruling" by taking turns in ruling and being ruled.[19] Eligibility to hold office is not seen as something a citizen is entitled to as a right; eligibility is merely the logical corollary of natural equality. Office holding is part of the condition of being a citizen, and status as a free man makes one equal to all other citizens.[20] Equality of citizens exists negatively in that neither the affluent nor the indigent dominate society, and positively in that freedom gives the same political weight to all.[21] The nature of this equality, its relation to freedom, and its implications are most clearly set forth in the second chapter of *Politics* 6:

> The idea underlying a democratic form of government is freedom. . . . The populist notion of justice is that no citizen is better than any other[22] in a quantitative and not in a qualitative sense. In the light of this notion of justice, the common people are necessarily sovereign, and what the majority decides is final and is just. For they maintain that each citizen must have an equal share;[23] as a consequence those without means enjoy greater authority in democracies than the affluent, for their number is greater and authority goes with majority decisions.[24]

Aristotle's idea of equality seems to me to go beyond anything stated in the American documents in two respects. While in American theory the equality derived from our Creator gives us a common moral sense from which the Declaration of Independence derives our title to liberty, the relationship is reversed in Aristotle: freedom, in the sense of already "having the status of free men," is the basis on which citizens can be regarded as equals. Freedom is the precondition for equality, not equality for freedom. Further, the equality guaranteed by the Fourteenth Amendment entitles all citizens equally to the protection of the laws; Aristotle, on the other hand, says very little about the relation of equality to the laws, except that, taking advantage of the double meaning of *isos* as both "equal" and "equitable," he calls *equality* a notion of justice valid only for "equals";[25] to the first kind of democracy he attributes an equality embodied in law (*nomos*), which demands that neither the affluent nor the indigent should dominate society.[26] In his view the equal status of all citizens as free men entails equality in appointments to office, and he believes that this is realized by the rota of taking turns at ruling and being ruled. The right of each citizen to equal treatment under the law[27] is of less interest to him as a manifestation of equality than the question of access to the various magistracies, which, in a *politeia* worthy of its name and especially in a democracy, is open to any free citizen on the rota principle. We have seen that this access is not envisaged in terms of a right but follows logically from the status of a citizen as a free man.[28]

The divergence of Greek from American thinking is even more glaring when it comes to defining "free" and "freedom." Greek uses *eleutheria* and *eleutheros* both in a social sense of individuals who are not slaves as well as in a political sense of states: the political meaning comes to the fore most prominently in Herodotus, according to whom the issue in the Persian Wars was the Greeks' defense of their *eleutheriē* against the Persians;[29] Aristotle, however, tends to give only a social sense to both adjective and noun in the *Politics* to contrast the status of a "free" man with that of a slave. Like Aristotle, both the Declaration of Independence and the Fourteenth Amendment predicate "freedom" of an individual. But the liberty they promise entitles a person to privacy by marking off an aspect of life in which the state cannot interfere; and, as a corollary, it extends the protection of the rights of the individual also to the protection of the rights of minorities. Aristotle, on the other hand, looks on freedom as the individual's membership card in society. There is, to the best of my knowledge, neither in Aristotle nor anywhere else in Greek thought any reference to the rights of minorities, simply because there were no minority groups recognized among the citizens.

Unlike "liberty," *eleutheria* is not expressed in terms of the "privileges or immunities" that the Fourteenth Amendment guarantees to the citizen; rather, all citizens, regardless of the kind of constitution under which they live, and regardless of economic condition, enjoy the status of free men which differentiates them from slaves.[30] The only "privilege" a free citizen can be said to enjoy is the *timē* (honor) of holding office.[31] But how much of a "privilege" can that be in a state, such as a democracy, where it is shared by all citizens? One of the essential definitions of *politeia,* a term that connotes both "citizenship" and "statehood," includes the way in which public offices are distributed;[32] and the art of citizenship (*politikē*) is the rule of and over persons who are equal in that they are all free.[33] In praising the principle of reciprocity, Aristotle says that

> since it is not possible for all to hold office at once, they do so either on an annual basis or on the basis of some other kind of term. . . . The better course would be to have always the same persons [*sc.,* seasoned professionals] as rulers, if possible; but where that is impossible because all are equal in nature, and where it is regarded as right that . . . all should have a share in ruling . . . those who are equal yield their office to one another in turn, and retain their equality even outside their term of office: some rule and others are ruled as if having changed their personality.[34]

In short, all citizens are equally privileged: the "privilege" is a privilege only to the extent that slaves and foreigners are excluded from it.

It is time to take stock of our inquiry so far: while the Declaration of Independence and the Fourteenth Amendment treat "citizenship" and the two notions of "equality" and "liberty" as rights, Aristotle sees none of the three Greek equivalents—*politēs, isotēs,* and *eleutheria*—as a "right" or a "title," although certain rights are implied when we try to translate these terms into our conceptual framework. How did Aristotle think of them?

To try to answer this question, we must begin with the linguistic evidence. Where we would use the word *right* to express the most important aspects of citizenship, Aristotle works with a number of expressions that, though they may incidentally connote "rights," primarily denote "sharing," "participation" (*metechein*), or "being in a position to do something" (*exeinai*). There is in his vocabulary nothing that corresponds exactly to our concept of "right" in the sense of "claim" or "entitlement."[35] To understand this way of thinking, we have to remember that for Aristotle the state is a compound entity, all of whose constituent parts "participate in" or "share in" it.[36] The standard way of describing the status of citizenship is "having a share in the social and political community" (*metechein tēs politeias* [or *tēs poleōs*"]).[37] The norm of this status is found in a democracy, where all citizens have an equal share, based on freedom and equality.[38] For Greeks freedom and equality, as well as the state itself, are entities that citizens share through the community to which they belong; they do not possess them as rights to which they feel individually entitled.

There is, however, a term that, at first glance, seems to come closer to describing what we understand by "rights." When we read, for example, that a specified amount of property determines eligibility for office in oligarchies and in some democracies, "eligibility," that is, the "right" to hold office, is expressed by the phrase *exousian einai metechein* (to have the possibility to share).[39] However, a closer look reveals that it is not a "right" that is expressed. Since we are told in the immediate sequel that without an income it is impossible to enjoy the leisure necessary to devote oneself to public affairs,[40] the key verb *exeinai* clearly refers to leisure not as a "right," but as a precondition for public service; it describes something "permissible," "allowable," that is open to a person, not something to which a person is "entitled."[41]

What applies to property qualifications applies to eligibility to office in general: it is not a "right" but a "sharing in office" or "sharing in honors" (*metechein archēs* [or *timēs*], *meteinai archēs*).[42] Like citizenship, public offices are thought of as forming a kind of pool owned by the political community to which those who are full members of the community have access, but to which they do not necessarily have a "claim." The political community as a whole, the *politeia,* assigns offices,[43] and the verb used for the distribution of this share is commonly a form of the verb "to give" (*didonai*) either in its simple form or in the compounds "to give away" or "to give a share in" (*apodidonai* or *metadidonai*).[44]

This "assignment" does not involve the granting of rights: the essential thing for the Greeks is that the corporate entity makes accessible to its members something it owns and controls: it opens to the citizen in actuality the enjoyment of a share in the corporation, which he already possesses potentially. R. K. Sinclair has examined some central aspects of this "sharing" in a work he entitled *Democracy and Participation in Athens.*[45] "Participation" is indeed the most suitable term in English, but it does not go quite far enough to capture what is involved in *methexis* and *meteinai.* To understand what is involved, we have to think of a "share" not in terms of the stock market, in which shares can be disposed of at will, but in the terms in which each limb has a share in the human body: my leg "shares" or "participates" in my body in the sense that whatever affects it affects my body, and whatever affects my body affects it.

"Rights" constitute for us only one aspect of citizenship, namely political and legal entitlements that are based on the fact of recognized membership in the corporation that is society and/or the state. They have a positive as well as a negative aspect: my rights define the space in which I can freely move without threat of outside interference; but they are also limited by your rights, which prevent me from encroaching on your territory. "Rights" are guaranteed by laws and are determined and enforced by a court of law. "Rights" need to be claimed or exercised in order to be valid: my "right" to vote makes me only a potential and passive citizen; while I do not lose my citizenship by failing to exercise it, I am not an active participant in the political process if I fail to vote.

Methexis, on the other hand, gives a citizen a full share in the society in which he lives. No act of his can make him an active member of the community: the degree to which he is a citizen is not determined by himself, but by the expectations of the community of which he is a part in terms of the contribution he can make to its functioning. When Solon divided the citizen-body into the so-called four "property-classes,"[46] he did not set up a system of graduated entitlements: his purpose was to determine the degree of service the state could expect of each group of citizens, since there was no public pay for public service: only the highest class, the *pentakosiomedimnoi,* whose estates had an annual production rate of five hundred bushels, could be expected to serve as treasurers and in other high offices; cavalry service, based on the ability to keep horses, was expected of the second highest class; ownership of a team of oxen was deemed a sign of the ability to provide one's own armor and thus to serve as a hoplite in the heavy infantry; and the unpropertied, the lowest class, could be called on only for attendance and voting at assembly and at jury meetings. Membership in each of these classes was not a precondition for graduated rights: the Athenian name for "property-class" was *telos,* derived from the verb *teleō,* which denotes the fulfilment of a public obligation, such as the payment of a tax. Thus, belonging to a given class did not describe a "right" ("what your country can do for you") but the expectation the community had of a member ("what you can do for your country").[47]

While "rights" describe only the political aspect of citizenship, "sharing" has facets that the term *rights* does not express. A citizen also "shares" in the social, economic, and religious life of his community not as an "entitlement" but by virtue of belonging to a group that recognizes him as its member. It is taken for granted and expected of him that he will participate in its life; it is not viewed as a "right" that outsiders do not possess. By sharing in the *politeia,* a citizen is part of the corporation that is the state: the "right" to participate and its implementation inhere inseparably in citizenship.

The meaning of this is perhaps best driven home by an observation on the place of religion in the modern American and classical Greek civic communities, respectively. By introducing the principle of separation of church and state, Americans banish religion from the political sphere and relegate it to an area that guarantees the individual his "liberty" of conscience against state interference. Greek religion is not a matter of conscience: it consists only in "doing the conventional thing by the gods" (*theous nomizein*). The "conventional thing" is, significantly, the verbal expression of *nomos,* the norms accepted by the state, including its statutes. This indicates concretely that religion is part of the civic order, that citizenship does not involve what we understand as "religious freedom" or "religious belief," even if, to the best of our knowledge, an individual was in the Greek world "free" from public constraints (other than social pressure) in his/her participation in divine worship. Tolerance of the religious convictions of others, which is for us part and parcel of the liberty a citizen enjoys, was not part of the freedom enjoyed by the citizen of an ancient Greek state.

I have chosen religion as an extreme example of what citizenship meant to the Greeks, bound inextricably to their individual communities and sharing with those communities every aspect of their lives. Citizenship was neither a right nor a matter of participation, but a matter of belonging, of knowing one's identity not in terms of one's own personal values but in terms of the community that was both one's possession and possessor. When he defined the human individual as a *zōion politikon,* Aristotle stated a profound reality of Greek society.

Acknowledgments

I happily acknowledge debts of gratitude to Professors Robert C. Bannister, A. John Graham, and Carol Nackenoff for valuable comments and criticisms, which have banished some mistakes of fact and judgment from this paper. Needless to say, responsibility for remaining imperfections is entirely my own.

Notes

1. Cochrane, *Christianity and Classical Culture,* 86–87.

2. For an excellent account of the problems involved, see Kettner, *Citizenship.*

3. A few words ought to be said about the possibility of differentiating *liberty* from *freedom.* None of the many attempts to distinguish between them has won universal acceptance. The *Declaration of Independence* speaks of "liberty" in detailing the rights with which we are said to be endowed but proclaims at the end that "these United Colonies are, and of Right ought to be, *Free* and Independent States," perhaps because "liberty" has no cognate adjective in English, so that the adjective derived from *freedom* has to be borrowed to express it. Even if that be the reason, it is true that the noun *freedom* occurs neither in the Declaration of Independence nor in the Fourteenth Amendment. Modern English translations of Aristotle's *Politics* use *liberty* or *freedom* indifferently as translations of *eleutheria,* presumably in order to express its relation to the adjectival *eleutheros,* "free." The only firm distinction between *liberty* and *freedom* I can think of in English is that *freedom* may be followed by either *to* or *from,* whereas *liberty* may be followed only by *to.*

4. The attempt of Wills, *Inventing America,* to see the Scottish Enlightenment rather than Locke and the English Enlightenment as the chief philosophical source of the *Declaration* (for which see Becker, *Declaration of Independence,* ch. 2) has been decisively refuted by Hamowy, "Jefferson and the Scottish Enlightenment."

5. For Jefferson's meaning, see the pertinent remarks of Wood, *Radicalism,* 178–79. For the status of women, children, and slaves, see Kettner, *Citizenship,* 197–98, 311–12.

6. Some aspects of this problem have been discussed by Rodgers, *Contested Truths;* on problems left unanswered even after the Constitution, see Kettner, *Citizenship,* 231.

7. For the transformation of the "pursuit of happiness" in the *Declaration* into "property" in the Fourteenth Amendment, see the remarks of Wills, *Inventing America,* 240–55, with the critique of Hamowy, "Jefferson and the Scottish Enlightenment," 516–19.

8. Arist., *Pol.* 1.2, 1253a1–3: ἐκ τούτων οὖν φανερὸν ὅτι τῶν φύσει ἡ πόλις ἐστί, καὶ ὅτι ὁ ἄνθρωπος φύσει πολιτικὸν ζῷον (These considerations make it evident that the city-state belongs to the group of things that exist by nature, and that man is by nature a social and political being). Cf. also *Eth. Nic.* 1.7, 1097b11 and 9.9, 1169b18–19. Note also the phrase διὰ τὸ τὴν φύσιν ἴσους εἶναι πάντας (because all are by nature equal) at *Pol.* 2.2, 1261a39-b2.

9. Arist. *Pol.* 3.16, 1287a10–18.

10. Ibid. 3.6, 1279a21; 3. 8, 1280a5.

11. Ibid. 1.13, 1260b15–20, esp. 18–20.

12. Ibid. 3.1, 1275a12–18.

13. This is already the case in the *Declaration of Independence,* which complains that

the King "has endeavoured to prevent the Population of these States; for that Purpose obstructing the Laws for Naturalization of Foreigners. . . ."

14. Arist. *Pol.* 3.1, 1275a13–14: ἀτελῶς μετέχουσι τῆς τοιαύτης κοινωνίας (They share in a community of this sort in an incomplete sense).

15. See γένος ἴσοις ἢ μείζοσι (than their equals or superiors in birth) at 3.9, 1281a6; and at 1277b8–9 the definition of πολιτικὴ ἀρχή as τῶν ὁμοίων τῷ γένει καὶ τῶν ἐλευθέρων (rule over persons of a similar rank in birth and free).

16. See Osborne, *Naturalization,* vol. I, 5–8.

17. Arist. *Pol.* 5.1, 1301a28–31.

18. See above, p. 52 with n. 8, and especially *Pol.* 2.2, 1261a39-b2: διὰ τὸ τὴν φύσιν ἴσους εἶναι πάντας. Here and in the following, I use "man" in its generic sense (= "mankind") and use the masculine to include both male and, where appropriate, female. It must not be forgotten that for the Greeks only the male can be a "citizen" in the full sense of the word.

19. Arist. *Pol.* 2.2, 1261a39-b5. The text is full of difficulties. I have adopted the version of W. D. Ross. The point made here is again made at 3.16, 1287a10–18, cf. n. 3 above.

20. Arist. *Pol.* 1.7, 1255b20: ἡ δὲ πολιτικὴ ἐλευθέρων καὶ ἴσων ἀρχή (rule of citizens is over persons equal and free).

21. Ibid. 4.4, 1291b31–37. "Political weight" seems to be an appropriate equivalent to κυρίους in this context.

22. I believe this to be the most accurate rendering of the idea underlying τὸ ἴσον ἔχειν, which literally means "to have the equal thing." Since, as I hope to show in the sequel, membership in the community is invariably described in terms of "sharing," "participating in" (μετέχειν, μετεῖναι), the only "thing" all citizens have equally is a share in the community.

23. See n. 21 above.

24. Arist. *Pol.* 6.2, 1317a40-b10.

25. Ibid. 3.9, 1280a11–12: οἷον δοκεῖ ἴσον τὸ δίκαιον εἶναι καὶ ἔστιν, ἀλλ᾽ οὐ πᾶσιν ἀλλὰ τοῖς ἴσοις (what is just is held to be and is equitable, not for all but for those who are equal).

26. Ibid. 4.4, 1291b30–34. Cf. n. 21 above.

27. The idea is partially expressed in the Greek concept *isonomia.* See Ostwald, *Nomos,* 96–136.

28. For a different approach to "equality," see Ian Morris's essay in this volume; for a different approach to the relation of "freedom" to "equality," see Mogens H. Hansen's essay in this volume.

29. See von Fritz, "Die griechische ΕΛΕΥΘΕΡΙΑ." But even here Demaratus' famous remark to Xerxes (Hdt. 7.104), ἐλεύθεροι γὰρ ἐόντες οὐ πάντα ἐλεύθεροί εἰσι· ἔπεστι γάρ σφι νόμος, τὸν ὑποδειμαίνουσι πολλῷ ἔτι μᾶλλον ἢ οἱ σοὶ σέ (for though they are free, they are not free in all respects: law is above them, and they fear it much more than your men fear you), seems to apply more to the Lacedaemonians as individuals than to the Greeks in a collective sense.

30. Arist. *Pol.* 3.8, 1279b39–1280a5.

31. Ibid. 3.10, 1281a31: τιμὰς γὰρ λέγομεν εἶναι τὰς ἀρχάς (for we say that "offices" are "honors"); cf. also 3.16, 1287a11–18, where the point is made that those who are equal by nature must necessarily have the same standard of right and wrong and nat-

urally accept the same values (τὸ αὐτὸ δίκαιον ἀναγκαῖον καὶ τὴν αὐτὴν ἀξίαν κατὰ φύσιν εἶναι), which are said to include also their attitude to τιμαί: consequently, they do not regard either ruling or being ruled as right, and take their turns (ἀνὰ μέρος) at both. See also the expression ἐν ταῖς τιμαῖς εἶναι as a synonym for τῶν ἀρχῶν μετέχειν at 4.4, 1290b12 and 5.6, 1305b4.

32. See ibid. 4.3, 1290a7–8: πολιτεία μὲν γὰρ ἡ τῶν ἀρχῶν τάξις ἐστί (for a régime is the ordering of public offices). Cf. also 3.4, 1277b7–16.

33. Ibid. 1.7, 1255b20: ἡ δὲ πολιτικὴ ἐλευθέρων καὶ ἴσων ἀρχή.

34. Ibid. 2.2, 1261a32-b5.

35. I owe to Mordechai E. Ostwald the observation that what I am trying to describe here comes very close to Leo Strauss's description of Greek society in his *Natural Right* 129–32. My fundamental disagreement with Strauss concerns his inclusion of citizenship among "classic natural rights."

36. Arist. *Pol.* 1.13, 1260b13–14. Cf. also 4.3, 1290a2–5.

37. E.g., ibid. 2.8, 1268a24, 27–28; also 10, 1272a16. Cf. 4.6, 1293a3–4; 8, 1294a12–14; 4.13, 1297b4–6; 5.3, 1302b26–27; 6, 1306b10–11; 13–14; 6.13, 1332a32–35; 7.10, 1329b37. It is not uncommon to find κοινωνεῖν, "associate in," in place of the relevant forms of μετέχειν, e.g., 2.1, 1260b38–42 and 2.8, 1268a18: κοινωνεῖν <τῆς πολιτείας >; cf. τὴν πολιτικὴν κοινωνίαν (to participate in the social and political community/in the community of the city-state) at 2. 10, 1272b14–15; 4.5, 1292b23–25: ἀνάγκη γὰρ ἢ πάντα τὰ εἰρημένα μέρη τοῦ δήμου κοινωνεῖν τῆς πολιτείας, ἢ τὰ μὲν τὰ δὲ μή (for either all the aforementioned parts of the people must participate in the social and political community or some do and others do not). For both expressions together, see 4.11, 1295a29–31: ἀλλὰ βίον τε τὸν τοῖς πλείστοις κοινωνῆσαι δυνατὸν καὶ πολιτείαν ἧς τὰς πλείστας πόλεις ἐνδέχεται μετασχεῖν (but a way of life that is possible for the majority to participate in and a social and political community that it is possible for most cities to share in). Occasionally, μέτεστι τῆς πόλεώς τινι is used in place of μετέχειν; see, e.g., 3.9, 1281a4–7. On the whole question, see Manville, *Origins,* 7–11.

38. Ibid., 4.4, 1291b34–37.

39. Ibid., 4.4, 1291b40–1292a4; cf. also 3.5, 1277b34–35. For oligarchies, see ibid. 4.5, 1292a39; cf. 6, 1292b29–32. So also at 4.6, 1292b35–41, 1293a14–15, 6.6, 1320b25–26. Similarly, 3.1, 1275b18–20.

40. Ibid., 4.6, 1292b32–33: τὸ δὲ δὴ ἐξεῖναι σχολάζειν ἀδύνατον μὴ προσόδων οὐσῶν (The possibility of enjoying leisure does not exist in the absence of income). The textual problem seen here by Ross is not apparent to me.

41. So also *exousia* in Aristotle's discussion of Plato's restriction of the amount of property a person can own cannot possibly refer to the "right" of a citizen to own no more than five times the amount of the smallest property; see ibid. 2.6, 1266b5–7: Πλάτων δὲ τοὺς Νόμους γράφων μέχρι μέν τινος ᾤετο δεῖν ἐᾶν, πλεῖον δὲ τοῦ πενταπλασίαν εἶναι τῆς ἐλαχίστης μηδενὶ τῶν πολιτῶν ἐξουσίαν εἶναι κτήσασθαι (When he wrote the *Laws,* Plato believed that increase should be permitted up to a certain point, but that no citizen should be allowed to acquire more than five times the amount of the smallest property).

42. Ibid. 2.11. 1273b12–13; 3.1, 1275a22–23, 28, 32–33; 10, 1281b25–26; cf. 2.11, 1274a21, 3.5, 1277b36. For τιμῶν μετέχειν, see 3.4, 1278a35–38, 4.11, 1296a15; 13, 1297b6–11; 5.7, 1306b23; 12, 1316b21.

43. Ibid., 5.3, 1302b6–9: ὑβριζόντων τε γὰρ τῶν ἐν ταῖς ἀρχαῖς καὶ πλεονε-κτούντων στασιάζουσι καὶ πρὸς ἀλλήλους καὶ πρὸς τὰς πολιτείας τὰς διδούσας τὴν ἐξουσίαν (Offensive behavior and graft on the part of those in office give rise to conflicts among them and against the regimes that give them license). The ἐξουσία here referred to is presumably the possibility the political system gives to officials to enrich themselves and act arrogantly. Cf. also 7.9, 1329a13–16: λείπεται τοίνυν τοῖς αὐτοῖς μὲν ἀμφότερα (sc., military duty and deliberation) ἀποδιδόναι τὴν πολιτείαν ταῦτα, μὴ ἅμα δέ, ἀλλ᾽ ὥσπερ πέφυκεν ἡ μὲν δύναμις ἐν νεωτέροις, ἡ δὲ φρόνησις ἐν πρεσβυτέροις εἶναι (what is left for the state is to grant both functions to the same persons, but not simultaneously, but, as nature wants it, strength is found in younger, and good sense in older men).

44. In addition to the preceding note, see 4.13, 1298a6–9. Also 5.6, 1306a25–26. Cf. also 6.7, 1321a26–29.

45. Listed in the Bibliography, this volume.

46. For the role these property-classes played in shaping the Athenian democracy, see V. D. Hanson's essay in this volume.

47. I discuss this problem in greater detail in "Public Expense: Whose Obligation?"

TRANSGRESSION, EQUALITY, AND VOICE

Sheldon S. Wolin

I

Thanks to the influence of ancient writers and of Aristotle in particular, it was long believed that the practices of governance and politics naturally grouped themselves into forms or constitutions, such as kingship or aristocracy, and that each form provided the norms that its type of regime should strive to realize.

That belief is reflected in contemporary liberal versions of democracy. According to one of the most influential theorists of liberal democracy, the "coercive political power which citizens exercise over one another when fundamental questions are at stake" is legitimate "only when it is exercised in accordance with a constitution the essentials of which all citizens may reasonably be expected to endorse in the light of principles and ideals acceptable to them as reasonable and rational."[1] This way of thinking eliminates the possibility that democracy may have been, and still is, a phenomenon that can be housed, but may not be realized, within a form.

The notion of "transgression" will be my way of representing a different location of democracy, while the notion of "voice" is meant to call attention to what ancient democracy most notably lacked, discursive traditions that emphasized, as the core of democracy, its demotic and participatory elements.

In discussing democracy, it is almost irresistible for students of ancient political theory to adopt Aristotle's starting point and to treat equality as the decisive mark of democracy and to assume that the meaning of democracy is exhausted in a description of the constitutional form given to equality. Democratic equality is usually conceived within, rarely apart from, a constitutional structure. This is not to suggest that ideas of equality have not been an important part of the ideology of democracy or that the role of constitutional forms is insignificant. My point is exactly the opposite: a constitution can be a potent means of shaping a particular kind of democracy by subjecting the demos to institutional constraints in the hope of preventing certain kinds of outcomes, such as the confiscation of the property of the rich. Similarly, the idea of equality can be articulated in a set of practices designed to delimit its possibilities, e.g., all citizens regardless of property may vote but only those with a certain amount of property may hold the higher state offices. Without resorting to legal disqualifications, constitutional practices may favor certain modes of action

(e.g., formal eloquence) and privilege certain acting abilities (mastery of legislative strategies) that disadvantage those with no formal education or legal
background.[2]

Notwithstanding the efforts of constitutionalists to shape actors, to domesti-
cate them to accord with the practices of a particular *politeia* (constitution),
there have been certain spectacular types of action that have broken with constitutional modes. The agonistic impulse of heroic actors is a familiar theme in
Greek literature and philosophy. The uneasy relationship of a demonic Alcibiades to Athenian democracy belongs to that same genre. Modern liberal constitutions have frequently been troubled, sometimes subverted, by men bred in
military modes of action, and have even more frequently been corrupted by
those schooled in the rule-bending ways of financial speculators. The nineteenth-century American *politeia* managed to elect a heroic but hapless general
(Grant), who managed to surround himself with clever and unscrupulous speculators, representatives of those great transgressors and heroes, the Robber
Barons of nineteenth-century capitalism.

Because the heroic has been claimed as an individualistic category, the idea
of an agonistic demos seems not only unfamiliar but oxymoronic. Why should
it seem intuitively absurd that an agonistic demos, like an agonistic Alcibiades,
might be driven by the needs of its nature to strain at constitutional restraints?
Or that the relationship of Alcibiades to Athenian democracy was vexing because two overreachers were confronting each other? The problem that democratic action poses for sensibilities bred to notions of heroic or individual actors is its anonymity.

From this perspective one can easily identify the modes of action, both in antiquity and modern times, by which one can say that a democratic agon has been
performed: revolution or popular uprising, collective disobedience, and mass
protest. These are typically regarded as destructive or disruptive of established
order and as either anticonstitutional or threatening to become such. Democratic action, or the demos as autonomous agent, might be defined as collective action that initially gathers its power from outside the system. It begins with the
demos constructing/collecting itself from scattered experiences and fusing
these into a self-consciousness about common powerlessness and its causes.
The demos is created from a shared realization that powerlessness comes from
being shut out of the councils where power's authority is located. The demos
becomes political, not simply when it seeks to make a system of governance
more responsive to its needs, but when it attempts to shape the political system
in order to enable itself to emerge, to make possible a new actor, collective in
nature.

Among the ancient writers most often consulted by political theorists
today—Thucydides, Plato, Aristotle, and Cicero—equality, like democracy,
was typically discussed in relation, first, to a ranked order of virtues or disabilities attributed to each social class, and, second, to the social or political contribution possible to each class in the performance of the various offices that

formed the constitutional structure.[3] The common assumption of the ancient commentators was that equality had to be qualified by the "objective" requirements of office in a system.

The most striking feature of political controversies in the contemporary United States is that while philosophers and social scientists have produced a vast literature on equality, the word itself is virtually taboo among practical politicians and in the rhetoric of politics. Talk about "discrimination," while widespread, works to confine public discussion of equality rather than to promote a conception of an egalitarian society. Discrimination is assumed, whether rightly or wrongly, to be a limited phenomenon, referring to discrete practices and specific groups (identified by race, gender, religion, etc.) and hence requiring only pragmatic adjustments such as equal pay for equal work. Equality, on the other hand, implies a general condition and hence is more threatening. In a competitive society with a volatile economy, members do not typically strive for equality but for differential rewards. Accordingly, today no politician dares run on a platform of equality and this despite the well-known fact that inequality, both social and political, is on the increase.[4]

When equality is invoked, it is most often associated with the denial of some status, right, or opportunity, which in turn diminishes the physical, material, and intellectual well-being of persons, their dignity, and their chances of living fulfilling lives. Neither the original American Constitution nor its Bill of Rights mentioned equality. However, Article I, section 2, establishing the basis for representation and direct taxation, sanctioned inequality by distinguishing "free persons" from Indians and "other persons," meaning slaves, and excluding those two categories from incorporation into the civic body. Although later amendments outlawed slavery, affirmed the right to vote regardless of race or "sex," and guaranteed "equal protection" of the laws, a century of struggle was required after the Civil War before African-American voting rights were assured, although that did not make equal protection under law a practical reality.

Unequal treatment is less a consequence of unequal rights than of unequal power. Unequal power is often, although not always, related to an inability to act effectively or at all. The question then arises, what kind of democracy is it where equal rights are formally guaranteed but where wealth and power are no less concentrated than poverty and powerlessness?

I propose to explore that question by way of a contrast between Athenian democracy, in which the demos was the major actor, and a democracy I shall call "electoral democracy," or a democracy without the demos.[5]

II

Aristotle's assertion that man is by nature a *politikon zōion* is so familiar that it is easy to overlook the extraordinary element in that characterization (*Pol.* 1253a1–6). To an antidemocratic writer as careful as Aristotle, a notion so sweeping could only make sense if there had been a powerful, undeniable experience of politicalness, an actual practice sufficiently widespread to justify claiming it not simply as a human possibility but as the teleological principle of human nature itself. What was captured, a posteriori, by Aristotle's formula was the revolution in the political accomplished by Athenian citizen democracy of the fifth century.

If space permitted, it would be possible to show that the *politikon zōion* formula was merely one of several instances in which the vocabulary of ancient Greek political theory implicitly accepted the broadening effects of the egalitarian, participatory politics pioneered by Athenian democracy. Plato's efforts to devise a conception of a polity that would promote the good of all social classes (*Rep.* 420b–421c); Aristotle's admission that justice had to respect the claims of equality, that a polity had to accommodate diverse claims, not merely those of birth or wealth, and that the common good should be the criterion for any form of governance (*Pol.* 1283a29–42), were all acknowledgements of the broadened understanding of the political which the achievements of Athenian democracy forced on the intellectualized consciousness.

But if these are the compliments antidemocratic theorists paid to democracy, they are also the source of tensions within theories that strove to preserve various forms of elitism or political exclusivism while simultaneously celebrating the comprehensive or inclusive character of the polis: only beasts or gods, according to Aristotle, had no need of the polis, though manual workers, women, metics, and slaves could never be full members. (*Pol.* 1262a1–6; 1277b33–1278a13.) He thus denied that the political community (*politikē koinonia*) was coextensive with the polis.[6]

If critics like Tocqueville may be believed, the ongoing crisis of postrevolutionary French politics was principally due to the failure of the bourgeoisie to become precisely what the Athenian demos did become, a politically committed class. That achievement, the self-transformation of the demos into the citizen body (*politeuma*), of the subject into the citizen (*politēs*), is given indirect confirmation by an antidemocrat, such as Aristotle, who acknowledged that whatever the shortcomings of individuals, the demos was better at deliberating public policies than were the few.[7] Or put slightly differently, deliberative politics was the crucial element in the experience by which a demos constructed itself as a political actor. Deliberative politics was for the demos a mode of political development, and by the same token certain other types of politics— bureaucratic, charismatic, or even representative government—arrest that development. A participatory and egalitarian politics that is deliberative serves the political education of the demos. It is the nurturing ground of a democratic *paideia* to which Plato's Academy was the self-consciously radical alternative.

III

The claim, then, is that Athenian democracy was not simply about the extension of something old but the creation of something new that enlarged the conception of the political, expanded the boundaries of political space, and transformed the practices of politics. It involved, above all, the construction of a new actor, autonomous, able to choose and to deliberate collectively. But for the demos to occupy a stage hitherto reserved for heroes, kings, and nobles, it had to overcome or destroy barriers of class, status, wealth, and expertise.

In attempting to establish the idea of the demos as actor, one runs up against certain difficulties created by the dramaturgical models that have strongly influenced conventions governing the understanding of action.[8] This was especially true at Athens, where theatricality was a powerful element in the culture, including the theoretical culture,[9] and where epic standards of action persisted.[10] Accordingly, a "true" political actor was portrayed as an individual who performs a notable individual deed or who utters something memorable.[11] It was as tempting to a Thucydides as it is to modern scholars to fix upon a Pericles and pronounce him to be the paradigm of the praiseworthy democratic actor and, from the same dramatizing impulses, to pounce upon a Cleon and portray him as the counter-paradigm, the actor who embodies the violence, passion, and crudity of the demos when it is unrestrained by "moderate" leadership. And later, when there is no Pericles, the rhetors stand in.[12]

Thus the formula of actor-action, with its clear-cut notion of agency, excludes the demos, always a somewhat shadowy, inchoate identity, always in need of the crystallizing energy of a "leader." But if the Athenian demos could not simply be dismissed, it might be reconceptualized as "audience," or spectators who shout their approval or disapproval, or as the buffoon in *The Clouds*.[13] As a result the novelty of the phenomenon of collective force tends to remain conceptually undeveloped. Dramaturgical categories, even those that have been "philosophized," have trouble dealing with a power that does not "act" as a discrete subject, that lacks an identifying genealogy such as birth or wealth or wisdom and the claims to power that accompany them. And it lacks the celebratory voice of the poet, philosopher, or historian that can lend dignity and awe to the bearers of those genealogies. The genealogy of lesser folk presents an exact contrast to genealogies of power: it is a tale of abuse and exploitation, not of great deeds; of powerlessness, not power; of inarticulateness, not voice. A fragment from Antiphanes preserves their protest: "'not democratic' = 'unfair'."[14] When they manage to exert power, it is only by inventing forms that pool individual weakness.

Accordingly the tendency of historians to link the expansion of equality to changes in the structure of the Athenian military forces seems to me too narrow and to fit more properly under Weber's category of "passive democratization."[15] Recall that during the English civil wars of the 1640s and the wars that followed shortly after the French Revolution of 1789 there were mass armies mobilized and their members exposed to radical political ideologies. Nonetheless, in the immediate postrevolutionary decades there was no significant expansion of popular participation in the major decision-making institutions of those societies. In the case of Athens, doubtless the military contributions of hoplites and thetes lent a certain logic to the extension of civic equality, but something more was needed to explain the hegemony of the demos. In a comparable case Aristotle conceded that slaves and manual workers were "necessary" conditions for the existence of the polls, yet he denied that this constituted grounds for including them in the *politeia.* In American history the descendants of African slaves served in every war fought by the United States but, though emancipated and legally citizens, they have yet to be admitted fully to the equivalent of the *politeuma.* Instead their formal status as voters is subject to the kind of parody that would have delighted Aristophanes: allegedly, during the 1993 gubernatorial election in New Jersey, efforts were made to pay Afro-Americans not to vote—and this by the party of Lincoln.

The tenuous character of modern democratic participation underlined in that incident helps to underscore as well the magnitude of the Athenian achievement of inventing a demos that would be a continuous political subject, one that took part in the operation of the major decision-making institutions of its society. Its presence meant the transformation of politics, from an activity monopolized by those whose property and status allowed them leisure time, to an occupation for those who had little property or leisure. Consequently, instead of the political being the private property of the few, it was broadened and became the property of a new subject, the public.

Historically, democratization has had an energizing effect on social strata whose previous political activity has been sporadic, such as protests, "murmurings," local uprisings, and acts of collective disobedience.[16] At Athens democratization was concentrated in political institutions. Citizens took part in assemblies, law courts, and a range of offices; the sheer volume of their activity has amazed later scholars, who found it incredible that citizens of little means would travel great distances and spend considerable time away from their own concerns to deal with public matters. But with the outbreak of the Peloponnesian War in 431 B.C., that energy would be directed outwards and expressed in new ways. Athenian democracy was admired or feared by contemporaries for its innovativeness, boldness, and *periousia,* or "superabundance" of energy, "adventurous beyond their power and daring beyond their judgment," and forever hopeful (1.13, 70). That energy and daring, according to Thucydides, remained focused singlemindedly on winning the war so long as Pericles could restrain the impetuousity of the citizens and persuade them to place the public good of winning the war above their private interests (1.74; 2.40, 61, 65).

Yet the public/private dichotomy that Thucydides has Pericles praise in the Funeral Oration was a standing threat to the leadership principle that Pericles allegedly embodied. In a democracy public concern might legitimately lead to pressures for greater involvement and thus encroach on that "government by the first citizen" admired by Thucydides (2..65). On the other hand, if citizens grew more preoccupied with private concerns, leadership might become more autonomous and democracy more attenuated, an eventuality not unwelcome to modern elites frustrated at the "ungovernability" of democracy.[17]

Following the death of Pericles, Athenian democracy—according to Thucydides—exhibited the excesses that Pericles had managed to contain. It squandered the resources he had carefully husbanded; its whims became the decisive element in public decisions; and its political predominance encouraged a politics of cabals among politicians vying for favor (2.65). Yet Thucydides unintentionally provides the most telling example of post-Periclean popular participation as intelligent, ultimately able to control its passions, and interacting with leaders who offered genuine alternative policies in the context of an illuminating debate concerning the necessary conditions for democratic deliberations—an example, in short, of what Pericles had called the singular achievement of Athenians, combining "daring and deliberation, each carried to its highest power, and both united in the same persons" (2.40).

IV

The episode of the revolt at Mytilene recounted by Thucydides best reveals the demos learning how to be an actor and, at the same time, the kind of experience by which the political was being democratized. It provides, I believe, a more revealing description of Athenian democracy than does Pericles' manipulative Funeral Oration.

When the Mytilineans revolted, the Athenians' first response was to order the killing of the whole male adult population and the enslavement of the women and children. Then, Thucydides relates, "the morrow brought repentance with it and reflexion on the horrid cruelty of a decree, which condemned a whole city to the fate merited only by the guilty" (3.36). A new discussion was begun as "most of the citizens" wanted a chance "to reconsider the matter." Cleon, whom Thucydides despised as "the most violent man at Athens" and "by far the most powerful with the commons," advocated enforcement of the original decree. Despite his alleged influence, he loses the debate and despite his alleged appetite for violence, his speeches contain numerous passages that aim to instruct the citizens on how they ought to deliberate, how grave matters should be pondered, and the situations in which democracy and empire conflict.

His speech begins by daring to pose the possibility Pericles had avoided, of whether "a democracy is incapable of empire" (3.37). Then, provocatively, he tells the Assembly that their empire is a tyranny—the form of political rule that democrats considered their exact opposite—and hence sentimentality has no place in deliberations about imperial rule because it produces confusion about policies. He reassures them that ordinary men are more capable of holding to a steady course than the orators who fit their policies to the prevailing popular mood (3.38). The issue, Cleon insists, is that Mytilene rebelled without cause and by that action challenged the very principle of empire. "For if they were right in rebelling, you must be wrong in ruling." Ruling requires a clear-eyed view of one's interests, "or else you must give up your empire and cultivate honesty without danger" (3.40).

Thucydides' portrait of Cleon was clearly intended as a contrast to Pericles, a judgment modern historians, repelled by the cruelty of the decree, tend to embrace. Yet Cleon's defense of the decree not only echoed a warning made by Pericles but one that was a standard criticism of democracy, now as well as then, that democracies are by nature fickle.[18] In advice that borders on self-subversion, Cleon urges the Athenians to display the steady virtues they have, to ignore the blandishments of orators, and to resist allowing politics to become primarily a contest between leaders (3.37). Like his opponent in the debate, Diodotus, Cleon attempts to instruct the citizenry about the political by emphasizing the distinctive character of the proceedings and the gravity of a setting that requires that they behave not like "the audience of a rhetorician" but like "the council of a city" (3.38).

Cleon's adversary, Diodotus, opposed the decree, but as his argument develops it becomes an analysis of the conditions necessary to genuine deliberation and encompasses a conception both of the democratic citizen and of the democratic, though not Periclean, leader. For Diodotus the issue of the decree does concern Athenian interest, but the context of empire requires that interest be considered on a long-run, enlarged basis rather than an immediate interest, such as punishing a rebellion. How, then, should a democracy go about consulting its long-run interests, and what are they?

As framed by Diodotus, the broad context is political education in democratic responsibility, not only for the assembled citizens but for the rhetor who is engaged in arguing the merits of one policy over another. Those who would serve the citizenry must impose on themselves a certain discipline if democracy is to act wisely. They should avoid calumnizing their rivals, for otherwise citizens will hesitate to stand forward and serve the polis. "The good citizen ought to triumph not by frightening his opponents but by besting them fairly in argument."[19] The crucial obligation is that the speaker ought not to encourage suspicions of the idea of speech (*logos*) or language itself, for that would be to deprive the actor of that which speech makes possible, namely, action informed by forethought (3.42).

Diodotus' rhetor may be said to serve the demos as Plato would later have his Socrates serve the nobility: by raising the particular problem to a more general level, a level, however, that was comprehensible to the Many rather than just the Few and that tried to teach them about the nature of the demands of democratic ruling.[20] The virtue with which Diodotus was concerned was that of the citizen, not, as for Plato, that of the good man. The citizen of Diodotus was man in his corporate capacity.

For their part the citizens should not punish a speaker who offers his best advice but proves unsuccessful in persuading them. (3.42) The relationship between the speakers, who should "make it their business to look a little further," and the citizenry who perforce "judges offhand" is depicted as delicate. It requires, when the counsels of the speakers turn out badly, that the citizenry not absolve themselves of complicity by blaming the speakers alone (III.43). The citizen should understand what the demands of the political are and what it means to think in a political context. "We are not in a court of justice, but in a political assembly; and the question is not justice, but how to make the Mytilineans useful to Athens" (3.44). Citizenship is a deliberative activity, a mode of thinking that deals in considerations and categories different from those used in one's own affairs or when one is a juror judging someone's guilt or innocence. Unlike a law court, a political deliberation means that "we are deliberating for the future more than for the present" (3.44).[21] Adopting the long view not only requires taking into account a wider range of considerations and forces than when a personal matter is involved or when a legal judgment is reached; it demands certain virtues just as surely as Plato's insistence that the search for truth is as much a matter of character as of intellect. At a minimum it requires repressing immediate gratifications, such as the desire for revenge, while recognizing the values of taking care of arrangements so that they will endure.

Diodotus' emphasis on the future as the necessary perspective for the political act of deliberation signals that he is entering that treacherous domain of imperial politics where Thucydides' Pericles had excelled. A modern critic has represented that entrance by Diodotus as an attempt "to break out of the careful rational limits" of politics as taught by Thucydides. Diodotus' speech is said to depict "a world of shadowy powers . . . of pure physis, of nature without limitations or restraint."[22]

The passages in the speech of Diodotus that seem to reflect a deep irrationalism are accompanied by some broad generalizations about the inefficacy of legal restraints that suggest a more analytical bent than he is credited with. There are, Diodotus held, certain driving forces in human nature that take different forms with different social classes. "[A]s long as poverty gives men the courage of necessity," they will defy the laws. That reference is clearly to the poorer classes, and it anticipates the notion of later writers, from Aristotle to Marx to Hannah Arendt, that those classes live in a "realm of necessity."[23] Diodotus does not exempt the upper classes: equally dangerous are those to whom "power gives . . . the ambition natural to the confident and the proud." (3.45)[24] The futile attempts to control those drives Diodotus named "legal terror." A city such as Mytilene will rebel because it refuses to believe that it can fail. Men and cities break the law or exceed their own capabilities because hope and cupidity feed on each other while fortune (*tuchē*) tempts them on:

> This is especially the case with communities because the stakes played for are the highest, freedom or empire, and, when all are acting together, each man irrationally magnifies his own capacity. 3.45

Diodotus has been charged with "imposing a rigid antithesis between the right and the expedient," and this despite the fact that his policy spared more lives.[25] In emphasizing the moral deficiencies of Diodotus' policy, an accompanying concern is overlooked: not only what is to be done but what is to be taught. Diodotus draws on familiar proverbial wisdom about man's temptation to overreach, but he uses it to orient the listeners to the unfamiliar, to give them some means of understanding the magnitudes of power and human emotions involved in empire, the most massive form of human power known to the times. Imperial power was at least as awe-inspiring to that age as science-based technological power is to our own. Hence, when Diodotus and others appeal to *expediency* and *interest,* those terms strike a certain deflationary, demythologizing note, humanizing what is otherwise inhuman, delimiting the effects of concentrated power without claiming to control it perfectly, much less being able to abandon it.

> It is far more useful [Diodotus says] for the preservation of our empire voluntarily to put up with injustice [i.e., the revolt] than to put to death, however justly, those whom it is our interest to keep alive. 3.47

Diodotus' appeal to interest against justice, although it offends the modern sensibility, is a more complex argument than is usually conceded. It can be construed as a claim on behalf of freedom against the coercive necessity now embodied in justice, a justice that leaves no room for political considerations but insists on enforcing what is justified, even if it results in horrendous human suffering. Diodotus makes plain what those political considerations should be. "[I]n all the cities the people is your friend." To butcher "the people of Mytilene . . . will play directly into the hands of the higher classes" [3.47]. What matters is the policy proper to a democratic imperium:

> The right course with freemen [who have revolted to protect their independence] is not to chastize them rigorously when they do rise, but rigorously to watch them before they rise, to prevent their even entertaining the idea, and, the insurrection suppressed, to make as few responsible for it as possible. 3.46

V

To discover the complete horizon of a society's symbolic
values, it is necessary to map out its transgressions.
—Marcel Detienne[26]

Spinoza aside for the moment, throughout the history of what might be called formal political theory, it is difficult to find a theorist who devoted much care to developing a conception of the "people" as actor. Save for some comments about a limited right of the people to revolt, as in the *Vindiciae contra tyrannos*

(1579), or in some of the pamphlet literature of the English Civil War and Locke's *Second Treatise,* it was not until Rousseau's *Social Contract* and its concept of the "general will" that collective action was located at the center of politics. However, Rouseau's "general will" was constructed so as to be "right" rather than populist.[27] Rousseau could not conceive of a self-fashioning people and so he invents, literally, a deus ex machina, a Great Legislator who is to transform human nature by giving it a collective cast and then prescribe the framework of beliefs and practice that ensures the proper operation of the *volonté général.*[28] Except for rare elections, the idea of a democratic practice, of how ordinary people might actually cultivate political skills, remained undeveloped by Rousseau.

Given the traditional silence on the matter, if we are to theorize about Athenian democracy and the emergence of a new conception of political practice, it is necessary to find appropriate ways of representing a new collective actor. A conception of the demos as an actor requires a theoretical equivalent to Hobbes's account of an actor whose passions and power drives, uncertainties and anxieties, fancies and hopes provide an account of a new and complex presence, and to a transformation in the terms of the political. Such a conception would have to allow, as Hobbes had, that the dynamic that leads to great achievments may also be its undoing.

I want to sketch an alternative, drawn from a contemporary of Hobbes, that would do for the democratic collective actor what Hobbes had done for the bourgeois individual. Then I want to show, first, how that alternative was prefigured in ancient Greek theory but given a negative formulation; second, how Athenian democratic practices helped to transform the democratic actor; and third, what the implications of that transformation were.

My alternative starting point is Spinoza.[29] My concern here is not with the qualifications he placed on democracy but with his delineation of a new kind of actor and its raw power. Specifically, his concept of *conatus,* which Spinoza was especially concerned to relate to his notion of "the multitude" (*multitudo*), identifies the Many with a certain elemental force. A similar characterization had been made by ancient critics of democracy and would be repeated by modern ones.[30] Everything, Spinoza declared, endeavors to persist in its own being; it opposes any other thing that would take away its existence. Accordingly, the essence of any thing is its power, "whereby, either alone or with other things, it acts or endeavors to act."[31] The multitude collectively embodies a *conatus,* but because its psychology is limited to what Spinoza called the realm of imagination (*imaginatio*) and unable to ascend to the level of reason, it remains ignorant, superstitious, prone to crude and fantastic religious beliefs. The *imaginatio* of the multitude leaves it vulnerable to violent emotions that breed conflict, violence, and other forms of social disorder. Even when it is not violent, the multitude is gripped by wildly fluctuating opinions that oscillate between fear and hope.[32]

Spinoza believed the multitude was incapable of achieving rationality, but he hoped that by establishing proper institutions, including a religion purified of superstition, the mentality of the multitude could be elevated to an imitation of rational thought. Without endorsing Spinoza's conclusion, which leads to a system of dual truth, one for the masses and the other for the rational few, we need to ask what was the dynamic that Spinoza perceived in the multitude and its *conatus* that led him beyond the ancient critics to a rare defense of democracy?

The dynamics of *conatus* are such as to require an external cause for a thing to come into existence: resistance brings with it a heightened sense of self-awareness, of distinctive identity. Nietzsche, who had a critical admiration for Spinoza, described it this way:

> The wish to preserve oneself is the symptom of a condition of distress, of a limitation of the really fundamental instinct of life which aims at the expansion of power and wishing for that, frequently risks and even sacrifices self-preservation.[33]

Applying these notions to ancient Athens, we might say that while the demos represents the existence and vitality of a natural entity, its *conatus* may also be the source of a problematic. The demos exists as striving, but that drive may be directed not at assuring duration to its existence but at challenging its own finitude. The tangible expression of that problematic would be the leap from polis to empire.

Spinoza's multitude, absent Spinoza's sympathies and hopes, is prefigured in Plato's "beast" and belongs to a chain of similar images: of Muentzerites, Luther's "murdering, thieving peasants," Shakespeare's Jack Cade, the "mob" or revolutionary sansculottes, and Alexander Hamilton's "great beast." The resort to physical or animalistic imagery to describe the multitude, or hoi polloi, recognizes, *malgré lui,* the actual condition of most people in premodern societies.

Farmers and craftsmen, Socrates tells Alcibiades, "know but the things of the body" (*Alc.* 1.131a–b). They lived and worked close to the earth; they were often the victims of scavenging armies; and they were the evidence for claims that some beings were not fully human. That their psychology should be typically described as "passionate" confirms Spinoza's ontology in which existence follows essence: they threaten because their existence is continuously threatened.

Although it is possible to catch anticipations of Spinoza's *multitudo* and its *conatus* in unfriendly comments by ancient critics of Athenian democracy, the Athenian demos seems to have evolved into a different being whose essence is civic: a full-fledged citizenry whose being is validated through the numerous institutions in which it takes an active part. The beast has somehow become a deliberating citizen.

VI

How to understand the transformation? A starting point is provided by one of the great modern Hellenists who was also a great antidemocrat and, perhaps coincidentally or not, a great icon among postmodernists.

I want to recall Nietzsche's contrast between "slave morality" and "aristocratic morality." Nietzsche's aristocrat is pictured as a vigorous warrior-type, a man who takes risks, provokes strife, overflows with vitality, in short, a natural transgressor of conventions.[34] In contrast, slave morality, the morality of the masses, is leveling, resentful of aristocratic superiority, artful in contriving meshes of law and morality by which to trap their superior and to devitalize him, and aspires only to secure small pleasures.[35]

If, in the context of Athenian politics of the fifth century, we were to turn the perspectivist trick against Nietzsche and reverse his account of the two moralities, a case might be made that transgression was crucial to the making of a democratic actor. The signs of a presence, transgressive but anonymous, have to be sought in those who were its foes, in those who looked on the demos as the embodiment of the antipolitical and the antitheoretical.

Recall Plato's portrait of Callicles in *Gorgias:* a transgressive actor,[36] a figure of primal energy and demonic will, who delights in images of "smashing" the restraints imposed by the masses in the name of "equal shares" and "trampling" on all of the cultural restraints designed to repress the worthy few. Yet Callicles is not proposing to imitate the Homeric hero who seeks to best another solitary champion; rather he is matching himself against the demos, tacitly acknowledging that they have defied the norms of nature to set up their own standards.

> Those who lay down the rules are the weak men, the many. And so they lay down the rules and assign their praise and blame with their eye on themselves and their own advantage. They terrorize the stronger men capable of having more. *Gorg.* 483b–c[37]

The identification of the Many with a natural power that is said, paradoxically, to transmute itself into artifical conventions, which equally paradoxically are described as the triumph of the weak, resurfaced in Plato's *Republic.* There the demos is likened to "a great strong beast" (493a–b) but its qualities are again embodied in its enemy, Thrasymachus, the sophist who panders to the many while exploiting their elemental power (336b). Thrasymachus is pictured by Plato as a crude man, physically threatening and verbally aggressive, and likened to a wolf. The position that Thrasymachus attempts to defend is equally crude and physical. The strong rule in their own interest and adopt injustice as their guiding principle. This leads initially to the claim that all forms of government operate according to those same principles and that democracy is the power of sheer numbers (338d6–339a4). Later in the dialogue, however, Socrates refines that characterization of democracy while at the same time retaining the elemental, physical quality of democratic power, but now condensed and institutionalized. In a passage where Socrates depicts the plight of the exceptional man in a democracy, the physical power of the Many has undergone a transformation without losing its coercive quality:

> Whenever the populace crowds together at any public gathering, in the Assembly, the law-courts, the theater, or the camp, and sits there clamoring its approval or disapproval, both alike excessive, of whatever is being said or done; booing and clapping till the rocks ring and the whole place redoubles the noise of their applause and outcries. . . . What sort of private instruction will have given him the strength to hold out against the force of such a torrent, or will save him from being swept away down the stream, until he accepts all their notions of right and wrong, does as they do, and comes to be just such a man as they are?[38]

In such hostile representations of democracy as the embodiment of a barely civilized, almost raw force—the demos as Id and crude Superego—there was the suggestion of a new political presence that had succeeded in developing its own political culture. The strength of that achievement can be measured by the nature of its threat. Plato conjures up horrific imagery as he contemplates the deformed Many invading "the shrine of philosophy": "a multitude of stunted natures, whose souls a life of drudgery has warped and maimed no less surely than their sedentary crafts has disfigured their bodies" [*Rep.* 495d–e]. As perceived by Plato, democracy was an invasion of the psyche, contesting for nothing less than the "soul" of all citizens. Plato's political philosophy and moral psychology were shaped as much by the cultural challenge of democracy as by its political claims, so much so that Plato felt compelled to defend the soul in political terms:

> And for the structures and orderings of the soul the name is "lawful" and "law," from which people become lawful and orderly; and these are justice and temperance. *Gorg.* 504d

Behind the achievement by which the beast became a political animal with its own *paideia* lay a long and dim history. It included institutions and practices of self-help by which ordinary people came to the assistance of their neighbors: interceding for those threatened with slavery; responding to the call for witnesses to crimes; shouldering communal responsibility for actions by its members; relying on violence, not for revenge or simple brutality but to redress wrong; and, not least, rebelling against unpopular authorities.[39] There is a long political anthropology by which the demos is prepared for the politics of the city. Corporate solidarity and self-consciousness are its responses to oppression. "The harshest and most resented aspect" of the pre-Solonian constitution, according to Aristotle, was the enslavement by the rich of the debt-ridden poor, who "had virtually no share in any aspect of government." When Solon later intervenes to mediate the "severe strife" between classes, it is apparent that the Many have acquired a measure of cohesion; they are one "side" to the struggle, and they "oppose the leaders of the state."[40] Thus the "essence" of the Many acquires more complexity as it invents itself in collective action and becomes— save for military formations—the principal collective actor.[41]

VII

The complexity of the collective actor is displayed not only in its adaptation to the institutions of the polis, such as the assembly and law courts, and by the adaptation of those institutions to demotic needs, but in its greatest monument, the empire dominated by the democratic polis of Athens and defended in a war that eventually resulted in its loss. The empire was testimony to both the transgressive and aggressive impulses of the Many and to an epical hero whose agon goes mostly uncelebrated by poets and philosophers and only ambivalently by ancient historians. The Many display a willingness to sacrifice and a seemingly inexhaustible energy that enables them to perform prodigies, to succumb to hubris, to rebound from defeats, even to continue to fight after abandoning their city. The beast has become the citizen without losing its vitality, truly a *politikon zōion.*

That actor is portrayed in one of Thucydides' most striking episodes, the so-called Melian dialogue that is commonly interpreted as a brutal, excessive display of the natural right of the stronger. Melos, a colony of Sparta, refused to capitulate to Athens and in the end its adult male population was slaughtered and its women and children enslaved. Because the doomed Melians, with an attractive naïveté, choose to die rather than surrender, the Athenian part of the dialogue is rarely discussed as an example of political sophistication strikingly at odds with the dismissive treatment of democratic capabilities by the philosophers. At the first discussions the Athenians display a confidence in their own abilities to conduct political negotiations: they accept the Melian proposal to discuss matters in private with "the few," thus waiving the advantage of a public setting where the democrat was most at home. The Athenians go a step further and propose that both sides abstain from set speeches, a format familiar to a rhetorical democracy, and proceed, instead, to deal with practical matters one at a time (5.85, 89). In the exchanges that follow, the Athenians instruct the Melians in how one should go about reasoning in public matters. They should attend to the facts and not allow hope to cloud reality and, above all, bear in mind always that the paramount consideration is the survival of the state (5.87). They should not attempt to plead principles of right so long as they are the weaker party (5.89) and expect that the stronger will risk the danger that its rivals might see that generosity as a sign of vulnerability. The world of gods and of mortals is a place, the Athenians explain, where those who can rule others do so. But that does not at all mean that power politics is devoid of principles. "It is certain that those who do not yield to their equals, who keep terms with their superiors, and are moderate towards their inferiors, on the whole succeed best" (5.111). At the end of the exchange, it is the representatives of the demos who urge their enemies to "think over the matter and reflect once and again that it is for your country you are consulting" (5.111). If we recall that the Melians were the representatives of a ruling aristocracy, the episode has the piquancy of a role reversal not unlike Sancho Panza lecturing Don Quixote.

The so-called radical democracy of the fifth century, the democracy of unparalleled popular participation, created an equally extraordinary release of energy that was sublimated into the political. This meant, among other things, a conception of the political sufficient to absorb the energies of a high proportion of the members of the polis, or, more precisely, a straining toward such a conception by extending its limits outward while destroying certain internal social boundaries erected in the name of birth or wealth or virtue.

Perhaps the most striking confirmation of this are the words that Thucydides attributes to a Corinthian who is part of a delegation sent to gain Sparta's support against the Athenians:

> The Athenians are addicted to innovation, and their designs are characterized by swiftness alike in conception and execution. . . . [T]hey are adventurous beyond their power, and daring beyond their judgment, and in danger they are sanguine. . . . [T]hey are never at home . . . for they hope by their absence to extend their acquisitions. Their bodies they spend ungrudgingly in their country's cause; their intellect they jealously husband to be employed in her service. . . . [T]hey were born into the world to take no rest themselves and to give none to others.[42]

The Aristotelian author of *The Constitution of Athens,* after describing the overthrow of The Thirty, asserts that that was the eleventh change of constitution for the Athenians (41.2). Not all of the changes, perhaps none, were the equivalent of a revolutionary overthrow of an entire social order. Yet most of them enlarged the power of the demos until, in this author's words:

> They have made themselves supreme in all fields; they run everything by decrees of the Ekklesia and by decisions of the dikasteria in which the people are supreme. 41.2

What is more remarkable is the language that Aristotle, no fan of democracy, uses in an immediately preceding passage to characterize the overthrow of The Thirty, the punishment exacted of them and their followers, and the restoration of democracy. "The Athenians appear to have handled their affairs, both private and public, as well and with as much statesmanship as any people have ever shown in a similar situation" (40.3). He goes on to praise the demos for their moderation and their scrupulous insistence on repaying the State debts incurred by The Thirty. He concludes that "it was just that the people should take control because they had secured their return by their own efforts" (41.1–2). It is not too much to say that what is being described is an unusual level of political maturity and self-confidence that had been acquired by the demos during the previous century.[43] That is, its political skills were "refined" by the constitutional conflicts of the period. Two things about those struggles should be emphasized, since they tend to be true of comparable events later on.

One is that there is always more politics involved than concrete results might suggest.[44] A new statute, a change in the powers of an institution, the abolition of certain established practices are all pitifully small testimony to the enormous amount of human activity, interaction, changes in consciousness, and acquisition of skills that brought about the changes in question. Significant political changes are the product of transgressive actions. They disturb the power relations, interests, expectations, and taboos that typically cluster around all laws and institutions. This leads into the second point.

No ruling group voluntarily cedes its power. "The only way in which oligarchy could be transformed into democracy," de Ste. Croix has written, "was by revolution. I know of no single case in the whole of Greek history in which a ruling oligarchy introduced democracy without compulsion and by a single vote."[45] Transgression provokes contestation because it is, in effect, a social invasion of a preserve from which the invaders had been previously excluded. Hobbes would later claim that something accessible to all is not by nature valuable—except, the democrat would demur, the status of citizen.[46] The triumph of the latter means the democratization of political values, because it entails a rejection of the fundamental aristocratic or oligarchic value of exclusivity.

The invention of a new actor was accompanied by a new conception of politics. Its radicalism can be best appreciated by recalling Aristotle's account of how the tyrant Peisistratus went about destroying the public realm and its demotic politics. While speaking to the people, he had his men collect the people's weapons.

> When he had concluded his speech, he told the crowd not to be surprised or alarmed by what had happened to their weapons; they should go home and look after their private affairs—he would take care of the state. . . . [Peisistratus also offered financial assistance to encourage farming.] He did not want them in the city but scattered in the country, and if they had enough to live on, and were busy with their own affairs, they would neither want to meddle with affairs of state nor have the time to do so. *Ath. Pol.*15.5–16.5

The new ideal involved not only reclaiming public space but rendering politics transparent. It would be a politics in which discussion and decision were open; where all citizens might speak freely without suffering the humiliation of a Thersites; where power was visible, audible, countable, accountable, and, above all, accessible to those without leisure. Transparent politics was the corollary of the revolutionary principle of full popular participation or, more precisely, of freedom understood as truly popular participation.

That politics also posited a contrast between the demotic politics of the Assembly (Ekklesia) and the selective politics of aristocratic factions (*hetaireia*). The central point of the contrast was captured by Aristotle's famous definition of the ideal citizen as one who knows how to rule and be ruled in turn.[47] That definition, though it seems democratic, is not. For it rests on the assumption that the good man, like the aristocrat and oligarch, not only wants to rule and would accept rule by others of his kind, but he would object to being ruled by inferiors. Now while it is true that the demos refused to extend democratic citizenship to women, metics, and slaves, that refusal, unlike the refusal of the aristocrat to admit the demos to high office, would contradict the idea of democratic equality. Or, stated differently, democracy was and is the only political ideal that condemns its own denial of equality and inclusion. This was recognized long ago, for example, in the speech Thucydides has a Syracusan democrat make:

> The demos includes the whole State, oligarchy only a part. . . . [N]one can hear and decide as well as the many; those talents receive their due in a democracy. 6.39[48]

VIII

The identification of democracy with "the whole State" was an effective trope because it drew attention to the paradox at the center of alternative systems. Monarchy, aristocracy, and oligarchy each claimed that ruling and citizenship should be restricted to a narrow social stratum; thus exclusion of the Many from politics was declared to be a necessary condition for ruling in the interests of all. The resulting idea of the political was of a good benefiting all and to which all should contribute without, however, sharing in power. Athenian democracy challenged the coherence of that formula by greatly broadening the base of power so as to identify the good of the whole with the benefits or advantages of those whose aggregated wealth, skills, and lives formed the greater part of the whole.

The demos might be said to be the carrier of an ideal political that was more inclusive than the class promoting it.[49] To counter that claim, without denying it or reasserting the claims of status or wealth, critics of democracy adopted a new, postdemocratic argument, that democracy could function effectively only when combined with strong leadership.[50] Pericles was the favored paradigm of the wise leader whose political genius lay in his ability to restrain the excesses/transgressions of democracy while rekindling hope when, in the face of reverses, the demos became disheartened.[51] That paradigm recurs in modern times, in, for example, Max Weber's notion of "leadership democracy."[52]

The idea of an "outstanding" leader involves a strategy of establishing "distance" between the demos and the individual who owes his position to popular choice or support. Distance was not meant as an idle metaphor but as the symbol of practices that might range from special education to indirect elections. The development of these notions owed much to the philosophers. Although Plato's *Republic* and *Laws* are familiar examples of the genre, one of the most striking is the neglected Platonic dialogue *Alcibiades I* or *(Alcibiades) Major*.[53] There virtue and knowledge are asserted to be the marks that set off leaders from the mob: You will be "deformed," Socrates tells the young Alcibiades, if you become a "lover of the people." Knowledge is likened to weapons that will protect the leader against the mob (132b).

Although in the dialogue Socrates uses the value of knowledge to establish distance between leader and led, he exploits that distance by introducing a strong manipulative element that assumes the demos has become an object in the thinking of the few. He describes an "eye" that sees into the eye of another but sees itself. This knowledge of self, which is declared to be beyond the powers of most humans, enables its possessor to understand not only the things that "belong" to himself but those of others (133a–c). The run of mankind, Socrates declares, does not even know its own "belongings"—a carpenter may know how to build houses but he does not know the nature of a construction or the meaning of tools—and so there can be no doubt that they have no knowledge of "affairs of state" (133d–e). At one point in the dialogue, Alcibiades responds to Socrates' argument that the noble and just should rule by saying that would mean that rule would be by "men who do business with each other and make use of one another, as is our way of life in our cities." Alcibiades' reference to the factious politics of the *hetaireiai* is then reformulated by Socrates by superimposing the true leader on top of the faction that is able to control the people. "Then," he says, "you speak of ruling over men who make use of men" and so rule over men who are fellow citizens (125c–d).

But perhaps the most complex stratagem for loosening the hold of the demos over the political—and one that has hardly been noted—was to separate democracy from the state. I am not referring here to the problem posed by Aristotle, of whether a change of constitution necessarily means a change in the identity of the polis (*Pol.* 3.1276b1–10). Rather, I want to call attention to a development in the thinking of critics of democracy that argued for, or appealed to, a metapolitical plane, higher and more enduring, which democracy had entered upon but could not democratize. A good example is provided by Pericles' speech following the second invasion, when the mood of the Athenian citizens was defeatist. Pericles appeals to them to place the safety of the polis above their personal misfortunes (Thuc. 2.61). Then he asks them to consider a new way of thinking about power, one so bold that he had not dared to pose it previously. It was: that while their city has been lost, their power is not tied solely to that place.[54] Sea power, which Pericles describes as "widely different," remains intact and Athenian vessels are free to go where they please (2.62). The power they had inherited from their fathers, who had defeated the Persians, and was now their responsibility to pass on, was constituted by their empire, not by their polis. That power was different in kind, tyrannical not democratic, and in magnitude, "a power greater than any hitherto known" (2.63–64).

In that formulation Pericles never once refers to democracy; he is representing the empire as the apotheosis of a power that has shattered its connection to the polis, to power structured by a constitution. Once that meta-plane has been charted, an Alcibiades can appeal to it at the same moment that he is betraying the city:

> I do not consider that I am now attacking a country that is still mine; I am rather trying to recover one that is mine no longer. 6.92

The culminating moment of this development occurs when the Athenians debate whether to allow Alcibiades to return. The question is put by Pisander in a form that reveals how much had been abandoned while cultivating power independent of a city or a constitution: "The safety of the state" is superior to the question of "the form of its government" (8.53).

Aristotle had asserted that the two essential elements of a polis were its citizen body and its territory (*Pol.* 7.1325b40). In Ehrenburg's phrase a polis was a "community of place."[55] The Long Wall built to protect Athens from the land forces of Sparta was a reflection of the importance to political identity of a "ground," as were the public architecture and layout of Athens. We might say that all of the elements of the political—the citizen-body, the main institutions of political and judicial deliberation, public festivals and rituals, in short, the constitution of state power—were associated with a place wherein the powers of the state were generated because confined, "a law and order," as Plato put it, "marked by limit" (*Phlb.* 26b).

But the growth of naval power and reliance on it by Athens during the Peloponnesian War attenuated the connection between power and place. Instead of the city representing the place where power was constituted, it served more as a naval base, that is, a launching point for a form of power that was to be projected abroad rather than embodied primarily in internal deliberations, policy decisions, or decrees.[56]

A democracy whose power is imperial and naval and described as continually "grasping at more" (Thuc. 4.41) is in symbiosis with, rather than the antithesis to, the Alcibiades who would, according to Socrates, prefer to die at once if he were prevented from pursuing ambitions that would take him beyond Pericles and anyone else who had ever existed, Greek or barbarian, and who ultimately aimed to "fill the whole world with (his) name and power" (*Alc.* 1.105a–c).

The symbiosis between democratic Athens and Alcibiades included a common element of deracination. When Alcibiades went over to the Spartan side and sought their support, he referred to democracy as a contingent fact, distinct from the identity of Athens. He explained that he had once served that democracy but only because "it was necessary in most things to conform to established conditions" (Thuc. 6.89). For Athenian democracy it was Athens that had become contingent. The apotheosis of power independent of place and political identity attained a certain pathos toward the end of the Syracusan debacle when Nicias tried to rally the Athenian forces by saying,

> Reflect that you are at once a city wherever you sit down . . . the one thought of each man [on a march] being that the spot on which he may be forced to fight must be conquered and held as his country and stronghold. Thuc. 7.77

IX

Plato and Aristotle both emphasize freedom as the basic principle of democracy, but, interestingly, both tend to characterize democratic freedom in social rather than political terms. For Plato democratic freedom is license to speak, dress, and behave in ways that violated traditional norms of deference. Aristotle simply absorbs democratic freedom into the demand for equality in matters that properly require deference to qualitative differences.[57]

The democratic conception of freedom is perhaps best preserved in an unexpected place, Cicero's *De Republica*. There freedom is identified with participation on a continuous basis. It is insufficient, the exponent of democracy declares, if the people merely vote, elect officials, and have bills proposed to them : "They are really granting only what they would have to grant even if they were unwilling to do so and are asked to give to others what they do not possess themselves" (1.31.47; tr. C. W. Keyes, Loeb). The case for democracy is about a partnership among political equals; it is not, the speaker emphasizes, about denying unequal talents or confiscating the fortunes of the wealthy (1.32.48–49).

This last point finds confirmation among historians today. Athenian democracy was guilty of few, if any, excesses against the wealthy.[58] The importance of this point is that the demos was not so much concerned with gaining forms of social recognition as creating a distinct political place where power was equally shared. In short, the ideal was political, not social. To my mind the best account of that kind of politics and of the essence of Athenian democracy is provided by the critic of Athenian democracy known as the Old Oligarch or Pseudo-Xenophon. He begins with the question of why instead of following the leadership of "the ablest" and "best," the demos insists upon heeding one of their own, even though he is uneducated and unvirtuous. The answer is masterful in conveying the flavor of Athenian democracy: The demos will prefer the unvirtuous man because he is better disposed to protecting their interests than the man of "virtue and wisdom."

Such practices do not produce the best city, but they are the best way of preserving democracy. For the common people do not wish to be deprived of their rights in an admirably governed city, but to be free and to rule the city; they are not disturbed by inferior laws, for the common people get their strength and freedom from what you define as inferior laws. If you are looking for an admirable code of laws you will find that the ablest draw them up in their own interest. . . . As a result of this excellent system the common people would very soon lose all their political rights.[59]

The passage is notable for its juxtaposition of a democratic theory of rule over against the conceptions that are more familiar to us from the political and constitutional theories of Plato and Aristotle. It is no exaggeration to say that modern prejudices against democracy still bear the imprint of those theories. Democracy never produced its own "word-smiths," but beginning with the intervention of Solon—the man who formulates the terms for understanding the first recorded contest between inchoate democratic stirrings and oligarchic power—and continuing down to Aristotle, it was the antidemocratic critics who developed conceptions of politics, constitutionalism, and governance that were intended to eliminate democracy, as in the case of Plato, or to qualify and contain it, as in the case of Thucydides and Aristotle.

Among the many achievements of Greek theory, one of particular consequence remains so much a part of our own thinking today as to be virtually an unconscious reflex rather than a considered choice. I am referring to what might be called "the intellectualization of the political and the relocation of politics from the assembly to the academy." By that I mean not only the reshaping of politics into a theoretical object and the power that technique makes available to those who can manipulate it, but the association of a higher political understanding with a higher education and a permanent dissociation of democracy from theory and intellect. The crucial figure in this development was Aristotle—although, here as usual, Plato cast a long shadow. Aristotle's achievement was to redefine aristocracy as meritocracy, downplaying the elements of birth and wealth and emphasizing the qualities of education, culture, and ability. To bring out further what the stakes were in this development, we might contrast two different pictures of politics, one sketched by the Old Oligarch, the second taken from Aristotle's *Rhetoric.*

It is right that the poor and the ordinary people should have more power than the noble and the rich, because it is the ordinary people who man the fleet and bring the city her power.[60]

In this formulation politics has a directness and immediacy: the power of the polis is, literally, the power of the people. That power runs, as it were, in a direct line from them to the major institutions. In the *Rhetoric,* however, a certain "distance" is evident between those who aim to play a leading part in politics, that is, those who now find themselves in the position the demos had previously been of seeking entry into politics, and the intellectualized form of the politics that is presented to them by the theorist who makes a virtue of remaining outside politics:

> But the most important and effective of all the means of persuasion and good counsel is to know all the forms of government and to distinguish the manners and customs, institutions, and interests of each.[61]

Aristotle concludes with a description of the political point of this education. Each form of government has "a character," and hence the political man will be most effective when he displays the characteristics appropriate to the political system in which he is vying for influence.[62] Here politics consists of manipulable beliefs and practices, with the self-manipulating actor standing to one side and surveying its possibilities. Clearly intellectualization promotes a community of understanding between the actor and the theorist: one manipulates concrete things abstractly, the other manipulates abstract ideas concretely.[63] But above all it is a community that is trying to generate a form of power different from the power of mere numbers represented by the demos.[64] To the theorist democracy represents the power/threat of the undifferentiated.[65] Aristotle attempts to deal with it, not as Plato's *Republic* had, by suppressing it, but by short-circuiting the power of the demos and by refusing to recognize democracy as other than quantitative. In his versions of acceptable constitutions, such as "polity" or a "law-abiding democracy," he acknowledges a simple numbers principle that allots to the demos the right to elect but not to hold office.

The evolution of theory from Solon to Aristotle might be summarized this way: Solon was not only, as Vlastos put it, "a man of the center" but a man at the center who actively intervened to redress injustice in order to forestall civil strife.[66] He is the man of words, the poet-theorist as mediator. Aristotle is the theory-man, standing outside but taking sides, prepared to assert that it is the virtuous few, not the many, who should rule and, moreover, the few are really justified in revolting when they are denied—although he hastens to add that they never do.[67]

X

The *conatus*-driven character of Athenian democracy achieved a democracy in which ordinary human beings overcame the barriers to power represented by wealth, status, education, and tradition and succceeded in inventing the practice of collective action on a continuing basis. Taking that achievement as a background, we can now address the question raised earlier, of the kind of democracy where equal rights are formally guaranteed but social and political inequalities are widespread and the demos is a negligible political actor. That system might be called electoral democracy.[68]

Electoral democracy is almost universally held to be the best form of government for the contemporary world. Its basic elements are formal provisions for equal civil liberties of all citizens; freely contested and periodic elections; mass political parties competing for the support of voters; elected officials who are accountable and removable by the electorate; a politics largely financed by powerful economic interests; and a constitution that specifies the authority and powers of the main governmental organs and stipulates the rules controlling politics and policy-making. To this list should be added the "free market." In a recent speech before the United Nations, President Clinton coupled "democracy and the free market" as the principal objectives of American foreign policy, a pronouncement that was meant to reaffirm this country's position toward the new societies emerging in Central and Eastern Europe and in the former Soviet Union.

The virtually unchallengeable status of the free market and capitalism in general in the contemporary public rhetoric of democracy is important to the theme of this volume, ancient and modern democracy. For whatever else one may want to say about free market capitalism, it is definitely not an arrangement for producing equality. Its principal motor force comes from the differentials in reward, status, and power that it makes available. In the United States evidence is substantial that various inequalities are increasing, especially along racial lines. It follows that contemporary democracy contradicts Aristotle's fundamental principle for identifying the distinctive character of a democratic *politeia,* that each citizen should be on an equality with the rest (*Pol.* 6.1317b5–7).

The contradiction between ancient and modern democracy is, however, only part of the picture. Contemporary democracies are in contradiction with modern conceptions of democracy, not simply with ancient ones. To take only the most striking instance, modern democracy adopted popular sovereignty as its first or defining principle. Power was supposed to be derived from the people, the people were supposed to exercise continuing vigilance over those using their powers, and the powers were supposed to "return" to the people at stated intervals. No one would take seriously such a conception as even remotely approximating the political realities of contemporary democracy.

Early modern doctrines of popular sovereignty are commonly interpreted by later commentators as posing a question of "will" and hence the political problem was conceived to be one of finding the constitutional or institutional means not of expressing, but of sublimating, the popular will, beginning with elections but reemerging as the legitimation of legislative, executive, or bureaucratic policy-making. What remained stillborn was the possibility of popular sovereignty as a will to power on the part of an actor struggling to be both collective and autonomous.

For "the people" to become an actor, not simply an elector, more than will was needed; a voice was also required. In the early gropings toward democracy during the English civil wars of the seventeenth century, one finds numerous references to "vox populi, vox Dei."[69] The remarkable idea was not so much the claim that the voice of the people was the voice of God but rather that the people had a voice at all. That notion implied a citizenry that expressed itself corporatively, that is, was able to frame its own understanding of its needs and, equally important, its own estimate of its situation. Three of the most important popular revolutions of modern times—of the 1640s in England, 1776 in America, and 1789 in France—were accompanied by an extraordinary outpouring of popular pamphlet and newspaper literature, a good part of it devoted to giving voice to the people.[70]

It is obvious that today—in the age of communication conglomerates, media pundits, television, public opinion surveys, and political consultants—the exercise of popular will, the expression of its voice, and the framing of its needs have been emptied of all promise of autonomy. Periodically American politicians and publicists claim that theirs is the world's greatest democracy. The reality is a democracy without the demos as actor. The voice is that of a ventriloquous democracy.

NOTES

1. Rawls, *Political Liberalism,* p. 217.

2. See the discussion of the role of rhetors in fourth-century Athenian democracy in Ober, *Mass and Elite,* especially chapter 3. For a more detailed discussion of democracy and constitutionalism, see my "Norm and Form."

3. See Paul Cartledge's contribution to this volume, especially the section "Use in Argument 1: Reference."

4. See Mansbridge, *Why We Lost the ERA.*

5. For an application of this notion to recent events, see my "Democracy without the Citizen" (180–91 of Wolin, *The Presence of the Past*).

6. The tensions between an inclusive view of the polls and an exclusive view of the political community are evident in Aristotle's efforts to justify slavery as being according to nature while admitting that that account does not always fit (*Pol.* 1255a21–b4). See the discussion in Nichols, *Citizens and Statesmen,* 19–24. On the general topic with some attention to Aristotle, see Finley, *Ancient Slavery and Modern Ideology,* especially 119–20.

7. *Pol.* 1281a40–1281b20.

8. "This is why the theater is the political art par excellence; only there is the political sphere of human life transposed into art." Arendt, *The Human Condition,* 188.

9. Plato *Rep.* 1, which has sometimes been called "The Book of Thrasymachus," and his *Gorgias* and *Alcibiades* I all give portraits of the actor frustrated by the politics of democracy.

10. Relevant here are the opening passages of Thuc. 1.1–3.

11. An influential example of this formulation is in Arendt, *The Human Condition,* 17–26, 188–94.

12. See Ober, *Mass and Elite,* 104ff.

13. Arendt, *The Human Condition,* 178–79.

14. Cited in K. J. Dover, *Greek Popular Morality,* 289.

15. *Economy and Society,* vol. 3, 984–87.

16. See the discussion in G. Wood, *Radicalism,* 229ff.; Maier, *Resistance to Revolution;* and the survey by Lintott, *Violence, Civil Strife, and Revolution.*

17. The classic discussion is by Weber, "Parliament and Government in a Reconstructed Germany," in his *Economy and Society,* vol. 3, pp. 2, 1381–1461.

18. For the Periclean echoes in Cleon's speeches, see de Romilly, *Thucydides and Athenian Imperialism,* 163ff. Also Connor, *Thucydides,* 79n. 1 and references cited there.

19. Connor, *Thucydides,* 87–88, charges Diodotus with "serious" misrepresentation of the facts. In support of his proposal of leniency, Diodotus had claimed that the common people of Mytilene had had no part in the revolt and had willingly turned the city over to the Athenians. Connor assumes that Thucydides provides the truthful representation of the facts (3.27). Although Thucydides' account does not squarely support Diodotus' claim, neither does it support the charge of serious misrepresentation. The commoners had been armed by the wealthy class for the sole purpose of launching an attack on the Athenians. Once armed, the common people "refused any longer to obey their officers" and proceeded to concert their own aims by insisting that the authorities "divide the provisions among all or they themselves would come to terms with the Athenians and deliver up the city." According to Thucydides, the authorities, knowing that they could not resist that demand and fearing they would be "left out of the capitulation," agreed to surrender to the Athenians (3.28). It seems clear that the Mytilinean authorities would not have surrendered in the absence of pressure from the commons. Connor also accuses Diodotus of having misrepresented the favorable disposition of subject people toward Athens. Again, his proof is what Thucydides said. But Thucydides also has Diodotus begin his speech with the broad assertion that any city would rebel because in such circumstances human nature invariably exaggerates possibilities (3 .45).

20. Connor has described Diodotus's speech as functioning at two levels, practical decision and "more general political discourse." (*Thucydides,* p. 83.) I would describe that generality as a "nonphilosophical theory." For further background on the Mytilinean incident, see de Ste. Croix, *Class Struggle,* 603–4n. 26.

21. For a discussion of the different oratory of the courtrooms, see Connor, *Thucydides,* 84.

22. Connor, *Thucydides,* 90. That Thucydides engaged an opaque world and tried to reinterpret it without however wholly emancipating himself from "prehistoric" or mythic modes was suggested nearly a century ago by Cornford, *Thucydides Mythistoricus,* especially viii.

23. Ar. *Pol.* 1278a13–26; Marx, *Capital,* vol. 3, pt. 4, ch. 20; pt. 7, ch. 48; Arendt, *The Human Condition,* 81ff.

24. Here and in all subsequent translated citations from Thucydides, I have followed John H. Finley's translation in *Thucydides,* 59.

25. Connor, *Thucydides,* 89, 90.

26. Marcel Detienne, *Dionysus Slain,* ix. See also the essays in Izard, *Between Belief and Transgression.*

27. Rousseau, *The Social Contract,* bk. 2, ch. 7. "One who dares to undertake to found a people should feel capable, so to speak, of changing human nature, of transforming

each individual, who by himself is a perfect and solitary whole, into a part of a greater whole from which the individual, in a sense, receives—his life and being."

28. Ibid., bk. 3 , ch. 4, 73.

29. I have found much that was suggestive in Yirmiyahu Yovel, *Spinoza,* esp. vol. 1, 128–37.

30. On the *conatus* see Spinoza, *Ethics* 2.6 (tr. R.H.M. Elwes, Dover). As James Madison wrote to Jefferson in 1787, "In a popular Government, the political and physical power may be considered as vested in the same hands, that is in a majority of the people." *The Complete Madison,* 254.

31. *Ethics* III.vii, tr. Elwes.

32. See especially Spinoza's Preface to his *Theologico-Political Tractatus.*

33. Nietzsche, *The Gay Science,* section 349. On Spinoza and Nietzsche, see Yovel, *Spinoza,* vol. 2, ch. 5.

34. Nietzsche, *Beyond Good and Evil,* sections 259–60; *On the Genealogy of Morals,* section S.

35. Nietzsche, *The Gay Science.* section 354.

36. Later commentators have described Callicles as a Nietzschean figure. See E. R. Dodds's introduction to his edition of *Gorgias;* Crombie, *An Examination of Plato's Doctrines,* vol. 1, p. 302.

37. Tr. Terence Irwin (Oxford). Also *Gorg.* 488c–489c. All subsequent translated citations from the *Gorgias* are Irwin's.

38. *Rep.* 492b–c (tr. Cornford, Oxford). See also *Gorg.* 483e–484a.

39. Here I have borrowed freely from Lintott, *Violence, Civil Strife, and Revolution,* 15–16,18, 19–23, 25, 28, 126.

40. *Ath. Pol.,* 2.2–3, 5.1–2. Here and elsewhere I have used the translation of J. M. Moore, *Aristotle and Xenophon,* p. 183 (41.2). See also the discussion by Wood, *Peasant-Citizen and Slave,* 94ff.

41. See Vidal-Naquet, *The Black Hunter,* 85–105. And see Plato's remark about how "the lean and sunburned" common men will notice that the pleasure-loving oligarch cannot endure the rigors of battle and will proceed to plot against him. *Rep.* 556 c–d.

42. Thuc. 1.70 (tr. R. Crawley, Random House).

43. The growing confidence of the demos is emphasized by W. G. Forrest, *The Emergence of Greek Democracy.*

44. See the discussion in de Ste. Croix, *Class Struggle,* 281.

45. Ibid., 288.

46. Hobbes, *Leviathan* ch. 8, 42.

47. *Pol.* 3.4.1277b8–13.

48. I have used Forrest's translation, *The Emergence of Greek Democracy,* 232. Aristophanes (*The Frogs,* 952) has "Euripides" claiming that it was democratic for him to have inserted parts for women and slaves in his rendition of tragic legends.

49. *Demos* might stand for the majority; or it might mean the poor; or it might signify those who supported democracy, including both the common people and the leaders from the upper classes; or it could stand for "the people as a whole." Lintott, *Violence, Civil Strife, and Revolution,* pp. 93–94; Fornara and Samons, *Athens from Cleisthenes to Pericles,* 48–49.

50. Plato of course, provides an exception. *Gorg.* 515a–516d.

51. Thuc., 2.65.

52. In our own day the Democratic Leadership Conference was formed by "centrist" Democrats to change the "populist" image of the Party. They pledged to limit social programs favored by the working class and poor, to hold down taxes, and to encourage high-technology corporations.

53. I have used the Loeb edition and translation by W.R.M. Lamb (Cambridge, Mass.: Harvard University Press, 1955).

54. Although this formulation is used earlier by a speaker identified only as the "Athenian," the implication is that abandonment of the city was abnormal, a measure of desperation (Thuc. 1.74). On this point it seems to me that in her splendid *Invention of Athens,* esp. pp. 53, 55, 57, 60, Nicole Loraux has treated "Athens" and democracy as virtually a single entity. My position would be that in the funeral oration the city tended to absorb democracy and then usurp its position.

55. Victor Ehrenberg, *The Greek State,* 28.

56. See Connor, *Thucydides,* 24–25; Thuc. 1.8, 143.

57. Plato *Rep.* 557b; Arist. *Pol.* 5.1310a30–34; 6.1317a40–bl6.

58. See Barry S. Strauss, "Aristotle's Critique."

59. *Ath. Pol.* 8–9 (tr. Moore).

60. *Ath. Pol.* 2 (tr. Moore).

61. *Rh.* 1.8.1–3 (tr. J. H. Feese, Loeb).

62. *Rh.* 1.8.6.

63. In *Pol.* 2.12. 1273b26. Aristotle refers to those who have only written about politics and those who have both written and taken part; there is no hint of incompatibility between the two groups. On the notion of manipulation, see Aristotle's discussion of how election requirements may be reshaped to produce desired outcomes (*Pol.* 4.13.1297al4).

64. *Pol.* 4.12.1296bl5 and the discussion of quantity and quality.

65. *Pol.* 4.9.1294a30–1294b14.

66. Gregory Vlastos, "Isonomia Politike," 175. See also Vlastos, "Solonian Justice."

67. *Pol.* 5.1.1301a39–b1. An argument could be made that democracy found in the rhetoricians of the fourth century (B.C.) its functional equivalents to the philosopher. I have criticized this view in my "Norm and Form."

68. Wolin, "Democracy: Electoral and Athenian."

69. Boas, *Vox Populi.*

70. The locus classicus is the Thomason Collection in the British Museum. There are also the Clarke Papers containing the Army debates during the English civil wars. Useful editions are Woodhouse, ed., *Puritanism and Liberty;* Aylmer, *The Levellers;* Hill and Dell, *The Good Old Cause.* For a survey of recent scholarship, see Dow, *Radicalism in the English Revolution.* On the American Revolution see Bailyn, ed., *Pamphlets of the American Revolution;* Wood, *The Creation of the American Republic.* On France see Hunt, *Politics, Culture and Class,* especially Part 1; and Chartier, *The Cultural Origins of the French Revolution.*

THE ANCIENT ATHENIAN AND THE MODERN LIBERAL VIEW OF LIBERTY AS A DEMOCRATIC IDEAL

Mogens Herman Hansen

As THE TITLE of my paper suggests, my intention is to compare Athenian *eleutheria* with political freedom in Western democracies, and to discuss differences and similarities between the ancient and the modern concept of liberty. For many years the fashion has been to emphasize the differences. The purpose of my paper is to advocate a swing of the pendulum and argue that the undeniable differences are overshadowed by the striking similarities. My paper must therefore be read as a plea, not as an attempt to present a so-called "objective" or "balanced" view of the problem.

Today the term *democracy* denotes both a set of political institutions and a set of political ideals[1]—ideals that are believed to be furthered by democratic political institutions more than by any other form of government.[2] As a set of political institutions, democracy is commonly defined as a political system in which power—directly or indirectly—rests with the whole of the people.[3] As a set of political ideals, democracy is connected first of all with liberty, next with equality.[4] It is remarkable how, in this respect, modern democracy resembles ancient Athenian *dēmokratia*.

In liberal democratic thought democracy, liberty, and equality form a triad and are often described as the three points of a triangle.[5] As for the ancient view, I will restrict myself to quoting two passages, one from a champion and one from an opponent of popular government. Let me begin with three lines from Aristotle's *Politics* which in one sentence condense what he repeats throughout this part of his treatise:

> For if liberty (*eleutheria*) and equality (*isotēs*), as is thought by some, are chiefly to be found in democracy (*dēmokratia*), they will be best attained when all persons alike share in the government to the utmost. And since the people are in the majority, and the opinion of the majority is decisive, such a government must necessarily be a democracy.[6]

Here we learn that *dēmokratia* was both a political system and a set of political ideals, that the two central ideals were *eleutheria,* "liberty," and *isotēs,* "equality," and that the concepts of *dēmokratia-eleutheria-isotēs* were commonly juxtaposed so as to form a triad.[7]

Now Aristotle disliked democracy, but his critical account of the democratic principles is confirmed, for example, by Pericles' praise of popular rule in the funeral oration as reported by Thucydides:[8]

> It has the name democracy (*dēmokratia*) because government is in the hands not of the few but of the majority (*es tous pleionas oikein*).[9] In private disputes all are equal (*pasi to ison*) before the law; and when it comes to esteem in public affairs, a man is preferred according to his own reputation for something, not, on the whole, just turn and turn about,[10] but for excellence, and even in poverty no man is debarred by obscurity of reputation so long as he has it in him to do some good service to the State. Freedom is a feature of our public life (*eleutherōs politeuomen*); and as for suspicion of one another in our daily private pursuits, we do not frown on our neighbor if he behaves to please himself or set our faces in those expressions of disapproval that are so disagreeable, however harmless.

In this famous passage we are supposed to be persuaded that Athens is a *dēmokratia,* that its political system is based on the principle *es tous pleionas oikein,* and that the basic ideals of democracy are *pasi to ison* and *eleutherōs politeuomen.*

It is important to keep in mind that the concepts of freedom and equality overlap—both in modern political thought and in ancient Athenian democratic ideology. Freedom of speech, for example, is seen sometimes as a kind of equality, but sometimes as a kind of liberty protected by the democratic constitution.[11] In Athens every citizen's right to address his fellow citizens is commonly called *isēgoria,* and the term indicates that the ideal is viewed as a kind of equality.[12] It is every citizen's *equal* right to speak that is stressed. But in Euripides' *Supplices,* for example, the same right is also described as a kind of liberty.[13] The situation is similar in modern liberal democracy. Discussions of equality invariably lead to the question, Equality of what? and to many liberal democrats the obvious answer has been, Equality of liberty![14] Thus liberty and equality tend to coalesce precisely as *eleutheria* and *isotēs* tended to coalesce in ancient Athens.

There is yet another similarity between modern and ancient democratic ideology that concerns the relation between liberty and equality: To modern champions of participatory or radical democracy, equality is more important than liberty, but to liberal democrats liberty matters more than equality.[15] The Athenians held similar views: In classical Athens—and as far back as the sources go—*eleutheria* eclipsed *isotēs.*

Many historians hold that the central aspect of democratic equality and of democratic ideology altogether was *isonomia.*[16] But the term *isonomia* is poorly attested in classical Athens.[17] First, it is not found in symbouleutic and forensic speeches, whereas the terms *eleutheria* and *eleutheros* are commonly used. Next, the names a state gives its warships often reflect its slogans and political values. In the Athenian navy several triremes were called *Dēmokratia* and *Eleutheria;*[18] one was called *Parrhēsia,*[19] but there is no sign of any trireme ever being called *Isonomia.*[20] Third, the political cults did not include *isono-*

mia: both *dēmokratia* and *eleutheria* were made divine and worshiped by the Athenians, *Dēmokratia* in its own right as a separate goddess,[21] *Eleutheria* in connection with the cult of Zeus Eleutherios;[22] but *isonomia* was never represented as a goddess and never connected with any form of worship. All three observations indicate that the key concept of Athenian democratic ideology was *eleutheria,* not *isonomia.*

So much for the close connection between *eleutheria* and *isotēs* and the similar connection between liberty and equality in liberal democratic theory. I now turn to the main question and ask, What is political liberty? and what was *eleutheria* in ancient Athenian democratic thought?

By way of introduction I will briefly point out that in sources describing classical Athens we can detect at least seven different uses of the noun *eleutheria* and the adjective *eleutheros.*

1. The most common use of *eleutheros* is in the sense of "free" as opposed to being a slave (*doulos*).[23] This sense of *eleutheria,* however, is not particularly democratic since slaves existed in all poleis independent of their constitutions.

2. *Eleutheria* was regularly invoked as a basic democratic ideal in debates that contrasted democracy and tyranny, cf. the famous dictum of Democritus: "Poverty under democracy is as much to be preferred to so-called prosperity under an autocracy as freedom to slavery."[24] The opposite of this form of *eleutheria* was being enslaved in a metaphorical sense, i.e., being subjected to a despotic ruler. Note that in Democritus *dēmokratia* is linked with poverty, *penia,* just as it is in the next case.

3. When status was at stake, *eleutheros* often had the meaning of being freeborn in the sense of being a born citizen.[25] In such a context one would expect *eleutheros* to denote both citizens and free foreigners as opposed to slaves (see 1 above), but there can be no denying that *eleutheria* used in a democratic polis about descent was restricted to citizens and excluded both free foreigners and slaves.[26] This type of *eleutheria* was a specific democratic value and formed the basis of one view of democratic equality: according to Aristotle democrats believed that since they were all *eleutheroi* (by descent) they ought to be equal in everything.[27] In Aristotle *aporos* is used synonymously with *eleutheros*[28] and the antonyms are *plousios* or *euporos.*[29] So in this case democracy is opposed to oligarchy, not tyranny.

4. In classical Athens all citizens were both entitled and expected to participate in the running of the democratic institutions—not, as one might have expected, as voters in the Assembly, but rather by taking turns in filling all the magistracies. "To rule and be ruled in turns" was described as *eleutheria* and conceived of as a kind of freedom to be found in democracies only.[30]

5. The most controversial form of democratic liberty, however, was the ideal that everybody had a right to live as he pleased (*zēn hōs bouletai tis*) without being oppressed by other persons or by the authorities.[31] It is sometimes stressed that a person's *eleutheria* in this sense was restricted by the (democratic) laws;[32] other sources emphasize that the principle *zēn hōs bouletai tis* applied to the private and not to the public sphere of life.[33]

6. Next, *eleutheros* is often used in the sense of *autonomos* as against being dominated by others (*hypēkoos*).[34] But again, *eleutheria* in the sense of *autonomia* applied to oligarchies—and sometimes even to monarchies—as well as to democracies. It was the freedom *of* the polis, whereas democratic liberty was freedom *within* the polis.[35]

7. Finally, *eleutheros* is sometimes taken by the philosophers to denote a person who is self-restrained.[36] *Eleutheria* in the sense of "self-control" is not far from some modern philosophers' view of positive freedom (cf. *infra*); but though often focusing on self-control, Plato and Aristotle hardly ever take it to be a kind of *eleutheria*,[37] and furthermore, *eleutheria* in this sense has no bearing on political and especially on democratic freedom.[38]

Only four of these seven uses are specifically connected with democracy, namely: *eleutheros* (a) in the sense of being a free-born citizen, (b) in the sense of being entitled to participate in the running of the political institutions, (c) in the sense of living as one pleases, and (d) in the sense of not being subjected to a despotic ruler. The four uses can in fact be reduced to two: the right to participate in political decision-making is inextricably bound up with being a full citizen by birth (a + b);[39] and the right to live as one pleases is often opposed to being ruled, especially by a monarch, and any kind of interference by others in one's private life is rejected as illegitimate and undemocratic (c + d).[40]

Now, how are these two types of freedom related to the notion of liberty advocated in Western democracies in the twentieth century? In contemporary liberal democratic theory liberty is commonly subdivided into negative freedom and positive freedom.[41] Negative freedom is freedom from oppression by the state or by other individuals. Positive freedom is harder to define in one sentence. Following Kant, Hegel, and Isaiah Berlin, philosophers take positive freedom to be some form of self-government or self-mastery, a notion that implies that one is divided into two selves, and that "positive freedom" consists in allowing one's true self to dominate one's other self.[42] Students of political theory take a somewhat different view: they interpret self-determination as an entitlement to participate in collective decision-making, i.e., in a democracy, to be politically active in a free society.[43] Since it is *political* liberty that interests us in our context, I will concentrate on the second line of thought and subscribe to the following description of positive freedom: "There is a link between liberty and democracy through the connection between self-government and self-determination: the self-determined—the free—individual is the self-governing individual. Here individual liberty is seen to involve participation in, rather than the absence of, government."[44] The negative and the positive aspects of freedom are essentially opposed: if we suppose that every aspect of life can be regulated by political decision-making, there is, in principle, no guaranteed freedom from political oppression, but if, on the other hand, we maximize freedom from public interference with the different ways citizens live, there is no political decision-making left in which citizens can participate. The negative and the positive aspect of freedom can only be reconciled if combined with a distinction between a public sphere, in which positive political freedom operates, and a private sphere, in which negative individual freedom is protected against interference from the state.[45] Freedom in the private sphere is connected with the concept of fundamental rights that protect one's person and property and guarantee that one can live as one pleases, as long as he or she respects the laws. Freedom in the public sphere is connected with free elections and with every citizen's right to participate in politics.

Like its modern counterpart, ancient democratic *eleutheria* had two aspects: freedom to participate in the democratic institutions and freedom to live as one pleased. The dual nature of *eleutheria* is most clearly described by Aristotle in the *Politics:*

> A basic principle of the democratic constitution is liberty. That is commonly said, and those who say it imply that only in this constitution do men share in liberty; for that, they say, is what every democracy aims at. Now one aspect of liberty is being ruled and ruling in turn. . . . Another element is to live as you like. For this, they say, is what being free is about, since its opposite, living not as you like, is the condition of a slave. So this is the second defining principle of democracy, and from it has come the ideal of not being ruled, not by anybody at all if possible, or at least only in turn.[46]

According to Aristotle liberty is partly political participation by ruling in turn, partly freedom from political oppression by not being ruled but by living as one pleases. A positive political freedom is contrasted with an individual negative freedom. Aristotle's description of democratic liberty is stated in general terms and there is no explicit reference to Athens, but all the sources show that in this respect the Athenians conformed to the norm.[47] The ideal "to live as one pleases" is praised as a fundamental democratic value by Otanes in the Constitutional Debate in Herodotus,[48] by Athenian statesmen in Thucydides' speeches,[49] and by the Orators in the speeches they delivered before the People's Court.[50] And to rule in turn is singled out by King Theseus in Euripides' play as an essential feature of Athenian democracy.[51]

The view I have presented here is one I have developed and advocated in two recent publications,[52] but it is not the prevailing view among students of ancient history and philosophy. The fashion today is to emphasize the differences between ancient Athenian *eleutheria* and modern democratic liberty: the Athenians, it is said, had no notion of individual rights; the polis was a type of society that permeated all aspects of life; consequently there was no "private sphere" out of reach of the polis, and no notion of what we call negative freedom, i.e., freedom from oppression by the state and its government. Furthermore, "positive freedom" in modern thought is far from the ancient notion of freedom as political participation. And, to top it all, an insuperable difference is that ancient *eleutheria* was intimately related to the opposition between the free and the slave, whereas, in the modern world, the absence of slavery places the concept of liberty in a very different setting.[53] I respond with five points.

1. The view of Isaiah Berlin and many philosophers that positive freedom is self-determination in the sense of self-control, is far from the Athenian view of political freedom as citizen participation in running the democratic institutions. But, as I noted above, political scientists prefer to see this aspect of freedom as individual self-determination *through participating in the creation of the social order*. When political freedom is connected with political participation, the similarity between ancient Athenian and modern political freedom becomes apparent.

2. To illustrate the gulf between modern negative freedom and ancient *eleutheria,* some scholars adduce Benjamin Constant's illuminating essay *De la liberté des anciens comparée à celle des modernes.* Here ancient *political* liberty is taken to consist of collective decision-making by all citizens in assembly, whereas modern liberty is *individual* and consists in guarantees against infringements of every person's right to live as he or she pleases. This type of freedom is, according to Constant, unknown in ancient Greece and Rome.[54] But those who adduce Constant usually forget to add that he explicitly excepts classical Athens from his general analysis of ancient liberty. In Athens, he says, the concept of freedom was very similar to the modern concept, allegedly because commerce was an important factor in the Athenian economy.[55] Whether Constant's explanation is right or wrong is debatable. The important point is that he detected the obvious similarity between ancient Athenian *eleutheria* and the "modern" type of liberty he experienced in his own age. What separates him from us is that he took Sparta and not Athens to be the model of a Greek polis and thus based his analysis of ancient liberty on Sparta and on the philosophers (who admired Sparta more than Athens), whereas he took Athens to be the exception. One of the first to take the opposite stand was George Grote, who maintained that in most respects Athens was the rule and Sparta the exception. Consequently he believed that the democratic ideal of every man's right to live as he pleased was typical of classical Greece.[56] I prefer to avoid generalizations, but following Constant and Grote, I would like to stress the similarity between the Athenian and the liberal notion of personal freedom.

3. The alleged difference between individual liberty in ancient Athens and in modern liberal thought lies in the principles and arguments used to justify it. In modern democratic thought liberty is about the protection of individual rights against infringements by the state or by other people, whereas, it is held, in Athens "the authority of the commmunity over individuals was relatively unrestricted." As Martin Ostwald has pointed out,[57] it is certainly true that the Athenians had no developed concept of "rights" as we have it today. But in practice they certainly knew about the privileges and liberties connected with their democratic constitution, and these rights were highly valued and crucial for their belief that democracy was the best constitution.

Several of the Attic Orators state with approval the rule that no citizen could be executed without due process of law.[58] Admittedly thieves and robbers were not included: they could be put to death immediately if they were caught in the act and had to confess.[59] But that limitation, though important, does not seriously alter the fact that "no execution without a trial" (*mēdena akriton apokteinai*) was felt to be a right that all citizens enjoyed.[60]

Another rule forbade torture of Athenian citizens.[61] It was warranted by a decree (*psēphisma*) probably passed immediately after the expulsion of the tyrants in 510–509 before the introduction of the democracy.[62] It was nevertheless adopted by the democrats and, like the expulsion of the tyrants, was later associated with democracy. The principle that free men are exempt from corporal punishment is closely connected with democracy in Demosthenes' speech against Androtion.[63]

The Athenian democracy further provided some protection of a citizen's home. Demosthenes was severely criticized by Aischines for breaking into a house and arresting the alleged traitor, Antiphon, without a warrant, i.e., a *psēphisma* of the People,[64] and in the Assembly Aeschines got his way and secured the man's release. Demosthenes, in his turn, accuses Androtion of having surpassed the Thirty in brutality: they had people arrested in the marketplace, but, when exacting arrears of *eisphora,* Androtion conducted the Eleven to the debtors' houses and had them arrested there.[65]

Finally, in Aristotle's *Constitution of Athens,* we are told that "as soon as the Archon enters upon his office, he proclaims through the public herald that whatever a person possessed before he entered upon his Archonship he will have and possess until the end of his term."[66] Like the ban on torture of citizens, this is probably a survival from the sixth century. It may even go back to Solon, a measure to reassure the Athenians that, after the *seisachtheia* (shaking off of burdens), no further infringements of private property would take place.[67] But even if the origin and original purpose of the proclamation are obscure, what we know for sure is that it was still valid in the fourth century and understood as a guarantee that no redistribution of property would take place in Athens, as happened in other Greek poleis.

In addition to the protection of person, home, and property, the most treasured of individual rights is freedom of speech, cherished by democrats but suppressed by supporters of authoritarian rule.[68] Once more we find the same ideal in democratic Athens,[69] as in Demosthenes' remark that a basic difference between Spartan oligarchy and Athenian democracy is that in Athens you are free to praise the Spartan constitution and way of life, if you so wish, whereas in Sparta it is prohibited to praise any other constitution than the Spartan.[70]

It is not enough, however, to have laws and regulations protecting the citizens: there must also be ways of enforcing them if they are infringed by the democratic polis itself and its officials. Consequently the Athenians provided for both public and private prosecution of magistrates and connected the democracy with the rule

of law and the protection of citizens against their rulers. An obvious example is
Aeschines' praise of the rule of law in democratic Athens: "As you are well aware,
Athenians, in a democracy it is the laws that protect the individual and the *politeia,*
whereas the tyrant and the oligarch are protected by mistrust and armed body-
guards. Oligarchs, and those who run the unequal states, have to guard themselves
against those who would overthrow the state by force; you who have an equal state
based on the laws have to punish those who speak or have led their lives contrary
to the laws."[71] Here legal protection of the citizens is singled out as the hallmark
of democracy. The comparison between the three constitutions in that passage
leaves no doubt that the laws Aeschines has in mind are laws binding the rulers,
not the ruled. In oligarchies and tyrannies citizens are exposed to the whims of
their rulers, in democracies the laws protect the citizens. Against whom? Obviously against the political leaders and the magistrates, who must respect the democratic laws in their dealings with the citizens.

4. It is often said that *eleutheria* was basically different from modern liberty because
   the connotation of being free in the sense of not being a slave lay behind any use
   of *eleutheria.*[72] It is true that *eleutheria* in the sense of self-determination was
   rooted in the opposition free/slave,[73] whereas the modern concept of liberty does
   not have slavery as its antonym (except in a metaphorical sense). But two considerations will suffice to show that *eleutheria* as a democratic ideal was viewed differently from *eleutheria* in its social sense (free *versus* slave). First, as a constitutional ideal *eleutheria* was specifically democratic and not a value praised in
   oligarchies or monarchies; the oligarchs[74] (and the philosophers[75]) did not have
   an alternative interpretation of *eleutheria,* as we shall see they had of equality; they
   simply rejected *eleutheria* as a mistaken ideal,[76] and that would not have been possible if the critics of democracy had felt that "not being a slave" was an important
   aspect of the democratic ideal. Second, as a democratic ideal *eleutheria* (in the
   sense of personal freedom) applied not only to citizens but also to metics and
   sometimes even to slaves. Thus, a slave, who in the social sphere was deprived of
   eleutheria, might well, in a democratic polis, be allowed a share in, for example,
   freedom of speech, though only privately and of course not in the political assemblies.[77]

   To sum up, the idea of self-determination may well be behind all uses of *eleutheria,*[78] but the sources show that Greek democrats distinguished constitutional liberty from liberty in the social sense, and imposed the distinction on the rest, by in-
   ducing aristocrats and oligarchs to hate *eleutheria* as a mistaken democratic value
   and, in this context, to ignore (or suppress) the notion of *eleutheria* as being opposed to *douleia.*

5. That the Athenians did distinguish a public sphere from a private sphere is now, I
   think, acknowledged by most scholars and to refute the opposite view would be
   to flog a dead horse. But a note of warning is in order: the Athenian distinction is
   between the private (*to idion*) and the public (*to koinon* or *dēmosion*), which is not

quite the same as our opposition between the individual and the state. First, in many modern discussions, e.g., of democratic freedom, the contrast individual/ state is itself somewhat twisted: the opposite of individual freedom is not state authority but public control.[79] Next, in the Greek sources, the public sphere is mostly identified with the polis,[80] whereas the private sphere is sometimes a social sphere without any emphasis on the individual: family life, business, industry, and many types of religious association belonged in the private and not in the public sphere. The Athenians distinguished between the individual as a private person and as a citizen rather than between the individual and the state. Thus, instead of *individual* freedom, it is preferable to speak about *personal* or *private* freedom, which was often individual in character, but not invariably so.

I conclude that Athenian democratic *eleutheria* in several important respects was strikingly similar to the concept of freedom in modern liberal democracies. As a democratic ideal *eleutheria* had two aspects: it was both freedom to participate in political decision-making (positive freedom) and freedom from political oppression (negative freedom). It was linked with the distinction between a public sphere (in which political freedom applied) and a private sphere (in which each individual was allowed to live as he pleased). Freedom of speech was perhaps the right most cherished by the Athenian democrats, as it is in liberal democracies. Together with *dēmokratia* and *isotēs, eleutheria* formed a triad, just as liberty, equality, and democracy form a triad in liberal democratic thought.

But why this similarity? It cannot be the classical influence on European political thought during the Enlightenment. Admittedly, the modern concepts of democracy, liberty, and equality have sprung from three sources: the American Revolution, the French Revolution, and the English utilitarians. But the positive view of democracy, and the triangle democracy-liberty-equality did not emerge until the mid-nineteenth century. And George Grote was one of the first to link it with the classical tradition. If we look for the influence of classical tradition on the modern concepts of democracy, liberty, and equality, we should probably shift the focus of interest from the American and French Revolutions to the mid-nineteenth century and on. But let me end with another warning: Tradition must not be overrated (it sometimes is, especially by classicists), and correspondingly we must not underrate our capacity in similar circumstances to develop strikingly similar but basically unrelated institutions and ideals. I am inclined to believe that liberty, equality, separation of the public from the private, and protection of personal rights are ideals fostered in the ancient Greek world by the development from tyranny over oligarchy to democracy, and, independently, in modern Europe by a somewhat similar development, from monarchy over republic to democracy. In my view the Athenian example was of little or no importance for those who in the nineteenth century developed the liberal view of democratic freedom, and there is no evidence of any *direct* tradition transmitted from Athens to Western Europe and America in the eighteenth century.[81]

ADDENDUM

The apparent disagreement between my paper and that of Professor Wood exists because we compare different things. I compare the ideals and views held by champions of Athenian democracy with the ideals and views of the liberal democrats of the nineteenth and twentieth centuries. Professor Wood chose to compare the views held by the critics of democracy, especially Plato and Aristotle, with the ideals and views of the American Founding Fathers of the late eighteenth century. I think that, in that case, Professor Wood is absolutely right in emphasizing differences more than similarities. The similarities I discuss become apparent only a century later, i.e., from c. 1850 onward, and are not between critics of democracy, but between professed democrats in the ancient and modern world.

Another difference between my paper and her response is that, following the democrats, I take *dēmos* in its political sense, as e.g. in the enactment formula of the decrees of the Assembly: *edoxe tōi dēmōi* (the people decided), whereas she, following the critics of democracy, emphasizes *dēmos* in its social sense, denoting a class, and more or less synonymous with *hoi aporoi*.

Again, I have no quarrel with her valuable observations but would like to point out that there are two modern traditions about ancient Greek democracy. One is the liberal tradition that focuses on Pericles' funeral oration, Euripides' tragedies, and the praise of democracy found in the orators. The other one is the Marxist tradition which, by and large, is based on Aristotle's account in books 3 through 6 of the *Politics* where he defines *democracy* as the rule of the poor over the rich whom they can outnumber in the Assembly. *Dēmokratia* is taken to be class rule rather than popular government, and *dēmos* is understood in the sense of the common people, not the whole of the people as Pericles, Demosthenes, and other Athenians preferred to believe. Aristotle's analysis of democracy in *Politics* books 3 through 6 fits in nicely with Marx's and Lenin's thoughts about democracy as the rule of the proletariat, but neither in Engels nor in Marx nor in Lenin is there any explicit reference to Aristotle as the source for this understanding of democracy. However, the parallel between the Marxist and the Aristotelian definition of democracy is often pointed out in Marxist literature, for example in C. B. Macpherson's books.[82]

NOTES

1. Sartori, "Democracy,"112; Hättich, *Begriff,* 10, 17; Burdeau, *Démocratie,* 10; Pennock, *Democratic Political Theory,* 14.

2. Dahl, *Democracy,* 88–89.

3. Pennock, *Democratic Political Theory,* 7; Holden, *Understanding Liberal Democracy,* 5; Naess, *Democracy, Objectivity, and Ideology,* 276–329.

4. Sartori "Democracy," 116–177; Pennock, *Democratic Political Theory,* 16.

5. E. Vacherot, *La Démocratie* (Paris: F. Chamerot, 1860) 7: "Démocratie, en bon langage, a toujours signifié le peuple se gouvernant lui-même; c'est l'égalité dans la liberté" [Democracy, properly speaking, has always signified the self-government of the people; it is the equality contained in liberty] = Tocqueville 2.2.1, but without his modifications. B. Holden, *Understanding Liberal Democracy,* 28: "Democracy, liberty and equality form, as it were, the three points or angles of a triangle."

6. Arist. *Pol.* 1291b34–38.

7. Cf. also Plato *Rep.* 563b; Isoc. 7.20; Dem. 10.4; Arist. *Pol.* 1310a28–33.

8. Thuc. 2.37.1–3.

9. For this interpretation of *es tous pleionas oikein,* cf. Thuc. 5.81.2, 8.38.3, 8.53.3, 8.89.2. Raaflaub, "Perceptions of Democracy," 60 and especially Harris, "Pericles' Praise of Athenian Democracy," 163–66.

10. Gomme, *HCT,* II, 108; Hornblower, *Commentary,* 300.

11. Rawls, "Basic Liberties," 55–57.

12. Wood, *Peasant-Citizen and Slave,* 130.

13. Eur. *Supp.* 438–41.

14. Plamenatz, "Equality of Opportunity," 84; Berlin, *Four Essays on Liberty,* 125; Sartori, *Democratic Theory,* 348.

15. Liberal democrats "put liberty at the top of their value hierarchy, above equality" (Pennock, *Democratic Political Theory,* 16).

16. Finley, "Freedom of the Citizen," 10; Mulgan, "Liberty in Ancient Greece," 12; Bleicken, *Die athenische Demokratie,* 32, 191, 263, 312. Meier, *Greek Discovery,* 55, 66–68, 162.

17. Hansen, *Was Athens a Democracy?* 42n.140.

18. Triremes called *Dēmokratia: IG* II^2 1604, line 24; 1606, line 59; 1620, line 32; 1623, line 326. Called *Eleutheria: IG* II^2, 1604, line 49; 1607, line 85; 1627, line 202; 1631, line 488.

19. *IG* II^2 1624, line 81.

20. Hansen; *Was Athens a Democracy?* 42n.142.

21. *IG* II^2 1496, lines 131–32; 2791, cf. Raubitschek, "Demokratia."

22. Agora I 2483 = Wycherley, *Agora,* no. 39; Xen. *Oec.* 7.1; Hdt. 3.142.4. Raaflaub, *Entdeckung der Freiheit,* 132–35.

23. Xen. *Hell.* 1.6.24; Arist. *Pol.* 1253b3–4.

24. Democr. fr. 251.

25. Dem. 57.69; Aeschin. 3.169; Arist. *Ath. Pol.* 42.1. Cf. *Pol.* 1281a6; 1283a33; 1290b9; 1291b26; 1301a28–35. I follow Wyse, *Speeches of Isaeus,* 281 *pace* Rhodes, *Commentary,* 499.

26. Arist. *Pol.* 1281b22–23.

27. Ibid., 1301a28–35.

28. Ibid., 1290b18.

29. Ibid., 1280a4–5; 1290b1–3.

30. Ibid., 1317b2–3; Eur. *Supp.* 406–8; cf. Isoc. 20.20.

31. Hdt. 3.83.3; Thuc. 2.37.2; 7.69.2; Lys. 26.5; Plato *Rep.* 557b; Isoc. 7.20.

32. E.g., Hdt. 3.83.3.

33. E.g., Thuc. 2.37.3.

34. Xen. *Hell.* 3.1.20; *IG* II² 126, line 16.

35. Cf. Raaflaub, *Entdeckung der Freiheit,* on *Polisfreiheit* (148), and *das innenpolitische Freiheitsbegriff* (258).

36. Cf., e.g., Plato *Tht.* 172c; *Phdr.* 256b; *Def.* 412d, 415a; Xen. *Mem.* 1.2.5.

37. In Arist. *Eth. Nic.* there is no discussion of *eleutheria* and *eleutheros,* and only *eleutheriotēs* and *eleutherios,* "generous" and "generosity," are concepts of any consequence.

38. Arist. *Pol.* 1325a19, referring to the philosopher who is *apolis.*

39. Dem. 9.3.

40. Hdt. 3.83.

41. Sartori, *Democratic Theory,* 282–87; Berlin, *Four Essays on Liberty,* 118–72; Taylor, "What's Wrong with Negative Liberty?" Gray, "On Negative and Positive Liberty," 321–48; Ryan, "Freedom," 163–66.

42. Berlin, *Four Essays on Liberty,* 131–34.

43. Kelsen, *General Theory,* 284–85: "Freedom is self-determination and political freedom is self-determination of the individual by participating in the creation of the social order." Sartori, *Democratic Theory,* 286: "It can be argued that political freedom has also a positive aspect. . . . Now, there is no doubt that political freedom cannot be inert, that it postulates some activity; in other words that it is not freedom *from,* but also *participation in.* No one denies this. But we must not overstress this latter aspect." J. Plamenatz, response to UNESCO's questionaire about democracy (1949): "Representative democracy is government by persons freely chosen by the great majority of the governed," in Naess, *Democracy, Ideology, and Objectivity,* 329. Cf. also Gray, Liberalism, 57; Dahl, *Democracy,* 89.

44. Holden, *Understanding Liberal Democracy,* 21. Cf. also Lucas, *Democracy and Participation,* 134: "Political freedom requires not only that a subject may hold opinions of his own and express them, but that he should have some real opportunity to ventilate his views, make common cause with those that are like-minded, and persuade others, who in turn may be able to persuade those to whom the decision is entrusted. Freedom of speech and the right of association are a beginning, but they need to be supplemented by some duty on rulers to listen, and some further provision that arguments and pleas are not only heard but sometimes heeded." Gray, "On Negative and Positive Liberty," 327: "Now both the understanding of freedom as consisting in the entitlement to a voice in political decision-making and the understanding of freedom as rational choice in accordance with standards that are one's own and which accord with a natural moral order are present in the modern liberal tradition but, as Berlin has emphasized, neither is distinctive of it." Dahl, *Democracy,* 311: "The democratic process . . . promotes freedom as no feasible alternative can: freedom in the form of individual and collective self-determination."

45. Berlin, *Four Essays on Liberty,* 124, 126; Holden, *Understanding Liberal Democracy,* 12–13, 140–41.

46. Arist. *Pol.* 1317a40–b17.

47. Plato *Rep.* 557b; *Def.* 412d; Isoc. 7.20.

48. Hdt. 3.83.2–3.

49. Thuc. 2.37.2; 7.69.2.

50. Lys. 26.5.

51. Eur. *Supp.* 406–8; cf. Isoc. 20.20.

52. Hansen, *Was Athens a Democracy?* 8–21, 25–28; *The Athenian Democracy,* 74–85.

53. Sartori, *Democratic Theory,* 292; Berlin, *Four Essays,* xl–xli; Gray, *Liberalism,* 1; Mulgan, "Liberty in Ancient Greece"; Bleicken, *Die athenische Demokratie,* 313.

54. B. Constant, *De la liberté des anciens comparée à celle des modernes* (1819) reprinted in M. Gauchet, *De la liberté chez les modernes: Écrits politiques* (Paris Livre de Poche, 1980), 491–515.

55. Constant, *Liberté,* 500: "Athènes était de toutes les républiques grecques la plus commerçante, aussi accordait-elle à ces citoyens infiniment plus de liberté individuelle que Rome et que Sparte"; [of all the Greek republics Athens was the most commercial, and furthermore it granted its citizens infinitely more individual liberty than did Rome or Sparta] cf. ibid., note 14: "Si le caractère tout à fait moderne des Athéniens n'a pas été suffisament remarqué, c'est que l'esprit général de l'époque influait sur les philosophes, et qu'ils écrivaient toujours en sens inverse des moeurs nationales." [If the Athenians' altogether modern disposition has not been sufficiently noticed, the reason is that the spirit of the time influenced the philosophers and that they always wrote placing themselves in opposition to the various national mores].

56. G. Grote, *History of Greece,* vol. 6, 180: "This portion of the speech of Perikles [§ 37] deserves peculiar attention, because it serves to correct an assertion, often far too indiscriminately made, respecting antiquity as contrasted with modern societies—an assertion that the ancient societies sacrificed the individual to the state, and that only in modern times has individual agency been left free to the proper extent. This is preeminently true of Sparta:—it is also true in a great degree of the ideal societies depicted by Plato and Aristotle: but it is pointedly not true of the Athenian democracy, nor can we with any confidence predicate it of the major part of the Grecian cities."

57. This volume.

58. Isoc. 15.22; Lys. 22.2; Hansen, *Was Athens a Democracy?* 13.

59. Arist. *Ath. Pol.* 52.1.

60. Lys. 19.7; Dem. 25.87.

61. Andoc. 1.43.

62. MacDowell, *Andocides,* 92–93.

63. Dem. 22.55.

64. Ibid., 18.132.

65. Ibid., 22.51–52.

66. Arist. *Ath. Pol.* 56.2. Mossé, "La Démocratie athénienne."

67. Rhodes, *Commentary,* 622.

68. Rawls, "The Basic Liberties," 55–79.

69. Eur. *Hipp.* 421–23; Dem. 45.79 and *Ep.* 3.13. Raaflaub, "Des Freien Bürgers Recht."

70. Dem. 20.105–8.

71. Aeschin. 1.4–5.

72. Mulgan, "Liberty in Ancient Greece," 8–9.

73. Meier, "Freiheit," 426; Raaflaub, *Die Entdeckung der Freiheit,* 29–70, 160–88.

74. Ps. Xen. *Ath. Pol.* 1.8; Theophr. 28.6.

75. Plato *Rep.* 557b–58c, 562b–64a; Arist. *Pol.* 1310a26–33; 1318b39–41.

76. Hansen, *Was Athens a Democracy?* 12, cf. Raaflaub, "Democracy, Oligarchy," 525–56 *pace* Mulgan, "Liberty in Ancient Greece," 18–20.

77. Dem. 9.3; Ps. Xen. *Ath. Pol.* 1.12.

78. Democ. fr. 251.

79. Taylor,"What's Wrong with Negative Liberty?" 175–77.

80. Isoc. 7.30; Dem. 20.57.

81. Hansen, *Was Athens a Democracy?* 26–28; "The Tradition of the Athenian Democracy," passim.

82. MacPherson, *Life and Times.* For a brief treatment of the liberal versus the Marxist version of ancient Greek democracy, see now M. H. Hansen, "The 2500th Anniversary of Cleisthenes' Reforms," 36–37.

LAW, FREEDOM, AND THE CONCEPT OF CITIZENS' RIGHTS IN DEMOCRATIC ATHENS

Robert W. Wallace

THE IDEOLOGY of personal freedom was a central characteristic of Athenian democracy, both praised by democracy's supporters and condemned by its critics.[1] The orator Lysias states that under the democracy "one can live as he will" (*hopoterōs bouletai zēn:* 26.5). In Thucydides the general Nikias calls Athens "the freest (*eleutherotatē*) of all cities, where all can live their daily lives subject to no control" (7.69.2). In the Funeral Oration Thucydides' Pericles remarks, "We govern our public affairs in a free manner (*eleutherōs*). As for suspicion about each other in our day-to-day lives, we are not angry with our neighbor if he does what he wants, nor do we not give him those black looks which, though they do no real harm, still are painful. In our private lives we live together in a tolerant manner, while in public affairs we do not transgress the law."[2] Of democracy's critics, Plato complains that under the democracy "the city is full of *eleutheria* and free speech and everyone in it is allowed to do what he likes . . . each man in it can plan his life as he pleases" (*Rep.* 557b). In *Areopagitikos* 7.20 Isocrates also attacks democratic freedoms, claiming that in earlier days "Athenians did not train citizens to consider unrestraint [*akolasia*] as democracy, lawlessness as *eleutheria,* freedom of speech [*parrhēsia*] as political equality [*isonomia*], and the power to do anything as happiness." According to Aristotle (*Pol.* 1317a40–b14),

> a basic principle of the democratic form of government is *eleutheria* . . . for every democracy has *eleutheria* as its aim. Ruling and being ruled in turn is one element of *eleutheria.* . . . Another is to live as you like. For this, they say, is a function of being free, since living not as you like is the function of a slave.[3]

Of the three freedoms, of speech, conduct, and thought, that are perhaps most clearly articulated in recent U.S. history, the ideology of free speech was also expressly articulated in Athens' democracy, as *parrhēsia* and also *isēgoria* (freedom to speak in the assembly). The practice of free speech is also well attested at Athens. For example, every assembly began with the herald's exhortation, "Who wishes to speak?" and many Athenians made use of this privilege. In his *Panathenaikos* (12.248), Isocrates says that sometimes the wisest speakers miss what is advantageous and one of the ordinary citizens, "deemed of little account and generally scorned . . . comes up with a good idea and is judged to speak the best."[4] Freedom of conduct at Athens is expressly attested in the statements I have quoted—for example in Isocrates' mention of individual Athenians' "power to do anything," or Plato's that in Athens "everyone is allowed to do what he likes." Freedom of thought, although not articulated as such, was abundantly practiced at Athens by the many writers and philosophers who worked in that city.

Yet despite Athens' well-developed ideologies of citizens' freedoms and also the practice of individual freedoms, significant violations of personal freedoms also occurred. Despite the ideology and practice of free speech, it appears to have been routine that in the assembly, for example, unpopular speakers were shouted down or even dragged off the orator's platform. According to Xenophon (*Mem.* 3.6.1), Glaucon was dragged from the *bēma* (platform), "an object of ridicule" because he insisted on addressing the assembly although "he was ignorant of what was said there." In Plato's *Protagoras* (319c), Socrates says that when dealing with a project like shipbuilding, the Athenians summon shipbuilding experts. "If anyone else tries to give advice whom they do not consider an expert, however handsome or wealthy or nobly born he may be, it makes no difference. The members reject him noisily and with contempt, until either he is shouted down and desists, or else he is dragged off or ejected by the police at the orders of the presiding magistrate." Despite the ideology and practice of the freedom of conduct, of "living as you like," from 451 onward the Athenians made it illegal for an Athenian citizen to marry any foreigner. In the fourth century, at any rate, citizens who broke this law were fined 1,000 drachmas and the alien was sold as a slave. As for the freedoms extended to philosophers, Socrates was actually executed in part for his religious beliefs. One of the two legal charges against him was "believing in deities of his own invention rather than the gods recognized by the city" (Plato, *Ap.* 24b).

These and other cases have raised the question of the extent to which the freedoms of Athenians, to live and talk and think as they wished, were ensured and protected—that is, in essence, to what extent these actually existed as freedoms.[5] In the U.S., individual freedoms are protected by the Bill of Rights, which guarantees the right to free speech, the right to assemble, the right to bear arms and to a fair and speedy trial, among other points. Any attempt to restrain public speech, for example, is typically countered by assertions of the right to free speech possessed by every American. In this context "right" is generally conceived to be a rigid, absolute term, implying a clear principle, often written down but in any case formulated as such, and "inalienable" except under specified circumstances. Thus in principle all U.S. citizens have the right to life and liberty, qualified only by the state's right to execute or imprison those adjudged to be criminals after the due process of law. In principle all citizens have the right to free speech, qualified only in cases where the government or courts have determined that the unrestrained exercise of free speech may be detrimental to the common good, for example in the areas of commercial speech, obscenity, and also "fighting words."

Although "right" in this sense is not an ancient Greek concept and ancient Greek lacks a word for it,[6] the term is often used in reference to Athens. Thus, for example, MacDowell has stated that "to establish his right to be a citizen, a man had to show only that his parents were citizens," and that an outlaw (*atimos*) "forfeited rights and privileges."[7] Wiltshire remarks that Solon "introduced the right of appeal of magistrates' decisions to the people," and that citizens had "political rights"; she calls *isēgoria* "the equal right to speak."[8] It is important to note that all of these statements reflect only what are called positive rights—in this case, the right to participate in the principal functions of citizenship and government.[9] Just so, in discussions directly addressing the question of Athenian citizens' rights, Finley and others have concluded that the Athenians did enjoy positive rights of this type.[10] However, this is not true of the so-called negative rights, the freedom of Athenians from oppression in their day-to-day lives, especially in matters of speech, conduct and thought. Most of those scholars who have directly addressed this question conclude that the Athenians did not have the right "to live as they wished," especially in these regards. Among recent writers, Finley states: "What was wholly lacking was a conception of precisely those inalienable rights which have been the foundation of the modern libertarian doctrine: freedom of speech, of religion and so on. . . . The Athenian state . . . could make inroads into freedom of speech and thought, and did so when it chose. . . . Provided the procedures adopted were themselves lawful, there were no limits to the powers of the *polis,* other than self-imposed (and therefore changeable) limits, outside the sphere in which deep-rooted and ancient taboos remained powerful. In 411 B.C., after all, the Athenian assembly voted to abolish democracy."[11] Mulgan notes that Athenians' "remarkable freedom of expression" was nonetheless one that "the community could override and punish at any point," as in the case of Socrates. "A society which could unquestioningly tolerate such a vague and general charge against one of its citizens can hardly be said to have believed in any fundamental right of free expression."[12] *Per litteras* (and see his essay, this volume), Martin Ostwald has written that in the United States "the primary factors in 'citizenship' are a number of 'rights,' regarded as 'entitlements.' . . . Although Athenian citizenship may also entail some of these rights, they are not the primary factors in the concept *metechein tēs politeias* (sharing in the polity), which rather regards the state as a corporation of which the citizen is an inseparable piece. This explains, for example, why there is little in Greek political thought about minority rights, rights to privacy, and several other 'rights' to which we regard ourselves 'entitled' as citizens."

As Finley and Mulgan indicate, the central reason for these adverse judgments on negative rights at Athens lies in what is perceived to be the absolute power of the Athenian state to interfere in virtually any aspect of personal life, as shown by a history of regulations and sometimes arbitrary punishments in matters pertaining to speech, thought, and conduct. The first detailed elaboration of this argument for Athens[13] was made in Fustel de Coulanges's *The Ancient City,* where he cites numerous examples of Athenian official interference in citizens' private lives: for example, compulsory military service to the age of 60; the obligation of "the owners of [sacred] olive trees to turn over gratuitously the oil that they had made"; a law against idleness; a law forbidding women to travel with more than three dresses; a law permitting no one to remain neutral in political conflicts; laws forbidding instruction without the magistrates' approval and the teaching of philosophy—"temporary measures," he admits, but which "not the less prove the omnipotence that was conceded to the state in matters of instruction." In addition, Fustel points out, the "state system of justice . . . could strike when one was not guilty, and simply for its own interest," as in the notable instance of ostracism.[14] "At Athens . . . a man's life was guaranteed by nothing so soon as the interest of the state was at stake." "It is a singular error, therefore . . . to believe that in the ancient cities men enjoyed liberty. They had not even the idea of it. They did not believe that there could exist any right as against the city and its gods. . . . To have political rights, to vote, to name magistrates, to have the privilege of being archon—this was called liberty; but man was not the less enslaved to the state. The ancients, especially the Greeks, always exaggerated the importance, and above all, the rights of society."[15]

By contrast, the consensus view that the Athenians had no "negative" rights or the freedoms that these entailed has recently been contested by Hansen.[16] Hansen adduces various provisions that he variously labels "rules," "principles," or "rights," which protected Athenian citizens from various forms of oppression: for example, the "rule" or "right which all citizens enjoyed" of "no execution without a trial"; the archon's guarantee at the start of his year of office that people will retain their property during that year; the "rule" or "principle" forbidding the torture of citizens; Aeschines' overturning of an arrest made by Demosthenes after he invaded someone's house, and Demosthenes' protests against Androtion for also invading people's houses, to collect back taxes. (These last two points, he suggests, amounted to "the individual right" of "the inviolability of a citizen's home.")[17] Hansen also cites Athens' "ideal" of free speech. He admits that Athenian citizens' rights were sometimes violated, but he regards such cases as exceptional or even (in Socrates' case, which he regards as a violation of free speech) unique. Finally, he counters the point that in principle the demos could at any moment do anything or strike at anyone, by observing that this is also true of the government in modern Britain, where nonetheless on a day-to-day basis citizens' rights are respected.[18]

As developed, these various arguments, both for and against the existence of (from our perspective) negative rights at Athens, have merit but also raise questions. Athens' restrictions and sometimes arbitrary punishments in matters pertaining to speech, thought, and conduct, and also the ability of the democracy generally to act as it wished, do indicate the democracy's great power to interfere in virtually any aspect of citizens' lives if it wanted to. Hansen mentions primarily the "exception" of Socrates, but not the other cases that Fustel thought violated individual freedoms or that are cited in the second paragraph of this essay—for example, the legal prohibition against marrying a foreigner. The protections that Hansen adduces—for example of no execution without trial—are important but do not add up to the protection of home, person, and property as he implies. And if Athenians except for Socrates had freedom of speech, what about those who were dragged from the *bēma?* In regard to Socrates, in fact his "rights" were not violated. He was brought to trial and legally condemned. However, despite these objections, Hansen has pointed to some valid protections of citizens' freedoms, both within the structure of the Athenian lawcode and elsewhere.

In this essay I shall argue that three factors worked to protect personal freedoms at Athens: laws and specific rules and regulations (such as no execution without trial); the *absence* of laws that regulated most aspects of private life; and finally, Athens' established democratic ideologies of personal freedoms. Infringements of these freedoms—the cases mentioned by Fustel, including that of Socrates—occurred only when the demos judged that it had been harmed or otherwise adversely affected as a result of some specific activity or required some benefit from a citizen. In principle this protection of individual freedoms is similar to that provided by one important part of the prevailing conception of citizens' rights and their restriction in the United States. That is, public restrictions of personal rights, both in Athens and in part in the United States, were, or are, intended to protect the community in accordance with prevailing public sentiment. Thus, in the United States, the protection of the community provides one part of the justification for restrictions on pornography and commercial speech, and in a less formal sense explains why, as in the 1992 police beating of Rodney King in Los Angeles, acquitted defendants may be retried until a "just" verdict is attained. In this respect, I shall argue, the case of Socrates is not exceptional, but consistent with the modern interpretation of rights and personal freedoms.

Of the three major differences regarding the actual protection of personal freedoms in Athens and the United States, two are differences of degree only. First, in Athens personal freedoms were not guaranteed by a specific document that stood above the law, as does the Bill of Rights. In various ways this served to make the protection of personal freedoms, as against the interests of the community, weaker and less systematic in Athens than in the United States. In theory—and sometimes in practice—the Athenian community could intervene in any area where it perceived its own interests lay. The statement by Raaflaub that by "the abolition of debt bondage . . . personal freedom became an inalienable right of the Athenian citizen," is thus too strong, since in Athens laws could always be changed.[19] U.S. history sometimes exhibits glaring discrepancies between constitutional guarantees or ideologies and actual practice—for example, in the internment of Japanese Americans during World War II, or the treatment of African-Americans. However, in both of these instances some redress has been forthcoming, based on the violation of constitutional guarantees.

Second, for political reasons the Athenian community was more sensitive to some areas (especially regarding its actual, physical survival) in which its interests might be affected than is the United States, whereas in other areas (such as pornography) this country is more restrictive. With dangerous enemies regularly both inside and just outside their gates, the safety of ancient cities was almost always more fragile and precarious than that of modern states. Ancient cities could not afford to take chances if one of its residents posed a threat to the community. If just one disloyal person opened a city gate during the night, all could die in their beds. In consequence, action to suppress such dangers was quicker and sometimes less consistent with political ideologies or the normal operation of justice.

The third major difference between Athens and the United States in the actual protection of personal freedoms is one not of degree but of substance, in that certain U.S. provisions limiting personal freedoms reflect essentially paternalistic purposes—for example, measures requiring the use of seat belts and motorcycle helmets. Such laws are intended to protect individuals against themselves. Athens simply had no laws of this type. Furthermore, important modern areas of legislation such as private sexual conduct and the consumption of alcohol, where restrictions can be justified on societal grounds, were in Athens almost entirely free of restriction, because such actions were not seen as harming society. In these areas Athenian sensitivities were much less pronounced than in the United States.

Therefore, in Athens many of the personal freedoms of citizens were protected as much as they are in the United States, and the infringement of those freedoms generally occurred for similar reasons. In other areas, especially relating to morality, the Athenians were much less sensitive to the social consequences of possibly harmful or socially undesirable private conduct and so left these areas unregulated. In these areas Athenian citizens enjoyed greater personal freedoms than do citizens of the United States.

As I have indicated, in this essay I shall argue that three factors worked to protect personal freedoms at Athens: specific laws, rules, and regulations; the *absence* of laws regulating private life; and Athens' democratic ideologies of personal freedoms. Of these three, laws, rules, and regulations functioned in two ways: they provided a defense against specific acts by restraining individuals' abuse of others' freedoms; and they established certain rights in a positive sense, for example the right to hold political office. The laws' protection of individuals is noted by Aeschines, as providing for the punishment of offenders: "As you are well aware, Athenians, the laws protect the individual and the *po-*

liteia. . . . You who have an equal state based on the laws have to punish those who speak or who have led their lives contrary to the laws" (1.5). Laws protected Athenians from being killed, imprisoned, enslaved, or otherwise harmed in their daily lives, except as a consequence of certain specified procedures by the demos or its agents the magistrates. These negative personal freedoms were also promoted by the so-called rule of law: jurors swore to "listen impartially to both sides and vote strictly on the issue at hand"; laws were to be equal for all (Dem. 10.4) and could not be retroactive (Dem. 24.42, 44, and 74) or directed against a single individual (Andoc. 1.87). Negative freedoms were also promoted by the accountability of magistrates, as Hansen notes (see, e.g., Aeschin. 3.18 and Dem. 22.38), and by the delimitation of magistrates' powers.

Although laws and other rules could protect individuals against a variety of specific abuses, they did not amount to general protection of personal freedoms. For example, did the Athenians have a rule, or recognize some form of guarantee, concerning the privacy of the home? As Hansen notes, Demosthenes protests that Androtion took the Eleven to people's houses to collect back taxes. But Demosthenes does not say that the Eleven were acting illegally or had to remit these taxes, or even that the offended parties protested this. The privacy of the home was a sentiment only: its infringement violated a sense of decency, but not people's legal rights.[20] Furthermore, even a rule against arbitrarily entering another Athenian's house is not the same as the (U.S.) right against illegal search and seizure. It protected Athenian property in one particular circumstance but not in others. Athenian laws and other rules were more limited than our rights in that they did not amount to general pronouncements and also could be changed by other rules or legal enactments. In contrast with the Bill of Rights, they did not stand above the law. In addition, the Athenian law code was notoriously vague, generally lacking strict or precise definitions of offenses such as "impiety." Such offenses, therefore, were open to interpretation by each member of the jury according to personal opinions and feelings.

As Finley and others have noted, laws also created a series of positive rights for Athenian citizens. Solon passed a law that treasurers were to be appointed from Athens' highest economic class, the "500-bushel men" (*pentakosiomedimnoi*). Thus, we may say, this group had a right to that office (Arist. *Ath. Pol.* 8.1). Most aspects of a citizen's participation in Athenian government were fixed by either written law or traditional rule. For example, barring certain legal disabilities (which will shortly be discussed), all citizens could speak in the assembly and participate in the jury-courts. Hence, we may say, qua citizens Athenians had these rights. However, these laws and rules were also weaker than the provisions of the Bill of Rights, in that they could be changed by formal amendment or else simply neglected. As examples of formal amendment, in 411 (as Finley notes) the Athenians abolished the democracy and in 403, in the restored democracy, they debated whether to restrict citizenship to those who owned land (Lys. 34). As an example of the neglect of rights, by law the right to hold the archonship was reserved for Athens' three highest census classes, and the lowest, the thetes, was excluded. In practice, however, according to Aristotle, by the later fourth century thetes served as archons without challenge (*Ath. Pol.* 7.4).

For protecting the personal freedoms of individual Athenians, even more important than laws and rules was the *absence* of laws and rules regulating purely personal actions. An examination of Athens' different types of public and private offenses, as listed for example in Lipsius's *Attische Recht,* and of the legal cases in the Attic orators and elsewhere, shows that the Athenian law code was concerned almost exclusively with matters of interpersonal relations in which there was or could be an actual victim (such as theft or inheritance cases), or in relations between the individual and the *polis* (such as military service and citizenship). Under the democracy, private conduct, conduct by an individual "against" himself—for example excessive drinking or male prostitution—was not regulated.[21] Fustel had listed Athenian legislation against idleness as an example of arbitrary intervention by the state in private life. In fact, according to the standard interpretation of the *nomos argias* (for example in Vinogradoff and Harrison), that measure was intended to ensure the continued cultivation of estates and thus protect the households that constituted the essential basis of the polis.[22] More recently, I have proposed an alternative interpretation of this *nomos* based on Herodotus' report of its wording, viz. that punishment was contingent on "the failure to declare the source of one's livelihood or the inability to prove that the source was an honest one" (2.177). This wording implies that people without visible means of support were thought to survive by stealing. If so, then the *nomos argias* was a measure against theft.[23] On any interpretation, however, this measure was not intended to regulate private life. To the contrary, a life of leisure, free from most work, was both an aristocratic ideal and also the reality for Athens' leisured class, which consisted of perhaps 4,800 to 8,000 heads-of-household and their families during most of the classical period.[24]

A second way in which the absence of laws promoted personal freedoms is exemplified by the Athenians' freedom from legal enslavement. That Athenians were legally immune from enslavement was not stated by any provision except in connection with debt (*Ath. Pol.* 6.1). However, enslavement was simply never enacted as a legal penalty for citizens, and therefore the Athenians were not subject to it.

Legal restrictions of private life in democratic Athens were invariably associated with the greater interests of the polis as the Athenian demos saw these. Thus, the obligation of all male citizens to perform military service, which Fustel rightly lists as an infringement of personal freedom, was obviously imposed to protect the city. Ostracism also illustrates the power of the community over individuals who had committed no offense, in its own interest. Those who were ostracized were almost invariably not private citizens but politicians, who in some way seemed to the demos a danger to the polis. Demosthenes (10.70) calls "the life of private citizens (*idiotai*) safe, uninvolved, and without danger, while that of the politician is precarious, open to attack, and full of trials and misfortunes every day." Male prostitution was not an offense in Athens: indeed, the polis collected a part of a prostitute's profits by means of a tax—the *pornikon telos*. However, male prostitutes were barred from speaking in the assembly or otherwise serving in government, on pain of either death or banishment.[25] The Attic orators directly justify this provision in that "one who has sold his own body . . . would not hesitate to sell the interests of the community as a whole" (Aeschin. 1.29, see also Dem. 22.30–32).

In democratic Athens, it appears, no one thought to enact laws regulating activity that caused no specific damage to other individuals or to the demos. In the light of the Athenians' well-developed ideology of personal freedom, this was apparently a conscious and also consciously democratic decision. By contrast, under the oligarchic government of Athens in 404 and in the more conservative democracy after 355 B.C., moralizing legislation was introduced. For example, in 404 the oligarchs enacted restrictions on the freedom to teach (Xen. *Mem.* 1.2.31, and see 4.4.3), and after 338 Lycurgus sponsored laws forbidding women to travel in carriages to Eleusis during the Mysteries. Some of these provisions are included in Fustel's list of democratic restrictions of personal freedoms. In fact, neither 404 nor the period of conservative reaction after ca. 350 was characteristic of Athens' democracy. In Thucydides' Funeral Oration, we have seen, Pericles distinguishes between private freedoms and public responsibilities. In 18.123 Demosthenes says, "The difference between abuse (*loidoria*) and accusation (*katēgoria*) I believe to be this. Accusation implies crimes punishable by law; abuse, such reviling as according to their nature enemies happen to say against one another. I assume that our ancestors built these law courts not that we should gather you [jurors] here to listen to us slandering each other with forbidden words about our private lives (*ta idia*), but that we should get convictions if someone happens to have wronged the city." In 1.195 Aeschines states that "the law examines not those who mind their own private business (*idioteuontes*), but those who are politically active (*politeuomenoi*)."

The principle of the greater interest of the polis was also in large part responsible for Socrates' trial. The demos's fascination with speculative philosophy is easily documented. Year after year, for example, thousands of ordinary citizens paid money to hear characters in Euripides utter the grossest blasphemy. Athens was a mecca for all sorts of philosophers, from the wider Greek world and beyond. The central issue in Socrates' trial was not immediately his "impious" beliefs. He had been broadcasting those same impieties in the agora and elsewhere for many years, before being brought to trial for them. Although the nature of the legal charge indicates that at least some Athenians were sufficiently offended by his religious perspectives that they might vote to condemn him on that basis,[26] for most a primary motivation in condemning Socrates was his students' participation in the murderous right-wing junta that had brutalized

Athens in 404. Aeschines expressly says that the Athenians executed Socrates because he was "the teacher of Kritias, one of the Thirty who put down the democracy" (1.173). This oligarchic coup finally convinced the Athenians that Socrates was a menace to the democratic polis and had to be stopped.[27] And just so, consistent with the Athenians' communitarian perspective, during his trial Socrates himself at first recommended as his "punishment" that he be given free meals by the polis for the rest of his life. This implies that he believed he had in fact benefited his community. In a modern context Socrates might be thought to represent the individual struggling for intellectual freedom against an oppressive state. The Greek perspective—and Socrates' own—was different. As I have argued elsewhere, of the various cases of intellectual persecution associated with Athens, only those of Socrates and the music philosopher Damon appear to be historical.[28] And Damon, a long-time friend and adviser of Pericles, is said to have attempted to manipulate the music of the polis and thus affect its behavior. As Plato's Socrates says in the *Republic* (424c), "Never are the styles of music disturbed without disturbing the fundamental rules (*nomoi*) of the city. So Damon says, and I believe him." Therefore, in this case also the demos suppressed an intellectual in order to protect the city.

The third important source of protection for the personal freedoms of speech, thought, and conduct at Athens were the established ideological principles of the democracy, principles that helped create Athens' democratic identity and that also shaped daily conduct. These included *parrhēsia, isēgoria,* the equality of all citizens before the law, and above all the freedom (as the Athenians said) "to live as you want." Finley has objected that even though all Athenian citizens expressly had the right of free speech, in practice most of them could make no use of it. "A fifth-century Athenian Thersites could not have been beaten by a nobleman for his presumption; he would usually have been shouted down by his equals."[29] As we have seen, the historical record shows that this is false. Among other points, in the courts the common use by speech writers of *ethopoieia,* or character writing, especially to represent a litigant as a simple man, indicates that the demos was well disposed toward ordinary speakers. However, ideologies of *parrhēsia* notwithstanding, a speaker in the assembly who was in some way unacceptable to the gathered community could quite properly be shouted down, since the interests and concerns of the community came first. As for freedom of conduct, the evidence is clear that Athenians allowed a wide range of personal behaviors, such as male prostitution, so long as the community itself was not harmed.

These ideological principles of the Athenian democracy were flexible both in themselves and as they functioned in society. Hence they were weaker protectors of personal freedoms than (for example) the Bill of Rights, and they do not themselves amount to rights in our sense of the word. Strikingly, nobody appeals to these general principles in court speeches. In Plato, Socrates nowhere says that the demos has no right to prosecute him for impiety. In fact, he says just the opposite.

Despite the weaknesses and limitations of the Athenians' ways to protect personal freedoms (laws, the absence of laws, and democratic ideologies), Fustel, Finley, and others press too hard their claim that nothing prevented the demos from intruding in any area of private life. It is not true, for example, that the demos could simply disregard the provisions of the law code. To be sure, after Arginousai some Athenian generals were tried as a group and executed. However, the Athenians realized that this action was illegal and later punished the proposer. Finley writes, "There were no theoretical limits to the power of the state, no activity, no sphere of human behaviour, in which the state could not legitimately intervene provided the decision was properly taken for any reason that was held to be valid by a legitimate authority."[30] In principle this was true, but as Hansen observes, principle here is not of primary importance—among other reasons, because in the United States as well, legal rights are routinely flouted despite the Bill of Rights.[31] The important question is whether, and how often, Athenians actually did restrict the personal freedoms of citizens. As we have seen, they did so only when the interests of the polis were judged to be of greater importance, and it seems that this did not happen often, or in many matters.

In these regards, as I have indicated, there are three essential differences between the United States and Athens. The first lies in the vaguer and less protective nature of such guarantees in Athens, as a consequence of the absence of express formulations of many freedoms and the vagueness of many laws and ideologies. Second, the greater emphasis of Greek society on protecting the community contrasts with the United States's greater orientation toward individual citizens. In Athens personal freedoms could be taken away at any moment by the demos when it thought its interests were at stake. Aristophanes, for example, was prosecuted for insulting the demos in front of foreign visitors. There cannot have been a specific law about this; hence Mulgan cites this case as an example of the restriction of personal freedoms.[32] As we have seen, however, for most Athenians and probably for most Greeks, the interests of the community took precedence over private interests, in part for immediate considerations of community safety. Thucydides' Pericles remarks, "When the city as a whole is on the right course, private citizens are better off than when the interests of each individual are faring well but the city as a whole is going downhill" (2.60.2). In Sophocles' *Antigone* (184–190), Kreon says: "Whoever places a friend above the good of his own country, he is nothing, I have no use for him. . . . Remember this: our country *is* our safety. Only while it voyages true on course can we establish friendships truer than blood itself" (trans. Fagles, Penguin). In the *Politics* (1337a27–30), Aristotle writes that "no one of the citizens must think that he belongs just to himself, but rather that everyone belongs to the city, for each is a part of the city, and the care of each part naturally looks to the care of the whole."[33] This community orientation of the Greeks inevitably meant the restriction of certain personal freedoms. In cases such as ostracism, individuals who were altogether innocent of any offense might have to leave the city, for what the Athenians thought were their own best interests. The community also restricted the conditions for membership in it, notably by limiting the categories of people who could marry. The democracy enacted numerous restrictions within the family; for example, in legal provisions specifying the order of inheritance, or against squandering one's patrimony to the detriment of one's heirs.[34] In such family matters modern law generally does not intrude. However, they pertain to interpersonal relations rather than private freedoms and hence were subject to regulation in ancient Athens. And although many types of social relations remained unregulated, such as religious associations, interest rates, agriculture, and many aspects of trade, the grain trade was controlled because the community depended on imported food.

This orientation toward community, however, had more directly positive aspects. People were both expected and required to participate in polis activities. As Finley points out, military service was obligatory for the hoplites, who also had to supply their own armor; their pay was sufficient only for food. For the thetes, by contrast, service in the fleet was voluntary. Hence (Finley writes), "the poorer Athenian had the freedom to choose between serving and not serving . . . , whereas the wealthier Athenian citizen had no freedom in this area."[35] Liturgies and *eisphorai* (exceptional taxations) also involved compulsory contributions to the community, requirements that pertained directly to the well-being of Athens. By contrast, the "positive" concept of individualism, that people might legitimately act in their own interest even when this harmed their community, is first attested in connection with Alcibiades, at the end of the fifth century. In this respect Alcibiades was a harbinger of fourth-century developments, especially in the rise of the great Hellenistic kingdoms, where individuals routinely took precedence over their communities. From this begins what is for us the noble tradition of civil disobedience to government by individual citizens. This concept was foreign to fifth-century Athenian democracy.

Finally, the third difference between the United States and Athens in protecting individual freedoms lies in the indifference of Athenians to regulating personal activities that did not represent a direct, physical threat to the community.

Therefore, on a day-to-day basis each Athenian citizen exercised and consciously valued a great range of personal freedoms, of which the demos could in principle deprive him though in fact it did not, except when it felt that its interests were threatened. Except for the supralegal guarantees provided by the U.S. Constitution and Bill of Rights, this general structure for rights and their limitations is apparent in the United States as well. Admittedly, the reasons for which the Athenian demos could deprive individuals of their freedoms might seem more spontaneous and even idiosyncratic than in the United States, as for example in the case of Aristophanes and the foreign visitors. Day by day, Athenians could act, speak, and speculate with great freedom and normally did so, but at any time something an individual said or did could be judged to have harmed the demos, and he might then suffer for it. On the other hand, in Athens actions were restricted only if they actually did harm to the community. In contrast to the United States, where laws restrict drinking, sexual activity, and gambling because of some paternalistic conception that in a general sense these are bad for people, no moralizing legislation of this kind restricted what Athenians could do in their private lives. Hence, an Athenian could feel reasonably free to do whatever he wanted, provided it did not affect anyone else adversely. In this respect his personal freedoms were greater than those of U.S. citizens.

ACKNOWLEDGMENTS

A version of this text was presented at the University of California, San Diego, in February 1995. I am grateful to David Cohen, to Avrum Stroll and George Anagnostopoulos, and to other members of the audience, for comments and suggestions.

NOTES

1. As Adkins points out, the semantic fields of "liberty" and "freedom" are not identical. "'Liberty' is characteristically associated with such ideas as equality and fraternity, when it should commend the co-operative association of free and equal persons . . . '[F]reedom' . . . denotes and commends the ability and the right of the individual to behave as he will" (*Moral Values,* 68). In Greek, however, *eleutheria* means both political freedom, i.e., not being ruled by others (e.g., Dem. 10.4), and personal freedom (e.g., Isoc. 7.20; for both senses, Arist. *Pol.* 1317a40–b14, quoted below): see Mulgan, "Liberty," 8; Hansen, *The Athenian Democracy,* 75–76, and Hansen's discussion in this volume. Accordingly, in translated Greek I have retained *eleutheria.*

2. Thuc. 2.37.2–3. Pericles' remarks about "black looks," i.e., the absence of social (rather than legal) coercion of behavior, cannot be entirely true: see n. 5 below. A third fifth-century text, Hdt. 3.83.2–3, is evidence not for the concept of "living as one pleases" (as, e.g., Hansen, *The Athenian Democracy,* 75) but for political liberty. Otanes states that he wishes "neither to rule nor to be ruled," but he and his family continued to obey Persian laws, and whether these affected private life is not specified. A non-Athenian fifth-century testimonium for personal freedom, however, occurs in Democritus (*DK* 68B245), that laws should not prevent people from living as they wish, provided they do not hurt one another.

3. See also *Pol.* 1310a35–36, where Aristotle says that in a democracy "freedom is seen in terms of doing what one wants. So in such a democracy each lives as he likes and for his 'fancy of the moment,' as Euripides [fr. 891 Nauck] says. This is bad. It ought not to be regarded as slavery to live according to the *politeia,* but rather as self-preservation."

4. Hansen ("Number of Rhetores") has calculated that from 355 to 322 B.C., between 700 and 1,400 Athenians actually made formal proposals in the assembly.

5. In this essay (on the law and citizens' rights), I am not concerned with the day-to-day realities of social control, from family pronouncements in table manners to the imposition of political views by peer pressure and the potential consequences of gossip. As Diogenes the Cynic most famously illustrates, in Athens these aspects of social control were not legally binding. (Diogenes decided he would do everything in the simplest and most direct way, and also in public—including masturbating and defecating.) In the present context, purely personal behavior that was either cooperative or deviant is only relevant when it was introduced as character evidence in court cases. See Hunter, *Policing Athens,* ch. 4, and Wallace, "Personal Conduct," 408.

6. This absence is not critical to the current discussion of whether Athenians possessed what *we* would call the right to various freedoms, although of course it means that we are asking a question formulated in modern terms. For a discussion of how the Athenians themselves regarded their relations and obligations to the polis, see Ostwald, this volume. Modern Greek has coined a word, *dikaiōma,* for "right" in our sense.

7. MacDowell, *Law,* 68, 73.

8. Wiltshire, *Bill of Rights,* 154, 121, 112.

9. In the distinction made famous by Isaiah Berlin, so-called negative freedoms are the freedoms of an individual from various types of oppression: in essence, that is, these freedoms constitute his right to be left alone. In a democratic context, positive freedoms refer to the right to self-government: see Hansen (this volume, p. 94n.44), who points out that negative and positive freedoms can be reconciled if they are distributed in accordance with the private and public sphere. Negative freedoms as represented by the libertarian position of J. S. Mill emerged in reaction to powers of the state that were judged excessive, so as to curtail the arbitrary authority in particular of monarchs or foreign powers.

10. It is universally and rightly agreed that the Athenians had no concept of inherent rights that were possessed by all individuals. This idea is commonly thought to have been a development of the seventeenth century; but compare, for example, Cicero *De officiis* 3.26. One consequence of the absence of this concept in classical Greece was that the Athenians could see no contradiction between their ideals of *eleutheria* and imperialism.

11. Finley, "Freedom of the Citizen," 92–93. Following Finley, Ober, *Mass and Elite,* 10, has also stated, "The Athenians never developed the principle of inalienable 'negative rights' (freedom from governmental interference in private affairs) of the individual or of minorities vis-à-vis the state—a central tenet of modern liberalism," despite the many texts attesting the ideology of citizens' freedoms in private life.

12. Mulgan, "Liberty," 15.

13. Constant's *Liberté* anticipated Fustel in its general description of ancient freedoms as freedoms not from interference but rather to participate in government. However, Constant thought that Athens was in part an exception to this.

14. In addition to these, Fustel alleged a number of restrictions on freedom at Athens that are not tenable: for example, that all Athenians were obliged to vote or to serve as magistrates, or that the democracy controlled education.

15. Fustel de Coulanges, *Ancient City,* 293–98.

16. Hansen, *Athenian Democracy,* 76–78; *Was Athens a Democracy?* 8–17; and his essay, this volume.

17. Hansen, *Was Athens a Democracy?* 13–14.

18. Hansen, *Athenian Democracy,* 79.

19. Raaflaub, "Homer to Solon," 71.

20. On the complex rules and standards of behavior in seizing property from people's homes, see Hunter, *Policing Athens,* 123–24.

21. See Wallace, "Personal Conduct," passim.

22. Vinogradoff, *Outlines,* 173; Harrison, *Law,* 79–81. Cf. now Hunter, *Policing Athens,* 12: the purpose of the *nomos argias* was to prevent the dissipation of property.

23. Wallace, *Areopagos,* 62–64.

24. On the size of Athens' leisured class, see Davies, *Wealth,* 6–14, 28–35.

25. See Dover, *Homosexuality,* 19–109, and Cohen, *Law, Sexuality, and Society,* 175–82.

26. In this case personal freedom of thought also came up against a conflicting ideology, that Athenians were expected to revere the traditional gods of the city. In the closing provision in the oath of the ephebes, as they received their armor, with hands outstretched above the altar and before the council of 500, Athens' soldier recruits swore, "I will respect the worship of my fathers" (Poll. 8.105, Stob. *Flor.* 43.48).

27. In the United States, I point out, speech merely advocating the overthrow of the government is outlawed, whether or not it has consequences.

28. See Wallace, "Private Lives."

29. Finley, "Freedom of the Citizen," 83.

30. Finley, *Ancient Economy,* 154–55.

31. Hansen, *Athenian Democracy,* 80.

32. Mulgan, "Liberty," 15.

33. See also Democritus *DK* 68B252.

34. See MacDowell, *Law,* 92, and Lipsius, *Recht,* 340, 353.

35. Finley, "Freedom of the Citizen," 88–89.

DEMOS VERSUS "WE, THE PEOPLE": FREEDOM AND DEMOCRACY ANCIENT AND MODERN

ELLEN MEIKSINS WOOD

THE PURPOSE of this paper is, like most of the others here, to *compare* "ancient" and "modern"; but perhaps I could add another possibility to the two modes of comparison outlined by Paul Cartledge. In responding to Mogens Hansen's comparison of ancient and modern conceptions of liberty, I am, like Cartledge in his discussion of equality, less interested in discovering universality than in emphasizing difference. This is both for the sake of preserving the historical specificity of the ancient case and for the sake of achieving critical distance from the modern one, in order to bring into focus what may be too close and too familiar to be visible. But there is another kind of comparison secreted in Cartledge's provocative proposition that *dēmokratia,* with its etymological connotation of "a unilateral, sectarian seizure of power" (suggesting a derogatory coinage by the democracy's opponents), may mean "something not far removed from 'dictatorship of the proletariat.'"

Without exploring the substance of this comparison, I simply want to note the question that it poses for the comparative method: taking account of the vast historical differences between ancient Greek society and modern capitalism—for instance, between ancient Greek farmers or craftsmen and the proletariat in a modern capitalist society—we might ask not only what is universally the same or what is different and historically specific in various "democracies," but what would have to change in modern capitalism in order to achieve effects, mutatis mutandis, analogous to those of Athenian democracy. I did not, in preparing this paper, set out to answer that question; but it does say something about the spirit in which I have written it.

ISĒGORIA

If the common practice among scholars now is to emphasize the differences between the ancient Athenian and the modern liberal views of liberty, Professor Hansen has done an effective job of swinging the pendulum by highlighting the similarities. I intend to swing it back the other way, but not just by reasserting the differences that, as he says, are emphasized in the prevailing view among students of ancient history and philosophy. Instead, I will focus on another kind of difference that tends not to appear in the prevailing view but seems to me more significant than all the other contrasts combined.

Let us start with two quotations, one from ancient Athens and one from a founding document of modern democracy:

> Now when we meet in the Assembly, then if the State is faced with some building project, I observe that the architects are sent for and consulted about the proposed structure, and when it is a matter of shipbuilding, the naval designers, and so on with everything which the Assembly regards as a subject for learning and teaching. If anyone tries to give advice, whom they do not consider an expert, however handsome or wealthy or nobly born he may be, it makes no difference: the members reject him noisily and with contempt, until either he is shouted down and desists, or else he is dragged off or ejected by the police on the orders of the presiding magistrate. That is how they behave over subjects they consider technical. But when it is something to do with the government of the country that is to be debated, the man who gets up to advise them may be a builder or equally well a blacksmith or a shoemaker, merchant or shipowner, rich or poor, of good family or none. No one brings it up against any of these, as against those I have just mentioned, that here is a man who without any technical qualifications, unable to point to anybody as his teacher, is yet trying to give advice. The reason must be that they do not think that this is a subject that can be taught. (trans. W.K.C. Guthrie, Penguin)

And then:

> The idea of actual representation of all classes of the people, by people of each class, is altogether visionary. . . . Mechanics and manufacturers will always be inclined, with few exceptions, to give their votes to merchants in preference to persons of their own professions or trades. . . . They are aware that, however great the confidence they may justly feel in their own good sense, their interests can be more effectually promoted by merchants than by themselves. They are sensible that their habits in life have not been such as to give them those acquired endowments without which, in a deliberative assembly, the greatest natural abilities are for the most part useless. . . . We must therefore consider merchants as the natural representatives of all these classes of the community.

Some of the most essential differences between ancient and modern democracy are nicely summed up in these two quotations. In the first, from Plato's *Protagoras* (319b–d), Socrates lays out what amounts to the Athenian conception of *isēgoria,* not simply freedom but *equality* of speech. It is illustrated by the Athenian practice of letting shoemakers and blacksmiths, rich and poor alike, make political judgments. In the second, from *Federalist* no. 35, Alexander Hamilton spells out the principles of what he elsewhere calls "representative democracy," an idea with no historical precedent in the ancient world, an American innovation. And here shoemakers and blacksmiths are represented by their social superiors. Now it should be made clear at the outset that the proposed contrast is not the conventional one between direct and representative democracy. There are more fundamental differences of principle between the two conceptions of democracy contained in these quotations, which I propose to unpack.

Like Professor Hansen, I single out the concept of *isēgoria* as a starting point, but not in order to point up the similarities between ancient and modern conceptions of liberty. On the contrary, this is the one concept associated with Athenian democracy that is the most distinctive, the most distant from any analogue in modern liberal democracy. Professor Hansen has emphasized the connection between freedom and equality in both ancient and modern ideas of democracy and cites *isēgoria* as a case in point. It is similar, he argues, to the modern concept of freedom of speech, which is sometimes seen as a kind of equality but sometimes as a kind of liberty protected by a democratic constitution. But the differences between *isēgoria* and the modern concept of free speech are at least as significant as the similarities.

The differences emerge when we contrast the two quotations. There can be little doubt, for example, that Alexander Hamilton was an advocate of free speech in the modern liberal democratic sense. In this sense "free speech" involves protecting the right of citizens to express themselves without interference, especially by the state. But there is in Hamilton's conception no incompatibility between advocating civil liberties, among which the freedom of expression is paramount, and the view that in the political domain the wealthy merchant is the natural representative of the humble craftsman. The man of property will speak politically for the shoemaker or blacksmith. Hamilton does not, of course, propose to silence these demotic voices. Nor does he intend to deprive them of the right to choose their representatives. He is, evidently with some reluctance, obliged to accept a fairly wide and socially inclusive or "democratic" franchise. But like many *anti*-democrats before him, he makes certain assumptions about representation according to which the laboring multitude must find its political voice in its social superiors.

These assumptions must be placed in the context of the Federalist view that representation is not a way of implementing but of *avoiding* or at least partially circumventing democracy. The argument was not that representation is necessary in a large republic but, on the contrary, that a large republic is desirable so that representation is unavoidable: the smaller the proportion of representatives to represented, and the greater the resulting distance between them, the better. As Madison put it in *Federalist* no. 10, the effect of representation is "to refine and enlarge the public views, by passing them through the medium of a chosen body of citizens. . . ." And an extensive republic is clearly preferable to a small one, "more favorable to the election of proper guardians of the public weal," on the grounds of "two obvious considerations": that there would be a smaller proportion of representatives to represented, and that each representative would be chosen by a larger electorate. Representation, in other words, is intended to act as a *filter.* In these respects the Federalist conception of representation—and especially Hamilton's—is the very antithesis of *isēgoria.* The system of representation envisaged by the Federalists was (to adapt Sheldon Wolin's formulation in this volume, p. 87) a ventriloquous voice for a "democracy without the demos as actor." And if, as Wolin suggests, citizens in modern democracy have been converted from "actors" to "electors," the point is not simply that direct democracy has been replaced by representation. The point is rather that the form of representation espoused by Hamilton et al. was intended not to give the demos a voice but to speak in its stead. Other, more democratic conceptions of representation were certainly possible; yet in the Federalist view, election became the essence of "representative democracy," not as a means of transmitting the *vox populi,* but rather as a means of tempering democracy with a touch of oligarchy. The Federalists operated on the very same principle as did Aristotle and other Greeks, namely that election was an oligarchic, not a democratic practice (even if democracies were sometimes obliged to resort to it), because it favored the *gnōrimoi,* the notables, the rich and well-born.

THE DEMOS VERSUS "WE, THE PEOPLE"

The Federalist argument is predicated on a conception of the "public weal" as more rather than less distant from the will of the citizens. This may help to put in perspective another contrast, drawn in more than one of the other papers here, between ancient and modern democracy: the contrast between the extreme particularism of Athenian citizenship and the greater universality of modern democratic, and especially American (or, more precisely, U.S.) citizenship, its greater distance from various particularisms of kinship, ethnicity, and so on. If U.S. citizenship has more in common with Roman than with Greek civic identity in its universality, its capacity for extension to "aliens," it may also have something else in common with (imperial) Rome in this respect, namely a greater distance between the "people" and the sphere of political action, a less immediate connection between citizenship and political participation. U.S., like Roman, citizenship may be more expansive and inclusive than the democratic citizenship of Athens, but it may also be more *abstract* and more passive.

If it was the intention of the Founding Fathers to create this kind of passive citizenship, or at least to temper the civic activism of the revolutionary culture, another revealing contrast might be proposed. W. R. Connor argues in his paper that in both the American and the Athenian cases, the emergence of democracy resulted from, among other things, "a preexisting democratic culture" outside the political realm, egalitarian habits in "civil society." Ian Morris too speaks of a "Strong Principle of Equality" that predated political democracy in Greece. The accomplishment of Cleisthenes, Connor suggests, was to transfer this democratic culture into the public space. This formulation may, as others have suggested, underestimate the radical break that the ancient democracy represented; but, in any case, if Cleisthenes' act of "foundation" had the effect of institutionalizing a preexisting democratic culture, the U.S. Constitution did so in a rather different sense. The founders of the U.S. Constitution were faced not only with a democratic culture but with fairly well developed democratic institutions; and they were arguably at least as much concerned to *contain* as to entrench the democratic habits that had established themselves in colonial and revolutionary America not only in "civil society" but even in the political sphere, from town meetings to representative assemblies. They achieved the desired effect in part by widening the distance between civic identity and action in the public space—not only by interposing the filter of representation between the citizen and the political sphere but even by means of a literal, geographic displacement. Where Cleisthenes made the local deme the basis of Athenian citizenship, the Federalists did their best to shift the focal point of politics from the locality to the federal center.

It says a great deal about the meaning of citizenship and popular sovereignty as conceived by the Founding Fathers that some anti-Federalists attacked the antidemocratic implications of the proposed constitution by rejecting the Constitution's opening formula, "We, the People . . ."[1] This formula, apparently the most unambiguous appeal to popular sovereignty, seemed to its critics as, on the contrary, a recipe for despotism, for an extensive empire ruled at the center by an unrepresentative and tyrannical state. For these critics, the more democratic formula, closing the distance between the people and the realm of politics, would have been "We, the States . . ." The Federalists' invocation of "the people" was, according to such anti-Federalists, simply a means of vesting true sovereignty in the federal government, giving it the stamp of popular sovereignty while actually bypassing institutions more immediately accountable to the people and converting republican into imperial government.

Americans were later to discover antidemocratic possibilities in the doctrine of "states' rights" that could not have been foreseen by either early critics or advocates of the Constitution; but to their contemporaries it seemed clear that the Federalists were invoking popular sovereignty in support of an effort to distance the people from politics and to redefine citizenship, shifting the balance away from republican activism to imperial passivity. The "people" was no longer being defined, like the Athenian demos, as an active citizen community but as a disaggregated collection of private individuals whose public aspect was represented by a distant central state. This redefinition may add another twist to the contrast explicated by Martin Ostwald in this volume between the American conception of citizenship as a matter of individual rights and entitlements and the Athenian conception of *sharing* in a political community. Today, the long-established American tradition of passive citizenship (or Wolin's ventriloquous democracy) is being carried forward by a majority of citizens who consistently fail even to function as "electors" (to use Wolin's formula again), let alone as democratic "actors"; while the current Republican "revolution," for all

its insistence on decentralization and devolution to the states, is less an affirmation of active popular sovereignty than the quintessential expression of popular passivity, the politics of impotence and anger.

A "People" without a Social Content

The "people" underwent another major transformation in the hands of the Federalists, which again sets their conception of democracy far apart from the democratic principles embodied in the idea of *isēgoria.* The very possibility of
reconciling Hamilton's particular conception of representation with the idea
of democracy required a major innovation, which remains part of our definition
of democracy today. The concept of "representative democracy" itself would
have been difficult enough for Athenians to absorb, but I can imagine conceptions of representation based on more democratic assumptions than Hamilton's
(not least, that of Tom Paine). What is more important here is the fact that
Hamilton's conception required the complete evacuation of any social content
from the concept of democracy.

Let us look at the ancient conception more closely first. Consider Aristotle's
classic definition of democracy as a constitution in which "the free-born and
poor control the government—being at the same time a majority" (*Pol.* 1290b),
as distinct from oligarchy, in which "the rich and better-born control the government—being at the same time a minority." The social criteria—poverty in
one case, wealth and high birth in the other—play a central role in these definitions. In fact they outweigh the numerical criterion. Aristotle emphasizes that
the true difference between democracy and oligarchy is the difference between
poverty and wealth (1279b), so that a polis would be democratic even in the unlikely event that its poor rulers were at the same time a minority.

In his account of the ideal polis, Aristotle proposes a more specific social distinction that may be even more decisive than the division between rich and poor
(*Pol.* 1328a–1329a). In the polis, he suggests, as in every other natural compound, there is a difference between those elements that are integral parts and
those that are necessary conditions. The latter merely serve the former and cannot be regarded as organic parts of the whole. In the polis, the "conditions" are
people who labor to supply the community's necessities, whether free men or
slaves, while the "parts" are men of property. The category of "necessary" people—who cannot be organic "parts," or citizens, of the ideal polis—includes
banausoi, those engaged in "base and mechanic" arts and trades, as well as others, including small farmers who must labor for a livelihood and lack the leisure
(and freedom of spirit?) to "produce goodness" and to engage in politics. This,
then, may be the critical dividing line between oligarchs and democrats:
whether "necessary" people should be included in the citizen body.

This is not to say that Aristotle's definition of democracy was the conventional one. If, as Paul Cartledge points out, even *dēmokratia* itself may origi-

nally have been an antidemocratic coinage, it was also antidemocrats who were likely to define democracy as rule by the demos in its social meaning, the lower classes or the poor. A moderate democrat like Pericles tended to define it as rule by the demos in its political meaning, something like the Roman *populus,* the whole people, rather than as a social category. Nevertheless, this usage itself had social implications. For Pericles no less than for Aristotle, a polis ruled by a political community that did not include the demos in its social meaning would hardly have qualified as a democracy. Pericles may not, like Aristotle, have defined democracy as rule by the poor; but it was rule by the many *including* the poor, a form of government in which social class is not a relevant criterion for public honors, and poverty or low rank is not a bar to office. It was a democracy precisely *because* the political community included the poor. In fact, the conflation of meanings in which the demos denoted both the lower classes and the political community as a whole is suggestive of a democratic culture. It is as if the Roman category *plebs,* with all its social connotations, had replaced the category *populus.* But even this analogy does not fully convey the democratic implications of the Greek usage, since the demos in its social meaning was more completely identified with the masses or the poor, not only the plebs as nonpatricians, but the plebs unambiguously *"sordida."*

In the Greek context the political definition of the demos itself had a social meaning because it was deliberately set against the exclusion of the lower classes, shoemakers and smiths, from politics. It was an assertion of democracy against nondemocratic definitions of the polis and citizenship. By contrast, when the Federalists invoked the "people" as a political category, it was not for the purpose of asserting the rights of "mechanics" against those who would exclude them from the public sphere. On the contrary, there is ample evidence, not least in explicit pronouncements by Federalist leaders, that their purpose, and the purpose of many provisions in the Constitution, was to dilute the power of the popular multitude, most particularly in defence of property.[2] Here the "people" was being invoked in support of less against more democratic principles. In Federalist usage the "people" was, as in Greek, an inclusive, political category, but here the point of the political definition was not to stress the political equality of social nonequals. It had more to do with enhancing the power of the federal government; and if the criterion of social class was to have no political relevance, it was not only in the sense that poverty or undistinguished rank was to be no formal bar to public office but more especially in the sense that the balance of class power would in no way represent a criterion of democracy. There would, in effect, be no incompatibility between democracy and rule by the rich.

There is another, more structural reason for these differences in the relation between political and social meanings of the "people" as conceived respectively in Athens and post-Revolutionary America. The Federalists, whatever their inclinations, no longer had the option, available to ruling classes else-

where, of defining the "people" narrowly, as synonymous with an exclusive political nation. The political experience of the colonies and the Revolution pre-
cluded it (though, of course, women and slaves were by definition excluded
from the political nation. In fact, the very existence of slavery was yet another
reason for creating an inclusive political nation of free white males, to form a
united front against a subject people). But another possibility existed for Americans which had not existed for the Greeks: to displace democracy to a purely
political sphere, distinct and separate from "civil society" or the "economy." In
Athens there was no such clear division between state and civil society, no distinct and autonomous economy, not even a conception of the state as distinct
from the community of citizens. There was no state of Athens or Attica, only
the Athenians.

The possibility of what is sometimes called "formal democracy," a democracy of rights and procedures devoid of social content, and the absence of any
such possibility in ancient Greece, has to do with the vast differences in social-
property relations between ancient Greece and modern capitalism.[3] To put it
briefly, the capitalist requires no juridical privilege or exclusive political rights
in order to exploit the power of property; and the modern wage-laborer can
enjoy the full rights of citizenship without fundamentally altering the power of
the capitalist to control production or to appropriate its fruits. But the Attic peasant who possessed the juridical/political identity of Athenian citizenship at the
same time and by the same token possessed certain economic advantages. There
was the obvious advantage of not being a slave, but there were also other advantages not enjoyed by free lower classes elsewhere throughout history, such
as the freedom from various forms of coerced labor and exactions by landlords
and states—exactions that depended on superior force and political privilege.
Political and economic powers and rights, in other words, were not as easily
separated in Athens as in the United States, where property was already achieving a purely economic definition, detached from juridical privilege or political
power, and where the economy was acquiring a life of its own. Large segments
of human experience and activity, and many varieties of oppression and indig-
nity, were left untouched by political equality. If citizenship was taking precedence over other more particularistic social identities, it was at the same time
becoming in many ways inconsequential.

For these reasons, too, Sheldon Wolin's point that the demos in Athens was
less interested in social recognition than in "creating a distinct political space
where power was equally shared," and that "their ideal was political not social"
needs to be qualified; for political space in the ancient polis could not be marked
off from the social or economic domain in the way that it is in modern capitalist societies. Equal rights of citizenship may not have depended on social equality, just as in modern democracy civic equality can coexist with social and economic inequalities; but the equal sharing of political power had social and
economic consequences in the ancient world which it does not have in modern

capitalist societies. It is also worth adding that while, as Wolin points out, "free market capitalism" is undeniably "not an arrangement for producing equality," neither is it unambiguously an arrangement for enhancing freedom, as it displaces so many spheres of life to an economic sphere beyond the reach of democratic accountability, subjecting them to the imperatives of competition, profit-maximization, and the rule of capital.

LIBERTY AND ELEUTHERIA

I have gone through rather an elaborate process of setting the stage for a discussion of ancient and modern conceptions of freedom. Starting with the distinctive conception of *isēgoria,* I have tried to unpack its underlying principles, as well as Athenian conceptions of democracy, the demos, and citizenship. I have also tried to identify how they differ from their American counterparts especially in relation to the connection between the political and social implications of their respective conceptions. These distinctions seem to me to shed a somewhat different light on the Greek concept of freedom, *eleutheria,* than is suggested by Professor Hansen. He argues that the social content of the idea is separable from its meaning as a democratic ideal. What he means is that the opposition free versus slave is not the relevant one in the constitutional ideal of democracy. For one thing, he says, the slave could have a share in freedom of speech—although with the all-important qualification that slaves could not speak in the assembly. Perhaps, incidentally, the freedom of speech enjoyed by the humble craftsman in Hamilton's democracy has something in common with the freedom of speech attributed by Professor Hansen to the slave in Athenian democracy, in the sense that his opportunity to speak does not necessarily extend to the *political* sphere of the assembly, where his representative is his political voice. But I shall not make too much of that, not least because Hamilton's conception would not involve a juridical exclusion.

Professor Hansen also argues that oligarchs and antidemocratic philosophers had no alternative conception of *eleutheria.* They just rejected it as a political ideal altogether. The social opposition between free man and slave was, of course, recognized by everyone, but as a political ideal, *eleutheria* was a purely democratic notion.

I agree that *eleutheria* was a distinctively democratic constitutional ideal. But the social distinctions drawn by Greek antidemocrats—between conditions and parts of the polis, or "necessary" and good or worthy people, for example, *banausoi* and *kaloi kagathoi* or *chrēstoi*—suggest that there are social divisions other than the one between free men and slaves that have political implications for oligarchs in their opposition to democracy. These oppositions do represent an alternative, oligarchic conception of *eleutheria,* in opposition to the democratic political ideal. Rejecting *eleutheria* altogether, typically by identifying it with license and social disorder, was just one of the strategies adopted by oligarchs and philosophical opponents of democracy. Another was to redefine *eleutheria* to exclude laborers, craftsmen, or traders who were not slaves. Aristotle in the *Rhetoric* (1367a), for instance, defines the *eleutheros* as a gentleman who does not live for someone else's sake or at someone else's beck and call because he does not practice a sordid or menial craft. This is why, he maintains, long hair in Sparta is a symbol of nobility, the mark of a free man: it is difficult to do menial labor when one's hair is long. What Aristotle has to say in the *Politics* about the ideal state suggests that this distinction between gentlemen and *banausoi,* as well as other "necessary" people, should have not only social but political and constitutional implications. Here, all those supplying the community's basic needs—farmers, craftsmen, shopkeepers—cannot be citizens at all.

The distinction between freedom and servility is even more emphatic in Plato, for whom bondage to material necessity is an irreducible disqualification for practicing the art of politics. In the *Statesman,* for example, (289c ff.) anyone supplying necessary goods and services, any practitioner of the "contributory" arts, is basically servile and unfit for the political art. Even agricultural labor should be done by foreign slaves. So, for both Plato and Aristotle, the distinction between freedom and servility (*douleia*) would then correspond not just to the juridical difference between free men and slaves but to the difference between those who are free from the necessity of labor and those who are obliged to work for a living.

That this conception of *eleutheria* was not so distant from at least some conventional usages is suggested by M. I. Finley's definition that "the free man was one who neither lived under the constraint of, nor was employed for the benefit of, another; who lived preferably on his ancestral plot of land, with its shrines and ancestral tombs".[4] But if this was indeed the conventional usage, there would have been some significant differences between how the ordinary Athenian citizen understood its implications and the meaning attached to it by Plato or Aristotle. For these opponents of democracy, not even the independent craftsman or small farmer could be said to be free if his livelihood depended on providing and selling necessary goods and services to others. I doubt that the Athenian craftsman or peasant-citizen would have been prepared to accept this extended definition of *douleia,* however metaphorical. But the main point is that it would not, for the democrat, be the relevant one in defining citizenship. For Plato and Aristotle, at least ideally, it would. Even in Aristotle's best practicable polis, there is some question about the status of craftsmen, let alone hired laborers.

In other words, for these opponents of democracy there is indeed an alternative conception of *eleutheria,* a conception with a social meaning that also has political and constitutional relevance. That alternative conception is not based on the opposition free versus slave but on something more like *eleutheros* versus *banausos.*

For the Athenian conception of freedom, then, social criteria are critical. The position of *banausoi,* or more generally, people obliged to work for a living, is a major touchstone of freedom as a democratic constitutional ideal for both its advocates and its opponents. This social content in general continued to be part of the concept of democracy at least until the eighteenth century, for both supporters and critics; but these social criteria are largely absent from the modern definition of democracy. This is not, of course, to say that modern democracy permits the exclusion of working people from citizenship. Nor is it to deny that social mobility, while still restricted, is greater in modern than it was in ancient democracy.[5] The point is rather that the criterion of democracy is not the distribution of social power, nor the relative positions of social classes, nor rule by the laboring multitude or the poor. The modern definition of democracy is hardly less compatible with rule by the rich than it was for Alexander Hamilton.

MODERN AGAINST ANCIENT DEMOCRACY

I have suggested that the social structure of capitalism changes the meaning of citizenship so that the universality of political rights, and, in particular, universal adult suffrage, leaves property relations and the power of appropriation intact in a way that was never true before. It is capitalism that makes possible a form of democracy in which formal equality of political rights has a minimal effect on inequalities or relations of domination and exploitation in other spheres. These developments were sufficiently advanced in late eighteenth-century America to make possible a redefinition of democracy devoid of social content, the invention of "formal democracy." This meant the suppression of social criteria in the definition of democracy and in the conception of liberty associated with it. It was therefore possible for the Federalists, for example, to lay claim to the language of democracy while emphatically dissociating themselves from rule by the demos in its original Greek meaning. For the first time, democracy could mean something entirely different from what it meant for the Greeks.

Since I am emphasizing the differences rather than the similarities between ancient and modern conceptions of democratic freedom, I am bound to differ with Professor Hansen about the historical connections between them. He has argued that, while there are important similarities between ancient and modern ideas, these similarities are not based on a continuity of tradition. In fact, he says, the Athenian example was of little or no importance to those in the eighteenth and nineteenth centuries who developed the modern conception of liberal democracy. He talks about similar ideas arising from similar circumstances, about the analogous developments in the ancient and the modern world from monarchy through republic to democracy.

Professor Hansen argues that there were similarities but discontinuities and that ancient ideas of democracy had practically no influence on their analogues in the modern world. I would (while agreeing in one sense) argue almost the reverse: There are major differences, but the ancient democracy *was* of some importance to the development of modern democratic ideas, because the ancient democracy served above all as a negative example.[6]

For the Federalists in particular, ancient democracy was a model explicitly to be avoided; it was mob rule, the tyranny of the majority, and so on. But what made this such an interesting conceptual problem was that, in the conditions of post-Revolutionary America, they had to reject the ancient democracy not in the name of an opposing political ideal, not in the name of oligarchy, but in the name of democracy itself. The colonial and revolutionary experience had already made it impossible to reject democracy outright, as ruling and propertied classes had been doing unashamedly for centuries and as they would continue to do for some time elsewhere. Political realities in the United States were already forcing people to do what has now, when all good political things are "democratic" and everything we dislike in politics is undemocratic, become conventional and universal: everyone had to claim to be a democrat. The problem then was to construct a conception of democracy that would, by definition, exclude the ancient model.

The constitutional debates represent a unique historical moment in which there is a visible transition from the traditional indictment of democracy to the modern rhetorical naturalization of democracy for all political purposes, including those that would have been regarded as antidemocratic according to the old definition. Here we can even watch the process of redefinition as it happens. The Federalists alternate between sharply contrasting democracy to the republican form of government they advocate and calling that very same republican form a "representative democracy." This ideological transformation takes place not only in the sphere of political theory but in the symbolism of the new republic. Just consider the significance of the appeal to Roman symbols—the Roman pseudonyms adopted by the Federalists, the name of the Senate, and so on. And consider the Roman eagle as an American icon. Not Athens but Rome. Not Pericles but Cicero as role model. Not the rule of the demos but SPQR, the "mixed constitution" of the Senate and the Roman people, the *populus* (or demos) with rights of citizenship but governed by an aristocracy.

REWRITING THE HISTORY OF DEMOCRACY

The modern redefinition of democracy has given it a new history, a new pedigree, and this applies in particular to the idea of freedom. The historical trajectory of modern democracy, according to this new ideology, runs from oligarchic Rome to Magna Carta, the Petition of Right, and the Glorious Revolution, not from democratic Athens through the Levellers to the Chartists, and so on. In this respect, it is at least partly true that the ancient idea had no importance for the modern one, because the modern ideas of democracy and freedom owe more, at least positively, to feudalism than to ancient democracy.

On these grounds, I would introduce a qualification into the proposition, suggested in various ways by Barry Strauss and Kurt Raaflaub, that ancient democracy extended traditional privilege, in contrast to modern democracy, which represents the abolition of privilege. I would make the point somewhat differently, not only because, like Sheldon Wolin and Paul Cartledge, I would be inclined to emphasize the discontinuties and struggles that divided the aristocratic polis from a hard-won democracy, but also because there is an important sense in which modern democracy owes a great deal to traditional privilege. And in this respect, too, the modern concept of liberty may owe more to Rome than to Greece, with echoes of the Roman *libertas* and its connotations of aristocratic privilege.

Modern conceptions of liberal democracy have roots in the early modern opposition to absolutism. But the principles of constitutionalism and limited government which we have come to associate with a body of ideas and institutions called liberalism can trace their pedigree even further back, to the Middle Ages and then especially to the processes of state-formation and monarchical centralization that brought feudalism to an end. Perhaps, then, we ought to attach more significance to the particular social and political origins of these constitutionalist ideas.

The constitutive ideas of modern constitutionalism and liberal democracy owe their origins to the assertion of lordship against the monarchical state. These ideas were not democratic in their intent or in their consequences. They represented the protection of the independent powers of the aristocracy against encroaching monarchies, the assertion of essentially feudal liberties, privileges, and powers, backward-looking claims to a piece of the old parcellized sovereignty of feudalism, not a looking forward to a more modern democratic political order. The association of these ideas with lordship persisted for a long time, well beyond the demise of feudalism.

The Western idea of freedom emerged from this process and has close historical connections with the notion of privilege. Even in seventeenth-century England, for example, gentlemen defending the rights of Parliament against the Crown invoked the concept of liberty in a sense that was virtually synonymous with privilege. They were asserting their right, their freedom to dispose of their property and their servants at will against interference from the king. Again, the classic documents in this history (e.g., Magna Carta or the Petition of Right) are always the charters of lordship. It is striking that these are the milestones that we, especially in the Anglo-American tradition of liberal democracy, celebrate as the landmarks of democratic development—never historic moments in the struggles of the demos for political rights, or more particularly, the struggles of the laboring multitude.

The tendency to identify the history of democracy with the history of lord-ship, whose defining moments have less to do with the increasing power of the demos than with assertions of lordly privilege against tyrannical monarchies, bespeaks a conception of democracy that is already vastly different from that of the Greeks. By the nineteenth century, this redefinition of democracy was firmly established in the discourse of liberalism, in which democracy is often treated as an extension of constitutional principles rather than as an expansion of popular power. It is not understood as the product of a struggle between com-peting social forces, such as *kaloi kagathoi* and *banausoi,* lords and peasants, or masters and servants, but as a contest between two political principles, be-tween (to use the formula of J. S. Mill) Authority and Liberty, or between the rule of violence and the rule of law or justice. The evolution from absolutist monarchy through oligarchy to democracy as it typically appears in nineteenth-century conceptions of political progress places the emphasis not on the eleva-tion of the demos to new heights of social power but rather on the limitation of political power and protection against tyranny, and on the increasing liberation of the individual citizen from corporate bonds, identities, and interests. Even the Athenian democracy itself was made acceptable to nineteenth-century lib-eral reformers by appropriating it to this narrative. Mill, for example, extolled its variety and individuality (though remaining vague about the role of "ba-nausics" in the democracy), while George Grote, parliamentary reformer and historian of Greece, praised the democracy not for giving peasants and "base mechanics" access to the political domain but for detaching the individual cit-izen from corporate allegiances and sinister interests.[7]

There is no doubt that the evolution of these "liberal" principles represented a major historic advance, but it is no less clear that the definition of democracy in these terms represented a significant change, and in some respects a retreat as much as an advance. If democracy appears in this narrative as the hitherto most advanced political form, the relevant criterion is not the degree of power enjoyed by the demos. Indeed, so profoundly has the definition of democracy been altered that a truly powerful demos (defined as a social category) is, in this liberal discourse, no less a violation of liberty than is absolute monarchy; and it even constitutes, as Mill insists in his *Considerations on Representative Gov-ernment,* a "false" and not a "true" democracy.

The Greek conception of freedom belongs to a very different history. Al-though it too contains elements of privilege, there are some interesting contrasts here between the idea of freedom as the privileges of lordship, a charter for mas-ters against both king and people, and the ancient democratic ideal of *eleuthe-ria* as the freedom of the demos. In the *Persians* (242), Aeschylus has a chorus of Persian elders tell us that to be an Athenian citizen is to be masterless, a ser-vant to no mortal man. In Euripides' *Suppliants* (429ff.), there is a speech de-scribing a free polis as one in which the rule of law allows equal justice to rich and poor, strong and weak alike. In a free polis, anyone who has something useful to say has the right to speak before the public (*isēgoria?*) and, moreover, the free citizen does not labor just in order to enrich a tyrant by his toil. There is something here that is completely absent from, and even antithetical to, the later European concept of liberty. It is the freedom of the demos from masters, not the freedom of the masters themselves. It is not the oligarch's *eleutheria,* in which freedom *from* labor is the ideal qualification for citizenship, but the *eleutheria* of the laboring demos and the freedom *of* labor.

There is little of this in the modern conception of democracy. In advanced capitalist democracies we have, of course, moved far beyond the aristocracies of early modern Europe. We (leaving aside excluded categories such as "guest-workers" or immigrant Turks in Germany) have not only constitutional government but also universal suffrage. Political rights and freedoms are more widely enjoyed than they were in the ancient democracy. But these rights and liberties may be less important than they were then—wider perhaps, but not, in some important respects, so deep. The social content of democracy is largely absent. It has been replaced as the main criterion of democracy by other criteria, by constitutional checks and procedural safeguards, derived from those postfeudal principles that were meant to protect lordship against the monarchical state. These checks and safeguards are a very good thing in themselves, and indispensable in any functioning democracy; but they have little to do with democracy in its literal sense. Yet we have allowed them to replace democracy in its literal meaning, to usurp the meaning of democracy.

Perhaps what the modern conception of democracy has done is neither to abolish nor to extend traditional privilege, so much as to borrow a conception of freedom designed for a world where privilege was the relevant category and apply it to a world where privilege, in its literal meaning, is not the problem. This is a world in which property, not lordship, is the ruling principle. In a world where juridical or political status is not the primary determinant of our life chances, where our activities and experiences lie largely outside the reach of our legal or political identities, freedom defined in these terms leaves too much out of account.

Liberties that meant a great deal to early modern aristocracies, and whose extension to the multitude then would have completely transformed society, cannot mean the same thing now. We live in an entirely different world, where, for example, the so-called economy has acquired a life of its own, completely outside the ambit of citizenship, political freedom, or democratic accountability. In this context, although we have found new ways of protecting "civil society" from the "state," and the "private" from intrusions by the "public," we have yet to find new, modern ways to match the depth of freedom and democracy enjoyed by the Athenian citizen in other respects.[8] And that finally brings us back to the original question: what would have to change in modern capitalism to achieve effects, mutatis mutandis, analogous to those of Athenian democracy?

ACKNOWLEDGMENTS

I am grateful to Paul Cartledge and Neal Wood for their comments and suggestions on an earlier draft.

NOTES

1. For a discussion of this point, see Gordon S. Wood, *American Republic,* 526–27.

2. Hamilton's views are fairly unambiguous, but even the more "Jeffersonian" Madison felt the need to dilute the powers of the popular multitude for the protection of property. See, for example, Wood, *American Republic,* 221, 410–11, 503–4.

3. I have discussed these points at greater length elsewhere, for example, in *Democracy against Capitalism: Renewing Historical Materialism,* esp. chs. 6, 7, and 9. (This book is based on a revised collection of my essays, which also incorporates sections from the present essay.)

4. M. I. Finley, *Ancient Slavery,* 90.

5. It is arguably becoming more restricted in advanced capitalist societies as they suffer from protracted recessions, and as even economic "growth" becomes increasingly compatible with poverty, homelessness, and mass unemployment.

6. Athens has throughout European history been used more often as a cautionary example by critics of democracy than as a model for the supporters of political reform. See Jennifer Roberts's article in this volume.

7. Mill presents a potted history of the struggle between Liberty and Authority in his introductory remarks to the essay "On Liberty." His essay on "The Subjection of Women" also contains some important comments on political progress as the replacement of the law of force by the law of justice, and the liberation of the individual from prescriptive identities. The contrast between a liberal Athens and a conservative Sparta appears in his review, published in the *Edinburgh Review,* of Grote's *History of Greece.* For an extremely useful study of how Greek history was appropriated to the purposes of political debates after the American and French Revolutions and especially during the debates on parliamentary reform in Britain, see Frank Turner, *Greek Heritage.* I have discussed other ways in which the history of Athenian democracy became a vehicle for conducting political debates in modern Europe, in *Peasant-Citizen and Slave,* ch. 1.

8. I am deeply skeptical of Brook Manville's suggestion that "postmodern" organizations in the "new knowledge society" contain the seeds of a modern analogue to Athenian democracy, a kind of democratization of the economic sphere. Among other things, his analysis not only exaggerates the extent of these new organizational forms while leaving out of account contrary but related trends, such as the expansion of low-paid service jobs and casual or part-time labor in increasingly oppressive and insecure conditions, but also because he neglects the ways in which the new technology has provided new means of surveillance and coercion in the workplace, closer monitoring of "productivity," more rigid control of the expenditure of time, and so on. The main point, however, is that even the most advanced "knowledge-based" industries are governed not by the self-determined objectives of those who work in them but by imperatives imposed on them from without, the interests of their employer and more particularly the coercions imposed by the capitalist market itself: the imperatives of competition, productivity, and profit-maximization. New modes of organization like the "team concept" are

conceived not as new forms of democracy, making the organization more accountable to its workers, but on the contrary, as means of making the workers more responsive to the economic needs of the organization. These "postmodern" organizations do not satisfy the most basic criteria of democracy, since the people, the workers, are not in any sense sovereign, nor is the primary purpose of the organization to "provide a better life for its citizens" or even to pursue goals that they have set themselves.

EQUALITIES AND INEQUALITIES IN ATHENIAN DEMOCRACY

Kurt A. Raaflaub

1. Democratic Equality

Equality and liberty were—and still are—the most important democratic values. Accordingly, equality figured prominently among the slogans used by the ancient Athenian democrats; it represented one of the crucial ideological battlegrounds in their struggle with oligarchs. Its realization, in a world traditionally—and again for many centuries to come—dominated entirely by monarchic and aristocratic forms of government, was a remarkable, if not sensational and revolutionary, accomplishment. It unleashed phenomenal energies in the citizens involved and caused bitter and widespread criticism and resentment. Modern scholars differ widely as to whether and to what extent ancient and modern concepts of democratic equality are really comparable. Most modern historians and political scientists probably tend to emphasize the differences, while at least some ancient historians point to close analogies in ideas and definitions. It is not my intention in this chapter to pursue such comparisons—fascinating and important though they are.[1] Comparison must be preceded by a thorough understanding of each of the *comparanda*. Surprisingly, given the centrality of the concept, neither the content and nature nor the origins of democratic equality are as yet fully understood. Much attention has been paid to *isonomia*—its origin, meaning, and relationship to *dēmokratia*—and to its relatives, *isēgoria* and *isokratia*.[2] But the more general notion of democratic equality has received only brief or partial but hardly any systematic treatments.[3] Of course, in this chapter I cannot provide a penetrating analysis either, but I discuss what the Athenians understood by "political equality," how and to what extent it was realized, and what it meant to the individual citizen. In order to put these issues in perspective, I also survey the origins of democratic equality and, more generally, the foundations and early history of equality in the Greek polis.

Although I focus mostly on the fifth century, it makes sense to begin such an investigation with Aristotle. He offers by far the most extensive, systematic, and informative analysis of the subject, hampered though it is by prejudices, inconsistencies, and a strong inclination toward conceptual simplicity, symmetry, and reliance on a single most important factor.[4] I briefly summarize his main

points, deliberately leaving aside variations, valuations, and theoretical considerations.[5]

Democratic poleis "are held to aim at equality above anything else" (*Pol.*
1284a19, tr. E. Barker, Oxford). In every constitution, equality in reference to
the distribution of goods—in this case, political rights and power—is linked
with the notion of justice. In democracy the criterion determining justice and
equality is simply free birth, as opposed to wealth in oligarchy and virtue in an
ideal aristocracy. Thus democrats embrace the principle of numerical or arithmetic equality and reject the distributive, proportionate, or geometric equality
favored by oligarchs and aristocrats. Due to the principle of majority decision,
democracy in fact is equal to rule by the poor (*Pol.* 1317b2–10). Moreover,
since in the real world constitutions serve not the common good but the self-
interest of those in power, democracy generally represents the rule by the lower
classes in their own interest. Ideally, though, this does not need to be the case:
in principle, numerical equality simply means that *all* citizens, poor *and* rich,
share in power and sovereignty (*Pol.* 1318a3–10).

Democratic equality is realized by giving each citizen access to political participation and office. Hence the well-known formula "ruling and being ruled in
turn," and hence the detailed list of features, of which democratic "liberty based
on equality" (*eleutheria hē kata to ison: Pol.* 1317b16–17) consists: all citizens
are eligible to all or most offices; all rule over each and each in turn over all;
the lot is used extensively, but property qualifications for offices only rarely; offices are held for short periods and repeated only exceptionally; jury-courts are
chosen from among all citizens and adjudicate on most and especially the most
important matters; the assembly has sovereign authority over everything; and
the principle of pay for political services prevails (*Pol.* 1317b18–38). Finally,
one possible justification of numerical equality is provided by the "summation
theory:"[6] "It is possible that the many, no one of whom taken singly is a good
man, may yet taken all together be better than the few, not individually but collectively, in the same way that a feast to which all contribute is better than one
given at one man's expense" (*Pol.* 1281a42–b3, tr. T. A. Sinclair, Penguin).

We now turn to the fifth century: what did the contemporaries of Euripides
and Thucydides mean by "democratic equality"? The terminology of equality
abounds in their writings: equality pure and simple (*isotēs, to ison*), to have
equal shares (*ison echein, isomoiria*), equality before the law, political equality (*isonomia*), equality of speech (*isēgoria*), equality of vote (*isopsēphia*), not
to mention combinations with other words expressing equality or sameness (*homoios, ho autos*),[7] community (*koinon*) or inclusiveness (all, the entire city:
pantes, pasa polis, etc.). References to democratic equality are found throughout the literature of the time.

I distinguish four categories of evidence. First, various authors mention this
concept directly and positively. In the Constitutional Debate, Herodotus emphasizes *isonomia*, then singles out the use of the lot, accountability, and decision-

making by the whole community.[8] Elsewhere, he explains Athens' rise to power
after the fall of tyranny with the introduction of equality of speech (*isēgoria*),
which symbolizes the newly won liberty of the Athenians in the Cleisthenic
"democracy."[9] In the *Suppliants* Euripides stresses equality of vote, equality of
justice guaranteed by common control over the laws and publication of the
laws, equality of shared power provided by the principle of ruling in annual
turns, and the supreme realization of equality, freedom of speech.[10] In the Funeral Oration, Thucydides focuses on equality before the law in private disputes
and on equality of chances and participation in politics.[11]

Second, negatively, the concept is attested directly or indirectly through criticism or refutation of democratic equality. Pericles' emphasis, in the Funeral
Oration, on recognition in democracy of achievement and excellence certainly
reflects such criticism,[12] and Athenagoras systematically refutes it in the Syracusan assembly in Thucydides, book 6. In response to the would-be oligarchs'
unwillingness to share political equality with the masses, Athenagoras points
out that it is only fair that citizens who are considered "the same" also have the
same privileges;[13] in defense of numerical equality, he cites inclusiveness and
a variant of the summation theory. He concludes that democracy gives all an
equal share and allows the elite to enjoy both equality and a greater share of influence.[14] The oligarchs' claim in 411 that full citizen rights should be restricted
to those who were best able to contribute "with money and bodies"[15] contradicts the democrats' insistence that *all* Athenians used their bodies to best serve
their polis.[16] Pseudo Xenophon's sarcastic remark that in Athenian social and
economic life freedom and equality of speech (*isēgoria*) were extended even to
metics and slaves[17] presupposes the fact that in political life these values were
shared by all citizens.[18] Finally, the insistence of some sophists, portrayed im-
pressively in Plato's *Gorgias,* that natural law entitles the stronger to rule over
the weaker and that justice consists of the right of the better to have more (*pleon
echein*), represents a strong reaction to democracy's pervasive egalitarianism.[19]

Third, some general statements on equality are not explicitly linked with
democracy but originate in the same context. A good example is Jocasta's praise
and Eteocles' refutation of equality in Euripides' *Phoenissae,* reflecting the
same tension between equality and the quest for individual power we find in
Plato's *Gorgias.*[20] Similar generalized echoes of contemporary debates about
democratic equality recur frequently in Euripides' plays and fragments.[21]

Finally, there are statements reflecting democratic equality without men-
tioning it explicitly.[22] Mostly, such testimonia vary the theme of "ruling and
being ruled in turn" or simply "taking turns"[23] or emphasize that *all* citizens
share in decision-making, offices, speaking in the assembly, and the qualities
essential to responsible civic participation. By manning the ships, says Pseudo
Xenophon, the lower classes contribute much more to their city's power than
the hoplites and the upper classes; thus "it seems just for all to have a share in
the offices . . . and for anyone among the citizens who wishes to do so (*ho*

boulomenos) to have the right to speak."[24] Not just a few specialists, declares Zeus in Protagoras' myth, but *all* citizens have to share in the basic civic virtues (justice and respect for others: *dikē, aidōs*); otherwise there could be no cities.[25] And Aeschylus insists in the *Suppliants* that *all* citizens, the entire polis, have to participate in decisions about questions that affect the safety of the whole community.[26]

In sum, fifth-century literature already reflects all the main elements occurring in Aristotle's discussion of democratic equality.[27] Such equality consists of the right of all citizens to participate on equal terms in voting and speaking in the assembly,[28] serving on the council, holding office through appointment by lot or election (that is, in ruling and being ruled in turn), and generally to contribute to the community according to ability; furthermore, democratic equality includes equality before the law and protection from aspiration to too much power or even tyranny by those unwilling to accept these principles.[29] Aristotle's definition of such egalitarian democracy as rule by the poor and lowly is anticipated by Pseudo Xenophon (*Ath. Pol.* 1.5–9) and the representatives of the sophistic theory of natural law; his emphasis on majority rule is stressed in Thucydides and Herodotus;[30] the importance of state pay for political functions is reflected in remarks by Pseudo Xenophon, and in the abolition of such pay by the oligarchs in 411,[31] while Thucydides' Athenagoras formulates the tension between numerical and proportionate equality and the justification of the former by the summation theory. Although no testimonium explicitly bases such numerical equality on the citizen's status as a free man, the importance of this status is emphasized strongly in other contexts.[32]

Moreover, as mentioned above, many sources attest that in the second half of the fifth century criticism of democratic equality was widespread and massive.[33] Not surprisingly, therefore, the fifth-century evidence provides several justifications of this principle. Apart from the summation theory, already mentioned, Protagoras seems to have promoted the theory that, with very few exceptions, all citizens shared—not all equally but all at least in an elementary way—in the basic civic qualities needed for successful communal life. "The importance of this doctrine of Protagoras in the history of political thought can hardly be exaggerated. For Protagoras has produced for the first time in human history a theoretical basis for participatory democracy."[34] We do not know to what extent more general sophistic theories concerning the equality of all humans[35] or the Athenian ideology of autochthony[36] were utilized for the same purpose. More pragmatically, the inclusion of the thetes rowing the fleet is supported both by Aeschylus' view that those who have to bear the consequences of communal decisions must participate in making them,[37] and by Pseudo Xenophon's insistence that the thetes contributed more than any other class to Athens' power.[38] A variant of this argument, justifying democracy by its military success, occurs in Herodotus, where equality is presented as one of the factors motivating the citizens to exert themselves for their city.[39]

Two additional comments are in place. First, as indicated before, many scholars believe that the Greek—or rather, Athenian—concept of democratic equality differs greatly from its modern counterpart.[40] Second, in his *Politics,* Aristotle defines the polis as "existing by nature" and as a community of citizens, and man as by nature a "political being."[41] The polis, essentially consisting of equals (whose equality consists of their free status), thus is founded on natural equality. This theoretical assumption collides with the empirical fact—of which Aristotle himself is very much aware elsewhere in the same work—that, whatever the origins of society and the polis, politically such equality was fully realized only in the democratic polis. The essential difference between "polis" per se and "democratic polis" thus tends to be blurred—a mistake made by modern scholars as well[42]—even though, as we shall see, there are indications that the polis did indeed evolve on a strong foundation of equality.

2. The Evolution of Democratic Equality

What was the origin of the concept of democratic equality, when did it emerge? The bulk of our testimonia comes from roughly the last third of the fifth century. While Protagoras' myth and Pseudo Xenophon's treatise perhaps offer earlier clues,[43] Aeschylus' *Suppliants* provides strong evidence that the issue was "in the air" in 463. By then, in fact, equality may have been a slogan for several decades, accompanying the rise of democracy since the days when, as many scholars think, Cleisthenes or his successors appropriated *isonomia* and *isēgoria* for Athens' new constitution. That they did use such terms, however, is by no means certain. Thus we cannot avoid the much-debated question of the origin of *isonomia* and related concepts. In addition, we should ask in what respects the Cleisthenic system was characterized by equality, how far and to whom such equality extended, and to what extent, if at all, this system realized, or anticipated, "democratic equality." Some of my suggestions in this and the following sections of my paper are controversial; I present them here in the hope of focusing future discussion on a few issues that seem crucial to our understanding of the development of democracy.

Isonomia, describing both legal and political equality (that is, equality before the law and equality of political participation), is attested in Herodotus and Thucydides and thus late in the fifth century. By then the term, although not confined to democracy and denoting any form of equality that was opposed to tyranny or narrow oligarchy, could almost be used as a synonym of *dēmokratia.*[44] It certainly is much older, but since only few direct and indirect testimonia survive from an earlier period, determining when and how it originated is difficult. Although important for its content, a fragment of the medical writings of Alcmaeon of Croton is variously dated between the late sixth and the late fifth centuries and thus of little assistance to our present inquiry.[45] Two *skolia* (drinking songs) are crucial: they praise Harmodios and Aristogeiton for hav-

ing killed the tyrant and made Athens "isonomic." Such songs point to an aristocratic environment. The question is whether we see in them, with Martin Ostwald and others, the expression of sentiments that were formulated close to the
events of 514/510, or, as Charles Fornara and Loren J. Samons argued recently,
a late echo of such experiences that was influenced by later views and terminology.[46]

Now *isonomia* is not the only term describing forms of political equality. In
related late-sixth-century contexts, Herodotus mentions *isokratia* and
isēgoria.[47] Writing several generations later, he naturally used the terminology
of his own time; unless there is independent evidence, we cannot know whether
such terminology was actually used at the time of the events he describes. In
the case of *isēgoria,* such evidence is provided by the name of Cleisthenes' opponent, Isagoras—a name that, for good reasons, later was no longer popular
in Athens. This appears to be a "political name,"[48] significantly given to a member of one of the important aristocratic families in Athens precisely around the
time when the value it expressed had assumed new importance. For equality in
the sense of participation in power, rule, and leadership—and thus also in the
right of speaking among the leaders and in front of the community—had been
a long-standing prerogative of the aristocracy (see below, section 3). They considered it their natural privilege and took it for granted; thus there was no need
to have a specific term for it. Tyranny deprived the aristocrats of such shared
control of power, which now became a value that needed to be formulated,
claimed, and fought for. This, most likely, is the context in which *isonomia* and
isēgoria were created and became prominent—occasionally even to be reflected in a name like Isagoras. In Athens this stage was reached in the second
third of the sixth century, elsewhere earlier.[49] If so, it need not surprise us that
the (exaggerated) praise of the Athenian tyrannicides' accomplishment focused
on their recovery of *isonomia* for their fellow aristocrats.

A couple of indirect testimonia, each by itself uncertain, can perhaps be
added as support. "Equal distribution" (*isos dasmos*) occurs in the corpus of the
Theognidea and has been interpreted as paraphrasing *isonomia*—but whether
this poem goes back to the sixth century, as much of the collection does, is completely uncertain.[50] The idea of balance and equality of justice in Anaximander's famous first fragment may well reflect the concept of *isonomia*.[51] While
strictly resisting the demand for *isomoiria* (in the economic sense of redistribution of land), Solon proudly emphasized his efforts to establish legal equality
for all: "I wrote laws for the lowborn and the noble alike, fitting out straight justice for each person."[52] This corresponds to one of the primary meanings of
isonomia—but the fact that Solon knew the concept, of course, does not prove
that he knew the word.

What all this amounts to, then, is rather little: *isēgoria* almost certainly, and
isonomia probably, in the sixth century were important terms for a highly valued aristocratic concept; possibly this concept was familiar and established

enough to be paraphrased in poetry, applied to philosophy/cosmology, and, if Alcmaeon is to be dated so early, used technically in medical literature. It is thus likely that Cleisthenes knew both the concept and the specific terms, but it remains unprovable that he actually applied these terms to his new system.

What is certain, though, is that this system contained strong elements of civic equality. It suffices here to mention three of its constituent elements: the demes with their "grassroots democracy" formed its foundation; the ten new tribes, each composed of demes from various parts of Attica, were designed to unite ("mix") different segments of the citizen body in common events and shared service in the army and council, and the new "Council of Five Hundred" was based on an exceptionally dense quota of representation, which made it impossible to restrict participation to the upper class.[53]

No doubt therefore: Cleisthenes had ample reason to apply *isonomia* and its cognates to his new system. This assumption has been vigorously opposed by several scholars, who consider it implausible and far-fetched that a concept, which seems to have been important to aristocrats in their struggle against tyranny, could turn into a slogan characterizing a new political order that reached far beyond the aristocracy and—at least later—could even be identified with democracy. A number of considerations, however, argue against such objections.[54] First, after the expulsion of Isagoras and his followers, we hear of no opposition to Cleisthenes' reform program; it thus seems to have received broad support in the citizen body. Accordingly, there is no reason to assume for that period a strong polarization between aristocracy and nonaristocracy:[55] Cleisthenes' reform was not directed against the aristocracy. Second, led by the Alcmeonids, many aristocrats both opposed tyranny and supported the new order. Particularly in view of the "oligarchic" aims of Isagoras' faction (see below), and of the continuing efforts by the tyrant family to be restored in Athens, this new order, emphasizing the opposition to exclusive (tyrannical or narrowly oligarchic) regimes, must in fact have appeared eminently supportable to most members of the elite. Third, as we shall see, the core of egalitarian tendencies such as those realized by Cleisthenes was very old; they are visible already in the early polis and, more generally, in early warrior societies; thus, they were not limited to the aristocracy.[56]

All in all we may feel confident in concluding, therefore, that through *isonomia* and its cognates political equality became a popular slogan in the aristocrats' fight against tyranny, figured prominently in their celebration of the overthrow of tyranny, and possibly was soon applied to the system introduced by Cleisthenes, which was characterized precisely by more broadly based civic equality and thus realized values shared at that time by aristocrats and nonaristocrats alike.

This raises the question of how far such equality reached, whether all citizens were entitled to participate equally, and to what extent power was transferred to the institutions in which such equality could express itself most forcefully. In a highly stimulating paper, Josiah Ober emphasizes the significance of what he calls the "Athenian revolution" of 508–507.[57] He interprets the spontaneous uprising of *boulē* and demos of Athens against Isagoras, Cleomenes, and their supporters, described in a well-known passage by Herodotus, as "a violent and more or less spontaneous uprising by large numbers of Athenian citizens," which in turn was the result "of a generalized and quite highly developed civic consciousness among the Athenian masses—an ability to form and act on strong and communal views on political affairs." In this "demotic action" and effort involving the entire demos, Ober sees the first expression of democracy: the demos took charge; control of power and politics by the demos therefore must have been realized in the subsequent reforms.[58]

Ober's suggestions merit detailed discussion.[59] He certainly is right in stressing that the demos acted with unexpected self-confidence and that these actions, in the context of the debate about Cleisthenes' reform proposals, created new realities. However, even if, as Ober maintains, the demos's action in this case was supported by many members of the lower classes, I doubt whether this would have been enough to create the preconditions necessary to enhance their political status and rights. After all, since its very beginnings, the polis had been a community of farmers and fighters (see below, section 3), characterized by a close link between the social, economic, military, and political status of its citizens. The thetes, unable to fight in the hoplite phalanx and thus not contributing to the defense of their city, were outsiders in their own community. Major changes would have been necessary for them to overcome this barrier. In 508–507, however, the thetes' involvement would have been short and exceptional, limited to the elimination of Isagoras' faction and the expulsion of the Spartan intruders—which meant that the domestic and political aspects of the event were inseparably intertwined with those of "national" pride. Once these goals were achieved, the community no longer depended on the thetes, and they had little to offer that would have justified their permanent political advancement. The difference to the crucial and permanent communal function assumed specifically by the thetes after the Persian Wars is decisive (see below at nn. 77–79). For in Cleisthenes' time, and for an entire generation thereafter, Athens relied on the strength of its hoplite army to ward off serious external threats: in 506 against a coalition of hostile neighbors and Sparta, in 490 against the Persians. This hoplite army was formed by the farmers; its creation—on a completely new social and organizational basis—was a major component of Cleisthenes' reform.[60] The fleet—whatever its size and organization—was still no major factor;[61] militarily, the thetes who did not meet the hoplite census continued to be of little significance. Why, then, would they have counted for much politically? A few decades later, distinguishing for the first time in our extant sources three types of constitutions, Pindar characterized the equivalent of democracy as a system in which the "turbulent army" (*labros stratos*) prevails. The poet, of course, is not referring specifically to Athens, but his choice of words seems to reflect a general awareness that the assembly used to be dominated by, if not restricted to, those who formed the army.[62]

There is general agreement that, as suggested by the extant sources, Cleisthenes' presentation of the principles of his reform program was decisive for his success in attracting the demos to his side and thus prevailing over Isagoras' faction. This reform began with, and was decisively based on, a reform of the demes. Its announcement, if not partial realization, preceded Cleomenes' intervention and the uprising of the demos. It seems plausible to conclude that those who were most interested in these reforms, who supported them most strongly and profited most from them, were primarily the farmers, large and small, including many members of the elite.[63] To this large group of citizens (perhaps at this time still a majority: n. 65) domestic peace and stability, a curb on violent and destructive rivalries among the leading families, the continuation of political developments begun under the tyrants,[64] and a proposal massively enhancing the role of the demes must have been most welcome.

Under Cleisthenes' *isonomia,* I suggest therefore, Athens essentially was a "republic" of hoplites and farmers. Indeed, in this system, political equality was greatly enhanced: active participation by large segments of the citizen body was encouraged and institutionalized. These same citizens were enabled to make use of *isēgoria:* primarily on the local level of the demes but also, slowly but increasingly, in the central institutions of the polis, especially the *boulē.* It is possible, however, that such equality did not fully extend to all citizens. With very few exceptions (such as property qualifications for high offices), political participation at that time probably was not regulated by law; rather, it was determined by social status and prestige. Just as in Homeric assemblies only the leaders (*basileis*) were entitled to speak publicly, while the people were limited to expressing their opinion collectively (see section 3 below), so too in the system introduced by Cleisthenes it was perhaps generally accepted and considered natural that only those were entitled to participate actively in politics (by holding office and speaking in council and assembly) who could boast sufficient social prestige—which was determined by (at least) hoplite status based on landed property.[65] The thetes were not excluded—perhaps they were even able to vote[66]—but we should consider the possibility that individually they still were "second class citizens," expected to be silent; they expressed their sentiments only collectively, by voting and presumably shouting.[67]

Despite its great importance and emphasis on equality, therefore, the Cleisthenic system was far from realizing *democratic* equality. Moreover, the potentially "democratic" institutions (assembly, council and law courts), probably were equally far from assuming the dominant role that characterized them in democracy. What little we know about the powers of council and assembly seems rather to indicate that initially they functioned as an institutionalized check or counterweight, balancing the power of the archons and the Areopagus council, who continued to represent aristocratic leadership and authority.[68] In other words the demos did not yet fully control, through the bodies representing the entire citizen body, the whole political process, from election to planning policies, supervising their execution and holding the officials accountable.[69] To put it simply, if Cleisthenes' system, as most scholars agree, was not yet democratic in the proper sense of the word,[70] "democratic equality" could not yet exist. Ober's "Athenian revolution of 508/7" (above, n. 57) thus was not a democratic revolution. But significant it was, creating the conditions for important reforms that did enhance equality, made it possible for large numbers of nonaristocratic Athenians to grow into their new political responsibility, and paved the way for later and even more momentous developments.

The decisive step toward creating a democracy in the full sense of the word was actually taken more than forty years later, by the changes implemented in the late 460s and 450s. This view is based on scant evidence but can be defended with plausible arguments.[71] Essentially, in 462 the Areopagus Council, the last bastion of institutionally supported aristocratic predominance, lost certain powers that were transferred to the assembly, the Council of Five Hundred, and the popular courts. Most likely, these powers concerned at least the examination of and control over the officeholders and perhaps other judicial functions, especially in state trials.[72] Subsequent measures, proposed at least in part by Pericles, included the introduction of pay, the reduction of property qualifications, and a new definition of citizen status (see below). All this represented a decisive shift toward enhancing the role and power of those institutions that represented the entire citizen body and in which now *all* citizens were entitled and enabled to assume their share of government and civic responsibility. As a result—and only then—the entire citizen body, the whole demos, was given control over the full range of politics. Many years later Euripides compared this power of the demos with that of a monarch or Homeric lord (*anax*). Whenever that stage was reached, I consider it significant that shortly before the reforms of 462 Aeschylus urgently emphasized the necessity of letting *all* citizens, the *entire* polis participate in the political process, and that the evidence currently available to us indicates that the word *dēmokratia* was coined in the early years of the same decade, perhaps in the context of heated debates that preceded those very reforms.[73]

Several additional points seem noteworthy. First, if this assessment is correct, it must have been at that time that equality was fully established as a central and comprehensive democratic value. Most of the measures initiated in subsequent years were explicitly designed to facilitate the realization of such equality in political practice (hence the introduction of pay for offices and service in council and *dikastēria*),[74] to minimize legal obstacles to such equality (hence the reduction, if not de facto elimination, of the property qualification for the archonship),[75] and to define precisely who was to share in such equality (hence Pericles' citizenship law of 451/450).[76]

Second, to extend full political participation to all citizens, without regard to descent, wealth, landed property, education, and other criteria that normally determined political rights in Greek poleis, was an unprecedented step into uncharted territory. It could be initiated only in Athens and was made possible by a set of uniquely Athenian circumstances.[77] These include the shared emergency and accomplishments of the Persian Wars, based on vital contributions by *all* Athenians, including the thetes; the continuation of the Persian Wars after 479, the foundation of the Delian League, and its transformation into an Athenian naval empire; the rise of the fleet that increasingly[78] and permanently assumed responsibility for the security, prosperity, and power of the polis; and the fact that thus the community came to rely on its lower-class citizens who mostly rowed the fleet.[79]

Third, scattered pieces of evidence suggest that this concept was hotly debated in the years before 463. If so, we might ask how it could be justified at that time. Certainly not by arguing that the poor should rule in the polis and have more power than the rich; nor by emphasizing that free status was the only requirement for full citizen rights. Rather, since democracy was a new and unique concept, realized only under exceptional circumstances, any proposal to extend equality to all citizens had to be based concretely on these circumstances: it had to emphasize the successes achieved by *all* citizens for their city and the continuing responsibility of *all* citizens for its well-being—including those who served on the fleet that had supported Athens' rise to power.[80] In other words, Ephialtes and his supporters probably fought with a combination of the arguments that we find used by Aeschylus, Herodotus and Pseudo Xenophon—although the latter's in a toned-down, less partisan version. Unlike Pseudo Xenophon, that is, they must have used *dēmos* in its comprehensive, inclusive sense. The opponents, on the contrary, may well have raised the spectre of lower-class domination, focusing on the partial, exclusive sense of the word.[81]

Fourth, I have argued that there was in Greece no democracy in the precise sense of the word before it was introduced in Athens,[82] and at least initially it was tied to conditions that applied uniquely to Athens. Once it was invented in Athens, however, democracies were installed, often under direct Athenian influence, in many other poleis.[83] However, since the Athenian original depended so closely on the city's imperial rule, other democracies can have corresponded only partially to this model.[84] The involvement, self-perception, and level of acceptance of the demos must have been different if this demos was not directly responsible for the security and power of its polis. And the leadership function of the elite must have differed radically if the polis conducted practically no foreign policy of its own.[85] Many problems here remain to be investigated, but it seems clear that democratic equality could not possibly be equal in all democracies.

Before we turn to the questions of how fully the Athenians succeeded in realizing democratic equality, and what such equality meant to the citizens, I
would like to pause for a moment, step back, and take a broader perspective.

3. FOUNDATIONS AND DEVELOPMENT OF EQUALITY IN THE GREEK POLIS

Long before the spread of democracies, constitutions characterized by some
form of equality were developed in many poleis. At least on the social level, as
current work by Ian Morris and others demonstrates, by the late sixth century,
egalitarian tendencies prevailed throughout large parts of Greece, quite independently of, and sometimes surprisingly similar to, phenomena we observe in
Athens.[86] How can we explain such widespread preference for equality? I suggest a twofold response: on the one hand, to some extent equality was inherent
in the early polis; on the other hand, certain developments in the archaic period
helped establish and formalize equality as a powerful stabilizing force.

I turn first to the early polis: to what extent and why was equality structurally
embedded in it, and how did such equality express itself? This is a complex
topic, tied in with the much-debated problems of the rise of the polis and the
polis in Homer. The following remarks are based on conclusions I reached elsewhere in a detailed analysis of the evidence.[87] In my view the Homeric polis
was a community of persons or "citizens" and as such more than an agglomer-
ation of almost autonomous households (*oikoi*) banding together only in times
of emergency. It was loosely organized, its institutions were not yet formalized,
and the individual was far from fully integrated in it. But all the components
essential for the polis were in place. Thus what Homer calls *polis* is indeed a
polis in the strict sense of the term: certainly an early forerunner of the classical polis, but more developed and complete than is usually assumed.

In this society equality is explicitly discussed with regard to a person's
prowess in war, ability to speak in the assembly, and status or rank in comparison with others. In all these respects, the leaders (*basileis*) draw a stark line between themselves and all the others—as Odysseus tells Thersites: "Sit still and
listen to what others tell you, to those who are better men than you, you skulker
and coward and thing of no account whatever in battle or council" (*Il.* 2.200–2,
tr. R. Lattimore, University of Chicago). In the *basileis'* self-perception and
self-presentation—which is enhanced by elite ideology and does not necessarily correspond with social reality—issues of equality only matter within their
group. This is what the conflict between Agamemnon and Achilles is all about:
Achilles, the greatest warrior, emphasizes the honor and respect he deserves and
complains about the unequal treatment he suffers on the part of Agamemnon,[88]
while the latter, insisting on the greater honor, privileges, and power he is entitled to as the overall leader, fiercely rejects any effort on the rival's part to present himself as equal.[89]

Despite these and other natural differences in rank and influence, however, basic equality among the *basileis* is essential and generally accepted. It is best visible in the "right" claimed by all to speak up in the assembly and council.[90] All this is well known, but it is worth emphasizing that such debates among leaders are much more than, as M. I. Finley puts it, mere "quarrels, . . . in which each side seeks to overpower the other by threats, and to win over the assembled multitude by emotional appeal, by harangue, and by warning."[91] Moreover, it is precisely this "right of equal speech," previously taken for granted, which would later prompt the Greek nobles to create a specific term for it (*isēgoria*) when they were fighting against the tyrants' efforts to monopolize power.[92]

On the basis of the "aristo-centric" picture presented by the epic poets, Finley concluded that the decisive dividing line in Homeric society indeed ran between the *aristoi* and all the rest, free and unfree alike. More recent scholarship has called this view into question.[93] The gap between the elite of *basileis* and the large class of free farmers seems to have been narrower and less marked than it appears at first sight, and the latter played a rather important role in the community. Thus, I suggest, the emerging polis was built on more egalitarian foundations than is usually assumed.[94] This thesis can best be tested by examining the role of the "commoners" in the assembly[95] and army. I focus here on the latter.

According to the view that predominated until very recently and was based essentially on Anthony Snodgrass's research,[96] in the epics the old, "heroic" mode of fighting prevails: the battle is decided by duels between the leaders, while the masses of their followers play an inferior background role. By contrast, the hoplite phalanx, not visible in Homer and fully developed after a century-long process by about 650, required the involvement of larger masses of equally equipped and trained soldiers. Thus a new class of citizens, the free farmers who could afford the panoply, were integrated into the polis army and eventually received political rights as well. This momentous change is often called the hoplite revolution and dated to the late seventh and sixth centuries.[97]

Joachim Latacz, W. Kendrick Pritchett, and Hans van Wees point out, however, that the battle descriptions in the *Iliad* contain much evidence for mass combat, sometimes even in relatively dense battle formations.[98] Some of the images are strikingly close to Tyrtaeus, who is often believed to sing about at least an early form of the phalanx.[99] The experience behind these images must be similar. Later authors, foremost among them Polybius who certainly was an expert, easily recognized the phalanx in Homer's battle descriptions.[100] The conclusion seems inevitable that we are dealing, not of course with the fully developed hoplite phalanx, but with its precursor: the common soldiers are fully involved in the fighting and, though less conspicuously than the leaders, share the responsibility for victory and defeat.[101]

Other indications suggest that in providing the details of his grandiose vision of a Panhellenic ten-year war against Troy—a vision passed on for generations in oral poetry but no longer imaginable concretely to singers and audiences of the eighth century—the poet of the *Iliad* drew on experiences more familiar to his own time: raiding expeditions on land and sea and wars between neighboring communities. I consider it hardly accidental that the earliest recorded cases of communal warfare—the conquest of Messenia and the war about the Lelantine plain on Euboea, among many others—date precisely to the late eighth century.[102] In such wars, all able-bodied and properly equipped men would help defend their own community or overpower the other. These wars greatly enhanced cohesion, solidarity, and shared responsibility in the polis. The connection, typical of the developed polis, between land ownership, military capacity, and citizenship or political rights must have existed already in this Homeric polis, albeit in an undeveloped and unformalized way.[103]

It is possible that public and private forms of warfare coexisted for a long time.[104] But by the second half of the eighth century in communal wars, mass fighting was common enough to be integrated in battle descriptions by the poet of the *Iliad*. Whatever the form of fighting in private raids, and whatever the historical reality of "heroic warfare," on the communal level, I suggest, once the polis began to crystallize, some form or other of mass combat in close formation soon prevailed, and this form gradually developed into the hoplite phalanx and tactics. Mass fighting thus evolved along with the formation of the polis: the masses of citizens providing the bulk of this prehoplite infantry army were an integral part of the emerging polis. By adopting the phalanx, the polis did not incorporate into the army a whole new class of citizens. Rather, along with the long and gradual process of perfection and homogenization of equipment, formation, and tactics, on the sociopolitical level, procedures and rights connected with the hoplite status were defined more clearly. In other words the polis, the phalanx, and the sphere of "the political" in the polis evolved in an interrelated process over a long time. Accordingly, there was perhaps less of a "hoplite revolution" than an evolution, starting on a more advanced level than is usually assumed.[105] All this helps to explain the relatively small gap between the mass of free farmers and the elite of wealthy landowners, mentioned earlier, and the latter's difficulties in establishing themselves as a sharply defined aristocracy, separated by effective class barriers from the rest of the population.[106]

The polis, therefore, was indeed built on a solid egalitarian foundation—and one that was essential for its survival. What, then, happened to this foundation in subsequent centuries and why does equality seem to have become a potent political force only much later? This again is a complex issue. I suggest, in a very preliminary way, that such an egalitarian substratum did not exclude continuing social, economic, and political differentiation; it remained in place, rooted in assembly and citizen army, but developed differently in each polis, depending on the specific conditions emerging in a given community and its re-lations with its neighbors. Generally speaking, it tended to be pushed back and weakened by the rise of the aristocracy and its specific preoccupations and feuds. But it was brought to the fore again as an integrating and stabilizing fac-tor in times of crisis and pressure.

For example, colonial poleis, which depended for their survival on the soli-darity of their citizens, at least initially emphasized egalitarian structures.[107] The social and political system of Sparta, which evolved in response to the challenges posed to the community by large-scale conquests and the enslave-ment of the defeated (helots), was based on strong elements of institutional-ized civic equality—here understood in the sense of similarity or uniformity (hence the Spartiates were *homoioi,* not *isoi*).[108] Elsewhere, the lack of outside pressure made such civic solidarity seem less urgent. Eventually, however, power struggles among aristocratic families, combined with economic and social crisis, at least in larger poleis provoked social conflicts and often ended in tyranny.[109] Threatened by the disintegration of the polis or the loss of power to a tyrant, the aristocrats were forced to discipline themselves; they discover-ed the importance of maintaining basic equality within their own ranks and in-troduced integrative measures capable of stabilizing the community. Hence, on the one hand, there emerged aristocratic value terms such as *isēgoria* and *isonomia.*[110] On the other hand, written legislation, equally binding on *all* citizens, was introduced to resolve problems likely to cause conflicts in the polis.[111] "I wrote down ordinances," says Solon, "for low and high (*kakos, agathos*) alike, providing straight justice for each man."[112] Hence, too, institu-tions were formalized; the role of the demos (whatever that meant in each case) in election, decision-making and jurisdiction was defined with increasing precision; and new institutions were created to meet such definitions. Eventu-ally, the polis began to speak in its own name,[113] institutions reflected their roots in the community of the demos,[114] and constitutions were characterized by *isonomia.*

When, how, and to what extent this happened, depended on the specific sit-uation in each community. Overall, as stated at the beginning of this section, by the end of the archaic period, egalitarian tendencies and "isonomic" systems of various types, integrating the hoplite farmers, must have been fairly common in Greece. Normally, however, the development toward formalization of polit-ical equality ended there, because of the link, in my opinion inherent in the polis, between land ownership, military capacity, and participation in commu-nal affairs. Hence, normally those who did not own sufficient land to serve in the army could not claim full political rights. Hence, too, no direct path and au-tomatic development led from Cleisthenes' *isonomia* to Ephialtes' and Pericles' *dēmokratia.* The realization of this final stage required a special stimulus: the military ascendancy of the thetes serving on the fleet of a polis that ruled over a naval empire.

4. Inequalities Despite Democracy

This brings us back to Athens and democratic equality. Two questions remain: to what extent was such equality realized and what were its limitations? And what did it mean to the citizens?

The democratic concept of equality was broad and comprehensive (above, section 1). In political practice, it was realized to an amazing extent: thousands of citizens attended the assembly once or more every prytany (that is, during one-tenth of the year; the number of regular assemblies eventually reached four per prytany), thousands manned the jury courts on every business day, hundreds served in offices in Athens and hundreds more abroad. Aristotle counts a total of more than eleven thousand peacetime jobs for citizens (though not all full-time or fully paid), not counting the crews of the ships on constant patrol.[115] The Athenian democracy was indeed built on broad and intense citizen participation.[116]

Still, there were limitations: Athenian society, of course, was far from completely egalitarian. Some of these limitations are well-known, often discussed in comparisons between ancient and modern democracy, and upsetting only to those who lack historical perspective and cannot think back more than 75 or 125 years.[117] The exclusion of women, foreigners, and slaves[118] concerns the concept of citizenship and thus, given the narrow definition of citizenship and restrictive enfranchisement policy typical of Greek societies in general and especially of Athens, does not affect the notion of democratic equality, properly speaking.[119] The latter was a strictly political concept intended to support the citizens' unique political status and identity. Thus different rules applied to everything outside the political sphere. True, due to empire and democracy, both metics and slaves enjoyed exceptional degrees of freedom and equality in the economic and social life of Athens; but, despite polemics and biting sarcasm, nobody thought seriously about extending citizen rights to them.[120] Sophistic theories about the essential equality of humankind had no impact on real life, let alone politics,[121] and comic fantasies about the women's political takeover were so funny precisely, though not uniquely, because they dealt with the impossible.[122] True, too, in rare cases of extreme emergency, large groups of slaves or allied citizens were enfranchised collectively; but this form of citizenship still did not make them politically equal to the "true" Athenians.[123]

On a different level, the insistence on property requirements—which by the fourth century (and probably earlier) mostly seem to have been dead letters anyway—or on election instead of sortition for certain high offices, though limiting equality, was well justifiable and hardly contested.[124] Moreover, although critics (e.g., Ps. Xen. *Ath. Pol.* 1.2) claimed, not entirely without justification, that in Athens the poor and lowly had more power than the rich and well-born, such power was not used to change the economic structure or massively redistribute wealth beyond the traditional and generally accepted framework of elite contributions to communal life (liturgies) and extraordinary taxation in times of emergency.[125] In other words, equality of property, *isomoiria* in an economic sense, was not a serious issue[126] and belonged in the sphere of comic surrealism or abstract theoretical schemes.[127]

On yet another level, there were inequalities that are difficult to assess and perhaps exist mostly in the perception of ancient and modern critics of Athenian democracy. According to this view, due to the exceptional size of Attica and economic necessities, participation was mostly limited de facto to those living in and near Athens and to those able to afford the leisure. In addition, speaking in the assembly was de facto limited to members of the elite and "professional politicians." This view is partly correct, partly mistaken or one-sided; to some extent, moreover, these are problems inherent in any direct democracy.[128] By providing a minimum of pay for most political activities, by distributing these widely, and by keeping the time required for such activities as short as possible, conscious efforts were made to secure the widest participation possible under the circumstances.[129] Probably few Athenians perceived such geographical or psychological limitations as objectionable restrictions of their democratic equality.

Rather than dwelling on these much-discussed issues, I would like to focus for a moment on another category of inequalities.[130] These are more hidden, somewhat uncertain but troubling, especially in view of strong prejudices against the thetes and their political rights—prejudices that persisted in parts of Athenian society and are well attested in our sources.[131]

First, in 411 the sympathizers of oligarchy proposed to restrict full citizenship to those who "would best be able to contribute with money and bodies." This formula referred exclusively to men of hoplite status and above.[132] It implied that only those fighting in open land battle as hoplites or horsemen properly used their bodies to benefit their community. Thus it directly challenged the democrats' claim that *all* Athenians used their bodies to best serve their polis.[133] This concept, related to another that emphasizes fighting and tilling the land as the only occupations truly worthy of the free and noble man, is equally based on long aristocratic tradition and intended to exclude the despised members of the lower classes.[134] This is but one of several ideological battlegrounds, on which the opponents of democracy directly challenged the democrats' efforts to justify a broad-based concept of equality and the inclusion of all citizens.[135] The present case is especially important because it concerned the lower classes' military contribution and thus the issue that initially and primarily supported their claim to full political integration.

Second, the Athenians maintained a central register of cavalry and, according to the predominant view recently challenged by Mogens Hansen, a catalogue of hoplites, but there certainly was no corresponding register of *nautai* (sailors). The hoplites were conscripted for each campaign by posting on the agora lists with the names of those called up to serve.[136] Thus it was easy to determine the names of those who did not come back. No such list existed for the thetes—whether they were conscripted or volunteered to serve on the fleet[137]—nor, of course, for the light-armed troops who, even if they were citizens, in the fifth century were not an organized part of the Athenian army.[138] No wonder then, that on various occasions Thucydides gives precise figures for the deaths of hoplites but is vague about those of members of the lower classes.[139]

Third, Antony Raubitschek suggested long ago that the thetes were not—or not always—recorded by name in the Athenian casualty lists.[140] Donald Bradeen and others objected—largely, it seems, because they considered it inconceivable that a heading stating "these Athenian men died," "could be put over a list from which the thetes were excluded."[141] As Nicole Loraux observes, however, "it is as if in matters concerning war, the word *Athenaios* was never used in its strict legal sense, but referred either to a wider group or to a smaller group than that of the soldier-citizens."[142] There is no conclusive proof either way,[143] and we should perhaps not put too much weight on what *we* consider probable or conceivable. At the very least, however, it is quite startling that we even have to discuss the possibility that at the height of democracy not all citizens were equally valued, let alone recognized, as citizens, and that at the state funeral (perhaps the most solemn patriotic celebration of civic unity) those who were most immediately responsible for the success of democratic Athens might have been valued, not as individuals, but only as an anonymous mass. At any rate, there is clear evidence that the death of hoplites was considered noble and taken far more seriously than that of light-armed soldiers, archers, and oarsmen, even if they were citizens as well.[144]

Fourth, the same uncertainty still clouds the much-debated issue of whether or not in the second half of the fifth century all thetes were registered in the lists of citizens kept by the demes (the *lēxiarchika grammateia*). The debate focuses on the interpretation of specific documents,[145] the meaning of *lēxis* and *lēxiarchikos,* the function of these registers, and the time by which all thetes were registered in them. This debate cannot be rehearsed, let alone resolved here: it is far from settled.[146] The main question is closely connected with that of the registration of the casualties among the thetes, mentioned above, and with the development of the notion of citizenship—an issue that, despite much recent discussion, needs further scrutiny.[147] Again, what seems normal and obvious to us may not have been so for fifth-century Athenians. Moreover, the discussion of whether or not thetes were included in this or that list or document usually operates with the Solonian census categories and thus perhaps uses distinctions that are too rigid and inappropriate in this case. Many thetes, although not meeting the appropriate (zeugite [i.e., a citizen of moderate substance]) census and thus not fighting as hoplites before the late fifth or fourth century, still owned landed property and thus probably were listed on the *lēxiarchikon grammateion* of their deme, while others, the truly landless, though still citizens, were not.

Fifth, in the late fourth century the *ephēbeia* (the training of the young citizens for their obligations as soldiers and citizens) supposedly was compulsory for male citizens who were fit for such service, and possibly included the thetes who were equipped at state expense; at the end of their two years of training and patrol duty along the borders, the ephebes received shield and spear.[148] The origin of this institution presents another of those vexed problems that cannot be resolved with the evidence presently available to us. Almost certainly, though, it was not, as was long believed, newly created after the battle of Chaeronea. Earlier forms existed at least since ca. 371 and probably much earlier (there is a substantial body of indirect evidence for the fifth century); essential parts of the ephebic oath undoubtedly are archaic, and the roots of the institution clearly lie in "ancient practices of 'apprenticeship,' whose object was to introduce young men to their future roles as . . . full members of the community."[149] At any rate, before the reforms of the late fourth century, and most likely even thereafter, participation was not mandatory for all young male citizens[150] and, in its military aspects, it always was exclusively a preparation for hoplite service.[151] Thus, as long as the thetes did not serve as hoplites, they were a priori excluded from the training and rituals that prepared the Athenian males for their function as citizens, and from the prestige, recognition, and esprit de corps that went with participation in those activities and rituals. Whatever training the Athenians underwent to prepare themselves for naval warfare, there is no indication that it served purposes equivalent to the comprehensive initiation of the ephebes.[152]

Finally, we cannot avoid the question—although we have no means to answer it—whether in the fifth century the war orphans, who received the panoply at the Great Dionysia after having been raised at public expense,[153] really included, as is always assumed, all citizens reaching adulthood and not perhaps only those whose fathers had qualified as hoplites (by meeting zeugite census).[154] Recognizing that this form of releasing the war orphans into adulthood and full citizenship clearly marked them as hoplites, Nicole Loraux draws the logical conclusion, "for those among them who were sons of thetes, social promotion was added to honor."[155] But is this necessarily correct? The origin of the institution is uncertain. It is clearly attested for the time of Pericles' Funeral Oration.[156] Epigraphic evidence gives a terminus ante of ca. 460; perhaps it is most reasonable to assume a connection with the origin of the state burial of the war-dead in the Kerameikos that was instituted soon after the Persian Wars.[157] At any rate, the institution seems to predate the fully developed "naval" democracy. With its emphasis on hoplites, it raises the same questions concerning inclusion of thetes as the *ephēbeia* and the other issues discussed above.

Many questions, but no certainty. It seems fair, though, to conclude that, as far as the social and institutional recognition of their military role was concerned, not all citizens were equal; despite their great merits, in status and prestige the *nautai* clearly were considered inferior to the hoplites and horsemen.

This discrepancy is perhaps visible in other areas as well. For example, if Jerome Pollitt's interpretation proves correct, at the height of Athens' naval power the larger part of the Parthenon frieze was designed to celebrate the most explicitly elitist segment of the Athenian armed forces, the cavalry.[158] As Loraux remarks concerning the roles of the thetes, "Could it be that someone was less of an Athenian if he specialized in nonhoplite warfare? Some Athenians thought so, and, without really taking back with one hand what it was giving with the other, the community was concerned to make the distinction."[159]

Cumulatively, the evidence I have adduced indicates that there may have been noticeable discrepancies between the ideology and the reality of democratic equality—discrepancies that corresponded to widespread and well-known aristocratic tendencies to exclude and denigrate the despised members of the lower classes. At the very least, this evidence illustrates what obstacles, rooted in century-old traditions and prejudices, may have made it very difficult to justify and fully realize a concept so revolutionary as that of almost unlimited civic equality. Nothing short of a complete overhaul of political values and ethics and a radical reeducation of the citizen body, it might seem to us, could have overcome these obstacles.

Some traces of such efforts at reeducation are indeed visible in Pericles' speeches in Thucydides.[160] But the new values, ethics, and behavior patterns needed in democracy could not easily be created from scratch, and there was no new class of citizens that, based on its own accomplishments and a marked sense of self-worth, had developed such ethics and was ready to impose them on society at large. Unlike, for example, the French bourgeoisie in the eighteenth century, the Athenian thetes had not risen independently to economic power and social prominence. All they could show was their military ascendancy—certainly no negligible feat and grudgingly acknowledged even by some adversaries,[161] but at the same time fiercely criticized and rejected by others together with the policies that had made it possible. Socially and economically, the thetes remained at the bottom, worse off than many metics. As Pseudo Xenophon (*Ath. Pol.* 1.10) observes, in appearance they were hardly distinguishable from the slaves. They therefore were unable to develop and support an alternative value system. Rather, in accordance with the gradual evolution of democracy and the gradual extension of equality to all citizens, inevitably traditional, mostly aristocratic ethics and behavior patterns were extended to, and adopted by, all citizens: the demos, so to speak, was "aristocratized."[162] Most notably, by being paid for political functions, they gained the leisure necessary for involvement in politics and running a polis. For this very reason, equality could not be limited to occasional elections and votes, nor delegated for extended periods to a small number of representatives. This democracy had to be lived actively and intensively, its equality realized to the fullest by involving the highest possible number of citizens from all classes in government and power, by ruling and being ruled in turn.[163]

And thus we arrive at our last question: what did such equality mean to these citizens? Members of the elite, of the hoplite class, and of the lower classes, and within these classes different groups, would have answered this question differently; I focus here in a general way on the thetes.[164] Precisely because, due to the exceptional conditions in imperial Athens, in social and economic life the status boundaries between citizens and noncitizens were blurred, there was only one sphere to distinguish the citizens from all the others: that of politics. There, as Aristophanes and Pseudo Xenophon illustrate vividly, despite the criticism and contempt he may have sensed from many members of the elite, the average Athenian belonged not to the "have-nots" but to the "haves"; he was equal and had to be taken seriously; there the rich and powerful, whether Athenians or foreigners, had to respect him and seek his approval.[165] For the lower-class Athenian, therefore, who otherwise lacked distinction and identity, his political status and function became exceedingly important. He developed, in Christian Meier's words, a strong and, in many cases, primary "political identity."[166]

This identity, however, was precarious, the status on which it rested unprecedented and contested. Hence the extant evidence presents a picture full of contradictions. In one moment, the masses, comparable to a violent beast, assert their power and crush their leaders; in the next, they allow themselves to be manipulated by the demagogues' clever rhetoric and flattery. There exist echoes of a strong sense of accomplishment and self-importance among the "rower-fighters who save the city," of the demos's self-confidence and pride in assuming the role assigned them in democracy, and there are indications of insecurity and diffidence.[167] These tensions and contradictions need to be explored further; they provide us with important clues to understand the democratic citizens' mentality. At any rate, their status, unique and under constant attack by elite circles, constantly needed to be defended and supported—and to be legitimized by continuous success. By enabling all citizens, even the poorest and lowliest, to participate in communal affairs, the concept of democratic equality encouraged, perhaps even compelled them to be active and involved. As Herodotus (5.78) observed acutely, democratic equality indeed was a powerful motivating force. This helps us understand the readiness of these citizens continually to devote themselves to the affairs of their city, both politically and militarily, in remarkable intensity and constancy, without slackening, over an extraordinary period of time.[168] Whatever the negative aspects of democracy—they certainly are not lacking—this side of it is quite astounding, unique in world history: these men understood that their job and responsibility—their "métier"—was to be citizens.[169]

ACKNOWLEDGMENTS

I thank Paul Cartledge, Josiah Ober, and several other participants in the "Democracy Ancient and Modern" conference for helpful comments on earlier versions of this article, and Gregory Bucher and Karen Lehr for indispensable technical assistance.

NOTES

1. See below, n. 40, for bibliography. Energies unleashed: Raaflaub, "Democracy, Power, and Imperialism." Criticism: below n. 33. In order to keep the footnotes reasonably short and avoid repetition, wherever possible I refer to other works of mine where the reader will find more detailed discussion and more bibliography.

2. See below, nn. 44 and 47.

3. Loenen, *Vrijheid,* is an early exception. See Hirzel, *Dike,* 228–320; Bengl, *Staatstheoretische Probleme,* 30–42; Grossmann, *Politische Schlagwörter,* 43–70; Müller, *Gleiches zu Gleichem;* Harvey, "Two Kinds"; Tarkiainen, *Demokratie,* 292–319; Jones, *Athenian Democracy,* 45–50; Guthrie, *Philosophy,* III.148–63; Euben, "Equality"; Thraede, "Gleichheit" (with bibliography); Kerferd, "Equality"; Thesleff, "Plato and Inequality"; Kullmann, "Equality in Aristotle"; de Romilly, *Problèmes,* 49–52; Loraux, *Invention,* see index s.v. *equality, isēgoria, isonomia;* Mossé, "Egalité"; Lengauer, "Gleichheitsdenken"; Hansen, *Was Athens a Democracy?* and *Athenian Democracy,* 73–74, 81–85; Bleicken, *Demokratie,* 287–310, 538–42; and the literature cited below in nn. 4, 5, and 44.

4. See Mulgan, "Aristotle's Analysis," esp. 310–11, 315–21. See also Mulgan, *Political Theory,* ch. 4, esp. 73–75; Dolezal, *Demokratie;* Schütrumpf, *Polis,* esp. ch. 7; Eucken, "Demokratiebegriff"; Aubenque, "Aristote et la démocratie."

5. See esp. *Nic. Eth.* 1131a25ff.; *Pol.* 1280a7–25, 1301a28–39, 1301b26–39, 1310a25–32, and the passages cited in the text and in Newman, *Politics,* ad loc. and IV. xxxvi–lxi. See also Harvey, "Two Kinds"; Mulgan, "Aristotle's Analysis"; Keyt, "Distributive Justice"; and M. Ostwald's contribution to the present volume.

6. Cf. Braun, "Summierungstheorie"; de Romilly, *Problèmes,* 66–71; Schütrumpf, *Polis,* 174–85, 356f. (with a critique of Braun's article); Voigtländer, *Philosoph,* 580–85. Other theoretical justifications include the "safety-valve argument" (*Pol.* 1281b21–38) and the "shoe-pinching argument" (1282a14–23).

7. See Paul Cartledge's contribution to this volume on the difference between *isos* and *homoios.*

8. 3.80.6: "The rule of the people is called by the fairest of terms: *isonomia.* . . . People hold office by lot, they are accountable for the actions of their administrations, and their deliberations are held in public (*koinon*). . . . In the many is all" (tr. W. Blanco, Norton, modified).

9. 5.78: "Athens really began to thrive now. It shows . . . that *isēgoriē* is a goodly thing, since under the tyrants the Athenians were no better than their neighbors in battle, whereas after they got rid of the tyrants they became by far the best; it shows that when they were downtrodden they slacked off, since they were toiling for a despot, but that when they became free, each and every one eagerly strove for his own success" (tr. Blanco, ibid.).

10. Eur. *Supp.* 350–53: "But if I state my reasons, I shall have more favor from the people, whom I made sole rulers when I set their city free and gave them equal votes (*isopsēphon polin*)"; 405–8: "This city is free. The people reign, in annual succession. They do not yield the power to the rich; the poor man has an equal share in it (*echei*

ison)"; 429–34: "Nothing is worse for a city than an absolute ruler. In the earliest days, before the laws are common, one man has power and makes the law his own: equality (*ison*) is not yet. With written laws, people of small resources and the rich both have equal recourse to justice (*dikēn isēn echei*)"; 438–41: "This is the call of freedom: 'What man has good advice to give the city, and wishes to make it known?' He who responds gains glory; the reluctant hold their peace. For the city, what can be more equal than that (*ti . . . isaiteron polei*)?" (tr. F. W. Jones, University of Chicago Press).

11. 2.37.1: "In name it is called a democracy, because we govern not for the few but the many; but, whereas before the law there is equality for all in private disputes, nevertheless regarding popular esteem the individual receives public preference according to his recognised achievement in some field—not by rotation rather than by excellence—and furthermore, should he be poor but able to perform some service for the city, he is not prevented by insufficient public recognition" (tr. J. S. Rusten). For the interpretation of this difficult sentence, I refer to the commentaries by Gomme, *HCT* I; Rhodes, *Thucydides II;* Rusten, *Thucydides II,* and Hornblower, *Commentary.*

12. Thuc. ibid. Cf. the commentaries cited in n.11 and, for example, Edmunds, *Chance and Intelligence,* 47–53.

13. 6.38.5: "Is it that you do not want to share *isonomia* with the *polloi?* But how could it be just that the same should be held unworthy of the same privileges (*tous autous mē tōn autōn axiousthai*)?" (tr. R. Crawley, Random House, modified).

14. 6.39.1: "It will be said, perhaps, that democracy is neither wise nor equitable (*ison*), but that the holders of property are also the best fitted to rule. I say, on the contrary, first, that demos includes the whole, oligarchy only a part; next, that if the best guardians of property are the rich and the best counsellors the wise, none can hear and decide so well as the many; and that all these talents, severally and collectively, have their just place in a democracy (*isomoirein*)." 40.1: "Reflect that in the country's prosperity the men of merit in your ranks will have both an equal and a larger share than the great mass of your fellow-countrymen (*kai ison kai pleon metaschein*)." For interpretation, see Gomme, Andrewes, Dover, *HCT* IV, *ad loc.*

15. Thuc. 8.65.3; cf. Arist. *Ath. Pol.* 29.5 and the parallels cited by Rhodes, *Commentary,* 382–83.

16. Thuc. 1.70.6, cf. 2.42 and 39.3.

17. Ps. Xen. *Ath. Pol.* 1.11–12: "In a state relying on naval power it is inevitable that slaves must work for hire so that we may take profits from what they earn, and they must be allowed to go free. . . . This, then, is why in the matter of free speech we have put slaves and free men on equal terms (*isēgorian . . . epoiēsamen*); we have also done the same for metics and citizens because the city needs metics because of the multiplicity of her industries and for her fleet; that is why we were right to establish equality of speech (*isēgoria*) for metics as well" (tr. J. M. Moore, University of California). Pseudo Xenophon here anticipates Plato's caricature of the *isonomikos* and *dēmokratikos anēr* (*Pol.* 561e, 562a, cf. 563b); a similar remark in Dem. 9.3.

18. Ibid. 1.6: "It may be objected that they ought not to grant all equally the right of speaking (*legein pantas ex isēs*) in the assembly and serving on the council. . . . As it is, anyone who wishes (*ho boulomenos*) rises and speaks." Cf. 1.2, cited below at n. 24.

19. Plato *Gorg.* 483b–c, 483e–484a, 488a–489b; see also 490a, 491a, 512cd. Reaction to democracy: for example, Dodds, *Gorgias,* 13–14; Guthrie, *Philosophy,* III.101–7, esp. 105–6; Euben, "Equality," 220–23.

20. *Phoen.* 501–2: "Nothing is like (*homoion*) or equal (*ison*) among men except the name they give—which is not the fact." 535–48: "It's better, child, to honor Equality who ties friends to friends, cities to cities, allies to allies. For equality is stable among men" (tr. E. Wyckoff, University of Chicago, modified). Cf. Mueller-Goldingen, *Phoenissen,* 101–8; de Romilly, "Phéniciennes"; Guthrie, *Philosophy,* III. 151.

21. Thus Eur. *Med.* 122–23; *Hec.* 306–8; *Erechtheus* fr. 362, 7–8 Nauck[2]; fr. 1048 (unknown tragedy); cf. also Eur. *Alexandros* fr. 52; Eur. *Pleisthenes* fr. 626.

22. This is an important category of evidence often neglected in terminological analyses that are based too narrowly on the uses of specific words (esp. through *TLG* word searches). Thus, for example, the fact that "no reasoned defence of this cardinal institution, the lot, has survived" is perhaps not only "a proof of the poverty of our information on democratic theory" (thus Jones, *Athenian Democracy,* 47) but due as much "to its obviously and incontrovertibly egalitarian implications" (Cartledge, in his comments on an earlier version of this paper).

23. Thus Hdt. 3.83.2; Eur. *Heracl.* 181–82, *Hec.* 1130–31, parodied in *Cyc.* 179–81.

24. *Ath. Pol.* 1.2, cf. 1.6 (above, n. 18).

25. Plato *Prot.* 322cd.

26. *Supp.* 365–69, 398–401, 483–85, 600–624, 963–65. See below, n.37 (with literature).

27. Incidentally, *pace* Hansen, *Athenian Democracy,* 83; "Anniversary," 28, I have no doubt that important passages dealing with democracy in general and not explicitly focusing on Athens still are primarily based on or concerned with the Athenian case. Herodotus' Constitutional Debate and Athenagoras' speech in Thucydides are obvious examples (on the latter, see Jones, *Athenian Democracy,* 43).

28. On the primacy and extremely high valuation of this right, see Bleicken, *Demokratie,* 290–98; Raaflaub, "Des freien Bürgers Recht," 41–46; Raaflaub, *Freiheit,* 277–83, 291–93.

29. Cf. also Ps. Andoc. 4 (*ag. Alc.*) 13, 16, 27. In other words, *isotēs* or *to ison,* as interpreted by the democrats, consists of *isopsēphia, isēgoria, isonomia, isomoiria* (the latter in the political, not economic sense of the word).

30. Thuc. 2.37.1; Hdt. 3.80.6, although this is not the only possible interpretation of *en gar tōi polloi eni ta panta:* for a different one, see, e.g., Apffel, *Verfassungsdebatte,* 33n.3; Bleicken, *Demokratie,* 300–1.

31. Ps. Xen. *Ath. Pol.* 1.3.—Thuc. 8.67.3 (cf. 65.3; Arist. *Ath. Pol.* 29.5).

32. Raaflaub, "Des freien Bürgers Recht," 14–21, 45–46; Raaflaub, "Free Citizen," 527–36.

33. See above at nn.12–19. Ps. Xen. *Ath. Pol.* 1.1–9; Thuc. 6.38–41, and the Constitutional Debates in Herodotus (esp. 3.81) and Euripides' *Suppliants* (399–455) are particularly important. Since the concept of democratic equality entails full citizen rights for, and active political participation by, all citizens, virtually all criticism of democracy directly or indirectly attacks this very principle; for criticism of democracy, see Larsen, "Judgment"; Jones, *Athenian Democracy,* 41–72; Raaflaub, "Perceptions"; Roberts, *Athens on Trial;* Ober, "How to Criticize Democracy."

34. Kerferd, *Sophistic Movement,* 144; Plato *Prot.* 320c–323a. Finley, *Democracy,* 28, considers it possible that Protagoras was the only thinker who developed a democratic theory. I follow Kerferd, Guthrie (*Philosophy,* III. 64, 265–66), and many others in accepting the authenticity of Protagoras' portrait and myth in Plato's dialogue. For in-

terpretation, see Guthrie, ibid. 63–68; Kerferd, "Protagoras' Doctrine"; Kerferd, *The Sophistic Movement,* 131–36, 139–47; Kerferd, "Equality," 9–10. See also Farrar, *Origins,* ch. 3.

35. Cf. Pachlatko, *Verschiedenheit;* Baldry, *Unity,* ch. 2, esp. 24–51; Kerferd, "Equality," 10–15; Guthrie, *Philosophy,* III. 152–63. For slavery, see n.118 below.

36. Cf. Plato *Menex.* 238e–239a: *isogonia* based on autochthony produced *isonomia.*

37. Aesch. *Supp.* esp. 366–69; see also 398–401, 483–89, 605–8, 621–22, 963–65; cf. Meier, *Political Art,* 84–97; Raaflaub, "Politisches Denken," 286–88.

38. See above at n. 24.

39. Hdt. 5.78 (above n.9). In Hipp. *Airs, Waters, Places* 16, 23, the same argument is used in a theoretical context to explain the positive attitudes of autonomous Greeks in Asia.

40. See, for example, Euben, "Equality," 208–10, 216–18; Hansen, *Was Athens a Democracy?* 21–25; Dunn, "Conclusion"; Bleicken, *Demokratie,* 290–91; Wood, "Democracy"; and Ostwald's contribution to the present volume.

41. See *Pol.* 1.2, 1252b27–1253a7 with Euben, "Equality," 214–16; the comments by Schütrumpf, *Politik I;* and the references cited in Ostwald's contribution to the present volume.

42. For example, Euben, "Equality," does not make the distinction sharply enough. The classic case, of course, is Ehrenberg, *Der Staat der Griechen* and *The Greek State,* respectively, where the polis "as the essential Greek state" ("der griechische Staat schlechthin") is seen as naturally culminating in the democratic polis; cf. Ehrenberg, "Grundformen." Critical discussions of Ehrenberg's views are listed by Meier, Review of Ehrenberg, *Staat,* 366n.1.

43. If we accept Bowersock's arguments for dating Pseudo Xenophon in the late 440s: "Pseudo-Xenophon," 33–38; cf. Sealey, *"Demokratia,"* 257–60; Fornara/Samons, *Athens,* 64–65 with n. 86. Most scholars, however, still prefer a date in the 420s: for discussion, see, e.g., Frisch, *Constitution,* 47–62; Treu, "Pseudo-Xenophon," 1947–95; de Ste. Croix, *Origins,* 307–10. It is unknown when Protagoras developed his theory of democracy; the fictive date of Plato's dialogue is 423 (von Fritz, "Protagoras," 909), but the 440s, when Pericles invited Protagoras to draft the constitution of the new Panhellenic colony of Thurii, might be more plausible; cf. Ehrenberg, "Thurii," esp. 168–69 = Ehrenberg, *Polis,* 313–14.

44. E.g., Hdt. 3.80.6. *Isonomia* does not fit poetic metres; hence paraphrases, such as Eur. *Supp.* 406–8, 429–41 (n. 10 above); see Raaflaub, *Freiheit,* 285–89. Hansen, *Was Athens a Democracy?* 23–24; *Democracy,* 81–85; "Anniversary," 27–28, points out that by the late fifth and especially in the fourth century the terms *eleutheria, dēmokratia, isēgoria,* and *parrhēsia* were more frequently used in Athens than was *isonomia.* The reason probably is precisely that the latter was not tied specifically enough to democracy. Hansen claims, moreover, that "by a closer scrutiny of the sources, much of the talk about equality being prior to liberty in early Athenian political thought vanishes into thin air" ("Anniversary," 27). This claim is based on the assumption that the terminology in passages that do not specifically refer to Athens has nothing to do with Athenian experiences (this assumption is clearly wrong, especially in the cases of Herodotus or Thucydides [see n. 27 above]; it would be a similar error to conclude, as is done not infrequently, that Aeschylus' *Suppliants,* because situated in Argos, is unrelated to contemporary Athenian concerns); moreover, Hansen does not consider paraphrases and in-

direct testimonia. On *isonomia,* see the bibliography cited in Raaflaub, *Freiheit,* 115–18, esp. 116n.16. Esp. important: Vlastos, *"Isonomia"* and *"Isonomia politikē"*; Ostwald, *Nomos;* Pleket, "Isonomia." More recently, Sealey, *Athenian Republic,* 99–100; Triebel-Schubert, "Isonomie"; Lengauer, "Gleichheitsidee"; Fornara/Samons, *Athens,* 42–50, 166–67.

45. See recently Triebel-Schubert, "Isonomie" (40n.3 gives a survey of proposed dates), who argues for the late sixth century, while most scholars prefer the first half or middle of the fifth.

46. Carmina convivalia 10, 13 (893, 896 Page, *Poetae*); Fornara, *Archaic Times,* 39. Cf. Ostwald, *Nomos,* 121–36 with bibliography; Fornara/Samons, *Athens,* 42–50 and 166–67 (without in principle excluding the possibility of a sixth-century origin of *isonomia*). See also Ehrenberg, "Harmodioslied;" Lavelle, *Sorrow,* esp. ch. 2.2.

47. *Isokratia:* Hdt. 5.92a.1; cf. Ostwald, *"Isokratia." Isēgoria:* Hdt. 5.78 (above n. 9); see Raaflaub, "Des freien Bürgers Recht," 23–28 with bibliography.

48. See Raaflaub, "Des freien Bürgers Recht," 23–24, 26–28. Beloch, *Griechische Geschichte,* I. 616–17, stresses the significance of the emergence of names with the *-agoras* component; Hirzel, *Dike,* 266n.5, the political importance of names with *Iso-.*

49. See Sealey, *Athenian Republic,* 99. Thus the terminology of aristocratic equality hardly originated in Athens.

50. Theog. 678; see Cerri, *"Isos dasmos."*

51. Anaximander, no. 12B1 *DK;* see Vlastos, *"Isonomia,"* 361–63, based on his "Equality," esp. 168–73.

52. Solon, fr. 24.18–20 Diehl (= 36 West, *Iambi* II = 30 Gentili/Prato). Cf. Vlastos, "Solonian Justice." It seems significant that Solon uses *homoios,* not *isos* (see above, n.7). On *Isomoiria:* see n.126, below.

53. The bibliography on Cleisthenes' reforms is vast. See, for example, Ostwald, *Nomos,* esp. part 3; Ostwald, "Reform"; Will, *Monde grec,* 63–76; Martin, "Kleisthenes," 5–22; Kinzl, "Athens," 199–210; Whitehead, *Demes;* Meier, *Politics,* 53–81; Fornara/Samons, *Athens,* 37–58, and the bibliography cited in nn. 41 and 52 of my "Kleisthenes."

54. See the bibliography cited in my *Freiheit,* 117n.220. I have presented my arguments ibid., 115–18; in "Des freien Bürgers Recht," 23–28, and again in "Kleisthenes," section V.

55. See Martin, "Kleisthenes," 18–22; Kinzl, "Athens," 202.

56. Cf. Detienne, "Grèce archaïque"; Borecký, "Equality."

57. Ober, "Revolution," further elaborated in "Revolution Matters."

58. Hdt. 5.66, 69–70, 72–73.1; Arist. *Ath. Pol.* 20; for other sources and discussions, see Rhodes, *Commentary* ad loc. The citation is from Ober, "Revolution," 222–23. He emphasizes the importance of "demotic action" in "Revolution Matters," based in part on Wolin's contribution to this volume.

59. See my "Power in the Hands of the People" and "Thetes," the latter in response to Ober's "Revolution Matters." Part of the difficulty is that Herodotus' narrative and interpretation of the event naturally are influenced by both the vocabulary and political experiences of his own time.

60. For detailed discussion, see Siewert, *Trittyen,* who, however, takes this aspect too absolutely.

61. See, briefly, Starr, *Sea Power,* 28–30; in more detail, Amit, *Athens and the Sea,* 18–20; Wallinga, *Ships,* 17–18, 21–22, 140–48; Gabrielsen, *Financing,* 20–26; more bibliography in Walter, *An der Polis teilhaben,* 186n.60; contra: Jordan, *Navy,* 5–16.

62. Pindar *Pyth.* 2.87 (dated to ca. 470); cf. *Ol.* 9.95; Aesch. *Eum.* 683. See Meier, "Drei Bemerkungen," 12n.33; Meier, *Begriff Demokratie,* 42. Lotze, "Begriff der Demokratie," 209, expresses doubts. Ostwald, *Sovereignty,* 23, and Whitehead, *Demes,* 23n.78, consider it possible that Cleisthenes' order was still influenced by this factor; see also Fornara/Samons, *Athens,* 64.

63. Hdt. 5.66.2, 69.2; Arist. *Ath. Pol.* 20.2, for the connection between reform plan and Cleisthenes' popularity. The *boulē,* slated to be abolished by Isagoras, led the resistance against Cleomenes and Isagoras. If this was the Solonian Council of 400, its members most likely belonged to the elite; this probably was true at least initially even of the new Council of 500—if it was already in place; see Meier, *Politics,* 71.

64. For this often neglected aspect, see, for example, Martin, "Kleisthenes," 20–21; Bleicken, *Demokratie,* 28–34, esp. 33–34; Stahl, *Aristokraten,* part III; Eder, "Self-Confidence"; Eder, "Polis und Politai," 28–31; Ober, *Mass and Elite,* 60–68; Manville, *Citizenship,* ch. 7.

65. They would have numbered above ca. 10,000, which at that time probably still amounted to rather more than one-third, perhaps even more than half of the entire citizen body. In 490 at Marathon, Athens fielded 9,000 hoplites, in 479 at Plataea 8,000. Hdt. 5.97.2 assumes 30,000 citizens for ca. 500 B.C.; cf. Beloch, *Bevölkerung,* 60. The latter is a round figure, probably based more on the realities of Herodotus' own time than on historical information or reconstruction (cf. Hdt. 8.65.1; Ar. *Eccl.* 1132; Plato, *Symp.* 175e). While we have fairly precise figures for hoplites in the period of the Persian Wars and before the Peloponnesian War (Thuc. 2.13.6–7), the number of thetes (like that of slaves and metics) is entirely uncertain. It probably was relatively small in the early polis (eighth and seventh centuries), increased substantially during the agrarian and social crisis preceding Solon's reforms, may have been reduced again by these reforms, increased probably slowly during the sixth century (as a result of Solon's encouragement of immigration, Plut. *Solon* 24.4, and prosperity under the tyrants) and then massively in the fifth century (Davies, "Society and Economy," 296–99). But what does that mean in absolute figures? For discussion of Athenian population figures, see recently Hansen, "Number," "Demographic Reflections," and *Demography;* Garnsey, *Famine,* part 3; Bleicken, *Demokratie,* 84–85, 470–72; more generally, Sallares, *Ecology,* part 2.

66. Arist. *Ath. Pol.* 7.3 assumes this already for Solon's reforms; see the discussion by Rhodes, *Commentary,* 140–41.

67. All this requires more detailed discussion; the whole problem obviously is tied in with that of the development of the assembly (Starr, *Birth,* is of little help; cross-cultural comparison might offer some clues) and that of citizenship and of a sharp separation between citizens and noncitizens; on these see the bibliography cited in n. 118; on citizenship, see Peremans, "Droit de cité"; Davies, "Citizenship"; Sealey, "Citizenship"; Manville, *Citizenship;* Whitehead, "Norms of Citizenship"; Boegehold/Scafuro, *Athenian Identity.*

68. See, e.g., Ostwald, *Sovereignty,* 19, 26–27; Ostwald, "Reform," 328; Meier, *Politics,* 71, 77. Meier, "Intelligenz," 91n.16, and "Umbruch," 360, considers the possibility that *isonomia* initially envisioned, among other things, a balance between aristocracy

and demos. By contrast, despite the lack of evidence, Larsen, *Representative Government,* 13–21; Woodhead, "Isegoria," 135–40; and others assume a powerful popular council. Rhodes, *Boule,* 208–10, argues against this view.

69. I consider this a minimal definition of democratic practice, based on the Athenians' own understanding of it (which is all that matters in this context); for further discussion see my "Power in the Hands of the People," section 2. Other definitions will of course produce different conclusions; thus Ruschenbusch, "Verfassungsgeschichte," is able to "prove" that both Solonian Athens and "Homeric society" were democratic. The use of the word *democracy* in discussions of popular or non-autocratic elements in the political systems of various ancient Near Eastern societies (thus especially Jacobsen, "Primitive Democracy" and "Mesopotamia," 128–29; on the phenomena involved, see, e.g., Evans, "Assemblies," and recently Crawford, *Sumer,* 20–28; Postgate, *Mesopotamian Society,* 79–87; Pettinato, *Ebla,* 74–95; Crüsemann, "Theokratie"; Cancik, "Herrschaft" [all with bibliography]) seems to me unfortunate and misleading; see also Ehrenberg, *Polis und Imperium,* 264n.2; Meier, *Politics,* 31; and Robinson, *Greek Democracies,* ch. 1.

70. Those who disagree include Lotze, "Entwicklungslinien"; Fornara/Samons, *Athens,* 39–40, 48–50, 52–57; Hansen, *Athenian Democracy,* 34; Ober, "Athenian Revolution" and "Revolution Matters."

71. For discussion, see Hignett, *Constitution,* chs. 8 and 9; more recently, Rhodes, *Boule,* 201–7, *Commentary* on Arist. *Ath. Pol.* 25–26, "Revolution," 67–77; Martin, "Kleisthenes," 29–40; Wallace, *Areopagos,* 81ff., esp. 83–87; Sealey, *History,* 257–64, "Ephialtes"; Ruschenbusch, *Innenpolitik,* 57–65; Davies, *Democracy,* ch. 4; Ostwald, *Sovereignty,* 28–83; Meier, "Umbruch"; Ober, *Mass,* 77–81; the commentary of Chambers, *Aristoteles,* on *Ath. Pol.* 25–26; Fornara/Samons, *Athens,* 58–75; Hansen, *Athenian Democracy,* 36–38; Bleicken, *Demokratie,* 44–46 with 454–59, and my "Kleisthenes," section IV, "Power in the Hands of the People," and "Thetes."

72. See recently Ostwald, *Sovereignty,* and Rhodes, "Revolution" (previous note).

73. Eur. *Supp.* 352, 406; cf. *Cyc.* 119. Aeschylus: see n. 37. *Dēmokratia:* see my "Kleisthenes," section V (arguing against Hansen's claim, *Democracy,* 69–71, that the term existed in Cleisthenes' time), and "Power in the Hands of the People," section 3.

74. See Arist. *Ath. Pol.* 27.3–4 with the comments by Rhodes and Chambers; Hignett, *Constitution,* 219–20; Fornara/Samons, *Athens,* 67–74; Rhodes, "Revolution," 75–76; more generally, Hansen, "Misthos"; Bleicken, *Demokratie,* 280–86, 534–38.

75. Arist. *Ath. Pol.* 26.2 with the comments by Rhodes and Chambers; Hignett, *Constitution,* 225; Ruschenbusch, *Innenpolitik,* 66–72 (who argues against interpreting this as a democratic measure); and Ryan, "Thetes."

76. Arist. *Ath. Pol.* 26.4 with the comments by Rhodes and Chambers; Hignett, *Constitution,* 343–47; Humphreys, "Nothoi," 93–94; Ruschenbusch, *Innenpolitik,* 83–87; Patterson, *Citizenship Law,* esp. ch. 4; Fornara/Samons, *Athens,* 74–75; Rhodes, "Revolution," 76–77; Boegehold, "Perikles' Citizenship Law."

77. See esp. Schuller, "Zur Entstehung," "Wirkungen"; Bleicken, *Demokratie,* 42–44.

78. Though not yet uniquely; the hoplites contributed heavily until most of the territories controlled by Athens on the mainland were lost in the early 440s and, as a result of Pericles' change of policy, Athens relied almost entirely on the fleet and the city's extensive fortifications; but see Ridley, "Hoplite," 522–27, for continuing reliance on the hoplites as well even in later decades.

79. On the crews manning the fleet, see Amit, *Athens,* 30–49, esp. 39ff.; Jordan, *Navy,* 210–40; Rosivach, "Fleet"; Wallinga, *Ships,* 169–85; Gabrielsen, *Financing,* 105–10. The question of whether the thetes were mostly conscripted (see also Hansen, *Demography,* 22–23) or volunteers (as Rosivach and Gabrielsen stress) is secondary here; but see below at n. 137.

80. Bleicken, *Demokratie,* 298, thinks that, in view of the splendid victories of the Athenian armies and navies, and of the spectacular rise of Athenian power, justification of democracy was necessary only much later. On the contrary: the reforms of Ephialtes provoked massive tensions and violence; thus there must have been intense discussions. See Thuc. 1.107.4–5; Arist. *Ath. Pol.* 25.4; Plut. *Cimon* 15–17 and *Per.* 10, with Meier, *Politics,* 82–87, and "Umbruch," 366–74.

81. See the passages from Herodotus, Ps. Xenophon, and Aesch. *Supp.* cited in nn. 9, 24, 26 above; Plut. *Cimon* 15.3. On *dēmos* see Donlan, "Changes"; Fornara/Samons, *Athens,* 48–49; cf. also Meier, "Bemerkungen," 25–29 (on frequent preference for *plēthos*). In "Power in the Hands of the People," section 3, I suggest that the exclusive sense of *dēmos,* focusing on the lower classes, emerged precisely as a result of the political ascendance of the lower classes, that is, of democracy itself. On echoes of contemporary debates in the extant sources, see Meier, "Umbruch," 359–74; Rhodes, *Commentary,* 314, and "Revolution," 70. Efforts to stress the hoplites' contribution to the great victories against the Persians, though probably somewhat earlier, reflect similar concerns; see Fornara, "Psyttaleia"; Loraux, "Marathon" and *Invention,* 161–62; Vidal-Naquet, *Black Hunter,* 90–91, 310–14.

82. For discussion of "forerunners" of democracy, see Zimmermann, "Ansätze"; Robinson, *Greek Democracies;* and O'Neil, *Origins.*

83. See Schuller, "Zur Entstehung," and *Herrschaft,* 82–100; Bleicken, *Demokratie,* ch. 15.

84. This conclusion, overlooked far too often (de Ste. Croix, *Class Struggle,* 283–85, is among the exceptions), is supported by the great variety of democracies included in the empirical material analyzed in Aristotle's *Politics,* his theoretical and schematic distinction between four types of democracy (on all this see Newman, *Politics;* Mulgan, "Analysis" [as cited in nn. 4–5 above]; Hansen, "Solonian Democracy," 96–97), and the variations indicated even in his list of elements of democratic equality (1317b16–38).

85. On the latter, see Ruschenbusch, *Untersuchungen,* 68–71, and *Innenpolitik,* 15–17; Schuller, "Wirkungen," 94–97.

86. Morris, this volume, and *Archaeology of Democracy.* See also, for example, the discovery of "egalitarian" row houses in several Greek poleis (Hoepfner/Schwandner, *Haus*) and the debate about their connection with democracy (Schuller/Hoepfner/Schwandner [eds.], *Demokratie und Architektur*), as well as works on "forerunners" of democracy (n. 82 above).

87. See my "Homer to Solon," which provides extensive documentation and bibliography. Ibid., 44–46, and in "Homer und die Geschichte," 207–15, I explain why I essentially accept the historicity of "Homeric society." For recent discussion of these issues, see also Ulf, *Homerische Gesellschaft;* van Wees, *Status Warriors,* esp. chs. 1 and 2; Bowden, "Hoplites."

88. See esp. *Iliad* 1.163–64; 16.52–54; cf. 9.318–19 (with Arist. *Pol.* 1267a1–2) and, on the level of the gods, 15.185–93 and 208–10.

89. See esp. *Iliad* 1.185–87, 277–79, with 280–81, 287–89, and 9.160–61.

90. See esp. *Iliad* 9.9–79, 89–172 (33: it is right [*themis*] for Diomedes to speak up against Agamemnon in the assembly); other meetings of the council are described in 2.53–83; 7.323–44; 14.27–134; and, on the Trojan side, 12.210–50; 13.723–48; 18.243–313 with 22.99–110. See, for example, Finley, *World,* 78–83, 108–17; Spahn, *Mittelschicht,* 29ff., esp. 34–37; Vernant, *Thought,* chs. 3–4, esp. 45–52; Gschnitzer, "Rat"; Carlier, *Royauté,* 182–87. Interestingly, equality even appears in names: Isandros (*Iliad* 6.197, 203), Isos (11.101).

91. Finley, *World,* 114.

92. See above at nn. 48–49.

93. Finley, *World,* 53. Contra: Starr, *Growth,* 123–28; Spahn, *Mittelschicht,* 47–58; Donlan, *Aristocratic Ideal,* ch. 1, and "Pre-State Community"; Gschnitzer, *Sozialgeschichte,* 35–38; Welwei, "Adel," and *Polis,* 51–53; Murray, *Early Greece,* ch. 4, esp. 68.

94. Nicolai, "Gefolgschaftsverweigerung," recently put much emphasis on this aspect; see also Donlan, "Changes," 387n.19; Morris, this volume. Contra: Spahn, "Individualisierung," esp. 347–54.

95. See the bibliography cited in the previous notes; in addition, Sakellariou, *Polis-State,* 366–71, and the bibliography cited in my "Homer und die Geschichte," 246n.137.

96. Snodgrass, *Early Greek Armour,* esp. chs. 8 and 9, "Hoplite Reform," *Archaic Greece,* 99–114.

97. The debate and literature on these issues are extensive; see the bibliography cited in my "Homer und die Geschichte," 225–30, and "Homer to Solon," 94n.49, 104n.178. Murray, *Early Greece,* chs. 8–10; Bryant, "Military Technology"; Cartledge, "Nascita degli opliti" offer good summaries. More generally on the hoplite phalanx, see recently Hanson, *War* and *Hoplites.*

98. Latacz, *Kampfparänese;* Pritchett, *War* IV, 7–33; van Wees, "Homeric Way of War." See also Krentz, "Hoplite Battle"; Bowden, "Hoplites"; Snodgrass, "Hoplite Reform Revisited." The following summary is based on my brief discussions in the articles cited in the previous note; it is intended to stimulate discussion. For a more detailed discussion of all the problems involved, see my "Citizens, Soldiers" and a forthcoming book on Homer and the early Greek polis.

99. E.g., *Iliad* 13.130–34; 16.212–17. Cf. Tyrt. 11.29–34 West, *Iambi* II.

100. Polybius 18.29.6, referring to *Iliad* 13.131–33; cf. Diodorus 16.3.2; Pritchett, *War* IV, 24n.78.

101. Hence, for example, great care is taken to ensure fairness and equality in the distribution of booty; Detienne, *Maîtres,* ch. 5; Nowag, *Raub,* 36–50.

102. On types of war in Homer, see my "Homer und die Geschichte" 222–25; de Polignac, *Naissance,* esp. 54–66; Jackson, "War." On historical wars in the eighth century: Messenia: Cartledge, *Sparta,* 113–20. Lelantine War: Murray, *Early Greece,* 76–79; Tausend, "Der Lelantische Krieg." See generally, de Polignac, *Naissance.*

103. See Snodgrass, *Archaic Greece,* 37–40 on the connection between the political phenomenon of the advent of the polis and the economic one of the increasing importance of landownership; Snodgrass, "Rise of the *Polis,*" 37–39, on the connection between the concepts of territoriality, landownership, and citizenship.

104. As they did in Italy and Rome: Timpe, "Kriegsmonopol."

105. See also Welwei, *Polis,* 51f.; Morris, *Burial,* 196–201. Snodgrass, *Arms and Armour,* 61; "'Hoplite Reform' Revisited," 60–61, offers some thoughts on organizational issues.

106. On the former: n. 93 above. On the latter, see generally Donlan, *Aristocratic Ideal;* Stein-Hölkeskamp, *Adelskultur.*

107. See Asheri, *Distribuzione,* 7–16, and "Osservazioni"; Vallet, "Cité," esp. 74–78, 94–107; Murray, *Early Greece,* 113–15.

108. See, among many others, Kiechle, *Lakonien,* ch. 4, esp. 187–88, 209–10, 255; Forrest, *Sparta,* 50–55; Spahn, *Mittelschicht,* 87–111; Cartledge, *Sparta and Lakonia,* 131–35; Hodkinson, "Social Order"; Murray, *Early Greece,* ch.10, esp. 173–79; and Cartledge, this volume.

109. For various aspects of these developments, see, for example, Heuss, "Archäische Zeit," esp. 45–53 and 68–80, respectively; Stahl, *Aristokraten,* part 2; Stein-Hölkeskamp, *Adelskultur,* 57–85. For this entire section, see also my "Homer to Solon," sections 3b and 3c (with extensive bibliography); and Morris, this volume.

110. See above, section 2, at nn. 48–49.

111. See, for example, Bonner/Smith, *Administration of Justice* I, ch. 3; Gagarin, *Law,* 58–80; and esp. Ruschenbusch, "Polis und das Recht"; Eder, "Codification of Law"; Hölkeskamp, "Written Law," "Arbitrators," and *Schiedsrichter;* Gehrke, "Gesetz," all of whom correct common misperceptions.

112. Solon, fr. 24.18–20 Diehl (= 36 West, *Iambi* II = 30 Gentili/Prato; Arist. *Ath. Pol.* 12.4, tr. Rhodes, Penguin).

113. Thus in a law of Dreros dated to the first half of the seventh century B.C. (Meiggs/Lewis, *Inscriptions,* no. 2; Fornara, *Archaic Times,* no. 11; cf. Ehrenberg, "Early Source") and in an early-sixth-century decree from Cyzicus (*SIG* no. 4 [3rd ed.]; see Ehrenberg, "Rise," 152 and 89, respectively). See now Hölkeskamp, "Written Law," 95–96; on the development of institutions, see Stein-Hölkeskamp, *Adelskultur,* 94–103.

114. Thus the *boulē dēmosiē* in a mid-sixth-century inscription from Chios (Meiggs/Lewis, *Inscriptions,* no. 8; Fornara, *Archaic Times,* no. 19); the magistrates called *damioi* in the Dreros inscription (previous n.) or *damiorgoi* in other places (cf. Murakawa, "Demiurgos," esp. 403–4), the *skēnē damosia,* the people called *hoi peri damosian,* or the *damosion,* all attested for Sparta (cf. Ehrenberg, "Early Source," 18 = *Polis,* 104, and "Damos," 293–96 = *Polis,* 208–11); see further Gehrke, "Gesetz und Konflikt." On *dēmosios* see now also Lewis, "Public Property."

115. Arist. *Ath. Pol.* 24.3 (not counting the military jobs), with the comments by Rhodes, *Commentary* and Chambers, *Aristoteles.* Ships on patrol: Plut. *Per.* 11.4 (doubted by Gabrielsen, *Financing,* 111 with n. 13). On the assembly: Hansen, *Assembly;* Starr, *Birth;* Bleicken, *Demokratie,* 161–83. On the jury-courts: Hansen, *Athenian Democracy,* ch. 8; Bleicken, *Demokratie,* 203–28; Markle, "Jury Pay"; Todd, "Jury." On officeholders: Hansen, *Athenian Democracy,* chs. 9–10.

116. Meier, "Besonderheit," explains why such broad participation was necessary; see also his "Bürgeridentität" and "Political Identity"; Martin, "Aspekte," 224–27. On broad citizen participation, see also Gomme, "Working"; Jones, "How Did Democracy Work?" Bleicken, *Demokratie,* 306–10 and ch. 6 with 555–64; Sinclair, *Participation;* Hansen, *Assembly,* and *Athenian Democracy;* Eder, "Who Rules?"

117. See the references, in Ostwald, this volume, to the Fourteenth and Nineteenth Amendments of the U.S. Constitution, validated in 1868 and 1920. For comparisons between ancient and modern democracy, see, for example, Dunn, *Western Political Theory,* ch. 1, and Conclusion to *Democracy: The Unfinished Journey;* Hansen, *Was Athens a Democracy?* Bleicken, *Demokratie,* 423–34.

118. See generally, e.g., Bleicken, *Demokratie,* 83–97, 474–77; Strauss, "Genealogy." Women: see below, n. 122. Foreigners and metics: Whitehead, *Metic* (with bibliography); more recently, Baslez, *L'Etranger;* Vatin, *Citoyens;* Whitehead, "Immigrant Communities"; Lonis (ed.), *L'Etranger.* Slaves: Wood, *Peasant-Citizen;* more generally: Schlaifer, "Theories of Slavery"; Guthrie, *Philosophy* III, 155–60; Vogt, *Slavery,* 1–25; Finley, *Slavery.*

119. On citizenship policy in Athens, see Osborne, *Naturalization;* Patterson, *Citizenship Law;* Whitehead, "Norms"; see also Sealey, *Republic,* 5–31; Euben, "Equality," 213–15. Important questions related to this issue are discussed in Boegehold/Scafuro (eds.), *Athenian Identity.* The contrast with Rome's open society and integrative policies is revealing: Gauthier, "Citoyenneté"; Sherwin-White, *Citizenship;* Drummond, "Citizen Community," 209–11; Cornell, "Rome and Latium," 269–71, and "Anachronism."

120. Ps. Xen. *Ath. Pol.* 1.10–12; cf. Ar. *Frogs* 948–52 (Euripides presents himself as especially democratic in letting women and slaves speak on stage); Xen. *Hell.* 2.3.48.

121. See above, n. 35.

122. See Auger et al., *Aristophane;* Henderson, "Lysistrate," esp. 185ff. passim, and *Aristophanes' Lysistirata,* XXV–XXXVI; Taaffe, *Aristophanes and Women;* more generally, among others, Loraux, *Children of Athena;* Keuls, *Reign;* Just, *Women;* Fantham et al., *Women.*

123. Slaves: Welwei, *Unfreie,* 96–107; see also Graham, "Crews." Plataea and Samos: Osborne, *Naturalization,* D1 (I.28 with II.11–16), D4–5 (I.33–37 with II.25f.), T10 (III.33–37); see further IV.145, 154, 173–83; Gawantka, *Isopolitie,* 174–97.

124. Election: Arist. *Ath. Pol.* 43.1, 44.4, 61 with Rhodes, *Commentary* and Chambers, *Aristoteles;* Hansen, *Athenian Democracy,* 233–35. Property requirements: *Ath. Pol.* 8.1, 47.1 with the commentaries and Hansen, ibid. 107–8. For reactions: e.g., Ps. Xen. *Ath. Pol.* 1.3.

125. See Thomsen, *Eisphora;* Davies, *Wealth;* and briefly Hansen, *Athenian Democracy,* 110–16. During the Peloponnesian War the burden imposed on the wealthy by these obligations increased massively; this contributed to upper-class dissatisfaction with democracy and ultimately to the oligarchic coup of 411 (Thuc. 8.48.1, 63.4, 65.3 with Arist. *Ath. Pol.* 29.5).

126. Solon's refutation of *isomoiria* (fr. 34.8–9 West, *Iambi* II = 29b.8–9 Gentili/Prato) probably aims in a different direction: Andrewes, "Growth," 382; Rosivach, "Redistribution." On democracy and redistribution, see, generally, Tarkiainen, *Demokratie,* 309–19; Bleicken, *Demokratie,* 206–8; Hennig, "Besitzgleichheit"; Ober, *Mass,* ch. 5. Things changed in the fourth century, though mostly outside of Athens; see, for example, Mossé, *Fin,* part I; Vernant, "Remarques"; Fuks, "Patterns"; Pečírka, "Crisis"; Humphreys, *Anthropology,* 144–46; and the contributions by Gert Audring, Reinhard Koerner, Siegfried Lauffer, and Claude Mossé, in Welskopf, *Poleis.* For a recent assessment of Aristotle's view of democratic class struggle, see Eucken, "Demokratiebegriff," 282, 286–91.

127. Thus in Aristophanes' *Ecclesiazusae* (cf. Rothwell, *Politics*) or in the scheme of an ideal state designed by Phaleas of Chalcedon (Arist. *Pol.* 1266a39–b5); see Mossé, *Fin,* 234–46; Guthrie, *Philosophy* III. 152. Cf. generally Tarkiainen, Bleicken, Hennig (as cited in note 126).

128. See, for example, Eur. *Supp.* 420–22. I have discussed these issues in some detail in my "Des freien Bürgers Recht," 39–46; to the bibliography cited there should now

be added, for example, Bleicken, *Demokratie*, 293–94, 306–10; Carter, *Quiet Athenian;* Sinclair, *Participation;* Ober, *Mass;* Starr, *Birth;* Hansen, *Athenian Democracy.*

129. Pay: see n. 74 above; in addition, Markle, "Jury Pay"; Todd, "Lady Chatterley's Lover." On assembly pay (after 400), see Hansen, *Assembly,* 46–48, and *Athenian Democracy,* 150. Time: Hansen, "Duration," and *Assembly,* 32–34. For other measures enhancing and protecting equality, see Bleicken, *Demokratie,* 306–10.

130. I have mentioned these very briefly in my "Democracy, Power and Imperialism," 139–42.

131. See, for example, Hdt. 3.81.1–2; Eur. *Supp.* 417–22; Ps. Xen. *Ath. Pol.* 1.1–9, and the bibliography cited in n.33 above.

132. Thuc. 8.65.3 (*chrēmasin kai sōmasin*); cf. Arist. *Ath. Pol.* 29.5 with Rhodes, *Commentary,* 382–83.

133. Thuc. 1.70.6; 2.42.4. Plato's scathing condemnation of military power based on naval strength (*Laws* 4. 707a–d; cf. *Gorg.* 519a) had its predecessors in the fifth century in the glorification of Marathon and its heroes: Ehrenberg, *Aristophanes,* 298–300, and the bibliography cited in n. 81 above.

134. See Vernant, "Travail"; Aymard, "Travail"; Meier, "Arbeit"; Descat, *Idéologie du travail.* For the *technē* involved in naval warfare that equates it to all the base occupations, which were characterized by technical skills and professionalism and thus disqualified as "unfree" or "unnoble" (*aneleutheron*), see Vidal-Naquet, *Black Hunter,* 93 with sources. For *aneleutheroi technai:* Raaflaub, "Freiheitsbegriff," 305–13, and "Democracy, Oligarchy" 531–32.

135. Other disputed issues include the interpretation of *dēmos* (at n.81 above) and political concepts such as equality (Harvey, "Two Kinds") or freedom (Raaflaub, "Democracy, Oligarchy"; *Freiheit,* 304–11).

136. For the register of cavalry, see Bugh, *Horsemen,* 52–55, and the bibliography cited there. For that of the hoplites, Vidal-Naquet, *Black Hunter,* 87–88; Jones, *Democracy,* 163; Dover, in *HCT,* IV, 264; Andrewes, "*Katalogos.*" Contra: Hansen, "Hoplites," 24–29, and *Demography,* 83–89; accepted by Hornblower, *Commentary,* 256.

137. Conscription: Jordan, *Navy,* 101–3; Hansen, *Demography,* 22–23. Rosivach, "Fleet," and Gabrielsen, *Financing,* 105–8, now argue that the thetes serving on the fleet were mostly volunteers. See also Schmitz, *Wirtschaftliche Prosperität,* 44–55.

138. Jameson, "Apollo," 220, and the bibliography cited by Loraux, *Invention,* 360n.123. See also Schmitz, *Wirtschaftliche Prosperität,* 44–47.

139. 3.87.3 (deaths caused by the plague); 4.101.2 (the losses at Delion; Gomme, *HCT* ad loc. is refuted by Loraux, *Invention,* 361n.127). See also Patterson, *Citizenship Law,* 47. Ridley, "Hoplite," 513n.19, points out, however, that even for hoplites Thucydides rarely gives casualty figures.

140. Raubitschek, "Inscriptions," 48n.102; cf. Mattingly, "Imperialism," 191. Ridley, "Hoplite," 513 seems to assume that the casualty lists referred only to hoplites.

141. *Athenaiōn hoide apethanon: IG.* I^2 943 = I^3 1162. Bradeen, "Lists" (1964), 25n.15; see also Bradeen, "Lists" (1969), 153–54. Vidal-Naquet, *Black Hunter,* 88, and Loraux, *Invention,* 34, accept Bradeen's view.

142. Loraux, *Invention,* 34.

143. Jordan, *Navy,* 222, 227, assumes that the appearance of trierarchs on some lists necessitates the presence of at least some *nautai.* Whether "plebeian-seeming names" must belong to sailors (Gomme, *HCT,* I, 311) seems uncertain to me, given the large-

scale promotion of thetes to zeugite status (on which, see Jones, *Democracy*, 7, 167–77). The matter is complicated by the fact that occasionally ships were rowed by hoplites: Jordan, *Navy*, 225–30. See also Schmitz, *Wirtschaftliche Prosperität*, 51–54.

144. See Loraux, *Invention*, 33–34, cf. n.126 on p. 361.

145. Especially *IG* I² 79 = I³ 138, lines 1–7.

146. See recently (with references to earlier bibliography) Hignett, *Constitution*, 132–42; Habicht, "Urkunden," 5–6; Jameson, "Provisions," 399–400, expanded in his "Apollo," 213–23, esp. 222 with 223n.1; van Effenterre, "Clisthène," 7–15; Patterson, *Citizenship Law*, 8–28, esp. 27; Osborne, *Demos*, 72–73; Whitehead, *Demes*, 34–35; Bugh, *Horsemen*, 55n.64. See also Schmitz, *Wirtschaftliche Prosperität*, 46–47.

147. See the bibliography cited in n. 67 above; for further bibliography, see Manville, *Citizenship*, and Whitehead, "Norms;" see also Boegehold/Scafuro (eds.), *Athenian Identity*.

148. For detailed discussion, see Pélékidis, *L'Ephébie;* Rhodes, *Commentary*, 494–95, 503–10 at *Ath. Pol.* 42. Ibid. 503 and 768 (additional note to p. 503) for bibliography on whether or not the thetes were included in the formalized *ephēbeia* of the late fourth century. See also Sallares, *Ecology*, 119–22.

149. Vidal-Naquet, *Black Hunter*, 106. On the date of the earliest epigraphic evidence see Reinmuth, *Ephebic Inscriptions*, no. 1 (361–360); Mitchel, "Earliest Ephebic Inscription" (334–333); scholarship supporting the early date is listed by Vidal-Naquet, *Black Hunter*, 122n.1, that opposing it by Rhodes, *Commentary*, 494n.35. On Aeschin. 2 (*False Embassy*) 167 (pointing to 371), see Rhodes, *Commentary*, 494, and Robertson, "Documents," 21. Vidal-Naquet, *"Philoctetes,"* interprets Sophocles' play of 409 in terms of the *ephēbeia* (contra: Di Benedetto, "Filottete"); Merkelbach, "Theseus," suggests that Bacchylides' dithyramb "Theseus" (no. 18 = dith. 4 Snell/Maehler) was created for an Athenian festival of the ephebes after 460, and McCulloch/Cameron, *"Septem,"* find an allusion to the *ephēbeia* in Aeschylus' *Seven against Thebes* 12–13 (performed in 467). For discussion of other possible fifth-century testimonia, see Pélékidis, *L'Ephébie*, part 1; Roscam, "Remarque" (who draws attention to numerous representations on fifth-century Athenian vases of young men with chlamys [short cloak], petasos [broad-brimmed hat], and two spears and identifies these with the *neōtatoi* mentioned in Thuc. 1.105.4; 2.13.6–7; and these in turn with ephebes or their forerunners; on *neoi* and *ephēboi*, see also Forbes, *Neoi*); Ridley, "Hoplite," 531–34 (who points out that *peripoloi*—the word used by Aeschin. 2.167 for the function of ephebes during his two years of service—are amply attested in fifth-century sources, and that *neōtatoi* served in similar functions), and Winkler, "Ephebes' Song" (1985), esp. 32–38, who (in the revised version in *Nothing to Do with Dionysos?* 42–62) postulates a close connection between the ephebes and the tragic chorus. A. Henrichs draws my attention to the ritual of "lifting the ox," which is connected with the *ephēbeia* in (late) Attic ephebic inscriptions (Pélékidis, *L'Ephébie*, 223) but attested on vase paintings of the fifth century; on the latter, see recently Barbieri/Durand, "Bue," esp. 13 (see also Bérard et al., *City of Images*, 59 fig. 83); Durand, "Boeuf," esp. 238 (both emphasizing the role of the ephebes); on the aetiological myth for this ritual (Paus. 1.19.1), see Graf, "Apollon," 14–15. On the connection between hunting and the *ephēbeia*, see Schnapp, "Pratiche," and Durand/Schnapp, "Sacrificial Slaughter"; on the connection, fairly well established by now and important, between dances in arms (such as the Pyrrhic) and *ephēbeia*, see Poursat, "Danse armée"; Scarpi, "La Pyrrhiche"; Borthwick, "P. Oxy.

2738"; Ridley, "Hoplite," 535–47; Wheeler, "Hoplomachia," 229–32; Lonsdale, *Dance,*
162–67; and esp. Ceccarelli, *Danza armata.* (If the connection between pyrrhic and
ephēbeia proves correct, some form of the latter seems confirmed in Athens for the first
half of the fifth century: Ceccarelli, "Pirrica di Frinico.") On the ephebic oath, its archaic
elements, and possible echoes in fifth-century literature, see Siewert, "Ephebic Oath."
Robertson, "Documents," 6–7 distinguishes between an old citizens' oath (in which all
the archaic language is found) and a much younger (fourth-century?) soldiers' oath, but
Vidal-Naquet, *"Philoctetes,"* 162 points out that the closing formula as much as the
opening clauses marks the entire oath as a hoplite oath. Reinmuth, *Ephebic Inscriptions,*
123–38, proposes that the *ephēbeia* was formally organized soon after the Persian Wars.
On the roots of the *ephēbeia* in archaic rituals of initiation: Vidal-Naquet, *Black Hunter,*
106, with bibliography (citation: 106); Winkler, "Ephebes' Song" (including some modifications of an earlier version of Vidal-Naquet's essay *"Ephebeia"* [*Black Hunter,*
106–28]). See now also Vidal-Naquet, "Black Hunter Revisited."

150. For discussion, see Gauthier, *Commentary,* 190–95 on Xen. *Poroi* 4.51–52;
Rhodes, *Commentary,* 502–10; Hansen, *Demography,* 48–50; Sallares, *Ecology,* 121; cf.
also Antiphon Fr. 61 Thalheim.

151. Thus correctly Rhodes, *Commentary,* 503. See Vidal-Naquet, *Black Hunter,*
106–28, esp. 120: "In historical terms, the ephebe in Archaic and Classical Greece was
a pre-hoplite. By virtue of this, in the symbolic enactments that are the rites of passage,
he was an anti-hoplite. . . . At the technical level, the ephebe is a light-armed soldier. . . .
Creature of the frontier area . . . , he guarantees in his hoplite oath to protect the boundary stones of his country, and with them, the cultivated fields, the wheat, barley, olive
trees, vines, and figs."

152. Naval training: Amit, *Athens and the Sea,* 49–50; Jordan, *Navy,* 103–6;
Gabrielsen, *Financing,* 111 with n. 13: "Not that training was unimportant (Thuc.
1.142.9), but, as contemporary sources insist, experience was gained through frequent
service on expeditions (Ps. Xen. *Ath. Pol.* 1.19–20; Thuc. 3.115.7–8; Xen. *Hell.*
6.2.27–30)." Gomme, *HCT* I, 460, observes that in the *Ath. Pol.* Aristotle describes the
training of the hoplites "but says nothing of the sailor's which was far more elaborate."
On the training of the hoplites: Pritchett, *War* II, ch. 11; Ridley, "Hoplite," 535–47.

153. See Pickard-Cambridge, *Festivals,* 59 with nn.1–2; Stroud, "Inscriptions,"
288–90; Loraux, *Invention,* 26–27; Goldhill, "Dionysia," 107–14 (all with sources and
further bibliography).

154. Goldhill, "Dionysia," 107–14, typically speaks only of hoplites and does not
consider fleet, rowers, or thetes. Similarly Snodgrass, *Arms and Armour,* 59: The "sons
of hoplites killed in action were armed at the state's expense." The "young hoplite, on
completing his training, was presented with shield and spear but had to find the rest of
his equipment at his own expense." On the latter aspect, however, see Hansen, *Demography,* 48–49. An inscription from Thasos (Sokolowski, *Lois sacrées,* vol. 2 supp., no.
64; Institut Fernand-Courby, *Nouveau choix,* no. 19), dated to the first half of the fourth
century, lists among the honors for those who died fighting for the polis, "Whoever of
them leaves children behind—when they come of age—the polemarchs must give them,
if they are boys, to each greaves, a cuirass, a dagger, a helmet, a shield, a spear, worth
not less than three minas, at the Heracleia, and they must proclaim their names" (lines
16–21). See also Diod. 20.84.3.

155. Loraux, *Invention,* 27; see already den Boer, *Private Morality,* 43.

156. Thuc. 2.46.1; see also Winkler, "Ephebes' Song" (1985), 32–33, on the chorus of the sons of the fallen heroes at the end of Euripides' *Suppliants.* Aristotle (*Pol.* 1268a8–11) wrongly attributes the idea to Hippodamus of Miletus, which is accepted by Ruschenbusch, ΣΟΛΩΝΟΣ ΝΟΜΟΙ, 44.

157. *IG* I³ 6, C 40–41 = *SEG* 10. 6, C 123–25. Stroud, "Inscriptions," 288 (but see Rhodes, *Commentary,* 309) assumes on the basis of Arist. *Ath. Pol.* 24.3 (end) that "the practice was known in the period *ca.* 478–462"; he also finds references to a sixth-century, even Solonian, origin credible; contra: Loraux, *Invention,* 355n.70, favoring the connection mentioned in the text.

158. Pollitt, as presented in a lecture at the National Gallery of Art in Washington, D.C., on Jan. 22, 1993. Pollitt's own explanation, that this was an expression of shared communal pride in a recently reorganized and important military institution, may, of course, be correct. A recent survey of interpretations of the Parthenon frieze in Jenkins, *Parthenon Frieze.*

159. Loraux, *Invention,* 34; cf. n. 126 on p. 361. See also Cartledge, "Nascita," at n. 63.

160. Prejudices: n.131 above. Reeducation: see my "Democracy, Power and Imperialism," 129–30. I do not mean to imply that democracy was introduced in Athens on the basis of long-term plans and abstract or theoretical considerations (see Bleicken, *Demokratie,* 47–54), but I do believe that the political constellations in the final phases of the evolution of democracy (from the 460s) were such that those who proposed democratic measures and reforms were bound to know what they were doing and forced to justify their proposals in open debate (see my "Kleisthenes," 44–46).

161. Notably Ps. Xen. *Ath. Pol.* 1.2.

162. Just as, to some extent, the aristocracy was "democratized." Cf. Bleicken, *Demokratie,* 289–92; Meier, *Politics,* 145 (with n. 19 on p. 272); Stein-Hölkeskamp, *Adelskultur,* 205–30; Ober, *Mass,* 290–91 and the bibliography cited there.

163. See n. 116 above. Typically, the critics found that type of democracy most acceptable, in which most citizens were prevented by their daily work from participating actively in politics (cf. Arist. *Pol.* 1318b32–36; Mulgan, *Political Theory,* 74–75).

164. On elite and democracy, see especially Ober, *Mass;* furthermore, Donlan, *Aristocratic Ideal,* chs. 4–5; Stein-Hölkeskamp, *Adelskultur,* 205–30; Raaflaub, *Freiheit,* 267–72; and "Democracy, Oligarchy." On hoplites and democracy, see Hanson, this volume.

165. See, for example, Ps. Xen. *Ath. Pol.* 1.6–9, 18; Ar. *Knights* and *Wasps.*

166. Meier, "Political Identity"; cf. his "Bürgeridentität"; Humphreys, *Anthropology,* 146–49.

167. Ar. *Ach.* 162–63 (*thranitēs leōs ho sōsipolis.*) On the demos as a "beast," see Wolin, this volume; on the demos's pride and self-confidence, Strauss, this volume; Ober, "Revolution Matters"; on assessments of the demos, Meder, *Demos.* Indications of insecurity: below, note 168.

168. On all this see my "Des freien Bürgers Recht," section 11; "Democracy, Power and Imperialism," section 5c. See also Meier, "Rolle des Krieges."

169. The formulation is taken from Nicolet, *Métier.*

COMPARATIVELY EQUAL

Paul Cartledge

> man
> Equal, unclassed, tribeless, and nationless,
> Exempt from awe, worship, degree, the king
> Over himself.
> —P. B. Shelley, *Prometheus Unbound*

I. Aim and Method

My aim here is not only, nor indeed so much, to respond directly to the admirably clear, diachronically arranged paper of Kurt A. Raaflaub, although I shall be taking issue with it on a couple of points. Rather, it is to give a preliminary sketch in miniature of a forthcoming work on ancient Greek political thought (not only democratic) and so to stake out a slightly more ample terrain of enquiry.[1] I wish first, and very briefly, to compare ancient and modern conceptions and practices of equality, more specifically ancient Greek and post-Renaissance "Western" conceptions. Second, and in more detail, I wish to draw some comparisons within the ancient world, between Greek and Greek.

Method

For the structural-functional anthropologist A. R. Radcliffe-Brown, it is the aim of comparison to discover the universal.[2] For disciples of the "Cambridge School" of "conceptual history," on the contrary, among whom I should count myself,[3] comparison ought to emphasize difference.[4] In the present case, at all events, it is hoped that comparison will serve, first, to make us "clearer about features of our own social and political environment, features whose very familiarity may make it harder for us to bring them into view";[5] and second, to help us specify the peculiarities of ancient Greek constructions of equality by contrasting the set of meanings then available to political actors with that available today.

The concept of "constructions" merits special emphasis, since all of us presumably—whether we are ancient historians, political philosophers, or just plain citizens—are mainly interested in explaining, or understanding, the twin processes of discursive negotiation and practical implementation of political concepts. Equality happens to be one of the two most fundamental of these (the other is freedom), both in ancient and in modern democratic discourse. Since, however, language is constituted in political action, and political action in turn conditions or determines language,[6] an ineluctable tension or dialectic subsists between political theory (or ideology)[7] and political praxis. This is especially likely to be so in an antagonistic, zero-sum political culture such as that (or those) of classical Greece.[8] It follows that we should expect the meanings of a core concept like equality to be especially unstable, and to become extraordinarily hotly contested in situations of civil strife or outright civil war. Thucydides' famous account of the civil war on Kerkyra does not either disappoint or confound that expectation (see further below). In short, "there can be no histories of concepts as such; there can only be histories of their uses in argument." In application of this methodological principle, three distinct "uses in argument" of the general term *equality* in ancient Greece are hereafter proposed for consideration.[9]

Use in Argument 1: Reference

In the first place, equality of what?[10] What kinds of equality were at stake, and within what value-system? To begin comparatively, and negatively, we are not dealing here with the—or a—liberal sense of the equality of individual rights against the State.[11] Even if the Greeks did recognize what might plausibly be called rights, they did not construe the individual in a modern way and they did not have the fortune to know the separately instituted "State" in any post-Hobbesian sense.[12] Nor, second, are we dealing with the equality of all humankind in the sight of God, in either some specifically post-Pauline Christian or some generically eschatological, transcendent, metaphysical sense.[13] At most, the pagan Greeks would have accepted that vis-à-vis the immortal gods all mortals were equally powerless.[14] Nor, finally, is there any question here of sexual or gender equality, in the sense that modern feminism according to one dictionary definition is "advocacy of women's rights on ground of equality of the sexes".[15]

For classical Greece as a whole, not just classical Athens, the meanings of equality in practical question are rather as follows: first, and most broadly, political (or civic) equality, meaning equality of status and respect within the conceptual framework of the Greeks' normative system of polarized sociopolitical hierarchy.[16] Inasmuch as, and to the extent that, the Greek citizen was by definition male not female, free not slave, native insider not stranger or outsider, adult not child, he was in those respects and to that extent equal to all other citizens, and deserving therefore of equal respect, privilege, consideration, and treatment. However, there were two further factors that might and frequently did frustrate the translation of formal citizen equality into universal equality of outcome: birth (aristocrat against commoner, *agathos* against *kakos*) and wealth (rich against poor, *plousios* against *penēs*). Different Greek communities in fact distributed the privileges of citizenship differentially, in accordance with their divergent evaluations of these two factors, especially the latter.[17]

Second, there was theoretically the possibility of equality of welfare, of the good life in a sense that is not narrowly materialistic or mathematically calculated: generalized *eudaimonia,* or "well-being."[18] This is not to be confused with the allocation of precisely equal shares of some or all privately as well as publicly owned goods.[19] Third, the Greeks, especially democratic Greeks, operated with an idea of equality of opportunity. This amounted to the notion that all relevant citizen contestants in the (often literally) life-and-death race of public, political activity should ideally start behind the same line and run across a more or less level playing-field.[20]

Use in Argument 2: Criteria of Application

It has been noted cross-culturally that equality has often tended to be urged as an idea or ideal against some perceived inequality, particularly in moments of revolutionary upheaval.[21] Classical Greece was no exception. In 427 the democratic revolutionaries of Kerkyra were loud in their demand for what they styled *isonomia politikē* (Thuc. 3.82.8).[22] For the disabused Athenian historian, this was but a specious slogan, a cloak for the selfish ambitions of a power-mad clique. The speciousness was due, however, not only to the alleged motives of its propagators but also partly to the slogan's inherent radical ambiguity, or vapidity. For what was to count in practice as an "equal" sharing of power, and, more importantly, which (of the) "people" were to constitute the relevant community of sharers, actual or imagined?[23]

Isonomia, that is, may have been "the fairest of names" (Hdt. 3.80.6), but it was the beginning, not the end (in a temporal sense), of a political argument.[24] In fact, it might just as well be appropriated by Greek oligarchs (Thuc. 3.62.3) as by Greek democrats, depending on who were to be counted as relevantly equal, and in what respects. Aristotle was not the only oligarch to propound a theory (or ideology) of distributive, proportionate or "geometric" equality, a relativist notion of equality based on moral evaluation according to which some citizens were literally "more equal" than others.[25] On the other hand, even democrats, who more honestly espoused the opposite "arithmetical" conception, were prepared to concede that in practice equality was not everything (see further below). It was not mere coincidence that *isonomia* was not an official slogan of the Athenian democracy, let alone its guiding principle, in the sense that "the strong principle of equality" may justly be held to underlie the United States' dominant construction of democracy today.[26]

Use in Argument 3: Appraisive Function

The Greeks did of course "have a word for" *equality,* in fact more than one: not only *isotēs* but also *to ison* (the equal thing), wherein "equal" bears its root meaning of "exactly, mathematically equal," as in an *iso*-sceles triangle. But they operated and negotiated as well with a wide range of compound nouns starting with the *iso-* prefix. I cite five. *Iso-nomia,* just mentioned, stood for the most general and unspecific principle of political equality, *iso-kratia* and *is-ēgoria* connoted, respectively, the oligarchic and the democratic constructions.[27] *Iso-timia,* not certainly attested before the third century B.C., captured the social notion of equality of consideration or respect, parity of esteem; and finally *iso-moiria* did the same for the economic idea of equal distribution of some communal goods.[28]

This verbal flexibility regarding civic equality, welfare equality and equality of opportunity may be considered in itself an improvement on our comparatively restricted and ambiguous vocabulary. But the Greeks went further. They not only employed *iso-* compounds in this acutely sensitive area of political semantics. They also realistically anticipated the "discovery" of modern political philosophy that, although equality "does, after all, imply sameness,"[29] in hard political praxis the operative criterion governing equality's implementation is not sameness or identity but rather similitude or likeness. Hence, *isotēs* was complemented by the concept of *homoiotēs,* especially in the familiar prepositional phrases meaning "on an equal and fair basis" (*en/epi tois isois kai homoiois, epi tēi isēi kai homoiāi*).[30] Equality by itself, in other words, was not considered to be in all circumstances fair or just, even in the eyes of hardline ideological egalitarians in democratic Athens. Yet of all ancient cities Athens was surely the one that most fervently preached the gospel of equality.

II. COMPARING ATHENS AND SPARTA: SIMILARS AND EQUALS

In comparing the political systems and ideologies of Athens and Sparta, it makes sense to start with Aristotle and his *Politics,* not least because it was his own basic principle of political-philosophical method to start from the received and reputable views (*ta phainomena, ta endoxa*) of the prudent (*phronimoi*) participant observers and practitioners of civic life in the Greek polis. For Aristotle a polis had to consist of similars (*homoioi*); indeed, the polis according to one of his definitions is "a kind of association of similars" (*Pol.* 7.1328a35–36). Yet earlier in the same work, where he had been explicitly seeking to define the citizen, he had apparently said just the opposite: citizens cannot all be similars, even *qua* citizens (*Pol.* 3.1276b28, 40; 1277a6–7). Contradictions are by no means unknown elsewhere in the *Politics,* and this one too surely reflects the tension between the Greeks' ideal aspiration toward equality and the failure of its perfect implementation in practice. A properly Aristotelian golden mean is struck in the formulation that "the polis aims at being composed, as much as possible, of similars and equals" (4.1295b25–26).[31]

The dyadic combination, "similars and equals" (*homoioi kai isoi*), is crucial. It is the concrete counterpart of the abstract prepositional phrases meaning "on a fair and equal basis" cited above. In a democratic context such as that of Athens, the original [32] and most developed of Greek democracies, the latter accurately reflected the combination of partial egalitarianism in theory with hierarchy and subordination in practice that characterized all ancient systems of direct self-rule of and for the demos. Indeed, the rhetorical negotiation of such phrases may well have been the strategic response of Greek ideological democrats at Athens or elsewhere to one of the strongest charges pressed against ancient democracy on principle by its diehard opponents, that it perpetrated the manifest absurdity and injustice of treating palpable unequals ostensibly equally.[33]

Athenian Democratic Equality

At any rate, in democratic Athens from about 460 B.C. onward, all Athenians were considered *qua* citizens to be officially equal on principle. That strong principle was grounded in the claim that the essence of democracy was freedom, so that all Athenian citizens were *ex hypothesi* free—by birth and by autonomous situation, being masters both of themselves and of each other's collective destiny. On the grounds that they were all equally free in this civic sense, in Shelley's oxymoronic phrase "kings over themselves," they were all equal.[34] That in turn gave rise to the democratic view that the lottery was the most appropriate way of apportioning among citizens the equality of *timē,* meaning both abstract "esteem" and concrete "office," to which they were theoretically entitled. Sortition of course had purely practical implications and consequences (such as the attempted prevention of bribery in the jury-courts), but its intrinsic ideological connotation of equality was of no less importance to the Athenians' collective sense of political self-definition and civic identity.[35]

In practice, however, Athenian citizens neither were, nor were considered for all purposes to be, exactly equal, identical, and the same, in all relevant respects. They were not so, most conspicuously, with respect to their executive capability, especially since active political capacity was deemed to depend crucially on wealth. Hence the Athenians' pragmatic resort to election rather than sortition for the great military and financial offices of government. For the tenure of these, the privileged elite few, the seriously rich—who were likely also to be exceptionally well educated and expertly knowledgeable—were adjudged differentially well qualified. The other side of this elitist pragmatism, perhaps, is the negative ideological discrimination against Athenians of the lowest socioeconomic status, the thetes.[36] In short, in democratic Athens the rules were as follows: *isotēs* in basic but not indefeasible principle was to be tempered by *ho-*

moiotēs for practical purposes. Citizens who were all "same-ish" (*homoioi*) were not necessarily "the same" (*homoi*) and should not therefore automatically be treated as "equals" (*isoi*) but rather "on a basis of equality and similitude."

Spartan An(ti)egalitarianism

Despite the impression that is all too easy to receive, Athens is not the equivalent of classical Greece; rather, it was one of over one thousand separate, often radically self-differentiated political communities. In Aristotle's day the regimes of most could be classified fairly straightforwardly as variants of either democracy or oligarchy, but both in antiquity and today when it comes to the classification of classical Sparta, Athens's "other" in many respects, confusion reigns.[37] The reason for bringing Sparta centrally into the present discussion is that the Spartans apparently identified themselves as citizens under the title of *Homoioi.*[38]

In light of what has been said above, it should now be clear why it is vital to avoid the standard English translation "Equals." Notwithstanding their universal and communally enforced educational system, Spartans did not graduate into civic adulthood as assembly-line *Homoioi* counting politically as *Isoi.* Rather, unless they were revolutionaries, they did not seek *isotēs* in any sense other than the ideal enjoyment of an equal lifestyle (*iso-diaitoi*: Thuc. 1.6.5).[39] Comparison and contrast of Athenian and Spartan methods of registering and counting legislative, electoral, and policy-making votes will make the same point substantively.

Democratic Athens, to borrow Euripides' strictly anachronistic phrase (*Supp.* 353), was an *isopsēphos polis.* In actual practice, raising the hand (*kheirotonia*) was more common than secret ballot (*psēphos* means "pebble"), and in the Athenian Assembly, to save time, votes were usually estimated rather than individually counted (as they always were in the Council and People's Court). But the principle was egalitarian in all cases: one citizen–one vote, with everyone counting for one and no one for more than one. The Spartan method of open voting by shouting (Thuc. 1.87) implicitly denied that principle and was thus the polar antithesis of Athenian sortition—a method that the Spartans, consistently, abjured altogether.[40] A supposedly Spartan *bon mot* nicely reflects this essential difference between the two cities: "In answer to the man who insisted that he establish a democracy in the polis, Lycurgus replied, 'Do you first create a democracy in your own household'" (Plut. *Mor.* 228cd [21]).[41] Greek male citizen democrats, in other words, inconsistently drew the line at equality in their own homes, which they ruled undemocratically, whereas the Spartans consistently preached and practiced inequality both at home and in public civic space.[42]

Spartan political actuality confirms the judgment of "Lycurgus." Toward outsiders, all Spartan citizens turned a uniformly homogeneous and resolutely exclusive face.[43] In terms of their internal civic capacity, however, Spartan citizens were self-differentiated along four axes of hierarchical discrimination: not only by birth and wealth, but also by age and attainment (*andragathia:* Hdt. 5.42.1). It might perhaps be said that the same kinds of discrimination existed in Athens too, but there they were far less "exciting,"[44] far less pronounced and of far less moment. What made the difference was, in a word, the Helots. Because of this servile yet native Greek, more numerous and politically motivated underclass, Sparta was an essentially military society, and multiple hierarchizing then as now suited the military way. There was no place for genuine equality in the ordered *kosmos* that Sparta was ideally represented to be (Hdt. 1.65.4). Spartans in a real sense could not afford to practice egalitarianism, except of the pseudo-egalitarian "geometric" variety favored by Athenian oligarchs. In Athens too the citizen was by definition a warrior, but he was not, like the Spartan, a full-time professional warrior constantly in training for war against the enemy within, and he was so to speak a citizen first, and warrior second: there was more space between his military and his other civic functions than was the case either institutionally or ideologically or psychologically at Sparta.[45]

III. CONCLUSION

I end, in accordance with the spirit of a collection that is concerned centrally with the dialectic between ancient and modern constructions of democracy, with two very different modern writers. First, there is Charles Beitz's identification of political egalitarianism, which he envisages underlying the modern concept of democracy, as the ideal that each of us should have an "equal say" in the determination of policy and choice of our political leaders. What is this if not a modern translation of ancient Greek, and especially ancient Athenian, *isēgoria,* reminding us that the "noble and substantial political ideal"[46] of egalitarianism is a living legacy specifically of classical Athens?

Then, finally, there is Primo Levi, perhaps the most compelling literary witness to the Shoah, or Holocaust, who included the following observation in a reply to questions from readers of his *If This Is a Man* and *The Truce:* "In every part of the world, wherever you begin by denying the fundamental liberties of mankind, and equality among people, you move toward the concentration camp system, and it is a road on which it is difficult to halt."[47] For all the undeniable institutional and ideological differences between ancient Greece and the modern worlds, these two quotations do in their disparate ways sufficiently indicate the desirability, and I would add the possibility, of making a conscious and pragmatic connection between them.[48]

ACKNOWLEDGMENTS

It was a particular honor for me to participate in a panel on Equality in the modern country that has the most wholeheartedly embraced "the democratic gospel of equality" (Aron, *Progress,* 87–88)—notwithstanding the rival claims of

France (Ozouf, "Equality"). My sincere thanks to our organizers and sponsors, above all Charlie Hedrick, Josh Ober, and Cathy Vanderpool, and the Classics Department of Georgetown University, the American School of Classical Studies at Athens, and the National Endowment for the Humanities.

NOTES

1. *Political Thought in Ancient Greece: Elite and Mass from Homer to Plutarch,* forthcoming in Cambridge University Press's "Key Themes in Ancient History" series.

2. Carrithers, *Why Humans Have Cultures,* 18.

3. Miller, "The Resurgence of Political Theory," 424–27.

4. See, in different contexts, Cartledge, "Rebels and *Sambos* in Classical Greece"; Golden, "The Uses of Cross-Cultural Comparison."

5. Miller, "The Resurgence of Political Theory," 427.

6. Hanson, R. L., "Democracy," 69 ("the constitution and reconstitution of meaning in politics").

7. Schofield, "Ideology and Philosophy."

8. Gouldner, *Enter Plato.*

9. Skinner, "A Reply to My Critics," 283. Three types of "use": Skinner, "Language and Political Change," 6–23, at 9–11.

10. Sen, "Equality of What?"

11. A "liberal egalitarian society" in one standard formulation (Gutmann, *Liberal Equality* 287n.35) is one "in which governmental authority is derived from and consistent with the autonomy of every individual." Modern construals of "State": Skinner, "The State," 90–131. Liberal democratic freedom and equality defined in relation to the State: Bobbio, *Democracy and Dictatorship.* (It may be of interest to report that in the past fifteen or so years more than two hundred books have been published on the subject of equality in English alone, any serious selection of which would include at least Baker, *Arguing for Equality;* Beitz, *Political Equality;* Green, *Retrieving Democracy;* Nagel, *Equality and Partiality;* Norman, *Free and Equal;* Phelps Brown, *Egalitarianism;* Roemer, *Egalitarian Perspectives;* Sen, *Inequality Re-Examined;* Temkin, *Inequality;* and Westen, *Speaking of Equality.*)

12. Ancient Greek claims to (e.g.) freedom and democracy at most implied or connoted "rights," but freedom and equality in any of the modern senses discussed by Dagger, "Rights," were not construed by the Greeks as rights in themselves. To illustrate the gulf fixed between modern liberal and ancient democratic individualism, one may observe that Hansen, *Athenian Democracy* (72), translates *ta tōn dēmokratoumenōn sōmata* (Aeschin. 1.4) as "the individual"; and cf. the essays by Hansen and Ostwald, this volume. Gawantka, *Die Sogenannte Polis* (cf. Lotze, "Die Sogenannte Polis") is clearly eccentric in its contention that the polis is a nineteenth-century fabrication, but noneccentrics do not yet perhaps appreciate sufficiently that with the partial exception of Sparta ancient Greek poleis were technically "State-less political communities." (I would like to acknowledge here especially the help I have received on this basic point from Dr. Moshe Berent of the Open University of Israel.)

13. *Galatians* 3.28 and the similar *Colossians* 3.11, it should be otiose to point out, have no bearing on this-world equality: Ste. Croix, *Class Struggle,* 107–8, 419.

14. For the incommensurable power of the immortal gods, see recently Bruit-Zaidman and Schmitt-Pantel, *Religion in the Ancient Greek City;* Williams, *Shame and Necessity.*

15. *Concise Oxford Dictionary,* 8th ed., s.v. "Feminism". Feminist construals of democracy: Mendus, "Losing the Faith"; Okin, *Women in Western Political Thought; Justice, Gender and the Family;* "Gender, the Public and the Private"; Pateman, "Feminism and Democracy"; *The Sexual Contract;* and Susan Cole in this volume. Modern types or instantiations of equality: Lukes, "Equality and Liberty," 58, with whom Lee (*The Cost of Free Speech,* 105) agrees that liberty and equality can in some respects be mutually reinforcing, not just rivals.

16. This polarized hierarchy, and especially its manipulation by classical Greek historians, are the informing themes of Cartledge, *The Greeks;* and see Carol Dougherty's paper in this volume.

17. Birth in the early polis: Ian Morris in this volume. Wealth in the developed polis: Fuks, *Social Conflict in Ancient Greece;* and Ellen Wood in this volume. Ste. Croix, *Class Struggle,* extends its purview beyond the exclusively civic.

18. Sen and Nussbaum, *The Quality of Life.*

19. As Kurt Raaflaub has observed in this volume, strict economic equality "was not a serious issue and belonged in the sphere of comic surrealism and abstract theoretical schemes." Borecký, "The Primitive Origin," is a historiographical curiosity.

20. Hansen, *Athenian Democracy,* 83–84.

21. Aron, *Progress and Disillusion,* 304; cf. Temkin, *Inequality.*

22. The standard discussion is Vlastos, "*Isonomia politike*"; cf. Borecký, "Die politische Isonomie"; one possible translation—or explication—of the phrase is "constitutional government with the equal sharing of power by all people" (Graham and Forsythe, "A New Slogan for Oligarchy"). Modern slant on justice and equality, from an ancient philosopher: Vlastos, "Justice and Equality."

23. Vapidity: Berlin, "Equality," 81. "Imagined communities": Anderson, *Imagined Communities.*

24. The choice of *isonomia* by "Otanes" (Hdt. 3.80.6) to describe an unambiguously democratic form of governance was discursively overdetermined by the imperative necessity of *not* using *dēmokratia,* a term that may actually have been coined by its opponents; cf. Meier, *The Greek Discovery of Politics,* 161ff. By its very etymology (*dēmos* in the sense of the poor masses, *kratos* in the sense of a forcible grip on the disempowered wealthy few) *dēmokratia* could be construed negatively to mean something approaching "dictatorship of the proletariat."

25. Harvey, "Two Kinds of Equality."

26. Hansen, *Athenian Democracy,* 82–83. Dahl, *Democracy.* See also Ian Morris's essay, this volume.

27. *Isokratia:* Hdt. 5.92a.1, with Ostwald, "Isokratia as a Political Concept." *isēgoria* (esp. Hdt. 5.78; Ps. Xen. *Ath. Pol.* 1.2, 6, 12: Eur. *Supp.* 438–441): Hansen, *Athenian Democracy,* esp. 83–84.

28. *Isotimia* (the reading at Xen. *Hiero.* 8.10 is uncertain): I am indebted to Nathaniel Ober for reminding me of the phrase "parity of esteem"; *isomoiria:* above, n. 19.

29. Bedau, *Justice and Equality,* 12; cf. Berlin, "Equality," 90, 92, 93.

30. *LSJ,* ninth ed., s.v. "*isos*" II.2, helpfully collects references, though it is important to distinguish uses of the phrase within a polis from its uses in relations between poleis:

e.g., Thuc. 5.79.1 (treaty between Athens and Argos; cf. Ostwald, "Isokratia as a Polit-ical Concept," 52n.20) may not bear the same connotations as Dem. 21.112.

31. Aristotle's method: Owen, "*tithenai ta phainomena*"; Barnes, "Aristotle and the Methods of Ethics." Aristotle on citizen equality: Von Leyden, *Aristotle on Equality and Justice.*

32. A textually corrupt clause of the not certainly authentic or authentically early Spartan document known as the "Great Rhetra" (Plut. *Lyc.* 6) may contain the words *damos* and *kratos* but, even if that is so, they should not be taken straightforwardly as denoting or even connoting anything like what the Athenians understood by *dēmokra-tia:* see Cartledge, "The Peculiar Position of Sparta."

33. The old canard that ancient democrats never formulated a theory of democracy should have been laid to rest by Ober, *Mass and Elite* (cf. already Myres, *The Political Ideas of the Greeks*)—even if "theory" is understood as abstract, ivory-tower philoso-phizing by politically disengaged intellectuals. Most but not all of the latter were anti-democratic: Roberts, *Athens on Trial.*

34. It is unlikely that at any rate the full-blown democratic ideology of freedom an-tedated by much if at all the Ephialtic reforms of 462–61.

35. The peculiarly democratic association of sortition is sufficiently demonstrated by Hdt. 3.80.6, Arist. *Pol.* 6.1294b8, and esp. Arist. *Rh.* 1.1365b32; cf. Whibley, *Greek Oli-garchies,* 35, 145; and esp. Headlam, *Election by Lot at Athens.*

36. See the essays of Raaflaub and Strauss, this volume.

37. Multiplicity of Greek political units: Gehrke, *Jenseits von Athen und Sparta.* Sparta: Cartledge, "The Peculiar Position of Sparta," and *Agesilaos,* 99–159.

38. Xen. *Hell.* 3.3.5; cf. Hdt. 4.3.4, 7.234.2. "Spartiatai," denoting full citizens of the polis officially called Lakedaimōn, was perhaps the formal counterpart of "Homoioi."

39. One failed revolutionary, Kinadon, allegedly wished "to be inferior to no one in Sparta" (Xen. *Hell.* 3.3.11). This presumably implies that he did wish to be superior to most, inasmuch as the Homoioi (to whose number Kinadon had apparently once be-longed) indeed were superior to Lacedaemon's other classes. Xenophon's rough equiv-alent of the Spartan "Homoioi" in the pseudo-Persian context of his fictional *Cyropae-dia* was "Homotimoi"—"the Same in Honour / Esteem / Privilege / Respect."

40. Spartan shouting: Ste. Croix, *Origins,* 348–49. Spartan absence of sortition: Rhodes, "The Selection of Ephors at Sparta." Origin (Athenian?) and significance of the counting (as opposed to other methods of measurement) of votes: Larsen, "The Origin and Significance of the Counting of Votes."

41. Compare the demand of the English Royalists in the seventeenth century that, if the House of Commons claimed powers from the people, it would then have to show that *all* the people, every woman and child as well as every adult male, had participated in granting them: Morgan, *Inventing the People,* 289.

42. I cannot, therefore, agree with Raaflaub, this volume, that Sparta's "political sys-tem was based on strong elements of institutionalized civic equality."

43. Unlike all other Greeks known to the widely traveled Herodotus (9.11.2, perhaps also 9.55.2), the Spartans alone refused to distinguish between Greek *xenoi* and non-Greek *barbaroi,* lumping Greeks and non-Greeks together as equally outlandish *xenoi* and practicing what they preached in the form of *xenēlasiai,* periodic "expulsions of *xenoi.*"

44. Plamenatz, "Diversity of Rights," 82.

45. Not all that much more space, perhaps: compare and contrast the related papers in this volume by Victor Hanson and Barry Strauss. However, I would draw attention once more to the apparent negative discrimination against thetes (above, and n. 36), and I would venture to suggest that, with respect at least to its distinction between Spartan militarism and Athenian politics (Thuc. 2.39–40), the Periklean Funeral Speech in Thucydides may be taken as an accurate representation of Athenian democratic ideology as well as practice.

46. Williams, "The Idea of Equality," 137. "Equal say": Beitz, *Political Equality.*

47. Levi, *If This Is a Man* and *The Truce,* 390–91. The original version of this paper was presented in Washington on Yom Hashoah (Holocaust Remembrance Day).

48. Terray, *La Politique dans la Caverne,* 13, concludes his Preface with a series of interrogatives, including "L'égalité est-elle une condition nécessaire de ces libertés?" To which he adds, "Sur tous ces points, soyons attentifs à la réflexion grecque: on le voit, les questions qu'elle pose sont aussi les nôtres." D'accord! As witness, e.g., Wood, *Democracy against Capitalism.*

ATHENIAN EQUALITY: A CONSTANT SURROUNDED BY FLUX

Jennifer Tolbert Roberts

IN THE CONTEXT of discussing what was then the Soviet Union in his study of Greek aristocracy, M.T.W. Arnheim observed astutely that "the more fundamental the disagreement on principle, the greater the agreement on the factual situation, and vice versa."[1] Perceptions of political equality in classical Athens in many ways exemplify this thought pattern. Equality throughout history has been a highly charged concept—perhaps never more so than in my own country at the present time. Co-opted by all sides in the so-called "culture wars" that rage in the United States, it plainly does not mean the same thing to Dinesh D'Souza as it does to Stanley Fish; it does not mean the same thing to the National Organization for Women as to the National Association of Scholars. Because of the passions engaged in the debate over the meaning and implementation of equality, it should occasion no surprise that writing about the nature and extent of equality in classical Athens should have been shaped throughout the last centuries by judgments and emotions of many different kinds. Paul Cartledge (this volume) does well to cite Quentin Skinner's observation that "there can be no histories of concepts as such" but only "histories of their uses in argument."[2] It is this history that I would like to examine today as it regards equality and the Athenian state.

Much of the dialogue among the ancient Greeks themselves about justice and the best state was predicated on competing views of equality—loosely speaking, the arithmetic and the geometric. Proponents of arithmetic equality wished political power to be shared equally among all male citizens; champions of geometric equality wanted an equal ratio between political power and the capacity for good decision-making. There existed in ancient Greece a constant tension between egalitarian and hierarchic thought patterns—the distinction that would one day be recast, as Sheldon Wolin points out, in Nietzsche's contrast between "slave morality" and "aristocratic morality."[3] For some, the most salient aspect of human nature was the common bond that tied people together; for others, the differences that set individuals apart. Some sophists went so far as to posit a continuum that linked people to animals and even to plants; at the other extreme Theognis was convinced that only a few families could produce people with *gnomē,* a special inborn capacity for good judgment. The primacy of differences among individuals underlay the work of Greece's most famous political philosophers, Plato and Aristotle. Aristotle in the *Nicomachaean Ethics* inveighed against friendship between *epieikeis* and *phauloi*—respectable folk and riffraff, gentlemen and slobs—and in his celebrated *Republic* Plato created an ideal state in which all participants knew their place and performed specialized tasks suited to their discrepant natures. The notion of specialization according to natural talent and disposition has reemerged in the past 150 years in arguments about men's and women's divergent temperaments and "separate spheres," a debate to which I return shortly. Strangely, however, it was also Plato who enthroned on the stage of history the compelling figure of Protagoras, whose curious tale about the origins of civil society has all the earmarks of the founding myth of Athenian democracy. There was a time, Protagoras recounts, when their lack of *politikē technē* prevented human beings from forging a successful civic life together. Zeus, consequently, resolved to prevent the destruction of the species by asking Hermes to bring justice and propriety to mortals. These, Zeus suggested, should be distributed not to a select few (like the specialized arts, such as medicine) but to everyone, "for cities cannot be formed if only a few share in these skills as they do in other arts" (*Protagoras* 322d). Because of this general distribution of *politikē technē,* Protagoras tells Socrates, the Athenians, "when they come together to take counsel on matters in which *politikē technē* is relevant . . . take advice from everybody, since it is held that everyone should partake of this excellence, or else states cannot exist" (322e–323).

What is striking about this story is not simply Protagoras' endorsement of democratic deliberation but also his refusal to suggest that all people possess equal capacity for political judgment. And in fact the Athenian system was premised not on a belief in the equality of individuals, but rather on the belief in equality before the law for nonslave, citizen males. Athenian democrats believed not that people were inherently equal but that, as inequalities were hard to measure, the law should treat all citizen males evenhandedly. This allowed merit— *axiōsis*—to shape the formation of a natural aristocracy, one that would be fluid and subject to constant revision. Leaders and followers there would be; but within the class of citizen males, roles would be allotted on the basis of interest and talent rather than of wealth or birth. Facile distinctions between active and passive citizens so dear to the heart of Aristotle and later of Kant were rejected by a system that stressed participation more than equality.

As Kurt Raaflaub and others have amply demonstrated, however, equality played an important part in Athenian rhetoric both democratic and antidemocratic.[4] Equality, as has been pointed out by modern political scientists, is today a "virtue word." This was equally true in Greece, where states as different as Athens and Sparta competed to be awarded the palm for equality, and thinkers as divergent as Euripides and Isocrates could put themselves forward as champions of an equality purer than that of their ideological opponents.[5] Democrats, uncertain of easy criteria that might divide better citizens from worse, advocated an arithmetic equality whereby each individual was allowed equal input into political decisions; antidemocrats, more confident about knowing who was who, preferred geometric equality, which maintained an equal proportion between merit and clout.

But the government forged by the Athenian democrats in their quest for arithmetic equality presents a powerful paradox to the modern mind. On the one hand, the Athenians created an eloquent and compelling rhetoric of equality. They also forged a state in which decision-making power was shared by (proportionally speaking) a very large group. That group was astonishingly large when compared with other ancient states. It was also large in practice, if not in theory, when compared with many modern states. Yet participants in policy-making accounted for only a fraction of Attica's inhabitants; the law denied a say in government to most residents. Slavery was endemic to ancient civilization, and abundant evidence suggests that many Athenian men held an exceptionally low opinion of women's capacity for judgment. As in all modern states, moreover, the bulk of political power in Athens was concentrated in the hands of those who were not poor. This was particularly true before the mid-fifth-century reforms of Ephialtes. But it persisted to a degree even afterward, because of the limitations of geography, leisure, and the low status of thetes noted by Kurt Raaflaub.[6] Economic inequality inevitably undermines high-sounding professions of equality in the political realm.

During the centuries since Cleisthenes' death, perceptions of Athenian democracy have varied dramatically. Renaissance thinkers such as Machiavelli and Guicciardini took a dim view of Athens, comparing it unfavorably with solid, stolid Sparta. Their unshakable belief in the instability of Athenian democracy had a profound effect on America's Founding Fathers, who rejected it decisively as a model for their own fledgling nation. On the whole, thinkers of the eighteenth century found Athens effeminate and decadent. Yet during the nineteenth century, Victorian liberals like Macaulay and Grote described the government and society of the Athenians in glowing terms. Meanwhile, the slaveholders of the American South put Athens forward as an admirable lesson in what slavery could accomplish. Americans of the 1940s, 1950s and 1960s—the age of World War II and the Cold War—eagerly identified with Athenian democrats against Spartan militarists and Macedonian monarchists, in whom they saw clear harbingers of Nazi Germany and the Soviet Union, whereas Americans of the later twentieth century are equally disposed to bemoan the status of Athenian women and the common ancient practice of slavery. For all these vicissitudes in the valuation and perception of the Athenian democracy, however, most commentators have viewed the Athenian system as egalitarian, and they have shared a strikingly "uniformitarian" conception of the demos.

Ancient writers, as Kurt Raaflaub convincingly demonstrates, agreed on the egalitarian nature of the Athenian democracy; there is no need to rehearse the documentation again here.[7] Both Plato and Aristotle were given to lamenting the leveling arithmetic equality that gave the good an equal voice with the bad—it is important to remember that the Greek word *kakos* meant both "poor" and "bad"—and the man known as Pseudo Xenophon, author of a short treatise on the Athenian constitution, suggested that the equality extended even to the slave population, complaining (1. 10) that it was impossible to distinguish slaves from free people walking down the street. In a flight of fancy, Plato caricatured the democratic state as one in which even horses and donkeys insisted on equal rights to space, refusing to yield the right of way to human beings (*Republic* 563c). Though slaves and animals are rarely included in the embrace of egalitarianism, modern thinkers also share a surprising consensus about equality within the citizen body. Issues of equality first became prominent in thinking about Greece during the age of revolution, when French cries of "égalité" directed attention to the egalitarian nature of society in both Athens and Sparta.[8] Britons (who Matthew Arnold would later insist practiced a "religion of inequality") were on the whole appalled by events in France and America, and William Young's *History of Athens* included a fierce indictment of the "leveling" that began with Aristides' extension of the franchise and culminated in the demagogy of Ephialtes and Pericles.[9]

Meanwhile the French backlash found a voice in Montlosier, who also lamented the leveling tendency at Athens, where no house or individual was permitted to become more glorious than any other, and decried the exile, proscription, and death with which Athenian politicians were so often rewarded for their public service.[10] Americans, on the other hand, were almost uniform in their determination to distance their experiment from democratic Athens. Insisting that "property is surely a right of mankind as really as liberty," John Adams recoiled from the egalitarian basis of Athenian democracy and agreed with other founders like Madison and Hamilton that the new American nation required protection from the encroachment of the masses. He was convinced that the Athenian masses had regularly affirmed equality by confiscating the property of the rich.[11]

Fostered by admiration for Aristotle, the founders' conviction that Athenian citizens had enjoyed equality was shared by many political thinkers in the centuries that followed. The equality that slavery promoted in the citizen class became a common topos in proslavery rhetoric throughout the antebellum era. Some adduced Sparta as a prime example of the phenomenon—Thomas Cobb of Georgia, for example, in his 1858 *Historical Sketch of Slavery from the Earliest Periods*. "True philosophy," Cobb maintained, confirmed the argument that slavery "is an element essential in a true republic, for the preservation of perfect equality among citizens."[12] Convinced that all wise men must think alike, he ascribed this view to Plato and Aristotle. Thomas Dew, president of William and Mary College, appealed to the classical example in identifying slavery as the source of liberty, equality, and cultural achievement and maintained that relegating menial offices to slaves removed the major causes of "distinction and separation of the ranks of society."[13] Dew's fellow Virginian George Fitzhugh, who had a particular fascination with Athens, recurred frequently to the classical example, arguing in his provocatively titled *Cannibals All! or Slaves Without Masters* that slavery would prevent poor whites from winding up "at the bottom of society as at the North." Rather, they would enjoy the lives of "privileged citizens, like Greek and Roman citizens, with a numerous class far beneath them." Southern society, he contended, would mimic antiquity in ensuring that wealthy citizens did not lord it over poor ones, "for all are equal in privilege, if not in wealth."[14]

It is significant that many of those who advocated slavery as the guarantor of equality within the citizen class were also exercised about feminist agitation in the abolitionist camp. This concern was not entirely lacking in the north; an editorial in the *New York Herald* of 1852 contended that woman had become subject to man "by her nature, her sex, just as the negro is and always will be, to the end of time, inferior to the white race, and, therefore, doomed to subjection."[15] But it was to become a fundamental article of faith among many Southern pro-slavery men. Fitzhugh, who had announced in *Sociology for the South* that "marriage is too much like slavery not to be involved in its fate," caricatured the platform of the reformers as one of "Free Women . . . and Free Negroes."[16] William Gilmore Simms associated abolitionism with feminism both in his misogynistic review of *Uncle Tom's Cabin* and in his attack on the abolitionist essay of Harriet Martineau, and Chancellor Harper of South Carolina contended that the superior chastity of Southern women could be accounted for by slavery, which somehow siphoned off promiscuity to members of another race.[17] Some day, Harper mused, England itself might be "overrun by some Northern horde—sunk into an ignoble and anarchical democracy, or subdued to the dominion of some Caesar—demagogue and despot." Civilization would then persist, he maintained, in the American South, where "there may be found many republics, triumphing in Grecian arts and civilization, and worthy of British descent and Roman institutions."[18] On close inspection his peculiar association of democracy and despotism reflects a marriage of the Aristotelian linking of tyranny and mob rule with championship of the Athenian democracy Aristotle so disliked. A footnote explains his meaning: "I do not use the word democracy in the Athenian sense, but to describe the government in which the slave and his master have an equal voice in public affairs." The ironic assumption put forward for rhetorical effect that in a modern democracy there would still be slaves underlines his endorsement of the Athenian system, where equality obtained only within the citizen class.

For U.S. proslavery activists, the connection between citizen equality among the Athenians and the subjection of women at Athens marked out the school of Hellas as an enviable society, a model for modern times. At the same time, however, a somewhat different position was evolving in Europe, as the movement for reform in Britain combined with the rise of Hellenic aesthetic ideals in Germany—and, in time, the Greek independence movement—to shape new ways of looking at classical Athens. Eager to set up ancient Athens as a model for modern Britain, British liberals like Macaulay and Grote put Athens forward as a cohesive society where a high level of education existed within the citizen body, facilitating responsible political decisions on the part of large numbers. Macaulay rhapsodized freely about the high tone of intellectual life in Athens. "Let us for a moment," he suggests,

> imagine that we are entering its gates in the time of its power and glory. A crowd is assembled round a portico. All are gazing with delight at the entablature; for Phidias is putting up the frieze. We turn into another street; a rhapsodist is reciting there: men, women, children, are thronging round him: the tears are running down their cheeks; their eyes are fixed; their very breath is still; for he is telling how Priam fell at the feet of Achilles and kissed those hands—the terrible, the murderous—which had slain so many of his sons. We enter the public place; there . . . Socrates is pitted against the famous atheist from Ionia. . . . But we are interrupted. The herald is crying. . . . The general assembly is to meet. . . . Pericles is mounting the stand. . . . Then for a play of Sophocles; and away to sup with Aspasia. I know of no modern university which has so excellent a system of education.[19]

Other Victorian thinkers were guided by the same principles that underlay this remarkable vignette. Many of the same assumptions undergirded the multivolume Greek history undertaken shortly afterward by the London banker George Grote. Disturbed by the particularism that seemed to be dividing the England of his day and determined that greater unity and cohesion could be attained by following an appropriate ancient model, Grote informed his Greek history with an Athens devoted to "equal law" and the "sentiment of the entire commonwealth as one indivisible" [sic]. Through the reforms of Cleisthenes, he contended, "the Athenian people, politically considered . . . became one homogeneous whole."[20]

The English liberals disagreed among themselves in many particulars. Grote, though he sympathized with the Southern states in the American civil war, was largely indifferent to both slavery and the status of women at Athens. The anonymous author of an essay on the national character of the Athenians published at Edinburgh in 1828, on the other hand, was convinced that the egalitarianism of the Athenians must have extended to both sexes, contrasting the Athenians' treatment of women with the chivalrous ambivalence that would follow in modern Europe. The Greek spirit, he maintained, "raised woman to an equal with man in mind and in fortitude, at the same time that it preserved to her the admiration due to the attributes of her sex. She was at once the companion of the philosopher, the counsellor of the statesman, the mistress of her lover, and the model of the artist—the Aspasia of Pericles, and the Phryne of Apelles."[21] A third position was taken by John Stuart Mill, who viewed slavery and the exclusion of women as a blot on Greek civilization.[22] In 1874, however, a genuinely sophisticated and analytical view was put forward by the Irish classicist John Pentland Mahaffy, who in 1874 offered the first known thoughtful formulation of the connection many have since perceived between the growth of democracy at Athens and a decline in the status of Athenian women. When the aristocratic tone of life gave way before democracy, he argued,

> the result of this equality upon the position of woman is obvious. . . . A common man, with an actual vote, would become of more importance than an Alcmaeonid lady, who might possibly of old have swayed her ruling husband; and so with the development of political interests, gradually absorbing all the life of every Athenian, there came, in that deeply selfish society, a gradual lowering in the scale of all such elements as possessed no political power. Old age and weaker sex were pushed aside to make way for the politician—the man of action—the man who carried arms, and exercised civic rights.[23]

The same connection between citizen equality and the denigration of women would be articulated fully a century later by Sarah Pomeroy, who in 1975 suggested in her groundbreaking history of women in Greece and Rome that "after the class stratification that separated individual men according to such criteria as noble descent and wealth was eliminated, the ensuing ideal of equality among male citizens was intolerable. The will to dominate was such that they then had to separate themselves as a group and claim to be superior to all nonmembers: foreigners, slaves, and women."[24] Similarly David Halperin has grounded Athenian laws against sexual violation in the egalitarian nature of the Athenian ethos, contending that "one of the first tasks of the radical democrats at Athens, who brought into being a form of government based (in theory at least) on universal male suffrage, was to enable every citizen to participate *on equal terms* in the corporate body of the community. . . . The transition to a radical democracy therefore required a series of measures designed to uphold the dignity and autonomy—the social viability in short—of every (male) citizen, whatever his economic circumstances." Along parallel lines, he argues that to assault a male citizen in nonsexual ways "was not only to insult him personally but to assault the corporate integrity of the citizen body as a whole and to offend its fiercely egalitarian spirit."[25]

Halperin's willingness to suggest that the equality of Athenian citizens may have been more theoretical than actual is something of a departure from the tendency to view the Athenian demos as monolithic. This view of the unity and indeed uniformity of the male citizens who made up the demos gained prominence with the growth of what Ellen Wood has aptly termed "The Myth of the Idle Mob"—a set of beliefs that grew up in the eighteenth century, gathered strength in the nineteenth, and has survived well into the twentieth.[26] In this popular construct, indigent Athenians disappear from sight and the world is viewed as a binary one populated only by slaves on the one hand and idle citizens on the other—men of leisure who spent the bulk of their hours in discussion and debate, with occasional time out for attending theatrical performances or admiring the temples on the Acropolis. (In this construct women often disappear altogether.) Some viewed the relegation of real work to slaves as the hallmark of Athenian greatness and idealism; others recoiled from the slave basis of all ancient society; and still others were troubled by ambivalence, nostalgic for the leisure of the Athenian citizen but disquieted by the moral problems posed by slavery. But throughout the nineteenth century, there was astonishing consensus that hard work and citizenship were mutually exclusive in Attica. It was this world that had captured the imagination of American slaveholders, and it was this world too that presented itself to Hegel.

Solon, Hegel insisted, "gave the Athenians a constitution, by which all obtained equal rights." Unfortunately, he argued, the demos's conviction that it could know what was right came to have a leveling effect, as "confidence in Great Men is antagonistic" to a "state of things—in which every one presumes to have a judgment of his own, and as soon as any of these great men had performed what was needed, envy intruded—i.e., the recoil of the sentiment of equality against conspicuous talent—and he was either imprisoned or exiled. Finally, the Sycophants arose . . . , aspersing all individual greatness, and reviling those who took the lead in public affairs." Slavery, Hegel maintained, provided citizens the leisure indispensable for participation in the business of the state, business that demanded "that the citizens should be freed from handicraft occupations," with the result that "what among us is performed by free citizens—the work of daily life—should be done by slaves." In Athens, Hegel contended, there existed "a vital freedom . . . and a vital equality of manners and mental culture; and if inequality of property could not be avoided, it nevertheless did not reach an extreme." Finally, he believed, shared values and easy consensus were indispensable: "The living together in one city, the fact that the inhabitants see each other daily, renders a common culture and a *living* democratic polity possible" in a way unthinkable in a large nation-state—in revolutionary France, for example, where tyranny "raised its voice under the mask of Freedom and Equality."[27]

While Hegel stressed the importance of the smallness that made possible the uniformity of manners and values indispensable to a democratic state, his contemporaries were lamenting the leveling tendencies of democracies in a very large state. Complaining in his travel journal of the sameness of American culture, de Tocqueville wrote that "the plane of uniform civilization has passed over it. The man you left in New York you find again in almost impenetrable solitudes: same clothes, same attitude, same language, same habits, same pleasures."[28] In this America, de Tocqueville argued, women enjoyed a freedom dramatically different from that of their European contemporaries. Hegel would no doubt have been rather taken aback to have his work compared with that of an American woman, but his notion of the monolithic unity of the free male population of Athens is also evident in the work of Page duBois, who was very concerned about the kind of distinction Paul Cartledge has identified between *isotēs* and *homoiotēs.* In her *Centaurs and Amazons,* she stressed the need of Athenian males to define themselves in contradistinction to what they were not, envisioning "humanness, maleness, Greekness, in terms of opposition."[29] Amazon myths, she argued, offered a forum for "discourse on the differentiation of kinds. How are human beings different from animals? How are women different from men? How are Greeks different from barbarians?"

"All these questions," she maintained, were posed "in the context of the city" of Athens, "where men understood themselves to be bound together by sameness, by *isonomia,* by a common destiny and space, by endogamy." Citing Vernant, she identified the hearth of the *oikos* as "the center of a democratic circle in which *equals* were contained." Opposed to the bestial, irrational, chaotic, "other" represented by women, animals, and barbarians was the unified citizen body. "The fifth century citizen," she contended, "gazes at his *equals,* to understand the principles which unite him with other citizens. The barbarian, female, animal are significant primarily in their contribution to that definition."[30] In duBois's construct, distinctions among male citizens disappear.

Marxist historians have construed the equality of the demos in a variety of ways. Marx himself vacillated between stern condemnations of slaveholding as the basis of the ancient economy and dreamy nostalgia for the shared sense of freedom and community that marked the Greek state.[31] In general, Marxist historians have construed the Athenian system on a binary model, dividing inhabitants into workers and their owners (though of course there are notable exceptions such as Geoffrey de Ste. Croix, whose monumental *Class Struggle in the Ancient Greek World* takes very much the opposite view.) Thus, for example, the Soviet *History of Antiquity,* assembled in the 1950s under the direction of Diakov and Kovalev, bills the Athenian citizens as a minority living off the thankless toil of the enslaved masses and sees the Athenian state as a structure designed to protect the interests of the slave-owning class led by Pericles. On the whole, "slave-owner" is the authors' standard label for those whom Western historians have normally termed "citizens." As in the writings of many Western historians, the slaveless Athenian working class disappears conveniently from view.[32]

Marx's own more romantic ideas of the egalitarian principles underlying the classical Greek state (despite its slave-holding) have also emerged in subsequent thinking about Athens. Engels's tract on *The Origin of the Family, Private Property and the State* built on work by the American anthropologist Lewis H. Morgan. Much taken with the egalitarianism of the Iroquois, Morgan insisted that early Greek government was organized on similar principles. The Athenians' outstanding intellectual accomplishments, Morgan contended, were the product of an essentially democratic and egalitarian system of values that had informed Greek thinking even before the emergence of Athenian democracy. Though on the whole Morgan admired Grote, he contended that his own American perspective enabled him to see what Grote could not—that even the earliest and most primitive of Greek governments were "essentially democratical . . . organized as self-governing bodies, and on the principles of liberty, equality and fraternity."[33]

The Marxist Robert Padgug formulated a similar construct a century later. Padgug viewed classical Athens as a restored commune, reconstituted after an "aristocratic interlude" on the ruins of an earlier, purer commune. In the restored commune, however, slavery and imperialism were required to enable "all members of the commune to live on an at least minimally acceptable level" and to help compensate for the comparatively small amount of land available in Attica. Like Fitzhugh and his cohorts, then, Padgug stressed the egalitarianism slavery promoted within the nonslave class.[34]

Naturally, professional historians who specialize in the Athenian state continue to explore the inequalities that divided groups within the state. The truth is, however, that to a remarkable degree Greek philosophers, Renaissance theoreticians, eighteenth-century politicians, antebellum slaveholders, modern feminists and Marxists, and Georg Wilhelm Friedrich Hegel have managed to find common ground in the conviction that for good or for evil the Athenian demos operated as a bloc. The elements of egalitarianism in the Athenian political system charmed both those committed to the universal dignity of humankind and those who prefer egalitarianism only within a privileged circle. Hence the enormous popularity of Athens in mid-nineteenth-century America: in the South the Athenians were admired for the egalitarianism within the citizen class fostered by slavery; in the north Lincoln modeled the Gettysburg address on the Periclean model in which the disfranchised were kept largely out of view. Meanwhile, the eminent classicist Edward Everett offered on the same day a companion address of greater length and lesser fame. He framed his speech between two Athenian *topoi*, beginning with Marathon and ending with the Periclean oration.[35] Marxists have vacillated between praising the egalitarian underpinnings of the system and lamenting the division of inhabitants between citizens and slaves; Marx himself had little concern about the exclusion of women, but many of his followers have censured it sharply.[36] The Athenian system afforded its poorer citizens a greater degree of *isonomia* than other ancient states, and this has prompted considerable praise of Athens' egalitarianism. But the existence of slavery and subsequently the discounting of women has fostered a "uniformitarian" view of the Athenian demos, whereby important distinctions among citizen males disappear and a binary "establishment versus underdog" construct becomes the ruling principle. In works for the general reader, it is difficult to find hardheaded analyses of the status of thetes, like that offered by Kurt Raaflaub, or comments like those of Stringfellow Barr, whose 1961 study of Greek culture included not only women, slaves, and metics among those who could not participate in "the dream of equal freedom under law" but also " the poor man, the man who was not well-fathered."[37]

The Spartans' success in persuading antiquity of the egalitarian nature of their government is well known. The myth of Sparta took shape already in antiquity, as the relegation of labor to noncitizens facilitated powerful fictions about the egalitarianism and communality of the society. What could be more equal than a state in which all voters were known as the nine thousand *homoioi*, the equals?[38] As Paul Cartledge has pointed out, the myth did not fully correspond to historical reality, but this did not prevent it from reigning supreme during the Italian Renaissance and living on to achieve its most exquisite elaboration in the hands of Rousseau.[39] The Athenians, I suggest, have been the object of a similar construct: The egalitarian principles of democrats, bitterness about leveling on the part of antidemocrats, and the presence of disfranchised classes such as women and slaves in Athens have combined to foster a view of a cohesive and homogeneous body. This view has survived dramatic permutations in the way Athenian democracy has been analyzed and valued. It has lent a strange consistency to thinking about the Athenian state, a surprising constant in a sea of flux sailed in their diverse crafts by nervous eighteenth-century men of property, antebellum slaveholders, Victorian reformers, Marxist critics, and indignant feminists. Even as we approach the end of the millennium, the myth of the idle mob lives on. Henry Phelps Brown's *Egalitarianism and the Generation of Inequality* appeared in 1988. Brown contended that the Athenians observed "equality of rights and treatment" among citizens—a "restricted class," to be sure, for "only those men were citizens," he maintained, "who had certain qualifications. Beyond them—it was taken for granted—were all women, but also all farmers, labourers, mechanics, freedmen, slaves and aliens. Within the pale of citizenship, however, there was this basis of equality, that there was no clash of interests between employers and workers. The manual work was done by non-citizens; the citizen depended on no one other man for his livelihood. It was natural, therefore, for citizens to enjoy equality—before the law, in the discussion of public affairs and in access to public office."[40]

The tradition of the cohesiveness, homogeneity, and equality of the Athenian demos is a venerable one and may be long in dying, common as it is to Athens' admirers and detractors alike. But recent developments tying together social activism and intellectual analysis have raised serious questions about the utility of the equality model for the achievement of justice. Thus, for example, Mary Midgley has argued that using the concepts of equality and freedom to right the wrongs done to women in society "is like trying to dig a garden with a brush and comb. The tools are totally unsuitable."[41]

Feminist theory and politics have shed new light on the role of equality within Athenian society and on Greek political thought. This is not merely a recent development, for the doctrine of "separate spheres" promulgated in the nineteenth century served as the focus for considerable debate over the issue of female suffrage. The principle that equality before the law can only operate for those who are "similarly situated" helped to shape decisions of the Supreme Court until the 1970s.[42] The debate over whether men and women are "similarly situated" with regard to such phenomena as pregnancy, rape, and military service not only evokes the geometric/proportional equality arguments of Plato and Isocrates, with qualitative concerns replacing their largely quantitative ones, but in fact draws on them; thus, for example, Elizabeth Wolgast's 1980 *Equality and the Rights of Women*, written from a theoretical and not a historical standpoint, contains numerous references to the views of equality found in the Greek philosophers.[43] The question of the relation of "sameness" to equality touched on by Paul Cartledge has also been engaged by feminist thinkers moving away from the facile "equality feminism" of the 1970s to a more nuanced "difference feminism." These thinkers were shaken by the insufficiency of "equality feminism" to shape solutions to such central life problems as the treatment of pregnant workers; for plainly nothing is accomplished by saying that pregnant women should receive precisely the same benefits as pregnant men.[44]

Meanwhile, the stresses occasioned by the increasing ethnic diversity in the United States have laid bare the inadequacy of early assumptions that justice could be served by demanding that the legal system support the equal right of all Americans to assimilate into the mainstream Anglo-Saxon culture; other countries are facing similar realizations. It is a truism that the ethnic uniformity of the Greek polis is prominent among the characteristics that set it apart from the modern nation-state, but one that bears repeating. James Madison had a solution to the *homonoia* problem, and it seems to have been born of interest in the Greek polis: faction could be prevented, he argued, only "by giving to every citizen the same opinions, the same passions, and the same interests."[45]

The exclusionary character of states like classical Athens has a great deal to teach us about the human community and its history. Works like Carole Pateman's *Sexual Contract* have lent new force to the old notion that both *isonomia*, whatever that was, and *dēmokratia*, whatever that was, were in reality based on the extension of the rights of noblemen to a somewhat larger class. As Kurt Raaflaub (among many others) has pointed out, the demos of free males simply co-opted the rights of aristocrats.[46]

I am intrigued by Raaflaub's contention that the exclusion of women and existence of slaves is "upsetting only to those who cannot think back more than 70 or 125 years."[47] First, the emphasis on the emotional and moral issues surrounding this exclusivity (signaled by the word *upsetting*) detracts from its significance on an intellectual level. Second, the conceptualization of the demos as an exclusive "club" dates back at least to Sir Ernest Barker's work on Greek political theory early in this century—it did not have to wait for its articulation at the hands of French intellectuals like Pierre Vidal-Naquet.[48] Increasingly scholars have come to suspect that the Athenians in their quest for equality and community were, in fact, "cheating." We all know that when you put a model together from your kit, whether you are building a toy car or a real polis, you have cheated if you claim the model is done even though a large number of pieces are left over. If the polis was defined by citizenship, it left out too many categories of people to be able to make an honest claim to have completed its model. But at another level, of course, nothing was left over, since the polis system could not have worked without the slaves and the disfranchised women, both *hetairai* and homemakers. It is crucial, I believe, to remember that the "cheating" was not only moral cheating but—and this is perhaps of more concern to us as historians—intellectual cheating as well.

Something important can be learned about the structure of "egalitarian" Athens from the naïveté of the so-called liberal feminism that maintains that it is possible for women to be doctors and lawyers and Greek historians without radical changes in the structure of society. As a variety of thinkers have pointed out, the existence of slaves and the exclusion of women from the body politic was not simply the product of the blinders of an earlier era; it was essential to the functioning of the system, which was both psychologically and economically dependent on the labor and suffering of the excluded. Thinkers like Pateman—who use gender relations as a model for other power relations—have argued that the "social contract" is in part an agreement among free males about how to protect their monopoly on authority by an equitable allocation of justice within their circumscribed group. Marxist studies of antiquity are also informed by the idea that institutions that appear to be grounded in basic principles of social justice—e.g., classical democracy—are based in reality on the desire of the most powerful class (men, nonslaves) to shore up their power against potential attacks from without. For Diakov and Kovalev, Pericles' role in Athens was to protect the interests of the slave-owning class. Yet in the history of antiquity assembled under their direction, the hardworking poor disappear mysteriously from view, just as stratification among males often receives short shrift from feminist approaches.

I have discussed the arguments of those who stress the unequal situation of women and slaves in Athens not primarily in order to call into question the Athenians' pretensions to equality but principally to emphasize the way in which energy focused on the "out-groups," the "leftovers," of the Athenian state, serves to distract from the structure of the "in-group." It is no coincidence that Kurt Raaflaub found himself using the word *upsetting* in discussing responses to the situation of women and slaves in Athens. Studies of slavery ancient and modern are notoriously entangled with emotional and moral overlay. To deny, for example, that slavery was crucial to the functioning of ancient society has frequently been taken as trivializing the evil of slavery or the suffering of slaves. To insist, on the other hand, that ancient society was based on

slavery is often to align oneself with the claim that the achievements of the ancients may be dismissed or substantially cheapened. Such insistence is also perceived as redounding to the moral credit of the speakers.

Equality is similarly charged.[49] Most often, *equality* has been a "virtue
word." Bryan Turner is mistaken, I think, when he contends that equality "is a
modern value" and "can actually be used as a measure of what it is to be modern and of the whole process of modernization."[50] For a wide variety of thinkers
in both antiquity and in modern times, equality—whatever its merits—has consistently been identified with the Athenians. In *Democracy in America*, de Tocqueville identifies two different kinds of equality. One sort is "a manly and lawful passion for equality that incites men to wish all to be powerful and honored";
but "there exists also in the human heart," he writes, "a depraved taste for equality, which impels the weak to attempt to lower the powerful to their own level,
and reduces men to prefer equality in slavery to inequality with freedom."[51] It
is this ambiguity that has made the belief in equality within the Athenian demos
proof against the wild vicissitudes that have affected thinking about Athenian
democracy in general.

ACKNOWLEDGMENTS

My own thinking about Athens has benefited enormously from participation in
the "Democracy Ancient and Modern" conference, and I would like to thank
the conference organizers, Charles Hedrick, Josiah Ober, and Catherine Vanderpool, as well as the American School of Classical Studies at Athens, the
Classics Department at Georgetown University, and the National Endowment
of the Humanities for coordinating this important venture. I am also indebted
to the conference participants for their thoughtful papers and for their comments on my own; I would most particularly like to thank Paul Cartledge and
Ellen Wood.

NOTES

1. Arnheim, *Aristocracy* 160.

2. From Skinner's "Reply to my Critics," 283, cited in Cartledge, this volume, 176.

3. "Transgression, Equality, and Voice," this volume, 75.

4. Raaflaub, "Equality and Inequalities," this volume.

5. For equality as a "virtue word" in (at least) contemporary thought, see J. R. Pennock's introduction to the volume (IX) of *Nomos* entitled *Equality*, ix, and the discussion in the preface to P. Westen, *Speaking of Equality*.

6. Raaflaub, this volume, 147 with notes 66–67.

7. Ibid., 139–43.

8. See, for example, Parker, *The Cult of Antiquity;* Palmer, "Notes on the Use of the
Word 'Democracy'"; Mossé, *L'Antiquité;* Vidal-Naquet, *La Démocratie*.

9. Matthew Arnold, "Equality," reprinted in *Mixed Essays,* 65; William Young, *History of Athens* (1786; there are several other editions, each with a different title).

10. Montlosier's remarks appear in the *Archives Parlementaires,* first series, 1787–1799, 11 (February 23, 1790), 684.

11. Adams's remarks are cited from C. F. Adams, ed., *The Works of John Adams,* 6. 9.

12. In *Historical Sketch,* vi–ix, cxiii–cciv.

13. In *Debate in the Virginia Legislature,* 9–10.

14. *Cannibals All!* 220.

15. *New York Herald,* September 12, 1852.

16. *Sociology for the South* (1854), reprinted in Harvey Wish, ed., *Ante-Bellum,* 205; Fitzhugh, "Black Republicanism in Athens."

17. Simms, *Morals of Slavery,* in *The Pro-Slavery Argument,* 248 and passim; Harper, *Slavery ,* in *Cotton Is King,* 601.

18. *Slavery,* 605.

19. Macaulay, "On the Athenian Orators," 8.153–55.

20. Grote, *A History of Greece,* cited in the 1869 edition, 4. 59–67. It is the cohesive aspect of the Athenian democratic community in Grote's thinking that Frank Turner chose to emphasize in his *Greek Heritage,* where these passages are cited (218–19).

21. *A Rejected Essay on the National Character of the Athenians* (Edinburgh: Cadell, 1828).

22. Mill, "Grote's History of Greece."

23. Mahaffy, *Social Life in Greece,* 137.

24. Pomeroy, *Goddesses, Whores, Wives and Slaves,* 78.

25. D. Halperin, *One Hundred Years,* 95–96.

26. In *Peasant-Citizen and Slave,* 5–41.

27. In *The Philosophy of History,* 251–56, 260.

28. Cited in M. Horwitz, "Tocqueville," 301.

29. Cartledge, this volume.

30. *Centaurs and Amazons,* 60–61, 122.

31. Marx's responses to the ancient world are generally cast in the form of broad generalizations that make it difficult to know to exactly what time and place he was referring; it is particularly hard to get a sense of Marx's specific response to Athens. On Marx and the ancient world, see Kain, *Schiller, Hegel, Marx;* Lekas, *Marx on Classical Antiquity;* de Ste. Croix, "Karl Marx and the History of Classical Antiquity"; Furet, *Marx et la Révolution Française;* McCarthy, *Marx and Aristotle,* and *Marx and the Ancients.*

32. V. Diakov and S. Kovalev, *Histoire de l'antiquité,* passim.

33. *Ancient Society,* 247; cf. 254.

34. "Classes and Society in Classical Greece," 201–2.

35. See Garry Wills, *Lincoln at Gettysburg* and my own "Thinking about Democracy."

36. For one Marxist linking of women and slaves at Athens, see Marylin Arthur, "Early Greece." One of many discussions of Marx's indifference to women's relation to their labor is Michèle Barrett, "Marxist-Feminism."

37. Barr, *Will of Zeus,* 125.

38. On the history of thinking about Sparta, see E. Tigerstedt, *Legend of Sparta,* and

E. Rawson, *Spartan Tradition,* as well as works on the use of antiquity during the French revolution cited above, n. 8.

39. Cartledge, this volume; on Rousseau see, for example, *Restoration of the Sciences and Arts,* paragraph 24, p. 10.

40. Brown, *Egalitarianism,* 16. This view is facilitated by Brown's conviction that in their view of equality Plato and Aristotle agreed not only with one another but with Athenian citizens generally, and he goes on to develop the "Athenian" view by citations from the philosophers.

41. M. Midgley, *Beast and Man,* 33.

42. See for example Wendy Williams, "The Equality Crisis."

43. E. Wolgast, *Equality,* passim.

44. Cartledge, this volume.

45. *Federalist* 10; see also the discussion in Rahe, *Republics Ancient and Modern,* 59–60, 583–84.

46. Raaflaub, in an earlier draft of his essay for this volume.

47. Ibid.

48. See E. Barker, *Greek Political Theory,* 16; H. Van Loon, *Story of Mankind,* 66; Vidal-Naquet, *The Black Hunter,* 207.

49. See, for example, Finley's discussion in *Ancient Slavery,* ch. 1, where he discusses the "habit of using the ancient world as a springboard for a larger political polemic" (63) and cites the observation of David Brion Davis that lately every "new interpretation of slavery has professed to be more antiracist than the one it replaces" (11, cited from "Slavery and the Post-World War II Historians," *Daedalus* 103 [1974]: 11).

50. B. Turner, *Equality,* 18.

51. *Democracy in America,* 1.56.

RESISTANCE TO CHANGE IN THE LAW AT ATHENS

Alan Boegehold

How did an Athenian of the fifth or fourth century B.C. look at the laws of his state? A survey of a few scenes from Greek literature, when considered in a sequence, identifies an attitude that was vital for the origins and maintenance of radical democracy. The survey also permits the inference that what we are pleased to call radical democracy was sustained even in its full form by a deep vein of conservatism.[1]

These vignettes begin with Lycurgus, an Athenian orator, who in prosecuting one Leocrates presents the court with a problematic assurance. Demosthenes is next, as he commends severe constraints on proposals of new legislation, and then Sophocles' *Antigone*, where Haimon, the son, and Creon, the father and legitimate ruler, face each other in a life-and-death argument. Cleon follows, as he addresses an Athenian assembly on the fate of the adult male population of Mytilene in the third book of Thucydides' *History of the Peloponnesian War*. The series ends with a conversation between two old friends, Socrates and Crito, in a prison, shortly before Socrates is put to death. On the way, notices from Aristotle, Old Comedy, inscriptions published on stone, and the city archives enter into the commentary. But first, a brief history of the Athenian constitution.

CONSTITUTIONS

Athens by tradition once had kings; they, however, disappeared before historical times to be replaced by an aristocracy composed of landowners. In the late seventh century B.C. Dracon gave Athens, which by this time had become a coherent state, a code of laws. Of that code, some phrases, and even some sentences concerning homicide, can be recovered from ancient quotations, but little else. Then early in the sixth century, Athenians had Solon compose a new code by which a new constitution was formed. This constitution, which included an assembly, a council, and a system of people's courts, eventually made possible Cleisthenes' restructuring of civic identities. During the years of Peisistratid tyranny, which intervened between Solon and Cleisthenes, Solon's laws (and Dracon's homicide laws) were not formally abrogated and replaced: they were simply (for the most part) ignored.

Cleisthenes' creation of ten tribes, arbitrarily defined, and a council of five hundred citizens, chosen by allotment, together with his other reforms, made a democracy at Athens possible. That democracy in its fully developed form perhaps came about gradually, beginning with the appointment by lot of chief administrative officers in 487 B.C., and then developing more quickly with the transfer of significant powers in 462 B.C., from a council of aristocrats (Council of the Areopagus) to the popular courts, where panels of judges ranging in number from two hundred to six thousand adjudicated a great variety of questions. Their independence of judgment was protected by the secret ballot; their generally democratic complexion was maintained by pay for judging. The wide range of matters that came before them provided access in time to all the official ways of determining policy and judging its outcome. It is really the time after 462 B.C. we mean when we speak of "democracy" in classical Athens, and this democracy lasted for about 140 years. It was interrupted in 411 B.C. briefly by an oligarchic takeover and then reestablished in the same year. And almost immediately after that, Athenians voted to collect, collate, and publish Solon's laws, which had become scattered and altered in the course of almost two hundred years. A second brief oligarchic regime, that of the so-called Thirty Tyrants, in 404 B.C., lasted for less than a year. Democracy was reestablished in 403, and revision of the Solonian laws, almost complete by that year, was in place a few years later. From then until 322–21 B.C., Athens was without interruption a democracy.

Now to define the word *law* as I use it in the present essay. A law is a general rule by which a given society agrees to be bound.[2] Law can be regulations for conduct at any and all levels and functions of human society. At Athens and elsewhere in Greece (but not at Gortyn in Crete), laws were often loose, general statements without any attendant cluster of particulars, as though lawmakers foresaw a long replication of instances where a judging body would need to assess the "dread individual case." Solon's laws, especially those on inheritance, and Dracon's homicide laws are good examples of this sort of formulation.[3]

The Greek words *nomos, psēphisma,* and *thesmos* can each be translated "law" in one or another context, although often the exact application requires an explanatory note, locating the time and place of use. Here I use the word *law* in its most general sense, not distinguishing the different ways Athenians had of creating these "laws" in the sixth, fifth, and fourth centuries. All three terms were in use at Athens throughout these centuries. When, below, it becomes necessary further to differentiate *nomos* (law) and *psēphisma* (statute or decree), I shall take a moment to do so. *Thesmos* we can think of as an archaic word for the broadly inclusive *nomos,* while *psēphisma* is a law or regulation or decree that has been presented to the *ekklēsia* as a *psēphisma* and duly ratified by vote (*psēphos*).

The laws, once in place, had great authority[4] and were expected to stay in place. When Solon gave Athens a new code of laws, he closed them for one hundred years, using an oath or an entrenchment clause to protect the laws' integrity.[5] He next left Athens to travel for ten years—only, however, after he had exacted from his fellow citizens a promise not to disturb any of the laws until he returned. He knew that he had to leave, because he knew that no one can sit down and review laws, even laws one has finished making a moment before, without seeing necessity for change in almost every sentence, and his fellow citizens could not have failed to persuade him to reconsider particular points.

LYCURGUS, *AGAINST LEOCRATES*

Now to the first (and problematic) vignette. Lycurgus, a legislator and orator at Athens, has indicted one Leocrates, an Athenian citizen, for having slipped out of the city one night in contravention of a law. In the course of assessing the place of a law in the community's life, Lycurgus says to a panel of 501 judges: "If a man walked into the Metrōon and erased a law (*nomos*) and defended himself by saying that erasure of the law had nothing to do with the city beyond the act itself, you would have him put to death."[6] A question arises here, because Lycurgus invokes the death penalty as natural and unsurprising for what seems to be no more than a misdemeanor, an act of vandalism. Where, anyone might ask, is the capital crime? It is not the act of defacing an official document. That sort of thing was done often at Athens, to judge from the complaints recorded in forensic oratory, and even in the heat of rhetoric no one asks for a death penalty in such instances. But, to try a different approach, can the crime be that of abrogating a law? The answer is no, because no matter what impression Lycurgus wants to create, his putative vandal does not abrogate a law when he erases a text of that law in the Metrōon. Consider the scene as a whole.

The jury-members number 501. They are Athenian citizens, over thirty years of age, and they are seated under the roof of a stoa or portico in the northeastern area of the Athenian public square, the Agora. When they look over to the west and a little south, they see the Metrōon, a sanctuary of the Mother of the Gods, situated at the base of Kolonos Agoraios, a low hill rising just west of the Agora. What lies in the space between lawcourt and Metrōon is a jumble of shops, bins, and stalls, where everything under the sun is for sale: cheeses, perfumes, puddings, witnesses, water clocks, summonses, and wine.[7] The jury-members see the building itself, and they are familiar with its interior: the Metrōon had been established some eighty years previously as official repository for texts of all sorts, including laws, ordinances, treaties, and accounts. In order to get your hands on the text of a law that was kept in the Metrōon, you applied to a functionary who was stationed inside the building. He would climb up to a sort of mezzanine, search the compartments or boxes in which public documents were kept, find the plaque on which the law was written, and bring it down to you.[8] The plaque was of wood, painted white, and the text of the law was printed in capital letters in black paint—water-soluble, presumably. There were no spaces between letters, possibly no paragraphs indicated. This is the physical composition of the document that Lycurgus' hypothetical villain will alter. Now, suppose he did have the plaque in hand. What would he do next? Wet his finger and rub out the letters of the law? Or would he have brought a wet sponge with him?

It does not matter, because those 501 judges know that you do not undo a law by erasing letters from a plaque in the Metrōon. There were to be sure transactions whereby a man's civic status could be changed by a mere swipe of a sponge. When you paid off a debt to the state, your name was wiped off from a list of debtors, and your civil rights were restored by that simple act. Alcibiades is said to have erased a lawsuit for a friend. He walked into the Metrōon and rubbed out the relevant entry from a notice board.[9] Aristophanes' wily antihero Strepsiades divined a way to deal with an unwelcome lawsuit. He would place himself behind the magistrate as notice of the suit was being written into a wax tablet by means of a stylus. He would produce a magnifying glass, focus the sun's rays on the tablet, and presto! The wax would melt and the indictment would disappear (Ar. *Nub.* 767–72).[10]

Laws, the judges knew, were published. Once a law had been ratified, the manner of publishing was as follows: the text, written out in ink on papyrus, would be given to a scribe who cut the letters of the text (but not always all of them) into stone or bronze. This durable text might be posted as a stele in a highly visible place like the Acropolis, or in front of the Bouleuterion, or it might be cut into the actual wall of an important building, like the Royal Stoa. And if an Athenian wanted to read what the law said, he went as readily to the published version as to the one stored in the Metrōon. These published versions were the texts that Athenians tended to cite in law court speeches. The man standing in the Metrōon therefore, wet sponge in hand or finger in mouth, did not pose a threat to any law at Athens. No matter what damage he did to that painted text, he knew (and his judges knew) that more often than not an authoritative text of the law could be consulted on a marble or bronze stele somewhere in the city, and that a papyrus text, equally authoritative, stayed in the keeping of the relevant magistracy.

But to return to Strepsiades, his comic fantasy is not so far removed from Lycurgus' awful example. Take the short, straight route to the solution of a problem. Make the immediate physical manifestation disappear, and maybe the thing itself will no longer exist. Or, to take another perspective, suppose it is not in fact the act of vandalism that Lycurgus sees as a threat. It is the imagined defense, which might run somewhat as follows: The erasure of a law is only that. It is some letters being wiped away from their evanescent seat on a painted board. It has no more meaning outside of itself, no force as precedent.

So, Lycurgus implies the man might argue, while he, Lycurgus takes the phrase "erase one law in the Metrōon" as metaphor for "destroy a law of

Athens." Lycurgus and the dikastic panel he addresses understand the danger of destroying a law. It can mean the destruction of all the rest. The miscreant, however, in the defense Lycurgus imagines he might offer, denies that the destruction of a single law brings other annulments with it. Is this then the offense for which Lycurgus invokes the death penalty, an insistence that violation of the law implies nothing more than that? But again, what is the crime? What law at Athens said that a defendant could not argue that his transgression had no broader consequences? There does not seem to be any such law. There was, however, at Athens a deep current of conservative feeling, one that worked to preserve laws just as they were established. And it is to this feeling in the dikasts that Lycurgus confidently appeals. If neither the act of erasing a text nor the argument in defense of that act was actually a crime, Lycurgus could feel that the dikasts nevertheless knew what he meant.

DEMOSTHENES, *AGAINST TIMOCRATES*

Lycurgus' prescription, when seen in this light, is an item in a long-lived and consistent attitude not only at Athens but elsewhere in the Greek world. Demosthenes, a contemporary of Lycurgus, in a speech written for Diodorus, cites with approval a Locrian custom: "I want to outline for you how the Locrians propose laws . . . especially it is an example of a city that obeys its laws. For there they think it so necessary to keep using the old existing laws and to sustain ancestral practices . . . that whoever wants to propose a new law does so with his neck in a noose. And if the law is judged good and useful, the proposer departs alive, but otherwise, they pull the noose and put him to death." (24.139–40).

Demosthenes has Diodorus recommend a radical Locrian practice around the middle of the fourth century B.C. and adds (not to anyone's surprise, I should think) that in two hundred years the Locrians have passed only one new law. There is a possible reflection of Locrian practice some seventy years before: Aristophanes' *Acharnians,* produced in 425 B.C., has Dikaiopolis make a separate peace with the Spartans, Megarians, and Boeotians, cities with which Athens was at the time actually at war. Dikaiopolis is threatened by a chorus of charcoal-burners who see him as traitor, and he, in response, offers to put his head on a chopping board, while explaining the usefulness of his actions. If he does not convince them, they are to chop off his head (Ar. *Ach.* 355–66). This comic invention could have had as its source the same Locrian practice that Demosthenes approves.[11]

If we can believe that in rhetoric and comedy an Athenian who tried to change the law in some idiosyncratic way could expect to be rewarded with a "short sharp shock," can anything be added by way of confirmation from mere laws and decrees? These documents should by their nature be free of embellishment by metaphor.

ENTRENCHMENT CLAUSES

There was more than one way to ensure stability of the law, for instance, the entrenching clause, a sanction against change written into a piece of legislation. An early entrenching clause can be found in a Locrian law concerning division of land:[12] it provides that "whoever proposes a <subsequent> division or puts it to a vote in the council of elders or in the city or among the select men or makes civil strife about the division of land, he himself and his family shall be accursed for all time, his property shall be confiscated, and his house demolished just as under the law about murder." The manifesto of the Second Athenian Confederacy in 377 B.C. presents an Athenian example of an entrenching clause: If anyone, official or private citizen, proposes or puts to a vote, contrary to this statute (*psēphisma*), a motion to abrogate anything that has been said, he is to lose his rights as a citizen, his money is to be confiscated by the state with a tenth to go to Athena, and he is to be judged among Athenians and their allies as disintegrating the alliance, and they are to impose a penalty of death or exile where Athenians and their allies are in control. If death is the penalty, he is not to be buried in Attica or allied territory (*IG* II² 43, lines 51–63).[13] Furthermore, "entrenchment clauses against entrenchment clauses" are found at Thucydides 8.67.2 and at the *Constitution of Athens* 29.4, where a motion is introduced that will allow people in that assembly to say whatever they want, i.e., to present any motion they want, in the interest of the city's survival. And anyone who takes a proposer to court on a charge of proposing illegalities is to be put to death. The leaders of the oligarchic takeovers in 411 B.C. and 404 B.C. relied on law to establish their authority and promptly set about changing those laws. The oligarchs who met at Colonos in 411 B.C. to establish a constitution with a limited franchise first of all proposed and passed a motion that anyone be allowed to propose a motion for the good of the city. The effect of this resolution was to void the power of entrenching clauses embedded in decrees (*psēphismata*) that guarded the democratic constitution.

THE INDICTMENT FOR LAW CONTRARY TO EXISTING LAW

Athenians could also prosecute persons who proposed and caused to be passed a law or decree that was subsequently shown to be inappropriate or in contradiction to an existing law, or not in the best interest of the state. The "indictment for law contrary to existing law" (*graphē paranomōn*), succeeded in the fourth century by the "indictment for an inappropriate law," is a way of protecting the demos from itself.[14] An unscrupulous demagogue can incite the assembly to catastrophic error (as was the case with the generals who in 406 B.C. were put to death after their great victory at Arginusae, a time when all protections failed), but the indictment for illegality or for proposing an inappropriate law did give the law courts a way of monitoring decisions made by the people in Assembly. A man found guilty of sponsoring a law that was inappropriate, or one that was contrary to existing law, might pay a small fine or a large one. On one occasion the penalty was death (Dem. 24.138).

SOPHOCLES, *ANTIGONE*

The prohibition of a burial (noted above as a sanction in the manifesto of the second Athenian Confederacy) leads to consideration of Sophocles' *Antigone,* and a famous confrontation between father and son. The issue here is not obvious at first as the result of an attack on established law, but this becomes a basic theme of the tragedy. The play was first produced a little after the middle of the fifth century B.C. The scene is Thebes; the time, just after Polyneices and his six recruited heroes have died in their attempt to storm Thebes. Toward the middle of the play, Creon and Haimon, father and son, contest the limits of civil obedience and the necessity for existing law to stand unchallenged. Creon, as recognized, lawful ruler, has the right to make the law at Thebes. In that capacity, he has declared Antigone's brother, Polyneices, an enemy of the state. Polyneices' corpse is to lie in the open, not buried. Any person who attempts to bury him will be put to death. Antigone, Haimon's wife-to-be, is caught in the act of covering Polyneices' body with earth. She justifies herself by appeal to a law established long before Creon's, which requires her to bury her dead. Creon, who believes he is secure in the primacy of his law, condemns her to death. When Haimon, argues for Antigone's life, Creon says that whoever the city appoints to govern must be obeyed in all, whether right or wrong.[15] By the end of the play, Creon is a ruined man: Antigone is wrongfully dead; his wife, Eurydice, and his son, Haimon, suicides. It is not, however, for his obstinacy: a ruler must safeguard the law he makes. Creon's tragic error is in having attacked established law. That law, as he confesses in his dearly won understanding, had been founded before him.[16] By his attack he has undone himself.

CLEON ON STABILITY OF LAW

Thucydides has Cleon, son of Cleainetos, and Diodotus opposed in the Assembly in debate. The year is 427 B.C., and the Archidamian war has been going on for four years. On the island of Lesbos, the oligarchs at Mytilene who tried to revolt from the Athenian empire have recently been contained and disarmed. Athens has voted in Assembly the day before to put to death not just the rebellious oligarchs but all adult male Mytilenaians.[17] On the day of the reported debate, the question of the Mytilenaians is reopened: a course other than wholesale slaughter is proposed. Cleon argues against change. "The thing to be feared most of all is if we do not establish as fixed whatever we decree, if we do not understand that one city is stronger than another when its laws, no matter that they are less good, are not subject to change, and the laws of the other, although they may be good, lack authority."[18] His insistence on the necessary immutability of a law once set in place, whatever that law may be, is something like Creon's. In this case, as it turned out, most of the Mytilenaians were saved at the last moment. The Athenians voted to change the law, a *psēphisma* here. It is interesting in this context to note that Greek did not have a noun for the undoing or revoting of a *psēphisma*.[19]

ARISTOTLE, *POLITICS*

A summary from Aristotle's *Politics* can serve as epilogue to Cleon's maxim. Aristotle has just introduced Hippodamus of Miletus, a city-planner and innovator who recommended some different ways of composing a government. After describing Hippodamus' proposed reforms, Aristotle considers the advantages and disadvantages of changing laws and concludes that it is better— even when magistrates are in error—to let them be. "Now there are instances and times when laws should be changed, but, looking at it another way, it would seem a matter requiring great caution. Because when the betterment is small, and since it is bad to habituate people to abrogate laws easily, it is obvious that some failings on the part of legislators and magistrates should be allowed to pass, since you do not help so much as you hurt by accustoming people to disobey their authorities" (Arist. *Pol*. 1269a12—18).

SOCRATES IN PLATO'S *CRITO*

Now it is time to consider the case of Socrates. Plato, writing early in the fourth century B.C. at Athens, presents in four dramatic dialogues the last days of his mentor, Socrates. In 399 B.C. Socrates was tried before a panel of five hundred judges, found guilty of impiety and of corrupting young men, and sentenced to die. Athenians later and the world generally since then have judged the proceedings a terrible miscarriage of justice. Socrates was imprisoned directly after the trial to await his execution. As it happened, his execution was delayed for forty days by the city's annual embassy to Delos. Toward the end of that forty days, in Plato's account, Socrates' old friend Crito comes to the prison where Socrates is being held and offers escape. He and his friends can open the way with money and influence, and Socrates can retire to Thessaly to live out his natural life.

Socrates' response to this offer, after almost 2,400 years, still prompts surprise and speculation. He says no to Crito. He will end his life as the court has determined, because—as he explains—for him to escape by the means that Crito proposes would be tantamount to an attempt to destroy the laws of Athens. He cites one conceivable defense of such an escape: he might argue that he was not given a fair trial. But that line of argument is not relevant, he decides, because the law in question is that which affirms a court's judgment as final authority. That is, whether right or wrong, the court's judgment is final.[20] For him to void a court's sentence by any means other than persuasion is an attack on the very existence of the Athenian law.

To complete his explanation, Socrates imagines a conversation in which he personifies the Laws of Athens. He calls them "the laws, which are Athens as State."[21] They remonstrate with him. If he does not die, as an Athenian court has judged he must, he will destroy them, who are his nurturers and sustainers, his parents. And he has agreed—from long ago his whole mode of life has made this apparent—to live by those laws. He must not now, although they may seem to have been misapplied, try to destroy them.

This is the basis of Socrates' position. But why does Plato not allow Socrates to consider the possibility of an educational resistance, one which might cause the Laws to suffer, but in the end to change for the better? Suppose Socrates had escaped from prison and gone to Thessaly; he could easily have anticipated a change of political climate. He knew how volatile Athenian politics, friendships, and political associations were, and what capacities for forgiveness Athenians had. Think of the murderous regime of the Thirty. They and their friends and supporters had exercised a tyranny just four years earlier, and from all accounts, many of them who survived could have been open to severe retaliations. The Athenians, however, in their wisdom found a way to fashion and maintain an amnesty. Why does Socrates then not acknowledge the inadequacy of the Laws, frustrate their immediate application, and put himself in a position to take advantage of a rationally foreseeable, benevolent reversal of judgment? The Laws as he imagines them accept persuasion as a legitimate instrument of change. Would the temporary elopement to Thessaly not be a kind of persuasion?

Socrates chose to accept death, when he had a chance to escape, to live in exile for a short time, and then to return honorably and legally to Athens. Standing firmly in a tradition, he protected the law. Law was the true constitution of a society, and any act that can be interpreted as a subversion of established law is in effect a physical attack on the society that the law informs. A judgment of death therefore levied on subverters of law is perhaps roughly equivalent to killing an enemy who is trying to storm your walls.

But this reconstruction of a context may not wholly account for Socrates' choice. He could truly have construed his temporary absence from Athens as a sort of persuasion, and persuasion was permitted. Why not persuade the laws? Give them some time to come to their senses? It may be that the chief operative reason for Socrates' own personal choice is one that he gives to Crito almost at the end of the Laws' imagined speech. It is that he cannot stand to become a figure of fun. The Laws tell him that he obviously cannot go to a city where people obey the law. He would have no place there. What then? Well, he might go to Crito's friends in Thessaly, where there is not much respect for law and order. "And if you go there," they say, "won't people find it agreeable to hear the funny story how you became a runaway, putting on some costume, with a goatskin or some other such thing as runaways use, and how you changed your whole appearance. And will there be no one who says that you had a lot of nerve, since you are an old man with not much time to live anyhow, to be so greedy for life that you break the most important laws?" And what after all will he do once he gets there? He will find abuse and perhaps a dinner or two. He will be seen as having run away to Thessaly for a dinner.

It hurts to be laughed at, and it hurt especially in Greece, since in Greek literature laughter is most often mocking, cruel joy at the discomfiture of an enemy. Socrates in his exaltation of law walks a traditional path. He does so also in refusing to let himself become ridiculous, and because he is Socrates, we understand that it is not in the eyes of others but in his own that he must not turn out to be a laughable creature. He never wavers in his clear-sighted perception of himself. He reaffirms his views on death and sees no way to reconcile those views with the act of running away. To have acquiesced in Crito's scheme might seem to almost anyone a natural response, no more than a minor passivity that serves a good end. But Socrates cannot compromise his principles and must accordingly say no.

It is relevant here to consider an assertion that Socrates makes in the course of his defense speech before five hundred judges. Suppose, he says, you the people of Athens were to acquit me but on the condition that if you ever catch me going about and asking the sorts of questions I do, philosophizing, that is, you will put me to death. To this supposition, Socrates replies, Thank you very much but I will obey God rather than you (Plato *Ap.* 29c5—29d4). Is this conditional sentence a deliberate assertion (as has sometimes been claimed) of his intention not to obey the law? Is the Platonic Socrates in the *Apology* consistent with the Platonic Socrates of the *Crito?* A brief glance at the actual powers and procedures of a law court at Athens should absolve Plato and Socrates of any charge of inconsistency here. The court can set him free, but the court cannot set conditions. An Athenian court had only two options. The judges could convict or acquit. If they voted to convict, they could in some cases determine what a guilty person had to pay or suffer. But on such occasions, the judges were again tightly limited in what they could do: they could only choose between whatever the prosecutor proposed as penalty and whatever the defendant proposed instead.[22] Here is Aristotle on the question of qualified verdicts (in his discussion, let it be said, of another topic entirely): "A qualified verdict is possible in an arbitration, even when several arbitrators are there, for they can confer with each other on a decision. But in a law court, no such judgment is possible, because most legal codes, far from permitting such conferences, have in them specific measures to keep judges from communicating with each other" (Arist. *Pol.* 1268b). The only way a judging panel could attempt to silence Socrates with the force of law would be for a prosecutor to propose that silence as his penalty and for the judging panel to vote that penalty. But records of Greek juridical proceedings do not suggest that specially imagined penalties were designed to suit the transgression of one special person.

CONCLUSION

In closing, a brief summary: Lycurgus could take the rhetorical position that Athenians would sentence to death anyone who tried to change the law of Athens by unauthorized means (and argued that such changes had no meaning beyond the act itself). Demosthenes illustrated the general principle with a radical practice from Locris. Sophocles' Creon provided a tragic example of obdurate confrontation with established law, and Cleon, son of Cleainetos, directed Athenians to follow the ordinance that has been set in place principally because it has been set in place, no matter that it is not as good as it could have been. Finally Socrates, amused and ironical as ever, shows what obedience to the law can finally exact, and that it is right to do so. When we speak of conservatives, we usually mean persons who are committed to preserving things as they are. Given this usage, it is hard not to give the name *conservative* to these protectors of laws, all of whom are quite different characters. They are Sophocles, Thucydides' Cleon, Plato's Socrates, Demosthenes' Diodotus, and Lycurgus, each of whom, resident in a "radical" Athenian democracy, responds in his own way to complex questions regarding stability of law.

NOTES

1. The citizen as landowner and hoplite might in any case have been expected to be conservative in general outlook, as people whose lives are bound to the land tend to be. Cf. the essays of Victor Hanson and Kurt Raaflaub in this volume. It is at the same time illuminating to compare a letter of Thomas Jefferson as quoted in B. R. Barber's "Misreading Democracy" (this volume). Jefferson writes in a letter: "I know also that laws and institutions must go hand in hand with the progress of the human mind. . . . We might as well require a man to wear still the coat which fitted him when a boy, as civilized society to remain ever under the regimen of their barbarous ancestors."

2. Dem. 25.16. "A common agreement of the city by which all in the city are required to live" (πόλεως δὲ συνθήκη κοινὴ καθ᾽ ἣν πᾶσι προσήκει ζῆν τοῖς ἐν τῆι πόλει). Cf. also Plato, *Crito* 50a6—54d1.

3. Ruschenbusch, ΣΟΛΩΝΟΣ ΝΟΜΟΙ; R. Stroud, *Drakon's Law;* M. Gagarin, *Early Law.* Ostwald, *Nomos,* p. 48 cites Aristophanes *Birds,* 1650, 1655–56 as references to Solon's inheritance laws. Ruschenbusch, "ΠΡΩΤΟΝ ΔΙΚΑΣΤΗΡΙΟΝ."

4. There is an often-cited exchange, generally relevant for Greece, that took place at Thermopylae between Demaratus, a Spartan king in exile, and King Xerxes, who was invading Greece. Demaratus, acting as Xerxes' advisor, describes the Spartans as free men who are not really free, because law is their master, and they fear that master more than Xerxes' subjects fear him (Hdt. 7.104). The strength of that metaphor, "law is master," is explicit at Plato *Crito* 50e2–51a2, and in Pericles' usage at Thuc. 2.27.2. It also

makes easy and natural a personification of the law, already established in Pindar's famous "law is king" (Fr. 169a Maehler).

5. Hdt. 1.29; Arist. *Ath. Pol.* 7.2 "He closed the laws for a period of one hundred years" (κατέκλεισεν δὲ τοὺς νόμους εἰς ἑκατὸν ἔτη). Cf. E. Ruschenbusch, ΣΟΛΩΝΟΣ ΝΟΜΟΙ F 93a/b.

6. Lyc. *Leoc.* 66. Cf. Deinarchus, *Against Demosthenes* 86.

7. Cf., e.g., Euboulos, fr. 74, *Poetae Comici Graeci* V.

8. Arist. *Ath. Pol.* 47.5. See Chambers, *Aristoteles* ad loc. on Sterling Dow's reconstruction of procedure.

9. Rhodes, *Commentary on Ath. Pol.* 47.5, notes some instances of erasure.

10. Dem. (20.35) does in fact use the same word, *erase,* to mean "repeal" or "abrogate," but in a different context, one that does not set the act in a sequence of exact circumstances. Cf. Socrates' figurative language at Plato, *Phdr.* 257b2–5 and Aesch. *Ag.* 1327 with E. Fraenkel's commentary.

11. A. Szegedy-Maszak, "Legends of the Greek Law-Givers," notes some laws that passed from the realm of history to that of myth. See p. 207 on Locris.

12. Meiggs-Lewis, number 13, Lines 9–14. Cf. Dem. 24.

13. See also Cargill, *The Second Athenian League,* 23.

14. "Indictment for passing an inappropriate law" (γραφὴ νόμον μὴ ἐπιτήδειον θεῖναι). Cf. Mogens Hansen, *Athenian Democracy,* 205–12.

15. Soph. *Ant.,* 666–67, Creon: "Whom a city appoints, him must you obey, even in little things both right and wrong" (ἀλλ᾿ ὃν πόλις στήσειε τοῦδε χρὴ κλύειν καὶ σμικρὰ καὶ δίκαια καὶ τἀναντία), and then at line 672: "There is no greater ill than absence of authority" (ἀναρχίας δὲ μεῖζον οὐκ ἔστι κακόν). Note also *Ant.* 634, where Creon asks Haimon, "Are you with me in everything I do?" (ἦ σοὶ μὲν ἡμεῖς πανταχῆι δρῶντες φίλοι). The implications of this question are a resonance of Odysseus' observation that "a multiplicity of direction is not a good thing": (οὐκ ἀγαθὸν πολυκοιρανίη Homer *Iliad* 2.204).

16. Soph. *Ant.,* 1113–14: "For your life, the best thing, I fear, is to keep the laws that are established" (δέδοικα γὰρ μὴ τοὺς καθεστῶτας νόμους ἄριστον ἦι σώζοντα τὸν βίον τελεῖν).

17. The decree has the form of a *psēphisma.* See Dover, "Anapsephisis." (rept. 1988, *The Greeks and Their Legacy: Collected Papers*).

18. Thuc. 3.37. Cf. the role assigned to Cleon by Sheldon Wolin in his essay in this volume. Note also Ar. *Wasps,* 102, where the Paphlagonian says he nourishes the heliasts "shouting right or wrong" (κεκραγὼς καὶ δίκαια κἄδικα).

19. See K. J. Dover, "Anapsephisis."

20. Plato *Crito* 50b9, "What is adjudicated has the authority" (τὰς δίκας δικασθείσας . . . κυρίας εἶναι).

21. οἱ νόμοι καὶ τὸ κοινόν, Plato, *Crito* 50a7–8. I construe the καί as explanatory, e.g., "the laws <by which I mean> the community." Cf., e.g., Plato *Rep.* 341d3, where κατὰ τὴν τέχνην καὶ τῶν ναυτῶν ἀρχὴν means "in accordance with his skill, which is that of directing sailors."

22. Cf. the discussion of A. D. Woozley, *Law and Obedience,* pp. 44–46; Richard Kraut, *Socrates and the State,* pp. 13–14; T. C. Brickhouse and N. D. Smith, *Socrates on Trial,* pp. 143–47.

PART TWO

Civic Ritual and the Education
of Citizens

CIVIL SOCIETY, DIONYSIAC FESTIVAL,
AND THE ATHENIAN DEMOCRACY

W. ROBERT CONNOR

THE TWENTY-FIVE HUNDREDTH ANNIVERSARY of Cleisthenes' reforms provoked a great series of celebrations, many of which have encouraged useful re-
assessments and fresh thinking about Athenian democracy. It may seem churl-
ish to complain, yet birthday parties are not a particularly Greek practice.[1] Nor
did the ancient Greeks pay more than passing attention to centenaries or other
anniversaries, scarcely even noting, for example, that the Second Athenian
Naval Confederacy was established almost exactly a century after the first.

Their avoidance of such folderol contains a useful warning. Such celebrations may encourage a view of democracy as a political "event," rather than as
a cultural process. They focus attention on the year 508—507 and on the political actors, the drama of Cleisthenes' confrontation with Isagoras, and the psychological question of his motives. Alternatively they may provoke further discussion of the already amply discussed questions about the form of Athenian
democracy and the consequent debates about its success or failure in antiquity
and its implications for modern societies. These debates, in my opinion, are
based on a flawed premise, one shared by defenders and critics of Athenian
democracy—that the *form* of ancient democracy provides a model or a lesson
for modern political organization. Yet surely it is overly optimistic to think that
this tiny city, this almost face-to-face society in which participatory democracy
was the rule, will provide useful advice for the modern nation-state, whose scale
demands representative government and whose decision making is carried on
through the filter of mass media. Lower expectations may be more realistic: perhaps the differences in scale and structure may alert us to a few features shared
by democracies of many different forms.

Scholars of classical Athens, moreover, may well benefit from a fresh exploration of the analogy between ancient and modern democracy. In particular
it is useful to note that the emergence of American democracy resulted from the
convergence of at least three factors:

1. Specific grievances, such as those reflected in the slogan "No taxation without representation."
2. The intellectual climate, one deeply rooted in the European Enlightenment.
3. A preexisting democratic culture.

The cumbersome phrase "preexisting democratic culture" is simply a way of alluding to certain patterns of discussion and decision-making in some quarters in colonial America—a consensus that certain topics were open for discussion, and that all free adult white males of a certain level of affluence within a given community might properly join in that discussion. There were, moreover, some widely accepted ground rules for discussion—"one speaker at a time," "take turns," in some cases even majority rule. In a colonial regime the topics discussed might be narrowly circumscribed, strictly local, and sometimes not even "political" in our sense of the term. The likelihood that the habit of democratic deliberation sometimes grows up outside the strictly political realm should not surprise us, but it does remind us to cast the net widely, and look not only at constitutional and legal changes but also at "civil society," that is, the network of shared activities, voluntary associations, religious and commercial undertakings, indeed all communal action not initiated by the state. In colonial America that would entail an investigation of associations of craftsmen and tradesmen, the governance of churches, the organization of self-help societies, volunteer fire companies, and all the institutions, large and small, that were not primarily the responsibility of the colonial governments. Civil Society creates the cultural patterns that create a vigorous democracy.

But what of ancient Greece? We can readily conjecture that a similar situation is likely to have prevailed in ancient Athens and conclude that in discussing the origin of Athenian democracy we would do well to look beyond the steps that led to the establishment of that form of political organization and pay attention to ostensibly nonpolitical activities. But where is the evidence? It is bad enough for strictly constitutional changes, and even worse for the developments in civil society whose significance we can more readily suspect than document. Yet we are not totally without evidence about associations of merchants, religious groups, and other voluntary activities and associations. These institutions, however "a-political" they may seem, deserve careful attention not only for their own sake but because the patterns of discussion and decision making within them ultimately affect political and constitutional patterns. To say that such institutions prepared the way for and eventually helped sustain democratic polities is not to deny the importance of constitutional changes nor of a skillful politician such as Cleisthenes. But it is helpful to be reminded from time to time that democracy is practice, not taxonomy. It is a way of carrying on political life, not just a way of classifying constitutions.

Democratic practice may derive from many sources, especially that zone between the individual and the state that we have come to call Civil Society. It is there that individuals can form their own associations, pursue their own interests, and make the state treat them as its proprietors, not its servants. The key to effective conduct within this zone is collaboration and group formation. Hence attention to Civil Society helps provide an alternative to the widespread presumption that democracy, ancient or modern, is a relationship between what

Robert Nisbet calls "the abstract individual" and the state. In recent decades the limits, practical and analytical, of abstract individualism have become increasingly clear. In political theory it eclipses the importance of mediating groups, families, neighborhoods, and associations. In political practice it has often encouraged the modern nation-state to dominate, sometimes even to eliminate, the associations of civil society.[2]

Aristotelian political theory took quite a different approach, beginning not with the abstract individual but with the associations of family, clan, and village as the true constituents of the polis. This is evident not only in the *Politics* but in an interesting passage in the *Eudemian Ethics:*

> All constitutions are some species of justice; for they are partnerships (*koinōniai*) and every partnership is founded on justice. . . . The other partnerships are a constituent part of the partnerships of the state—for example that of the members of a brotherhood (*hē tōn phraterōn*) or a priesthood, or business partnerships (*hai chrēmatistikai*).[3]

Here Aristotle calls attention to some of the principal forms of associations within the early Greek polis. His observations parallel (and he may well have had in mind) the Solonian law cited in Justinian's *Digest* 47.22.4:

> If a deme or members of a phratry or *orgeōnes* of heroes or members of a *genos* or messmates [*sussitoi*], or funerary associates, or *thiasōtai,* or pirates, or traders make arrangements among themselves, these shall be binding unless forbidden by public texts.[4]

This law, despite the late source on which we depend, and doubts about some of the phrasing, closely corresponds to the passage just cited from the *Eudemian Ethics.* Each emphasizes the abundance and importance of kinship groups, real or fictitious: the *phratriai,* and the genos, and religious groups: we might translate *orgeōnes* and *thiasōtai* as "confraternities." In addition there are those who dine together or provide one another with a decent funeral. And there are, as any reader of Thucydides might expect, "pirates," out for profit in their time-honored profession, and the perhaps less reputable practitioners of overseas trade.[5] One can suspect, moreover, that the law marks an effort on the part of the polis to regulate preexisting organizations, much as the polis gradually regulated or in some cases took over long-established religious cults.

This law leaves us, however, with many questions. Of these, for present purposes, the most important is how these groups governed themselves. Since the point of this decree is to validate a wide range of practices among them, we should not expect to generalize. But it seems equally implausible that they were all nicely democratic or that they were all strictly hereditary and hierarchical. Many are associations among ostensible equals: brothers and partners. It seems unlikely then that they were patriarchal or that authority was vested in those with the best genealogies. More likely individuals within these associations negotiated ways of governing that allowed a voice to all and developed ways of making decisions and resolving disputes that seemed fair to all. In Aristotle's phraseology, "every partnership is founded on justice" (Arist. *Eth. Eud.* VII.1241b15, trans. H. Rackham, Loeb).

Such associations, then, are important constituents of ancient civil society. Let us begin with the closest of primary attachments, that of the family. Normally any glimpse of the family is blurred by ancient reticence or refracted through myth. Yet the transcription of Draco's law on homicide provides a revealing glimpse of decision making among kin: "Pardon is to be granted, if there is a father or brother or sons, by all, or the one who opposes it shall prevail. And if these do not exist, pardon is to be granted by those as far as the degree of cousin's son and cousin, if all are willing to grant it; the one who opposes it shall prevail. And if there is not even one of these alive . . . then let ten members of the phratry admit him to the country, if they are willing."[6]

If we try to envision the process implied in this law, family members must gather, and discuss, whether *aidēsis* is to be allowed. Any one of them can stand up against the others and say no. There is no "patriarchal authority" in the strict sense of that term, nor mere ratification of what the elders have to say. Rather, the decision is explicitly shared among specified male members of the family. Within that most primary of all attachments, the family, the habit of discussion seems already established in Draco's day. Implicit in these procedures, moreover, is a rudimentary but crucial sense of equality: that the son might veto what the father had proposed; that one recalcitrant cousin might block all the other relatives within that degree of kinship.

What, then, of another primary attachment—the neighborhood or the village? We have already seen that the decree cited in Justinian's *Digest* recognizes the authority of the deme to conduct, within broad limits, its own business.[7] Before Cleisthenes the organization of the city of Athens was not based on these units, and we may readily conjecture that they had considerable latitude in the conduct of local affairs. But although they might be to a large extent outside the constitutional structure of the polis, they were very important in the daily life of the residents of Attica. The ancient sources indicate clearly that these settlements were deeply rooted: "Under Cecrops and the first kings, down to the reign of Theseus, Attica had always consisted of a number of independent townships, each with its own town hall and magistrates. Except in times of danger the king at Athens was not consulted" (Thuc. 2. 15, trans. Crawley, Modern Library).

King Theseus, Thucydides notes, changed the old political structure that was based on independent townships, centralizing the government in Athens. Yet, even at the outset of the Peloponnesian war, "old habit still prevailed. . . . Deep was their trouble and discontent at abandoning their houses and the hereditary temples of the ancient constitution, and at having to change their habits of life and to bid farewell to what each regarded as his ancient city" (Thuc. 2. 16, trans. Crawley).

In a similar vein Hecataeus (*FGrHist* 1 F 126) refers to the town of Thorikos as a polis; and Homer refers to Eleusis in the same way. The cluster of four townships near Marathon, moreover, is the Marathonian *tetrapolis,* not "the Marathonian *tetrakōmoi*" or "the league of the demes near Marathon" or some such.[8]

The names of some of these towns, Daidalidai, for example, suggest the importance of associations of craftsmen. In other cases, Philaidai for example, they may have been dominated by individual *genē* in the archaic period. That conclusion, however, entails a further question: Was each *genos* so completely in the control of a single leading family that it had little or no shared decision-making? More likely these *genē* were from time to time sites of contestation and contention for prestige among various individuals and family groups.[9] In outlying areas, moreover, smallholders must often have made routine decisions about local matters.[10] These would include questions of shared access to grazing land, water, and wood, the adjudication of some local disputes and the administration of some cults, and some legal proceedings.[11] Unquestionably these towns had an important role in the life of archaic Attica.[12]

In classical times these townships spent much of their effort, it would seem, on the administration of local cults. But religious life, as is well known, was not entirely in the control of the demes or the polis. Even at a relatively late date, private religious associations were of great importance. Here we enter the network of *thiasōtai, orgeōnes,* et al., to which both Aristotle and the Solonian law in the Digest allude. The *orgeōnes,* to focus on one type of association, were, according to one ancient authority, "persons holding meetings centering on various heroes or gods," that is, they sacrificed to divinities in privately established cults.[13] To judge from the evidence preserved in much later periods, these were voluntary associations, composed most often of prosperous and respectable citizens—"middle class," we would say.[14] While the general pattern of their worship might be defined by tradition, countless practical issues—succession, sacred lands, division of the sacrificial meat, disposition of hides, etc.—were open to dispute and decision-making within the organization. The earlier history of such associations is far from clear, but there is good reason to think that they were prominent and often the site of contention throughout early Greece.

So far, we have looked at several types of private associations in which the habit of shared decision-making is likely to have prevailed—the extended family, the neighborhood, the religious confraternity. These and commercial and trade associations all contributed to a civil society antedating and facilitating, in my view, the Cleisthenic reforms. Each located authority not in centralized hierarchies but in circles where consensus could be hammered out through discussion and debate among ostensible equals. Many of these associations ante-date Athenian democracy and persisted long after it was established. Yet, since Attica had no monopoly on them (though they were perhaps more prominent there than elsewhere), they do not provide the answer to the two questions that most perplex historians who investigate Athenian democracy: Why did this form of government emerge just then—in the late sixth century—and why just there, in Attica?

To answer these questions, I believe we need to look at another aspect of Athenian life, what the historian Maurice Agulhon calls "the folklore of a regime"—customs, practices, ceremonies that are as necessary to rule as any set of constitutional measures or the ever-elusive statements of democratic ideology that political theorists are constantly seeking. This inquiry suggests a hypothesis which I will present in the remainder of this paper—that Cleisthenes brought together the habits of equality and shared decision-making that had long been present in Attica and other parts of the Greek world and combined them with what I propose to call a "Dionysiac social imaginary." The separate elements of this "imaginary" all existed elsewhere in Greece before Cleisthenes, but in Attica they fused together in a new way.

The growth of Dionysiac worship in sixth-century Athens has often been described, though its significance in my opinion is frequently misrepresented. It seems to me neither a part of an elaborate religious policy imposed from above by the tyrant Peisistratus and his sons nor a movement toward "personal religion." Rather, it is best understood as the first imaginings of a new type of community. Those imaginings did not spring from the mind of the Athenian leadership, but they were recognized and used by Athens' leaders. Peisistratus in this, as in many other matters, is not a bold sherpa leading his people into lofty mists, but a skilled surfer who knows how to ride the waves of popular feeling.

In his *Bacchae* Euripides refers to Dionysus as a god who "in equal measure to rich and humble gives the griefless joy of wine" (421–23). Dodds in his commentary on these verses emphasized the democratic nature of Dionysiac worship: "Dion. is a democratic god: he is accessible to all, not like the Pythian Apollo through priestly intermediaries, but directly in his gift of wine and through membership of [sic] his *thiasos*. His worship probably made its original appeal mainly to people who had no citizen rights in the aristocratic 'gentile state' and were excluded from the older cults associated with the great families."[15]

Or to put it another way: Dionysiac worship tumbles into carnival and carnival inverts, temporarily, the norms and practices of aristocratic society. While these inversions may provide a temporary venting mechanism and thereby help stabilize repressive regimes, in the longer run they can have quite a different effect. They make it possible to think about an alternative community, one open to all, where status differentiations can be limited or eliminated, and where speech can be truly free. It is a society that can imagine Dionysiac equality and freedom.[16]

Benedict Anderson's book *Imagined Communities* implicitly challenges classicists to think more closely about the role of social imagination in the constitution of ancient societies.[17] It is especially important to examine more closely how such imagination works. It does little good to think of it in abstract terms. Rather it is a highly metaphorical activity, in which specific practices from one realm are envisioned as operating in another realm. There is always a *tertium comparationis* between present reality and imagined alternative.

In late-sixth-century Athens that comparison, I believe, involved the transference of certain features of Dionysiac cult from the sacral sphere into the realm where day-to-day decisions about the polis were located.[18] The Dionysiac *thiasos* then becomes "one of the 'figures' that render society visible to itself."[19]

We are still trying to think our way into this "imagined community" of the Dionysiac *thiasos* now, twenty-five hundred years later. The effort is an important one, for our society as well as for classical scholarship. But for the Greeks of the classical period, the *thiasoi* of Dionysiac worship had a more immediate relevance, for they helped demonstrate in action the equality of people sharing an activity of great intensity and commitment. Perhaps ancient peoples were more attuned to the potentially revolutionary nature of participation in such worship. One thinks, for example, of Herodotus' story of the Scythians' reactions to their King Scylas when he joined in the Dionysiac *kōmos* in Borysthenes:

> The Scythians are wont to reproach the Greeks with their Bacchanal rage, and to say that it is not reasonable that there is a god who impels men to madness. No sooner, therefore, was Scylas initiated in the Bacchic mysteries than one of the Borysthenites went and carried the news to the Scythians. . . . The chiefs of the Scythians went with the man, accordingly, and . . . regarding the matter as a very great misfortune . . . came and told the army what they had witnessed. [80] When, therefore, Scylas, after leaving Borysthenes, was about returning home, the Scythians broke out in revolt. (Herodotus 4. 79 f., trans. Rawlinson, John Murray)

Scylas was soon beheaded, and the Scythians galloped away from any departure from their traditional governance.

In Attica the story was, of course, quite different. There we see a system that institutionalized in the political realm some features that probably originated in religious practice, for example, "outspokenness," *parrhēsia*, and *isēgoria*, "equality of speech." They are the two progenitors of what we consider a basic human right, freedom of speech.[20] As Martin Ostwald points out in this volume, the Greeks never spoke of such "rights," but they did recognize that practices that existed in one context might influence other parts of life.

This, I suggest, is exactly what happened in the establishment of Athenian democracy. Practices that existed outside "the political" realm—in everything from bands of freebooters to religious confraternities, from groups pitching in to deal with a local problem—when combined with Dionysiac worship, provided a basis on which democratic institutions could be built. The transference of these religious practices into public space, and their modification into acceptable forms, was, I believe, Cleisthenes' accomplishment. His recognition of the political implications of Dionysiac worship gave him a new rationale for imitating his grandfather, Cleisthenes of Sicyon, who "took away from Adrastus the sacrifices wherewith he had till then been honoured. . . . Besides other ceremonies, it had been their custom to honour Adrastus with tragic choruses. . . . Cleisthenes now gave the choruses to Dionysus, transferring to Melanippus the rest of the sacred rites" (Hdt. 5.67, trans. Rawlinson).

Given the importance of Dionysiac cult groups in this social imaginary, it is not surprising then that Athenian democracy once established would express itself in a Dionysiac festival. The establishment of the City Dionysia has most often been dated to the middle third of the sixth century, a view based on what turns out to be a serious misreporting of the inscriptional evidence. I hope a previously published discussion has convinced some scholars at least that this festival was established not under the Peisistratid tyranny, as the traditional date implies, but in the time of Cleisthenes or soon thereafter.[21] It is, in my view, best understood as "a freedom festival" in celebration of the fall of the tyranny. In its fully developed form at least, as the late Jack Winkler most eloquently showed, it represents and reinforces the structure of Athenian democracy.[22] It also helps sustain the social imaginary out of which came the successive approximations of democracy during the fifth century in Athens.

The festival helps us understand why our texts contain no elaborate statement of Athenian democratic theory. One can reconstruct such a theory from oligarchic and other criticisms of democracy, but the democrats never provided anything like the texts our Founding Fathers left for us. The ancient Greeks did not write theory; they enacted it. They enacted it in particular through the City Dionysia. And as they acted, they not only affirmed the current form of their democracy, they also helped themselves to begin imagining a different kind of community than any the politicians had yet devised. It was one, to be sure, that they never attained, indeed never fully articulated. Many of them would have feared the messages of equality and of the elimination of repression implicit in a celebration that pointed toward a festival society, one whose goals were not the coordinating of human effort for economic aggrandizement, nor the marshaling of human bodies for war and the glory of the state, nor the imposition of some Utopian order on a subservient population, but delight, enjoyment, and for a few days at least, the integration of all members of the community.

NOTES

1. There were, however, sacrifices on the birth of a child and these were sometimes repeated annually: Eur., *Ion* 653, 805; Plato *Alc.* 1.121c. Ammonios *Peri homoiōn kai diaphorōn lexeōn*, s.v. *genethlia*. Other passages are cited in Jacoby, "Genesia," 74f.

2. Cf. Nisbet, "The Contexts of Democracy," 15–23.

3. Arist. *Eth. Eud.* 7.1241b14–27, following H. Rackham's Loeb text and translation. Dietsche, however, has strong justification in printing *orgeōnōn* (of the orgeones) rather than *orgeōn* (or a priesthood) to maintain the parallel with *phraterōn*. For the error, cf. Lysias fr. 112 and the book text of Justinian's *Digest* discussed below. The parallel to the passage in the *Digest* is especially suggestive, since Aristotle may be paraphrasing this law.

4. The translation is based on Ferguson, "The Attic Orgeones," 64f. Cf. Whitehead, *Demes,* 13.

5. On piracy as a respectable undertaking in early Greece, see Thucydides 1.5.

6. *IG* I³ 104, lines 13–18; trans. Stroud, *Drakon's Law,* 6.

7. Much has been written about whether the demes before Cleisthenes enjoyed official recognition "as constitutional entities." The skeptics have a strong case: see Whitehead, *Demes,* 3–13. But the lack of official recognition does not preclude considerable local autonomy.

8. Cf. Parker, "Festivals of the Attic Demes," 137.

9. Cf. Connor, "Lycomedes against Themistocles?"

10. By the sixth century it appears that many well-born residents of Attica preferred to live in the city of Athens rather than on their country estates. That is perhaps why Peisistratus found it desirable to set up judges in the villages and from time to time himself made inspection tours around the countryside, settling local disputes (Ps. Arist. *Ath. Pol.* 16.5), for the traditional authorities were now hard to consult.

11. Cf. the selection of *parasitoi* discussed in the quotation from Themison cited in Athenaeus 6.235a. See Schlaifer, "Cult of Athena Pallenis," esp. 37f. and 43 for reasons to believe that the selection of *parasitoi* by the demes was "of great antiquity."

12. Rihll, "The Attic *naukrariai,*" 10, suggests that the "*naukraries*" attested in some of our sources were residential groupings. They had, if this is correct, nothing to do with the word for "ship," *naus.* Rather, the etymology was from the verb *naiō,* "dwell." Hence the "presidents of the *naukraries*" were likely to have been the official link between these local settlements and the city that, officially at least, ruled all Attica. Is it possible that a truly public realm first grew up in these settlements and, if so, did the local residents organized in a civic community, a demos, provide a model and a name for the civic form called democracy?

13. Cf. Seleucus of Alexandria, *FGrH* 341 F 1. See also Ferguson, "Attic Orgeones," 62f.

14. See the discussion by Ferguson, "Attic Orgeones," 126f. Ferguson concludes, "The old Attic orgeones were not 'kleine Leute' in the sense that thetes were; nor were they aliens. If I were to classify them in Solonian terms I should call them zeugitai."

15. E. R. Dodds, *Euripides Bacchae,* 2d ed. (Oxford: Clarendon Press, 1960), 127–28.

16. The myths about Dionysus' intervention in civic life reinforce the effects of this practice. Myths such as those about the fall of Pentheus, King Lycurgus (Apollod. *Bibl.* 3.5.1), or King Thoas of Lemnos (Val. Fla. 2.242–302) suggest that the introduction of Dionysus' worship meant the end of monarchical rule. In practice it seems more likely that the hierarchical differentiations of aristocratic society, not monarchy, were most strongly challenged by the growth of Dionysiac cults. I have benefited greatly from dis-

cussions with Richard Seaford on issues concerning this and other implications of
Dionysiac worship.

17. Anderson, *Imagined Communities.* See also Castoriadis, *Imaginary Institution of
Society.*

18. In Athenian terms this could be represented as a relationship between *ta hiera,* the
distinctively sacral, and *ta hosia,* the realm where decisions involving practical justice
were made. Cf. Connor, "'Sacred' and 'Secular.'"

19. Castoriadis, *Imaginary Institution of Society,* 130.

20. On *parrhēsia* see Peterson, "Zur Bedeutungsgeschichte von *parrhēsia*" and Martin, "Metanastic Poetics." The term is sometimes a hallmark of democracy, as in Polybius 2.38.6, and frequently associated with Athens, as in Eur., *Hipp.* 422, *Ion* 672, and
cf. Plato *Gorg.* 461e.

21. Connor, "City Dionysia and Athenian Democracy." In this respect Cleisthenes of
Attica was following the lead of his grandfather Cleisthenes of Sicyon (Hdt. 5.67).

22. Winkler, "Ephebes' Song."

OATH RITUAL AND THE MALE COMMUNITY
AT ATHENS

Susan Guettel Cole

The ancient Athenian political system was successful because it allowed for
the development of a stable yet responsive political community. Individuals
were successfully integrated into a variety of different social structures, and
from these the larger political community continually recreated and reshaped
itself. Aristotle understood that this process was political (*Pol.* 1276a–b), but it
was a political process that could be expressed in ritual language and by means
of ritual acts. Because modern political theorists have tended to minimize the
ways in which Athenian political life was defined, managed, and ordered by religious ritual,[1] they have rarely noticed the ways in which their modern terminology obscures social relationships and social stratification within the Greek
polis. There has been some recent discussion of political rituals, but this discussion has been focused on public festivals and public spectacles as the primary instruments of social and political cohesion.[2] Massed public displays,
however, reveal more about the shape of group ideology than the way the group
was formed or how the group encouraged and maintained the commitment of
individual participants. Public festivals were certainly important, but there were
other rituals, no less significant, that emphasized the dynamic relationship between the political community and its participants.

Creating Political Identity

One particular ritual, concerned with identifying individual commitment and
defining group solidarity, was the swearing of oaths, an important marker in
many traditional or transitional societies and a basic ritual of the Greek city-
state. As ancient political communities increased in complexity, oath rituals became more rather than less important. Oaths functioned not as a relic of a primitive past, but as a powerful public expression of collective approval and
disapproval, required by the increasing complexity of political life in the growing Greek city. Public performance of oath ritual was directly related to the expansion of the electorate and the expansion of political responsibility. Athenians, in fact, were famous for the number of oaths they swore.[3] Athenian
democracy differed greatly from modern democracies, and the nature of that

difference will remain opaque unless we try to understand how traditional expressions of obligation defined and marked political responsibility in Athenian
contexts. In order to do this, we need to look closely at the content of oath ritual, not reduced to modern terminology, but in the language and actions of the
participants and performers themselves.

The Athenian citizen belonged to a whole network of groups, with the polis
as the largest of the many communities (family, phratry, deme, tribe, demos)
that claimed attention, allegiance, time, and interest.[4] We often use the term *citizenship* to identify the relationship of the individual to the polis, but the Athenians of the classical period, with their restrictive notions of citizenship, would
not have understood what the post-Roman Western world means by this term.
Pericles was the first to define the Athenian requirements. The fourth-century
Constitution of the Athenians tells us that the only people who had a share in
the *politeia* were people whose parents on both sides were *astoi* (belonging to
the city of Athens; [Arist.] *Ath. Pol.* 42.1). *Politeia* in this context is usually
taken to mean something like "citizenship," "body of citizens" or even "government," but the term also includes the idea of "political community."[5] In fifth-
century Athens, where metaphor had a more powerful explanatory role than abstraction, the nature of what we call citizenship was expressed by metaphors of
kinship. The myth of Athenian autochthony, by which Athenians claimed descent from a king born from the soil, defined Athenians as members of a single
family.[6] Pericles' citizenship law of 451, by defining membership in the political community in terms of family relationships, emphasized ties of kinship and
sharpened the distinction between insiders, men with Attic mothers and fathers,
and outsiders, men with a foreign parent.[7]

In practical terms, participation in the political community was marked by
ritual; these unifying activities permeated every aspect of Athenian public life.
Rituals involved recognition of divine protection, and they also provided procedures to draw individuals together and to mark distinctions of gender and status within the larger group. Aristotle recognized that the political community
was created from a community of families, each family represented in the larger
world of the polis by its male head (*Pol.* 1259a37–1260b20). The Athenian
democracy required the cooperation of a larger group of male participants than
did other city-state forms of government. The system therefore needed to create expressions of unity, but it also required mechanisms to regulate the inevitable competition and conflict resulting from the ever-widening pool of political actors in the expanding Athenian democracy.[8] Natural ties to family were
stronger than ties to peers or ties to the city. Ritual expressions of unity were
consequently required in order to maintain the artificial bonds that brought and
kept the male community together. The language of oaths and the actions of
oath sacrifice functioned as part of a network of public rituals that symbolized
obligation to the collective power of the whole group. Any description of Athe-

nian political structures remains meaningless without the language and codes of ritual action that defined male identity and bound the Athenian male to his political community.

In the poleis of ancient Greece, those who had an active share in political life were always assumed to be male. Men who belonged to the Athenian political community were described as *epitimoi*, "possessing honors and privilege"; and men expelled from that group were described as *atimoi*, "without honors and privileges."[9] Athenian language defining this community reflects the exclusivity of these honors and privileges. Women could be called *Attikai* (belonging to the territory of Attika) or *astai* (belonging to the city of Athens), but not by terminology that signified membership in the political community.[10] Women and men both derived their identity from the land (*Attikai / Attikoi*, "belonging to Attika") or the place (*astai / astoi*, "belonging to the town"), but only men could regularly be described by terms that defined political relationships (*Athenaioi*, "Athenian"; *politai*, "citizens"). At Athens women were not seriously called *politai* or even the infrequent feminine *politides*, and the feminine *Athenaiai* was a rare term, used collectively of females only when eligibility for public service as priestess in public cult was an issue.[11]

The author of the *Constitution of the Athenians* was aware of these distinctions. After describing the Athenian qualifications for participation in the political community, he goes on to describe the activities of the male *politeia*. His first topic is how a boy became a man, according to the regular procedures for acceptance in the political community of adult males ([Arist.] *Ath. Pol.* 42). The author describes this process in terms of the requirements for membership in the local geographic unit of the polis, the deme, because membership in the deme was equivalent to membership in the *politeia*. The first stage of the procedure had two parts. First there was a vote under oath in each of the 139 demes, to determine whether local candidates met the requirements of age (eighteen years), status (free, not slave), and kinship (born from parents who were both *astoi*, "belonging to the city"). The second stage of the procedure required another vote under oath, this time in each of the ten tribes, to choose three men from each tribe to train the young men in the military skills considered necessary for their adult life of political activity and political participation. Our author does not tell us the content of these oaths, but it is likely that they included an appeal to one or more gods to bear witness, a promise to act in accord with a specific law or decree, and a short curse inviting self-destruction if the sworn oath was not kept.[12] The young men themselves marked the beginning of the acculturation process that would eventually define them as full citizens by swearing an oath to the community, called at Athens the "oath of the ephebes."[13] This oath bound young men to the territory of Attika at the time of the beginning of their eligibility for military service and identified that service with loyalty to comrades, obedience to the laws, and protection of the boundaries of the land of Attika. Other oaths marked the undertaking of other stages of political responsibility: the heliastic oath, the bouleutic oath, and the oaths of the magistrates and archons.

OATH RITUAL

Oaths were used in two basic contexts: to mark promise or contract and to mark assertion or denial. The first guaranteed agreement, the second defined dispute. The oaths that bound the citizen to the community were of the first type and, like oaths used to mark private financial agreements, provided a mechanism for marking agreement. In the archaic society in which the form originated, a society without written contracts, an obligation to the gods was believed necessary to ensure fidelity to sworn oaths. Oaths were ranked according to their significance; important oaths were called "great" (*megas*), "strong" (*krateros*), or even "greatest" (*megistos*).[14] Oaths were accompanied by ritual, and like the language of oaths themselves, the ritual varied with the significance of the situation. The implicit hierarchy of oaths was expressed by the degree of complexity of the ritual.

Homeric descriptions of oath ritual indicate significant differences from the standard forms of animal sacrifice in content, form, and desired effect. Both rituals required the killing of an animal, but the standard form of sacrifice, called *thusia,* usually resulted in communal banquets and was associated with festivity.[15] In some oath rituals, however, the animals had to be male, were cut up in a special way, and seem not to have been eaten.[16] The purpose of oath sacrifice was not always a shared meal, but the performance of a ritual designed to bind the swearer to the other party of the oath (either another individual or a group), and to obligate both parties to the gods. In *thusia* only part of the animal was burned, the rest cooked for consumption. In oath sacrifices the entire body of the animal could be burned,[17] buried,[18] or thrown into the sea.[19] The fate of the sacrificial victim represented the potential destruction of the person swearing the oath and was a visual and tangible sign of human powerlessness in the face of the gods.[20] The flesh of the animal could be treated in several ways. The usual formula describes oaths as sworn "over" (*kata*) the victims, with the preposition implying that the oath swearer made a downward motion. In particularly stressful situations it is clear that the oath swearer had to touch the flesh of the animal[21] or take the pieces of the victim in his hands.[22] Special treatment of the body of the victim was characteristic of oath sacrifice, and procedures show some variety. At Kos, for instance, in an oath sacrifice to the Charites, the priestess poured the blood of the victim (a goat) three times on the altar and a fourth libation on a special oath stone. Then the sacrificial officials (*hiaropoioi*) divided the meat into portions for each goddess and placed them on the altar, so that those swearing the oath could touch the stone and the entrails while pronouncing the words.[23]

The most formal type of oath sacrifice required three adult male victims, which could be a bull, boar, and ram (Dem. 23.68), a boar, a billy goat, and a ram (schol. Ar. *Pl.* 820), or a bull, a billy-goat, and a boar (Istros *FGrH* 334 F 51).[24] The vocabulary of oath ritual is quite specific about the gender and sexual maturity of these victims. This type of sacrifice was called a triple or "triplet" sacrifice (designated in Greek by *trittus, trittua, trikteua, trikteira,* or *triktoia,* and at the Attic deme Thorikos, by *trittoa*). The generic name for the oath victim was *horkōmosion,* used for both the ritual and for the victim, in the singular for a single animal,[25] and in the plural for triple victims.[26]

There is no single account of oath sacrifice in Greek literature that describes the sequence of events from start to finish. The available evidence indicates that there was probably considerable variation in practice, depending on the divinities, the situation, and what was being sworn. Homer is our best source for a detailed description of oath ritual. His description is embedded in the account of the oath sworn by Agamemnon and Priam when they determined the conditions for the duel between Paris and Menelaos at Troy. After pronouncing the terms of the oath, Agamemnon cut the throats of three young sheep (*Iliad.* 3.246), and the two kings poured libations on the ground (295–96). They prayed that, like the wine they poured, the brains of any violator be spilled out on the ground, together with the brains of his son, and that his wife be left as loot for the enemy. The analogy between the destruction of the sacrificial victims and the potential destruction of those who violated the oath, together with their families, was crucial to the ritual action.

The Homeric expression for the performance of oath sacrifice, "to cut oath victims" (*horkia tamein*),[27] alludes to, but does not give the details of, a central action of oath sacrifice, the cutting up of the sacrificial victim.[28] Some oaths required that the victims for sacrifice be male,[29] adult, and not castrated. A Hellenistic treaty of *sumpoliteia* ("co-citizenship") between Kos and Kalymnos defines the strict requirements that could govern some situations protected by traditional oath ritual.[30] The regulations for sacrifice in this case prescribe the status of both oath swearers and animal victims in very precise terms. The oath swearers, eligible for citizenship, had to be male (*andres*) and sexually mature (*hēbadon*). The three victims slain, specified in the texts as oath victims (*horkōmosia*), had to be "bull, billy goat, and ram, all *telea.*"[31] In the epigraphical vocabulary of Greek sacrificial regulations, where animals were often carefully selected for a precise age,[32] *telea* (in dialect spelling; neuter plural to refer to the victims, *horkōmosia*) describes the age status of the victims and specifies mature adults.[33] The oaths between the citizens of Kos and Kalymnos therefore were protected by a rite where the age status and sexual status of the animal victims had to correspond to the age status and sexual status of the oath swearers. The ritual required a correlation between adult male animals destroyed and the males who swore because the destruction of the animal represented the enormity of the conditional curse implied in the oath.

Hesychius describes such triple victims (which he calls *trikteira*) as victims "with testicles" (*hiera enorcha*).[34] These two requirements, triple adult victims and triple uncastrated victims, would mark the triple oath sacrifice as unusually expensive and especially significant, in that the animals slain were killed not for their meat but for their meaning. The economics of Greek livestock-rearing, geared toward breeding of animals for production of milk and wool, required the disposal (and therefore consumption) of surplus young males.[35] The most frequent sacrificial victims were therefore young, castrated males, wethers in the case of sheep and steers in the case of cattle. Sacrifice of fully adult males was not common. Because livestock raising always required fewer males than females and because it was expensive to feed unnecessary animals, surplus males would normally have been sacrificed (and eaten) before reaching full maturity. Such males, not needed for breeding, were usually castrated to make them easier to handle (Hes. *Op.* 786, 791). Adult, uncastrated males would therefore have been exceptional sacrificial victims, possibly raised to adulthood especially for rituals like oath sacrifice,[36] where they were required for their symbolic value.

Oath ritual was performed in specially defined situations. Deme inscriptions give some idea of the nature of the public oaths accompanied by oath sacrifice. The fourth-century deme calendar from Thorikos in Attika provides the best example.[37] This inscription, although not complete, lists at least three different oath sacrifices during the year: a single animal for the public examination (*euthyna*) of the accounts of retiring magistrates in the month of Metageitnion (August), three animals to Pythian Apollo in Mounichion (April), and a single animal for an oath sacrifice in Skirophorion (June). We know the oath for the public scrutiny of accounts in Metageitnion,[38] because the oath for the public examiner and the assessors is appended to the calendar. The Attic deme functioned as a miniature polis, and the demarch (the elected leader of the deme) presided over the oaths required by the deme's procedures; he was the "authority of the oath" (*ho kurios tou horkou*).[39] Oaths promising honest votes were required whenever the demesmen voted on the annual examination of young candidates for membership (*dokimasia*),[40] examination of magistrates (*euthyna*),[41] or scrutiny of membership lists (*diapsēphisis*).[42] Victims were sacrificed and the oaths were sworn over the victims according to established procedures. The rules and regulations of the demes assumed that the gods sanctioned the procedures for determining qualifications for citizenship.

Because we lack a complete state calendar of sacrifices for Athens, we must rely on partial evidence to reconstruct oath sacrifice at the level of the polis during the classical period. Political oath-taking at Athens was a male activity. Important oaths at Athens were sworn at a special stone in the agora. These were the oaths of the nine archons, the oaths of arbitrators, and the oaths of summoned witnesses who denied that they had any testimony to give ([Arist.] *Ath. Pol.* 55). The nine archons took their oath twice, once in the agora and a second time on the Acropolis. The procedure at the stone in the agora is described as follows: "They go to the stone on which are the cut pieces (*tomia*) . . . and going up on this (stone), they swear that they will rule justly."[43] Demosthenes, describing a similar procedure before the Areopagus, says that any man accusing another of deliberate homicide had to swear a special oath "standing on the cut pieces (*tomia*) of the victims."[44]

Tomia clearly refers to the pieces of the dismembered animal, but precisely which pieces is not clear. Burkert, following Stengel's interpretation of the term *tomia* as "testicles," describes the ritual as follows: "Essential is the dismemberment of the victim: the person swearing the oath treads with his foot on the 'severed parts,' namely, on the sexual organs of the male victim; bloodshed is compounded with the horror of castration."[45] Not everyone agrees. Faraone has assembled the Near Eastern evidence for similar rituals used in crisis situations, and though he thinks that "some sympathetic curse is involved with the employment of *tomia*," he finds no parallel elsewhere to support Stengel and Burkert.[46] Rudhardt argues that *tomia* refers to the inner organs (*splanchna*), sliced for sacrifice.[47] Casabona takes them for the dismembered limbs of the sacrificial victim.[48] As with most issues concerning Greek sacrificial procedure, Greek writers assumed that their readers did not need to be told the details. It is possible, however, that in those situations where the oath ritual required adult, male, and uncastrated victims, the term *tomia* carried a special meaning.

The Language of Oaths and Curses

The content of oath language provides a clue to the meaning. Like other forms of ritual expression, Greek oaths were carefully structured, with three distinct parts: 1) an invocation to a god or gods (often three in number) to bear witness; 2) a claim or a promise, and, in solemn or "great" oaths, 3) a self-directed curse if the claim were not true or the promise not kept.[49] In "great" oaths the main statement, either a promise or assertion, was framed by two ritual pronouncements: the invocation, addressed to the gods, and the curse, directed at the oath taker and his family. At Athens the three gods most often invoked in oaths were either Zeus, Demeter, and Apollo, or Zeus, Poseidon, and Apollo. The content of the curse could vary. The most frequent form of curse threatened destruction in the primary areas of male productivity: agriculture, raising of livestock, and begetting of children. One of the most complete Greek versions on record is the curse from the oath of the Delphic Amphictyony, quoted in Aeschines (3.110–11) as follows:

> If anyone violates these conditions, whether as polis, private individual, or ethnic community, let them be under a curse (*enagēs*) of Apollo, Artemis, Leto, and Athena Pronaia. . . . May their land not bear fruit; their women not bear children

resembling their fathers, but monsters; nor their flocks bear young according to nature; and may they have defeat in war, lawcourt, and agora and complete destruction for themselves, their family and their race.

A summary form, also frequent, often appeared in a formula that specified, "For
the man who keeps his oath, many good things, but for the man who doesn't,
complete destruction (for himself and his household)."[50] Curses like these,
originating in the Mesopotamian cultures of the Sumerians and Akkadians,
were widespread in the region of the eastern Mediterranean,[51] and similar patterns occur in the oaths of other Greek cities.

The man who broke his oath destroyed not only himself, but all the fruit of
his property and all the children born from his body.[52] The curse and the oath
sacrifice, where the swearer pronounced the curse in contact with the *tomia,* expressed identical ideas. The oath as speech act was reinforced by a powerful ritual action that mirrored the curse and at the same time represented the result of
that curse, directed at the oath-swearer himself. Not every oath included a curse
and not every oath was accompanied by oath sacrifice, nor did every oath sacrifice require uncastrated victims, but the potential violence of the actions was
expressed even in the milder form of oath accompanied only by libation, described by Euripides with the metaphor of cutting in the expression "cut libations" or "cut a truce" (*spondas temnein, Helen.* 1235; *Supp.* 376).

The contents of the curse are the reverse of the blessings associated by Hesiod with the city of right judgments. For Hesiod, agricultural security depended on political success and judicial fairness. Hesiod's just city is a city of
peace, a place where the earth gives forth its bounty and where men "reap the
tilled land that is their care . . . the oak in the mountains bears acorns at the tips
of its branches and honey in its midst, the woolly sheep are heavy with fleeces,
the women bear children resembling their fathers, and these people flourish forever with good things" (*Op.* 228–36). We can extend this idea to the imagery
of oath ritual and the language of curses. The success of the community was
considered to be reflected in the success of its individual citizens. Failure to uphold sworn oaths damaged the political community and produced disaster.
The imagery of Hesiod's just city retained its significance in the period of the
Athenian democracy, where the language of the self-directed curse, used in political, judicial, and diplomatic contexts and appearing regularly in courtroom
speeches and epigraphical documents, shows that these issues were still very
much alive in the fifth and fourth centuries B.C. The divinities invoked as witnesses in the oath of the Athenian ephebes included not only the gods of war,
manhood, and agricultural increase, but the products of the land itself: the
wheat, the barley, the vines, the olives, the figs. The imagery of the oath of the
ephebes, emphasizing agricultural production, is not unlike the imagery of Hesiod's description of the just city.

Paternity and citizenship, like paternity and patrimony, were closely connected. Membership in the political community, like property, was passed from citizens to their male descendants, in the paternal line from fathers to sons, in the maternal line from a mother's male relatives through her to her sons. Even after Pericles' law of 451 B.C., when the status of a mother became a determining factor of citizenship, it was actually the status of the males in her natal *oikos* that ultimately determined the status of her son.[53] The tradition of the self-directed curse recognized the anxiety associated with paternity (as opposed to maternity) and the necessity of the preservation of the family as a unit of the city. The performance of political duties required individual and collective swearing of oaths by male citizens in public contexts. For Demosthenes the three foundations on which democracy depended were the people, the laws, and curses.[54] Punishment for breaking public oaths was directed by gods and community at the individual and his family. Punishment for contempt of public as well as private oaths was expressed in terms of personal failure and public humiliation, and by loss of descendants, symbolized in oath ritual by images of mutilation.

In defining citizenship and political privilege, the Athenian polis recognized these principles of paternity and male identity and exploited the emotional content of the traditional self-directed curse to guarantee loyalty to the political community. The family became security for the citizen's fidelity to the polis. Citizens who failed to live up to the requirements of membership in the political community were punished by exclusion, and that punishment extended to their families. One special issue that cut to the core of the democracy was treason (*prodosia*). Convicted traitors lost their lives, their property, their homes, and the ability to confer citizenship on their children. Like the children destroyed by a father's betrayal of his oath, the children of traitors were publicly destroyed, not by real death, but by political death, expressed in the language of the self-directed curse. In 411–410 B.C. Antiphon and Archeptolemus, betrayers of democracy, were condemned by the city with such a punishment. The sentence pronounced by the court, quoted by Plutarch from a published inscription, sounds like a curse.

> The sentence was passed on these two to be given over to the Eleven (for execution); their belongings to become public property with a tenth part given to the goddess; their houses to be torn down to the ground;[55] and boundary stones set up on their fields with the inscription "Belonging to the traitors Archeptolemus and Antiphon"; the demarchs to inventory their property; and it shall not be possible to bury Archeptolemus and Antiphon at Athens or any place where the Athenians rule; and Archeptolemus and Antiphon shall be deprived of rights of citizenship, and the descendants of these, both bastard and legitimate children; and if anyone adopts any of the descendants from Archeptolemus and Antiphon, let the adopter be deprived of rights of citizenship.[56]

The city itself could become partner to a curse and function as the instrument by which it was carried out.[57] A citizen owed loyalty to his city, and oaths of loyalty took precedence over oaths sworn with other groups.[58] A city could even assume priority over oaths wrongly sworn against itself. A Thasian law on conspiracy, for example, released from both oath and self-directed curse any man who informed on the traitors with whom he had previously sworn a treasonous oath.[59]

OATHS TO MARK EQUALITY

Oaths tied citizens to the Athenian democracy at all levels. When the orator Lycurgus castigates Leokrates for breaking an oath taken on behalf of the city, he claims that the oaths of its citizens were the glue that held the Athenian democracy together.[60] He distinguishes the three types of oath especially important to the Athenian democracy: the oath of public officials, the oath of the juryman, and the oath of the individual citizen. His first category included the oaths of the nine archons[61] and the other major officials at Athens,[62] the bouleutic oath,[63] the oath of public arbitrators,[64] the oaths of the *stratēgoi*,[65] and the oaths of priests and priestesses of city cults.[66] His second category included the heliastic oath, an oath sworn by the six thousand residents of Attika selected to serve annually on the panel of jurors.[67] By distinguishing the oath of jurors from the oaths of officials, Lycurgus shows that he understood the distinction between magistrates, who swore to perform their duties in accordance with the laws, and jurors, who not only swore to obey the law, but promised as well, in cases where there was no law, to vote according to what was most just.[68]

Lycurgus' third category included all oaths sworn by private citizens, whether in public or private contexts. It included oaths sworn in bringing a case to court, oaths sworn in private contracts, and oaths sworn in public or private arbitration.[69] It also included the oaths required of all citizens by the city for political participation, sworn collectively, but pertaining to each man individually. The oath of the Athenian ephebes, the oath that marked the Athenian male's initiation into political life, belonged to this group. In addition, the third category included oaths in the deme and oaths in the phratry, especially the oath sworn by witnesses attesting to the legitimacy of sons when fathers introduced them to their phratries.[70] It also included oaths asked of citizens as individuals, such as the oath to obey the laws of Solon;[71] the oath Athenians were asked to swear (by tribes and demes) against tyranny when democracy was restored in 410,[72] or the oath after the reconciliation and restoration of democracy in 403.[73] An appeal to the strength of oaths was expected to impress a jury. Like Lycurgus, Andocides also builds a triadic cadence when he appeals to the power of oaths, emphasizing the oaths "common to the whole polis: the one that all citizens swore in 402, the bouleutic oath, and the oath of the jurors" (Andoc. 1.91–92).

In constructing his catalogue of important oaths, Lycurgus ignores an important distinction, one that we drew earlier, that between oaths of promise and oaths of assertion. This distinction is crucial for understanding the way oaths worked. Oaths provided a means of resolving disputes. At Athens, private and public arbitration outside the courts and litigation inside the courts involved contests of opposing oaths. Consequently oaths sworn in judicial contexts contained not promises, but claims of assertion or denial. In the male culture of litigation, oaths of assertion or denial helped to fix the issues. The Greek legal terminology for tendering and receiving such oaths, reciprocal but opposite actions, is difficult to render intelligibly in the English vocabulary of oath taking. That is to say, to tender or offer an oath was expressed by the Greek verb "to give" (*didonai*), and to receive an oath given by someone else was expressed by the Greek verbs meaning "to take," or "to receive" (*lambanein, dechesthai*).[74] Like prayer, sacrifice, and the giving of gifts to the gods, and like the Greek terms for giving and exacting judicial penalties (*dikēn didonai, dikēn lambanesthai*), oath giving and oath taking were forms of exchange.[75] Homer's Hector makes an assumption of equality when he offers to Achilles an exchange of promissory oaths with these words: "Let us exchange gods with each other."[76] Achilles denies the equality and, by exploiting an image that connects himself to hunter and Hector to his prey, refuses the exchange: "There are no trustworthy sworn agreements (*horkia pista*) for lions and men, nor do wolves and lambs have a like-minded spirit. . . . There is no *philia* between you and me" (*Iliad* 22.261–263).

Homer provided a model, but the Athenian environment of litigation was far more complex. Judicial procedures in democratic Athens assumed similar contests of power between males, and oath challenge was one of the means by which one citizen could take the measure of another. In legal disputes one person could demand an oath from another, with the expressions for this action implying an element of force as well as challenge.[77] An opposing party might ignore a challenge, but to fail to respond was a source of shame and could weaken a case. The offer of an oath could therefore impress an audience even if the oath was never sworn. In the grand political competitions for gaining honor (*timē*) and assessing dishonor (*atimia*), Greek males used oath challenge as a test of power. Just as a litigant could offer to swear an oath he himself had no intention of actually swearing,[78] he could also try to weaken an opponent's case by offering an oath he knew would be refused.[79] Even if a challenge was accepted, there was still a chance for duplicity. Aristotle quotes Xenophanes to indicate that in cases where both parties did agree to swear, a pious man would be at a disadvantage with an impious opponent.[80]

OATH SWEARING AND POLITICAL STATUS

By examining the way oaths were used, we can see the games men played to establish ascendancy, and we can measure differences in status between various groups within the population of Attika.[81] Two, perhaps three, categories of

individuals were excluded wholly or in part from direct participation in litigation: women, metics, and slaves. Limitation of access to the complete ritual language of oath and oath sacrifice is one of the measures of disability with respect
to political status.[82] At one time metics had access to the court system only
through a citizen, who acted as sponsor (*prostatēs*).[83] Women had access to the
judicial system for redress of injury only through a guardian (*kurios*); access
for slaves depended entirely on their owners. Women and (privately owned)
slaves did not participate directly in a trial at all. Women could be asked to provide sworn testimony in arbitration, testimony that could be presented in court
if a case resulted later.[84] Women (and children) appeared at jury trials only as
mute characters, part of the standard repertory of emotional appeals for pity by
their male relatives. The testimony of slaves, because they were thought to be
unreliable, was considered valid only if tested by physical torture.[85]

Female behavior in private life is almost entirely hidden from us, but we can
see from the plays of Aristophanes that women could make exclamatory oaths
in casual conversation.[86] This sort of oath is very different, however, from the
promissory oaths sworn by Athenian males in public life or the reciprocal oaths
sworn by males in arbitration and litigation. Exclamatory oaths like "by
Artemis!" "by the two goddesses!" or "by Aglaurus!" had no legal status and
served only to provide emphasis and punctuation in normal conversation.
Women did take promissory oaths, but only in clearly defined situations, for instance, when accepting ritual responsibility in the priesthoods of the city's public cults.[87] This was the only context in which women were designated as
"Athenian," because this was the only place where a woman could represent
the polis.

Greek tragedy shows that in private situations women could swear two-party
oaths[88] and could even request oaths,[89] but we should distinguish oaths of private life from the kinds of oaths men swore in public life. Women rarely (perhaps never) participated in public oath ritual. In Athenian public life, even as
plaintiff in a lawsuit,[90] a woman always had to be represented by a male authority (*kurios*), who initiated action for her and represented her interest. A
woman could offer an oath or be challenged to swear an oath in private arbitration, a procedure used as alternative or preliminary to a public trial,[91] but
women did not swear the oaths required for public trials themselves. A woman
swore in litigation only when she had a direct connection to a male relative involved in a dispute, or, possibly, when a case directly concerned her.[92] A
woman's testimony was sought only when no one else could have known what
she knew. Women's experience was confined to family life; women were therefore consulted only in cases and procedures concerned with family affairs.
Recorded disputes involving a woman's oath concern kin, and issues revolve
around property.[93] Women could participate in family meetings, where they
could offer to swear oaths later in a formal setting (Lys. 32.13), or they could
participate in private arbitration where they swore before an arbitrator.[94] We

know of such oaths only from trials resulting later. A contestant in court could appeal to a woman's oath sworn during an earlier stage, in arbitration, but women themselves appeared at trials only as silent witnesses to a male speaker's plight. The issue most frequently requiring a woman's testimony was paternity and legitimacy of children, the sort of thing that only a mother could have known for sure.[95]

Women could be challenged in pretrial litigation to swear an oath, but they could not issue a formal public challenge themselves. There are three disputes that illustrate this point. In the first case, Demosthenes' mother was said to have been willing to swear oaths about the status of the freedman Milyas and the status of her own dowry, but the first oath had to be offered by her son, and the second demanded in challenge by Aphobus, his opponent. Neither the offer nor the challenge actually materialized, and she swore neither oath.[96] It was the possibility of offering an oath or the threat of accepting a challenge that was supposed to indicate the moral highroad and impress a jury, and when women were involved, men tried to use women's reputations to score judicial points.

The second case where women's oaths were an issue was a dispute about property rights that illustrates very clearly the way in which a woman's oath might be manipulated in a dispute between males. The issue at hand was the building and moving of a wall between two pieces of adjacent property. The only witnesses (beside the defendant) to the original boundary were the mothers of the two neighboring families; at the time of the trial both were advanced in age (Dem. 55.3). The plaintiff claims that he had proposed an oath for his opponent's mother to swear, an oath about the location of the original boundary, and maintains that he had challenged the other family to have his own mother swear the same oath. Neither woman responded, but it is clear that only the sons, as *kurioi* of their mothers, could offer the challenges. The plaintiff says, "*I* was ready to tender (*edidoun*) an oath to his mother and *I* kept challenging (*proukaloumēn*) him to have my mother swear the same oath" (55.27). Each mother could be asked to respond, but neither could act directly by proposing or demanding an oath herself.[97] The situation shows us how women, as instruments in men's disputes, could be silent players in a game where the speaking parts were all played by men.

The third example demonstrates how a woman could trick a challenger, even though she herself could not actively challenge someone else. In a famous case, a certain Plangon upset the applecart when Mantias challenged her to swear about the paternity of her sons. She upstaged him by accepting the oath, even though according to his opponent he believed he had offered her enough money to refuse to swear, if challenged, that her sons were his.[98]

Before any case went to trial, the plaintiff and defendant had to swear an exchange of oaths (*antōmosia*) before a magistrate at a preliminary session. Murder cases, especially those conducted before the Areopagus, required special laws and special procedures, including the procedures for the oath of denial,[99] special sacrifices (*tomia*), and a ritual proclamation banning the accused from public places until the trial took place.[100] The use of the term *tomia* to describe the pieces of the oath victim indicates that this was a special situation and an unusually solemn affair, belonging to a special class of oath and oath ritual. *Tomia,* used of the sacrificial victim, do not appear in all types of oath ritual, but only in those special situations marking especially important male activities: the oaths of athletes at Olympia (Paus. 5.24.9), the oaths of the Athenian magistrates taken on the stone in the agora, the oaths sworn in murder trials, and probably the oaths associated with treaties.[101] We may never know the precise meaning of *tomia,* but in the most solemn of oaths, homologies between the oath taker, the sacrificial victim(s), and the reference of the male-centered curse indicate a ritual language that marked special boundaries of gender identity, political status, and familial responsibility.

This ritual language had consequences for those excluded from its use. When a woman was accused of homicide, she would not have sworn the oath of denial herself, even though this inevitably weakened her case. In the only case on record of a woman accused of murder, it was not the defendant but her son who swore the oath. Because he had not been present at the time of the alleged crime, he could not swear that his mother had not committed the deed, but only that he was certain that she had not (Ant. 1.8, 28). This distinction becomes a point of contention for the prosecutor who asks, "How could anyone know certainly what he himself did not witness?"

OATHS AND THE POLIS

In his catalogue Lycurgus omits another category of oaths, one no less important for fifth- and fourth-century Athenians: the oaths of treaty and alliance that bound Athens to other cities and ethnic communities.[102] The language and ritual action of oath taking and oath giving was part of the network of inter-city and international diplomatic relations in the eastern Mediterranean. These oaths differed from oaths within the polis because they required the mediation of the gods of both parties and required oath by representation. That is, the swearers of this type of oath did not swear in their own names or person, but in the name of their city or political community. They were delegated as representatives of the demos and polis to act as part for the whole.

Each city swore through its representatives a form of its own traditional (*nomimos*), local (*epikhōrios*) oath (Thuc. 5.47.8). Such exchanges of oaths could be symmetrical or asymmetrical. Asymmetrical oaths could be sworn between a metropolis and her colony,[103] between Athens and a member of the Athenian League, or between a monarch like Philip II and a group of Greek cities. Symmetrical oaths between cities as equal partners were more common, especially in alliances. The agreements certified by such oaths were symbolized in pictorial representations by *dexiōsis,* the shaking of right hands.

Dexiōsis could be depicted on documents of alliance where a major divinity of one city is shown shaking hands with a major divinity of another.[104] Oaths sworn by representatives of a city, especially symmetrical oaths, usually did not contain self-directed curses.[105] If such an oath were broken, it was the city, not the individual, that suffered penalties.[106]

We have considered the situations where oaths played a role in the political and private life of Athenian citizens. Athenians used the same rituals of oath and oath-sacrifice as did other Greeks. In the classical period, oaths and their self-directed curses were not outmoded survivals of archaic ritual, but part of the living political discourse by which citizens made agreements and competed with each other, and by which they recognized obligations within and between cities.[107] Within the political community the language of oaths provided metaphors of unity. Promissory oaths bound the citizen to the city and identified areas of duty and obligation. The self-directed conditional curse represented the risks of breaking an oath to the community or to another individual, and the curse used by males shows us what citizens especially valued: their land, their agricultural produce, their animals, their children. Children are not listed as objects of affection, but as physical products. In the formulaic curses used by males, wives are symbols of production, identified with the land and with the farmer's domesticated animals, the means of agricultural production.

Oaths also marked important groups within the political community. Athenian men swore oaths in many groups: phratry, deme, tribe, annual jury panel, council, and, as ephebes, in their own age cohort. The Athenian assembly, the collective group of all citizens, called "the people (*dēmos*) of the Athenians," was the only group not distinguished by a public oath. Every meeting of the assembly began with a prayer and a curse, but there was no collective oath sworn by the assembly as a group.[108] The "Old Oligarch" saw this as a flaw in the Athenian political system. He thought that Athenian political discussions and decisions were, as a consequence, not bound by the religious obligations he claimed for oligarchic administrations (Ps. Xen. *Ath. Pol.* 17). But he ignores the ways in which the various oaths of obligation that Athenians *did* swear created a structure in which public speech and collective decision-making could express the collective will of the demos. It is the movement from that deep structure to political decision-making that constitutes the real contribution of the Athenian political system.[109]

Because a democratic *politeia* not only required collective decision-making but also distributed political responsibility to so many individuals at so many levels, more promissory oaths were required in a democracy than in other forms of political organization. Lycurgus even calls oath the "guardian of democracy." This does not mean, however, that the institution went uncontested. Athenians knew how to manipulate assertory oaths for personal and political advantage, and cynicism could breed contempt. Contestants and competitors knew how to use oaths for personal advantage. Oaths were an object of discussion in Greek tragedy, an object for parody in Greek comedy, and an object for criticism by intellectuals.[110] When Medea appeals to the power of oaths and asserts a right to *dexiōsis*, she breaches a boundary between male and female, a boundary sanctified by ritual and protected by custom.[111] Lysistrata can turn an oath designed to initiate war into an oath to end a war; for the Athenian audience the humor of the situation derived from her violation of the same boundary.[112] Xenophanes may have doubted the inviolability of oaths, but Thucydides recognized the consequences of ignoring their power (3.83). The traditional language of offering and receiving oaths was one of the many forms of political discourse recognized at all levels, both inside and outside the immediate polis, a language that marked identity and defined individual and group responsibility, and a language that mediated between competing individuals, competing groups, and competing cities.

ACKNOWLEDGMENTS

The material presented here is part of a larger project on gendered ritual in the ancient Greek polis. For sharpening the issues, I would like to thank audiences at the conference, Democracy Ancient and Modern, and audiences at SUNY Buffalo and Cambridge University. For particular suggestions, I am indebted to Jan Bremmer, Brock Cole, Christopher Faraone, Paul Kimball, Lene Rubinstein, Adele Scafuro, and the referees of the Press.

NOTES

1. Most recently Murray, "Cities of Reason," esp. 19–22.

2. Connor, "Tribes"; Goldhill, "Great Dionysia"; Winkler, "Ephebes' Song."

3. Hesychius, s.v. *Ardettos;* Hirzel, *Der Eid,* 124–25, 132–33. See now Rauh, *Sacred Bonds,* 137–38.

4. See Connor's paper, this volume.

5. Loraux, "Reflections," esp. 35, on πολιτεύεσθαι; Hansen, "*Polis* as City-State," 16–18. For a clear discussion, see Ober, "*Polis* as a Society," 130–33.

6. Loraux, *Children of Athena,* 37–71.

7. Patterson, "Those Athenian Bastards," 61.

8. For the consequences of the rapid expansion of this political community in the fifth century B.C., see Victor Hanson's essay in this volume.

9. For notions of honor and dishonor as they related to citizenship, see Murray, "Solonian Law," 140.

10. Patterson, "*Hai Attikai,*" 50–57.

11. Meiggs-Lewis, *Greek Historical Inscriptions,* I no. 44.4. Patterson, "Neaira," argues persuasively about the many ways in which wives of Athenians shared in the larger community, but her (mis)translation of *hai gunaikes tōn Athenaiōn* as "the Athenian women" (201) proves my point.

12. For oaths in the demes, see *IG* II² 1174, lines 15–17; 1183, lines 11–16: appeal to

Zeus, Apollo, and Demeter, followed by a short curse, and a list of obligations concluding "and to vote whatever seems to me to be most just."

13. Tod, *Greek Historical Inscriptions* II, no. 204; Robert, "Acharnai"; Siewert, "Ephebic Oath."

14. Hirzel, *Der Eid*, 8–9. Plescia, *Oath and Perjury*, 12, attempts to describe the ranking of oaths, but does not understand the relationship of ritual to the whole process of oath-taking.

15. For festivity and commensality, see Schmitt Pantel, *Cité*, 53–105. There is a lack of precision in Greek terminology for sacrificial ritual. Theophrastos, for instance, uses the expression *thuein ton horkon* (*Peri Sumbolaiōn* fr. 97, in Wimmer, *Theophrasti Opera*, 441, line 38; Stobaios *Anthologium* IV.129, line 10).

16. Homer *Iliad* 3.310, 19.267f. Pausanias, 5.24.10, regrets that he forgot to ask about the disposal of the animals used in oath sacrifice at Olympia. The sacrifices performed in the phratry of the Demotionidai were accompanied by an oath, but the meat of other animals sacrificed was distributed to phratry members. See *IG* II² 1237, lines 34–38, 108–13; Hedrick, *Demotionidai*, 8, 10; cf. Dem. 43.82. For a summary of oath sacrifice, see Nilsson, *Geschichte*, 139–40 and Burkert, *Greek Religion*, 251–52.

17. For a possible early example, *IG* I³ 14, line 17.

18. Paus. 3.20.9.

19. Homer *Iliad* 19.267–68.

20. Vivid examples are discussed by Faraone, "Molten Wax," 65–67.

21. Aesch. *Sept.* 44 (G. O. Hutchinson, *Aeschylus. Septem contra Thebas*, edited with introduction and commentary [Oxford: Clarendon Press, 1985], 2, 48–49).

22. Aeschin. 1.114. The mother of the Spartan king Demaratus, forced to swear about her son's paternity, held the inner organs (*splanchna*) of the victim in her hands: Hdt. 6.68. See Plescia, *Oath and Perjury*, 10, for other gestures accompanying oath ritual.

23. F. Sokolowski, *Lois sacrées des cités grecques* (Paris: E. de Boccard, 1969), no. 151 D.5–17; it seems that those swearing had to taste the *splanchna*. For another complex sacrificial procedure, possibly also an oath sacrifice, see ibid., no. 96.35–39 (Mykonos). Witnesses in the Attic phratry of the Demotionidai held on to the altar when they swore their oath; *IG* II² (1237, lines 108–13).

24. Epich. 187 (Kaibel, *CGF* p. 88) for two sheep and an ox (*trittys*). Not all triple sacrifices were oath sacrifices; see *IG* I³ 4, line 5, 78, line 37; I² 845, lines 9–10.

25. Daux, "Thorikos," 153–54, lines 12, 52 (deme calendar); F. Sokolowski, *Lois sacrées de l'Asie mineure* (Paris: E. de Boccard, 1955), no. 13.28 (sacrifice accompanying oath of magistrates about the priesthood of Asclepius at Pergamon, after 133 B.C.). For swearing an oath with only one goat, cf. ibid., no. 30 (Ephesus, sixth century B.C.).

26. Schmitt, *Staatsverträge*, 285 no. 545.9–10; Stengel, *Opferbräuche*, 82n.2.

27. *Iliad* 2.124, 3.73, 4.155; *Od.* 24.483. Cf. Hdt. 7.132, 4.70 (for the middle voice used of both parties to the oath). The expression becomes standard in Greek; see Pollux 21.24.3, 21.32.15, etc.

28. Stengel, *Opferbräuche*, 78–85.

29. Dem. 23.68; scholiast on *Iliad* 19.197, for Athenian practice.

30. Schmitt, *Staatsverträge*, III.285 no. 545. For the imposition of an oath of loyalty to Athens on the Chalkidians, to be sworn by all adult citizens, see IG I³ 39, lines 32–33.

31. Schmitt, *Staatsverträge* III 285 no. 545, lines 9–10.

32. The age of the animal can even indicate precise correlation of normal breeding cycles with season of sacrifice; see Jameson, "Sacrifice and Animal Husbandry," 102–3.

33. The meaning of *teleios* (lexical spelling) has been much debated. Depending on the context, the term can mean "complete," "full-grown," or "perfect." Aristotle does use the term to denote a "perfect" victim (*Fragmenta,* 98 no. 101, lines 18–19), but in sacrificial regulations *teleios* usually denotes age. The problem has now been solved by Rosivach, *Public Sacrifice,* 91–93, 148–53, who shows that in such regulations animal age was calculated by the growth of teeth. *Teleios* describes the victim as having a complete set of teeth, therefore "full-grown."

34. Hsch., s.v. τρίκτειρα, a sacrifice to Enyalios; *Suda,* s.v. τριττύς· θύεται πάντα καὶ ἔνορχα.

35. Jameson, "Sacrifice and Animal Husbandry," 88–91.

36. Rosivach, *Public Sacrifice,* 90–91, argues that it is unlikely that meat was consumed outside the sacrificial system of Attika.

37. Daux, "Le Calendrier de Thorikos," 153 lines 12, for ὁρκωμόσιον offered ἐς εὐθύνας in Metageitnion, and 52, for another ὁρκωμόσιον offered in Skirophorion; Whitehead, *Demes,* 117. For a ὁρκωμόσιον sacrificed in oaths to Zeus Soter in the agora at Pergamon to accompany an oath of magistrates about the priesthood of Asclepius, see Sokolowski (above, n. 25) 13.28, second century B.C., before 133 B.C.

38. Daux, "Le Calendrier de Thorikos," 154, lines 57–60: "I swear to direct the office which I have received by lot according to the decrees by which the office was established." The officials swore by Zeus, Apollo, and Demeter and pronounced a curse of destruction on themselves if they did not abide by the oath (ἐξώλειαν ἐπαρώμενον, line 61).

39. *Dem.* 57.8; Whitehead, *Demes,* 93.

40. [Arist.] *Ath. Pol.* 42.1; Whitehead, *Demes,* 93, 101.

41. *IG* II² 1174, lines 15–18; 1183, lines 11–13, for oath to Zeus, Apollo, and Demeter and an abbreviated curse. For three of the men named in this text appearing on curse tablets, see Whitehead, *Demes,* 112n.130.

42. Dem. 57; Whitehead, *Demes,* 105.

43. [Arist.] *Ath. Pol.* 55.5 (cf. Dem. 23.68). At *Ath. Pol.* 55.5 I follow Kenyon's reading of the papyrus ἐφ' ο[ὑ̑]; see Rhodes, *Commentary* ad loc.

44. Dem. 23.67. The crucial phrase is στὰς ἐπὶ τῶν τομίων.

45. Stengel, *Opferbräuche,* 78–85; Burkert, *Greek Religion,* 251–52. The Greek verbs "to cut" (τέμνειν, ἐκτέμνειν), used by Homer and others to mean figuratively "make an oath sacrifice," when used by Hesiod with masculine nouns for domesticated livestock mean "castrate" (Hes. *Op.* 786, 791).

46. Faraone, "Molten Wax," 65–72, esp. 68n.37.

47. Rudhardt, *Notions fondamentales,* 283–84.

48. Casabona, *Recherches,* 220–25, 323–26.

49. For the formula, see Rudhardt, *Notions fondamentales,* 202. Plescia, *Oath and Perjury,* 83–85, discusses the difficulties of equating English notions of perjury with the Greek terminology for two separate actions: swearing false oaths and breaking oaths once sworn.

50. Described in the inscription from Thorikos as "imprecating utter destruction"; Daux, "Le Calendrier de Thorikos," 154, line 61: ἐξώλειαν ἐπαρώμενον.

51. Strubbe, "'Cursed Be He,'" 51n.35 for the Near Eastern material, and n. 34 for the Greek material.

52. See Plato *Laws* 931b–c for the idea that the most powerful curses were those of parents on their children.

53. Made clear by Scafuro, "Witnessing," 165–70, especially 169: "Although the polis gives no formal civic identity to a woman, nevertheless it is in her interest to establish one. She does this through her father and husband, through their phrateres and fellow demesmen, by their testimony to her betrothal and marriage and to her participation in public cults and by their acceptance of her husband's oaths on various occasions that his children are born from an aste and *enguete*."

54. Dem. 20.107. Watson (*Arae,* 18) argues for "attrition" of the force of curses in the fifth century B.C., but the frequent use of oaths in formal documents right through the Hellenistic period indicates continuing public use of oaths and curses. See J. and L. Robert, "Kybarissos."

55. For this punishment as the object of a curse, see Connor, "Razing of the House," 80–88.

56. Plut. *Vitae decem oratorum* 833e–834b, from Caecilius, who probably quoted from the collection of decrees made by Krateros *FGrH* 342 F5; Harp. s.v. Ἄνδρων). The translation here follows C. W. Fornara, *Archaic Times,* 178–79, no. 151. Cf. Andoc. 1.96, for quotation from the inscribed law against tyranny of 410, where the city releases from pollution the man who kills one who commits treason.

57. In archaic Teos the city regularly performed public curses of those who interfered with the grain trade; Meiggs-Lewis, *Greek Historical Inscriptions,* I no. 30. At Athens those who profaned the mysteries were cursed by the priests and priestesses of the city "according to an old and ancient custom"; Lys. 6.51. Alcibiades was cursed in absentia by all the priests and priestesses; Plut. *Alc.* 22.5 (on which, see Sourvinou-Inwood, "Priestess").

58. For expressions of loyalty to the polis, see the citizen's oath in the new inscription from Teos: Herrmann, "Teos und Abdera," 7, lines 13–22; and Graham, "Abdera and Teos," 55–56.

59. Meiggs-Lewis, *Greek Historical Inscriptions,* I no. 83; Graham and Smith, "An Elipse," 405. Ties to the city take precedence over ties to conspirators against the city; compare the oath of citizenship at Chersonesus: "and if I have conspired with anyone, and if I am bound to anyone by oath or curse, may it be better for both me and for mine if I break the oath, and if I keep it may it be the opposite" (*SIG*³ 360, lines 40–44, trans. Graham and Smith, "An Elipse," 411). For an official oath-cleansing ceremony to erase oaths of loyalty to a previous government, publicly announced in Kenya in 1983, see Kratz, "Power," 654n.12.

60. *Leoc.* 79: τὸ συνέχον τὴν δημοκρατίαν ὅρκος ἐστί. For oath as the guardian of democracy, see Lys. 25.28.

61. Who swore to perform the duties of their office with justice and according to the laws and not to receive bribes, the penalty for which was dedication of a gold statue at Delphi; [Arist.] *Ath. Pol.* 55.5, for content of oath and penalty. On the penalty, see as well Plut. *Solon.* 25.3.

62. The oath varied according to the office; Din. 3.2, 10; Rhodes, *Commentary,* 620–21, for sources.

63. [Arist.] *Ath. Pol.* 22.2; Xen. *Mem.* 1.1.18; Andoc. 1.91; Lys. 31.1; Dem. 24.144. For discussion, see Rhodes, *Boule* 194; *Commentary,* 538.

64. Sworn on the *lithos* at the Stoa Basileus before the decision was given; [Arist.] *Ath. Pol.* 55.5.

65. Lys. 9.15; Din. 3.2.

66. The *boulē* had the responsibility of establishing public offices and of writing out the necessary oaths of office; see [Arist.] *Ath. Pol.* 29.5 and Lys. 20.14.

67. Quoted, sometimes in part, in several speeches: Andoc. 1.91; Dem. 19.179; 20.118; 24.149–51. See Fränkel, "Heliasteneid," and Hansen, *Athenian Democracy,* 18–19, 170, 182–83.

68. A clause in the heliastic oath said, "I will cast my vote in consonance with the laws and with the decrees passed by the Assembly and the Council. But if there is no law [on a point], I will give judgment in consonance with my sense of what is most just" (trans. Hansen, *Athenian Democracy,* 170, 182). On the definition of "law" after 403, see Hansen 170, for a principle of fourth century democracy: "The magistrates are *under* the law, but the jurors, being guardians of the law, though normally required to follow it, can in certain circumstances be regarded as *over* the law." For the distinction between juror and magistrate elsewhere, see Ziehen, "Eid," 2080.

69. Isaeus 5.32, where the contenders in a private arbitration swore oaths, but the private arbitrators did not have to.

70. *IG* II² 1237, lines 108–13; Hedrick, *Demotionidai,* 10.

71. Hdt. 1.29.1; [Arist.] *Ath. Pol.* 7.1; Plut. *Solon* 25.3.

72. . Sworn over adult victims (*kath' hierōn teleiōn*); [Arist.] *Ath. Pol.* 29.2, 5. Preserved in decree of Demophantos, later inscribed on a stele in the Bouleuterion; Andoc. 1.96–98. Lyc. *Leoc.* 124–27 wrongly associates the decree with the events of 403 B.C. The law of 337–336 against tyranny did not require the swearing of an oath; Meritt, "Greek Inscriptions," 355–59.

73. Andoc. 1.90; see Rhodes, *Commentary,* 135, for a list of other cities where communal oaths of all citizens were sworn.

74. Hdt. 6.23: *horkous dous kai dexamenos,* "after giving his oath to them and receiving theirs." Cf. *IG* I² 54, lines 19–20; Arist. *Rh.* 1377a7. The vocabulary of oath giving and oath taking is really far more complicated than this simple summary. See Mirhady, "Non-technical *Pisteis,*" 21–22.

75. Issues of reciprocity in oaths are discussed by Karavites, *Promise-Giving,* 65–66.

76. *Iliad* 22.254, θεοὺς ἐπιδώμεθα.

77. ὅρκους ἑλέσθαι τινός. ὅρκους ἐπελαύνειν τινί. ὅρκους προσάγειν τινί.

78. Hermes in *Hymn. Hom.* 4.274–76, 393–84; Callaway, "Perjury," 22–24.

79. Aristotle understands this quite well when he divides oaths into four categories; *Rh.* 1377a. For the ritual of oath challenge as a social measure, see Herzfeld, "Pride and Perjury."

80. *Rh.* 1377a19–20: οὐκ ἴση πρόκλησις αὕτη τὰσεβεῖ πρὸς εὐσεβῆ.

81. For the performance of oaths and curses as indicators of power, see Kratz, "Genres."

82. On the issue of the limitations of equality at Athens, see Raaflaub and Roberts, this volume.

83. The evidence is not clear on this point; for a recent summary, see Whitehead, *Ideology,* 90–97.

84. Mirhady, "Oath-challenge," 80–82; Todd, "Evidence," 25–28. This explains why a woman, who could not speak in court, directly initiate a suit herself, or offer an oath challenge, could be the object of a curse designed to make her mute when testifying. The procedure is not understood by Gager, *Curse Tablets,* 119–20. For judicial curses directed at women, see Gager, 126–27, nos. 39–40. In both examples the women are listed with a group of men and are therefore not necessarily the principal litigants or the primary targets.

85. Thür, *Schwürgerichtshöfe;* Aristotle has no confidence in evidence obtained under torture, but his criticism is due to reservations about its validity (cowards are likely to say anything to avoid pain) rather than to any feeling that it might be wrong; see *Rh.* 1376b–77a.

86. Gender bias in exclamatory oaths was noticed originally by Ziebarth, *De iureiurando quaestiones,* 10–14. Ziebarth describes exclamatory oaths as oaths "in daily life" (*in vita cotidiana*).

87. Oath of the *gerarai,* administered by the wife of the *basileus;* [Dem.] 59.78, Athens. Elsewhere: Sokolowski (above, n. 23), 65, Andania (where the priests swear their oath before administering a different oath for the priestesses to swear); ibid. 175, Antimacheia; Sokolowski, *Lois sacrées,* no. 127, Athens, imperial period (priestess swears oath on taking office that she will protect the temple furnishings).

88. Creon asks Ismene to take an oath (Soph. *Ant.* 535); Deianeira thinks Lichas swore an oath at her request, but he did not actually do so (Soph. *Trach.* 314–19).

89. Iphigeneia asks Pylades to exchange oaths; he swears by Zeus, she swears by Artemis (Eur. *IA* 735–65).

90. Women were plaintiffs in suits mentioned in Dem. 43.3 (also Isaeus 11.9); Isaeus 3.2; and the case for which Isaeus 7 was delivered (see 7.3). All of these cases concerned property; see Hunter, *Policing Athens,* 53 (where there is no distinction made between the case at hand and an earlier dispute or arbitration mentioned in the speech).

91. Mirhady, "Oath-Challenge," 79–80, 82–83.

92. Lys. 32.13; Diogeiton's daughter offers to swear on her children that her husband had deposited money with Diogeiton. In [Dem.] 47.50 a women whose husband is party to a dispute is said to have sworn at the Palladion about the mistreatment of a freedwoman by the prosecutor. For a woman's sworn testimony at the Delphinion, see Isaeus 12.9. Evidence for women's oaths in legal actions is discussed by Leisi, *Der Zeuge,* 13–15 and Lacey, *Family,* 160, 174.

93. Humphreys, "Kinship Patterns."

94. Dem. 29.26, 33, 56; 39.3–4; 40.2,10–11; 55.27; Isaeus 12.9. See Hunter, *Policing Athens,* 36.

95. Isaeus 12.9: "Who was more likely to know this than she?" Arist. *Rh.* 1398b, for the belief that women can be counted on to identify the fathers of their children.

96. Dem. 29.26, where Demosthenes says that at an earlier stage of the dispute with Aphobos his mother was willing to swear on her children that Milyas was not a slave, as Aphobos claimed, but a freedman manumitted by her husband on his deathbed. At Dem. 29.33 Demosthenes' mother was willing to swear on her children that Aphobos had received her dowry in accordance with her husband's will. In the earlier arbitration Demosthenes challenged Aphobos to swear on his daughter that he denied admitting that Milyas was a free man.

97. Cf. Isaeus 12.9 for another mother and an offer to swear an oath. The fact that a

woman could not issue a challenge for an oath of assertion or denial does not mean that a female could not request a promissory oath. The nurse in Euripides' *Hippolytus* asked Hippolytus for an oath he did not keep; Eur. *Hipp.* 610, 612, 657.

98. Dem. 39.3; 40.10–11; with comments by Carey and Reid, *Demosthenes,* 170–71. Plangon swore before an arbitrator in the Delphinion. As Todd, "Evidence," 35 points out, because Mantias himself had challenged Plangon to swear, he could not deny her testimony.

99. Harrison, *Law,* II.99.

100. Antiphon 5.88; Dem. 23.67–68.

101. Variations of the Homeric formula *horkia pista tamein* (*Iliad* 2.124, etc.) appear in early treaties from Chios (Schwyzer 1960, 687d), Kyzikos (ibid., 732b.8), and Halikarnassos (*SIG*[3] 45, line 44). Casabona, *Recherches,* 214, stresses the public character of the oaths involved.

102. Collected in Bengston and Schmitt, *Staatsverträge,* II–III.

103. Meiggs-Lewis, *Greek Historical Inscriptions,* I, no. 20, between Locris and her colony at Naupaktos, 500–470 B.C.

104. Herman, *Friendship,* 45ff.

105. The alliance between Philip II and the Chalcidians (357–356 B.C.) includes a curse with short formula; Bengtson, *Staatsverträge,* II.308.

106. Thucydides suggests that the Spartans suffered reversals in the Archidamian War because they had violated their oath of alliance with Plataea; 7.18.2 (cf. 2.71.2–3, 74.2). See also Mikalson, *Honor,* 262n.62; Schmidt, "Fluch und Frevel."

107. Siewert, *Eid,* 21 for oaths on Athenian documents of the fifth and fourth centuries B.C.

108. The size of the ekklesia could not have been an issue. All Athenians swore the oath against tyranny, by tribes and demes, over adult victims, before the Dionysia in 410 B.C.; Andoc. 1. 97–98. For the issue of voting by tribal groups, see Stanton and Bicknell, "Voting."

109. In his attempt to privilege political action, Murray, "Cities of Reason," 19, puts this the wrong way around.

110. Mirhady, "Non-Technical *Pisteis,*" 8, suggests that oaths were considered old-fashioned by Aristotle's day.

111. Burnett, "Revenge"; Rickert, "*Akrasia*"; Boedeker, "Vanity."

112. Ar. *Lys.* 181–239; Casabona, *Recherches,* 323–26.

DEMOCRATIC CONTRADICTIONS AND THE SYNOPTIC
ILLUSION OF EURIPIDES' *ION*

Carol Dougherty

IN BOOK FIVE (66) of his *Histories,* Herodotus describes the famous Cleisthenic reforms of the Athenian political system in 508–507 B.C. as follows: "He [Cleisthenes] then changed the Athenians from four to ten tribes, and he replaced the old names—previously the tribes had been named after the sons of Ion: Geleon, Aegicores, Argades, and Hoples—and discovered instead the names of native heroes, except Ajax, whom he included even though a foreigner since he was a neighbor and an ally." As Herodotus acknowledges more explicitly a little later in his history, Cleisthenes' restructuring of the Athenian tribal system—shifting the basis for political access from one of aristocratic birthright to a system based on locality—is often considered the "founding moment" of Athenian democracy.[1] In fact, the conference from which these papers emerge celebrates the twenty-five hundredth anniversary of the Cleisthenic reforms and the revolution that made them possible as the focal point for our own discussions of democracy ancient and modern. Foundation tales of all kinds tend to respond to the needs of the present as much, if not more, than they accurately record the past, and Herodotus' account of Cleisthenes' political restructuring represents and encodes a fundamental shift in the way Athenians defined themselves as citizens in the fifth century.[2] Furthermore, as this paper suggests, Cleisthenes' reforms are very much implicated in the continuing debate over Athens' origins—the ideology of Ionia versus that of autochthony—a debate that both structures Athenian civic identity and provides the narrative and metaphoric framework for imagining the simultaneous development of Athenian democracy and empire.

"All communities," Benedict Anderson claims in his book on the origins and spread of nationalism, "larger than primordial villages of face-to-face contact (and perhaps even these) are imagined."[3] In other words, the sense of community or civic identity that binds together disparate individuals into a coherent group is not inherited but is constructed, fashioned with the help of preexisting rituals, religious systems, and patterns of belief. Anderson contends that we must understand nationalism "not with self-consciously held political ideologies, but with the larger cultural systems that preceded it, out of which—as well as against which—it came into being."[4] I would argue that much of Anderson's discussion of how a sense of nationalism emerges in modern societies, espe-cially the ways in which it borrows from preexisting cultural systems and mythologies, applies equally well to the construction of a sense of civic iden-tity in Athens in the fifth century B.C. Athens' success in imagining itself as a democratic state coincides, as many have noted, with its development as an im-perial power: both civic identities are reflected in and promoted by the com-peting stories of Athens' origins. One story claims that the Athenians are related to the Greeks of Ionia, and contained within the larger concept of this Ionian ideology is the framework for setting the terms for Athens' role as head of an empire. Yet another version, however, celebrates the Athenians as continuous inhabitants of Attica—self-sufficient, born from the very earth—and within the topos of autochthony lies the rationale for the emergence of a democratic form of government. As we can see from Herodotus' account of the Cleisthenic re-forms, the story of the foundations of Athenian democracy must confront and reconcile both these narratives of Athens' past.

This paper, then, will explore the larger parameters of these competing ide-ologies—their mythologies and their metaphors—to see how they operate to help Athenians structure their sense of what it means to be Athenian. We will see that in spite of the Cleisthenic reforms, Ionian connections fail to disappear completely; in fact, a sense of renewed Ionian interest—the repurification of Delos, the rebuilding of the altar to Apollo Patrōos, Euripides' *Ion*—appears to resurface in the last quarter of the fifth century. Euripides' *Ion,* in fact, explic-itly addresses the tensions between democracy and empire, autochthony and Ionia, and a close look at the play in the final sections of this paper will suggest that Euripides uses the interpretative space of Attic theater to imagine a new world in which Athenians emerge as both autochthonous and Ionian, simulta-neously democratic and imperial.

But first, a word about methodology. The competing versions of Athens' civic origins and of the foundations of its political system structure the Athenians' narratives both as a set of oppositions (democracy vs. tyranny; autochthony vs. colonization; native Athenian vs. Ionian identity) and as a series of analogies (autochthony and democracy; democracy and empire). Faced with this over-lapping and conflicting evidence, we might be tempted to normalize these nar-ratives in order to create a unified theory of the origins of democracy and its relationship to Athenian civic identity. Certainly, one way to reconcile these competing accounts is to look to history, and I will begin by sketching the story of Athens' connections to Ionia and the city's subsequent self-promotion as au-tochthonous. But while it is instructive to recognize the chronological devel-opment of these events, the narratives that describe them take on explanatory force outside the specific historical context from which they emerged. For this reason, it is equally valuable to read these cultural narratives in all their incon-sistencies and repetitions. To help explain why, I draw on some of Pierre Bour-dieu's observations about what he calls the synoptic illusion.

In *Outline of a Theory of Practice,* Bourdieu remarks that in questioning native informants (a luxury classicists will never have) about the nature of a classificatory system such as the Berber calendar, he acquires a mixture of knowledges drawn from a multiplicity of traditions. As soon as he tries to draw up an inclusive calendar that would combine the most commonly attested features and account for prominent variants, he is confronted with a difficulty: identical periods of time are often given different names or vice versa, identical names cover variable time periods, situated at different parts of the year depending on region, tribe, village, or informant. The same informant may even provide different names for the same time of the year at different points in the interview— one Berber, one drawn from the Islamic tradition. As a result, competing systems of opposition will emerge depending on the nature of the event in question, the social status of the agent, and the precision with which the event is described.[5] Bourdieu thus warns us: "There is a great temptation to amass and collate these different productions in order to construct a lacuna-free, contradiction-free whole, a sort of unwritten score of which all the calendars derived from informants are then regarded as imperfect, impoverished performances. The problem is that the calendar cannot be understood unless it is set down on paper, and that it is impossible to understand how it works unless one fully realizes that it exists only on paper."[6]

This is our challenge, too—to read the multiplicity of narratives that represent Athenians as Athenians in such a way that we preserve their contradictions, for they provide us with a view that transcends historical developments and individual experience. As Bourdieu suggests, we need the big picture to help us understand the conflicting parts of the story, but we must also remember that no matter how useful or persuasive, this synoptic view is no more real or "true" than any one of the individual stories. When Cleisthenes replaced the Ionian tribal system with one based on native heroes, Athens' ideological identification with Ionia does not completely disappear. The continued prominence of the phratries and of festivals like the Apatouria in Athenian civic life are proof that Ionian influence endured in spite of formal systems that organized citizens into demes and trittyes based not on birth but on locality. As with the contemporary Berber calendar, so too Athenians of the fifth century B.C. identified themselves differently at different times, and these multiple identities were reflected in and negotiated through the stories of their civic origins.[7] The diachronic approach helps us identify how these different identities emerged over time; the synchronic approach sheds light on how these competing identities continue to articulate the parameters of Athenian civic identity.

While classicists may not have native informants to interview, we do have a rich tradition of contemporary political discourse in the form of drama and oratory that can be interrogated and investigated in much the same way, and thus the principles of contradiction and synthesis that Bourdieu articulates for the Berber calendar can provide a useful supplement to the more traditional, historical approach to understanding fifth-century Athenian sources as well. Furthermore, since our "native informants" are in fact highly stylized literary products, we must also acknowledge their literary qualities—their tropes, metaphors, and narrative patterns.[8] For these reasons, in order to focus on the political issues that Athens' originary tales continue to articulate, my project is twofold. I begin by sketching briefly the ideologies of Ionia and autochthony in their historical context in order to determine what each contributes to a sense of Athenian civic identity. Then I turn to Euripides to see what the synoptic view adds to the picture.

IONIA

At the beginning of the sixth century, Solon boasts that Athens is "the oldest land of Ionia" (Fr. 4a West, *Iambi* II), and while it is unclear whether Solon was specifically referring to the Attic colonization of Ionia, we can be fairly certain that at least by 500 B.C., Athenians and Ionians alike credited the Athenians with the settlement of Ionia.[9] Thucydides tells us that while the Peloponnesians founded most of the colonies in Italy and Sicily, and some in other parts of Hellas, "the Athenians colonized Ionia and most of the islands" (1.12). And later on in book 1, he attributes the founding of the Delian League to the tradition of Attic colonization of Ionia.[10] Pherecydes may have been the first to celebrate Athens as the mother city of Ionia; according to Strabo, "he [Pherecydes] says that Androclus, the legitimate son of Codrus the king of Athens, was the leader of the Ionian colonization movement . . . and that he became the founder of Ephesus" (14.1.3). Pausanias gives a more detailed version. He begins by explaining that the land of Achaea used to be called Aegialus, and when Xuthus was expelled from Thessaly he went to Athens, where he married the daughter of Erechtheus and had two sons, Achaeus and Ion. When King Erechtheus died, Xuthus was asked to choose the king's successor, but when he chose Cecrops he was expelled by the rest of Erechtheus' sons. Xuthus reached Aegialus where he died; his son Achaeus went to Thessaly, and Ion became king of the Aegialians (who were then called after him the Aegialian Ionians). Pausanias then tells how the Dorians invaded Argos and Lacedaemon and expelled the Achaeans, who subsequently arrived in Aegialus and in turn expelled the Ionians. The Ionians then fled to Athens, where they were received by King Melanthus. A few years later, Medon and Neleus, the eldest sons of Codrus, quarreled over the throne. Neleus refused to let Medon rule him since he was lame, and so they consulted the Delphic oracle. There the Pythia told them that Medon should rule, and Neleus and the other sons of Codrus set out to settle Ionia (7.1–7.2).

The Athenian colonization of Ionia was invoked by Athenians and Ionians alike. Herodotus explains that Aristagoras of Miletus used this colonial connection to persuade the Athenians to help defend the Ionians against the Persians. He argued that "the Milesians were Athenian colonists and since the Athenians were very powerful, they should certainly protect the Milesians" (5.97). Later on in his *Histories,* Herodotus has Themistocles appeal to the Ionians fighting on the Persian side to defect on the grounds that they would be fighting against their own. In his famous message inscribed on the rocks, Themistocles argues, "Ionian men, you do not deal justly in making war on us your fathers and in enslaving Greece" (8.22.2).

Herodotus also gives us a slightly different, noncolonial version of the close relationship between Athenians and Ionians: he says that originally the Athenians were themselves Pelasgians and called Cranai. "But when Cecrops was king, they were called Cecropidae, and then when Erectheus inherited the rule, they changed their name again, to Athenians; and when Ion, the son of Xuthus, became their commander-in-chief, they were called, after him, Ionians" (8.44). Ion is acknowledged as the eponymous father of the Ionian race, and his sons gave their names to the four tribes that determined Athenian citizenship until the time that Cleisthenes replaced them with the ten tribes named for local heroes.

In addition to these mythic connections, Athenians shared many cultural practices with the Ionians.[11] According to Thucydides, it was just recently that Athenians stopped wearing Ionian dress. "Indeed it has not been long since the elder men of the prosperous families, who had luxurious tastes, gave up wearing linen undergarments and tying their hair behind their heads in a knot fastened with a clasp of golden grasshoppers; the same fashions spread then to the elders of Ionia, on account of kinship, and lasted there for some time" (1.6.3).[12] Furthermore, Athenians and other Ionians participated in common festivals such as the Apatouria, which celebrated Apollo Patrōos as their common ancestor.[13] Herodotus explains that those that consider themselves the bluest-blooded (*gennaiotatoi*) Ionians are those who came from the prytaneum of Athens (1.146). All, he continues, are Ionians who came from Athens and who, like the Athenians, celebrate the Apatouria (1.147). Indeed it seems clear that there was close contact and mutual borrowing between Athens and Ionia with respect to social and religious customs, names of calendar months, festivals, dialect, dress, and cults.[14]

But what exactly does all this mean? It is not necessary to read as historical fact the myths that describe the Athenian colonization of Ionia in order to appreciate the significance of the connection between Athens and Ionia that they preserve. Although the Ionians certainly get a good deal of bad press in the fifth century (especially in comparison with the supposedly stronger, more morally upright Dorians), Athens, in its formative stages as an emergent polis, drew heavily on Ionia to define itself as a city in very basic ways: the tribes that organize its citizenship and the festivals that regulate the city's religious life.[15] As W. R. Connor has suggested, in the time before the Persian invasion, Ionians were extremely prosperous, both economically and intellectually: "When

viewed in this light, the power and appeal of Ionian civilization are evident. Ionian identity, moveover, provided a comprehensive approach to the world, a set
of attitudes that encompassed everything from style to wealth and social distinction, to politics and theology. It was in effect, an ideology, and a powerful
one."[16]

In addition to providing "a comprehensive approach to the world" and organizing basic structures of civic life in Athens, this Ionian ideology was extremely helpful in constructing the empire. In the subtle but inevitable shift
from Delian League to Athenian Empire, the myths and rhetoric of Athens' relationship to Ionia, in particular its role as mother city, prove powerful imaginative tools. It provided the model whereby Athens treated its Ionian allies as
colonies, demanding that they offer panoplies and sacrifices annually· at the
Panathenaic games.[17] This Ionian ideology was also, however, an aristocratic
ideology, and the growing dissatisfaction with aristocratic rule coupled with the
increasing power and politicization of the people may help explain why Ionian
appeal waned in the face of Persian opposition at the beginning of the fifth century.[18] Whatever the reasons, this ideological shift away from Ionia made room
for a competing narrative that described Athens' origins as completely local and
ultimately more democratic.[19]

AUTOCHTHONY

Autochthony as an Athenian myth of origins surfaces both in art and literature
in the fifth century B.C., and its appearance is surely prompted by the political
and imperial developments of the time.[20] Since all citizens are born equally
from the earth, all have equal access to political power, and Athenian public discourse linked democracy explicitly to autochthony. This rhetorical stance thus
suppressed Athens' period of tyrants and in its place represented Athens as a
progressive, egalitarian city from birth.[21] Furthermore, as V. Rosivach has recently argued, once the Athenians begin to describe themselves as continuous
inhabitants of their land, their preexisting chthonic origins, in particular those
of the early king Erechtheus, take on new value and begin to function as a
metaphor for their continuous occupation of Attica.[22] Whether we read the motivation for this invention as a response to the myths of Dorian invasion or as
an alternative to the Ionian connection, the word *autochthōn* does come to describe Athenians as native inhabitants of the land.[23]

Rosivach shows that the compound *autochthōn* was invented to describe
people who live in their homeland forever, whether they are literally born from
the earth or not. More specifically, its meaning is articulated in contrast with the
word for "foreigner," *epēlus*.[24] Lysias uses this native/foreigner opposition to
praise the Athenians in his funeral oration. First of all, he points out, since they
are born from the earth, Athenians are not immigrants, nor have they colonized
other peoples' lands: "They had not been collected, like many, from every quar-

ter, and had not settled in a foreign land after driving out others" (17). These are also the terms with which Praxithea praises Athens in her speech from the lost Euripidean play, the *Erechtheus*. She boasts: "I could not have had a better city than this; first our people were not brought in from outside, but rather we are born autochthonous. Other cities are divided as if by throws of the dice, while others are imported from other cities. Whoever moves from one city to another is like a peg badly fixed on wood; in name he is a citizen, but not in his actions."[25] Implicit in this dialectic is the advantageous comparison of autochthony with the problematic nature of colonial origins that by definition entail civil war, imperialism, and the potential for conflict.[26]

Not just anticolonial, the ideology of autochthony describes Athens' local origins as specifically non-Ionian even though, as we have seen historically, Athenian-Ionian connections remain strong, the two cultures bound together by common dialect, ritual, and ancestry. A key theme in Cleisthenes' democratic reforms of 508 was to refound Athens' political identity on its own ground, as non-Ionian. Named for the early Athenian kings, the new tribes define Athenian citizenship in terms of local heroes; the ideology of autochthony establishes this new democratic identity as self-sufficient and not, therefore, dependent on Ionia.[27] In the fifth century, this distancing of Athens from Ionia downplays its imperialist role in Ionia as well. As Lysias points out (2.17–18), Athenians live a clean life: since they did not come from anywhere else, they did not displace any previous occupants of Attica. Athens' autochthonous origins thus help define democracy as anti-Ionian, both coming and going—as both anti-immigrant and anti-imperialist.[28]

Plato, too, suggested that a heterogeneous population is somehow more easily disposed to tyranny or oligarchy—the inherent differences among peoples leads to a diverse and hierarchical politics. Consider, for example, the following passage from the *Menexenus:* "Other states [i.e., other than Athens] are composed of different people from all over, so that their constitutions also are heterogeneous, both tyrannies and oligarchies, some of them considering one another as slaves, others as masters" (238e).[29] By extension, then, it is precisely the sameness inherent in autochthony (since all citizens are equally born from the earth) that produces fair and just forms of government, specifically democracy.[30]

While the myth of autochthony certainly emphasizes the equality of Athenian citizens, it just as persuasively justifies their nobility. To be earthborn means to be well-born. As Lysias argues, "Being born nobly (i.e., from the earth) and knowing comparable things, our ancestors accomplished many noble and remarkable things" (2.20).[31] In this context, the ideology of autochthony helps justify Athens' highly exclusive citizenship laws and is articulated in opposition to peoples of mixed origins.[32]

Rosivach has already suggested that the concept of being earthborn, mythologically embodied in the serpentine Athenians kings Erechtheus and Cecrops, functions as a metaphor or symbol for Athenian autochthony.[33] Taking the generative component of the compound "earthborn" literally, we find within fifth-century political discourse an additional set of metaphors that describe the relation of an Athenian citizen to his country as that of a son to his mother (or nurse).[34] Returning to the *Menexenus,* the argument continues by claiming that since all Athenians are born from one mother, the Attic soil, they are all brothers: "But we and our people, on the contrary, all born as brothers to a single mother, consider ourselves deserving to be neither the slaves of one another nor the masters; rather our equal birth (*isogonia*) forces us to seek equality of law (*isonomia*) according to the law, and to yield to one another not at all except in reputation for virtue and thought" (238e–239a). If all Athenians are born from the same mother, they are all brothers to each other, and it is this image of fraternal equality that dominates public discourse of the fifth and fourth centuries and links authochthony to democracy.[35] As a rhetorical *topos,* the image of citizen-brothers, with their collective and inherently equal origins, guarantees their political equality as well.[36]

As this brief overview shows, both the Ionian and autochthony myths join the founding of democracy and empire together with the origins of Athens itself. Furthermore, both tales—each in its own historical context—embed a series of competing and complementary themes that structure Athenian political discourse and describe the city's past. As in the Berber calendar, so in Athenian civic mythology, different legends emphasize different issues and so will be told at different times and in different contexts. I want to suggest that in the *Ion,* however, Euripides reconciles many of these contradictory democratic themes, and he does so precisely by restaging Athens' foundation. In particular, by fusing Athens' autochthonous origins with its Ionian connections, Euripides creates what Bourdieu might call "the synoptic illusion" of an Athenian democratic empire.

EURIPIDES' *ION*

Euripides' *Ion,* produced sometime in the last quarter of the fifth century B.C., opens with a prologue by Hermes who previews the action of the play for the audience.[37] First he explains what has already happened: Apollo raped Creusa, daughter of Erechtheus, in a cave beside the long cliffs of Athens. Fearing her parents' reaction, she hid her pregnancy and exposed the child. Creusa subsequently was married to Xuthus, a foreign ally from Achaea, but they have no children and so have come to Delphi to consult Apollo about their infertility. Hermes explains that meanwhile Apollo has been looking out for the son born to him by Creusa—the child was saved and now lives as a slave to the god at his temple at Delphi. He then goes on to predict the future: the boy will be called Ion, and he will become the founder of the Asian land.

As Nicole Loraux and others have pointed out, Euripides' *Ion* addresses autochthony and Ionian kinship as two competing representations of Athenian civic identity.[38] As elsewhere in Athenian public discourse, the Ionian colonization myth helps legitimate Athenian imperialism while the autochthony story sets the terms for Athenian citizenship as highly exclusive and endogamous. Loraux's discussion of the *Ion* focuses on Creusa as the sole survivor of Athens' founding family; she suggests that she functions as a kind of *epiklēros* or heiress. As the daughter of Erechtheus, king of Athens, her filial obligations to preserve her father's household merge with the needs of the city. Consequently, her dowry is autochthony, legitimacy, and Athenian political identity.[39]

I want to elaborate on Loraux's reading of the play by showing that in addition to using the language of legal relationships and the rhetoric of the funeral oration, Euripides draws on the poetics of colonization to rewrite Athens' autochthonous origins.[40] For it is none other than Apollo, both as patron deity of colonization and in his role as Patrōos, co-ancestor of Athenians and Ionians, who rapes the autochthonous princess in this play and thereby physically unites Athens' Ionian imperial identity with its democratic autochthonous one. Traditionally in Athenian mythology, Xuthus is Ion's father, and the fact that Euripides makes Ion Apollo's son here and sets the play at Delphi (the starting point for all colonial expeditions) suggests that we consider the *Ion* in light of the themes and strategies of city foundation literature.[41]

Pierre Lévêque and Pierre Vidal-Naquet have already suggested that Cleisthenes was influenced by the themes and strategies of the archaic colonial movement when he set about refounding Athens as a democracy.[42] Cleisthenes' position as a political outsider, emblematized by the Alcmaeonid curse, is consonant with the marginal status of the political exiles and murderers who are often said to found colonies in the archaic period. Syracuse, Acarnania, and Rhodes all tell stories of their city-founders as murderers sent into permanent exile by the Delphic oracle; still other cities claim to be founded by political exiles.[43] Furthermore, before embarking on colonial expeditions, city founders first consulted the Delphic oracle, and many colonial tales record these oracles as part of a city's founding tradition.[44] Cleisthenes, too, consulted Delphi when he decided to reorganize the Athenian tribal structure. [Aristotle] in *Athenaiōn Politeia* tells us that he submitted one hundred names of native Athenian heroes to the Pythia for her approval and that she chose the ten that gave their names to the new tribes.[45] Furthermore, the tribal heroes are called *archēgetai,* the specific title of a colonial founder as well as the cult title of Apollo in his role as city founder, and the eponymous heroes' statues, like the tombs of city founders, are centrally located in the agora.[46] To imbue his actions with revolutionary meaning, Cleisthenes borrows details from the colonial narrative and appropriates many of the gestures of a city founder.

Colonial ideology drives the plot of Euripides' *Ion* as well. Colonial narratives usually describe the founding of a city in terms of a crisis, personal or civic, that prompts the consultation of Apollo's oracle at Delphi. Myscellus of

Rhype (like Xuthus and Creusa) wanted to know if he would have children and was told instead to found a colony: "Myscellus, short-in-the-back, Apollo the far-darter loves you and will give you offspring. But first he commands this for you, that you make your home in mighty Croton among the fair ploughland" (Diod. 8.17.1). This conflation of agricultural and human fertility is in fact common to colonial discourse and thus the question Ion asks Creusa upon her arrival at Delphi—"Have you come on account of fruit of the earth, or children?" (303)—sets the scene for the act of civic foundation that will follow.

This tripartite nexus of civic, human, and agricultural production appears most prominently in another common version of the colonial tale, one that tells the story of city foundations as the marriage or rape of a young girl by an Olympian deity. The nymph then gives her name or the name of her offspring to the new city. Zeus, for example, rapes a local girl named Thalia (or Aetna) in Aeschylus' play the *Aetnaeae,* and from this act of sexual conquest are born twin boys and a new city named after the nymph, Aetna.[47] This narrative pattern obviously depends on the tendency to associate women with elements of nature, particularly with the land itself; it disguises the imperial flavor of military and political domination and figures it instead as erotic conquest.[48]

Apollo's rape of Creusa in the *Ion* should be read in light of this particular narrative tradition. In fact, the plot of the *Ion* is similar in several respects to the version of Cyrene's foundation that Pindar tells in *Pythian* 9 as the marriage of Delphic Apollo, the patron deity of colonization, and a young eponymous nymph Cyrene: hence it is worth looking briefly at the poem. *Pythian* 9 represents the founding of Cyrene as a rape or a marriage, casting Apollo in the dual role as bridegroom and colonial deity, with the nymph Cyrene as symbol of the land—she gives it her name. The poem begins with a transition that moves seamlessly from Pindar's praise of the victor's home city, Cyrene, to its eponymous nymph, Cyrene, "whom the long-haired son of Leto once took from the valleys of Pelion which echo in the wind, and he brought the wild maiden in a golden chariot and made her mistress there and caused her to live in the lovely, flourishing third root of the many-flocked and much-fruited land" (5–8).

Later in the poem Pindar uses a harsh agricultural metaphor to characterize this marriage as a kind of rape when Apollo asks if he can "cut down the honeyed flower from her bed."[49] Scholars have flinched at the crudeness of this phrase, but they fail to recognize that it is the colonial context of this poem that generates this particular metaphor. The violence of marriage, as represented through this agricultural image, evokes the violence of colonization as well—violence to the landscape and to the native populations.[50] Pindar's use of agricultural imagery here to describe the sexual deflowering of Cyrene is meant to remind the listener that this is no ordinary marriage, but one that represents a greater civilizing project—the colonization of a Greek city in Libya. A successful marriage is measured in terms of legitimate children, and the prosperity of a colonial settlement similarly depends on the colonists' ability to transform the virgin territory into a productive landscape—a city.

Similar strategies are at work in the *Ion* as well. Apollo's rape of Creusa is described several times in the play, each time more graphically and in more detail. Finally in her powerful and emotional monody, she accuses the god himself of rape: "You came to me, your hair radiating with gold, when I was gathering the yellow flowers in the folds of my robe, the flowers that bloomed like golden suns. You caught the white wrists of my hands and drew me screaming 'mother, mother' to the bed in the cave. Divine seducer, you drew me there and shamelessly you worked the pleasure of Cypris. And I, poor me, bore you a son, and in fear of my mother I cast him upon your bed, upon the wretched couch where wretchedly you seduced me, a miserable girl. Poor, poor me!" (887–902) Like the rape of Cyrene, this is clearly an act of violence—Apollo takes her by force, his hand on her wrist, the language calling to mind the convention in vase-painting which characterizes marriage as a kind of rape.[51] Creusa's cries of "mother" remind us of Persephone's similarly ineffectual cries as the flowers she is picking recall Persephone's similar act, symbolic of her own imminent defloration.[52] Like the rape of Cyrene, this is a founding act: it will produce a son who will give his name to the Ionian people and whose own sons will colonize Asia Minor in the name of the Athenians. And like the rape of Cyrene, the agent of this founding rape is Delphic Apollo; his direct participation here stands in for the important role the Delphic oracle traditionally plays both in the colonial movement itself and in the narratives that record it. Of course the *Ion* is not just another colonial legend—this is Athens, after all—and that is what makes it so interesting.

The rape of Creusa in the *Ion* sets off a complicated narrative scenario, one that uses the concepts of mother and fatherhood metaphorically to weave together the threads of autochthony and Ionian colonization into a single network of family relationships. Creusa, while not an eponymous nymph like Cyrene, functions metonymically in the play as the symbol of Athenian autochthony. As the only surviving heir, daughter of the noble Erechtheid family, she represents the legitimate transfer of citizenship and political power within the family structure, a role traditionally embodied by the legitimate wife and mother. But even more significant, her character brings motherhood as metaphor for autochthony to the stage and enacts the dialectic between legitimate and adoptive parent that operates prominently in Athenian political discourse. In the *Menexenus,* Plato explains that to be Athenian is not to be of immigrant stock, but to be "autochthonous, dwelling and living in their own true fatherland; and nursed not by a stepmother, as others are, but by that mother country in which they live. She bore them, reared them, and receives them even now, when dead they lie in their own places" (237b–c). Similarly Lysias boasts that to be autochthonous is to possess the same mother and fatherland, and Lycurgus in his speech against Leocrates uses family language to describe one's relationship to one's country:

he claims that men do not hold foster parents as dear as their own fathers and so have analogous feelings about adopted countries.[53]

Plato's argument in the *Menexenus* proceeds to develop the analogy of Athens as mother in even closer detail. Other lands have produced monsters, but Athenian land sent forth citizens: "And in this way it is clear whether a woman is truly a mother or not: [she is not] unless she has springs of nourishment for her child, which, both our land and our mother, provide as sufficient proof that she brought forth men; for at that time she was the first and only to produce as human nourishment the fruit of wheat and barley, by which the race of humankind is most beautifully and well nourished, since, in truth, she herself gave birth to this creature" (237e–238a).[54] The Athenian land is thus represented as the only true mother; the authenticity and political legitimacy of other cities is called into question insofar as they are mere stepmothers or adopted parents. I want to suggest that one way to read Creusa's role in the *Ion* is as a narrative enactment of this metaphorical complex. Her maternal identity in this play—in all its permutations: unwed mother, barren mother, stepmother, and finally legitimate mother—dramatizes the range of possible relationships between citizen and country. The integrity of Creusa as metaphor for autochthony is then violated by the colonial and Ionian themes embodied in Apollo Patrōos and Delphi. The colonial rape problematizes Creusa's position as legitimate autochthonous mother and sets the action of the play in motion.

When we first meet Creusa, she is married but unable to produce children. Unsure about the fate of the child she bore as an unmarried girl to Apollo and then exposed, Creusa now comes to Delphi with her foreign husband in search of more children. Although they have been trying for a long time, Creusa explains to Ion, she and Xuthus have been unable to produce a child (304), and Euripides offers her own infertility as a sign of the inadequacy of autochthony as an aetiological myth.[55] Within Athenian mythology, children of the earth are famous for their lack of offspring—Cecrops, Cranaus, Amphictyon all died childless—and the narrative problem becomes how to continue to perpetuate the race of autochthonous peoples. Hephaestus' famous frustrated sexual encounter with Athena which produced Erichthonius from the earth is one way to address the difficulties of moving from an autochthonous origin myth to the more traditional manner of sexual reproduction, but in this play Euripides suggests that this was just a temporary solution—it only lasted one generation since Erechtheus, Erichthonius' son, also died without a male heir. And so he offers the Apollo and Creusa story as another answer. What is missing from this autochthony narrative, he proposes, is the father—and we will return to that problem, but first let us continue with Creusa's identities as mother.

When Xuthus first claims Ion as his son, Creusa is cast temporarily in the role of stepmother, and it is precisely this family configuration that raises for Ion the very real problems of his qualifications for citizenship in Athens. He points out to Xuthus that if Creusa is not his real mother, then in Athens, as the bastard son of a foreigner, he will not be accepted: "They say that those famous, au-tochthonous (*tas autochthonas kleinas*) Athenians are not a race that has come from elsewhere (*epeisakton genos*), and there I will enter with two strikes against me, being born from a foreign father (*patros t'epaktou*) and being a bas-tard (*nothagenēs*)" (589–92). Thus he prays to discover his mother and to find that she is Athenian in order that he might enjoy the right of free speech (673–5).[56] Creusa as stepmother defines Ion as an illegitimate son—not the rightful heir to the land, but a hostile usurper who will deprive the native sons of their patrimony.[57]

The play's conclusion then reverses these roles and reestablishes Creusa as the legitimate mother and symbol of Athenian land.[58] Xuthus is revealed as the adoptive father, a role that mirrors his status as inhabitant of an adopted coun-try. When Creusa describes her husband to Ion, she explains that he is not a citizen, but that he comes from another land (290). In fact, Xuthus' own words betray his nonautochthonous roots; in response to Ion's claim to be born from the earth, he exclaims increduously: "The earth does not bear children" (542). Finally at the end of the play, Euripides unites the family and reveals Apollo, colonial god and Ionian god, as the progenitor who can make Athenian au-tochthony work.

Let us focus now on Apollo's role as the father in this family drama, for the Apollo who sires Ion is, in fact, the same Apollo who functions as co-ancestor of all Athenians and Ionians, Apollo Patrōos.[59] The cult of Apollo Patrōos is one that celebrates the relations between Athenians and Ionians in family terms. Apollo is the mythical ancestor of both peoples, and members of this Athen-ian/Ionian family are called brothers, organized into phratries.[60] Each year at his festival, the Apatouria, future Athenian citizens are registered at birth and again on coming of age. In spite of the Cleisthenic reforms, the phratries and Ionian kinship ties continue to play an important role in restricting Athenian cit-izenship to free, native males born (at the time of Pericles' citizenship law) of two Athenian parents. In the *Euthydemus*, Plato explains that the Athenians and the Ionians worship Apollo as Patrōos precisely because Ion is born of Apollo and Creusa (*alla Apollōn Patrōos dia tēn tou Ionos genesin*, 302c–d). Thus, just as Creusa functions as symbol of Athenian civic motherhood, Apollo is father to Athenians and Ionians alike, and I want to suggest that Euripides literalizes the metaphor built into this cult title when he makes Apollo Ion's father. Eu-ripides thus establishes the genealogy of these Athenian/Ionian connections in Athena's speech at the conclusion of the play. She explains: "The sons born to him, four from a single root, will give their names to the tribes of the land of those who dwell upon my cliff. Geleon will be the first, next Hopletes, and Ar-gades, and Aegicores, the tribe named from my aegis" (1575–81). By placing Ion at the head of the family tree, Euripides makes the Ionians descendants of Athenians.

Furthermore, in addition to this paternal role, just as in *Pythian* 9, Delphic

Apollo functions here as representative of the colonial movement. In fact, the plot of the *Ion* resembles the colonial legend of Myscellus of Rhype. Xuthus and Creusa consult the oracle about their childlessness; Apollo's response produces both a son and the future Athenian colonization of Ionia. Ion's very name, in true colonial fashion, is significant here.[61] In addition to its obvious function designating him as the eponymous founder of Ionia, the name is etymologized in the play from the verb *eimi,* "to go." Xuthus is told that his son will be the first person he meets as he exits the temple, *exionti,* and this person is of course Ion, whose name thus prefigures and legitimates his expansionist role as Athenian colonizer of Asia Minor.[62] Hermes describes Ion in the prologue as the founder, the *ktistōr,* of the Asian land, and we learn from Athena at the end of the play that Ion's descendants will in fact found cities in Asia Minor: "Moreover, the children of these men [Ion's sons] shall at the appointed time settle the Cycladic island towns and the shore of the mainland, which gives strength to my land. Facing across the straits, they will inhabit the plains of two continents, of Asia and of Europe. They shall be named Ionians because of the name of this boy and they shall acquire fame" (1581–88).

The family dynamics are finally clear: Xuthus, the adoptive father, disappears from the story, and Apollo Patrōos, mythical co-father of Athenians and Ionians, together with Creusa the autochthon, true legitimate mother of all Athenians, combine to produce Ion, a son who is both Ionian and autochthonous, foreign and native, imperial and democratic. The metaphorical union of mother and father creates the framework for imagining the political compromise of autochthony and Ionia, and in conclusion, I would like to suggest that this family portrait could only be painted at Delphi.[63]

DELPHI

W. R. Connor, in his contribution to this collection, emphasizes the importance of the City Dionysia and of drama in general as a format for the "social imaginary," and he discusses the role this social imagination plays in the development of democracy in Athens. Drawing upon recent discussions of the carnivalesque aspect of Athenian drama, Connor suggests that the inversions typical of Dionysiac worship do more than provide a temporary venting mechanism for a highly rigid society. They also make it possible to imagine an alternative community—an inclusive one without status differentiations and with truly free speech. Others have noted as well the role drama plays in political life in Athens. The theatre functions as a second agora, or public space, in which the community at large can discuss its political options, and in the conclusion to this paper I follow up on Connor's formulation of the political possibilities for the Dionysiac theater, to explore specifically how the topography of dramatic space works within this institution of social imagination.[64]

Froma Zeitlin has shown that the topos—and by "topos" she means both a geographical locale and a recurrent concept or "commonplace"—of Thebes plays a specific role in Greek tragedy. "Thebes," she argues, "provides the negative model to Athens' manifest image of itself with regard to its notions of the proper management of city, society, and self. As the site of displacement, therefore, Thebes consistently supplies the radical tragic terrain where there can be no escape from the tragic in the resolution of conflict or in the institutional provision of a civic future beyond the world of the play."[65] In other words, in the dramatic world of Thebes, Athens can imagine, enact (and thus preclude) its own destruction as a functioning political community. What I want to suggest here is that Delphi functions in Greek tragedy as a dramatic topos with the opposite effect from that argued so persuasively by Froma Zeitlin for Thebes— Delphi is the place where things work out, where civic futures are plotted. It is the imaginary site from which new institutions (like the court of the Areopagus in the *Eumenides*) can be founded and at which contradictions (like those inherent in conceptualizations of democracy) can be reconciled through a kind of Delphic logic.

Of all the Greek tragedies that survive, only two are actually set at Delphi, Aeschylus' *Eumenides* and Euripides' *Ion*, and it is no coincidence that both plays enact a movement from Delphi to Athens and that both plays celebrate civic foundations.[66] The *Eumenides* links the origins of the Areopagus court to the House of Atreus and Orestes' trial for the murder of his mother. Likewise, the *Ion* generates the story behind the Ionian tribes at Athens and Athens' colonization of Ionia. In the Greek topographic imagination, Delphi occupies the center of the earth, its navel, and consequently it functions as a metaphorical birthplace for cities, legal codes, and civic institutions. All beginnings must come from Delphi. Thus, as a dramatic topos, Delphi's value lies in its role as the place from which new things are born, particularly with respect to Athens.[67] The *Ion* (and the *Eumenides*) is set in Delphi precisely so that the action of the play can move—a transition that is prefigured in the play's conclusion by the substitution of Athena for Apollo—from Delphi to Athens. If Thebes destroys the possibility of constructing a "civic future beyond the world of the play," Delphi provides both the originary site and the interpretative space for just such an imagination.[68]

In addition to functioning as a point of origin, Delphic space centers on interpretation. The typical Delphic narrative starts with a state of categorical confusion that demands to be interpreted, and the point of the narrative is rarely the solution, but rather the act and terms of the interpretation itself.[69] When Herodotus, for example, recounts the story of the wooden walls oracle in book 7 of his *Histories,* he devotes a significant part of his narrative to the process by which the Athenians correctly interpret the reference to wooden walls as a metaphor for ships. Similarly in the *Ion*, Hermes, at the close of his prologue, explains that he has come to Delphi "to learn about the prophecy of the child (*to kranthen hōs an ekmathō*)."[70] In other words, he wants to discover how the oracular story about the boy's identity will be interpreted. The verb *manthanō*, "to learn or discover," is often used to characterize the process of solving a riddle, a process that involves a kind of creative learning, an ability to see the world in new ways and thus to solve the puzzle of the riddle.[71] The entire plot of the *Ion* is presented in oracular terms—set at Dephi, framed by the absent presence of Apollo, whose representatives (here Hermes, the Pythia, and Athena) mediate between the god's omniscience and the partial knowledges of mere mortals.

Characters and situations in the *Ion,* like the metaphors on which enigmatic Delphic oracles depend, appear at first to be other than they are: slaves are free men, stepmothers are real mothers, native Athenians look like foreign invaders. The final recognition scene between Ion and Creusa is in fact presented as an oracular consultation—the swaddling clothes are called *symbola* (1386) that Ion and Creusa must correctly interpret to ensure Ion's proper identity. In this focus on Delphi, as in many other ways, Ion's story is similar to that of Oedipus. Both characters are unsure of their identity; both confront the oracular language of Delphic Apollo in search of their true home and father. But the *Ion* takes place at Delphi, not Thebes, and so, unlike the enigmatic oracles of the *Oedipus Tyrannus,* which are solved too late and ultimately destroy Thebes, the resolution of this play (like most colonial oracles), avoids murder and restores all participants in timely fashion to their proper and productive identities.[72] In fact, thinking about the play's allegedly "happy" ending in Delphic terms, as the correct solution to a significant civic problem, we avoid the pitfalls inherent in reinventing the genre of the play as melodrama or tragicomedy. The *Ion* is a tragedy set at Delphi, and so the logic of its *dénouement* is radically different from that of the *Antigone* or the *Bacchae,* but nevertheless it shares with those plays tragedy's characteristic focus on essential issues of Athenian civic identity.

Euripides moves Athens to Delphi temporarily to take advantage of this foundational, interpretative space and stages the synoptic illusion of an Athens in which the contradictions of contemporary politics can be reconciled.[73] The *Ion* has been called "a drama that tells of all the ways to be an Athenian outside Athenian orthodoxy."[74] It is precisely because of its ambiguous setting at Delphi, that in merging Ionian ancestry with autochthony the *Ion* is able to address and imagine a solution to many of the contradictions inherent in democracy—slave versus free, autochthony versus Ionia, native versus foreign, legitimate versus bastard.[75] The play's conclusion thus moves from Delphi to Athens to establish the Athenians simultaneously as the sons of Apollo and the fathers of the Ionians. As sons of Delphic Apollo, they are the founders of Athenian democracy; as the parents of Ionia, they establish an empire.[76]

ACKNOWLEDGMENTS

I would like to thank the organizers of the conference from which these papers emerged: Josh Ober, Charles Hedrick, and Cathy Vanderpool. I also want to thank Paul Cartledge, W. R. Connor, Joel Krieger, Leslie Kurke, Nicole Loraux,

Ian Morris, Gregory Nagy, Andrew Szegedy-Maszak, and Froma I. Zeitlin for their generous help and useful criticisms of this and earlier drafts of this paper.

NOTES

1. For an ancient view of Cleisthenes as founder of the Athenian democracy, see Herodotus 6.131.1; he explains that Cleisthenes was the one "who established the tribes and democracy in Athens."

2. Foundation tales are particularly persuasive ways to ground political innovations in a sense of the conservative past. See Sahlins, *Historical Metaphors,* for a discussion of how cultures negotiate a place for what is new within their traditional cultural framework. For a collection of papers that discuss the novelty that is often masked by the rhetoric of tradition, see Hobsbawm and Ranger, eds., *Invention of Tradition.*

3. Anderson, *Imagined Communities,* 6

4. Ibid., 12. See also p. 5 on the difference between the larger concept of "Nationalism" and individual manifestations of how communities imagine their own identity: "It would, I think, make things easier if one treated it [nationalism] as if it belonged with 'kinship' and 'religion,' rather than with 'liberalism' or 'fascism.'"

5. See also Bourdieu, *Outline,* 104–5: The "linear diagram of the agrarian year (like all discourse) at once masks and reveals the difficulties that are encountered as soon as one ceases to take practical relations of analogy or homology singly (or in pairs) and successively, and endeavours instead to fix them simultaneously so as to cumulate them systematically."

6. Bourdieu, *Outline,* 98.

7. See Alty, "Dorians and Ionians" for a discussion of the nature of ethnic identity in the fifth century; he focuses particularly on the Dorians and the Ionians and the problematic boundaries between loyalty to ethnos and loyalty to the mother state. Perhaps a useful parallel can be drawn with the current events in the former Yugoslavia or Soviet Union where, as we have seen recently, the political construct of the Republic of Yugoslavia or the Soviet Union could not permanently replace or erase longstanding ethnic identities.

8. Cf. Ian Morris's paper in this volume for a similar warning about the need to recognize the generic conventions of archaic poetry before using such poetry as a source for historical analysis.

9. Barron, "Milesian Politics," 6; "Religious Propaganda," 46–48. For more general discussions of the relationship between Ionians and Athenians, see Sakellariou, *La Migration grecque;* Emlyn Jones, *Ionians and Hellenism;* Prinz, *Gründungsmythen,* 314–76; Huxley, *Early Ionians;* Hanfmann, "Ionia"; Connor, "Ionian Era"; Cook, "Ionia and Greece."

10. Thuc. 1.95.1. Further evidence of the prominence of this tradition might be deduced from the *Ionica* of Panyassis (see the *Suda,* s.v. Panyassis), which may have treated this topic.

11. On the close ties between Athens and Ionia, see Huxley, *Early Ionians,* 30–35; Connor, "Ionian Era," 194–204.

12. Cf. Geddes, "Rags to Riches," for more detailed discussion of the political significance of clothing styles in fifth-century Athens.

13. On the cult of Apollo Patrōos at Athens and its role in fostering connections between Athens and Ionia, see De Schutter, "La Culte d'Apollon"; Hedrick, "Temple and Cult of Apollo Patrōos."

14. On the complicated nature of these interactions, see Hanfmann, "Ionia"; Connor, "Ionian Era," 197.

15. On negative connotations of "Ionianism," see Alty, "Dorians and Ionians," 7–11; Connor, "Ionian Era," 199.

16. Connor, "Ionian Era," 200. Cf. Hanfmann, "Ionia"; Cook, "Ionia and Greece."

17. Meiggs, *Athenian Empire,* 293. Cf. The Assessment Decree of 425 in which (if the supplement is correct) the allies are to escort their offering in procession like colonists ([καθάπερ ἄποι]κ[οι); Meiggs and Lewis, *Greek Historical Inscriptions,* 69.57–58.

18. Obviously, what I have described here as an Ionian, aristocratic ideology at work in Athenian political discourse is closely linked to a larger Panhellenic phenomenon. See, for example, Ian Morris's paper in this collection for an excellent discussion of the elitist ideology associated with Lydia and manifested particularly in sympotic poetry. Athens' Ionian ideology is both part of this larger Panhellenic trend, yet it also has particular force in Athens in the beginning of the fifth century in light of Athens' dismissal of its Ionian ties and the establishment of local democratic traditions.

19. See Connor, "Ionian Era," 201–4 for reasons that Athens repudiated its Ionian connections; see Kurke, "Politics of Habrosyne," for the aristocratic associations with Ionia and for a discussion of its decline in popularity in Athens in the fifth century.

20. For a much more thorough discussion of autochthony as Athenian ideology, see Loraux, *Invention of Athens; Children of Athena;* Rosivach, "Autochthony." As Loraux has shown (*Invention of Athens; Children of Athena,* 41), the funeral oration in particular roots democracy in Athens' autochthonous origins.

21. Loraux, *Invention of Athens,* 193.

22. Rosivach, "Autochthony," shows that while as early as the *Iliad* the Athenians were called chthonic, the adjective *autochthonous* is probably a late invention, and it is not until the fifth century that to be born from the earth comes to be equated with continuous occupation of the same land.

23. Rosivach, "Autochthony," 296 (Dorian invasion); Connor, "Ionian Era," 204–6 (Ionian connection).

24. Autochthony versus *epēlus:* Hdt. 4.197.2; 8.73.1–2. Isocrates 4.63; 12.124. Plato *Menex.* 237b; Ps. Dem. 60.4. Autochthony versus *epaktos:* Eur. *Ion* 589–90; *Erechtheus* fr. 50.7–8 (Austin).

25. Euripides *Erechtheus* fr. 50.5–13 (Austin).

26. Cf. Thuc. 1.2. Attica is free of political disunity because its inhabitants are of the same race; migrations cause political inequality elsewhere.

27. Lévêque and Vidal-Naquet, *Clisthène,* 50–51.

28. Cf. Isoc. 4.24–25.

29. We must, of course, acknowledge that the funeral oration embedded in the *Menexenus* is surely a parody of the genre. See Loraux, *Invention of Athens,* 325, for more on the tone of the speech. Nevertheless, even (or especially) as a parody, the speech will include the kinds of metaphors and rhetorical gestures that are particularly characteristic of the genre, and it is the rhetoric, not the tone of the dialogue, that is of significance here.

30. Cf. Thucydides 6.17 for mention of the political and moral weaknesses created in Sicily because of the heterogeneity and instablity of the populations there. See Paul Cartledge's paper in this collection for a discussion of the ideological role of "sameness" and its connection to notions of equality in democratic discourse.

31. Lysias' speech (2.17–19) shows how a eulogy of democracy, the ostensible goal of the funeral oration, is grafted onto Athens' autochthonous origins and then presented as proof of Athenian nobility. See also Plato *Menex*. 239a7. As Nicole Loraux (*Invention of Athens*, 149–50) observes in her discussion of autochthony as a topos of the funeral oration, "Its main task is to give Athenians an aristocratic image of themselves." In fact the orators often use *eugeneia* as a synonym for autochthony. See also Walsh, "Rhetoric of Birthright," on this same association of *earthborn* and *well-born* in the *Ion*.

32. Cf. [Dem.] (*Against Neaira*) 59.74

33. Rosivach, "Autochthony," 301.

34. See also Isoc. 6.124; Lyc. *Leoc*. 100; Plato *Rep*. 414e.

35. Plato *Rep*. 415a. See Rosivach, "Autochthony," 301–5.

36. Furthermore, as Anderson points out, the vocabulary of kinship lends an air of naturalness, or inevitability, to political relationships; see Anderson, *Imagined Communities*, 143. See also Hunt, *Family Romance*, for a discussion of how various images of the familial order (good father, bad mother, brothers) underlie and structure French revolutionary politics.

37. For a discussion of the problems involved in dating the play, see Owen, *Ion*, xxxvi–xli.

38. Loraux, "Kreousa," 178–79; Saxonhouse, "Myths and Origins of Cities." See also Owen, *Ion*, xi–xii and Barron, "Religious Propaganda" on the theme of imperialism in the *Ion*.

39. Cf. Loraux, "Kreousa," 186–90 for a discussion of Creusa as *epiklēros*.

40. By "poetics of colonization," I mean the complex of myths and metaphors that combine to structure the Greek memory of the archaic colonization movement. See Dougherty, *Poetics of Colonization*.

41. Herodotus (7.94; 8.44) names Xuthus as Ion's father.

42. Lévêque and Vidal-Naquet, *Clisthène*, 68–75.

43. Syracuse: Plut. *Mor*. 772e–773b; Acarnania: Thuc. 2.102.5–6; Rhodes: *Iliad* 2.653–70; Pindar *Ol*. 7; Strabo 14.2.6. See also Dougherty, *Poetics of Colonization*, 31–44, for a discussion of the significance of the murderous founder in colonial discourse.

44. For collections of colonial oracles, see Parke and Wormell, *Delphic Oracle;* Fontenrose, *Delphic Oracle;* Malkin, *Religion and Colonization*. For a discussion of how oracles work in colonial discourse, see Dougherty, *Poetics of Colonization*, 45–60.

45. [Arist.] *Ath. Pol*. 21.6.

46. See Martin, *Recherches sur l'agora*, 197–201 for a discussion of the burial of city founders in the agora. Malkin, *Religion and Colonization*, 189–240 collects the literary and archeological evidence for the cult of the founder.

47. Aeschylus *Aetnaeae* fr. 6 (Radt).

48. This narrative pattern and metaphor, although common in Greek myth and legend, is not unique to it. Livy's version of the rape of the Sabine women follows this same plot. For further discussion of the theme in Greek colonial literature, see Dougherty, *Poetics of Colonization*, 61–80. For other literary and artistic traditions, see Carroll, "Erotics of Absolutism"; Kolodny, *Lay of the Land*.

49. The Greek: ἐκ λεχέων κεῖραι μελιαδέα ποίαν (37).

50. It is worth noting the larger semantic range of the verb (κεῖραι) Pindar uses in Apollo's question about Cyrene. It can mean to cut short or clip, as one shears hair as part of the rite of mourning; it can also refer to the process of ravaging a landscape. In Herodotus the verb is used to describe the clearing of a plain for cavalry action prior to battle (5.63), the destruction wrecked by the Persians on the uncooperative people of Carystus (6.99), and Xerxes' army hacking away at the Macedonian mountains so that his men might move through them (7.131).

51. For more on the iconographical convention of "hand upon wrist," see Jenkins, "Life after Marriage"; Sourvinou-Inwood, "Erotic Pursuits"; Oakely and Sinos, *Athenian Wedding,* 79–81.

52. The *Homeric Hymn to Demeter* shows many similarities to both *Pythian* 9 and this passage from the *Ion.* Cf. Loraux, "Kreousa," 201–3; Zeitlin, "Mysteries of Identity," 159–64 for the significance of the Kore myth in the *Ion.*

53. Lysias 2.17; Lyc. *Leoc.* 48: Cf. Dem. 60.4; Isoc. 4. 24. Cf. Loraux, *Children of Athena,* 65.

54. Notice the imagery here: just as the true mother feeds her children with milk from her breast, Athens nourishes her children with wheat and barley. This same dichotomy between true and false mothers appears at *Ion* 318–19 when Creusa asks Ion who nourished him with milk, and he replies that he did not know the breast, but that the Pythia nourished him.

55. Loraux, "Kreousa," 191–92. Cf. ibid. note 78 for list of the uses of *apaidia* and *ateknia* in the play. See also Peradotto, "Oedipus and Erichthonius," 92.

56. Cf. *Ion* 1058–60; 1069–73.

57. Creusa herself is aware of the hostile behavior of stepmothers (1025); cf. Ion's speech at 1330.

58. To push the images of motherhood a bit further, we can recognize the Pythia (who lives at Delphi, the navel of the earth) as the surrogate mother in this family drama. Ion refers to the priestess as his mother "although she did not give birth to me" (1324). Cf. *Ion* 313–19 and 1370–79 for a similar distinction between the mother who bore him and the one who nursed him.

59. Hdt. 1.147: Athenians and Ionians observe the Apatouria. Cf. Diod. 16.57.4, who explains that the Athenians boasted Apollo as their tutelary god and progenitor.

60. De Schutter, "La Culte d'Apollon."

61. Colonial legends, especially those that include Delphic oracles, often use etymological wordplay to generate narratives to explain the meaning of the city's (or founder's) name. Cf. Dougherty, *Poetics of Colonization,* 46–48.

62. *Ion* 535; 661–62.

63. I do not, however, mean to suggest that this play is a "Delphic tragedy," in the sense that it promotes Delphic propaganda or in any way celebrates the humanity of the Delphic religion. Cf. Loraux, "Kreousa," 177, n.27.

64. For discussions of the political nature of tragedy, see the essays collected in Winkler and Zeitlin, *Nothing to Do with Dionysos?* especially those by Goldhill, Longo, and Redfield.

65. Zeitlin, "Thebes," 131. She continues, "There [Thebes] the most serious questions can be raised concerning the fundamental relations of man to his universe, partic-

ularly with respect to the nature of rule over others and of rule over self, as well as those pertaining to the conduct of the body politic."

66. The *Eumenides,* of course, is only partially set at Delphi; the second half of the play moves the action to Athens. There are other plays, of course, in which Delphic Apollo and his oracle figure prominently and often negatively (e.g., Euripides' *Andromache*) but these plays are not actually set at Delphi, nor do they enact a movement from Delphi to Athens. It is the Delphic topography on stage that is significant.

67. Cf. *Ion* 1364, where the Pythia even tells Ion that he must begin his search for his mother at Delphi.

68. In her article on this play, Froma Zeitlin appreciates the *Ion* as an Athenian play and contrasts its joyful ending with the destructive power of Theban plays: "It also releases generative power for the future in the genealogies to come, as well as in pragmatic ways of treating various forms of kinship. The play indoctrinates us therefore not only into the complexities of ideological mythmaking but also into the sources and resources of the theatre itself that stages the myth" (Zeitlin, "Mysteries of Identity," 154–55). I would add that it is precisely the act of setting the play at Delphi and its subsequent movement *from* Delphi *to* Athens that enables both the "generative power" of the play and its ability to mobilize what she calls "the dense network of signs and designs necessary for matching the unknown self to the identity it is asked to claim."

69. For an excellent essay on the role of Delphic prophecy in Greek thought and politics, see Vernant, "Mute Signs."

70. The Greek: τὸ κρανθὲν ὡς ἄν ἐκμάθω, 77. I disagree with Owen's (*Ion,* 74) interpretation of this line. He argues that "We must take τὸ κρανθὲν of what is actually accomplished or shortly will be so, not what is fated, as Hermes, though wrong, claims to know that." The logic of the play, I want to suggest, is to enact the process of intepreting "τὸ κρανθέν," what has been prophesied.

71. Athenaeus (10. 455f) shows us that the conventional way to ask, after posing a riddle, whether the listener has understood is "μανθάνεις;" or "do you get it?" For the similarities between metaphors and riddles as two ways to engender creative knowledge, see Arist. *Rh.* 3.10.1410b10–15.

72. Enigmatic colonial oracles are more often correctly interpreted in time to be useful than other enigmatic Delphic oracles that, like those of Oedipus, are only solved in retrospect. This distinction, I think, reflects the way that the Greeks represent founding a new city as an act of interpretation itself; cf. Dougherty, *Poetics of Colonization,* 45–60. See Peradotto, "Oedipus and Erichthonius" for structural comparison of the myths of Oedipus and Erichthonius. There are, of course, some very important differences between the two myths as well, and it is interesting to note how they continue to articulate the important distinctions that are drawn between Athens and Thebes on stage. In Thebes autochthony produces civil war; Oedipus fails to solve the Delphic puzzle, and he becomes a parricide. In a suspiciously antonymic fashion at Athens, autochthony produces democracy; Ion is successful at Delphi, and he avoids killing his mother.

73. Vidal-Naquet, *Black Hunter,* in his discussion of the Marathon statue base erected at Delphi (312), makes a similar point about the interpretative value of Delphi: "Although Delphi was not a *center* for propaganda, from which there would be disseminated a doctrine—it is hard to see what organization would have invented and maintained such dogma—it was undoubtedly a *site* for propaganda where cities, and

sometimes their citizens, could try out new ventures that they would not have risked at home. By organizing the finances for the new temple at Delphi, Cleisthenes and the Alcmeonids secured for themselves a base for returning to Athens."

74. Cf. Loraux, "Kreousa," 180: "Enacted on the stage is the story of a child with two fathers but whose mother alone is Athenian; an Athenian drama but one which takes place in Delphi; a drama about autochthony but one in which there are no *andres Athēnaioi;* a drama about citizenship in which not a single character is a citizen, and in which it is the women who embody legitimacy and slaves speak for the city, while the eponymous hero has no name, as befits the child of a woman."

75. Furthermore, Euripides successfuly combines the Theseus founding story with autochthony. In this play Ion plays the role of Theseus, similarly cast as an outsider, a foreign threat, a bastard who attempts to invade Athens and wrest political control from the native, ruling autochthonous kings. In the *Ion,* just as in the Theseus myth, Creusa, temporarily playing Medea's role as stepmother, attempts to poison the invader but is foiled at the last minute. What is different about the *Ion* is that here at Delphi the outsider is really a native; the bastard, really legitimate; and the slave, really an authentic citizen.

76. The question of the play's overall tone, of course, still remains, and I do not mean to suggest that Euripides is without irony in presenting this perfect, synoptic solution. Perhaps, just as in the late-twentieth-century United States, so too in Athens at the end of the fifth century, with both democracy and empire similarly at risk, Euripides' audience was looking for miracles.

ARISTOTLE AND THE IDEA OF LIBERAL EDUCATION

CARNES LORD

I

The importance of education for responsible democratic governance is a persistent theme in the American political tradition, from Benjamin Franklin and Thomas Jefferson to Horace Mann to recent critics of American public and higher education like William Bennett and Christopher Lasch.[1] It is, nonetheless, striking to what extent the issue of education is slighted in contemporary theorizing about politics.[2] Evidently, the extrusion of the issue of education from the public sphere effected by the founders of modern liberalism—notably, John Locke—remains powerfully if subliminally influential today.[3]

The encounter with classical antiquity is particularly valuable in this regard. Education was not only a theme, it was a central theme of the political thought of the ancient Greeks. The prominence of the question of education in the political philosophy of Plato and Aristotle plainly reflected in some measure the historical realities these thinkers faced: the classical polis differed dramatically from the modern nation-state in the relative weakness of its institutional or bureaucratic structures and the corresponding prominence of individuals—citizens in the mass as well as outstanding statesmen—in its day-to-day governance. At the same time, it is far from clear that the institutions of modern democracy have solved in a convincing manner the problems the ancients believed could only be solved by educating individuals—that is to say, by educating them in individual or civic virtue. A powerful strand of contemporary democratic theory has recently called attention to the neglect by traditional liberal thinkers of the cultural preconditions of liberal democracy, reviving in the process an older understanding of democratic citizenship as a form of community and a way of life.[4] This "communitarian" critique of liberalism and the response it has generated have begun to restore the issue of education to the agenda of contemporary political argument. A fresh and serious examination of ancient views of education would seem especially desirable in view of the use that is made by contemporary communitarians of the tradition of classical or civic republicanism in general, and of Aristotle in particular.

Even the most cursory survey of the history of education must pay tribute to Aristotle, who has an excellent claim to being considered the founder of the modern university as well as a good number of the intellectual disciplines that

find a home in it. Nevertheless, Aristotle cannot be said to be a conspicuous figure in the ranks of theorists of education. No separate treatise on education survives under his name (although he apparently composed a now-lost dialogue
on the subject), and his other pertinent writings do not speak clearly or directly
on education as a whole or its role in human life. Moreover, to the extent that
Aristotle does have a theory of education, it is often assumed to represent little
more than an adaptation of the traditional ideas and practices of classical
Greece.[5]

It is always hazardous to assume that formidable thinkers are merely children of their times; the assumption is particularly risky in the case of Aristotle,
who insists on approaching any intellectual inquiry by interrogating current
opinions—and attempting to do justice to the truth that may be contained in
those opinions—before offering his own account. Aristotle's thoughts on education would be of considerable interest even if they amounted to little more
than a systematization of Greek educational practices of his day, given the absence of a specialized literary tradition devoted to the subject. In fact, however,
an excellent case can be made that Aristotle does have a distinctive theory of
education, and one exhibiting greater coherence, subtlety, and originality than
is generally recognized. Moreover, this theory is one of more than passing relevance to the contemporary debates on citizenship, community, and culture in
a democratic society.

In the United States today, education at all levels may be said to be increasingly under pressure from forces in the wider society to conform to, or serve as
the instrument of, a particular political agenda. Some lament the increasingly
evident failure of American schools to create responsible citizens, and call for
greater instruction in traditional morality and civic or democratic values. Others seek to advance a different understanding of democracy focusing on greater
equality or preferment for groups constituted by race, ethnicity, or gender. At a
more theoretical level, what one may describe as the received liberal approach
to education, with its professed neutrality toward "values" and its emphasis on
the promotion of individual autonomy or self-realization, has come under sustained attack in the name of individual virtue and community. On all sides, it
seems to be increasingly assumed that schools and universities, whether public
or private, exist to serve essentially public purposes, and that those purposes
must fulfill in more or less direct fashion the ideological and political requirements of a democratic society.

At first sight, Aristotle—indeed, the classical republican tradition generally—would seem altogether sympathetic to this trend, at least in principle.
Aristotle emphatically supports the necessity for public education in every sort
of regime, including democracy, and appears to embrace the idea of a moral and
civic education designed to inculcate the values of particular regimes.[6] While
clearly not a democrat, Aristotle has much in common with contemporary democratic critics of liberal individualism and its social consequences. On in-

spection, however, Aristotle's communitarianism proves to be more problematic than is sometimes supposed. Aristotle is very far from accepting an organicist view of political society, or a belief that political conflict is anything other than a natural and ordinary condition of political life; in particular, he does not rely on a concept of civic or political friendship as providing an essential bond of political communities, as is now often argued.[7] So far from defining virtue in terms of its social or political utility, Aristotle rather underlines the tension between human virtue in its most elevated forms and the requirements of ordinary political life.[8] Finally, contrary to what many argue or assume, Aristotle does not unambiguously endorse the full and active participation of the citizenry in politics or the value of political activity for its own sake, or simply subordinate the private to the public.[9]

For all of these reasons, Aristotle's embrace of the idea of civic education, as that term is generally understood in the American political tradition, is at best qualified. Aristotle's reservations about the value of democracy as such lead him to doubt the value of political or cultural homogeneity in ordinary political life or for most practical purposes, attractive though he finds it to be in theory. This necessarily complicates the task of elaborating a public education designed to foster civic virtue. I argue that this accounts for the hesitations and ambiguities in Aristotle's theory of education and shapes its fundamental character. Aristotle may be justly considered the founder of liberal education, in a sense of that term that is still intelligible if not entirely familiar. Liberal education in this sense transcends civic education yet is something other than the specialized, scientific, or scholarly education that is today so frequently confused with liberal education. Rather, it is a practical education designed to form good citizens and free men, to train potential statesmen, and to support a life of cultured leisure.

II

Some initial observations are in order on the notion of "education" itself in the Greece of Aristotle's day. The Greek word for "education," *paideia,* derives from the Greek word for "child," and education in its original meaning was essentially limited to the upbringing or education of children. By Aristotle's time, however, *paideia* had taken on broader connotations. For Aristotle's contemporaries, education extended to higher forms of learning and increasingly referred not only to the process of education but to its outcome—to the learning, cultivation, or "culture" of an educated individual.[10] Taken in this larger sense, education involves more than the education of children, yet something less than a thorough knowledge of the specialized arts and sciences. Moreover, it implies something beyond mere intellectual accomplishment. "Education" in Greek usage is always distinguished from mere "learning" or "instruction" (*mathēsis*) by its relationship to human character and behavior.[11] For the Greeks, the education of children was always conceived much less as a training of the mind than as a training of the character or the soul; and this remains true in significant measure of *paideia* in its extended sense as well.

The principal thematic treatment of education in the surviving works of Aristotle occurs in the context of his discussion of the best political order or regime (*politeia*) in books 7 and 8 of his *Politics*. This treatment concentrates on the education of the young, thereby creating the impression that Aristotle holds to a distinctly old-fashioned conception of *paideia*. This impression is misleading, however, and has helped obscure what is genuinely distinctive in Aristotle's thought in this area. In the first place, there is considerable evidence that the discussion in the final books of the *Politics* is incomplete as it stands—and some indications that higher education was specifically addressed in the material now lost.[12] Second, there are important (though generally neglected) references scattered throughout the *Politics* that show quite clearly Aristotle's acceptance of the contemporary and broad sense of *paideia* as encompassing the education or culture of mature persons.[13]

That this should be so is hardly surprising given the prominence that Aristotle (following the example of Plato in his *Republic* and *Laws*) accords education in his overall political teaching. Education is properly part of political science as Aristotle conceives it because education is a factor of critical importance in forming men's political outlook and determining their behavior in society. The political importance of education for Aristotle is apparent in the first instance in his very understanding of the nature of the political community. The "city" (*polis*) or the "political community" (*politikē koinōnia*) is distinguished from other forms of human community or association by a commonly shared perception of the good and the bad and the just and the unjust—that is, by a certain understanding of the moral requirements of human life or of what we might speak of today as fundamental values. The city, Aristotle says, exists not only for the sake of living—of mere survival—but rather "primarily for the sake of living well" (*Pol.* 1252b27–53a18), that is to say, for the sake of a humanly fulfilling, virtuous, or happy life. Anyone concerned with the proper functioning of a city therefore "gives careful attention to civic [*politikē*] virtue and vice," and the laws of the city must be designed to foster virtue, not simply to guarantee protection against injury, as the sophist Lycophron (anticipating modern liberal individualism) would have it (*Pol.* 1280b5–81a7).

Because Aristotle famously holds that man is by nature a political animal, it is often assumed that he considers the polis a natural and inevitable product of human society. Aristotle is at considerable pains, however, to distinguish the city from the simple natural community of the family or household as well as from other social structures that do not appear to rest on a comparable moral foundation. While "there is in everyone by nature an impulse" toward this kind of community, "the one who first founded [a city] is responsible for the greatest of goods" (*Pol.* 1253a29–31). This is so because the city is "in its nature a sort of multitude," one made up of a large number of human beings "differing in kind"—that is, economically and socially differentiated individuals, households, and classes. The attempt to overcome these differences on the plane of politics—Plato's procedure in the communitarian thought-experiment of the *Republic*—is unworkable. Rather, as Aristotle says, the city, "being a multitude, must be made one and common through education" (*Pol.* 1261a18–25, 63b36–37).

Cities are in need of founders because the city is not simply natural; the city is not simply natural at least in part because morality or virtue is not simply natural. Education in virtue or in a particular understanding of virtue is therefore the critical constitutive act for any city. The true founder of a city is not necessarily its original founder, but the one who constitutes it as a moral community—a Solon (in the case of Athens) or Lycurgus (in the case of Sparta). Once constituted as a moral community, however, the city must be preserved as such through continuous acts of statesmanship. Education is thus a critical function of the statesmen or politicians (*politikoi*) charged with preserving freedom and community for a city's inhabitants.[14]

Education in the broad sense used in this context encompasses, as Aristotle puts it, "habits, philosophy, and laws" (*Pol.* 1263b37–64a1). What needs to be noticed first about this formulation is that it completely transcends schooling in a formal sense. By "habits" (or "customs": *ethē*), Aristotle means the shaping of character and behavior primarily in the young, through parental upbringing as much as through any kind of formal instruction; the contemporary term *socialization* tolerably captures the sense of the expression. By "philosophy," he seems to mean here not philosophy in its narrow sense but a range of disciplines concerned with the intellectual formation of young and old alike. As will be seen shortly, philosophy in this sense is not only and perhaps not even primarily the business of educational institutions but reflects rather a society's larger intellectual heritage or culture. By "laws" (*nomoi*), finally, Aristotle refers to the impact both of formal laws and less formal conventions of public or political behavior; the contemporary term *political culture* is not overly misleading in this regard.

Aristotle's analysis is of more than passing interest from a present-day perspective in the way it frames the issue of education in this larger context. It can be argued that one of the major weaknesses of much contemporary discussion of education is its overemphasis on, or the unrealistic expectations it invests in, formal schooling, coupled with its neglect of the educational relevance of such things as cultural or religious ritual, civic ceremonies, law and legal practice, military service, political participation, and popularized intellectual doctrine.[15] Not only Aristotle but most Greeks of the classical age saw matters differently. When Thucydides' Pericles called Athens the "school [*paideusis*] of Greece" (2.41), he had in mind not its educators nor its educational institutions but its way of life as a whole. Education in the true classical sense is indistinguishable in the last analysis from the culture of a society, and more particularly, from its common or public culture. Where, as in Athens of the classical age, the common or public culture dominates society, where citizens are continuously exposed to powerful collective experiences in the law courts and the popular assembly, in religious gatherings and in the theater, *paideia* in its broad and informal sense must be expected to dominate *paideia* in a narrowly institutional sense.

III

Before proceeding to consider in greater detail Aristotle's own view of the structure and requirements of education so understood, some attention needs to be given to the implications for education of the moral psychology of Aristotle's ethical writings. Briefly, Aristotle holds that the soul is divided into a reasoning and a nonreasoning part, the latter being the locus of desire or emotion and therefore also of moral virtue, understood as a habitual disposition toward the various emotions. The reasoning part of the soul is in turn divided into two parts, a "practical" part and a "theoretical," or contemplative, part. The practical part is also called by Aristotle *phronēsis,* "practical wisdom" or "prudence."[16]

A grasp of what Aristotle means by "prudence" is essential for understanding his view of higher education. For Aristotle as in current usage, prudence is a kind of intellectual virtue closely tied to experience. For Aristotle, though, prudence is a key component of moral virtue in the fullest sense of the term. It complements or completes moral virtue by supplying the intellectual element necessary for a virtuous disposition to express itself effectively in action. Effective moral behavior depends decisively on an understanding of circumstances and persons; it is this understanding that prudence supplies. Prudence requires, then, at least in the best case, a sophisticated knowledge of a wide range of human traits and social phenomena. Because such knowledge is inescapably tied to experience, prudence can only develop in relatively mature persons. Prudence is preeminently the virtue of the statesman or legislator. While prudence as such may not be teachable, Aristotle appears to hold that education of the proper sort can assist or complete its development.[17]

Aristotle begins his thematic discussion of education in the final book of the *Politics* by taking note of a general uncertainty concerning the nature and purpose of education. It appears that there are disagreements concerning both the end education should serve and the sorts of subjects that ought to be taught. "Not everyone conceives that the young should learn the same things either with a view to virtue or with a view to the best way of life, nor is it evident whether it is more appropriate that it be with a view to the mind or the character of the soul. Investigation on the basis of the education that is current yields confusion, and it is not at all clear whether one should have training in things useful for life, things contributing to virtue, or extraordinary things" (*Pol.* 1337a35–42).

This remark is a salutary warning against unwarranted assumptions about the uniformity of Greek educational ideas; it is also in a way a reassuring testimony to the persistence through history of genuine human problems.[18] There appear to be three basic alternatives. Education could simply be instrumental to the needs of life—education in basic skills that can serve a variety of personal ends, particularly economic ones. Or education can be moral education—education of the character particularly with a view to the requirements of civic life. Or education can consist in the mastery of unusual and difficult subjects that are in themselves useless yet prepare children for a greater enjoyment of life when they are mature.

It might seem that only the last alternative should qualify as liberal education, at least in any tolerably modern sense of the term. Throughout his analysis, Aristotle lays great stress on the contrast between things that are merely "necessary" and "useful" and things that are "liberal" (*eleutheria*) and "noble" (*kala*). What is merely necessary or useful belongs to the business of ordinary life, while the liberal or noble is peculiarly at home in "leisure" (*scholē*). And it is a mark of the liberally educated man—the "free man" (*eleutheros*) in the emphatic sense of the term—to prefer leisure to occupation, the noble to the necessary.

Aristotle is reluctant, however, to endorse the idea that the pursuit of extraordinary or difficult accomplishments (*ta peritta*) is the proper grounding for a liberal education. He does not object to the pursuit of such things—which in one place he seems to equate with "liberal sorts of knowledge" (*eleutheriai epistēmai*)—up to a certain point. But he cautions that "to persevere overly much in them with a view to proficiency" is "vulgar" and liable to have harmful effects (*Pol.* 1337b14–17). Aristotle is no doubt thinking primarily of proficiency in singing and the playing of musical instruments, the major preoccupation of much of this discussion. But the point is a more general one. In the traditional aristocratic outlook that Aristotle is here echoing, proficiency or precision (*akribeia*) in any pursuit is to be viewed with a certain suspicion. It is a quality appropriate to mastery of a craft or trade (*technē*) and to those compelled to make their living by such means, but not to an education associated with refinement, judgment, and personal distinction.

Aristotle's argument as a whole cannot be fully understood apart from its social and political context. Much of the uncertainty and disagreement Aristotle finds among his contemporaries concerning the purposes of education clearly reflects the fact that the culture of democratic Athens, far from being simply a common one, was an amalgam of distinct and in part divergent attitudes and traditions reflecting its long-standing social makeup.[19] Aristocrats, traditionally the primary patrons and consumers of education, tended to see the purpose of education as the support of their distinctive way of life, a life devoted to noble or beautiful pursuits. Democrats—ordinary citizens who had to work for a living—tended by contrast to see education in primarily utilitarian terms. Aristotle's own solution to the question of the purpose of education emerges only gradually from a discussion whose complexity seems to owe something to a desire not to offend unnecessarily either of these contending parties. Aristotle goes out of his way to stress his agreement with the traditional aristocratic view of education. On closer inspection, however, his agreement with that view turns out to be highly qualified. Aristotle agrees that certain things should be learned with a view to leisure in later life, or because they are liberal and noble rather than useful. But he indicates that the primary rationale for the education of the young lies rather in its contribution to virtue. And he lets the reader see that the aristocratic view tends to slight the importance of education in virtue—in part because it misunderstands the relationship of virtue to the best way of life and the nature of the leisured activity that should be central to it,[20] but in part also, or so it would seem, because it underestimates the virtue required to sustain democratic community.

To judge at least from Thucydides' analysis of Athenian political culture, however, Athenian democrats were hardly champions of public education in support of civic virtue: they believed that virtue was a natural or spontaneous outgrowth of the Athenian character (2.39). The real champions of education for virtue in the Greek world were rather the Spartans—and their aristocratic admirers in Athens and elsewhere. This, then, is the third party in Aristotle's dispute. There can be no question that the Spartans in some ways better reflect the spirit of democratic communitarianism that is abroad today than do the Athenians, with their fierce individualism and tolerance of aristocratic ambition and distinction. Yet it would also be a mistake to suppose that Aristotle uncritically embraces the Spartan alternative.

Aristotle's indirect and subtle criticism of traditional aristocratic as well as Spartan views of education cannot be developed in detail here, but the most salient points must be mentioned. According to Aristotle, there are four subjects that are customarily taught to the young: letters, gymnastics, music, and drawing. He indicates that it is generally agreed that both letters—that is, reading and writing—and drawing belong to the category of things useful for life. Gymnastics, on the other hand, is generally considered to inculcate the virtue of courage. Finally, there is the crucial case of "music" (mousikē)—a term Aristotle uses in its traditional sense to refer not only to instrumental music but to poetry or literature generally. It seems that there is a disagreement about the purpose of music. At present, Aristotle says, most people engage in it for the sake of pleasure, although music was originally brought into education in order to support the enjoyment of noble leisure later in life. Aristotle proceeds to defend the old-fashioned or aristocratic view against the view evidently prevailing in democratic Athens. As the argument continues, however, it becomes apparent that Aristotle actually disagrees with both views and holds instead that the central purpose of education in music is to inculcate virtue (*Pol.* 8.3, 5–6).

Aristotle also makes clear an important difference between his view of gymnastic education and the traditional view—in this case, a view reflecting the Greek consensus. He criticizes certain cities that publicly superintend education for training their young to be professional athletes in order to compete in the Olympics (another instance of a perennial human problem?) on the grounds that it interferes with the normal growth of the body. And he delivers a harsh condemnation of the Spartans for subjecting their youth to a regime of physical training so severe that it produces "savagery" rather than virtue. Aristotle's view is that the purpose or result of gymnastic education is not in fact to inculcate courage or any other virtue, but merely to contribute to the proper development of the body.[21]

Aristotle distinguishes two principal stages in the education of the young. Primary education, extending from ages seven to fourteen, is apparently to be taken up wholly with training in letters and gymnastics. Secondary education proper, extending from fifteen to eighteen, is devoted primarily to music. The final four years of adolescence is then to be given over to a kind of national service geared primarily to developing physical and technical skills for war, though also involving certain types of civic or political training.[22]

By modern standards, the demands of education at both of these stages are extraordinarily light, at least in terms of the acquisition of knowledge or intellectual skills. This underlines the extent to which Aristotle conceives of the education of the young generally as an education of the nonreasoning part of the soul in the "habits" of moral virtue. While Aristotle gives no direct description of the curriculum to be followed in music education, he makes a strong argument for training in singing and the playing of musical instruments. It may be assumed that he also envisioned extensive literary studies, particularly in the epic poetry of Homer (representing in many ways the common education or culture of the Greeks generally) and in lyric poetry of various kinds (representing more particularly the outlook of Greek aristocrats). It should also be noted that Aristotle does not endorse the study of any and all types of music but goes to considerable effort to distinguish the moral effects of different musical modes or styles and recommends only one of these—the so-called Dorian mode—for use in the education of the young. Indeed, much of the reason for his insistence on the actual learning of musical skills by the young—as distinct from mere passive exposure to music performed by others—appears to lie in his assumption that this is the most effective way to assimilate the moral characteristics of particular musical modes (*Pol.* 8.7). Aristotle's preoccupation with music as the central medium of moral education is likely to strike us as quaint or even bizarre, until we begin to reflect on the enormous appeal—and moral authority—of consciously subversive styles of popular music among adolescents in the contemporary world.[23]

IV

We come finally to the question of Aristotle's view of higher education. Unfortunately, in the absence of a thematic discussion of this subject in the *Politics* or elsewhere, any discussion of it must be largely speculative; yet it seems possible to reconstruct Aristotle's thinking with at least reasonable plausibility.

As indicated earlier, Aristotle emphatically endorses the notion that education should be public and uniform, not only in the best city but in any city deserving of the name. In so doing, he recommends a radical enhancement of public authority in Greek political life: even among more traditional or aristocratic cities, only Sparta had a serious system of public education. In an important passage in his *Nicomachean Ethics* (1180a24–b28), however, Aristotle qualifies his commitment to public superintendence of education by noting that private instruction of one's children or friends can be superior to public education because—as in the case of medicine—it is able to take account more fully of the unique requirements of individual human beings. Most obviously, individuals have differing intellectual endowments, and these could be expected to come into play in higher education much more than in secondary education, at least as Aristotle conceives it. Further, at least in societies with a semipermanent ruling element, there may be a divergence between the education that is appropriate to the political class and that suitable for ordinary citizens. Aristotle appears to hold that in such cases at least there should be a differentiated education geared to the training of potential rulers in the political or legislative art and the virtue of prudence.[24]

In a key passage in book 5 of the *Politics* (1310a12–27), which is devoted to the question of the sources of stability and revolution in regimes, Aristotle asserts that "the greatest of all things . . . with a view to making regimes lasting—though it is now slighted by all—is education relative to the regimes. For there is no benefit in the most beneficial laws, even when these have been approved by all those engaging in politics, if they are not going to be habituated and educated in the regime—if the laws are popular, in a popular spirit, if oligarchic, in an oligarchic spirit." This remark appears merely to restate Aristotle's commitment to a uniform system of public education. But he then adds: "But to be educated relative to the regime is not to do the things that oligarchs or those who want democracy enjoy, but rather the things by which the former will be able to run an oligarchy and the latter to have a regime that is democratically run." In harmony with his overall analysis, Aristotle here indicates that there is a fundamental tension between education in the spirit of a regime and education designed to enable a regime to preserve itself and prosper. Education in the spirit of a regime is, or tends to be, narrowly partisan, its object merely the perpetuation of the power of the ruling group. But most cities need a ruling class or element that can transcend partisan concerns as well as the ordinary temptations of political office, and at the same time can provide positive leadership in the difficult task of fostering genuine community. Moreover, precisely because most cities consist of disparate and potentially hostile social or political groups, and because these groups tend to behave in partisan fashion, the attempt to impose a uniform public education in the spirit of the regime narrowly conceived could well arouse antagonism among the nonruling strata of the regime, and thus actually foster political instability.

These considerations seem to point to the need for a system of education in ordinary cities that is not simply uniform, and one that in significant part transcends civic education. What is called for is a special sort of higher education tailored to those specially favored by nature or fortune—those Aristotle variously refers to as "the refined," "the respectable," "the notables," "the gentlemen" (hoi kaloikagathoi), or simply "the best men" (hoi aristoi). Aristotle appears to hold that an aristocratic class constituted by inherited wealth, good breeding, and/or exceptional natural ability can play a key political role, even—indeed, especially—in regimes where it is far from politically dominant. All regimes stand in need both of prudent statesmen and of men who are willing to undertake the burdens of public office out of a sense of duty or honor rather than a desire for personal aggrandizement. Aristocrats like Pericles could and did loyally serve Athens' democratic regime while counteracting some of its immoderate tendencies.[25] It is evidently in the long-term interests of the people (or, in oligarchic regimes, the wealthy few) to make use of not only such men, but the political support that the aristocratic class as a whole can provide their regimes.

It is essential to bear in mind the traditional association in classical Greece of education with the aristocrat's way of life—indeed, its role as a defining element of that way of life. As indicated earlier, it would be a mistake to assume that Aristotle uncritically embraces the perspective of the traditional aristocracy in his account of education or, indeed, more broadly.[26] Nevertheless, the aristocratic perspective certainly figures importantly in the background of Aristotle's thinking in this area, if only because of its role in shaping the outlook of what no doubt formed the preponderant part of the audience for Aristotle's own teaching and writing. At the least, one may say that, in spite of certain appearances, Aristotle is committed to preserving ideological space for an education of an elite or elites within ordinary (that is, socially and politically differentiated) regimes.[27]

What, then, is the character of higher education so understood?

It is, to begin with, sometimes suggested or assumed that Aristotle, like the Plato of the Republic, favors a later training in the higher sciences for public purposes. But there is little reason to suppose that Aristotle envisioned the creation of public universities on the model of Plato's Academy or his own

Lyceum, and no reason to assume that he considered the theoretical sciences or philosophy an essential part of any educational system.[28] When Aristotle describes the instruments of public education in the broad sense as "habits, philosophy, and laws," and when he indicates that the citizens of the best city will require "philosophy" for the right use of leisure, he is very far from endorsing Plato's vision of the "philosopher-king." Rather, I believe, what he has in mind is intellectual culture generally, and in the first instance the leisured enjoyment of "music."[29]

Music in its original and broad sense—the study of music, poetry, and literature generally—provides the clearest and most direct link between secondary and higher education for Aristotle. His emphasis on the education of the young in music is repeatedly justified by reference to the leisured enjoyment of music by older persons, and there is every reason to suppose that the liberal or noble pursuits of leisure alluded to in the *Politics* preeminently involve the enjoyment of music broadly understood. Aristotle no doubt thinks, not of any kind of formal instruction, but rather of public performances of poetry, of which instrumental music was often an integral element; and he probably thinks in the first instance of tragedy and comedy.

In a famous passage in his *Poetics* (1451b5–7), Aristotle remarks that "poetry is more philosophic and more serious than history, for poetry narrates rather the universals, while history narrates the particulars." Aristotle does not mean that poetry simply presents universals, for that would make it indistinguishable from philosophy; rather, poetry narrates the universals as they manifest themselves in particulars, but shorn of the unique and contingent features that complicate our understanding of historical events. The universals of poetry are the universals of moral and political action. Aristotle regards poetry as "imitation" (*mimēsis*)—imitation of human life as it is or should be, and not as an exercise of imaginative creation that has no necessary relationship to a shared world of human experience. Because poetry necessarily shapes or reinforces the shared perception of good and bad and just and unjust that underpins the political community and human social life generally, it is a matter of critical interest for education. For Aristotle, it makes sense to suppose that poetry, or the right kind of poetry, can contribute to the education of men's moral sensibilities through presenting the interplay of universal moral imperatives with the recalcitrant particulars of human experience. As such, it may be added, poetry serves as an education in "prudence" in precisely the Aristotelian sense of that term.

Nor is that all. No education can guarantee that the emotional part of the soul will become completely responsive to the requirements of virtue. Aristotle gives us to understand that even those well brought up in youth will be susceptible to the influence of passions of various sorts—particularly passions that, while not inherently disreputable, can have adverse and even catastrophic consequences when unchecked. In another famous passage of the *Poetics* (1449b24–28), Aristotle tells us that tragic poetry "effects through pity and fear a catharsis of passions of this sort." Interpretation of Aristotle's notion of tragic catharsis is notoriously contentious, but at least it is plausibly understood in fundamentally moral or educational terms. On such a view, catharsis is a purification of pity, fear, and possibly other passions resembling them, the effect of which is to blunt their force, purge their potentially harmful tendencies, and reduce them to their proper place in the economy of the human soul.[30]

If this interpretation is correct, poetry, and in particular tragic poetry, may be said to represent at once the culmination of civic education and a key component of liberal education generally. Tragedy is a central feature of the noble or serious leisure that Aristotle regards as a key feature of any civilized way of life; it is routinely if not essentially a public and communal activity, of general interest, and accessible to all regardless of their capacities or any specialized training. Tragedy was, of course, an invention of Athens.[31] Though deeply rooted in the aristocratic culture of archaic Greece, it became in an important sense the literary expression of Athenian democracy and the chief vehicle of democratic education. Aristotle does not emphasize the relationship between tragedy and democracy as such, or the highly political character of much contemporary tragedy. Nevertheless, he appears to accept the centrality of tragic poetry in the communal life even of the best city, to judge at any rate from some scattered indications in the discussion of music and education that concludes the *Politics*.[32]

Of particular importance for the present discussion, however, is the extent to which Aristotle thinks that tragedy, or poetry broadly, transcends the city and its purposes. Tragedy above all connects human beings in a powerful way with the nonpolitical sources of their happiness and misery, the gods and the human soul. Plato had recognized the potential tension between tragedy and the city and banned tragic poetry from the best regime of the *Republic*. Aristotle's theory of catharsis clearly responds to this Platonic concern, though whether or to what extent it might require reform of existing tragic practice is quite uncertain. If it is indeed the case (as seems very likely) that catharsis as Aristotle understands it involves moral or political and not merely aesthetic effects, obviously these effects are assumed to be broadly humane in nature, and not directly supportive of any particular political order. The key point is that tragedy for Aristotle, while serving important public purposes, can in no sense be understood simply as a vehicle of civic or political education. This is the critical difference between Aristotle and the most influential forms of modern communitarianism in approaching the question of the political management of literature and the arts.[33]

V

As noted above, Aristotle seems to differentiate between two sorts of liberal or higher education, one designed primarily to form good citizens, and another designed primarily to form good political leaders or statesmen. If poetry or literature may be said to be the core of the public or common form of higher education for Aristotle, the core of this more restricted education is evidently rhetoric.

Aristotle's interest in rhetoric, the art or expertise of public speaking, is well-attested. One of his earliest writings (now lost) was a dialogue on rhetoric; he is reported to have given lectures on rhetoric as a young man in Plato's Academy; and his surviving treatise on the subject reveals a keen awareness of the utility of rhetoric and its political importance. All of this is worth emphasizing in light of the general eclipse of rhetoric today, and in particular, the loss of a sense of its centrality in liberal education. The rhetorical tradition in education, which remained powerful in the West until well into the nineteenth century, is usually traced to Aristotle's (and Plato's) great rival, Isocrates. Insufficient attention has generally been paid, however, to the evidence for Aristotle's early interest in rhetoric and its significance. Cicero attests to a radical break effected by Aristotle with the previous handling of rhetoric in the Academy, and it makes sense to assume that this development reflected his recognition of the need for a practically oriented approach to the teaching of rhetoric along the lines pioneered by Isocrates.[34]

Rhetoric for Aristotle has two directly political functions. It contributes to deliberation on the public good as carried out in public assemblies or political bodies of various kinds; and it contributes to the adjudication of legal cases. In some ways more important, however, is the kind of "display" rhetoric (the technical term is *epideiktikē*) in which Isocrates in particular specialized. Such rhetoric can have broad if indirect political influence through its articulation of basic moral and political principles, its affirmation of the shared outlook and experiences that form the identity of a political community or culture, and its shaping of attitudes toward fundamental public issues like war and peace.[35]

Americans today tend to be at once dismissive and suspicious of rhetoric. Aristotle is far from insensitive to the power of rhetoric, and to the danger that it can degenerate into sophistry and be made to serve questionable political purposes. He makes clear that rhetoric has a certain innate tendency to usurp the place of knowledge, and for this reason, he insists (in opposition to Isocrates) on defining rhetoric as a purely instrumental or technical expertise, one that stands in need of substantive guidance from another discipline.[36] At the same time, Aristotle indicates that the positive benefits of rhetoric can be substantial. Rhetoric serves a unique function because it deals with those things "about which we deliberate but do not have arts [*technai*]" (*Rh.* 1357a1–2)—that is to say, matters that cannot be decided on the basis of technical information because they are not reducible to techniques or sciences but rather belong to the realm of prudence or practical judgment. Like poetry, then, rhetoric is concerned with the application of universal moral and political principles to the circumstances of the moment and is therefore a prime vehicle for the development and exercise of prudence.[37]

The substantive discipline that supplies guidance to rhetoric is called by Aristotle political science (*politikē*). The art, science, or expertise of politics—the Greek expression is an elastic one encompassing all of these meanings—differs from present-day political or social science in a number of fundamental respects. Above all, it is a "practical" rather than a "theoretical" science: its overriding purpose is to benefit political practice rather than simply to increase knowledge about political phenomena. Accordingly, its central concerns are the central concerns of citizens and their political leaders; it is geared not to the formulation of general laws of political behavior, but to the solution of commonly acknowledged problems as they are encountered in the context of particular political orders. In this respect, it bears a certain resemblance to what would today be called "policy analysis" or "public policy" as distinct from political or social science strictly speaking.[38]

Aristotelian political science is presented in two treatises that must be accounted among his greatest works, the *Politics* and the *Nicomachean Ethics*. That ethics is a major component of a practical science of politics is a second feature that strikingly distinguishes Aristotle's approach. Unlike contemporary social science, Aristotelian social science is unabashedly concerned with moral values and unafraid to render moral judgments. Beyond this, however, ethics is for Aristotle an essential part of political science because or insofar as human character and the formation of character remain a key dimension of politics. As indicated above, moral education is for Aristotle a critical instrument in creating that commonality of outlook which gives a society its fundamental identity. A thorough understanding of morality and the importance and requirements of moral education is therefore an essential aspect of the education of potential political leaders.

More broadly stated, the education of potential political leaders is one centering not on the acquisition of information, but on the development of prudence or practical judgment, a quality that is at once inseparable from moral virtue in those who possess it and essential for the flourishing of political communities. Aristotle appears to be convinced, to repeat what was indicated earlier, that political leadership—the leadership of an elite few or even of a single individual—is an indispensable aspect of decent political life. Appropriate political institutions and the rule of law are of course also necessary, but as Aristotle likes to remind us, in the final analysis not laws but men must rule.[39] Aristotle thus opposes both modern liberalism's emphasis on institutions and modern communitarianism's emphasis on an egalitarian and partisan civic education, in the name of something that is not misleadingly described as liberal education in the original sense of the term.

More extended comparison of Aristotle's educational ideas with later views cannot be attempted here.[40] What has been said thus far is perhaps sufficient to make the case that Aristotle's contribution to the long historical debate on these issues is important in its own right, and of greater relevance to contemporary concerns than is generally recognized. Aristotle's comprehensive vision of liberal education as a moral and practical education should commend itself to all who are concerned at the loss of moral compass so evident in education today, as well as the continued drift toward ever more technical and specialized instruction at the expense of what Aristotle would call the liberal and the noble. To say, as many no doubt will, that such an education is impossible today, or fundamentally at odds with the spirit of contemporary democracy, is to betray a short-sighted view of democracy's genuine interests.

NOTES

1. Bennett, *The Devaluing of America;* Lasch, R*evolt of the Elites,* 141–93. A brief overview of older American discussions of this theme may be found in Pangle, *The Ennobling of Democracy,* 163–82.

2. Consider, for example, the virtually total silence on this subject in Sartori, *Theory of Democracy.* It is surprising that there has not been more discussion of education in current debates over the prospects for popular rule in the newly emergent democracies of the former Soviet bloc.

3. See Tarcov, *Locke's Education* .

4. See, for example, Sandel, *Liberalism;* Barber, *Strong Democracy;* and for a recent overview, Kymlicka, *Political Philosophy,* 199–237.

5. Aristotle receives no systematic treatment in the most authoritative modern works on this subject: Jaeger, *Paideia,* and Marrou, *History of Education.* Marrou makes the following remark: "The fact is that Aristotle's educational work does not seem to me to have the same kind of creative originality as Plato's and Isocrates'. His ideas and his actual practice as the founder of a school, a brotherhood of philosophers supported financially by the generous benefactions of Philip and Alexander, simply reflect the ideas and practice of his age." (381n.2). On the Lyceum, see Lynch, *Aristotle's School,* which is more appreciative of the distinctiveness of Aristotle's contribution. Frankena, *Historical Philosophies,* is a useful account.

6. See especially *Politics* 5.9 1310a12–18, 8.1 1337a7–20, as well as *Nicomachean Ethics* 10.9. Citations translated from the *Politics* in this paper follow Lord, *The Politics of Aristotle.*

7. See especially Yack, "Community and Conflict," "Reinterpretation." Cooper's interpretation ("Political Animals") of civic friendship in Aristotle is cogently criticized by Annas.

8. Consider Aristotle's treatment of magnanimity (*megalopsuchia*) and theoretical virtue in the *Nicomachean Ethics,* and of the political claims of "the one best man" in the *Politics,* well discussed by Newell, "Superlative Virtue."

9. See Mulgan, "Aristotle," as well as the discussion of *Pol.* 7.1–3 in Lord, *Education and Culture,* 180–96. Swanson, *The Public and the Private,* is a valuable corrective to the widely shared assumption that Aristotle ignores or depreciates the importance of the "private sphere" recognized by modern liberalism.

10. See, for example, Marrou, *History of Education,* 98–99.

11. Consider Plutarch's treatise *On the Education of Children,* with the remarks of Marrou, *History of Education,* 147–48.

12. *Pol.* 1336b20–27, 1338a30–37, 1341b38–40.

13. These passages are collected and discussed in Lord, "Politics and Education," on which this paper draws throughout. For a detailed interpretation of *Pol.* 7–8, see Lord, *Education and Culture.*

14. On the question of the naturalness of the polis and its evolution from prepolitical society, see Lord, "Aristotle's Anthropology." Swanson, *The Public and the Private,* 132–42, offers a useful account of Aristotle's view of civic or political virtue in the basic sense just discussed; cf. Yack, "Reinterpretation," 30–33.

15. Consider, for example, Lasch's comments (*Revolt of the Elites,* 151–54) on the limitations of Horace Mann's educational thought. A fine analysis of the political significance in the United States of popularized academic doctrine is Ceaser, *Liberal Democracy* .

16. *Eth. Nic.* 1.13, 6.5.

17. Ibid. 6.5; cf. 1.3.1094b22–95a11.

18. "[A] brief overview of writings about 'liberal education' and about its history reveals contradiction and confusion; and the more that is written, the more confounded things become" (Kimball, *Orators and Philosophers,* 9). The terms of the debate over the purposes of education in nineteenth-century America (see Veysey, *American University*) were essentially no different from the terms of the debate as it appears in Aristotle.

19. For a discussion of the evolution of aristocratic and popular attitudes in Athens and elsewhere in the Greek world, see Morris, this volume.

20. This interpretation is developed at length in Lord, *Education and Culture,* 68–85.

21. *Pol.* 8.4. The inculcation of courage as well as the other virtues belongs instead to the education in music.

22. *Pol.* 7.17, 8.4 1338b39–39a10, 8.6.1341a4–8. The "military and civic training" (*polemikai kai politikai askēseis*) mentioned by Aristotle in the latter passage should almost certainly be assumed to reflect the Athenian *ephēbeia,* though Athenian youth served in this institution for only two years.

23. Consider Bloom, *American Mind,* 68–81. Any honest analysis of the political implications of contemporary popular music would have to take account not only of its decadent and antinomian features but of its increasingly open flirtation with the symbols and attitudes of fascism.

24. Compare *Eth. Nic.* 10.9 with *Pol.* 3.4, especially 1277a16–20, b25–30.

25. See, for example, Kagan, *Pericles,* 11–45, and more generally, Ober, *Mass and Elite.*

26. Consider the critique of Aristotle's "aristocratic conservatism" in Wood and Wood, *Class Ideology,* 209–53.

27. Cf. Swanson, *The Public and the Private,* 144–45.

28. Lynch (*Aristotle's School,* 69–70) rightly emphasizes the lack of congruence between Aristotle's practical approach to education in the best regime of the *Politics* and his own teaching activities; but he goes too far when he asserts that "the realization of the politically ideal state as Aristotle explored it in his *Politics* would in effect be the death of philosophy as practiced in the Lyceum," which overlooks the elaborate comparison developed by Aristotle in *Pol.* 7.1–3 between philosophy understood as the best way of life for the individual and the best way of life for the city; moreover, given the evidently incomplete condition of the text of the last book of the *Politics,* Lynch ignores

the possibility that Aristotle's original argument was more explicit in holding open the door to the (private) study of philosophy in the best city (compare the "Nocturnal Council" of Plato's *Laws*).

29. *Pol.* 2.5.1263b37–64a1, 7.15.1334a22–23. See Lord, *Education and Culture,* 199–202, and for an alternative interpretation, Depew, "Politics, Music, and Contemplation." Aristotle's broad use of the term *philosophia* (note especially *Rh.* 1394a5) is perhaps best understood as reflecting a partial appropriation of Isocrates' critique of Plato and the Academy.

30. General discussion in Lord, *Education and Culture,* 119–41, 159–74, and Halliwell, *Aristotle's Poetics,* 168–201.

31. Important for Aristotle's overall view of tragedy is the frequently misread passage in *Poetics* 4 on its origins and development; see Lord, "Aristotle's History."

32. I believe *Pol.* 1342a11–15 unquestionably alludes to tragedy (cf. Lord, *Education and Culture,* 119, 138–41). Consider Salkever, "Tragedy and the Education of the Dēmos;" (274–303); Euben, "Introduction" (1–42) as well as other essays in his collection *Greek Tragedy and Political Theory;* and see Dougherty, this volume.

33. The difference is nicely captured in this remark by the Marxist literary critic and philosopher Georg Lukacs: "In all artistic questions, classical aesthetics . . . saw public issues, questions of social pedagogy. By contrast, modern aesthetics represents, with few exceptions, a step backward. Partly this is because this aspect of art's effect was entirely or largely disregarded and art was essentially reduced to a specialized connoisseurship, but partly too because it was indeed recognized that art exercises such a societal effect, but this effect was understood to operate in a much too direct and too concrete and substantive a fashion—as if art existed simply in order to achieve the implementation of particular concrete societal tasks" (*Ästhetik,* 1:810).

34. The evidence is assembled in Chroust, *Aristotle,* 1:105–16. The key role of rhetoric and of Isocrates in particular in the origins and development of the idea of liberal education is properly stressed in the fine study of Kimball (*Orators and Philosophers,* especially 13–39, 237–41); but Kimball (like Jaeger) fails to appreciate the extent of the kinship between Isocrates' rhetorical *paideia* and Aristotle's project of "practical philosophy."

35. On the different types of rhetoric and the relationship of rhetoric to politics, see Arist. *Rh.* 1.3–4, 9–10.

36. *Rh.* 1.2.1356a25–33, 4 1359b2–16. See further Lord, "Intention."

37. An interesting treatment of this issue in Aristotle and writers influenced by him is Kahn, *Rhetoric.*

38. On the "practical" character of Aristotle's political and ethical writings and their relationship to contemporary social science, see Salkever, "Aristotle's Social Science," and for a fuller discussion, Salkever, *Finding the Mean;* Ceaser, *Liberal Democracy,* 41–69.

39. Consider especially Newell, "Superlative Virtue," as well as Nichols, *Citizens and Statesmen.*

40. Perhaps most noteworthy is the marked resemblance between Aristotle's approach to education as outlined here and the tradition of genteel education deriving from Renaissance humanism, which remained powerful in the United States until well into the nineteenth century. Consider especially the educational program of Sir Thomas Elyot in *The Boke Named the Gouernour* (1531), with the discussion in Kimball, *Orators and Philosophers,* 75–113.

HOPLITES INTO DEMOCRATS: THE CHANGING IDEOLOGY OF ATHENIAN INFANTRY

Victor D. Hanson

DRAMA, festivals, and oratory were public fora where Athenians witnessed and questioned democratic ideology. Smaller, more elite discussions over politics took place frequently at symposia, gymnasia, and in personal debates. Private higher education organized by the sophists, Isocrates, Plato, Aristotle, and others examined democracy as part of larger interests in political rhetoric and natural law. Yet the real democratic education of the Athenians, in the broadest sense of that word, was more amorphous and insidious, involving a remarkable transformation in the thought of the traditional polis dweller himself, the middling agrarian who was induced by Athenian democracy to accept practices entirely antithetical to those found in the normative Greek city-state of two centuries past.

BEFORE DEMOCRACY: THE NORMATIVE POLIS

The Greek polis that crystallized after the Dark Ages in the seventh and sixth centuries B.C. was in most places a community of small agriculturalists.[1] At Athens, for example, Solon's census rubrics of the early sixth century B.C. were expressed in nothing other than agricultural produce (e.g., Arist. *Ath. Pol.* 7.3–4). Much of his legislation was agrarian in nature (e.g., Arist. *Ath. Pol.* 6.2; Plut. *Solon* 15.2–16.4; 23–4), reflecting at this date both the primacy of farming in the life of the Athenians, and the gradual movement away from pastoral aristocracy to landed timocracy (e.g., Arist. *Ath. Pol.* 5.2; 6.1–2). Politically, by the early fifth century B.C., most Greek city-states reflected their agrarian geneses and so had often evolved a constitution that was timocratic in that full participation in representative government was limited to those who farmed their own land.

Yet it is not easy to characterize the political organization of Greek agricultural communities in simple terms as either "oligarchic" or "democratic" (e.g., Aris. *Pol.* 3.1279b20–1280a7; and cf. 4.1290a30ff.). As Aristotle knew, early agrarian poleis (such as Solonian Athens) could be in some sense quasi-democratic: if the property qualification was quite low and made allowances for individual changes in status, there was always some fluidity between cen-

sus rubrics, ensuring that a great many middling farmers, or *mesoi,* could qualify for citizen rights.[2] Under enlightened "oligarchies" only the very poorest
with either insubstantial plots or no land at all were liable for their entire life-
time to be excluded from full participation in the government of the polis.[3]

But there was also the other political extreme. When the property qualification for full citizenship was quite substantial, and the ruling body was thus limited only to a small group of larger (and often aristocratic) landowners (e.g.,
Arist. *Pol.* 4.1293a23–34), then the oligarchical regime of the agrarian city-
state approached near autocracy. Aristotle himself seems to envision (and prefer) the existence of a moderate timocracy, neither radically democratic nor op-
pressively autocratic, a regime run by small landowners which he dubbed
"polity" (*politeia*). This was a middle form of constitutional government that
must have been common among the poleis in classical times, one that sought
through a variety of mechanisms (inheritance laws, restrictions on land trans-
fers and the accumulation of wealth) to preserve agricultural egalitarianism.

Almost always after the eighth century B.C., those residents of the Greek city-
state who qualified (by both birth and property) as full citizens organized themselves for battle as hoplite infantry in the phalanx, a mass formation of heavy-
armored equals who fought on flat agricultural land, most often against other
similarly equipped bodies of agrarian militia: the state's entire apparatus of warfare reduced to a single battle between farmers, on farmland, often over farmland.[4] There has been some controversy (which we will return to shortly)
whether or not by the late fifth century B.C. hoplite participants were still always
a distinct social "class," one composed strictly of yeoman farmers. Yet, before
the Peloponnesian War there is no reason to doubt the traditional view that
heavy infantrymen of the phalanx were originally drawn from the surrounding
landowners of the polis. Aristotle, for example, even in the late fourth century
B.C. stated that "it is often the case that the same men are to be both hoplites and
farmers."[5]

True, the wealthy were always present on the Greek battlefield. At Athens
they probably owned between seventy and one hundred acres, which allowed
them to purchase and maintain horses. But the mounts of the Greek *hippeis*
(cavalry) were small ponies, without stirrups, and consequently of little value
against the pikes of heavily armed infantry squares. Unless they rode to battle
and dismounted to join their social inferiors, or simply marched out as hoplites
altogether, even the elite horsemen increasingly found their role as cavalry
proper only incidental, never essential, to the original agrarian phalanx. This is
surely a reflection of the inability of a very few to dominate the early political
life of most of Greek communities.[6]

The less fortunate, those without land in the community, were even more
marginal on the hoplite battlefield, relegated to ravaging and light-armed skir-
mishing (e.g., Arist. *Pol.* 6.1321a14–15). Under the intricate protocols of the
original agrarian city-state, their role during wartime was to harass and mop up

before and after battle, or, by the fifth century B.C. and later, to serve as rowers in the fleet of the maritime poleis.[7] At least until the mid-fifth century, then, the political status of the polis resident of Greece was reflected in his particular role on the battlefield, with the frequency and exclusivity of hoplite battle a sure indication of the social and political superiority of this rather broad landowning class. In short, the serried ranks of the phalanx had become a reflection of the agrarian solidarity of polis membership. As Aristotle put it, "The men who fight have the most power, and those who possess the arms (*kektēmenoi ta hopla*) are the citizens" (*Pol.* 3.1279b3–5; cf. 3.1288a12–15).

Economically, the aim for each of these small agrarian Greek city-states was *autarkeia,* the cherished ideal of self-sufficiency in food production (e.g., Thuc. 6.20.4), which helped to ensure a larger independence (*autonomia*) and freedom (*eleutheria*) to set one's own laws of governance, without outside intervention.[8] This reliance on locally grown grain, olives, and vines further reinforced the privileged political and military position of the resident landowners surrounding the polis. So, until the fifth century B.C., the glue that held most Greek city-states together, the true distinguishing characteristic of a polis, was precisely this triadic equation shared by a broad group of its people: voting citizen = hoplite infantryman = small food producer.

But it is unpopular in academic circles currently to speak at any era of an ancient Greek "middle class." It is rare now to envision a broad-based agrarian citizenry neither wealthy nor poor in either absolute or relative terms. Hoplites of the early polis, nevertheless, seem to fit that rubric perfectly.[9] For example, at the beginning of the sixth century B.C. under the old Solonian rubrics at Athens, the "yoked" (*zeugitai*)—who were nearly always associated with hoplite infantry—were sandwiched between the large producers and horsemen above (*pentekosiomedimnoi* [500 measures of liquid or dry produce] / *hippeis* [300 measures]), and the landless *thētes* (less than 200 measures) below.[10]

Similarly, the Athenian tyrant Peisistratus nearly a half-century later seems to have championed emerging rural interests neither rich nor poor, by encouraging farm residency, the planting of trees and vines, and the expansion of hardworking yeomanry onto marginal lands.[11] At Athens these early efforts at agrarianism were successful: truly large farms never existed during the four centuries of polis culture, just as at the other extreme land redistribution schemes of the landless mob never became too widespread. Far more commonly there (and throughout the Greek-speaking world until the Hellenistic era), archaeological and epigraphical evidence reflects a common-sized "hoplite" farm of about 8 to 12 acres.[12]

Too poor to maintain slave-labor gangs, the hoplite-farmer nevertheless often possessed a servile worker or two to labor intensively alongside him on his farm, and to carry his equipment while on campaign.[13] Slave ownership helps to belie the notion that agrarian infantrymen were subsistence "peasants." Thucydides at any rate could break down the losses in the Athenian plague not in terms of a dichotomous rich and poor, but rather by employing three separate categories of fatalities: wealthy cavalrymen, hoplites, and the "mob" below (Thuc. 2.31.2).[14]

Although it was standard practice in antiquity for aristocratic thinkers (e.g., Ps. Xen. *Ath. Pol.* 1.2; 2.14; cf. Xen. *Hell.* 2.3.48) to lump hoplites in with rich people like themselves (logical enough given the fact that two census groups above the *zeugitai* might also serve as hoplites in the phalanx, the muster-lists usually not listing *thētes* at all [e.g., Thuc. 6.43.1]), we often hear that *zeugitai* infantrymen were considered to be of moderate means. In the fourth century some farmers could not meet their assessments of the war tax (Dem. 22.65). Others, even poorer, could not afford to provide their own food on campaign (e.g., Dem. 21.95; Lys. 16.14). No wonder then that earlier during the Peloponnesian War they sometimes openly joined the landless against the wealthy. At Corcyra, for example, hoplites clubbed and stabbed to death the captured wealthy aristocrats, whom apparently they saw as inimical to their own interests (e.g., Thuc. 4.47). Likewise, in colonization schemes, the wealthy were often expressly excluded, the state emphasizing that it was the *zeugitai* and the *thētes* who needed sole opportunity to win new land (e.g., *IG* I³ 46, lines 43–46).

This occasional and unsystematic inclusion of hoplites with either the poor or the elite characteristically reveals their traditionally moderate stance. So, under most ordinary circumstances during the history of the polis, the presence of this independent "middle" entity within the Greek polis was real, not a mere philosophical construct (e.g., Phoc. fr. 7.1–2; Solon fr. 4.5–8; Eur. *Supp.* 238–42), a group aligned politically and socially neither with the hereditary affluent nor the growing urban poor.

The problem, then, at all times for any would-be reformers at Athens—or any other Greek city—was to find a mechanism to win over this large group of middling farmers, the *mesoi.* Democracy sought to convince conservative Attic yeomen that their own interests lay with the gradual extension of political protection to the landless and less fortunate, that they must not ally themselves with the reactionary wealthy, who were so resistant to Athenian democracy. Aristotle, for example, wrote that "the lawgiver must always in his constitution take in the middle class (*proslambanein tous mesous*); if he is making oligarchical laws he must keep the middle in consideration, and if he desires democratic [laws], he must legislate to bring them in." (*Pol.* 4.1296b35–38).

THE DISTORTION OF THE OLD REGIME

Athens altered the economic, political, and military triad on which the Greek state was based in the fifth century B.C.[15] The wars with, and eventual victory over, Persia (490, 480–479 B.C.), and the subsequent creation of a maritime empire presented economic and political possibilities unimaginable in the sixth century B.C., offering Athens resources beyond the capabilities of most other poleis (Thuc. 1.89–96). Athenian imperialism hastened the democratization process begun by Cleisthenes (507 B.C.). It enhanced the status of social groups that held no land, providing jobs for more than twenty thousand citizens outside agriculture (e.g., Arist. *Ath. Pol.* 24.3; Ar. *Vesp.* 709). Besides adding new-found prestige to these landless *thētes* who had served so well against Persian ships, the formal creation of a vast navy from the tribute of allied states turned Athenian attention permanently seaward (Thuc. 1.99.1; Plut. *Cimon* 11), away from purely landed aspirations. The erection of the long-walls and the fortification of the Athenian port at Piraeus only cemented this new reliance on naval strength, rather than infantry power alone (Thuc. 1.107.1–108.1; 2.13.7). Citizens of Athens in a psychological sense walled themselves off from their own farmland to connect with the sea.

Likewise, as early as the mid-fifth century, grain was imported in sizable quantities into the Piraeus.[16] Despite the controversy over the exact date and degree of dependence on overseas foodstuffs,[17] Athens' well-known concern for foreign cereal supplies represented an interest in pricing, availability, and commerce that was ostensibly at odds with the old ideal of absolute self-sufficiency in food products (e.g., Arist. *Pol.* 7.1326b29–30).

Finally, the exploitation of the silver mines at Laurion in southern Attica, the growth of some small factories (*ergastēria*) in Athens, and the manning of a huge Aegean fleet drew slaves into Athens proper in enormous numbers. With them came the metics, resident alien businessmen, bankers, and traders, an entire shadow city of outsiders who had no formal political rights in the polis.

By the fifth century B.C., there were somewhere between 10,000 and 40,000 metics (adults and children), and between 80,000 and 150,000 slaves.[18] As if the official attempts at diversifying the economic, political, and military resources of Athens were not enough, this less-organized migration of foreigners and slaves into the polis further diminished, by their sheer numbers, the traditional exclusivity of the hoplite landowner at Athens (e.g., Plut. *Per.* 12; Ps. Xen. *Ath. Pol.* 1.10–12).

We are not sure how many residents were not middling agriculturalists of Attica by the middle of the fifth century B.C., but it is a safe guess that at least half the citizens themselves might no longer possess a hoplite-sized farm, that is, land that would have met the traditional yeoman census. Of the total resident population of adults in Attica, hoplites liable for military service now probably constituted no more than a seventh to a tenth (i.e., about 20,000 hoplites out of a total population [male citizens, women, slaves, and metics] of well over 150,000 adults). Yet the entire ideology of the Greek polis had once derived from that increasingly small minority.

The result of what we may legitimately now call the Athenian experiment, this catalyst of polis deviancy among the Greek city-states should have been, I think, constant friction between old-guard hoplites and landless citizens, who were traditionally limited in their rights but were now performing important economic and military functions for the state—with occasional outright fighting between the two groups as landed broad-based oligarchy and timocracy sought to suppress landless democracy. Radical democracy of the Athenian kind, after all, was in theory inimical to broad-based agrarian government. No matter how low the property qualification for full-citizenship under egalitarian agrarian governments might extend, did not Athenian-style democracy go even further? Ostensibly (though not always in practice), Athens put a man with little or no land on roughly equal political and military footing with a farmer-hoplite, a citizen whose plot had provided the fountainhead of family privilege for generations.[19] Money, a far more fluid and volatile standard of privilege than land (e.g., Arist. *Pol.* 5.1308a35–1308b8), could quickly widen the gulf between wealthy and poor and destroy the agrarian middle.

Yet between 507 and 338 B.C. convolution more often than revolution prevailed at Athens. As more democratic institutions took hold in the century after Cleisthenes (507 B.C.), the agrarian exclusivity of Attic farmers was transformed or at least partially reinvented. Although there was always growing tension between Athenian landed and nonlanded, no overt fighting broke out between hoplites and the poorer during this long process of democratization. Instead, what occurred at Athens throughout the fifth and into the fourth century B.C. was actually a gradual diminution of hostility between the two groups, yeomen (*zeugitai*) and landless (*thētes*). Farmer-hoplites increasingly accepted the tenets of Athenian democracy, as privileged classes reinvented the nature of the traditional whole in order to save at least some of its parts.

How and why could so-called radical democracy at Athens become palatable to hoplite-farmers? Was not democratic government a revolutionary institution? Did it not threaten the old economic, political, social, and military domain of small landowners? Clearly, the Athenian polis took special care to educate and incorporate its farmers into the cultural life of the polis, rather than to marginalize them, even when democratic institutions were at odds with the traditional farming agenda of most Attic hoplites.[20] Just as important, however, hoplite-farmers as individuals came to learn that their own social, economic, and political status could (for a time) be selfishly enhanced under Athenian democracy, not inevitably diminished as we might expect. If Athenian farmers could be taught to give up a belief in their absolute and traditional military, political, and economic precedence, some growers therein might find even greater advantage—at least in the immediate short term.

The Transformation of Athenian Yeomanry

The Democratic Hoplite

As pitched battles between phalanxes were becoming more and more irrelevant in late-fifth and fourth century B.C. Greece, Athens most successfully sought to refashion the entire military role of the heavy-armed hoplite. Of course, duty outside formal phalanx battle doomed the hoplite as exclusive protector of the polis. But fighting away from the mass also gave Athenian agrarians new responsibilities, albeit in very different roles. During fifth-century B.C. Athenian democracy, hoplite infantry were used more frequently than during the period before the Persian Wars under either agrarian oligarchy/timocracy or Peisistratian tyranny (i.e., 700–480 B.C.)—although in guises antithetical (and so in the long term disastrous) to the notion of traditional one-day, agrarian wars.

Despite the emphasis on naval operations in the Athenian Empire, there were many occasions throughout the fifth century B.C. when autonomous hoplite forces played a less dramatic, but nevertheless vital military role in the defense of the polis as amphibious troops and besiegers.[21] The ever-conservative Aristotle may have had these hoplite operations in mind when he complained that constant infantry service abroad had incurred high casualties among the landed and thus in his opinion strengthened the aspirations of the poor at home (e.g., *Ath. Pol.* 26.1; *Pol.* 5.1303a7–10). Although these battles outside the agrarian arena were precisely part of the process that destroyed hoplite warfare in Greece, at Athens heavy infantrymen were not left idle. Rather they were used outside pitched battles and integrated into the city's multifarious defense forces, becoming key agents in a new, more dynamic, democratic warfare far more murderous than anything the Greek city-state had experienced in the prior two centuries.

True, there are numbers of anecdotal passages in Greek literature attesting to "NAVAL MOB" the growing friction between landed conservatives and the "naval mob" (the nation of hoplites now supposedly being replaced by a rabble of rowers).[22] But under closer scrutiny these observations usually reflect the disenchantment of the more wealthy at Athens. There was probably not much complaint from the Athenian hoplite farmer himself, who after the Persian Wars increasingly was seeing his traditional military interests oddly protected by democratic change.

A more accurate representation of Athenian hoplite ideology is found in Aeschylus, and even in the conservative comedy of Aristophanes and the often-bitter drama of Euripides. These playwrights had no real sympathy for aristocratic (or Spartan) oligarchs, but rather praise for the egalitarian nature of Athenian democracy. They acknowledge the great contribution of the rowing-class of Athenian poor but somehow see in it no obstacle to their innate pride in the achievements of their own class of hoplite farmers in both a military and agricultural sense. The integration of moderates into democracy, and those whom they represented, is in stark contrast to the shrillness of the Athenian fourth-century philosophers. Those dissidents posed as nostalgic spokesmen for the Athenian hoplite class of which they were not always part in either sympathy or practice.[23]

During the late fifth century B.C., there were only a few instances where hoplite armies collided head-on in any great number (e.g., Delium [424 B.C.], Mantineia [418 B.C.], and to a lesser extent at Solygeia [425 B.C.] and before Syracuse [415 B.C.]). Yet at Athens hoplites were busy for a while yet. There were numerous occasions, for example, when Athenian hoplites marched out on purely infantry expeditions and attempted to engage the enemy (not always successfully) in decisive encounters. Here one thinks of the twice-yearly invasions of the Megarid, when the Athenian hoplite force mustered in full strength during the Archidamian War (Thuc. 2.31; 4.66.1; Plut. *Per.* 30.3). Two thousand hoplites also marched north against Spartalus in 429 B.C., forcing the Chalcidian infantry into the city proper, and then falling back before enemy missile-troops and cavalry sorties. Deployed traditionally on flat ground against an enemy who had no intention of deciding the issue with similar heavy infantry, over 430 hoplites perished (Thuc. 2.97.7).

Athenian hoplites also played a vital role in more complex, combined operations during the Peloponnesian War. In these situations they were transported by sea and then expected to occupy ground alone or seek out enemy light and heavy infantry. While ostensibly marines in the sense that they arrived in enemy territory on ships, rather than independently by land, it is better to describe these new hoplites as "expeditionary forces." Often, for example, their activity was far from the coast, independent, and not always supported by combined naval strategy.[24]

Hoplites in the fifth century B.C. were also used by the democracy in smaller numbers as amphibious marines or as more daring, seaborne raiders (e.g., Plato *Laws* 4.706b–c). During the Archidamian War, they skirted the coast of the Peloponnese, disembarked, ravaged, plundered (e.g., Thuc. 2.17.4; 2.23.2; 2.25.30; 2.26; 2.32; 2.56; 2.58.1), and then, in the wake of enemy reprisals, fled to the safety of the ships. Although these troops probably rarely formed up in the phalanx for decisive, single battles or engaged in drawn-out sieges, there is little doubt they were employed as hoplites proper, not armed as light-armed skirmishers.

More controversial still is the actual status of the trireme's standard seaborne contingent of ten *epibatai*, the naval "marines" permanently attached to many Athenian vessels quite independent of any accompanying hoplite forces that were being transported from theater to theater. Given their exalted status in the literary and epigraphical sources, the nature of their training and armament, and their apparent recruitment from the hoplite muster-roll, it is logical—if these strict census differentiations still always applied in the late-fifth and fourth centuries B.C.—that most *epibatai* should not have been landless *thētes.* Marines were often instead those who were eligible and liable to see service as hoplites proper.[25]

From the record of their employment during naval engagements, Athenian marines were not mere adornments. Often they became the decisive element in battle as both naval boarders and defensive troops who kept the enemy from gaining access to the decks of their own ships.[26] Even more striking, on some occasions in the Peloponnesian War, farmers may not have fought as hoplites at all but rather served as rowers in the fleet alongside the landless.[27]

What we see at Athens during the entire course of the fifth century B.C. is not quite—as is argued by the Old Oligarch, Plato, Isocrates, Aristotle, Plutarch, and others—an abridgement of the hoplite presence, but some increased opportunity and need for its service, albeit in new and untraditional ways. Although these novel military roles ultimately contributed to the demise of agrarian warfare in Greece, they did no immediate damage to Athenian yeomanry itself. This integration and complementary use of Athenian hoplites and rowers were exactly what Pericles was referring to in his funeral oration when he bragged that the Athenians were usually successful at war because of "simultaneous attention to the navy and the expedition by land of its citizens to many lands" (Thuc. 2.39.3), a practice that "made every sea and land the highway of our daring" (Thuc. 2.41.4; and cf. especially 1.142.5).

Elsewhere, among other Greek democratic and maritime powers, there was nothing comparable to Athens' success in balancing naval and land defense. Hermocrates of democratic Syracuse, for example, blamed the Sicilians' initial loss to the Athenian phalanx on his fellow-citizens' utter lack of familiarity with hoplite warfare (Thuc. 6.72.3–5). His comment may indicate that by the end of the fifth century B.C. some democratic seafaring poleis had little need of either the old or new hoplite protocols. In short, the number of conventional single-day encounters that were purely hoplite in character may have decreased under Athenian democracy, but the occasions where fighters saw some type of hoplite service surely multiplied. The ubiquity of heavy infantry was due both to a greater frequency of warfare in general during the fifth and fourth centuries B.C. (as opposed to seventh and sixth, for example), and to the expansion of the Athenian hoplite horizon to include new responsibilities as marines and as seaborne hybridized troops.

Even the notorious (from a farming point of view) Athenian policy of avoiding pitched battle in Attica during the Peloponnesian War (e.g., Thuc. 2.14.1; 2.21–22; Plut. *Per.* 33.7) did not guarantee the destruction of native farms by enemy ravagers. While forced evacuation of landowners inside the walls of Athens should be seen as democracy's rebuke of traditional Greek agrarian ideology, it was still not necessarily fatal to Athens' own indigenous hoplite farmers. The issue is more complex: the Athenians offered some help to agriculturalists in ways that were consistent with the new democratic thinking, rather than old-fashioned timocratic ideology.

The five enemy invasions between 431 and 425 B.C.—and even the Spartan occupation of Decelea outside the walls of Athens (413–404 B.C.)—did not harm Athenian farms irrevocably. Planting continued throughout the Archidamian War, and perhaps sporadically even during the occupation of Decelea. Serious damage to capital crops such as trees and vines simply did not occur. Many farmers never evacuated their families into Athens at all. Athenian land forces were not idle in Attica and did not allow ravagers to attack with impunity the property of fellow hoplites. The democracy took pains to ensure that cavalry patrols, light-armed sorties, and overseas actions were designed to relieve pressure from local farmers' property.[28]

True, most rural folk surrounding Athens were completely opposed to the evacuation, inasmuch as it was an affront both to their hoplite pride (e.g., Thuc. 2.20.1–2.21.3) and to the integrity of their property (e.g., Thuc. 2.59.1–2). But the real suffering of Attica's agrarians occurred because of the plague inside Athens, not because of enemy ravagers (e.g., Thuc. 3.87.2). Understandably, we hear of no organized or sustained hoplite resistance to Pericles' strategy of forced evacuation. Despite the private grumbling, there was little, if any, civil insurrection over his policy—a plan that the historian Thucydides (no radical democrat) at any rate felt made for good strategy (e.g., 2.61.2; 2.65.7,13).

Periclean defense was, in fact, palatable to its citizens (even if strategically unsound) partly because of the belief of Attic hoplites in their leaders' ability to protect their farms by means other than pitched hoplite battle—a promise in retrospect for the most part kept. And as hoplite landowners, they must have realized also that enemy devastation was aimed at drawing out other hoplites, not in canvasing the entire countryside and rendering the rural infrastructure of a polis desolate. Consequently, if anyone profited from the radical, antiagrarian strategy of deliberately avoiding hoplite battle in Attica—the old Themisto-clean ideology once more promulgated by Pericles and his followers—it was the Athenian farmer-hoplite (even if not always the wealthy cavalry elite).

It is possible to suggest that, apart from psychological considerations of the hoplites' martial ethic, a further benefit accrued to hoplites from the Periclean strategy. Pitched battle in 431 B.C. on the Athenian plain between Athenians and the Peloponnesian and Boeotian intruders would probably have led to at least one or two thousand dead Attic farmers (about 10 percent of a 10,000- to 20,000-man infantry force in the field), and thus to a greater loss of military prestige among local landowners. The Peloponnesian and Theban enemy invaders, we should recall, marched into Attica in 431 B.C. with perhaps 20,000 to 40,000 men—the largest assembled hoplite force since the combined Greek army at the battle of Plataea (479 B.C.).

In short, under imperial democracy Athenian hoplites for a time enjoyed bizarre trade-offs: highly visible military service, but an actual avoidance of all-out (and lethal) battle between national armies in Attica; evacuated farms but little long-term destruction of the Attic countryside. Pitched fighting in Attica and constant protection of isolated homesteads were the ostensible trademarks of hoplite agrarianism. But they were also the very military situations where high hoplite casualties were certain, and where defeat and accompanying loss of military reputation before formidable Peloponnesian and Theban infantry were possible. At the beginning of the Peloponnesian War, the landless Athenian *thētes* were numerically equal to the other citizens who fought in the phalanx (about 20,000 men each). But by the end of the war it was a different story. During the twenty-seven years of fighting, landless *thētes*, the supposed beneficiaries of Athenian liberalism, died more than twice as frequently as hoplites, the purported losers under radical democracy.[29] If the Peloponnesian War was a tragedy for all Athenian citizens, then it became an abject slaughter of its landless population.

The multifarious use of Athenian hoplites as amphibious troops was a dramatic marriage of traditional infantry and growing naval power. Aside from the acknowledged military advantages that mobile infantry brought to the defense requirements of the Athenian empire, there were also less apparent social and political benefits to democracy as well: landowners were transported by, and could fight alongside with, their social inferiors, blurring traditional census rubrics and cementing the notion—as the shared experience of danger offered by military service so often does—of political equality (e.g., Arist. *Pol.* 6.1321a17–19). The role of heavy infantry at Athens, then, was not rejected in the fifth century B.C., but rather transformed. This revolutionary development tended to strengthen the social foundations of Athenian democracy, just as it undermined agrarian protocol and drastically changed the nature of Greek warfare in general. The policy went forward apparently without much objection from farmers themselves—despite the knowledge that the precious equation between small landowner and heavy soldier was being lost.

The Democratic Farmer

With the steady growth of Athenian imperialism in the fifth century B.C. and the continually rising population in Attica, occasional import of foodstuffs—essentially wheat and to a much lesser extent barley—became necessary. Controversy rages about the exact degree and date of the Athenian need for foreign grain. The argument pits traditional positivist reliance on literary and epigraphical references to overseas grain-dealing against contemporary agronomic and demographic models that argue for near Attic self-sufficiency. No clear resolution of the debate is possible. But it is certain that in the fifth or fourth century B.C. local farmers of Attica were never entirely displaced in an economic sense by growers overseas, just as it is also true that "Athens could exist without farmers better than she could without imports."[30]

It is likely that all produce, home-grown and imported alike, was in the fifth and fourth centuries B.C. in even greater demand at Athens (cf. Xen. *Mem.* 3.6.13). Foreign supplies only helped assuage the increased appetite for a variety of foods among the growing Attic population. Consequently, the notion that Athenian democracy paid little heed to the hoplite agriculturalist, or did not require his local foodstuffs, is simplistic. This need for foreign supplementation might as well argue for increased local demand, as for a decision to replace domestically grown food. "Those of you involved in mining," the speaker of a Demosthenic speech against Phainippos (about 320s B.C.) reminded his audience, "have experienced setbacks, but you farmers are profiting beyond what is fitting" (42.21; cf. Diod. 18.18.6; 16.83.1). Xenophon's Ischomachus says, "No business gives greater returns than farming" (*Oec.* 20.22).

The earlier dynamism and growth of Athenian democracy enhanced the economic position of the local Attic farmer in a strictly financial sense. At just the same time, however, it was ending his traditional and privileged role as single food guarantor of the polis: short-term enhancement for individual growers accompanied long-term destruction of the agrarians as a privileged class. If Athens was ultimately dismantling Greek agrarian ideology of two centuries past, that upheaval resulted from an effort to protect her own farmers as citizens at large, by transforming Athenian custom and practice beyond the original, confining, agricultural ideology of the Greek polis. Attic farmers seeing gain in the fifth and fourth centuries B.C. forsook long-term (and parochial) interests.[31]

The farms of Attica were not actually sacrificed during the Peloponnesian War. Despite the rhetoric of Attic comedy, local agriculture was not destroyed. In the ensuing fourth century B.C., moreover, the Athenians spent vast sums on interior fortification, ostensibly now intent to keep secure the countryside of Attica.[32] This military conservatism may not have been so much a reaction to the agrarian damage of the Peloponnesian War (which we have suggested was in fact minimal), as an acknowledgment of three new realities: (1) the need to curb overall defense expenditure and avoid costly offensive campaigns of the past; (2) the realization that the Athenian hoplite phalanx, by both its changing composition and spirit, was no longer eager to face down enemies in the old style of pitched battle—fights that in themselves were becoming increasingly rare in Greece; and (3) the presence of an enormous (and expensive) variety of military contingents on the evolving Greek battlefield.[33]

The increasing appearance of mercenary bands and organized groups of light-armed raiders demonstrated that peril lay not simply in columns of heavy infantry, but in war waged by any means at an enemy's disposal. In this environment, even expensive rural construction made some sense and at least showed the democracy's intention not to neglect the Athenian landowner. The new self-interested Athenian hoplite wanted the psychological security of keeping foreign armies off his farm—without the need to march out to meet the aggressor in a pitched battle. To a large extent the democracy—through roads, forts, rural patrols, and garrisons—granted him his wish.[34]

But there were even more advantages than the mere avoidance of agricultural loss. Democratic government ostensibly hostile to agrarian broad-based oligarchy brought clear profit to the farmers of Attica. This paradox developed in a number of ways. At its most basic it was simply a question of greater opportunity for theft. After describing the Theban plundering of rural Attic estates, the fourth-century anonymous Oxyrhynchus Historian explains that this was lucrative because the Athenian countryside was "the most lavishly furnished" in Greece (12.4–5; cf. Thuc. 2.14–16). His commentary on the wealth of the Attic countryside ends in fragments. But a partially restored phrase concludes, "whatever they took [when fighting] from the Greeks they brought into their [own] fields." The subject of that incomplete sentence is unexpressed, but almost surely it is the Athenians: apparently Attic farmers in the fifth century B.C. often took rural property from conquered subjects and then reemployed it on their own farms. This pilfered cargo resulted in an agrarian infrastructure that was the most "lavish" among all the Greek city-states. At the end of the Peloponnesian War, the Thebans replundered what the Athenian farmers themselves had plundered. Here we should imagine stock, slaves, tools, woods, and metals, items the Athenians had probably looted from years of overseas campaigns and local intrusions into nearby agrarian Megara.[35]

When a right-wing thinker of the fifth-century B.C., the so-called Old Oligarch, claimed that Athens' wealth in part derived from the sea, he perhaps was thinking of both plundered and legitimate riches of every type that came into the Piraeus—and then were dispersed throughout Attica (Ps. Xen. 2.7, 11). The impression once more is that beneficiaries of Athenian maritime power were often the farmers inside Attica. Less overt than simple theft and plunder must have been private dealing by Athenian officials. Many found ample opportunity to acquire cheaper products across the Aegean even after the formal end of the empire. For example, in a fourth-century oration of Demosthenes, Meidias is accused of diverting ships while on official Athenian business to pick up stock and slaves for his farm back in Attica (Dem. 21.167–68; Plut. *Mor.* 785c). That charge of seizing property and using it for one's own needs in Attica must have been a frequent complaint (cf. Dem. 51.13; also Dem. 4.24, 45, 47; 8.24).

Perhaps equally important to Attic farmers was the introduction of pay for hoplite military service, probably sometime around the mid-fifth century B.C.— a phenomenon inimical to the amateurism of agrarian warfare. Yet military compensation was no doubt welcomed by Athenian farmers themselves, who in the twilight of the old agrarianism were discovering the attractions democracy had to offer. That monetary incentive lies behind the purported (and, in the traditional agrarian sense, blasphemous) advice of Aristides after the Persian Wars that the Athenians "should strive for hegemony, and after coming in from their farms, live in the city. For that way there would be compensation for everybody: for those who were serving in the army, for others who were posted as frontier guards, and in general for those attending to public affairs" (Arist. *Ath. Pol.* 24.1–2; cf. Plut. *Arist.* 22, 25).

Under the traditional agrarian regime of the past two centuries, the Athenian farmer presumably had left his plot, formed up in the phalanx, and advanced his polis's claim to a strip of disputed borderland—inferior farmland more valuable in terms of community prestige than as a source of agricultural bounty. Most losses during these old-style wars, in both time and lives, were the agrarian community's alone. But in the new regime, the burden was shifted to the entire polis. Now if Athenian farmer-hoplites were to fight, they must be paid.

For most of the fifth century, the money came not from taxes on farmers' property or harvests, but from overseas tribute and commercial excise revenues.

Under Athenian democracy the burden of polis defense was not only shared with the landless, but it also could prove for a time much more lucrative to the landed. Given the mobility of ships and government support, many Attic farmers were now paid salaries (at least three obols a day) to range over the Aegean, and in the process they were given greater opportunity to carry valuables back to their own ground. The tradition that Attic agrarians had enjoyed state pay from both military and public service under the Athenian democracy led Plutarch to say they had been "corrupted" by Pericles' offers of cleruchies (settlements abroad), theater-subsidies, and jury pay (Plut. *Per.* 9.1). In a sense Plutarch may have been correct: all were activities that took a man away from his farm and curtailed the city's reliance on his own ability to grow food. That surely constituted "corruption" in the old agrarian sense.

But even if Plutarch exaggerated (many rural Athenian hoplites found few opportunities for state cash), generous polis entitlements to others (e.g., Aristides' "everybody") could only expand the economy. Trickle-up economics, as it were, enhanced the assets of those who were not poor to begin with. Athenian expansionism, then, was not a zero-sum format where someone's gain was another's loss, but rather an inflationary and expansionary process that actually benefited most people involved in it.[36]

The Democratic Timocrat

The creation and evolution of democracy through the fifth and fourth centuries B.C. have sometimes been interpreted as a political affront to the power and privileges of the old hoplite regime in Athens, since any extension in political participation was conceivably antithetical to the traditional influence of the farming class and a challenge to the foundations of the traditional agrarian polis. Cleisthenes, for example, purportedly brought in non-Athenians and freed slaves to be enrolled in the citizen rosters of the newly constituted demes (Arist. *Pol.* 2.1275b34–40; cf. *Ath. Pol.* 21.4). Likewise, the introduction of ostracism (e.g., Plut. *Arist.* 7.3–8; Philochorus *FGrHist* 328 fr. 30; Arist. *Ath. Pol.* 22) allowed any prominent figure to suffer from the jealousy and hostility of his social inferiors. In the 460s B.C., in the wake of increased naval prominence and growing imperialism, the popular leader Ephialtes also reduced the power of the aristocratic Areopagus, leaving it as a mere homicide court for murdered Athenians (Arist. *Ath. Pol.* 25.1; 28.2; 41.2). The transference of its formidable political influence to the Athenian assembly, council, and law-courts (Arist. *Ath. Pol.* 25.2) was traditionally felt (perhaps wrongly) to have been practicable only when Cimon, accompanied by 4,000 conservative hoplites, was away from the city, assisting the Spartans in suppressing her helot revolt. Pericles' subsequent inauguration of pay for citizens' public service, his building program, and his reliance on an Athenian naval presence of at least 330 ships, were seen as efforts to increase the power and visibility of the landless *thētes* at the expense of the rich and the middling hoplite classes.[37]

Opposition among the yeomen to the expansion of Athenian democracy should have been apparent in the only real revolutionary movements in the history of Athenian democracy: the oligarchical insurrections of 411 ("The Four Hundred") and 403 B.C. ("The Thirty Tyrants"). The extreme rule of the so-called Four Hundred in 411 B.C., a revolutionary body of 400 elite Athenians, failed. It gave way after only four months to a government dominated by Theramenes and his more moderate followers. As part of a "hoplite" proposal passed in the assembly, government participation was now to include only citizens who could afford the panoply (rather than possession of land alone). This meant that a group called "The Five Thousand," but more likely numbering nine thousand or more (Thuc. 8.97.1–2; Arist. *Ath. Pol.* 33.1–2; Lys. 20.13), took over power from the rightist cabal.

In 411 B.C., then, there was the ideal environment at Athens for a return to broad-based agrarian timocracy of the old style (cf. Thuc. 8.97.2; Arist. *Ath. Pol.* 33.2). Permanent overthrow of radical democracy and a return to "hoplite democracy" along the lines of Aristotle's ideal "polity" or—better yet—a regression to Solon's reforms of nearly two centuries prior, could recreate a sixth, rather than a fifth-century B.C., Athenian polis: moderate leaders and a middle constitution of (no doubt largely agrarian) holders of heavy weaponry.[38]

Yet the fortunes of the so-called Five Thousand transitional reformers in 411 B.C. were no more successful or lasting than those of the more reactionary "Four Hundred" revolutionaries earlier in the year. Why was this so? Neither insurrectionary group could count on the support of Attic hoplite agrarians. Just as the "hoplites" (or whoever the "Five Thousand" actually were) had been instrumental in dethroning the ultra-right-wing "Four Hundred" (e.g., Thuc. 8.92.4; 8.98.1), so, too, many of these hoplite landowners in power now actually acted as custodians for, not usurpers of, democracy. When the danger of aristocratic revolutionaries was over, in a matter of months power returned from agrarian hoplites to the original radically democratic government.

While the exact sequence of political events of the year 411 B.C. has been endlessly debated, it is clear that in both stages of the revolution, Athenian agrarians had openly opposed the wealthy aristocratic "Four Hundred." They also had little enthusiasm over the idea of a permanent hoplite government of "Five Thousand"—even though that latter body probably would have been composed of men identical to themselves. Clearly, the gradual erosion of the old tenets of Greek agrarianism was proving lucrative to Athenian *mesoi*, farmers who were beginning to see that radically democratic government and Aegean imperialism could pay dividends (at least for a while) to landowners in Attica.

Little need be said of the more radical and murderous aristocratic coup that ensued in 403 B.C. at Athens. Then Attic hoplites were even less sympathetic to the wealthy ideological zealots on their right (largely horse owners who had expelled hoplites from their farms).[39] Given the recent losses of landless rowers in sea battles and a navy demoralized over recent defeats, democratic resistance to the rightists once more counted on the support of the moderate hoplites, who were now led by the hero Thrasybulus. His efforts culminated in a dramatic hoplite battle at the port of Piraeus, where the radical oligarchs, led by the aristocratic "Thirty Tyrants," were routed. Democracy was restored for the second time in a decade.

Nor in the aftermath of the downfall of the Thirty did the Athenian citizenry have much sympathy with a third resurgence of antidemocratic fervor. A conservative named Phormosius proposed to confine citizen rights to those who owned land (a variant on Theramenes' earlier idea of restriction of citizenship on the basis of arms). That reintroduction of a property qualification (*politeian mē pasin alla tois tēn gēn echousi paradounai*) would have reasserted the tenets of the old agrarian polis and would have disenfranchised some five thousand Athenian citizens immediately (Dion. Hal. *hypothesis to Lys.* 34). Yet it failed to become legislation. Apparently, the Athenian hoplite constituency had no desire to balkanize a society in which they had done quite well, and which they had just defended with their own lives.[40]

After a century of gradual dilution of their old agrarian privileges, at the end of the fifth century B.C., Athenian hoplites fought unwaveringly on behalf of democratic institutions. In the fourth century B.C., they continued their staunch support. Several military and economic explanations for the attractiveness of Athenian democracy to the agrarian hoplites of Attica have already been offered. But we must keep in mind that Greek military service itself was changing so much that, by the middle of the fourth century B.C., a man's equipment and manner of fighting were no longer always an accurate representation of his social status: many fourth-century hoplites may not have been farmers and some may not even have owned their own arms.[41]

Aside from military and economic self-interest—and the drift into irrelevance of the hoplite census itself—there were also political reasons that likewise indicate precisely how Athenian agrarians had been transformed in the course of the fifth and fourth centuries B.C. First, old-style agrarian timocracy was in itself the forerunner to Athenian democratic government. The original hoplite reaction against the wealthy landowning clans in the seventh and sixth centuries B.C.—whether dramatic or incremental—had instilled in Greek farmers no love of aristocrats, but instead a natural affinity for broad-based constitutions. Consequently, the innovative Athenian decision to expand the franchise to an additional class of native-born residents was a far less radical move for hoplites than their own destruction of hereditary aristocracy and monarchy centuries earlier. The heritage of Athenian democracy can be traced directly back to agrarian timocracy of the seventh and sixth centuries B.C.

Aristotle, for example, claimed that the earlier agrarian oligarchies (wrongly, he felt) had dubbed themselves "democracies," a logical enough notion given that political participation was considerably broadened to include a sizable group of relatively small-scale farmers (e.g., *Pol.* 4.1297b24–26). Similarly, Herodotus argued that once the democratic regime of Cleisthenes was established, the Athenian land army had fought far better than under Peisistratian tyranny (Hdt. 5.78)—again another suggestion that even at the beginning agrarians had felt more at home with democratic government than with narrow authoritarianism.

As we have seen, the reactionary "Four Hundred" of the revolution of 411 B.C. vainly sought the protection of a hoplite constituency: the former believed that a broader-based agrarian constitution might garner considerable support among the farming citizenry and thus stave off popular reprisals from the landless demos. Most revealingly, the aristocrats of the "Four Hundred," like their ancestors centuries earlier, had little real empathy for the idea of a genuine "hoplite" polity, thinking "that so many sharers in power would be essentially the rule of the people (*antikrus dēmon*)" (Thuc. 8.92.11).

The rightist "Four Hundred" of 411 B.C. were, of course, absolutely correct in their belief that the succeeding government of "Five Thousand" hoplites would be more palatable to the Athenian democrats as "essentially the rule of the people." But they were entirely wrong on the more critical issue: if Attic hoplites rejected a return to agricultural government, they had even less desire to protect aristocratic autocrats intent on attracting the landless citizens. For agrarian militiamen of Athens, the inclusion of the *thētes* was far more paltable than the exclusion of all nonaristocrats. For the life of the autonomous Athenian democracy, no property qualification was reestablished to disenfranchise the landless. "Many of the hoplites," G.E.M. de Ste. Croix has remarked of these two Athenian right-wing revolutions at the end of the fifth century B.C., were "inclined to waver—as one would expect of *mesoi*—but eventually [came] down firmly on both occasions in favor of the democracy."[42]

Second, for all the complaints of later elites, the public symbolism and popular ideology of Athenian democracy was largely hoplitic—not, as we might suppose from the groaning of rightists such as the Old Oligarch and Plato, exclusively dominated by themes of the landless *thētes*. The conservative Plutarch thought that Cleisthenic democracy, far from marking the beginning of radical democracy, had actually been "an aristocratic regime" (*Cimon* 15). The fifth- and fourth-century B.C. military muster-lists (*katalogoi*) that listed Athenian citizens in their demes for military service—even if more and more symbolic than regulatory—were essentially hoplite registers. They omitted poor *thētes* altogether, men who, incidentally, no doubt aspired to become yeomen *zeugitai* (i.e., to possess some capital and own land) whenever they could.[43] Class differences remained under Athenian democracy. But as is usually the case where factors other than birth and property reign, distinctions were more along emulative American, rather than resentful European, lines. Far from destroying it, the Athenian poor often envied and thus sought to reconstitute the "hoplite mirage."

Officially, the magistracies and major public offices at Athens were rarely opened to the landless until the fourth century B.C. (e.g., Arist. *Ath. Pol.* 7.3–4; 26.2; 47.1). They remained, at least theoretically, the domain of the upper three classes, of which the yeomen *zeugitai* were by far the numerically superior.[44] The late-fourth-century Athenian orator Lycurgus thought it important to mention an old precedent according to which the proposer of legislation had to prove land ownership (Lyc. 22). Another fourth-century orator, Dinarchus, said that Athenian generals had to have landed property inside Attica (*ag. Dem.* 1.71). These echoes suggest that, even under democracy, property still continued to lend symbolic prestige and social status, and the transformation of the agrarian polis to a landless institution was spiritually and psychologically incomplete.

The occasional call to "make the *thētes* into hoplites" (e.g., Ant. fr. B6), in the strictly political (rather than military) sense of granting all citizens in democracy equal access to office-holding, was also a phenomenon of the late-fifth and fourth century B.C., a time when class distinction and the census rubrics themselves were becoming ever more incidental. Yet we never hear of a wish "to make the hoplites into *thētes*." Ideologically, hoplites were made to feel that the landless *thētes* were becoming more like themselves, rather than vice versa. This "big-tent" notion that others were brought up, rather than insiders pulled down, was important to the Athenian experimentation with democratic polis transformation. Infantrymen, not (the militarily more important) rowers, were most frequently portrayed on Attic vases. Dramatists and historians continued to laud infantry service. Public sculpture and painting emphasized hoplite bravery.[45] Popular myth magnified infantry prowess. Hoplites were commemorated in public decrees, casualty lists, and in public orations.[46] When the Athenians wished to punish and humiliate their captured adversaries, they voted to cut off the prisoners' right thumbs, making them incapable of using the hoplite spear, but not the oar—even though the greater military threat to Athens at the end of the Peloponnesian War was from enemy triremes, not landed hoplites (Plut. *Lys.* 9.5).

Just as the growth of Athenian democracy had reconstituted the need for infantry and enhanced the private prospects of many farmers, so too it deliberately cultivated hoplite tradition and pride. Athens gave its landed infantry a sense of magnified (if not always lasting) political preference as well—even as the whole exclusionary and parochial notion of the agrarian hoplite was itself slowly eroding. This ideological deference to hoplites in the fifth century B.C. can also explain why their continued incorporation and loss of independence at Athens went on unheeded during the fourth century B.C. In short, hoplitic symbolism was adopted by the democracy not as a device to divide, but to unify the various elements of the multifaceted democracy. It was never, as is sometimes argued, an aristocratic ethos that subverted the hearts and minds of the poor.

Third, the large number of slaves and resident alien metics at Athens, and the careful restrictions between citizen and noncitizen also helped to draw hoplites into line with democratic thinking. The inclusion of landless *thētes* in the Athenian citizenry left many social and political inferiors outside the citizen body. Hoplite landowners realized that democracy provided sharp demarcations between free and slave, citizen and noncitizen, female and male, and even at times propertied and propertyless. Adult Athenian males who enjoyed voting privilege and full access to political office were still a distinct minority of the adult resident population of Attica. Inclusion of the landless at Athens in the citizenry may have resulted in a society that was no more egalitarian in demographic terms than that which existed during more conservative agrarian regimes. Those rural city-states of Greece may have insisted on the tradition of a property-qualification for their native-born, but they also lacked large numbers of disenfranchised aliens and slaves engaged in trade, commerce, and mining.

At Athens there were also instances—military service, colonization schemes, *cleruchies*—where yeomen *zeugitai* and propertyless *thētes* shared common enterprises and aspirations. These occasions were reflections of Athenian hoplite ease with, rather than distrust of, the landless poor. Nowhere was the radicalization of democracy accompanied by wholesale attacks on hoplites. Athenian farmers were not routinely ostracized. They were not as a group singled out and hauled into court or subjected to land confiscations and redistributions. Emulation and admiration, not class warfare, was the rule. Athenian hoplites' political loss was largely relative, rarely absolute: if there was political diminution, it occurred through the sharing, not the curtailment, of rights and privileges.

CONCLUSION

We have now seen that during the fifth and fourth centuries B.C. the old rigid structures of the agrarian polis were gradually transformed on a variety of fronts at Athens, without much opposition from farmers themselves. Hoplite service was no longer a peculiarly agrarian experience. Nor did it now comprise the totality of Greek warfare. The expansion of the Athenian economy, the growth of the fifth-century B.C. population, and the bureaucracy of government in the fourth—all fatal to the centuries-old idea of polis agrarianism—actually for a time favored local Attic agriculturalists.

Through frequent paid military service and overseas plunder, money and capital accrued to farmers in an economy that had grown beyond agricultural alone. The veneer of hoplite ideology in turn was preserved in the hearts of all Athenians, and politically its yeomen representatives often continued to receive preferred treatment over those without property—the supposed beneficiaries of the new radical democracy. It is no surprise that hoplite farmers always supported, never attacked, democracy in time of crisis.

In sum, the old idea of the Greek polis that its local landowners alone were to be makers of its laws/protectors of its people/producers of its food gradually was forgotten at Athens, but that rethinking was not accomplished by wholesale exiles, executions, or confiscations. There was no need for these coercive measures under an insidious system such as Athenian democracy, which could reconstruct—symbolically, ideologically, spiritually—hoplites as stalwart defenders of the democratic order. While hoplites had become democrats, democrats had, in some equally important sense, become "hoplites."

ACKNOWLEDGMENTS

I would like to thank Josiah Ober, Charles Hedrick, and an anonymous reader for helpful remarks on an earlier draft. Some of the ideas expressed in the paper derived from a chapter, "The Erosion of the Agrarian Polis," in *The Other Greeks*.

NOTES

1. Hes. *Op.* 23–24; 40–41; 240–47; 225–36; Arist. *Pol.* 5.1302a13–16; 6.1318b8–15; and cf. 6.1319a7–10.

2. Cf. *Eth. Nic.* 8.1160b16–20; *Pol.* 4.1291b38–41; 6.1318b10–1319a19.

3. Increases in wealth and income that might change (and raise) one's status under the census rubrics: Arist. *Pol.* 5.1306b10–15; *Rh.* 1387a21–26; *Ath. Pol.* 7. 4; Ps. Dem. 42.4; Plato *Laws* 754d; Rhodes, *Commentary,* 145–46; Raubitschek, *Dedications,* no. 372; Hignett, *Athenian Constitution,* 226–27. General informality of census standards: Arist. *Ath. Pol.* 7.4.

4. Hoplite warfare and farmer participation: Hanson, *Western Way,* 27–39, *Hoplites,* 3–11; Grundy, *Thucydides,* vol. II, 246–58; Snodgrass, *Arms and Armour,* 62; Osborne, *Classical Landscape,* 138–39, 144; Adcock, *Art of War,* 7. On posthoplite appreciation for a lost system: Aeschin. 2.11.5; Dem. 9.49; Isoc. 8.48–54; Plato *Rep.* 5.469b–471b, *Menex.* 242d; Polyb. 13.3.4; 18.3.3. Kurt Rauflaub in this volume has characterized Athens after Cleisthenes' reforms as a 'republic' of hoplites. He has demonstrated quite clearly that the egalitarian foundations of Athenian democracy had a long pedigree prior to Cleisthenes; drawing on additional archaeological evidence, Ian Morris (also in this collection) would agree with an egalitarian creed preexisting well before Athens. I have argued similarly elsewhere (*The Other Greeks*) that Athenian democracy was the last stage in a centuries-long evolution toward equality throughout the Greek poleis, an alternative to, not a replacement of, agrarian hoplite egalitarianism in the majority of the other city-states.

5. *Pol.* 4.1291a31–33; cf. Xen. *Oec.* 5.12–18; and cf. Xen. *Oec.* 5.4–5; 6.6.7. 9–10; [Arist.] *Oec.* 12. 1343b2–6; Plato *Rep.* 2.374c; on the superb nature of agrarian infantry, cf. too, Varro *Rust.* 3.1.4; *Vegetius* 1.3; Pliny *HN* 18.26.

6. Small size of ancient horses: Anderson, *Horsemanship,* 16–39; Sallares, *Ecology,*

398–400. On the relative subordination of horses and cavalry to hoplite infantry: Lys. 16.13; Dem. 19.169–70; Xen. *Hell.* 6.4.11; Anderson, *Horsemanship,* 145–154; Bugh, *Horsemen,* 36–37. Mounted hoplites of the seventh and sixth centuries B.C.: Greenhalgh, *Early Greek Warfare,* 84–145; Delbrück, *Art of War,* 58–60. Growing subordination of cavalry to hoplite infantry reflecting the new economic realities of the culture of the Greek polis: Arist. *Pol.* 4.1289b33–41; 4.1297b16–28.

7. Relationship between light-armed infantry and navies with the landless demos: *Pol.* 4.1321a15–22; *Ath. Pol.* 24; 26.1; Ps. Xen. *Ath. Pol.* 1.2. See Barry Strauss's article in this volume on the solidarity created among the *thētes* by shared naval experience. Light-armed troops and inferior social status: Garlan, *War,* 127–33; Kromayer and Veith, *Heerwesen,* 87–88.

8. Agricultural *autarkeia* and the ideal of polis self-sufficiency in food production: Sallares, *Ecology,* 297–300; Osborne, *Classical Landscape,* 17–18. For the political *autonomia* of the polis: Bickerman, "Autonomia," 330–38; de Ste. Croix, *Origins,* 98–99.

9. Hoplite agrarians as a distinct middle group: Finley, *Early Greece,* 98–99; Andreyev, "Aspects," 23; Fuks, *Social Conflicts,* 41; Hansen, *Athenian Democracy,* 115–16; Spahn, *Mittelschicht* 123–82. Some (wrongly, I think) have suggested Aristotle's *mesoi* (e.g., *Pol.* 4.1289b31; 1295b2, 7–35, 1296a4–19; 1296b36–38; 1297b1–31302a14; 1306b11; 1319b14; cf. 4.1294b5–18; 1296a6–10; 1296b) were neither an important entity within the polis nor a significant part of Aristotle's methodology of social classification. Cf. de Ste. Croix, *Class Struggle,* 69–89; Ober, "Sociology," 119–210; Cartledge, "Hoplites," 11–27; esp. 24. True, we do not know exactly the nature of the majority of constitutions in the Greek city-states before the fifth century (or even later), but the existence of hoplite warfare, references in Hesiod, Phocylides, Solon, Theognis, and other lyric poets to middling farmers, and Aristotle's *Politics* suggest widespread landowning timocracies. The amply documented public organization and state administration throughout the Greek world (as outlined, for example, by Jones, *Public Organization*) lead to the same conclusion. See Hanson, *Other Greeks,* 181–214.

10. Arist. *Ath. Pol.* 7.3–5; Plut. *Solon* 18.1–2; Poll. *Onom* 8.129–32.

11. Cf., e.g., Arist. *Ath. Pol.* 13.4–5; 16.3; *Pol.* 5.1305a23–24; Hdt. 1.59.3; Dio. Chrys. 7.107–8; 25.3.

12. On the standardization of 40–60 plethra plots (8.9–13.3 acres), cf. Andreyev, "Aspects," 1–15; Burford, *Land and Labor,* 27–28, 67–72; 110; Burford, "Family Farm," 168–72; Finley, *Land and Credit,* 58–60; Lewis, "Rationes Centesimarum"; Jameson, "Agricultural Labor," 144. See, too, Pečírka and M. Dufkova, "Excavations," 134–36. On the absence of large farms in Attica, cf. Finley, *Economy and Society,* 64–66; de Ste. Croix, "Estate"; Pritchett, "Attic Stelai," 275–76; Jardé, *Les Cereals,* 120–22; Amouretti, *Le Pain,* 205–6; Isager and Skydsgaard, *Agriculture,* 120–29. See especially now Jameson, "Class," for the identification of the hoplite middle in the ancient countryside, and the increasing difficulty of identifying many free poor as farm owners in the countryside of the polis.

13. Slaves in Greek agriculture and attached to Athenian hoplite households: de Ste. Croix, *Class Struggle,* 506–9; Jameson, "Agriculture and Slavery," 122–45; "Agricultural Labor," 140–46; Garlan, *Slavery,* 63–65, 56–57; Hervagault and MacToux, "Esclaves"; Amouretti, *Le Pain,* 212–14; Sargent, *Slave Population,* 82; Hanson, "Thucydides," 226–28; contra Wood, *Peasant-Citizen,* 188n.10; Gallant, *Risk and Survival,* 33; Sallares, *Ecology,* 55–58; Ober, *Fortress,* 22–23; Ober, *Mass and Elite,* 24–27. On one

slave per hoplite: Thuc. 3.17.3; Ar. *Ach.* 1097, 1136; Antiphanes 16 (Kock); Theophr. *Char.* 25.4; Pritchett, *War,* I, 49–51; Sargent, *Slave Population,* 206.

14. On the problems of using the term *peasant* for the hoplite landowners of Attica: Osborne, *Demos,* 41n. 84, 142n.47; Garnsey, *Famine,* 44–46. I have argued elsewhere against the use of *peasant* in describing the typical ancient Greek rural citizen (*Other Greeks,* 107–68, 467–8, 497).

15. E.g., Ps. Xen. *Ath. Pol.* 1.2; 1.7–9; 2.1–6; 2.14–16; Plut. *Them.* 19.

16. Thuc. 6.20.4; Isoc. 17.57; Ps. Xen. *Ath. Pol.* 2.2–3; *IG* I³ 61, lines 32–41.

17. Degree of Athenian dependency on foreign grain: Garnsey, *Famine,* 131–33; 150–64; Pritchett, *War,* V, 465–72.

18. Metic numbers in the fifth century: Gomme, *Population,* 25–26; Hansen, *Athenian Democracy,* 92–93. Population of slaves at Athens: Hansen, *Athenian Democracy,* 93; Gomme, Population, 24–26. Cf. also Jones, *Athenian Democracy,* 165; Guiraud, *La Propriété foncière,* 156–59.

19. E.g., Arist. *Pol.* 4.1292a10–12; 4.1293a1–13; Ps. Xen. *Ath. Pol.* 1.2.

20. On the growing divide between the prestige of landowning and the power of money at Athens: Finley, *Ancient Economy,* 48; Cohen, *Athenian Economy,* 86–91. Contradictions, tension, and structural rigidity in the polis confronted with economic expansion and military opportunity beyond hoplite warfare: de Ste. Croix, *Class Struggle,* 295–300; Fuks, *Social Conflicts,* 17; Pečírka, "Crisis," 19–21; Runciman, "Doomed to Extinction"; McKechnie, *Outsiders,* 16–29.

21. Thuc. 1.98.2–4; 1.100.1; 1.100.2; 1.102.1–2; 1.104. 2; 1.105.1–2; 1.106; 1.114; 1.115–17; Plut. *Per.* 23.4.

22. E.g., Ps. Xen. *Ath. Pol.* 1.1–2; Hdt. 7.144.4; Thuc. 1.93.3; Plut. *Them.* 7,19; Nepos *Them.* 2.3; Plato *Laws* 4.706b–c; 707c; Arist. *Ath. Pol.* 27.1; cf. Isoc. 8.48, 64, 69, 75, 79, 101.

23. Representation: Eur. *Supp.* 238–45. No sympathy: Eur. *Andr.* 445–53; 595–601; 724–26; *Supp.* 187; cf. Aesch. *PV* 1069–70. Praise for democracy: Eur. *Supp.* 352–3; *Ion* 670–75; *Phoen.* 535–45. Contribution of the rowing class: cf. esp. Aesch. *Pers.* 373–81; Ar. *Ach.* 162–63; *Frogs* 1072–73; *Vesp.* 909; *Eq.* 1065–66; 1186; 1366–67; *Birds* 108. Achievements of hoplite farmers: Aesch. *Pers.* 85–86, 147–49, 238–45; Ar. *Ach.* 179, 625, *Eq.* 1334; *Nub.* 986; *Pax* 353–56; *Vesp.* 711; Eur. *Andr.* 681; *Vita Aesch.*; Eur. *Or.* 920; Ar. *Pax* 603, 511. Affinity for hoplites by right-wing aristocrats: Carter, *Quiet Athenian,* 97–98; de Ste. Croix, *Origins,* 183–85; 355–76; Gomme, *HCT,* I, 314.

24. E.g., Thuc. 3.98.4; 4.44.6; 5.2.1; 6.43; 7.20.7; 7.87.6; Diod. 12.65.6; 13.2.5, 8, 9.

25. Controversy over the status of *epibatai:* Jordan, *Athenian Navy,* 184–202; 193–95; Ostwald, *Popular Sovereignty,* 230–31, contra Gomme, *HCT,* II, 42, 80, 271, 367.

26. E.g., Hdt. 8.90.2; Diod. 13.40; 45–46; 77–80; Thuc. 7.70; 8.104–5; cf. especially Plut. *Cimon* 12.2.

27. Rosivach, "Athenian Fleet," 54–56.

28. E.g., Thuc. 2.19.2; 2.22.2; 7.27.5; cf. Xen. *Hipp.* 7.4; *Vect.* 4.47. On the general consequences of devastation during the Peloponnesian War: Hanson, *Warfare and Agriculture,* 111–43; Harvey, "New Harvests." On the role of Attica in Periclean and Spartan Strategy: Bugh, *Horsemen,* 81–119; Kelly, "Thucydides and Spartan Strategy"; Brunt, "Spartan Policy." Ober, "Thucydides"; Spence, "Perikles," 106–9. We should recognize that the rise of an imperial and democratic Athens changed the entire nature

of Greek warfare (cf. the complaints of Isocrates about generic democratic bellicosity [8.64–66]), ending the confining protocols of land-based hoplite battle, and offering little in its wake other than what was militarily efficacious. It is a sobering thought that more Greeks probably died fighting for or against democratic Athens than those killed during the entire earlier military history of the Greek city-states.

29. Strauss, *Athens*, 5, 58, 71, 75–76, 80–81, and especially 179–82.

30. Ehrenberg, *People*, 93.

31. Greek farmers always seemed to have had an especial fascination with the chance to land on unexpected riches, even when newly found monies eventually destroyed their agrarian tranquillity [e.g., Hdt. 7.190.1].

32. Ober, *Fortress*, 51–101; Munn, *Defense*, 3–33.

33. Curb expenditure: e.g., Lys. 34.10; Lycurg. 1.42–3; cf. Arist. *Pol.* 2.1267a32–36; *Rh.* 1.1359b-1360a; Xen. *Vect.* 5.13. Phalanx no longer eager: e.g., Ar. *Eq.* 1369–71; Xen. *Mem.* 3.5.19; cf. Ps. Xen. *Ath. Pol.* 2.1; cf. Andoc. fr. 3.1; Ar. *Nub.* 987–990; *Frogs* 1014–16; Andoc. *Against Alcibiades* 22. Evolving Greek battlefield: Xen. *Oec.* 8.6; Plut. *Mor.* 440b; Dem. 9.48; Polyb. 13.32–4; cf. Thuc. 1.83.2.

34. New ideology of defense: Garlan, *Recherches*, 19–86; Hanson, *Warfare and Agriculture*, 78–83; Ober, *Fortress*, 69–86; Munn, *Defense*, 32–33.

35. E.g., Diod. 12.44.3; 12.76.3; Thuc. 1.98.1–2; 2.26, 32, 69.1; 3.51, 96; 4.41, 45.2; 5.56.3, 116.2; 6.105.2; 7.18.3; 8.35.1–2.

36. No doubt a greater number of small landowners under the expansion of the Athenian economy might meet the hoplite census; cf. Patterson, *Pericles' Citizenship Law*, 67–68.

37. Helot revolt: Thuc. 1.102; Ar. *Lys.* 1138–44; Plut. *Cimon* 15.2; 16.8–17.3 ; Pay for public service: Arist. *Ath. Pol.* 27.3; Plato *Gorg.* 515e; Plut. *Per.* 9; Ar. *Ach.* 66, 90; Thuc. 8.67.3; Ps. Xen. *Ath. Pol.* 1.3. Building program: Plut. *Per.* 13–14. 330 ships: Thuc. 2.13.

38. On the somewhat obscure aims of the "Five Thousand": Whibley, *Oligarchies*, 192–207; de Ste. Croix, "Constitution," 1–23; Mossé, "Le Rôle"; Rhodes, "Five Thousand"; Bisinger, *Agrarstaat*, 44–45; Ostwald, *Popular Sovereignty*, 398–99; Gomme, Andrewes, Dover, *HCT*, V, 328–29. By the mid-fourth century B.C., even the Reaganesque reactionary Isocrates could bristle at the thought of a property requirement to restrict participation in democracy (Isoc. 4.105).

39. E.g., Xen. *Hell.* 2.4.2, 4–7, 24, 26–27, 31–32; cf. 3.1.4.

40. Agrarian support for democratic restitution: de Ste. Croix, *Struggle*, 292; Markle, "Farmers," 158–59. Right-wing support for The Thirty: Xen. *Hell.* 2.4.2, 4–7, 24, 26–27, 31–32; cf. Xen. *Hell.* 3.1.4; Arist. *Ath. Pol.* 38.2; Rhodes, *Commentary*, 415–82; Krentz, *Thirty;* Ostwald, *Sovereignty*, 475–96. See Lysias for the idea that Athenians were neither naturally democratic or oligarchic but supported "the political order that serves one's interests" (25.8).

41. Assumptions of nonfarmers in phalanx: Plato *Ap.* 36d, 37c, 38b; Ar. *Pax* 1181–90; Plato *Rep.* 2.374d; 8.556d; Dem. 1.27; cf. Plut. *Mor.* 214a72; knights and hoplites used interchangeably and also as rowers and light-armed: Thuc. 3.16.1; 3.18.3–4; Ps. Dem. 50.6,16; Arist. *Pol.* 7.1327b13–15; Lys. 14.7, 10, 11; Xen. *Hell.* 1.6.24; metics, allied noncitizens, and slaves in infantry and navy: Xen. *Vect.* 2.3; Thuc. 2.13.6; 2.31.2; 4.28.4; 5.8.2; 7.57.2; Paus. 1.32.3; 7.15.7; Dem. 4.36; mass-arming of populace; public fabrication and issue of arms; private gifts of weapons; public confiscation of pri-

vate arms: Thuc. 6.72.4; 8.25.6; Xen. *Hell.* 3.4.17; 4.4.10; Diod. 14.41.3–4; 14.43.23; cf. 14.10.4; 12.68.5; 15.73.2; 16.10.1; Aen. Tact. 10.7; 13.1–2; 17.2–4; 29.4–30; Lys. 16.14; 31.15; growing irrelevance of census qualifications for public and military service among citizens: Arist. *Pol.* 5.1303.a9–11; *Ath. Pol.* 7.5.

42. *Struggle*, 291–92; cf. Holladay, "Hoplites," 94–103.

43. Thuc. 6.43.1; Ar. fr. 232 Kock; Harpocration s.v. *thētes kai thētikon.*

44. On the hoplite *katalogoi* and the exclusivity of the top three classes: Andrewes, "Hoplite Katalogos," 1–3; Smith, "Casualty Lists," 351–54; Jones, *Athenian Democracy*, 79–81. No central hoplite list: Hansen, "Athenian Hoplites," 24–30.

45. E.g., Paus. 1.115.1–3; 10.10.4 Nepos *Milt.* 6.3–4; Aeschin. *In Ctes.* 3.186.

46. Cf. the hoplite scene at Marathon prominently displayed on the Stoa Poikile (Paus. 1.15.3; Nep. *Milt.* 6.3–4; Aeschin. *In Ctes.* 3.186), and scenes from the victory at Oenoe (Paus. 1.15.1). Mythic nature of hoplites at Marathon: Vidal-Naquet, *The Black Hunter*, 91–92; Loraux, *Invention*, 161–64; 170–71. Fabricated nature of the hoplite contribution during the battle of Salamis: Fornara, "Hoplite Achievement"; cf. Wardman, "Tactics and Tradition," 59–60. Prominence of hoplites in burials and on casualty lists: Loraux, *Invention*, 34–36; 360–62nn.124–33; cf. 151.

THE ATHENIAN TRIREME, SCHOOL OF DEMOCRACY

Barry S. Strauss

ATHENIAN DEMOCRACY began with the Cleisthenic revolution of 508–507 B.C. At the time, however, the poorest citizens lacked the leisure or mindset needed to make the most of the new possibilities of political participation: they lacked such qualities as self-confidence, a knowledge of the world, and less tangibly, the ability to imagine themselves as part of an active political community. Half a century later, by the time of the Ephialtic revolution of 462–461, those Athenians were well on their way to acquiring those qualities. The main catalyst of change was the growth of the Athenian fleet, in which their manpower played an important role.[1]

The connection between sea power and democracy in Athens has long been recognized. Ancient critics of *dēmokratia,* perhaps anticipating contemporary political arguments, concede a rough justice to the political power of the poor or landless citizens of the Athenian fleet—the power of the thetes. The purpose of this paper is to go beyond that argument in order to discuss the actual experience of serving on a trireme. Service in the fleet, I shall argue, ignited the thetes' political consciousness by offering them a practical education.

In order to address the political consequences of the thetes' maritime experience, it is necessary also to address a paradox facing the student of classical Athens. On the one hand, the student confronts texts asserting the military power and visibility of Athens' triremes (warships) and the political power of the citizen thetes who helped man them. These texts include literary evidence (history, tragedy, comedy, oratory, philosophy), epigraphical evidence (particularly the fourth-century naval lists), archaeological evidence (the Piraeus shipsheds in particular), and now, the *Olympias,* a hypothetical reconstruction of an Athenian trireme. However eloquent this testimony of Athens as a maritime democracy, it is matched by an equally impressive set of texts indicating the invisibility of the Athenian navy and its thetic seamen. Classical funerary oratory, for example, emphasizes the hoplite as the ideal Athenian male; it gives the thetes short shrift. Casualty lists inscribed on stone generally record hoplites, not thetes. Demes kept official records of hoplites, not thetes. Classical art displays a marked absence of representations of triremes and oarsmen, with the Ionic frieze of the Parthenon representing perhaps the most striking case of a missing presence. If the navy was indeed the backbone of Athens' military might, if the thetes possessed considerable political power in fifth-century

Athenian democracy, and if there was indeed a strong connection between
thetic naval service and political strength, then it is necessary to explain the si-
lences in the sources.[2]

The two subjects of this paper, then, are (1) the nature of naval service as political education for Athenian thetes and (2) the meaning of the lacunae in the
evidence. Modern scholarship tends to neglect the Athenian thetes, perhaps
even more than one might expect from the paucity of surviving evidence. Much
work needs to be done. This essay is by no means a comprehensive treatment
of the subjects; it aims, rather, to stimulate discussion and debate.

Let us begin with the evolution of the ideology of democratic self-
confidence. To become free and equal, ordinary people must first believe they
deserve to enjoy liberty just as the rich or well-born do; in other words, they
must accumulate self-confidence. It is not easy to explain how poor people in
the ancient polis acquired such self-confidence. Grave source problems make
it notoriously difficult to reconstruct popular ideologies in the ancient world.
Some points are nonetheless clear. In the later fifth and in the fourth century,
the equation between *dēmokratia* and *eleutheria* became a commonplace, as
Hansen notes in his paper in this volume. It had not always been so.

The notion of personal liberty antedated the notion of political liberty. Sixth-
century Greece witnessed simultaneously the growth of chattel slavery and the
insistence, best documented in Athens, that citizens be demarcated as free men
in a free land.[3] Citizens asserted personal liberty: they were not slaves but free
men. Political liberty was another matter. In the first half of the fifth century
B.C., as Raaflaub has demonstrated, *eleutheria* referred not to the power of the
demos but rather to the independence of a polis from rule by a tyrant or by the
Great King or by Athens. Alternatively, *eleutheria* referred to the free hand that
Athens enjoyed as an imperial power. Although by the 430s *dēmokratia* was
represented as the regime of liberty, originally it was not liberty but equality
(*isonomia*) and popular power—the *kratos* of the *dēmos*—that were considered
to be the hallmarks of the *dēmokratia*. Raaflaub suggests that it was the oligarchic reaction and challenge to democracy, crystallizing in the 440s, that pro-
pelled *eleutheria* into the position of leitmotif of *dēmokratia*. Only then did
democrats come to think of their political power as liberty: a liberty as precious,
and as in need of vigilant defense, as the liberty of the polis threatened by tyrants
or the Great King.[4]

Ober has convincingly reconstructed the mechanism whereby ordinary Athenians put into effect the eternal vigilance needed to guard their liberty against
elite ambitions. What, however, was the original source of mass self-
confidence? It may well be, as Ian Morris argues in this volume, that *dēmokratia* would never have come about without a crisis of confidence on the part of
Greek elites as to the legitimacy of their monopoly on political power. Yet unless ordinary people were ready to seize the opportunity when it presented itself, unless they were already convinced that they deserved a share of freedom

equal to that enjoyed by their self-proclaimed betters, then the crisis of the Greek elite would have been a mere quiver, a momentary hesitation before the torch of power was picked up by a new generation of aristocracy.[5]

Conditions fostering popular self-confidence were already present by 508–507 B.C. Developments in the fifth century, however, were to provide even greater support. The collapse of Athens' land empire in central Greece in 446 and the relative increase in the importance of the fleet to Athens' power no doubt boosted thetic self-confidence at the expense of Athens' hoplites.[6] That self-confidence, however, had begun to be forged decades earlier, as the outgrowth of an activity whose participants enjoyed the knowledge that they made Athens great and free, to use a phrase that Lysias employs in a general context (Lys. 25.32, 28.14).

In *Republic* 556c–557d, Plato's Socrates caricatures the process whereby a poor man comes to understand that the rich have no grounds to despise him. When serving with a rich man in a common pursuit—be it at an embassy or festival, in the army or aboard ship—the poor man would have occasion to compare his own fit and lean body with the wealthy man's overweight and out-of-shape physique. "'These men are at our mercy; they are no good,'" one poor man might say encouragingly to another (556e). In time the result would be a revolution and the establishment of democracy.[7] Satire indeed, but Plato's sketch points to the importance of military service as a crucible of social relations. Naval power in and of itself does not necessarily entail the creation or strengthening of democracy.[8] In fifth-century B.C. Athens, however, it did, as we shall see. The military importance of poor or landless citizens in the fleet was used to justify their political power under *dēmokratia* (Ps. Xen. *Ath. Pol.* 1.2; Arist. *Pol.* 1304a21–24; Arist. *Ath. Pol.* 23–25). Although popular testimonia are nonexistent, the justification may well have been used by thetes themselves. Old men in Athens looked back to their days behind the oar as a time of valor (Ar. *Vesp.* 1091–1101, 1119). When in the fifth century Athenian thetes gained a new outlet of prestige, a new way to fight for their country, a way to make a military contribution as important, if not more so, than that of their wealthier neighbors, they are likely to have felt proud. Perhaps they felt like the black sergeant in the Union army who asked rhetorically in 1864, "What has the colored man done for himself in the past three years? Why, sir, he has proved . . . that he is a man."[9]

The Athenian upper classes would not have rewarded "the demos who pull oars in the ships and impart power to the polis" (Ps. Xen. *Ath. Pol.* 1.2) unless the demos had made them do so.[10] In theory, the Athenian elite need not have employed citizen thetes as oarsmen at all. It could have—and *should* have, according to Aristotle (*Pol.* 1327b4–15)—used noncitizen farmers as oarsmen, supervised on board by citizen hoplite marines (*epibatai*), thereby sparing itself the worst excesses of *dēmokratia*.[11]

But the Athenian polis did use citizen thetes on its triremes. Athens used

316   BARRY S. STRAUSS

noncitizen labor at sea as well, as we shall consider presently: metics, allied mercenaries, and occasionally slaves. Citizen thetes nonetheless made up a significant proportion of the oarsmen and the petty officers. *Pace* Plato, it was not the presence of corpulent plutocrats on ship that gave thetes the confidence to turn their military power into political power. Rather, it was five other circumstances that proved decisive. First, however much he may have sneered, no hoplite, no cavalryman could deny the critical military importance of seapower to Athens. Knowledge of seamanship was widespread in Athens, and not only among the poor: among those Athenians with at least an elementary knowledge of how to row were (a) hoplites and (b) men who could afford to own a slave.[12] Second, as the striking arm of what came to see itself as a nation of rulers, thetes would not easily accept political subordination at home. Third, by the time the permanent military importance of thetic rowers began to become clear in the 470s and 460s, *isonomia* had been a dominant motif of Athenian ideology for two or more generations. By requesting a due share of honor and power for their vital labor, thetes were merely following contemporary protocols. Fourth, by creating and maintaining the Athenian empire, the navy generated the public income that financed state pay and the indirect forms of education (drama, festivals, etc.) that made possible political participation by the poor without bleeding wealthy Athenians dry.[13]

The fifth point, and our primary concern here, is that service on a trireme was an experience that created its own social imaginary (to use W. R. Connor's phrase in his essay in this volume). Participation in the community of rowers created new identities for the participants. Year in and year out, the thetes, the backbone of the democracy, sat on triremes and pulled oars, or served as petty officers or, less commonly, as marines or archers. The experience shaped their collective consciousness; it made *dēmokratia* and *isonomia* and *eleutheria* into not merely slogans but living realities. Communities are bound by symbolic, ritual, and emotive ties as much as by a rational and contractarian calculus. In Plato's *Laws* the Athenian Stranger asserts a direct relationship in every polis between the character of children's games and the quality and stability of serious customs and laws (797a). We might add that in adult activities too, the element of play bears a relationship to the character of the *politeia*. The symbolic, emotive, ritual, and ludic dimensions of the trireme have much to say about the character of Athenian democracy.[14]

Critics of democracy such as Thucydides or Aristotle sometimes dismiss the rowers as a mob, the *nautikos ochlos*.[15] A closer look, however, reveals a different picture. Although Thucydides criticizes seamen (*nautai*) for their violent emotions (8.84.3), even he concedes the discipline, order, and obedience of Athens' trireme crews in the Archidamian War (2.89.9). In *Persians*, Aeschylus describes the large mass of rowers moving in unison at the command of the timekeeper (395–97). Herodotus' Ionians learn just how much labor is required to turn civilians into disciplined oarsmen (6.11–13). Xenophon's Socrates castigates his young aristocratic followers by arguing that the thetes were better disciplined than either the hoplites or the cavalry (*Mem.* 3.5.18–19). And, returning to Thucydides, we learn that the rowers were trained to go into battle silent. Important in all warfare, silence was especially important at sea: quite a contrast to civilian affairs in Athens, a city famous as a talkative place.[16]

In an earlier day the thetes, the poorest of citizens, would not have had the opportunity to become part of so disciplined a military team; to be, as the general Phormio addresses them, *andres stratiōtai.*[17] As rowers in the Athenian fleet, however, they garnered prestige and self-confidence. They were now the *thranitōs leōs ho sōsipolis,* "the top-flight oarsmen who save the city" (Ar. *Ach.* 162–63), and a city famous for its fine triremes (Ar. *Av.* 108). It is small wonder that thetic seamen were usually volunteers rather than conscripts.[18] As a small part of a large enterprise—one man among 170 oarsmen and 30 additional crewmen per ship, in a fleet that might include thousands or even tens of thousands of men—the individual rower might develop a sense of allegiance to the group. The rowers went into battle silent but attentive, each bent to an individual oar but committed to the success of the whole boat and the entire fleet. Their group solidarity manifested itself most dramatically at Samos in 411, when the Athenian seamen in effect declared independence from the oligarchy in Athens and went their own way.[19] Although the thetic seamen were in general anti-oligarchic (Thuc. 8.72.2), they probably did not vote en bloc on more specific issues in the Athenian assembly.[20] A more interesting possibility, however, is that service on a trireme encouraged thetic seamen who might otherwise have stayed home to attend the assembly at all. Without such service, thetes might have lacked the confidence, the knowledge of what common effort could achieve, and most of all, the valorization of liberty (see below) to participate in politics. Not a mob, but a disciplined community, the seamen were a force to be reckoned with.

In asserting themselves, whether in the crisis of 411 or in the quotidian assembly meeting, the seamen no doubt made calculations based on the interests of their socioeconomic class. Let us not rule out, however, the possibility that they were equally motivated by their sense of belonging to the team. When, for example, concord, *homonoia,* was evoked as an Athenian political ideal, as it frequently was, a rower might think of his ship as a paradigm of *homonoia.* Aristotle says that it is education (*paideia*) that makes a polis "common and one" (*koinēn kai mian, Pol.* 1264a36–37). The experience of rowing was an important part of the political education of the Athenian thete, one that created a community—although, to be sure, not the kind of political community that Aristotle prefers (*Pol.* 1304b22–24, 1327b8–14; *Ath. Pol.* 27.1).[21]

Manning an oar on an Athenian trireme was largely a communitarian and egalitarian effort. Unless every oarsman kept to the same rhythm, unless every oarsman listened to the commands of the pulling master (*keleustēs*) and to the sound of the flute, then the ship could not be moved efficiently. The *kōpēs xunembolē,* "the regular dip of all the oars together" (*LSJ*), as Aeschylus calls it (*Pers.* 396) was crucial. In the close and cramped quarters of the vessel, the oarsmen knew each other. They shared their fears on the eve of battle (Lys. 2.37). They shared a competitive ethos, egging each other on to see who was the best rower (Ar. *Vesp.* 1094–97), which might mean being able to endure a longer stint of pulling but could hardly involve fighting a private battle, Achilles-style. As in a modern eight, some oarsmen contributed more than others to "getting a ship off the mark and keeping up the rate of striking" (Thuc. 7.14.1).[22] The key to success, though, was coordination and order (Xen. *Oec.* 8.8). The trireme was no place to march to the beat of a different drummer.[23]

Yet, although individualism was not a characteristic of the social imaginary of the trireme, liberty was; that is, liberty as it was understood in classical Greece: less the liberty of the individual than of the group. In this case the liberty in question was that of the thetes, the poorest Athenians who manned the ships.[24]

Athenians were at pains to associate liberty with their fleet. Let us consider several examples and then assess their political and symbolic significance. First, as Hansen notes in his contribution to this volume, several triremes were called *Eleutheria* and one was called *Parrhēsia* (freedom of speech). Second, one of the distinctions of the state trireme *Paralos* was that all of its rowers were *eleutheroi,* that is, freeborn men and citizens.[25] Third, as Pericles proudly reminded the Athenian assembly in 432, every helmsman (*kubernētēs*) and all the petty officers (*hypēresia*) were *politai* (citizens) (Thuc. 1.143.1).[26] They were, therefore, *eleutheroi.* Fourth, there is Plutarch's well-known statement that in response to the challenge in the 440s by Thucydides, son of Melesias, Pericles sent out sixty triremes annually in which many citizens (*polloi tōn politōn*) gained nautical skill and earned eight months' pay (Plut. *Per.* 11.4; cf. Arist. *Ath. Pol.* 24.3). Although the numbers of months and of ships are questionable, the basic notion that Pericles gave citizens a special status as oarsmen is plausible.[27]

In practical terms, the emphasis on *eleutheria* and *eleutheroi* represents bad faith, since the plain fact is that many of the oarsmen on Athenian triremes were metics, allied merecenaries, or, far less often, slaves.[28] In symbolic terms, however, the terminology is quite accurate, because it legitimates the power of the thetes. The "Good Ship Eleutheria" responds, as it were, to elite criticism that "real Athenians" do not serve on ships but on land, as hoplites or cavalrymen. The response is that, on the contrary, service on a trireme is an appropriate activity for a free man and a citizen.[29]

In this context it may be interesting to note Hansen's observation in this volume that both Democritus (fr. 251) and Aristotle (*Pol.* 1290b18) link democratic freedom with poverty. Plato, an egregious opponent of *dēmokratia,* despised seapower precisely because it liberated the canaille (*Laws* 707a-b). A sign of his brilliant pettiness, he has his Athenian Stranger rewrite history so that only the hoplite efforts at Marathon and Plataea save Greece from the Persians; Salamis and Artemisium, sea battles, are written out (*Laws* 707b–d).

As Raaflaub has pointed out, liberty and power were often connected during the heyday of the Athenian empire.[30] The service of the demos in the fleet was the basis of the power that made them free from rule by the elite. The "Old Oligarch" states explicitly that what the Athenian demos wants is to be strong and to be free. The demos is strong because it holds office, and it holds office because it imparts power to the city through its service in the fleet (Ps. Xen. *Ath. Pol.* 1.2, 8–9).[31]

Liberty and freedom of speech were inseparable for Athenians, as Hansen notes. Athenian seamen exercised that freedom: too professional to voice complaints while rowing, they were ready to speak up for themselves once off the ship (Xen. *Oec.* 21.3; cf. Ar. *Ran.* 1069–76). Two incidents in Thucydides are revealing. During the naval campaign in the Corinthian Gulf of 429, when the Athenian fleet was under the command of Phormio, the seamen were afraid of the prospect of attack by a numerically superior Spartan fleet. Their response was to gather among themselves (*kata sphas autous xunistamenoi*, Thuc. 2.88.1) and to discuss the situation. Noticing their action, Phormio called the men together to give a "pep talk" (Thuc. 2.88.1, 2.89.2). In other words the seamen behaved like free men: they engaged in free speech that provoked persuasive oratory on the part of their commander. The situation was different in 411, when seamen in the Peloponnesian fleet, many of them *eleutheroi,* responded to delinquencies in pay (Thuc. 8.83.2–84.2). Once again the seamen gathered together to discuss their grievances (*xunistamenoi kat'allēlous,* Thuc. 8.83.1). Unlike Phormio, however, the Spartan commander Astyochus responded with a threat of physical violence, which provoked an even more violent response from the seamen (Thuc. 8.84.2–3). Many lines of text separate the two incidents, but juxtaposition reveals a blunt message: Athenian triremes are sites of free and rational debate, while Peloponnesian triremes subject *eleutheroi* to emotion, compulsion, and violence.

That seapower afforded influence to Athenian thetes was bad enough, from the point of view of the elite, but the clout that seapower gave to slaves and metics was truly intolerable (Ps. Xen. *Ath. Pol.* 1.11–12). The presence of metics, allied mercenaries, and slaves as oarsmen might, therefore, have undercut the pride that citizen thetes felt in their contribution to the greatness of Athens. Two things prevented that outcome. First, no one forgot for a moment who aboard ship was a citizen and who was not (Thuc. 1.143.1, 7.63.3, 7.64.1). The *hypēresia* tended to be citizens; as for the oarsmen, citizen thetes are likely to have responded to the presence of outsiders in the same way the citizenry as a whole did: by the tried-and-true strategy of clubbiness. Some degree of fraternization among different kinds of oarsmen was, however, inevitable, given the need for cooperation on a trireme. Rather than generating thetic status anxiety, however, fraternization might have bred security. Thetic seamen learned that they were not alone in having a strong, pragmatic stake in *dēmokratia;* that, should a segment of the Athenian elite turn to oligarchy, the thetes had able-bodied allies in their shipmates. As it turned out, in 404–403, metics and slaves rallied to the democrats against oligarchy (Arist. *Ath. Pol.* 40.2).[32]

To sum up, service at sea was a fundamental part of the political education of the Athenian thete. The experience of the oarsman or petty officer forged thetic ideology. The trireme was a paradigmatic community. As a locus of equality, it gave the lie to the notion that to merit *isonomia* one had to own hoplite armor. As a locus of order, it countered the slander that seamen were a mob. As a locus of power, it taught poor men how to be free. As a locus of solidarity, it taught the thetes how to defend their interests in the assembly. In short, service at sea made an essential contribution to the politicization of the Athenian thete. If Athenian *dēmokratia* meant extending political power to the poorest citizens, then although *dēmokratia* survived the (temporary) loss of Athenian seapower, it would never have become a reality for so many poor people without Athenian seapower. Finley argued that the Athenian navy was a necessary condition for the creation of Athenian democracy because it created the material conditions—the wealth—needed for state pay.[33] This paper argues that the Athenian navy was necessary (though not sufficient) to solidify *dēmokratia,* but less because the navy generated income than because it generated ideology. The navy educated the thetes in solidarity, equality, and freedom.

There has been some recent discussion as to the ability of thetes to shape the discourse of democratic Athens. It may be objected that, although their importance in the fleet gave the thetes a brute power in Athenian politics, their education at sea otherwise left little mark on land. Tocqueville argued long ago that whereas the culture of Jacksonian America was proudly plebeian, even under *dēmokratia* Athens enjoyed a largely aristocratic culture. Athens, therefore, was less a democracy than an aristocratic republic. More recently, Loraux and, in his contribution to this volume, Raaflaub, argue that in the public discourse of classical Athens, seamen were considered inferior to hoplites and cavalrymen. Whether in funeral orations or casualty lists, thetes received second-class treatment. Raaflaub also notes the absence of thetes from ephebic rituals, those important tools of integration into Athenian manhood. Loraux argues more generally for the supremacy of aristocratic values and for the lack of a specifically democratic language in Athenian discourse. Victor Hanson makes a similar argument in his contribution to this volume, but with an important difference. Hanson emphasizes the predominance in Athens of middling, hoplite values rather than aristocratic values. In his argument, Athenian public culture did not ignore the thetes but absorbed them in the "big tent" of hoplitic imagery.[34]

Without doubt, the surviving evidence of classical Athens, with the possible exceptions of Thucydides and Aristophanes, does not give thetic seamen their due. The question is, how representative is the surviving evidence? In this context it is worth reiterating a point made by Rosalind Thomas: the extant texts of classical Athens represent only the tip of the iceberg of contemporary public discourse. Not only is what remains only a small part of the original literary or artistic production; it represents an even smaller part of the entire cultural production of what was primarily an oral culture. The thetes in particular were mainly illiterate, and not in a position to hire speechwriters or commission grave reliefs or purchase fine, painted pottery. Hence, the absence of a fully elaborated thetic ideology in extant ancient evidence does not mean that such ideology never existed. In fact, it may be a tribute to the one-time potency of that ideology that it leaves as many hints in the sources as it does.[35]

We must, therefore, be wary of generalizations about the nature of thetic discourse and about what "everybody" in Athens did or did not think. The people in Athens who were in a position to commission private art or to write fine literature are not likely to have held a high opinion of the "naval mob," which helps explain the paucity of references to ships and seamen in the extant products of classical culture—that is, at least in its privately commissioned products, for one might have expected to see more such references in public art and oratory, both domains in which the thetes should have been able to exercise power. We are given pause by such examples as the absence of seamen and the prominence of knights on the Ionic frieze of the Parthenon or the near absence of seamen from funeral oratory. These cases do demonstrate real limits to the ability of the thetes to stamp their image on Athenian public culture. Here too, however, caution must be the scholar's watchword.

The political message of a work of art is rarely easy to ascertain. For example, the prominence of cavalrymen on the Parthenon frieze, compared to the hoplites (who are underrepresented) and the thetes (who are absent), may say more about Athenian fondness for equestrian events in the Panathenaic games than about the knights' clout. The emphasis on hoplites in funeral oratory may bespeak the persistence of tradition, not contempt for thetes. The meaning of the absence of thetes from ephebic rituals would be easier to assess if we knew much about the training of thetes for service on a trireme. As Gomme notes, that training is likely to have been elaborate, but our sources, perhaps out of elitist bias, remain silent.[36]

It would make an interesting exercise to place alongside the Parthenon frieze certain other examples of classical Athenian art that have not survived: ships' markings.[37] These objects, along with the Piraeus shipsheds, loomed large in the Athenian visual imagination (see, e.g., Ar. *Ach.* 93–97, 544–54; Dem. 22.76). There was, too, the tomb of Themistocles on the Akte promontory in Piraeus (Plut. *Them.* 32.5–6). Consider also the so-called Lenormant Relief, a sculptural depiction of the rowers of a trireme. Standing on the Athenian Acropolis, the relief may have been part of a monument commemorating the support for democracy in the revolution of 411 on the part of the men of the state trireme *Paralos.* Who is to say that such things did not mean more to thetes than did the Parthenon or funerary lists emphasizing hoplites (the latter likely to have particularly limited impact on illiterate thetes)?[38]

To sum up, were the surviving evidence better, classical Athenian public culture would not look so one-sidedly hoplitic: thetic imagery would play a greater role. Yet hoplite symbolism would probably predominate nonetheless. With Hanson, historians should take the fact less as evidence of class conflict than of compromise and political maturity. Rather than storm the citadel of tradition and attempt to impose thetic images on all customary practices of Athenian culture, the thetes chose instead to respect the hoplites. No doubt many a thete aspired to a hoplite's prosperity and prestige. No doubt few hoplites aspired to the poverty or the dangerous and difficult military duty of a thetic seaman. Neither motive is reason for us to deny that most thetes felt pride in their glorious contribution to the greatness of their polis.

Reconstructing the culture of Athenian thetes—oral, communal, and improvisational as it may have been—is extraordinarily difficult, perhaps impossible.[39] That is hardly reason to deny its very existence, however. If the democratic discourse of Athenian thetes is no longer entirely visible, the problem may be the historians' and not the thetes'. These last words paraphrase the writing of the American historian Lawrence Levine, whose work on African-American culture in the nineteenth century demonstrates clearly the ability of poor people, even slaves, to create their own culture.[40]

Athenian thetes, of course, were not slaves, but citizens and politically powerful. The theory of ordinary people is sometimes best found not in treatises but in practice. Many scholars maintain that Athenian citizens received informal training for politics through the institutions of Athenian public life: deme assemblies, choruses, theater, magistracies, oratorical displays, military service. This paper examines one small aspect of that public life, the thetes' experience as oarsmen and petty officers in the Athenian fleet. That experience contributed significantly to the political education of the thetes. It contributed to democratic politics and to democratic discourse. It contributed to liberty.[41]

ACKNOWLEDGMENTS

Many people have encouraged, challenged, and helped me sharpen the ideas in this chapter. I would particularly like to thank Danielle Allen, Daniel Baugh, Paul Cartledge, Charles Hedrick, Lisa Kallet-Marx, Sandra Kisner, Josiah Ober, Boris Rankov, Kurt Raaflaub, Vincent Rosivach, Anthony Snodgrass, Rosalind Thomas, Margaret Washington, and Princeton University Press's reader.

NOTES

1. I take a middle ground in the debate on whether Athenian democracy began in 508 (see Ober, "Athenian Revolution") or only in 462 (see Raaflaub, this volume). Their naval service was necessary to make the thetes full participants in Athenian democracy, but without the groundwork laid in 508, naval service alone would not have created democracy for the thetes.

2. Naval lists: for bibliography, see Casson, *Ships and Seamanship,* 77n.1. Piraeus shipsheds: see ibid., 363–64. Olympias: see especially Morrison and Coates, *Athenian Trireme;* Shaw, *Trireme Project;* Meijer, *History of Seafaring,* 36–45. Funerary oratory, casualty lists, deme records: for details, see essay by Raaflaub in this volume. Classical art: see Morrison and Williams, *Greek Oared Ships,* 169; Johnston, *Ships and Boat Models,* 75. For classical images of triremes and seamen see Morrison and Williams, *Greek Oared Ships,* 170–79; Basch, *Musée Imaginaire,* 270–301. Parthenon frieze: see below.

3. Solon cited in Ps. Arist. *Ath. Pol.* 12.3; Finley, "Greek Civilization . . . Slave Labour," 71–72; Raaflaub, *Entdeckung der Freiheit,* 54–70; Manville, *Origins of Citizenship,* 133–34.

4. Here I follow the arguments of Raaflaub, *Entdeckung der Freiheit,* 264–77.

5. Mechanism: Ober, *Mass and Elite,* 163–65, 240–47, 332–39. Ordinary people seize opportunity: see, for example, Ober, "Athenian Revolution."

6. Raaflaub, *Entdeckung der Freiheit,* 275; "Contemporary Perceptions of Democracy," 36.

7. *Plato's Republic,* 306, translation Grube.

8. As several scholars have noted, most recently Schuller, "Attischen Seebunds . . . athenischen Demokratie," 90–91 and Ceccarelli, "Sans thalassocratie?" 446n.11 (with citation of earlier work); see also Sheldon Wolin's essay in this volume. Ceccarelli correctly concludes that the connection between seapower and *dēmokratia* was an ideological construct (p. 470), but she underestimates its grounding in reality and fails to consider the ideology of Athenian thetes.

9. Black sergeant: cited in Litwack, "Free at Last," 132. In ancient Greece too, nothing succeeded like military success when it came to boosting self-confidence and belief in one's manliness: see Xen. *Hell.* 7.1.23–25. Prestige and self-confidence of thetic seamen: Schuller, "Attischen Seebunds . . . athenischen Demokratie," 91.

10. Translation Morrison, "Hyperesia," 55.

11. Although Athenian *epibatai* were sometimes thetes (e.g., Thuc. 6.43.1), they were normally drawn from higher census classes (e.g., Thuc. 8.24.2): Jordan, *Athenian Navy,* 195–98; Dover, *HCT* ad Thuc. 6.43; Morrison, "Hyperesia," 55. Aristotle on the political sociology of seamen: see the valuable comments of Ceccarelli, "Sans thalassocratie?" 456–60.

12. Thuc. 3.16.1, 3.18.3–4 with Gomme, *HCT,* and Hornblower, *Commentary* ad loc.; Ps. Xen. *Ath. Pol.* 1.19–20; cf. Thuc. 1.142.5, 9; Xen. *Hell.* 1.6.24, 7.1.4.

13. Manpower on trireme: see below. Critical importance of seapower to Athens: Welwei, *Unfreie,* 71. Thetes not accept political subordination at home: Raaflaub, "Contemporary Perceptions of Democracy," 36. Nation of rulers, *isonomia* as dominant motif: Raaflaub, *Entdeckung der Freiheit,* 115–17, 262–64, 268. Navy and public income: Finley, *Democracy Ancient and Modern,* 81–88. Schuller, "Attischen Seebunds . . . athenischen Demokratie," 94–97 also notes that the need to administer navy and empire stimulated the organizational skills that Athenians also used to create the institutions of the new democracy.

14. Communities bound by symbolic, ritual, emotive ties: see Strauss, "Ritual, Social Drama, and Politics." Earlier work by Connor (especially "Tribes, Festivals, and Processions") is fundamental to the study of symbolic politics in Athens. On the democratic nature of certain aspects of the Athenian hoplite army, see Ridley, "Hoplite as Citizen."

15. Thuc. 8.72.2, cf. 8.48.3, 8.86.5; Arist. *Pol.* 1304a22, 1327b7–8, cf. 1291b20–24; cf. Isoc. 12.116.

16. Thuc. 2.89.9, cf. 2.84.3; cf. Plato *Laws* 641e. Morrison and Coates, *Athenian Trireme,* 75n.13; note the importance of silence aboard a trireme during battle.

17. Thuc. 2.89.1; cf. Ar. *Ach.* 546. On *stratiōtēs* as synonym for *nautēs,* see Morrison, "Hyperesia," 53. There may have been a gibe at the thetes' ineligibility to serve as infantrymen in Aristophanes *Banqueters* (fr. 248 Kassel-Austin). Thetes also served as light-armed troops, but such service did not require as much time (Schuller, "Attischen Seebunds . . . athenischen Demokratie," 91–92) and perhaps not as much skill as did service at sea, and so probably exerted less of an ideological and political impact.

18. So Rosivach, "Manning Athenian Fleet," 53–54; Gabrielsen, *Financing,* 106–8, 248n.6. Jordan, *Athenian Navy,* 101–3 and Hansen, *Demography and Democracy,* 22–23, argue that conscription was more common.

19. Thuc. 8.48.2–3, 8.72.2, 8.74.3–8.77, 8.81.1, 8.86.2–5, cf. 8.48.5–6.

20. Seamen at Samos in 411: see comments of Kagan, *Fall of Athenian Empire,* 121, 168–73. No bloc voting: see Amit, *Athens and the Sea,* 57–71.

21. On *homonoia,* see Ober, *Mass and Elite,* 297–99; on Aristotle and education, see Lord, this volume.

22. Translation Morrison, "Hyperesia," 51.

23. On these details, see Rankov, "Rowing Olympias" and "Operation of Trireme Reconstruction." "Rowing Olympias," 53 illustrates the view from the seat of a thranite (rower on the top deck): a vivid picture of the communitarian nature of rowing on a trireme.

24. Group rather than individual liberty: see the succinct remarks of Berlin, *Four Essays on Liberty,* xl–xli, cited by Hansen in his essay in this volume. Zeugites (Thuc. 3.16.1) and hoplites (e.g., Thuc. 3.18.3–4) sometimes rowed in Athenian triremes, but less regularly. See the interesting discussion of Rosivach, "Manning Athenian Fleet," 54–55. On noncitizens as Athenian oarsmen, see below.

25. Thuc. 8.73.5; Ar. *Ran.* 1071 with Dover's commentary. Triremes: Hansen, *Was Athens a Democracy?* 23, 42n.142. On this meaning of *eleutheros,* see Hansen in this volume. On the state triremes *Paralos* and *Salaminia,* see Miltner, "Paralos." On triremes' names, see the summary of epigraphic evidence in Miltner, "Seewesen," and the analysis in Casson, *Ships and Seamanship,* 350–54.

26. On this interpretation of the Greek, see Morrison, "Hyperesia," 55; Gomme, *HCT* ad Thuc. 1.143.1, is less sure of the meaning.

27. On the scholarly debate see Stadter, *Commentary on Plutarch,* ad loc.; Rosivach, "Manning Athenian Fleet," 57n.5; Gabrielsen, *Financing,* 111 and 249n.3.

28. Welwei, *Unfreie,* 65–104; Morrison and Coates, *Athenian Trireme,* 108–18.

29. On the elite bias in favor of land fighting, see Raaflaub's contribution in this volume.

30. Raaflaub, *Entdeckung der Freiheit,* 215–48.

31. Not all scholars accept Ps. Xenophon's testimony as evidence that the thetes could hold office in the late fifth century, although there is general agreement that they had secured that privilege by the late fourth century: see Rhodes, *Commentary,* 145–46.

32. See Welwei, *Unfreie,* 104–7; Krentz, *Thirty,* 83–84. On the question of the respective participation of citizens and others on Athenian triremes, see the interesting suggestion of Rosivach ("Manning Athenian Fleet," 51–53) that citizens tended to serve

on short voyages in the summer months while noncitizens predominated on longer voyages and those in the marginal sailing season of spring and fall. Note also the suggestion of Ruschenbusch ("Besatzung athenischer Trieren") that the sixty-two oarsmen per ship seated on deck, the *thranitai,* were usually citizens; with arguments against by Gabrielsen, *Financing,* 109, 249n.10.

33. Finley, *Democracy Ancient and Modern,* 82–87.

34. Tocqueville, *Democracy in America,* vol. 2, 65. See Hanson and Raaflaub in this volume and Loraux, *Invention,* e.g., 33–34, 180–202, 217–20, 361n.126 (with references to earlier scholarship). Important responses include Seager's review; Ober, *Mass and Elite,* 289–92, 339; and Thomas, *Oral tradition,* 213–21, who notes that the studied anonymity of the *epitaphios* imposes "democratic anonymity" (218) on a substratum of aristocratic values. Thetes and second-class treatment: Raaflaub also discusses in this volume the possible absence of thetes from the fifth-century *ephēbeia,* and the possibility that only hoplite orphans were supported at state expense. The evidence, however, is inconclusive.

35. Not give thetic seamen their due: see Gomme, *HCT,* I, 460, 266–67. Tip of the iceberg: Thomas, *Oral Tradition.*

36. Parthenon frieze: Osborne, "Viewing and Obscuring," 103–4, attributes the prominence of cavalrymen to an "aristocratic image of Athenian democracy" (104), made accessible to the ordinary citizen through the anonymity and lack of individuality of the individuals sculpted on the frieze. Tracy, "Panathenaic Festival," 148–51, attributes the prominence of cavalrymen to the prominence of equestrian events in the Panathenaic Games, a simpler and therefore more convincing argument. Thetic training: Gomme, *HCT,* I, 460.

37. Both bow decoration and stern ornaments, Thuc. 6.31.3; Hdt. 8.88; Ar. *Ran.* 933; Diod. Sic. 13.3; Plut. *Them.* 15; and gilded statues of Pallas Athena, Ar. *Ach.* 547; Eur. *IA* 239–76.

38. Ships' markings: Torr, *Ancient Ships,* 65–69; Casson, *Ships and Seamanship,* 344–48; Morrison and Williams, *Greek Oared Ships,* 133–34, 197–98. Tomb of Themistocles: Gomme, *HCT,* II, 445–46. Lenormant Relief: Beschi, "Rilievi votivi attici," 117–32.

39. Although, in spite of pioneering work by such scholars as Amit, Jordan, and Morrison and Williams, by no means have historians exhausted their treatment of the very considerable number of references to seamanship and rowing in Attic tragedy and comedy: see Morrison and Williams, *Greek Oared Ships,* 194–202.

40. Levine, "Slave Songs," 125; cf. more generally Levine, *Black Culture and Black Consciousness.*

41. Finding theory in practice: Strauss, *Fathers and Sons,* 30–33, with references to anthropological and sociological discussions. Ober, *Mass and Elite,* 338–39 argues that that elusive matter, Athenian democratic theory, is best to be found in democratic practice. Informal training: Ober, *Mass and Elite,* 159–60, with earlier literature cited.

READING DEMOCRACY: "SOCRATIC" DIALOGUES AND THE POLITICAL EDUCATION OF DEMOCRATIC CITIZENS

J. Peter Euben

I

Debate over the nature and purpose of public education has once more become a significant issue in the continuing contest to define American identity and the possibilities of American democracy. The end of a Cold War that had provided a definition of who we were and what we were not (totalitarian, godless, unfree) and what education should be for[1] made thinking about national purpose and international aims a pressing task. At the same time the dominant narrative about "America" was becoming loudly contested by groups who saw in the story of progress, the melting pot, the land of the free and the home for huddled masses a coverup, a hoax or a half-truth that elided the imperialist underpinnings of such a self-congratulatory narrative. As the lines of the Cold War became blurred, the lines of this new culture war became clearer. It was as if we had lived so long in a bipolar world that we could not live without it, even if that meant shifting the battle lines from the international to the national arena.

The new war is being fought on many fronts. On one it involves the debate over voucher systems and affirmative action, prayer in the schools and calls for a more exclusivist immigration policy, textbook politics and multicultural curriculum, the correlation of race and IQ and standardized tests and the level of support of public education generally. The battles are fought in local school boards and in Congress, by those who have removed their children from public schools, by those who would like to but cannot, as well as those who remain committed either by default or in principle to public schooling. Whatever their respective politics and diagnoses, almost all participants agree that the public school system is failing whether because of the skills and values it has failed to inculcate or the ones it has, because it has been asked to do too much or cannot even do the rudiments. Either in despair or with relief, more and more people are coming to regard the schools as places of discipline and confinement not unlike prisons.

On another front the war is taking place in institutions of higher education between "multiculturalists" and "canonists."[2] Surely the most striking thing about this version of the culture wars is its apocalyptic posturing. We are warned that the "Barbarians" (by which is meant an ill-defined conglomerate of feminists, Marxists, radicals, and postmodernists) are in the citadel and leading us into a new dark age, and that civilization itself is in the balance when the "great" works of Western culture chosen for their intrinsic virtues of literary merit, aesthetic achievement, and moral sensibility are displaced by texts selected on the basis of some political agenda. Because of all this, everything "we" value—freedom, reason, individuality, and democracy—is being lost. (The unspoken assumption among many conservative canonists is that literary works chosen for their intrinsic value happen to have admirable political consequences: a fortunate fact since choosing them for political reasons would be politicizing the university, a charge they level at their multiculturalist opponents.)

Almost as striking is the equally unpersuasive assumption that reading the right books or reading them rightly will help end oppression and ameliorate real-world wrongs.[3] Given the radically contingent connection between reading specific books in a university and actions done outside it,[4] it is implausible to suppose that one can create the politically correct students of the 1990s any more than one can recreate the supposedly deferential ones of the 1950s so admired by conservatives.

But whatever side one takes in these battles, what is startling is how debates over curriculum normally decided by desultory compromises reached in the relative privacy of faculty committees has suddenly become the focus of such heated public controversy. A clue as to why this has happened can be found in Paul Gray's plaintive question in a recent *Time Magazine* essay, "Who Are We?" As he saw it, the "customs, beliefs, principles that have unified the U.S. for more than two centuries are being challenged with a ferocity not seen since the Civil War." Surveying the multiculturalist critique, he wondered whether Americans still had any "faith in the vision of their country as the cradle of individual rights and liberties" or were, on the contrary, relinquishing "the teaching of some of these freedoms to further the goals of the ethnic and social groups to which they belong?"[5] At stake was the existence of the Union. But this civil war was not a battle between North and South but between "America" and its parts.

Improbable as it may seem, Plato plays a role in this debate, symbolically as well as substantively. As perhaps the quintessentially Dead White Male, his authority, as well as that of the democratic Athens he criticized, has been challenged by those who regard him (and it) as constitutive of a hegemonic discourse that delegitimates the "subjugated" voices and practices of non-Western peoples, women and the poor. Though there is evidence to suggest that Plato is not so much being removed from the canon as having to share his authority with others previously excluded from it, it is true that one now must make strenuous political and intellectual arguments for including the *Republic* in a required core course. Given that Socrates demands such arguments from his own interlocutors and given the long-standing controversies over the meaning of Socrates' life and death as well as over the *Republic,* this seems reasonable enough. Just ask whose Socrates is definitive: Xenophon's, Aristophanes', or Plato's? And which Platonic dialogue should we take as definitive of Plato's Socrates: the *Apology* or the *Parmenides,* the *Protagoras* or the *Phaedrus,* the *Republic* or the *Meno?* Whose reading of the *Republic* should be canonical: Karl Popper's or Leo Strauss's, Gadamer's or Terence Irwin's, Gregory Vlastos's or I. F. Stone's, Julia Annas's or Allan Bloom's?

Whatever side one takes in the culture wars or on the role Plato should play in the education of the young, there is virtual unanimity that he is no democrat. No one committed to radical democracy[6] looks to Plato for support for her commitment to the task of educating her fellow citizens—even if she agrees that confronting astute political critics makes her defense of democracy stronger and even supposing Josiah Ober is right in arguing that a robust democracy must respect systemic critics who are themselves marginalized by the dominant political culture.[7] But was Plato really an implacable foe of democracy?[8]

While the verdict on Plato is nearly unanimous, the jury is still out on Plato's Socrates. If there is a case to be made for Socrates as a democrat[9] and for the compatibility of democracy and philosophy, it must, so it seems, be based on Plato's *Apology of Socrates.* Here Socrates is portrayed as walking the streets talking to anyone he meets (including women and slaves) in a common language about the actions and thoughts of their everyday lives. Though he speaks to all, he is especially concerned with his fellow citizens since who they are and what they do create the community in which he lives his life as an Athenian and a philosopher. That is why he is so incredulous when his accusers claim that he is purposefully corrupting the young.

Socrates is not interested in idle chatter but in whether his fellow citizens know what they are doing and saying. Thus each conversation is an encounter in which he asks them to give an account of the kinds of lives they lead (or do not yet lead), of the claims and choices they do make (or do not make), and of the politics they have or do not know they have. Born into a language, institutions, and practices that have the comfortable feel of being natural and reflecting the order of the cosmos, polis, and soul, they are oblivious of the way these things shape who they are and so of the meaning(s) of their lives. Socrates wants to disturb that comfort so that the language and the practices it implicitly commends become available for reflection and reconstruction.[10] If every action or project we undertake aims at something we think is good or good for us, and if such a good remains unavailable to scrutiny, then we are condemned to live irrationally, since we will not know or even ask whether our attachment to that implicit good is in fact good. We will not know whether the work we do, the goals we strive for, the actions we undertake, the friends we have, and the authorities we respect enhance or diminish the capacity for judgment, thought,

and reflection distinctive to a human life. When Socrates says that "the unexamined life is not worth living," he is suggesting that such a life is not a human
life at all but a series of random motions that lack purpose and coherence. He
suggests that people are thoughtless in the sense Hannah Arendt means when
she characterizes Adolph Eichmann as an ordinary man who lacked the capacity to see what he was doing because he lacked the moral imagination to see the
world and so himself from another's point of view. "He was not stupid," Arendt
writes. "It was sheer thoughtlessness—something by no means identical with
stupidity—that predisposed him to become one of the greatest criminals of that
period."[11]

What is challenging for us is Socrates' assumption that everyone *can* be
thoughtful, that the ability to be self-aware and self-critical emerges out of, and
is a prerequisite for, the practices of democratic citizenship. When Socrates insists that the unexamined life is not worth living, he is making a claim that he
expects to be intelligible to his fellow citizens. He is also providing a framework for a contemporary distinction between a politicized education and a political one. It is a distinction that can clarify even as it moderates the Culture
Wars and provide some guidance for how to educate democratic citizens democratically.[12]

By *politicized education* we often mean *indoctrination,* where what can be
taught, who can teach it, and where it can be taught to whom is determined by
a partisan agenda with little regard for truth, or for encouraging independence
of mind and reciprocity. A politicized education regards the relationship between teacher and student as paradigmatic, so that some class or certain individuals are defined as being in need of perpetual moral tutelage due to political
incapacity. "[W]e have," Hannah Arendt writes, "been accustomed in our tradition of political thought to regard the authority of parents over children, of
teachers over pupils, as the model by which to understand political authority."
This model, which she finds in Plato and Aristotle, is "based, first of all, on an
absolute superiority such as can never exist among adults and which, from the
point of view of human dignity, must never exist."[13]

Any distinction between a politicized and political education must attend to
the way something is taught as well as to its explicit content. Context and subtext can work against a text, as when someone teaches radical democracy in an
authoritarian manner or defends authoritarianism in a way that encourages disagreement. There is a sense in which we teach who we are as well as particular views, which is why we distinguish moral rules from moral exemplars. More
amorphously but not less significantly, any distinction between the two kinds
of education must refer to the larger political and cultural context in which relationships and institutions of education are located. Even the most intimate
conversations and most abstract philosophical exchanges are structured by inequalities of power (as well as oppositions of sensibility and position), and these
too must be articulated and be subject to debate—as they are in the *Gorgias.*[14]

A political as opposed to a politicized education recognizes the temporariness and institutional particularity of the inequality between student and university teacher and the paradox of having authority over students who are already adults and so are our political equals. Such an education aims to teach such students to be thoughtful in a way that exemplifies, as it cultivates, the capacity for independent, yet collegially sustained, judgment that is essential for the active sharing of power and responsibility that should define democratic citizenship. As teachers in institutions of higher learning, our simple task is to help students think about what they are doing while acknowledging that, however well informed or expert we may be, remaining a student of one's students is crucial. It makes one a better teacher of them, because no matter how well-educated we may suppose ourselves to be, there are significant things about the world that we have missed, distorted, or evaded. As I shall argue in regard to the *Gorgias* and about the Platonic corpus generally, when one engages in dialectic the positions and languages of the participants cease to be fixed. Being a teacher is then no longer a professional role one assumes, but marks a changing position in a dialogic encounter.

Democratic political education must be dialogic whether the dialogue is with our student/citizens within the university or our fellow students outside it. In both contexts "real" dialogue must be about its own preconditions. It must acknowledge how the will to power frames the will to truth, and how inequalities of power shape the "positions" of interlocutors in ways that turn proclaimed dialogues into covert monologues. Such a two-level dialogue is a way of accepting the combination of authority and inequality present in the classroom, of responding to Arendt's warning not to confound politics and education, and of being alert to subtext and context as well as text. The insistence on dialogue is also an unembarrassed admission of our own historicity, mortality, and partiality even if that admission helps us to be less partisan. Dialogue presupposes that truth is neither wholly subservient to political imperatives nor deduced from ontological or metaphysical foundations. Truth may be generated politically but politics need not be a matter of who gets what when and how, need not be the art of the possible or simply power in a Hobbesian sense.[15]

But even if all this can be dragged out of the *Apology,* Socrates in almost every other dialogue and Plato in all of them is antidemocratic. Nowhere does this seem more obvious than in the *Gorgias* where Socrates is contemptuous of the multitude and the idea that it could have its own will and voice, rejects jury pay and majority rule, is indifferent to the question of who enjoys the political rights and prerogatives of citizens, endorses expert political knowledge, sees leadership as a form of "psychic engineering," and perversely disparages the revered democratic leaders of Athens[16]—all as part of a misbegotten project of substituting philosophical truth for the contingencies and uncertainties that mark all politics, but democratic politics most of all.

While I have no desire to explain away these antidemocratic sentiments or dismiss the conventional readings of the *Gorgias,* I will, in Section II, read the dialogue against the grain[17] to complicate the picture of Socrates as antidemocratic. At a minimum I will argue that Socrates is more of a democrat than he seems and that much of what he says about democracy in the *Gorgias* is directed at the way democracy is being construed by the interlocutors in the dialogue and by those in Athens who agree with or honor them. If such putative friends are in fact enemies of democracy, then Socrates' critique of them raises the question of who are democracy's true friends and whether the real friend may be the seeming enemy. This question has special urgency for a society in which, as Ian Morris emphasizes in his essay, citizens thought of themselves as tied together, restrained, and made equal by *philia.* If, like Polemarchus in the *Republic,* one is confused about who one's true friends and enemies are, then such ties and any politics based on them become deeply problematic. And unless one is clear on this, it will be difficult to distinguish between critics of democracy attempting to recall or inspire their fellow citizens to the highest possibilities of their culture,[18] whether it be by argument, example or provocation—from those who are antidemocrats.[19] Let me take Socrates' criticism of Athens' political leaders as an example of why the distinction is not as obvious as it seems. Below I say how that criticism involves a contest over the way that Pericles and so Athenian democracy is to be understood.

There is no question that Socrates' criticisms of the Athenian leaders are ungenerous at best, simpleminded and moralistic at worst. In assuming that leaders are in complete control of events, he ignores the contingencies that accompany all collective endeavors, and the inevitable discrepancy between intentions and results. But let us suppose Socrates (or Plato) knows that such revisionist representations, though they might find favor in a few militantly conservative circles, would be taken as provocative. Suppose the point is to stimulate argument and debate, to have Athenians become more thoughtful about what they had done and could do in the future. In this regard consider Sheldon Wolin's argument in this volume that during the Peloponnesian War the connection between power and place was attenuated as Athens became a naval base from which power was projected outward rather than being embodied in internal deliberations, policy decisions, and decrees. Should we regard sharp criticism of such developments and the leaders responsible for them as being antidemocratic? Perhaps, if the critiques go far enough, we should. But how far? Though I am not sure of the answer, I am sure that the *Gorgias* poses the question with unique force and subtlety and that a case can be made that part of Socrates' critique is directed against the unforeseen consequences of Athenian imperialism.

Those consequences are foregrounded when Socrates pointedly asks Callicles what will happen to him, to Athens and, by implication, to his assessment of Athenian leaders, when the city loses its empire—as of course it had by the time the dialogue was written. Indeed the tension between the dramatic and historical dates of the *Gorgias* presents Socrates as more politically prescient than the more "realistic" and pragmatic Callicles.[20]

There is another way of getting at the complications involved in making a sharp distinction between sympathetic critics of democracy and antidemocrats. Socrates dismisses majority rule as an absurd way of deciding on the best way or life or even the best policy. Since such rule is seen as essential to (if not distinctive to) democracy, such rejection seems strong evidence of Socrates' hostility to the equality and antifoundational epistemology democracy presupposes.[21] But majority rule is not distinctive to democracy, and so Socrates' criticism is not directed just at democracy but at any regime—including oligarchy—in which some group of citizens, no matter how exclusive, decide things by majority vote. What is distinctive to democracy is the elements comprising the majority when it votes. Even democracy's friends have often worried about what majority rule can mean in the face of elite manipulation. As C. Wright Mills put it some years ago, "We cannot assume today that men must in the last resort be governed by their own consent" because of the "power to manage and manipulate the consent of men. That we do not know the limits of such power . . . does not remove the fact that much power today is successfully employed without the sanction of reason or the conscience of the obedient."[22] For all the dangerous ideas such claims can lead to (such as false consciousness and need for something like democratic centralism), and for all the attempts by writers on popular culture to find local resistance where Mills finds manipulation, his concerns remain salient and echo Socrates' concerns about rhetorical manipulation and the manufacturing of consent.[23]

I offer one final way of complicating the distinction between being a sympathetic if critical friend of democracy and being antidemocratic. Though there are obvious and significant dissimilarities between modes of communication employed in the relatively face-to-face society of classical Athens and our own electronic mass media, Socrates' concern in the *Gorgias* with democracy's susceptibility to rhetorical manipulation anticipates contemporary concerns about the debasement of public discourse, the disappearance of public spaces, and the danger of the "system world" cannibalizing the "life world."[24] In its complete indifference to truth, our political discourse has become, in Neil Postman's view, "dangerous nonsense." "By favoring certain definitions of intelligence and wisdom and by demanding a certain kind of content," television has created "new forms of truth-telling."[25] When he goes on to insist that television fosters "misplaced irrelevant fragmented superficial information that creates the illusion of knowing something which in fact leads one away from knowing," we can hear Socrates' response to Gorgias' claims about the power of rhetoric overwhelming the truth about medicine or politics.

For Socrates rhetoric as practiced by Gorgias is committed to manipulation and misinformation, since his power (and that of the kind of rhetoric he practices) depends on the ignorance of the people.[26] In this sense Gorgias reveals his antidemocratic tendencies. Moreover, Socrates suggests that a participatory egalitarian politics requires that people be able to judge the character of the speaker and the general veracity of what is said, as well as being able to distinguish speech that is narrowly strategic and primarily manipulative.[27]

The political deficiencies and dangers of rhetoric do not lead Socrates into a wholesale rejection of rhetoric for at least two reasons. One reason is that philosophy too is rhetorical, even manipulative, a fact Socrates implicitly and the dialogue explicitly acknowledges (as I argue below). The other is the need each has for the other. Socrates ends the dialogue with a rhetorical display—the telling of a myth—intended, among other things, to convince the dialectically unpersuaded Callicles of the benefits of philosophy.[28] Nor do the deficiencies drive Socrates into an epistemologically rather than a politically grounded notion of political knowledge and wisdom. Rather he explores, both by what he does and what he says, the possibilities of a philosophically informed and politically grounded rhetoric that could help constitute a political education for a democratic citizenry. In this dialogue at least, Socrates does not transform politics into a theoretical object requiring elaborate education as a prerequisite for the sharing of power as he is said to do in the *Republic*. He does not separate democracy from theory and intellect. What Socrates (or Plato) does is detach aristocratic values of the sort Callicles embraces from social class and reattach them to intelligence and philosophy, while holding out the possibility that such intelligence can be inclusive, that knowledge, like power, might be widely distributed. It is this vision of an aristocratic democracy that Socrates explores persistently, though inconclusively, in the *Gorgias*.[29]

As this implies, Socrates assumes democracy as a context for his argument and his criticisms of politics would be beside the point and unintelligible if the demos was not a significant political actor. The democratic context is manifest in the *Gorgias'* thematic preoccupations with freedom, power, and empire, in its stress on the need for open frank speech, accountability, and responsibility, and in its insistence on assessing what someone says by the merits of his advice rather than on his birth, status, or wealth. It is also present in the dialogue's intellectualism (by which I mean a concern for the preconditions of what it is doing)[30] and in the way these thematic preoccupations become the stated preconditions for successfully engaging in philosophical dialogue. It is evident in the dialogue's commitment to and dependence on the idea of what Ian Morris (following Robert Dahl) calls a strong principle of equality, where all members of a community are regarded as sufficiently well qualified to participate in making binding collective decisions on all issues that significantly affect their good or interest. (Though Socrates proposes the idea of expert political knowledge, the dialogue he has with his interlocutors in the *Gorgias* neither illustrates nor claims it.[31]) As I read the dialogue, no one (including Socrates) is presented as so superior that he should be entrusted with making the collective decisions about what to talk about or who is entitled to speak about what to whom.

Though the matter is complex, I would argue that each participant/interlocutor in the *Gorgias* is accorded the dignity and respect that ideally helped define democratic citizenship.

Socrates not only assumes democracy as a context for his critique of politics, he elaborates democratic practices into a philosophical/political vocation.[32] Both the form and content of his criticism of Athenian democracy could build on a tradition of democratic self-critique found in drama and in the demand for accountability represented by the *dokimasia* and *euthunai*.[33] If, as Benjamin Barber argues in his essay, reflexivity conditioned by civic education turns out to be democracy's greatest virtue, if democracy is debate about what democracy is, then what better example can we have than the *Gorgias* and Socrates, who embodies, or at least helps constitute, a democratic culture of this kind? It is for these as well as other reasons (adduced above and elaborated below) that I believe that Socrates of the *Gorgias,* like Socrates of the *Apology,* remains a teacher of how to politically educate a democracy democratically, even if, as I would not deny, he remains skeptical of certain practices we regard as essentially democratic.

Finally, I want to offer a way of reading the *Gorgias* that opens up its democratic possibilities against the confluence between conservative canonists who find congenial political pronouncements in the dialogues like the *Gorgias* and their critics who condemn Socrates and Plato because of those pronouncements. The agreement between canonists and their critics relies on a flat and deflationary reading of the dialogue. It ignores the riddles posed by Socratic irony, the way Socrates' knowledge is, to use Gregory Vlastos's language, "full of gaps, unanswered questions," "invaded by unresolved perplexity in a way that makes Socrates strange" (*atopos* is what Callicles calls him), as well as the need to keep faith with Socrates by saving "both the assertion of his ignorance and his implied negation" of it.[34] It misses how the tensions, contrasts, or even contradictions between text(s) and context(s), argument and drama, form and movement, and characters (such as Socrates and Callicles) create generative spaces from within which the issues and conclusions of the dialogue are continually reframed. This is not so much a contrast between surface and depth or low and high (as in the *Republic*) as between shifting points of reference. And this means that questions of consistency and inconsistency are fluid and multiple for the same reason that the Funeral Oration in Thucydides' *History* reads differently depending on which other speeches it is compared with, which other Athenian leaders he is compared with, and which incidents (Melos, the Plague, the Mytilenean debate) are juxtaposed to it. If, as I will argue, these multiple points of view remain unresolved by any "normalizing" narrative, then the dialogue contains a superabundance of energy and transformative impulses ancient critics and modern defenders associate with Athenian democracy.[35]

In her essay in this volume, Carol Dougherty argues that the Athenians did not try to resolve the multiplicity of narratives by which they represented themselves as Athenians. Instead, competing narratives about the origins of democracy and its relations to Athenian identity, as well as contradictory views of specific historical events, were allowed to remain unrationalized. She goes on to suggest that the competition over origins was part of a contemporary controversy over the construction of citizenship and civic identity. As she puts it, "foundation tales of all kinds tend to respond to needs of the present as much if not more than they adequately record the past." Her point applies to the *Gorgias* and helps us make sense of the debate over Periclean leadership. That debate is not only about whether Pericles was a good leader, but about how "Pericles" is to be represented and what sort of politics various representations legitimate. Her point also helps us make sense of how and why the contest over "Plato" and "the" "Western" tradition[36] he comes to stand for is involved in contemporary debates over democratic citizenship and American civic identity.

II

Socrates' antidemocratic sentiments in the *Gorgias* seem clearest in his disparagement of the revered democratic leaders of Athens and in his conception of leadership as "psychic engineering." His most vehement criticism is aimed at the most democratic leader, Pericles, who is accused of making his fellow citizens worse by indulging their desires rather than educating their souls. How can someone who made those in his charge lazy covetous chatterboxes, who had a worse reputation among those he led at the end of his tenure of office than in the beginning, and who complained about his unjust treatment at the hands of the people he purportedly led, be considered a good political leader? If Pericles was a horse trainer who trained his horses to be even more unruly than they were before, or a doctor whose prescriptions made his patients worse, would we praise his art and accomplishments?

As an alternative, Socrates offers the true political art (*alēthōs politikē technē*) and himself as the one living practitioner of it. This political art aims at improving the souls of citizens, transforming their ill-formed aspirations and ill-informed unself-conscious commitments. In its assumption of a radical inequality between the competent authority of the true statesman and the actual lives of people, in the discrepancy it posits between the judgment of the people and the knowledge necessary for moral self-knowledge (which is itself a necessary condition for participation), it is a view of leadership incompatible with even a tepidly liberal view of democracy. The case against Socrates as democratic seems both powerful and closed. But as is by now obvious, I do not think it is either.

The antidemocratic Socrates argument depends on a kind of reading the dialogue itself warns against. The *Gorgias* is concerned with deception and self-deception. It shows Socrates using tactics he explicitly excoriates and failing to achieve what he repeatedly says he must in order to answer the central question of the dialogue ("Which is the best life?"). Moreover, it incessantly calls attention to what is absent or problematic in the argument and drama. The preconditions for dialogue become the dialogue's subject. In the end, it leaves the great dialectician talking to himself.

There is also the question I posed earlier, of when being a critic of democracy makes one antidemocratic rather than a prophet recalling his or her people to what is best in their past and most promising in their future. This is a particularly pressing question if, as the juxtaposition of the dramatic and historical contexts of the dialogue suggest, that democracy has become so corrupt that critique must be systemic. The question is particularly difficult if we read the *Gorgias* against the background of Euripidean or Aristophanic drama, whose criticisms of Athenian democracy can make Socrates' criticisms of his native city seem tame by comparison. Even if we acknowledge that philosophy was never part of the city's democratic institutions, as drama certainly was, it is worth emphasizing that popular juries awarded prizes to tragedies that challenged the evolution of their cultural forms and practices and to comedies that pilloried popular democratic leaders and current intellectual fashions.[37] One could even say that the dramatic festivals were a form of political and moral education, as was participation in other political institutions, but with this difference: drama alone provided the space and time to reflect on the patterns of action and cultural transformations that were difficult to discern in the urgency of daily decisions. In these terms, Socrates (and Plato) can be seen as extending a tradition of institutionalized critical reflection that had (perhaps) become corrupt. That might explain what seems Socrates' preposterous assumption in the *Apology* that every person who claimed power (which in Athens meant every citizen) should be called on to give an account of his life and be made fully aware of the ends otherwise implicit in his unself-conscious choices.

The dialogue presents the general corruption as one of language,[38] a corruption of particular significance in an oral culture and in a democracy that relied on speech as a mode of political education, common deliberation, and judgment. It is in this regard that Socrates appears more committed to democratic culture than the popularly acclaimed Gorgias and the putative democrat Callicles. For the Gorgias of this dialogue,[39] language is a form of manipulation and the necessary as well as sufficient condition for power, freedom, and happiness. The rhetorician's mastery of language enables his students to master anyone, anytime, any place, and for any ends. So what if the condition of their success is systematic miseducation?[40]

Where speech becomes mere words, when, as with Callicles (and some contemporary political leaders), protestations of affection and respect for the demos disguise contempt for it,[41] democratic citizens may well become cynical or passive. They may act impulsively or in ignorance—which then justifies elite claims to superiority. When masters of speech like Gorgias are disconnected from a living community of fellow citizens, so that their sons will not have to fight in a war their words may have helped begin, the separation of words and things becomes the separation of power and responsibility.[42] If political judgment rests on the anticipated communications with others with whom I share a world and with whom I have to come to some agreement, then "distorted communication," which Gorgias boasts of and perpetuates, is a threat to it. The fact that he is uninterested in listening to what others say (he claims he has already heard every question that could possibly be asked him), and that he is a foreigner, makes him less aware of the highly contextualized discriminations and attentive to particular ties of place and time that remind Athenians of their shared past and future. But Gorgias also dissolves the enlarged mentality political judgment requires, a mentality that enables citizens to think in place of others, to consider their perspectives. "The more people's standpoints I have present in my mind while I am pondering a given issue" Hannah Arendt writes, "and the better I can imagine how I would think and feel if I were in their place, the stronger will be my capacity for representative thinking and the more valid my final conclusion, my opinion."[43] This does not entail either erasure or reification of self, interest, or will. Nor is it a matter of altruism, following the dictates of an ontology or adhering to a stable vision of community. What it does entail is political and moral imagination, the ability to take, at least momentarily, the part of others, to see as they see, and so to see more of the world one shares with them. Like an actress, one has to play more than one role to avoid "type-casting." Like a member of an audience, one is able to see how the parts make up the whole. This is not a claim for objectivity or universality but for impartiality, in which we think as fellow actors, in representative ways.

The example Gorgias sets, the view of politics as domination he assumes or espouses, and the sort of citizens likely to emerge from that example and view (i.e., Polus and Callicles) endanger the always-fragile negotiations that characterize democratic deliberations. But this is not a matter of undistorted communication, since the *Gorgias* presses the ubiquity of power on us, even in philosophical discussions where it seems least present and most inappropriate. Nor, given the contest over the representations of Athenian democratic leaders and Socrates' own manipulations, does it permit a sure line between fact and fiction.

One could say that the dialogue presents two principles in tension (if not at war) with each other: The first is a Habermasian ideal of a communicative reason in which dialogue and deliberation are governed by ideas of frankness, mutuality, consensus, and rational argument derived from the formal structure of communication itself. The other is the Foucauldian suspicion that this discursive practice is a particularly insidious way of concealing power's "regime of truth" with its normalized productions and perpetuation of exclusions and hierarchies, both of which problematize any ideal of manipulation and coercion-free "conversation." For the former principle, dialogue provides a paradigm for political theory and politics. For the latter, it is another instance of hiding power amid the rhetoric of rationally motivated agreement.[44]

Thus the *Gorgias* holds out the hope and vision of dialogue as an exchange that excludes extraneous concerns beyond the desire to understand, clarify, reflect, and achieve agreement on the animating questions of individual and collective life. Here is a need for frankness and precision, friendship and consistency. But the dialogue challenges that vision by politicizing philosophy through its own semantic complexity. According to Mikhail Bakhtin, "The word, directed toward its object, enters a dialogically agitated and tension-filled environment of alien words, value judgments and accents, weaves in and out of complex interrelationships, merges with some, recoils from others, intersects with yet a third group: and all this may crucially shape discourse, may leave a trace in all its semantic layers."[45]

There is a third complication about Socrates' allegedly antidemocratic views, this one involving his criticism of Pericles. By the time we get to Socrates' critique, Pericles has been assimilated to tyrants. For Gorgias the connection is implicit, emerging from his definition of politics as deceit and domination for selfish ends. In these terms no political leader, including Pericles, could have shared responsibility with relatively free and equal citizens, since all leaders aim to be powerful, free, and happy and above the law. They aim to do what they want, when they want, to whomever they want. What is implicit with Gorgias is made explicit by Polus, who identifies the democratic leaders with the tyrant Archelaus. It is left to Callicles to provide a metaphysical justification for this identification and to praise Xerxes and Darius as having acted according to the nature of what is just (483e2)—in their attacks on Greece! So when we get to Socrates' critique of Pericles, the democratic sympathies of the latter are portrayed as an ingenious cosmetic ploy to insinuate himself with the demos in order better to dominate them. But if Socrates is criticizing *this* Pericles, then it is not so clear that his criticism of the Athenian pantheon is a criticism of "democracy." Rather, it may be a criticism of the way democracy and leadership have come to be construed by men like Gorgias, Polus and Callicles (and the society that has called them forth). If I am correct, then the contest over "Pericles" is a contest over how to represent the Athenian past in order to legitimate a contemporary political agenda.[46]

In addition, despite the claim that he alone possesses the true art of politics which should presumably ensure that his students are just in the way Gorgias' are not, Socrates was tried for corrupting the young. He was blamed then, as he is now (e.g., by I. F. Stone), for having taught students who were responsible for a violent antidemocratic coup. Thus the accusations Socrates levels at Gorgias were brought against himself. The question becomes why Socrates was as inept at "educating" his students as he accuses Gorgias and Pericles of being.[47] What makes things even more peculiar is that Socrates prominently invokes Alcibiades, who was both one of those people he was accused of corrupting and a ward of Pericles. Thus Socrates and Pericles share responsibility for their students' excesses. And that creates a certain kinship between Socrates and the man he accuses of being the worst political leader of all and against whom he offers himself as corrective. To top it off, there is Socrates' own inability to "control" Callicles. In the end he is left talking to himself, which is, Callicles implies, what he has been doing all along.

But what about the charge of "psychic engineering," the claim that Socrates endorses the idea of a political *technē,* and rule by experts whose special unshared knowledge entitles them to tell others how to live or, at a minimum, establishes a relationship of teacher and student inappropriate for the citizens of a democratic polis?[48]

There is no question that such an idea is present in the *Gorgias. If* politics is a *technē,* as shoemaking, horse training, or medicine are, and those who possess the political art can "make" people better, prescribing for their soul as a physician does for their body in accordance with some agreed-upon procedures and ends, then political issues can be dealt with rationally by professionals indifferent to the blandishments of men such as Gorgias. *If* there is such an art, no accidents of character or situation can thwart its success, since it is the absence of such an art that leaves someone like Gorgias unable to control the consequences of his teaching as they appear in the form of unjust actions by his students.

As with Socrates' criticisms of Pericles, we confront complications that leave us less certain of Socrates' endorsement of any such political *technē.* Of course any such uncertainty affects the degree to which Socrates' arguments for a *technē* can be grounds for his being considered antidemocratic.

To begin with, it is worth noting that Socrates presents his claim as a counter to Gorgias' assertions about the power of rhetoric to give one person absolute domination over everyone else and every situation. The old rhetoric promises mastery over others as a means to achieve the satiation of desires. It persuades by flattery rather than on the basis of facts or common deliberation since its success depends on manipulation. And it magnifies the divisions within the soul and the city. But the new philosophic rhetoric, the true political *technē* Socrates claims to practice, promises mastery for shared ends, treats others as ends, convinces these others on the basis of knowledge and dialogue, and lessens the divisions within the soul and the city. Making a man a friend to himself is, for Socrates, the precondition for making him a friend to others, and so a good citizen.

However strategic Socrates' claims for a political *technē* may be, he does make them. Of the three analogies Socrates introduces by way of justifying his art/artisanship—shoemaking, horse training, and medicine—the latter is the most plausible and most often invoked. A political educator or leader is like a doctor of the soul who prevents or cures political and psychic illness as the doctor does physical ones. Unlike inert materials (leather or wood) that artisans work on or the irrational beasts that concern trainers, in medicine the "material" participates in its own physical regeneration. The question is how? It had been one of Gorgias' boasts that the rhetorician is more powerful than the doctor even on medical matters since if a patient refuses to heed a diagnosis or to take a prescription, all the doctor's skill goes for naught, whereas a rhetorician can convince someone to do what makes him worse because of *his* skill with words. This is the ground for his claim that rhetoric is the master art. But for Socrates a good doctor-patient relationship entails the doctor's persuading his patient to accept treatment by explaining the cause of his symptoms and the reasons why he is prescribing the medicines he is. More significantly a healthy man would do whatever he wants, and so the political authority of the expert would be at most temporary.[49]

But this is still a *technē*. What evidence is there for the stronger claim that, despite all appearances, Socrates does not endorse even this kind of a *technē* for politics? If there is any ultimate authority in the dialogue, it is not a *technē* as Socrates has defined the term, but dialectic or dialogue itself. Dialogue, however, is a peculiar form of authority. For one thing, it is neither personal, contained in a body of knowledge, nor derivable from transcendent norms but is, like politics, constituted and reinterpreted by the participation of human agents in ways that do not happen even in a doctor-patient relationship. For another thing, even dialectic is contested and politicized, either by Callicles who challenges it directly, or indirectly by Socrates who pointedly departs from it, again unlike medicine.[50] Finally, Socrates' criticism of Callicles' elitism suggests the possibility that dialectic, unlike *technai* (including medicine), could be taught and practiced by anyone. If that is indeed his belief, if he is hoping to create a citizenry capable of thinking for itself and thus immune to rhetorical manipulation, a citizenry, moreover, that is willing or even anxious to accept the responsibilities of power which democracy requires, then the criticism of "Pericles" may constitute a general warning against democrats relying too much on *any* leader. Then the point of Socrates' philosophical rhetoric would not be to educate a few great leaders but to educate all Athenians to be leaders, at least to the degree that they will not have their judgment deformed by a Gorgias or a Callicles.[51] In these circumstances philosophical education becomes political education and Socrates' concern is with us as choosers rather than with any particular choice.

Consider the parallels between this view of a democratic political "leader" and Socrates' own role as a "teacher" and dialectician.[52] Socrates does not want us to think what he thinks or as he does unless we persuade ourselves by thinking for ourselves. There can be no passive acceptance of doctrinal instruction, whether the source be philosophers or political leaders. Thus the *Gorgias* finds Socrates questioning the authority of tradition, the many, self-styled political experts, pretenders to moral superiority and self-proclaimed aristocrats, all the while insisting that he has "no more knowledge than you do when I ask and speak but rather join in a common search with you" (506a). Socrates claims that he does "not know how it is that these things (the subject of the dialogue) are so" (508a–b).[53] Rhetoricians and sophists tell people what they want to hear as a way of gaining power over them. Socrates calls even the most obvious things and accepted views (about Pericles, wisdom, power, happiness) into question as a way of sharing power with them, whether in the dialogue or the city.

Or consider the way philosophical conversation, construed as a common search for a shared good that enhances an individual's and a dialogical community's good, stands as an ideal of political deliberation. In these terms, Socrates' insistence that "if my opponent has any substance in what he says I will be the first to acknowledge it" (506b), provides a standard for a political debate over the best policy. Moreover, citizens, like participants in the dialogue, should take responsibility for what they say, and in this respect they are educators of each other. To be a good citizen requires that one be a friend to oneself, which is a precondition and end of dialogue. When Socrates argues that truth is larger than particular interests of those engaged in its pursuit, or claims he cares for the argument that is their shared enterprise rather than being victorious, he is proposing a political as well as philosophical ideal. In these terms "philosophical" choices have direct consequences for how one acts politically, indeed for how one thinks about politics and action. Finally, the process of talk in both philosophical discussion and political deliberation changes how one talks. In both instances there is a move from what is private, selfish, or merely taken as given to a situation where reasons in terms of common purposes must be offered and defended.

The idea that participation in dialogue or deliberation changes participants is one reason why Benjamin Barber can describe what he calls the civic bond as "dialectical."[54] In his view individuals become involved in government by participating in the common institutions of self-government and become involved with one another by virtue of their common engagement in politics. They are united by the ties of the common activity and common consciousness—ties that are willed rather than given by blood or heritage or prior consensus of beliefs and that thus depend for their preservation and growth on constant commitment and ongoing political activity. With appropriate substitutions this is true of philosophical argument as well. Now this suggests that the question of whether and how Socrates is a democrat is not only a matter of what is said, but of how it is said. It is not only a question of explicit argumentation of dialectical "method" and the dramatic movement of the dialogue. Thus, it would be possible for the way democracy is criticized—provocatively, frankly, inconsistently, ironically, dialectically, polyphonically—to be "democratic" even as the particular argument was not.

I want to elaborate these ideas by articulating three voices in the *Gorgias*. Each voice is also a way of considering the relationship between philosophy and politics. I then want to recast these voices and these relationships as they are played out in the drama between Callicles and Socrates, which will lead to the question of Plato as a democrat and the third part of this essay.

The first voice, which I have called Habermasian, is the possibility of philosophical dialogue as an idealized analog for democratic deliberation. The idea that political debate should emulate dialectic as Socrates celebrates it rebukes Callicles' views of politics as a war of all against all, against the idealization of tyranny, and against the equation of power with domination. Here "communicative rationality" would be free from deceptions and self-deception, strategic manipulations and domination. The second voice is what I called Foucauldian. It politicizes philosophy, making it clear that establishing a dialogic community no less than a political one involves fiercely contested negotiations of power. Politicized philosophy confronts power as much as it does reason. Its search for truthfulness, in the sense of a mutually established ground for speech against rhetorical debasement, is disrupted by the play of interest and advantage within the dialogue, which echoes a similar play outside it. In this second voice, dialogue, like the democratic polis, rests on consent that is continually reworked and perpetually liable to politicization. If the first voice is the will to truth, the second confronts truth with the will to power.

There is a third voice that problematizes any analogy between philosophy and politics. It is a voice that reminds us of Socrates' death and anticipates the animus between philosophy and politics. Occasionally foregrounded, as when Callicles pointedly warns Socrates that his preoccupation with philosophy will leave him politically helpless and susceptible to false accusations that may well lead to his death, it mostly exists on the margins as a frame, or at the center as a subtext.

III

Fifty years ago Werner Jaeger wondered whether "we have not given enough thought to the possibility that in his own character Plato had so much of that unruly will to power as to find, and fight, part of himself in Callicles." Though such a will to power lies "deeply buried" in Plato's other writings, its presence in the *Gorgias* may explain why Socrates was so powerful an influence on him. For if Plato "had by nature been only a second Socrates, the real Socrates would hardly have had such an overwhelming effect on him as he had."[55] Though I would quarrel with parts of this formulation, Jaeger is right to emphasize the singular energy and passion of Callicles' challenge to Socrates and philosophy, and the deep ambivalence toward politics this challenge portends.

Callicles is bewildered by his reaction to Socrates. "I do not know how it is that your speech attracts me, Socrates. Yet I share the common feeling (*pollōn pathos*) of being unconvinced" (513c). On the one hand he admires Socrates' courage and tenacity, his independence and largeness of sensibility in adhering to something beyond petty pleasures and mundane preoccupations. If not convinced, Callicles seems at least worried by Socrates' argument that tyrants and those who would advise or support them are the least powerful, free, and happy because they must necessarily exhibit a slavelike hypersensitivity to what others think and might do. One could say that it is Socrates, not Callicles, who demonstrates the natural superiority that the latter so admires.

Yet for Callicles what makes Socrates powerful also makes him vulnerable to unjust accusations and prey for ambitious politicians. While Callicles respects philosophy as an essential ingredient in the education of a good man, to *be* a philosopher in the sense of making philosophical considerations paramount is a kind of insanity. It trivializes one's talents, marginalizes one's significance in life,[56] is ultimately self-defeating, and leaves one with a severe case of vertigo. At the very outset of their conversation, Callicles recognizes that if Socrates is serious in his arguments with Gorgias and Polus human life "will have to be completely turned upside-down" (*anatetrammenos*) and "everything we do seems the exact opposite of what we should do" (481c).

"One chooses dialectic," Nietzsche wrote in *Twilight of the Idols,* "only when one has no other means. One knows that one arouses mistrust with it, that it is not very persuasive. Nothing is easier to erase than a dialectical effect; the experience of every meeting at which there are speeches proves this. It can only be *self-defense* for those who no longer have other weapons."[57] Perhaps Plato shared some of Nietzsche's sentiments and so Callicles might have had the same effect on him that Socrates had on Callicles. Perhaps Jaeger is right in assuming that the *Gorgias* is a dialogue between two parts of Plato's soul (which would give yet another dimension to the *Republic).* What we would need to know to answer these questions is Plato. But in the most obvious ways we simply do not have him.

I begin with an obvious but sometimes unappreciated fact: nowhere in any dialogue does Plato speak in his "own" name. This makes the charge that Plato is authoritarian, antipolitical or antidemocratic, indeed the attribution of any doctrine to him, deeply problematic—unless one believes that Socrates is Plato's mouthpiece or that there is a straightforward way of distinguishing the democratic Socrates from the authoritarian Plato. Let me suggest why I do not think Socrates is the mouthpiece of Plato and why, even if he is, it will not advance the argument for the latter's authoritarianism, and why, even if we could establish such a separation, it is not very consequential for the question of a democratic Socrates or Plato.

In a recent essay Michael Frede distinguishes various forms of Platonic dialectic.[58] One form is didactic, where the respondent, ignorant of certain truths as shown by his false statements, confronts a questioner who already knows the answer and asks questions that will induce him to give the right one so they can proceed to the next step of the argument. In these exchanges the respondent has no influence on the course of the argument since the questioner will not go on until she has received the right answer. This view of dialectic assumes that Socrates is "advancing an argument he already has and espouses, because it is an argument Plato has and endorses and which Plato just puts into Socrates' mouth; an argument over the course of which the respondent has no real influence, except that, for dramatic purposes, he can be represented as stubborn or misguided and this as making it more or less difficult for Socrates to get to the conclusion of his argument" (209). This is how most undergraduates understand the Platonic dialogues on first reading, and how some of their teachers understand them after many.

But, Frede goes on to say, this form is never present in the early dialogues and, I am arguing, is also absent in the *Gorgias*. All the early dialogues are aporetic, representing Socrates as engaging in "elenctic, rather than didactic, dialectic" (210). An aporia is a situation in which one no longer knows what to say or do about an issue or question.[59] Like Callicles, one is befuddled, torn between the conclusions one has reached and what seems to be the case, at a loss as to how to get out of the difficulty presented by the contradiction between one's original claim and the conclusion of the ensuing argument. If it was a situation where Socrates provided a proof for the contradictory claim, then Callicles would be embarrassed as were Gorgias and Polus. But being at a loss as to what to say and do is a different matter.[60]

How does elenctic dialectic achieve *aporia?* Take Callicles as an example. Callicles presents himself as an expert on politics and human nature. Socrates proceeds to test the knowledge on which this claim to expertise rests. If Callicles (or Thrasymachus or Protagoras) contradicts himself on the very subject on which he claims expertise, then his authority is in question. Socrates is less concerned to refute directly any particular answer or claim than he is to refute Callicles himself. Indeed we might go further and argue, as I have in respect to leadership, that no claim to authority seems to withstand Socratic critique, so that expertise itself is suspect. The situation is analogous to the one in which we find equally reputable experts testifying on the opposite sides of an issue in a law court. It is not so much their individual expertise that gets called into question as the very idea of expertise itself.

If Frede is right about elenctic dialectic and I am right in applying it to the *Gorgias,* then Callicles contributes significantly to the movement and substance of the dialogue. It is true that Socrates poses the equations and in that sense shapes the argument. But since, as Frede points out, he does so to clarify the views and life of his interlocutor, "it does not matter in the least what the questioner himself knows or believes to be the facts about the subject in question."[61] Thus, even if Plato were to identify with Socrates, he is committing himself only to the elenctic dialectic itself, not to any particular argument, which means that if we are to make any inference about the position of the character Socrates or Plato it has to be highly indirect. Even in what are regarded as nonaporetic dialogues as different as the *Phaedo, Timaeus,* and second part of the *Parmenides,* the commitment of the questioner is often qualified, and even where it is not, "nothing follows about the commitment of the author."[62] So, even in his most dogmatic dialogues, "Plato" maintains "a radical distance from the views and arguments of the characters of the dialogue"[63] that is a work of fiction anyway.

But why does Plato take such pains to avoid being committed to particular arguments of the dialogue, and how and why do dialogues achieve this purpose? Surely one reason is to impress on us how hard, even impossible, it is to speak legitimately with authority, how few of us are justified in our confidence about the meaning of our actions and speech, how easy failure of understanding is, especially in those matters that effect and affect us most deeply. Human knowledge seems unable to master any subject, let alone subjects such as virtue, reality, justice, power, happiness, and freedom. These are not issues that are easily bounded by disciplines, for they help to determine our whole life as citizens and individuals.[64]

Perhaps this is the kind of ignorance that led Socrates to characterize himself as someone who cannot pronounce on the questions he is inquiring about and who denies that he is a teacher in the sense of being an expert or an authority. But what about Plato? Did he have the knowledge Socrates claimed not to have? Certainly nothing prevented him from presenting his arguments as treatises that would have amounted to a claim to speak as the author and from authority.[65] But he doesn't. At a minimum, dialogue seems to have afforded Plato the opportunity to present his views without endorsing them more strongly than he thought justified. But it affords something more. The dialogues, Frede points out, go "to great lengths to specify a fictitious context out of which the argument arises: it is individuals with a certain character, general outlook, a certain social position, certain interests, ambitions and concerns, individuals in a certain situation, who enter the debates, and this background noticeably colors their views."[66] What we see in the *Gorgias* (or *Protagoras* or *Republic*) is that to know about power, justice, friendship, happiness, freedom, or courage entails knowing about one's character, outlook, social position, interests, ambitions and concerns; that beliefs and experiences are deeply yet unobviously connected; that arguments emerge out of and remain more or less embedded in one's way of life; and that philosophy is tied to interest. What we see is, again, the politicization of philosophy.

Frede concludes by indicating how the relationship between respondent and questioner in the dialogue anticipates and is paradigmatic for the relationship between reader and author outside it. If Plato's concern is for our becoming clear about our ideas, commitments, and lives, then he must thwart our temptations to adopt his views for the wrong reasons; for instance, the view that an idea comes from a great mind like Plato's. Instead Plato pushes us to sort out our own views in order to come to what Frede calls "the correct view." If there is any lesson, teaching, or moral in the Platonic corpus, this is it: "nothing but our own thought gains us knowledge."[67]

Yet most of us do not think for ourselves, at least not in the way Socrates commands we must. Socrates is no more successful with us than he is with Callicles in the dialogue or with Critias, Alcibiades, and Charmides outside it. Nietzsche is right when he dismisses dialectic as the last refuge of resentful impotence. Most of us most of the time agree with him and Callicles that philosophy "emasculates" those of exceptional abilities by seducing them away from public life where there are real stakes to "live out their lives skulking in some corner, whispering with three or four boys, never saying anything worthy of a free, powerful and notable man" (*Gorg.* 485d). It is not only that philosophers are useless in terms of their own moral or moralistic principles—as Vlastos once asked: where was Socrates when the Athenian assembly debated the fate of the Mytileneans—but that in the end we simply walk away from them. At best we are like Crito, who acquiesces to arguments he has no doubt heard many times before and which manage to silence rather than convince him. Or we are like Protagoras, who praises Socrates as an excuse to get away from him (all other stratagems having failed). Or like Euthyphro, whose last words, "For right now, I am in a hurry to get somewhere, and it is time for me to leave" (15e), are astonishing given that *he* initiated the discussion and is continuing with an action whose morality and motives have been shown to be profoundly suspect. In these terms Socrates' concluding myth in the *Gorgias* is a monologue whose impact is emblematic for us as readers of the Platonic dialogues. Even when we do not accept all of Socrates' arguments, we almost always accept the superiority of his position to those of vanquished interlocutors like Crito, Protagoras, Euthyphro, or Callicles. Yet it makes little or no difference in our lives. Having taken Socrates' side, we close the book and, like the interlocutors, proceed to go about our business, perhaps amused by Socrates' cleverness or feeling edified in an abstract way that allows us to be self-righteous and amoral at the same time. We do not do what agreement with Socrates should entail: live the examined life by devoting ourselves, as he did, to the search for the good life.

No doubt what Socrates and Plato ask is extremely difficult. But if we agree that the search for goodness, justice, and truth is the right thing to do and we do not do it; if we know that it constitutes a better life than the one we lead yet we continue to live as we do; we are, as Plato's readers and Socrates' admirers, in what Alexander Nehamas calls "a very peculiar situation indeed." For "to believe that Socrates' effect, either on his own interlocutors or on the readers of the dialogues is generally beneficial is to be taken in by Platonic irony and to show ourselves to be missing the point in our very claim to see it. It is nothing other than displaying our ignorance of our ignorance."[68]

But perhaps Plato could succeed where Socrates failed, even if that success entailed abandoning Socrates in his name, a theme familiar to anyone who has read Dostoevsky's "Legend of the Grand Inquisitor." Perhaps Plato could take Socrates' paradoxical ignorance and systematically articulate the view that the life of knowledge and philosophy is the best life for humans to live. Perhaps he could take Socrates' goodness, his motivation, character, and activity, and make it more than a matter of luck or "divine accident"[69]—make it the product of a *technē.* If there were a way to ensure that there would always be few people like Socrates around, who would be honored for what they are, then one would likely turn to systematic education to "produce good people and the ability in those who are not good to recognize them."[70] One would produce the *Republic* as a response to Socrates' failure with Callicles, Protagoras, Euthyphro, as well as Alcibiades, Critias, and Charmides.

On Nehamas' account Platonic philosophy entails the separation of knowing from doing. It entails the adoption of a method that makes entirely possible the kind of political *technē* Socrates of the *Gorgias* sometimes endorses, but which elenctic dialectic ultimately undercuts. Plato wants to show us what the good life is, while separating the ability actually to live that life from the lesser (if still admirable) ability to recognize the superiority of that life and those who live it. Not only could Plato define what the good life was, he became "rapt" with "a method of learning which itself does not depend on luck and good will, but only on ability and persistence—a method which offers no choice but imposes the obligation to accept its conclusions once you begin to follow it."[71] It was on this basis that he devised a system for the direct education of every person's soul. Plato's method is "in its higher reaches mathematical."[72] We can have a political *technē* that produces the right kinds of students and citizens. Here is the missing ground for Socrates' criticisms of Gorgias' inability to control his students, and Pericles' inability to control the citizens he led. It is also the way a future Socrates can control a future Callicles or Alcibiades, thus exonerating philosophy from the charges of failure and complicity leveled at Socrates.

But all this is, Nehamas suggests, premised on a belief that philosophy constitutes the best way of life. When this sense is lost, as it is now, the "idea that philosophers are particularly qualified to understand the nature of the good life and show it to others must lose much of its hold."[73]

But I am not wholly convinced by the undemocratic Plato that emerges from Frede's and Nehamas's readings. I am not sure "Plato" wanted us to come to "the correct view," which sounds more didactic than elenctic. Nor am I sure that he regarded dialectic as instrumentally as Frede seems to when he sees it as a way of arriving at truth rather than a way of representing it. If the choice of writing dialogues (and arguing dialectically) "expresses a sense of life and of value, of what matters and what does not, of what learning and communicating are, of life's relations and communications";[74] if life is never simply presented by a text but always represented as something; then dialogue becomes exemplary and intrinsically valuable. A dialogue like the *Gorgias,* then, is a way of expressing the surprising variety, complexity, and impenetrability of the world, its flawed beauty and furtive orders that, however revered or longed for, yield to fissures and contingency. It suggests that even the most ingenious schemes of political and linguistic containment cannot erase division and conflict and that any mode of philosophical prose less allusive and attentive to particularity than dialogue would flatten the political and intellectual landscape. The rhythm of dialogues like the *Gorgias* and *Protagoras,* with their inversions and sub-versions, their movements of attraction and repulsion, of friendship and enmity, trust and suspicions, embody a surplus that exceeds any single position or interpretation.

This does not preclude Socrates from holding particular views that Plato may have shared, at least in the aporetic dialogues: views about the good life, about its being better to suffer injustice than commit it, about virtue's being knowl-edge and sufficient for happiness. That he holds these views matters to the suc-cess of dialectic, whether it is the dialectic within the dialogue or between the dialogue and its readers. But what also matters is how he came to those views, the sense in which he "holds" them, and whether he risks them in a dialogic encounter. Unlike Frede and Nehamas, I think he does.

As Vlastos argues, this has to do with the idea that because a particular po-sition has survived in the past there is "absolutely no certainty that it always will in the future; it may have been vindicated in a thousand elenchi in the past and prove false in the very next one after that."[75] But it also has to do with some-thing that emerges from Socrates' discussion with Callicles about whether it is better to suffer or commit injustice, something that bears both on Socrates' crit-icism of Pericles and the issue of political expertise.[76] Doing and suffering in-justice are ineradicable features of human life because the consequences of any action—whether done by Pericles or Socrates himself—escape prediction and containment. Since none of us can live in a completely controlled environment and are thus likely both to (inadvertently) cause suffering and experience it, the issue is how to live, politically and philosophically, in a world where our best efforts must partially fail.[77] In these terms Callicles' defense of the tyrannical life is also a Nietzschean insistence that only by cultivating the widest range of passions most intensely can one live life to the fullest. This endorsement of the sublime over the ordered life, this impiety toward conventions that impose un-natural limits on the forces of desire, this celebration of the sheer joy of im-posing one's own order on that which is other is what Callicles admires both in Socrates and in Pericles.

It is not only particular views that are at stake in Socrates' dialectic counters. Something far more is at risk: the status of dialectic itself. As I have argued, the *Gorgias* dramatizes the contest of power present in the constitution of dis-course, how winners erase what they have vanquished even as they deny there has been a war. Whatever Socrates' protestations about dialectic operating above the fray, he and dialectic are portrayed as very much part of it. This is true not only of the *Gorgias* but of the *Protagoras,* where the sophist argues that Socrates' insistence on dialectical argument is his way of forcing an opponent to fight on unfavorable ground. In these dialogues, as elsewhere, Socrates de-parts from his own dialectical strictures, using the antidialectical tactics of his opponents.[78] This is usually seen as Socrates showing that he can play his op-ponents' game better than they can. It is taken to show that his choice of di-alectic is really not aimed at vanquishing them since he can do that without di-

alectic. I think something more than that is at stake: the status of dialectic and
of Socrates. Dialectic demands that one be willing to open oneself up to a refutation of one's life and character as well as to the arguments that manifest it.
Few are willing to do so—certainly Callicles isn't, though he recognizes that
not doing so is a kind of cowardice—because we could discover that we are not
who we think we are and are not doing what we think we are doing. The courage
required to face the risk of discovering commitments acquired inadvertently
and wrongs done unintentionally is not only something Socrates displays in regard to his exchanges with the interlocutors in the dialogue, but something Plato
is also undertaking in regard to Socrates. This means that in the *Gorgias* (as in
other dialogues such as the *Protagoras* and *Republic*) Plato may be discovering the commitments he has more or less inadvertently made to Socrates as well
as the injustice he has suffered or is perpetuating as Socrates' student and rival.

  Nor am I convinced that Plato "provides the sort of Final Answer and Full
Disclosure that can resolve doubt by submitting all problems to the regime of
a mathematical world model."[79] Even in the *Republic* these arguments are embedded in a dramatic context that persistently challenges its readers to reexam-
ine not only its particular theses but the frame within which they become claims
to being true or false. What we make of any such claim depends on what we
make of Socrates' interrupting the discussion to warn the interlocutors that they
have been hasty in their agreement, gullible in their confidence, impatient in argument and have failed to recognize the significance of what they ask and fail
to ask. It depends too upon what we make of the dialogue criticizing what it is
(poetry and drama), extolling virtues it ignores (that one should play a single
role in life), and positing analogies between soul and state it gives ample evidence to reject.[80] Sometimes Socrates is explicit about these interruptions, but
not always. Insofar as Socrates is a character in a drama written by Plato, there
is a set of signals Plato provides readers which seem unavailable to any of the
interlocutors, including Socrates. Interpretations that fail to materialize within
the imaginary encounters of what Harry Berger calls "the field of dramatic play"
are conspicuously featured in the "field of textual play." Thus the *Gorgias, Protagoras,* or *Republic,* like other dialogues (Berger's example is the *Ion*), can be
read as a dialogue or agon between its speakers and its text. "For the text tells
us something about itself in adumbrating the limits of a form of discourse—Socratic logos, constrained by its oral conditions—which only textual representation can recuperate, or supplement, or transcend."[81]

  If the Platonic dialogues abound in so many contradictions and inconsistencies, then trying to elicit the "presence of the master, the coherence of his meaning and the disclosure of his mind"[82] seems a daunting if not impossible task—
impossible unless one is as confident as Terence Irwin that on the basis of textual
evidence one can easily distinguish the views of Socrates from those of Plato,
document the successes and failures of Plato's defense and his rejection and revision of Socratic ethics, and recognize that many of those views are "false, confused, vague, inconclusive and badly defended."[83] Or, by contrast though sim-

ilarly, the task is not impossible if one believes that rigorous attention to the dramatic context of an argument is a "key to Plato's intentions." Then an "attentive reader" can reveal Plato's intentions and provide us with Plato's teaching.[84]

If I am right about the *Gorgias* and Plato, then I was wrong to begin by saying Plato does not appear in his dialogues. He is all over them. "Perhaps," Aryeh Kosman writes, "we should not be discussing Plato's silence but his ventriloquy; the displacement of speech, its projection into a created other, a dummy, a mute substitute who is truly a silent partner in the act despite the fact that it is he who 'speaks.'"[85] These voices remain unstilled, provoking and inspiring, repellent yet seductive even for Callicles and Nietzsche "in spite of themselves" (in both senses of the phrase).[86] This is an astonishing fact given the general rejection of Socratic intellectualism as defined by a trust in reason, a belief that ignorance is the ultimate evil, an identification of virtue with knowledge and happiness, and an indifference to the affective side of human life and the need for habituation. Surely Socrates has his feet planted firmly in the *Clouds*. And yet he moves us even as he fails to convince us, perhaps because Plato's dramatization(s) of Socrates' life transmutes his teacher's intellectualism into something more arresting and affecting.

Nehamas and Nietzsche are right when they claim Socrates was unsuccessful in persuading friends and enemies alike of the truth of the statement that it is better to suffer injustice than commit it. But when he staked his life on that truth by refusing to escape the death sentence,[87] that became, in Plato's hands, a story of passion and pathos and Socrates became a man of Achillean courage who died for the life he led. This myth of a man who was at once a courageous citizen of a democracy and an independent thinker in part because of it, frames the arguments of the *Gorgias* and continues to agitate those who think of themselves as educators in a democratic polity. Mostly these are philosophers and political theorists whose professional responsibilities include teaching classical authors. But sometimes the question of whether Socrates (or Plato) was a democrat matters to them more than usual and to more people than usual. I think that is true now because of the ongoing debate between multiculturalism and canonists over the meaning(s) of America, a conflict that, not coincidentally, mirrors that between Socrates and his interlocutors in the *Gorgias* over the meaning of Periclean leadership and Athenian democracy. The peculiarities of this debate discussed in Part I suggest a need partly to recast the terms of my argument.

IV

Suppose we ask not about Socrates or Plato being democrats but about the resources for democratic readings and culture contained in dialogues like the *Apology, Crito, Gorgias, Protagoras,* and *Republic.* Such a shift would, to begin with, turn our attention away from the historical Socrates and authoritarian Plato to the interplay between an evolving text and the generation of sometimes divided interpretative communities who care about and for them. Then analysis of "the" text would include some study of how these interpretative communities are constituted and sustained, their place in the larger culture, how they "use" the text while learning from it. When, as in the nineteenth-century debate over the reform laws in Britain or in the current controversy over Great Books and core curriculum in the United States, these communities are wider than the academy, the issue of the relationships between democratic readings and democratic citizenship has more salience than it otherwise might.

Historicizing a text does not absolve us from making arguments for our readings of them: closely reading passages, contesting translations, detailing the interplay of what used to be called form and content, text and context. It means that, as Socrates suggests in the *Apology*, mortality inflects any understanding of events and texts, and eternal verities are always worked out in local circumstances.

If we attend to the democratic potentialities and democratic readings of works like the *Gorgias*, something curious emerges; some of Plato's most implacable critics become his allies, while some of his most strident defenders turn out to be the wolves in sheeps' clothing. If, as I believe, what makes texts like the *Gorgias* (or *Republic* or *Protagoras*) "great" is their capacity to generate the kinds of moral and political controversies canonist defenders such as William Bennett and Lynn Cheney would silence or circumscribe, then feminist, postmodernist, and Marxist critics of "Plato" may be giving his texts the life and energy his friends exhaust (providing, of course, that the critics do not themselves come to form a new orthodoxy). This gives a paradoxical cast to the charge by conservatives that various radical critics are "politicizing the university." If politicizing something is, as Aristotle argues, to regard it as "man" made and thus subject to human design (in contrast to what is natural and necessary), then the conflicting views of human nature and goodness prominent in dialogues like the *Gorgias* (for example, in the unresolved conflict over what is natural and conventional) are inscribed in the plots, themes, arguments, and dramatic settings of the texts canonists honor.[88]

Thus the *Gorgias* (like other dialogues) is polymorphous, exactly what Plato objects to about democracy in the *Republic* when he describes it as a bazaar of constitutions. The hearers most likely to respond to Jaeger's tensions and Bakhtin's semantic complexity are likely to be "democratic" readers. Readers committed to a single interpretative methodology, political standpoint, or philosophical approach and who aggressively insist that each character and term is fixed, are tone-deaf. They are deaf to the kind of irreducible paradoxes the *Gorgias* sustains, which are so often the substance of Greek tragedy. They play over the polyphony of shifting meanings (including those of democracy, politics, and philosophy) and miss the degree to which the interlocutors push each other (or us) to continual reassessment of our political and philosophical commitments. They miss how the dialogue pushes democratic citizens to be alternatively (if not simultaneously) political educators of each other. Such readers are like those individuals who embrace what Stuart Hampshire calls "a morality without perpetual regret, because it is without any sense of the possibilities lost, unnoticed."[89]

If I am right, then Callicles is not just a villain. Nor is he erased by what can be construed as Socrates' victory over him. He lives on as an agitating presence and thematic counterpoint waiting for restitution or revenge, for Nietzsche or Grote, for Foucault or Lyotard to take up his cause. Indeed the very difficulty of the effort to defeat him makes him a live cultural option and constitutes part of the power and provocation of the *Gorgias.*

But Callicles is no friend of democracy despite Socrates' ironic (or spiteful) punning of his love for a man named Demos. That he is not, is a useful reminder to those who romanticize the quasi-Nietzschean arguments he makes. We would not want him to rule either within a dialogue or in the world outside it. Yet for all this his voice disrupts the comfort of conversation in a way that creates an interpretative space, incites us to participate in the construction of the dialogues' meaning(s), and pushes us to reinvent Socrates and Plato as contemporary interlocutors.

The contest over who Socrates and Plato were, like the contest in the *Gorgias* over who Pericles was, is partly a contest over the identity of democracy including the role of philosophy for a democratic citizenry. I do not doubt that philosophy is often contemptuous of democracy, despising it for its ordinariness and grossness, its lack of grace and virtue. But I do not think that describes Socrates in the *Gorgias,* for as I have argued there is evidence that he is critiquing those he cares for so that they will not rest content in an unreconstructed understanding of who they are but will take the risk and find out what they could become.[90]

We are told by the Corinthians in Thucydides that the Athenians were "born into the world to take no rest themselves and give none to others."[91] The daring innovation and constant transformation they attribute to this most democratic of cities are imitated by the generative power of Platonic dialogues, whose resilience lies less in the prescriptions they offer or the harmony they commend than in the way their irreconcilable tensions keep open the question of what it means to be human. It is the responsibility of those citizens in a democracy charged with the care and teaching of such works to insist that this openness to struggle is one of the most valuable parts of a legacy we need to pass on to our citizen students.[92] Doing so, we can help recover the cultural heterogeneity of the West in ways that can ease the rigid polarities that mark the contemporary cultural wars and enhance the political education of our compatriots.

NOTES

1. Much of the case for school reform was made in terms of our need to combat the Russians, keep up with the Japanese and Germans, and generally maintain our political

and economic hegemony in the world. I have argued this in Chapter I of *Corrupting Youth.*

2. These are crude terms that have become straitjackets forcing people into alliances they do not want and positions they do not respect; see Euben, "The Debate of the Canon."

3. See Gates, "Whose Canon?"

4. As Katha Pollitt ("Why Do We Read?" 210–11) has pointed out, "Books are not pills that produce health when ingested in measured doses. Books do not shape character in any simple way, if indeed they do so at all, or the most literate would be the most virtuous instead of just the ordinary run of humanity with larger vocabularies. Books cannot mold a common national purpose when in fact, people are honestly divided about what kind of country they want." And books will not matter much to people for whom books do not matter.

5. Gray, "Whose America?"

6. On the notion of radical democracy, see the "Introduction" in Mouffe, ed., *Radical Democracy.*

7. Ober, "How to Criticize Democracy."

8. Several critics point to the *Protagoras* as an example of Plato's sympathy with democracy. No one, it is argued, with a total animus against democracy would have permitted or could himself have put such a powerful defense of democratic education as we have from Protagoras in the dialogue. But I think Plato's Protagoras a doubtful democrat, an unprincipled teacher, and a self-serving, even cowardly man, none of which make him evidence of Plato's sympathies for democracy.

9. The most powerful advocate for a democratic Socrates is surely Gregory Vlastos. See his "Historical Socrates," *Socrates: Ironist and Moral Philosopher,* and "Socrates' Disavowal of Knowledge." While Plato was no democrat, Socrates was in Vlastos' terms *philodēmos* and *dēmotikos.* Vlastos makes Socrates a democrat by making him a moral philosopher rather than a political theorist. He is not a political theorist because his doctrine is "properly speaking a moral one though it clearly has far-reaching political implications." (See *Socrates: Ironist and Moral Philosopher,* 13, 237.) Though I agree with much of what Vlastos says, I think he begs the question Socrates was raising: the relationship between politics and morality and philosophy and democratic citizenship.

10. See Kastely, "In Defense of Plato's Gorgias," 109.

11. Arendt, *Eichmann in Jerusalem,* 287–88.

12. I do not mean to argue that the political education of democratic citizens is the only thing colleges and universities should do or that political education is primarily done there. Institutions of higher learning have many more tasks than political ones and an overemphasis on the university's role in cultivating political judgment and thoughtfulness is likely to underestimate how much development of these traits are independent of academic learning and how much they depend on experience that occurs outside academic institutions.

13. Arendt, "The Crisis in Education," in *Between Past and Future,* 190–91.

14. For all the criticisms directed against it, Paolo Freire's *Pedagogy of the Oppressed* makes the most powerful and elaborate case for how this can be done.

15. Socrates' view of thinking largely (though not completely) ignores the role of habit and convention in education. (See Lord's essay on Aristotle in this volume.) One can argue, as Plato perhaps came to do, that the unexamined life is not livable or livable

only by a few and at a cost of dangerous deracination. One could also argue that Socrates' thought is gendered or distinctively Western. All of this must be entertained, since not to do so has the paradoxical consequence of refusing to "think" about thinking.

16. See Neal and Ellen Wood, "Socrates and Democracy"; Vickers, *In Defense of Rhetoric,* ch. 2.

17. I have done such a reading in much more detail in "Democracy and Political Theory," in Euben, Wallach, and Ober, *Athenian Political Thought,* 198–226.

18. It is perhaps worth remembering that radical democratic movements were often generated by attacks on the dominant culture for failing to adhere to their own declared principles or to extend them to all. (That is one lesson of E. P. Thompson's *Making of the English Working Class* as well as C.L.R. James's *Black Jacobins.*)

19. For reasons elaborated by Josiah Ober, *Mass and Elite,* such a polarity misdescribes the complicated ideological negotiations between elites and nonelites.

20. E. A. Havelock, *Liberal Temper,* argues that Plato lacked any understanding of the practical world with which the rhetoricians dealt. It is this political stupidity masked by high-flown pronouncements that Havelock suggests alternately annoy and enrage Callicles. I am suggesting the dialogue offers an implicit response to such charges (though they are only implicit and not conclusive).

21. As the essays by Morris, Raaflaub, Roberts, and Cartledge make clear, the relationship between democracy and equality is far more complex.

22. C. Wright Mills, *Sociological Imagination,* 40–41. For the political implications see Steven Lukes's discussion of "the third dimension of power" in his *Power: A Radical View* and John Gaventa's elaboration of it (and of manufactured consent) in his *Power and Powerlessness.*

23. In *All-Consuming Images.* Stuart Ewen talks about the "engineering of consent" where public relations experts "conflate ideological management techniques with the idiom of social and political liberty" and goes on to quote Edward Bernay to the effect that "the engineering of consent is the very essence of the democratic process, the freedom to persuade and suggest." The various freedoms in the Bill of Rights—speech, press, petition, and assembly, "the freedoms which make the engineering of consent possible"—are among the most cherished guarantees of the Constitution of the United States (267).

24. There is the added similarity of each dealing with the promises and danger of "enlightenment." Paul Cartledge (in his essay in this volume) rightly warns against easy comparisons that make the Greeks overly familiar, thus obscuring their distinctiveness and our own. But of course such an argument presupposes sufficient similarity to make a difference. And there are good political and interpretative reasons for being skeptical about some of the claims of the "Cambridge School." See Margaret Leslie, "In Praise of Anachronism." The phrases "life world" and "system world" are Habermas's. He first introduced them in *Legitimation Crisis* but develops them at great length in *The Theory of Communicative Action.*

25. See his *Amusing Ourselves to Death.* A similar argument is made by Roderick P. Hart in *Seducing America.* Ewen, *All-Consuming Images,* argues that advertising, public relations, and other "industries of image and hype" are creating "a jerry-built material world with provocative, tenuous meanings suggesting fathomable value, but occupying no clear time or space" (159).

26. Michael Berubé argues that the persuasiveness of critics like Richard Kimball

and Dinesh D'Souza depend on the ignorance of their audience. See his "Public Image Limited," 124–49.

27. I say narrowly and primarily because I do not think one can, practically speaking, establish a hard line between strategic and nonstrategic, manipulative and nonmanipulative

28. Kastely, "In Defense of Plato's Gorgias," argues that rhetoric and philosophy are partners because the former can help us distance ourselves from what we are most attached to and therefore assist the dialectic examination of our lives.

29. I made this argument some years ago (in "The Battle of Salamis"). Though I still think the conclusions sound, I do not think that the argument I made was fully persuasive, given the critique of such arguments by Nicole Loraux in her *Invention of Athens*.

30. See Martin Ostwald's discussion of the evolution of *nomos* in his *Nomos and the Beginnings of the Athenian Democracy*. One can see the same self-consciousness in Pericles' preamble to his Funeral Oration (in Thucydides), when he reflects on why the institution he is about to embrace came to be and whether it is better for it to exist than not to exist.

31. See Woodruff, "Plato's Early Theory of Knowledge."

32. I think Socrates' argument in the *Crito* that Athens is father to the man and vocation and his insistence that if he is to be understood his fellow citizens are the most likely to do so is a recognition of this fact. Irving Howe ("The Value of the Canon," 162) seems to me very close to Socrates when he writes that "Serious education must assume, in part, an adversarial stance toward the very society that sustains it—a democratic society makes the wager that it's worth supporting a culture of criticism. But if that criticism loses touch with the heritage of the past, it becomes weightless, a mere compendium of momentary complaints."

33. I argue this in detail in "Democratic and Socratic Accountability," in Euben, *Corrupting Youth*.

34. Vlastos, *Socrates: Ironist and Moral Philosopher,* 3.

35. See Wolin, "Norm and Form."

36. I use scare quotes around "the" and "Western" because I think that tradition is more polyphonous and less Western than many of its defenders conceive of it.

37. One could argue that these critics were also conservative in the sense Plato was. But I think this is probably wrong and certainly one-sided.

38. I am not endorsing Plato's understanding of Athenian political corruption. Rather, I am pointing out that the theme is present in Socrates' questions about what Athenians will do when they have lost the power by which they had defined themselves and suggesting that the theme is played out in what is said and done with language.

39. If we regard *Gorgias* as a prismatic focus, then the danger to democracy lies less within him than with the cultural forces that have made him popular and powerful. We make similar analyses of our political leaders when we see them against larger cultural frames.

40. There is a wonderful example of this in the "Gene industry" as analyzed by Hubbard and Wald, *Exploding the Gene Myth*.

41. In his second speech in favor of natural superiority, Callicles hardly disguises his contempt for the demos and later calls it a "mob of slaves" and a "rabble of worthless men" (489c).

42. Rhetorical ability *is* a necessity for a democratic political leader but it must be linked, Thucydides' Pericles tells us, with the ability to discern the appropriate policy, patriotism and integrity (2.60.5). If one "despises rational argument and wishes, like Gorgias, to win fame and fortune by some other means, what more convenient doctrine to espouse in the process than Gorgias' view that there is no truth anyway and it's all a matter of manipulation, more or less like drugging? Then one's failures to exhibit the traditional relational virtues will look daring rather than like sloppiness" (Nussbaum, *Love's Knowledge,* 221).

43. Arendt, "The Crisis of Culture," 219–24, and "Truth and Politics" (241–42), in *Between Past and Future.* She draws her notions of judgment from Kant and Aristotle.

44. See Habermas's "Further Reflections on the Public Sphere."

45. *The Dialogic Imagination,* 276.

46. This is not an unfamiliar situation given the continuing debate over the significance of the 1960s, which surfaces in every contemporary controversy over politics and education (nowhere more bizarrely than on the editorial pages of the *Wall Street Journal*).

47. Thomas Pangle sees the depth of the irony when he notes that "Socrates thus predicts his doom at the hands of the citizenry soon after having laid it down as *the* criterion of an effective statesman that in the course of his rule he make those he rules more tame and submissive to his rule than they were before he undertook to rule them!" ("Plato's *Gorgias,*" 6.)

48. Or so Hannah Arendt argues in "The Crisis in Education," in *Between Past and Future,* 143–73.

49. As Terence Irwin notes in his (Oxford) translation of Plato's *Gorgias,* 216.

50. Medical relations can become politicized. See, for instance, Ehrenreich and English, *For Her Own Good,* and Bledstein, *Culture of Professionalism.*

51. "Too long have the workers of the world waited for some Moses to lead them out of bondage," wrote Eugene Debs. "He has not come; he will never come. I would not lead you out if I could; for if you could be led out, you could be led back again." This is quoted by Mark E. Kann in "Challenging Lockean Liberalism," 214.

52. Socrates denied he was a teacher. The fact that he became one of the great moral teachers in the West is an irony discussed by Alexander Nehamas in "What Did Socrates Teach." Most commentators consider Socrates' demurral ironic. I think he was opposing himself to the sophists who claimed to have a doctrine they could give to their students. Socrates did not "have" a doctrine in the sense they claimed to have it, was very much aware of the disjunction between intentions and consequences, and thought teachers were supposed to have students who thought for themselves.

53. As Vlastos points out, he often says this after what seem unambiguous victories and compelling arguments.

54. Barber, *Strong Democracy,* 223.

55. *Paideia,* vol. 2, 138.

56. See the discussion in Nehamas, "What Did Socrates Teach," 279.

57. Nietzsche, "Twilight of the Idols," 476.

58. Frede, "Plato's Arguments and the Dialogue Form."

59. Frede is too parsimonious in his description of *aporia.* According to Liddell and Scott, *aporia, aporeō,* and *aporos* can mean being left without resources, being in difficult straits, having trouble passing through some place, or difficulty in dealing with

someone, embarrassment and hesitation, scarce or hard-to-get, and can refer to people who are intractable or in need.

60. This is one reason why I think Richard McKim may overstate his case in his otherwise insightful essay "Shame and Truth in Plato's *Gorgias.*"

61. Frede, "Plato's Arguments and the Dialogue Form," 212.

62. Ibid., 214.

63. Ibid.

64. Ibid., 215. See Martha Nussbaum's parallel discussion of the way the choice of *technē* reconstitutes what it means to be human in her chapter 4 on the *Protagoras* in *Fragility of Goodness.*

65. Charles L. Griswold, Jr. ("Plato's Metaphilosophy," 157) argues that "if reflection on the 'beginnings' of philosophy is unavoidable, if the fundamental question of metaphilosophy concerns the 'quarrel' between the proponents of philosophy and its various critics, if philosophy cannot be attacked or defended directly, and finally if the defense of philosophy requires a conversation with the critics of philosophy (and not just with abstract formulations of their 'positions'), then it makes sense for a philosopher who agrees to all this [which Griswold thinks Plato does] to write *dialogues.*"

66. Frede, "Plato's Arguments and the Dialogue Form," 216.

67. Ibid., 217, 219. Frede argues that because dialectical debate has a "public character," it assures an amount of rationality "which is not guaranteed when the soul is left to discourse with itself. Left to itself, the soul is not only hampered by its idiosyncratic views, it is also too easily derailed in its reasoning," 218.

68. Nehamas, "What Did Socrates Teach," 298.

69. *Rep.* 492a.

70. Nehamas, "What Did Socrates Teach," 304.

71. Ibid., 305.

72. Ibid.

73. Ibid., 305–6.

74. See Martha Nussbaum, "Introduction: Form and Content, Philosophy and Literature," in *Love's Knowledge,* 5.

75. Vlastos, *Socrates: Ironist and Moral Philosopher,* 114.

76. *Gorgias,* 509c–10a, which elaborates 469a–c.

77. Kastely, "In Defense of Plato's Gorgias," 100–101.

78. Perhaps the most bizarre is Socrates' long, contrived interpretation of Simonides' poem in the *Protagoras.*

79. The language is Harry Berger, Jr.'s in "Levels of Discourse," 78.

80. See Diskin Clay, "Reading the Republic," and Euben, "Justice in the Republic."

81. In Berger, "Levels of Discourse," 83. Like Berger, I think Plato is aware of the kinds of criticisms Derrida makes of him.

82. Berger, "Levels of Discourse," 83.

83. Irwin, *Plato's Moral Theory,* 3. For reasons why the rigorous attention to dramatic context of an argument by an "attentive reader" will not provide a "key to Plato's intentions" and reveal Plato's teaching either, see Berger, "Levels of Discourse." I think Kosman, "Silence and Imitation in the Platonic Dialogues," overstates his case insofar as he excludes the possibility that Socrates (but not only him) also creates the "author" or text that creates him.

84. See Berger's critique of Stanley Rosen in "Levels of Discourse," 87–89.

85. "Silence and Imitation in the Platonic Dialogues." In "Facing Sophists," Berger shows how in the *Protagoras* Plato's Socrates ventriloquizes a voice that blocks objections to a hedonistic position Socrates seems to endorse even though it contravenes how he lived and died.

86. As Nehamas suggests, Nietzsche's "repugnance for Socrates" was "indissolubly mixed with admiration." "What Did Socrates Teach," 279.

87. See Arendt's "Truth and Politics" in *Between Past and Future,* 247–48, where she argues that this teaching by example is the only form of persuasion that philosophical truth is capable of "without perversion or distortion." She goes on to suggest that it is the only way such truth can become practical and inspire action "without violating the rules of the political realm."

88. This is the argument of Kenneth R. Johnston in "The NEH and the Battle of the Books."

89. Hampshire, *Thought and Action,* 241, and Barber's discussion in *Strong Democracy,* 258–59.

90. Kosman, "Silence and Imitation in the Platonic Dialogues," 107.

91. Thucydides 1.70–79.

92. Johnston, "The NEH and the Battle of the Books," 132.

MISREADING DEMOCRACY:
PETER EUBEN AND THE *GORGIAS*

Benjamin R. Barber

I want to address Peter Euben's provocative essay "Reading Democracy" but before doing so must enter a caveat by way of an apology. I am a political theorist rather than a classicist, and I do not have the classicist's command of ancient Greek or of the complete cultural context from which the original texts spring. I approach our subject in a fashion that serious classicists, if they are polite, will deem at best casual. On the other hand, all productive political philosophy involves the intentional or inadvertent misreading of earlier works, and in this endeavor I can do as well as my rivals, including Euben.

Let me then come to Peter Euben's effort to read democracy into the *Gorgias*—a text that, as he acknowledges, is generally regarded as unfriendly to the democratic enterprise—by rendering Socrates himself as a democrat *malgré lui:* I offer three quite distinct arguments.

First, I look briefly at the textual argument directly in order to examine Euben's reinterpretation of Socrates as a stealth democrat; here I find his position thought-engendering as well as thought-exploding, but finally both astonishing and unconvincing.

Second, because this is the only way I can really confront what I believe is the fundamental flaw in his reading of Socrates, I speak to the problematic relationship between cognitive foundationalism and democratic politics; between democracy as rhetoric and conversation on the one hand, and democracy as common action in the face of conflict and ignorance on the other. My point here is to demonstrate that Peter Euben gives a brilliant reading of Socrates that works, however, only because he gives a brilliant misreading of democracy. That is to say, he is able to make Socrates look like a democrat only by thoroughly muddling democracy's meaning.

Third and finally, I say something about political education as it arises out of and conditions my understanding of democracy, because to do so may illuminate my differences with Euben about the relationship between rhetoric or dialectical (dialogical) method in Socrates, and the premises and entailments of what I understand to be democracy.

EUBEN AND THE *GORGIAS*

Euben offers his novel reading of Socrates by addressing the standard reading of the *Gorgias*. The dialogue is famous for Socrates' apparent attack on democracy as represented above all by Callicles' Thrasymachean realism, and Euben has no quarrel with this part of the standard critique. He cannot and does not try to install Socrates as a Periclean democrat. Rather, he recognizes the attack on democracy but construes it as a form of democratic revisionism. Deploying the very tactic he assails in liberal criticism, he suggests that "Socrates' critique may be an effort to save his native city from a corrupting vision of itself." This is at best an imprudent move. When in the unhappy 1960s the United States Air Force was targeting "friendly" strategic hamlets infiltrated by the Viet Cong and bombing them back into the Stone Age, Department of Defense publicists insisted they had to "destroy the towns in order to save them." The job Socrates does on democracy in the *Gorgias* seems conditioned by the same logic: in suggesting that Socrates is "a prophet recalling his or her people to what is best in their past and most promising in their future," thereby saving it from itself. Euben seems to want to argue that real democracy must be annihilated to save it. In this spirit, I might claim that in critiquing Euben's position I am only trying to save Euben from himself.

In truth, the central question is not so paradoxical. It is simply this: does Socrates' critique address contingent features of a deformed democratic practice that can be remedied by surgery—so that he can cut away the diseased portion and restore the healthy, thus recalling democracy to its best past? Or does he regard democracy itself as a generic deformation of a well-ordered constitution, the only cure for which is to remove it from the list of just governmental regimes? My own reading suggests the latter. Callicles is not, as Euben would have it, a perverse product of a democracy whose perversity Socrates and philosophy seek to reverse, he is democracy's essence—its ineluctable alter ego. As Socrates sees it, he is its logical entailment. Alcibiades does not "epitomize a democracy gone wrong"; he represents how, for Socrates, democracy must go wrong—how, inevitably and unavoidably and necessarily, it does go wrong; for democracy is precisely the privileging of common voting, however dumb, over philosophical learning, however smart, and as such it is intrinsically offensive to philosophy and to those who care for truth as something more than the provisional byproduct of a permanent conversation.

As Euben eventually acknowledges, "finally Socrates does regard majority rule as an absurd way of deciding any issue of import." But majority rule is not a contingent feature of democracy that can be sheared away in order to save democracy from itself. Majority rule is democracy; that is to say, it is a reductio of one of democracy's defining principles: the equality of human beings and thus the equal weighting of the votes by which they present themselves in the political process.

Euben is not, however, merely calling into question the adequacy of this rendering of democracy. He is suggesting Socrates wants to save popular rule from such crass formulas in the name of a far truer democracy. In addition to his skeptical reconstruction of Periclean democracy, Socrates is putatively offering an affirmative alternative. Euben believes that Socrates espouses a species of philosophical discourse and dialectical rhetoric that is akin to and thus compatible with—actually nurturing to—democratic deliberation. Indeed, Socrates emerges in Euben's portrait as a kind of deliberative democrat by virtue of his commitment to "the demands of reasoned argument" as well as to a form of dialectic that is "an idealized analogue of democratic deliberation." Hence, Socrates becomes a "true practitioner of political art" to be preferred to such "counterfeit democrats" as Pericles, a charlatan who only "insinuates himself with the city" in order "to dominate it."

Now Euben of course knows that any argument that makes Socrates the democrat and Pericles the tyrant is likely to be greeted with some suspicion by democrats, and it may be that Euben is more interested in deliberation per se than in democratic deliberation. Yet Euben's slightly scandalous penchant for outrageousness is one of his most attractive features as a theorist. So rather than take issue with the delightful claim that Pericles is not a democrat, let me suggest that the real problem with Euben's argument is that Socrates is not a dialectician, deliberative or otherwise, and therefore can hardly be regarded as a dialogical democrat even in some abstract epistemological sense.

Euben questions pious attitudes toward and easy assumptions about Pericles the democrat while uncritically accepting the still more pious attitudes toward and assumptions about, Socrates (or his puppeteer Plato) as a dialogic thinker. I am much less impressed than Euben by the supposed "polyphony" of Socratic dialogue, either in the *Gorgias* or elsewhere. I tend rather to share some of the cynicism of Callicles and Thasymachus, who often find themselves written into a conversation with Socrates which he constantly manipulates and dominates to his own advantage. The mood of the dialogues is monophony masquerading as polyphony. Callicles and Gorgias, very much like Thrasymachus in *The Republic,* do not so much find common ground with Socrates: rather, they argue and argue and finally fall silent. They are not won over, they go away or, as modern parlance has it, are "disappeared."

The common ground secured by Socratic inquiry usually turns out to be the turf Socrates was occupying all along, even as he affects to invite others to explore their turf. One can certainly credit Plato with giving Socrates' adversaries some good lines, but in the crux they rarely win arguments. Socrates' dialectical strategy is actually rather like that of the clever trial lawyer who uses apparently innocent questions seemingly aimed at bringing out objective truth to prod witnesses into impugning their own credibility. Getting other men to hang themselves with their own words is not exactly what democratic deliberation means to those who believe it discloses genuinely common ground. Democracy

treats conflict as an appropriate expression of distinct interests in need of reconciliation or compromise; Socrates treats conflict as a sign of error in need of
correction.

Because of their dramatic form, we tend to view Socrates' dialogical engag-
ments not only as dialectical exchanges but as actual dramas. But I know
Sophocles, and Socrates is no Sophocles! Plato's authorial voice may at times
be fragmented for tactical reasons into several discrete voices of which Socrates
is only primus inter pares, but I can discern no deep dialectic, no agon, no irre-
solvable paradoxes of the kind from which human tragedy is constituted or that
define the contestable interests of real citizens engaged in a pluralist democratic politics. Whatever else we may say of Socrates, he seems to lack the true dialectic of tragedy, where paradox and error are less deformations than the very
essence of what it means to be human. The affinity of both tragedy and democracy for a fallibilist view of human nature and human knowledge tied them together politically in the ancient world; just as the affinity of philosophy and aristocracy for virtue or excellence (*aretē*) made them natural allies against the
parity of democracy. Socrates looks past the muddled agon toward a domain of
immovable truth; to reach that domain, he may embark on the road of discourse,
but this hardly gives him a talent for the genuine polyphony that is the sine qua
non of democratic politics since, as I shall show presently, democratic politics
is not the least bit interested in truth. It is not discourse on the way to truth, but
discourse as a substitute for truth, discourse in the absence of truth, discourse
as an endless voyage that must chart direction without the aid of known
destinations.

I do not wish to hang my argument on whatever case can be made for demot-
ing Socrates from dialectician to demagogue, however. Many careful readers
take Socratic humility at face value, and Euben is certainly as persuasive as any
critic I have encountered in teasing a multivocal message from the (to me) uni-
vocal authorial voice of Socrates in the *Gorgias*. Let us then assume for the moment that Socrates is not himself the villainous manipulator he pillories in Pericles and that his dialectic is genuine. Our question then becomes this: Is Socrates'
philosophical rhetoric qua dialectic really an "idealized analog of political deliberation," so that Socrates himself can be understood to be a kind of epistemological democrat? In other words, even if we allow that Socrates is a genuine dialectician, what bearing does dialectic have on the politics of democracy?

I will argue here that it has little or no bearing. Whether or not he offers us a
paragon of authentic dialogue, Socrates is no democrat, and to think that philosophical discourse somehow provides an analog to democratic talk is to quite
misunderstand the true character of democratic talk, as well as of democratic
decision-making and democratic action. Euben claims Socrates renders the borders between philosophy and democratic politics "far more permeable than it
seems" and that he demonstrates in the *Gorgias* that philosophy "is political."
After all, Euben reminds us, Socrates' conversation with Gorgias and his asso-

ciates commences with Socrates' assurance that—in Euben's paraphrase—"what matters is that the discussion is committed . . . to truth no matter where it leads." Both philosophy and politics, Euben concludes, seek a "collective triumph over ignorance and confusion." It may be that philosophy does, but politics surely does not. Indeed, it is no exaggeration to say that democratic politics embraces and lives with confusion, while trying to render it productive. Both Michael Walzer and Hannah Arendt have made this point in telling political ways.

Philosophy betokens a love of knowledge, while politics signals an acknowledgment of ignorance and the conflicts it occasions. If there is any *philia* to be found in democratic regimes, it is a species of *polypragmosunē* (or "philopoliteia"), love of politics understood as action in the face of love of confusion and dissent, love of the rough-and-tumble of debate and confrontation in a setting of interests that are both equal to, and in conflict with, one another. Now Socrates, according to Euben, thinks "voting to decide which way of life or policy is best is moral and political suicide." If the issue is to determine the truth about a best way of life—Socrates' challenge in *The Republic,* for example—philosophy is necessarily the key to an adequate politics. But that is precisely not the issue in a democracy. In politics, whether it is conducted in ancient Athens or modern Greece, to seek a 'best policy' is not a matter of disclosing a cognitive truth, but a matter of reconciling adversarial interests, of forging common values, of deciding what to do in common at the very moment we cannot agree on the "truth" or even on whether there is such a thing. That is to say, democratic politics proceeds precisely in the absence of the kinds of common standards or mutually agreed-on truths that philosophy wishes to discover.

Socrates' dialectical rhetoric seeks to establish a science of the political soul such that its pathologies can be diagnosed and remedied by political doctors. Euben thus argues, "It makes no sense to allow a diseased soul to decide on what is good for it." This is a perfect formulation from the point of view of philosophy: it posits perfect humans with paradigmatically well-ordered souls whose primary enemy in life is error. But it is a radically imperfect formulation from the point of view of democracy, which takes imperfect humans as they are and, indeed, discovers in their common imperfections (their base appetites and animal natures) a source of their equality. The problem is not error but conflict, and the remedy is not truth but provisional agreement on courses of common action in the face of conflict. To elaborate this part of my argument, I need to move beyond the confines of the *Gorgias.* For I am trying to show that however well Euben reads Socrates and the meaning of Socratic dialectic, he badly misreads democracy. Thus, even though he may persuade some that Socratic philosophy is akin to democracy, he will not persuade me that he has understood the idea to which he says Socratic philosophy is akin.

My real quarrel, then, is less with Socrates than with Euben and with the peculiar construction of democracy he advances by which he convinces himself that Pericles and Themistocles are not democrats and that Socrates is a democrat. Because Socrates and I agree on what democracy is, we agree (or would agree, were he here) that Socrates is an aristocrat; because Euben and I disagree on what democracy is, he can persuade himself that Socrates is a democrat. In what follows I want to reflect on the relationship between philosophy and politics, in particular between the foundationalist philosophy that in Plato ties politics to cognitive norms and a democratic politics that, I shall argue, is antifoundational.

EUBEN AND DEMOCRACY

Pursuing the Platonic conviction that politics rests on knowledge and that, consequently, prudent doing necessarily derives from adequate knowing, Euben compares Socratic dialectic and democratic political deliberation.[1] But it is the character of politics in general, and of democratic politics in particular, that it is precisely not a cognitive system concerned with what we know and how we know it but a system of conduct concerned with what we *will* together and *do* together and how we agree on what we will to do. It is practical not speculative, about action rather than about truth. It yields but is not premised on an epistemology and in this sense is necessarily pragmatic. Where there is truth or certain knowledge, there need be no politics, even though (as Plato warns) politicians and citizens may wantonly ignore truth and certain knowledge in pursuit of base interests or raw power. But democratic politics begins where certainty ends. As I suggested in *Strong Democracy,* the political question always takes a form something like, "What shall we do when something has to be done that affects us all, when we wish to be reasonable, yet we disagree on means and ends and are without independent grounds for making the choice?"[2] For Socrates the point is to secure the independent ground—whether through dialectical discourse or pure speculative reasoning. Neither leaves room for politics. After all, as Hannah Arendt has warned, "The modes of thought and communication that deal with truth, if seen from the political perspective, are necessarily domineering ["despotic," she says earlier]; they don't take into account other people's opinions, and taking these into account is the hallmark of all strictly political thinking."[3]

To believe in democratic politics is to renounce foundational sources of conflict resolution. In this sense politics is ineluctably pragmatic and so, as William James says of pragmatism, turns its back resolutely and once and for all "upon a lot of inveterate habits dear to professional philosophers . . . away from abstraction and insufficiency, from verbal solutions, from bad *a priori* reasons, from fixed principles, closed systems, and pretended absolutes and origins."[4] As democratic politics is pragmatic, so pragmatism is democratic: "See already how democratic [pragmatism] is," James rhapsodized; "her manner as various and flexible, her resources as rich and endless."[5]

Politics occupies the domain of practical action and, as Dewey suggests, "the distinctive characteristic of practical activity . . . is the uncertainty that attends it."[6] The philosophical quest for certainty inspires a longing "to find a realm in which there is an activity which is not overt and which has no external consequences. 'Safety first' has played a large role in effectiving preference for knowing over doing and making." Like the Greeks Euben admires, modern foundationalists continue to believe that the "office of knowledge is to uncover the antecedently real, rather than, as is the case with our practical judgment, to gain the kind of understanding which is necessary to deal with problems as they arise."[7] But Euben seems to think that the quest for certainty can be assimilated to the politics of uncertainty as long as both employ some form of discourse. However, what Bertrand Russell said ruefully about the quest for mathematical truth seems to me to fit perfectly the quest for political truth in the form of foundations antecedent to democratic politics: "Real life is, to most men, a long second-best, a perpetual compromise between the ideal and the possible; but the world of pure reason knows no compromise, no practial limitations, no barrier to the creative embodying in splendid edifices of the passionate aspiration after the perfect from which all great work springs. Remote from human passions, remote even from the pitiful facts of nature, the generations have gradually created an ordered cosmos, where pure thought can dwell as in its natural home, and where one, at least, of our nobler impulses can escape from the dreary exile of the actual world."[8] Politics is not an ordered cosmos in which our nobler impulses can be given expression; it is how we try to govern ourselves in 'the dreary exile of the actual world.' Here we are, to use a metaphor favored both by Charles Saunders Peirce and Michael Oakeshott, afloat on an open and endless sea where, in Peirce's words, we must rebuild our ship "on the open sea, never able to dismantle it in dry dock and to reconstruct it out of the best materials."[9] Socrates pretends to argue the principles of navigation while on the open sea, but in truth he has his own charts and coordinates and a clear sense of his destination. He is not really trying to adjudicate different notions of an ideal port or to facilitate a consensus among the crew about how to navigate; he is merely educating them (by the circuitous but pedagogically and rhetorically sound path of question posing) to the truth of his destination and his coordinates. He is out to correct error, not forge provisional agreement; he wants to get to his home port, not live on the open sea. Or perhaps as a true philosopher, he wants merely to contemplate the starry firmament; he certainly does not wish to do anything in particular or in common with his fellow voyagers.

Because philosophy always seeks to "create the world in its own image" (Nietzsche), its despotism involves a coercive reduction: the transformation of the discussion of politics into a discussion of knowledge, even among those wishing to defend the autonomy and sovereignty of politics. This means that even citizens in search of a provisional basis for action may be seduced into a discussion of the foundations of the criteria for decisions. This is the turf of philosophy, where the politician and the citizen cannot but acquiesce to its mode of argumentation if not its actual substantive arguments. Euben invites us to admire the manner in which Socrates pursues truth and, since he claims it is dialectical, suggests that it models the dialectical strategy of politics—as if politics too were a form of truth seeking. Daniel Webster is closer to the mark, however, when he reminds us that governments are instituted for practical benefit and not for subjects of speculative reasoning. The question is not which politics is legitimated by a certain dialogical epistemology, but which epistemology is legitimated by a certain democratic politics. In taking "men as they are and laws as they ought to be" (Rousseau in the *Social Contract*), politics takes their interests and opinions as givens rather than errors to be overcome.

Epistemological concerns enjoin a definition of democracy in terms of its root values and antecedent normative foundations and then asks us to assess the methods by which they can be discovered and affirmed. A strictly political construction of democracy, on the other hand, focuses on active citizenship and ongoing deliberation. It assumes a regime in which we make (will) common decisions, choose common conduct, and create or express common values in an ever-changing practical context of conflicting interests and competition for power—a setting, moreover, where there is no necessary agreement on prior goods or certain knowledge about justice or right and where we must proceed on the premise of the base equality both of interests and of the interested.

Voting is not a discretionary option for determining what is to count as true; if it were, majority rule would, as Euben suggests, certainly be absurd. In practice it is, rather, a compulsory entailment of the need to choose in common under conditions where interests are equal and where objective (i.e., nonnormative) standards do not obtain. This political definition suggests certain attributes of democratic politics that help explain why democracy cannot and does not rest on "foundations" in the way that (say) natural law or Platonic justice does, and why, whatever kinship they enjoy when they share a 'dialectical' technique, philosophical discourse and political debate are essentially distinctive modes of human intercourse. Among democracy's most central attributes is its revolutionary spirit, which is tied to its spontaneity, its creativity, and its responsiveness to change. Sheldon Wolin's essay in this volume offers powerful testimony to these crucial features of democracy.

Plato may have been a dialogician and Socrates may have sought a conversational form of truth-seeking that has something in common with democratic discourse, but who would regard either of these classic heroes of philosophical inquiry as a revolutionary? Not even Euben, surely. Yet democracy is animated by a spirit of revolution and spontaneity that to ancient aristocratic philosophers could only have appeared as profoundly corrupt and corrupting—the very opposite of that "well-ordered commonwealth in speech" that Plato hoped to establish in *The Republic*. Democracy always brings with it a whiff of revolutionary self-assertion: that sense of fresh ownership that each generation brings to a constitution or political order by reembracing (or rejecting) its principles.[10] Democracy is in this respect arrogant, even solipsistic, wanting to install the *now* as the permanent arbitrator of the past and the future, wanting to make revolution a *permanent* feature of the political landscape rather than just a founding mechanism for a new, more legitimate politics of law and order.

Benjamin Rush reminded would-be democrats that though in the American system "all power is derived from the people, they possess it only on the days of their elections."[11] Thomas Jefferson loved "dreams of the future more than the history of the past."[12] Can Euben say the same of citizen Socrates? Jefferson warned against looking "at constitutions with sanctimonious reverence, and deem(ing) them like the arc of the covenant, too sacred to be touched."[13] Does Socrates urge his interlocutors to show less reverence for the *politeia* and the *nomoi?* Even when he challenges the *nomoi* of Athens, does he not insist (in the *Crito*) that what they represent be treated with deep respect? Finally, Jefferson is known famously for his insistence that "the tree of liberty must be refreshed from time to time with the blood of patriots and tyrants. It is its natural manure."[14] Could Socrates share such sentiments? Would his rhetoric lead him to boast that a "little rebellion now and then" was a "good thing" in and of itself?[15] And if not, how democratic is he? If we are to put Socrates' beliefs to a democratic test, surely Jefferson's revolutionary ardor and not some abstract notion of dialogical discourse is the proper standard.

Euben might suggest that both Socrates and Jefferson were constitution builders, but there is a paradox here. To be sure, a revolution is always a founding and thus a foundation, as well as the kindling of a certain spirit of spontaneity hostile to foundationalism. As Hannah Arendt has observed, in America the revolutionary spirit founded a constitution that in time came to be at odds with that spirit—as social contracts and fixed laws are always likely to grow at odds with the spirit of innovation that creates and ratifies them.[16] Jefferson saw democracy itself, more particularly ward government and active participation by citizens in self-governance, as the remedy to the ossification of the democratic constitution. To the ancient philosophers of truth and justice like Plato, ossification (that is to say, predictability and government by law) was the whole point of a *res publica,* and change itself might appear as a synonym for corruption and decay. To Jefferson, the call for ward government and full participation by citizens "not merely at an election one day in the year, but every day" was a way to put the demos in the place of a constitution.[17] To Socrates, a constitution was a way to put law in the place of government by the demos; it was, to him, a way to replace the despotism of opinion (*doxa*) with the rule of truth (*epistēmē*). To democrats, on the other hand, truth is the potential despot and true (unsensual) opinion offers the way to democratic common willing and hence to nontyrannical common action.

The lesson taught by Jefferson is that original consent derived from the foundational principles of natural right (the essence of social contract reasoning) is inadequate to the democratic mandate. Even a supposed natural rights theorist like Rousseau insists that while "the social order is a sacred right which is the basis of all other rights . . . nevertheless, this right does not come from nature" but from convention.[18] Rights are outcomes, not premises, of political life. For this reason democrats often become "strong" democrats and (as I have done) trumpet the benefits of participatory democracy. By this logic it is not just foundationalism, but foundings themselves that imperil the democratic orders they establish. The tension between constitutional order and the revolutionary spirit has been the subject of two recent books that pointedly capture the contradictions between founding and democracy: Gordon Wood's *The Radicalism of the American Revolution* and perhaps even more suggestively Bruce Ackerman's *We the People: Foundations.*[19] In the latter book, Ackerman offers a provocative version of "dualist democracy" in which "Rights Foundationalists" face advocates of the actual exercise of popular sovereignty in an ongoing contest over the meaning of democracy and of the revolution that made it. Ackerman sees in historical moments like the Founder's rejection of the Articles (and the procedural principles the Articles mandated), or Roosevelt's New Deal, revolutionary emblems of the nation's true democratic spirit. Foundationalism, even where it represents an authoritative establishing of the credentials of democracy, tends then to undermine democracy, and democracy both requires and entails an immunity to its own foundations in order to flourish.

Euben, Democracy and Education

Michael Oakeshott once said rationalists are "essentially ineducable," by which he meant that, wedded to formal models of truth and cognition, they are closed to the evidence of their senses about the here and now, and the commonsense conversation of those around them.[20] It was presumably Socrates' aim to buttress the soul against the misleading prejudices of the senses and to replace ordinary conversation with the dialectical discourse of truth seekers. Socrates was indisputably an educator, but just as indisputably, he was himself essentially ineducable, and thus immune to democracy. Others may need his dialectical help, but he knows his truths up front. Socrates has nothing to learn from others or the democratic process they fashion to steer themselves through what they regard as an opaque world of shadows and uncertainty. For those who despair of an exit from the Cave, survival means learning how to grope along in the dark, trying hard not to bump into others. Democrats do not just engage in democratic dialectic: they learn. Democracy enjoins constant, permanent motion—a gentle kind of permanent revolution, a movable feast that affords each generation room for new appetites and new tastes, and thus allows political and spiritual migration to new territory. Does this really describe the temper of Socrates or the object of his dialectics?

The democrat also insists that democracy itself along with its discourse and rules and provisional agreements all remain subject to ongoing correction—that they be seen as provisional not permanent. Democratic principles originate in historically important, psychologically pertinent, and morally admirable grounds and may be helped along via some form of rational discourse. But their legitimacy—how we know them politically—depends on the democratic process itself. Political knowing here meets Dewey's standard: "Knowing," he writes, "is not the act of an outside spectator but of a participator inside the natural and social scene (so that) the true object of knowledge resides in the consequences of directed action."[21] Not in Socrates thinking and discoursing about a problem, but in engaged, affected participants trying to do something about its consequences, lies the secret of what makes a politics democratic. The criterion by which this form of knowledge is judged "lies in the method used to secure consequences and not in metaphysical conceptions of the nature of the real."[22] Dewey's "method" turns out to be democracy itself. Dewey thus concludes that "the method of democracy . . . is to bring . . . conflicts out into the open where their special claims can be seen and appraised, where they can be discussed and judged in the light of the more inclusive interests than are represented by either of them separately."[23]

Dewey is portraying something like a general will, where the coincidence of particular wills describes a common good that can be willed on behalf of the community. The process modifies and legitimates as "public" not only the interests and the principles that adjudicate those interests, but the process itself. Hence, Article V of the Constitution renders the Constitution itself subject to revision via a difficult but specified set of democratic procedures. The operating principle of democracy produced by the imperative of autonomy is reflexivity. Democratic rules, the definition of citizenship, the character of rights —however they may originate—become legitimate only when subjected to democratic deliberation and decision.[24] Would Euben want to suggest that Socrates makes reflexivity the chief principle of his mode of discourse? Surely its test is how effectively it arrives at a truth already established in some ontological sense. Socratic discourse neither yields nor wills truth; it discovers or discerns or reveals truth, already-made by some other means. Will simply does not come into it, and so common willing has no relevance.

Democracy, on the other hand, is self-correcting: its insufficiencies are corrected democratically rather than by the imposition of externalities on the democratic process. The process is dynamic because it is self-transforming and educative. Dewey not only links democracy and education but suggests that "popular government is educative as other modes of political regulation are not. It forces a recognition that there are common interests, even though the recognition of what they are is still confused; and the need it enforces of discussion and publicity brings about some clarification of what they are."[25] Clarification can take a long time, but democracy holds out to those with the patience to struggle through rather than against it the promise of reform from within. It took nearly 150 years for American citizenship to be extended from propertied white males to all adult American residents by birth. But the struggle that led to the gradual expansion of the civic ambit was a democratic struggle in which the procedural rules of democracy were both modified and used to modify the outcomes produced by earlier applications of the procedural rules of democracy. A benevolent king or a Platonic Guardian would have acted far more quickly and decisively, but at the expense of the liberty of those in whose name democracy was evolving. Liberties given weigh less and perish faster than liberties taken. Those who win rights through engagement and struggle understand their meaning better than those who are passive beneficiaries of a benevolent patriarch's gift. Jefferson's notion that the remedy for the ills of democracy is more democracy speaks to its essentially self-correcting character.

Perhaps the clearest way to differentiate democratic from foundationalist reasoning is to contrast cognitive judgment with political judgment and to compare the differing forms of education they entail. Foundationalism reverts to epistemological modes of understanding and sees in education the necessary cultivation of cognitive faculties: Plato's account of education in *The Republic* is the paradigm. Democracy is firmly rooted in politics and publicity and understands education as what Tocqueville called the apprenticeship of liberty. Civic education means the acquisition of public judgment—something for which politics itself is a useful training. I will not rehearse the arguments I have offered elsewhere in defense of political judgment as an enterprise distinct from other forms of judgment,[26] but there is much to be said for the view that political judgment is defined by activity in common rather than thinking alone and is hence what democratic politics produces rather than (as with foundations) what produces democratic politics.

Democratic political judgment can be exercised only by citizens interacting with one another in the context of mutual deliberation and decision-making on the way to willing common actions. What is required is not foundational mandates or individual mental acumen in rigidly applying fixed standards to a changing world, but such political skills as are necessary to discovering or forging common ground. What is right, or even what a right is, cannot in itself determine political judgment. Rights themselves are constantly being redefined and reinterpreted and are hence dependent for their normative force on the engagement and commitment of an active citizen body.[27] Bills of Rights, Madison warned, are paper parapets from which real liberty cannot be defended. They are so many more exemplars of Hobbes' covenants without the sword. In any case, the citizen wishes only to act in common in the face of conflict, not to know with certainty or to uphold ancient norms that claim to be foundational. The object is to resolve or find ways to live with conflict, not to discover the grounds of bliss or a path to eternity. Civic judgment is thus always provisional, constrained by a sense of uncertainty. It is made uneasy by every form of absolutism, including foundational rights absolutism. Democratic politics is what men resort to when metaphysical foundations fail, rather than metaphysical foundations reified as a constitution. Democratic education is thus always part socialization in democratic norms like tolerance and reciprocity and part lesson in skepticism and subversion. It means learning to live with uncertainty and its posture is necessarily critical. It prefers challenging truths to imparting them. Its demeanor is humble rather than hubristic, social rather than solipsistic: where philosophy posits, democratic education questions. Democracy is government without metaphysics: the Greeks who established democratic institutions had the good fortune to live before metaphysics. We have the good fortune to live after metaphysics; political judgment and not abstract reason are our means to solving common problems.

My earlier argument is apposite here: "If political judgment is understood as an artful political practice conducted by adept citizens, then to improve our judgment we must strengthen our democratic practices. To think aright about politics, we must act aright, and to act aright calls for better citizens rather than better philosophers. If we find our political judgment defective, it may be the fault of too little rather than too much democracy."[28] Democracy may be established by a foundational logic but it is sustained only by a logic of citizenship and the requirements of civic education. It is made in Athens but enacted and practiced in Sparta—at least in the Sparta of political theory if not in the historical polity. The Athenians, said Rousseau, knew how to think aright; the Spartans how to act aright. It is not clear to me that Euben ever made the short but daunting journey from the image of Socrates' Athens to that of Rousseau's Sparta.[29]

Citizens are men and women who have learned to live freely and in common under rules they make for themselves, and who are thus capable not just of survival but of flourishing both in spite of the foundations that have supported their birth and in the absence of all foundations. Like every political system, democracy too has a birth mother and thus rests on foundations. Unlike every other political system, however, democracy is necessarily self-orphaned, the child who slays its parents so that it may grow and flourish autonomously. This may dismay those like Burke, who believe that in hacking up its aged parents, democracy destroys its soul, and it will be reviled by Plato if not by Peter Euben, because it abandons the founding forms and embraces the flawed copies. But democracy is government for, by, and of the flawed and the fallible so that, paradoxically, its strength lies in its acknowledgement of weakness and its adequacy derives from its recognition of insufficiency. That very insufficiency, because it is shared, becomes the basis (if not exactly the foundation) for our equality.

Reflexivity conditioned by civic education turns out to be democracy's great virtue. Democracy is the debate about what democracy is; education for democracy provisionally establishes its changing meanings; citizenship entails an argument about whom democratic citizenship includes; democratic politics debates and ultimately defines the limits of the democratic polity, thus adjudicating issues of private and public, society and state, individual and community. Popular sovereignty means common ground trumps truth. Truth's jealous lovers (philosophers) can hardly be expected to befriend common ground or provide discursive models for securing it: which leaves unanswered the question why Peter Euben thinks the father of all philosophers might possibly have wanted to do just that.

NOTES

1. This section of the paper draws on my earlier analysis in "Democracy without Foundations."

2. Barber, *Strong Democracy,* 120–21.

3. Arendt, "Truth and Politics," in *Between Past and Future,* 241. Arendt is as sympathetic with the perspective of the philosopher as with the perspective of politics, however, and worries about the status of truth in a world of opinion—a typically Platonic preoccupation, although one towards which she is compelled by the role of lying in the case of Adolf Eichmann. Arendt's epigraph to her *Life of the Mind* returns to the cleavage between philosophy and politics, citing Heidegger's aphorism, "Thinking does not produce usable practical wisdom.... Thinking does not endow us directly with the power to act." For a pertinent discussion see Canovan, *Hannah Arendt,* 253–74.

4. James, *Pragmatism and the Meaning of Truth,* 31.

5. Ibid., 44.

6. Dewey, *The Quest for Certainty,* 6.

7. Ibid., 19.

8. Russell, "The Study of Mathematics."

9. Peirce cited in Scheffler, *Four Pragmatists,* 57. Michael Oakeshott, *Rationalism in Politics,* 133, uses imagery that is equally captivating: for him, too, we are sailors "on a boundless and bottomless sea; there is neither harbour nor shelter nor floor for anchorage, neither starting-place nor appointed destination. The enterprise is to keep afloat on an even keel."

10. I am working on a project on the revolutionary origins of democracy that discriminates between at least four distinctive moments in revolution, of which the one highlighted here is only one. I call it the moment of "release."

11. Cited by Arendt, *On Revolution,* 239. Also see Michels, *Political Parties.*

12. Letter to John Adams, August 1, 1816; note that this was later in his life when, some will claim, his revolutionary ardor had cooled.

13. Letter to Samuel Kercheval, July 12, 1816

14. Letter to Colonel William Stephens Smith, November 13, 1787.

15. As Jefferson suggested in his letter to James Madison of January 30, 1787. In another place Jefferson writes: "I know also that laws and institutions must go hand in hand with the progress of the human mind.... We might as well require a man to wear still the coat which fitted him when a boy, as civilized society to remain ever under the regimen of their barbarous ancestors." Letter to Kercheval, July 12, 1816.

16. "Paradoxical as it may sound," wrote Arendt (*On Revolution,* 242), "it was in fact under the impact of the Revolution that the Revolutionary spirit in this country began to

wither away, and it was the Constitution itself, this greatest achievement of the American people, which eventually cheated them of their proudest possesion."

17. Letter to Joseph Cabell, February 12, 1815.

18. Rousseau, *The Social Contract,* 182.

19. Gordon Wood, *Radicalism;* and Bruce Ackerman, *We the People.*

20. Oakeshott, *Rationalism in Politics,* 32.

21. Dewey, *The Quest for Certainty,* 196.

22. Ibid., 220.

23. Dewey, *Liberalism and Social Action,* 79.

24. This suggests, to take a revealing current example, that Speaker Newt Gingrich's program of term limits, budget balancing amendments, and tax-policy supermajorities, far from being the "revolutionary" populist principles he labels them, are actually anti-populist, even Platonic, in their goal of curbing the will of today's simple majorities in the name of abstract principles like electoral turnover, fiscal harmony, and nontaxation.

25. Dewey, *The Public and Its Problems,* 201–2ff.

26. In *The Conquest of Politics.*

27. The political dimensions of this argument about rights in their relationship to democracy, illuminated by theorists from Rousseau to T. H. Green, are elaborated in some detail in my "The Reconstruction of Rights," so I will not rehearse the argument here.

28. Barber, *Conquest of Politics,* 211.

29. I *do* mean "image." The Spartan allusion points to certain images of laconic action, not to classical historiography. I do not wish here to enter into the debate about Sparta's historical status as a democratic or tyrannical slave state. Certainly Paul Cartledge and others have shown how romanticized and unfounded Sparta's reputation as a democracy may be. See, for example, Cartledge, *Hellenistic and Roman Sparta,* as well as his definitive history *Sparta and Lakonia.* Nonetheless, even if we question its institutional commitment to democracy, Sparta stands as a symbol of action versus reflection and of the laconic versus the grandiloquent.

ANCIENT GREEK DEMOCRACY AND THE MODERN KNOWLEDGE-BASED ORGANIZATION: REFLECTIONS ON THE IDEOLOGY OF TWO REVOLUTIONS

Philip Brook Manville

THE PREMISE of the conference that yielded this collection of essays was that valuable insights would arise from comparing and contrasting ancient and modern democracies. For the ancient case my fellow contributors have primarily used classical Athens, and for their modern cases the nation-state, mostly the United States of America. I follow their lead for the ancient example, but I propose to focus on a different contemporary case: the modern organization, both for-profit (companies, corporations) and not-for-profit (charities, public organizations, etc.) entities. I believe that there are some interesting perspectives to be derived from this particular juxtaposition of ancient and modern, each case in fact representing an important revolution in the structure of human societies. In the case of Athenian democracy, the revolution was born out of, and thereupon further developed, a new concept of the citizen's role and place in society, or as we might say a new "ideology"—a coherent, interdependent system of processes, habits, social relations, and mind-set based on (literally, in the case of *dēmokratia*) "the rule of the people."[1] The modern organization is midway through a comparably significant transformation and the creation of an analogous new ideology—driven by the increasing importance of knowledge in work. This ideology is changing the way people think about their jobs, the workplace, and their own place in society. In its own way, this too is a democratic revolution, though it is by no means over.

The skeptic will object that such an effort breaks the traditional rules governing historical comparisons and so risks becoming an apple-and-orange exercise in futility. Our skeptic will note that, whereas comparisons of ancient and modern states may be justified because both have a similar goal of "government," the comparison of a state with modern profit or not-for-profit organizations is troubled; modern organizations clearly aim at ends that are very different (e.g., for the profit-making company, creating wealth). Our skeptic may also object that the modern revolution, if not yet finished, cannot yet be examined for its implied analogies to anything in the completed historical past.

These are fair points, but let us indulge in a little creative thinking for the sake of carrying this conversation through the present and into the future—a fu-

ture in which (as many people agree) nation-states will not be the only important "political entities." Though there are some important differences between
our two cases (which I will also treat), there are some intriguing commonalities, based on the similar natures of the respective revolutions. And though the
revolution of the modern organization is not yet over, its general direction is
clear enough, at least for the purposes of our comparison. Both revolutions represent significant discontinuities with prior structural forms and processes; both
the ancient democratic and the modern knowledge-based organization are outcomes of collapsing hierarchical structures; both reflect a fundamentally expanded and different social role for the individual and that role is, in both cases,
based on the twin ideals of liberty and equality. Both the ancient democratic
polis and the modern knowledge-based organization are entities held together
and defined as much by shared values of its members as by any institutional
structures of decision-making or leadership. Finally, both organizational forms
depend vitally on debate and the free exchange of ideas to develop programs of
action and at the same time to create personal fulfillment and growth for their
members.

My purpose in exploring some conceptual links between ancient Athens and
the modern knowledge-based organization is twofold. First, because "democratic processes and culture" are increasingly a topic of discussion and experimentation in modern organizations, some new perspectives and new challenges
for democratic theorists may be provided. Second, and probably of more immediate practical value, this effort may shine some unexpected light on the issues that modern managers are wrestling with in their "more democratic" work-
places. I would assert (as an underlying assumption of the following discussion)
that political models are useful for managers, and that the ancient democratic
model of organization is more instructive—even as it is less familiar—to
today's managers than the traditional, post-Enlightenment concepts of (representative) democracy known through our experiences with the nation-state.[2]

ATHENIAN DEMOCRACY

Most of what we know about ancient democracy is based on the experience of
the people of Athens in the classical age. However, scholarly debate has long
raged about exactly when Athens became a democracy, that is, the form of political organization characterized by the rule of the demos, or "people." There
is a similar controversy about whether the democratic form of government can
be studied as a coherent whole over an extended period of time. For our purposes, however, we can date the "full" Athenian democracy to the years between (approximately) 460 and 320 B.C; similarly, though many changes in constitution and society occurred during these years, we can treat this period as a
relatively stable and thematically consistent "democratic era."[3]

This democratic era marked a significant discontinuity with the past—for all its consistency and coherence, it was the outcome and reflection of a "revolution."[4] During the democracy—for the first time in history—the multitude of all citizens, regardless of economic status or nobility of birth, come to govern themselves in a self-conscious and fiercely independent way. They take group-accountable responsibility for their decisions, and ultimately, at certain historical moments, they are responsible for the very survival of their state and themselves. Such had not always been the case.

In earlier times Athenians had been ruled by kings, aristocrats, tyrants, and/or economically powerful men. The majority of the civic population (i.e., free Athenian males) played little or no significant role in the decision-making of the society as a whole. That changed during the sixth century, and particularly at its end, during the conflicts surrounding the reformer Cleisthenes (c. 508–507 B.C). One can trace an evolutionary process of leveling of status distinctions, and the growth of popular power back hundreds of years, but the "Cleisthenic revolution" gave rise to a whole new way of thinking that manifested itself as the demos—the collective body of citizens—acting in a different, unprecedented way. Over the course of the following century, institutions and processes were developed which articulated and codified the new "power of the people"—laws and procedures for more clearly defining and maintaining citizenship, an open and accountable popular assembly, all inclusive popular courts, pay for public service, and lottery and rotation of public offices across the whole citizen body.[5]

But the origin and nature of the real change was not so much institutional as ideological. In other words, the democratic laws and decision-making bodies of classical democracy can be seen as artifacts of a larger sociological and cultural transformation, rather than vice-versa. On this view, though the democratic revolution included the development of the various well-known institutions of Athens in the classical age, it was at the same time something more. At the core of the revolution was the suddenly catalyzed development of a self-conscious, group identity of the demos—a collective understanding and set of behaviors that exemplified the rule of the people. It was a change whereby "the demos stepped onto the historical stage as actor in its own right and under its own name."[6] If such a metaphor points to the new ideology, how can we better understand what the new way of thinking and behaving really was?

The ideology of classical democracy—if we define that as a somewhat intangible amalgam of processes, behaviors, mind-set, etc.—is difficult to describe in a way that is at once simple and accurate, especially for nonspecialists unschooled in the language and traditions of classical Athens. Ideally one discusses Athenian democracy in the context of a wide familiarity; and of course, even with such context, any representation will inevitably distort or oversimplify the truth, just as a map represents helpfully but misleadingly the real landscape that it attempts to draw. Given such caveats, one way into the topic may be to identify some "key principles" of ancient democratic ideology, understanding that a static, summary list cannot capture every dimension of a complex and dynamic phenomenon.

Principle 1. *In the democratic era the polis was the citizens and the citizens were the polis.* Unlike modern states, in which governmental authority represents an abstract and impersonal bureaucracy against which members of society must be given rights to protect inalienable freedoms, the polis was an organization that existed simply as an association of people. Their membership—that is, their citizenship—defined the organization per se. The state did not exist separate and distinguishable from the Athenians themselves.[7]

Principle 2. *Membership in the polis was not a passive, legal status, but rather intimately bound up with active participation in "public life."* This principle follows closely from number 1, above. Aristotle (*Pol.* 1276b1–2) defined the polis as the community of citizens "who were arranged in respect to their *politeia*," a term we may approximate in translation as "citizenship." Here again, the modern concept—with its juridical, bureaucratic overtone—"citizenship as a passport"—is in fact only an approximation, for it misses the richer, more ambiguous texture of the ancient case. As any reader of Pericles' famous funeral oration (Thuc. 2.34ff.) will understand, *politeia* mingled various concepts including polis membership, "constitution," and even "way of life"; it was a sociopolitical concept directly linked with the spirit and behaviors of participation in public decision-making, and service to the polis. Aristotle's definition of the citizen reflects the essence of the idea: it is he "who shares in deliberative or judicial offices" (*Pol.* 1275b18–20).[8]

Principle 3. *Every citizen, regardless of birth, wealth, or property, was seen to have the ability, and the freedom, to make a public contribution to the polis. He was also expected to do so, through active participation and the exercise of free speech and debate in the assembly, courts, councils, or other offices.* This principle also follows closely those above and reflects the dual, intimately connected democratic pillars of freedom and equality.[9] On the one hand, it was assumed that every citizen, regardless of his particular background or calling, had equal capability to contribute to the body politic, at least in certain fundamental ways—public debate, voting for officials and resolutions, casting ballots in jury decisions, etc. Every citizen was free to do so and could not be denied the opportunity by some rich or aristocratic bully. Thus the famous passage in Plato's *Protagoras* (319b–d): in contrast to those unschooled in construction or shipbuilding who try to advise skilled craftsmen in these fields and are shouted down, "in affairs of the state . . . everybody is free to get up and give advice, and no one reproaches him."

But capability and freedom were not the end of the story—the citizen was also *expected to* participate in public life, and one's citizenship exemplified the obligation. It was not so much impersonal law that required it, but rather a deeply felt cultural norm. Athenian oratory of the period is rich with references to the public service attitudes and deeds of petitioners seeking favor from the democratic audiences they addressed.[10] Institutions reflected the same set of values, with universal military service being the most obvious example. In the same spirit, Athenians appointed no standing prosecutors for crimes against individuals or the polis; suit was brought by *ho boulomenos*—"anyone wishing to do so"—i.e., the community expected itself to be self-policing.[11] In general, as Pericles proclaimed (Thuc. 2.40.2), "we Athenians alone consider the man who takes no part in public life not as one minding his own business, but rather a good-for-nothing."

Principle 4. *Membership in the polis was a privilege, not a right, and could be conferred or taken away on the authority of the demos.* Though most Athenians were born into their citizenship, the democratic polis developed clear definitions of who was and who was not a citizen; similarly, there were procedures for approving native citizens, granting the honor to selected outsiders, and expelling unworthy citizens or those who were perceived as undermining the democracy. The last, for example, was accomplished through such mechanisms as ostracism (a public vote to send a troublemaker into ten-year exile) and *atimia* (legal "disenfranchisement" from membership in the polis).[12]

This principle also represents an important counterpoint to the concepts of freedom and equality; it implies a limit to both, for one's status and prerogatives within the community were ultimately subordinate to the overall interests, judgments, and sovereignty of the multitude—as the trial and conviction of Socrates painfully demonstrated.[13] Classical democratic citizenship did not embody the modern concept of "inalienable rights."

Principle 5. *Citizens took turns in "ruling and being ruled," in order to maximize opportunities for public service and minimize the monopoly of power by any particular elite.* The majority of offices in the democracy—service in the bouleutic council of 500, public courts, various magistracies—were rotated frequently, involving election by fellow citizens and/or random selection through the use of the lot; pay for public service helped support the participation of poorer members of the polis. And in fact, though full statistical data is lacking, there is ample evidence to suggest that the vast majority of Athenian citizens did participate in public democratic processes and institutions, albeit to varying degrees, and with varying frequency.[14]

Principle 6. *Citizens held each other mutually accountable for their actions and decisions in public life, and each citizen was accountable for what he said and did in the democratic polis.* Accountability as a theme runs through Athenian democratic processes and institutions. Some representative examples include the scrutiny of officials by all members of the demos before and after their term of service; the procedure of *eisangeleia* (or impeachment) against improper governance; and the procedure of *graphē paranomōn*, whereby a citizen could bring to trial anyone who proposed legislation in contravention of existing laws or the democratic ways of the polis.[15]

Principle 7. *The citizens, through debate and common discussion as a mul-*

titude, were able to reach sounder, more sensible decisions than could individ-uals or any elite. This central tenet of the democracy—embodied in almost all the structures and processes of the classical constitution—was constantly at-tacked by elitist critics who raved against the "craziness" and "emotions of the mob." But even critics of the "wisdom of the demos" occasionally acknowl-edged the power of collective versus individual judgment. Though Aristotle in the *Politics* was hard-pressed to praise the character of men among the masses, he noted that the sum of individually inferior parts could be great (*Pol.* 1281a39ff). He conceded that it could be appropriate to have the demos control the assembly, council, and courts—which of course they did during the fifth and fourth centuries.[16]

Principle 8. *The polis was an autonomous entity in which the demos was the sovereign decision-maker, responsible for its own destiny.* Historians have long debated the details of the political authority of the popular assembly—its spe-cific prerogatives, their development in this or that historical moment, the rel-ative separation of powers with other democratic bodies (e.g., the Council of 500), etc. But by the mid-fifth century (if not before), the assembly of all citi-zens represented the source of ultimate decision-making authority in all im-portant matters for the polis.[17] From the standpoint of ideology, the important point is the full coincidence between the will of the plenitude and the policy of the polis—again, reflecting that the "state was the citizens and the citizens were the state." To maintain the equivalence, the polis had to remain free from any kind of external domination; without its autonomy, the polis could not be a democracy.

Principle 9. *The equality in public affairs did not extend to other realms of society, nor did the democracy seek to level other nonpolitical distinctions, e.g., class, economic status, gender, birth origin, etc.* This principle, the source of endless commentary both ancient and modern, has at its center the fundamen-tal paradox of classical democracy—an organizational structure and philoso-phy that was at the same time exclusive and inclusive. On the one hand, it was a form that did not discriminate among citizens of diverse backgrounds, birth, or wealth; on the other hand its citizens rigidly excluded women, immigrants, resident aliens, allies of the polis, and slaves. The democracy also did nothing to redistribute property or otherwise "equalize" other barriers of status. Many scholars have argued that the democratic polis of adult male citizens was en-abled by the burdens borne by all noncitizens; others have held that without the various differences within society, the political equality would not have been as compelling and intense an experience for the citizens themselves.[18]

These are not issues that can be resolved here. For our purposes, we need only recognize that citizens of the classical Athenian democracy were not equal in what we might consider all modern dimensions, nor was that an ideal for which they strived. To at least some degree, we must assume that the citizens directly or indirectly benefited from other inequalities in the broader socioeconomic environment. On the other hand, it is also clear that the society was generally able to balance and accommodate the underlying tensions for the duration of democracy's history.[19]

Principle 10. *The polis, as the sum of citizens, was bound together by "civic spirit" and a striving for higher purpose.* Civic spirit of Athenians and pride for the democracy run throughout the literature of the period; again the locus classicus is Pericles' funeral oration, but it is by no means the only witness to the fierce pride of the demos for their polis.[20]

Over time, pride for the polis came to be linked to more philosophical questions about the purpose of membership in it. During the democracy, philosophers—Socrates, Plato, Aristotle, and others—developed various conceptions of "the good life" as a defining goal for the city-state and in turn identified them with the concept of justice. But the topics of justice, moral improvement, and the polis were not confined to philosophers; there are good indications of debate about such themes among a wider audience throughout the democratic period.[21] The vigor of the debate, coupled with the active participation of citizens in the practical institutions of justice, suggest that Athenians came to see their polis as a source of more than just common defense, economic benefit, or social collaborations. It was also seen as an association that made the individual citizen a better person. Witness, for example, the fourth-century speaker who told his fellow citizens that every law of the polis "is a discovery and gift of the gods, decided on by wise men, a corrector of errors both voluntary and involuntary, and a common agreement of the city-state as that by which every citizen should guide his life." (Dem. 25.16)

To sum up the ten principles sketched above, the ancient democratic polis was characterized by citizenship, based on active participation in, and adherence to, particular guiding principles of an autonomous, decision-making organization defined by the citizens themselves. Ideas were explored and refined through open debate and communication, and the governance of the organization was based on rotating responsibilities among the citizens, who held each other mutually accountable for their actions. The organization, sharing a certain spirit and common values among all members, aimed at a higher purpose—defined eventually as justice—that guided the political life of the community.

How did the democratic polis—and its defining ideology—arise? Historians, including many contributors to this volume, offer a range of various answers: economic revolution (new forms of wealth and the rise of "new men");[22] changes in warfare (equality fostered by new forms of fighting);[23] transformation of underlying "local" social processes through the intermediation of ritual (civil society extended and redefined via the Panathenaia);[24] etc. The ultimate causes need not detain us here as long as we realize the central thrust of the changes embodied in the principles discussed above: the creation of a bold and self-conscious demos that overturned the previous governing prerogatives of a traditionally superior class of aristocratic families. The democratic revolution broke down the hierarchy of aristocratic rule, and the new order was based on the premise that the body of citizens collectively had the talents and skills to govern themselves as a polis and do so better than when they were dominated by well-born and/or rich superiors.

THE DEMOCRATIC REVOLUTION IN MODERN ORGANIZATIONS

Modern organizations are in the midst of their own revolution that is overturning a different kind of hierarchical structure, that of "command and control" management. Like the Athenian transformation, business and not-for-profit organizations are reinventing themselves amidst the development of workforces that are self-consciously more powerful, and finding their way to center stage as "actors in their own right." The stimulus to this change is the increasing shift in the nature of work, from an activity in which value is primarily derived from capital assets, labor, and/or natural resources to one in which human knowledge is the critical resource.

This democratic transformation has been less prominent in the modern headlines than the political democratization of countries around the world in the aftermath of communism's collapse. Long term, however, it may be no less significant. In any case, the two trends are probably not unrelated, particularly as economic activity and the workplace expand as arenas for individual expression and social change.

The clearest articulation of the "knowledge revolution" has been made by Peter Drucker, particularly in his book *Post-Capitalist Society*. Drucker argues forcefully that this revolution, transforming our contemporary world to a society of knowledge, is potentially of the magnitude of the Renaissance or Industrial Revolution. Its core idea is that success in all endeavors will increasingly be based on intelligence, innovation, and productivity—knowledge and the fruits of applied knowledge—rather than scale or scope of tangible assets.[25]

This transformation can be traced historically through three phases. In the first, the Industrial Revolution, the focus of knowledge changed from its traditional application of "being" to its new role in enhancing "doing," that is, knowledge began to be applied systematically to tools, processes, and products. The end of the nineteenth century marked a second era that Drucker calls the "productivity revolution," in which knowledge began to be applied to work as its own endeavor; i.e., study, analysis, and engineering aimed at increasing the yield of industrialized processes. The last phase, and one we are still living with, is for Drucker the management revolution: using knowledge not only to understand how existing knowledge can be applied to maximize results, but also to systematically determine what new knowledge is needed and what will be required to continuously increase the effectiveness of knowledge in current and future processes. Knowledge per se is becoming its own topic and discipline of inquiry and application.[26]

To appreciate the democratizing effect of all this, we need to pursue the implications of the revolution one layer deeper. If indeed knowledge is becoming the new means of production, we must understand that organizational structure is required to apply and translate it to productivity and action. Whether we are talking about the intelligence needed to design better and cheaper microchips, perform Beethoven's *Ninth Symphony,* or further the cause of environmentalism, a person's particular expertise has no value alone: some organization is required to focus and apply the knowledge and provide the setting for its coordination with other forms of expertise. As knowledge becomes more and more specialized, and markets for ideas steadily increase in competitive intensity, organizational structures multiply, each providing productive context for the knowledge to be applied. Society thus is becoming increasingly a pluralism of organizations, each one focused around a particular purpose or objective, and thus harnessing (or attempting to harness) the increasing array of specialized knowledge that is everywhere evolving.[27]

The development of the new knowledge-based organization is requiring managers and other leaders to engage in a new kind of thinking fundamentally democratic in its philosophy. Many of the ideological principles of the democratic polis—mutatis mutandis—lurk beneath the changing behaviors and management approaches in contemporary enterprises.

For example, it is an axiom of today's management literature that organizations are "flattening" or becoming more "horizontal," that is, becoming less hierarchical. Management jargon talks of "empowered" workers, and like all clichés, this can be exaggerated. But the fact remains that in modern organizations, working people on the "front line" are increasingly moving to center stage in the process of adding value to customers, and the relative contribution of "elites"—i.e., supervisors—is declining (cf. Principles 1–3). Not surprisingly, thousands of middle managers are being laid off in companies around the world.[28]

Two complementary forces are causing this. Firstly, the proliferation of computer technology and other forms of electronic communication are making the ranks of middle management redundant. Traditionally, a major role of middle managers was to gather information from the layer above, and transmit it, selectively, for application in the next layer down. So the senior vice president learned from the president, told the vice president, who directed the senior manager what to do, and so on. The process also worked in reverse, as information was filtered up the hierarchy for decisions by the boss where the "buck finally stopped here." Today, with the aid of information and communication technology, front-line workers—or "knowledge workers" as they have been dubbed—have access to management information coming from the field. A company doesn't need an assistant director of sales to gather and package data about revenue by department or region for the vice president when the vice president himself can collect the data on his own pc directly from the salespeople. In one prominent example, Bill Gates, the billionaire founder of Microsoft, helps manage the development of his software products through direct e-mail communication with junior programmers in his company, bypassing what in former times would have been layers of managers and supervisors.[29]

Second, the knowledge-based organization reflects a democratic trend by giving lie to the old assumption that every manager must know how to do all the jobs of the people working for him or her. As knowledge becomes more specialized, and specialists and experts increasingly are joined together to achieve a common end for their enterprise, managers are slowly acknowledging that their expertise will almost inevitably be less than other more "junior" members of the organization working on any specific problem. The relationships between manager and worker are changing in the direction of co-equal associates, with every member of an organization increasingly dependent on the knowledge of others around him/her (cf. Principle 5). We are witnessing the transformation of elites governing the processes of work to a more collaborative environment that draws on the collective wisdom of the "multitude" (cf. Principle 7).

One of the best-known voices articulating this kind of change is Jack Welch, CEO of General Electric:

> More and more we're cutting back on useless titles, and we're rewarding people based on what they contribute—the quality of their ideas and their ability to implement them, rather than on what they control. . . . In an environment where we must have every good idea from every man and woman in the organization, we cannot afford management styles that suppress and intimidate.

> We had to dismantle the multiple layers of management that so smoothly ran the company in a more predictable era. . . . The cool efficiency of leaders must give way to *empowering, listening.* . . . We are talking about redefining the relations between bosses and subordinates. I want to get to the point where people challenge their bosses every day: "Why do you require me to do these wasteful things? Why don't you let me do the things you shouldn't be doing so that you can move on and create?" That's the job of a leader—to create, not control.[30]

The metaphor often used for the new, less hierarchical organization is that of a symphony or jazz orchestra[31]: many different musicians of specialized expertise, guided collaboratively by a conductor who need not be—and in many cases will not be—more skilled than all or even most of the musicians. The conductor may be able to play this or that part and perhaps play very well the cello or piano, but whatever he or she does, every specialist must be given his or her due in any decision making that is binding on the whole, particularly if it relates to the specialist's area of expertise. The conductor, then, must be willing to both rule and be ruled (Principle 5), depending on the circumstances, and so must every member of the orchestra.

To continue the musical metaphor, there are some additional requirements needed to make the orchestra work. Despite all the individual expertise of the members, performance requires that they all follow an agreed-on score. The cellist cannot be playing Mozart when everybody else is playing Beethoven. Accordingly, it is an axiom of the new knowledge-based organization that the group must have a clearly articulated set of goals and objectives (cf. Principle 10); the larger the organization, the more important the common goals and their articulation becomes, since each specialist's contribution becomes less directly attributable and visible in the overall output of the entity.

The articulation and discussion of common goals is becoming increasingly standard procedure for companies. However, not-for-profit organizations are also seeing its value. A well-known example is the U.S. Girl Scouts, whose (former) executive director, Frances Hesslebein commented: "Everything flows from the mission [of the organization]. . . . The real leader redefines or defines the mission in a very powerful way so that people understand it; it permeates the organization. . . . The more power you give away, the more you have. I truly believe in participatory leadership, in sharing leadership to the outermost edges of the circle."[32]

Closely related to this is the growing awareness among managers that knowledge-based organizations must develop, embody, and follow a core of shared values. These provide guidelines for the way the organization will work, respond to change, and manage itself through crisis and discontinuities. Without shared values, external pressures or internal dissension can easily destroy the organization and decouple the productive network of relationships based around specialized pieces of knowledge. As Margaret Wheatley writes: "In human organizations, a clear sense of identity—of the values, traditions, aspirations, competencies, and culture that guide the operation—is the real source of independence from the environment. When the environment demands a new response, there is a reference point for change. This prevents the vascillation and random search for new customers and new ventures that have destroyed so many businesses over the past several years."[33] The sentiment is echoed by Levi-Strauss CEO Robert Strauss, whose company is known for its focus on values. In stressing the importance of communication across the enterprise, he noted its role in creating a desirable "common vision, sense of direction, and understanding of values, ethics, and standards."[34]

There are also other trends visible in new knowledge-based organizations, suggestive of democratic ideology. For example, organizations must be, in some sense of the word, autonomous, or to follow contemporary jargon, must be "self-managing." As Drucker comments, even if the organization is a government agency, a subsidiary of a larger holding company, or the business unit of a corporation, "in actual operations [they] must be able to do their own thing."[35] If not, the goals and objectives that are critical to harnessing the knowledge of the members can be distorted or muddied, and performance will often suffer. The test case of this proposition is any of the multitude of examples of a successful company or enterprise bought or taken over by another, with a net effect that overall value is destroyed.[36] Self-management is not just a freedom but is actually critical to the success of most organizations.

Further, we are increasingly observing that membership in a knowledge-based organization represents a conscious decision—first on the part of the individual, reflecting a willingness to participate within the organization, in line with its shared values and goals; second, on the part of the organization: its acceptance of membership is its own decision, reflecting a collective understanding among the current members that there is a role for the knowledge and expertise by the individual to be contributed to the collective enterprise (Principle 4). An extreme example is provided by the W. L. Gore Company, makers of the waterproof fabric Gore-tex®. Unlike traditional organizations, Gore has no real central personnel function; people become "associates" of the company (in their nomenclature) by finding existing associates who will sponsor their joining and vouch for the value that they can add to the company.[37] Other companies are similarly seeing the value and importance of "cultural fit" in recruiting new staff and have developed personnel policies reflecting that dimension.[38] Many managers today speak of maintaining the values of their organizational "community" through such practices.

A close corollary to policies about membership, again evocative of classical democratic ideology, is how new-style organizations stress individual responsibility. Members must take "ownership" for the way in which they can contribute to the mission of the organization—the "community"—and must understand how that contribution fits with those of the other members of the organization. In some cases, organizations are addressing the human need of the individual to see his/her impact and strengthen members' sense of responsibility, by deliberately keeping themselves small. As one example, consider the not-for-profit service organization City Year: "City Year's success [is] making people prize communitarian values. It is small. The teams are 11, the whole core here in Boston 220. It works as the Greek philosophers thought the city state should work: with every individual feeling a responsibility for the whole."[39]

In knowledge-based organizations, an individual's responsibility is so critical that it rises ultimately to the level of the organization itself; that is, members must be mutually accountable to each other to ensure that everyone is operating for the common goals of the enterprise (Principle 6). Members must also manage themselves in accordance with this mutual accountability to ensure that individual knowledge and aspirations, while being respected and nurtured, are nevertheless congruent with the good of the overall organization. If not, the organization's efforts will be diluted and the organization will ultimately break apart. Freedom in the knowledge-based organization, to borrow from Aristotle, is not absolute but is always limited by the broader interests of the collective enterprise. Charles Savage, chronicler of new organizational forms, summarized these ideas in his book *Fifth Generation Management:* "Suppose we were to think of ourselves and our positions within the organization not as fixed little empires but as resources available to others. If we were to see ourselves not as boxes but as nodes in the network, not as cogs in a gear but as knowledge contributors. . . . In the network enterprise, each position . . . represents a person with capabilities, skills and experience. Instead of mutually exclusive tasks and departmental assignments, enterprises blend the talents of different people around focused tasks."[40]

One of the most provocative analogies between ancient democratic ideology and that of the modern knowledge-based enterprise is the central role of debate and communication in shaping the life of organizational "society" (Principle 7). Such things enable members to develop and internalize shared values, negotiate and understand each person's contribution, and develop new combinations and recombinations of knowledge that create innovation. The essential tools of the new knowledge organization are language and words—whether written, electronic, or face-to-face. These are the tools whereby consensus is achieved, ideas are voiced and incorporated, and mission, purposes, and goals are challenged, tested, and refined. Alan Webber articulated the point in a now well known article in the *Harvard Business Review:* "It used to be that if the boss caught you talking on the phone or hanging around the water cooler, he would have said, 'Stop talking and get to work.' Today if you're *not* on the phone or talking with colleagues or customers, chances are you'll hear, 'Start talking and get to work.' In the new economy, conversations are the most important form of work."[41]

Many new organizations have "town meetings" and open forums—sometimes electronic, sometimes face-to-face—for debating issues facing the company. The candid and open exchange of views across the "community" is encouraged and even expected. The culture of knowledge-based organizations is literally—in the Greek sense of the word—becoming political: "Organizations today are more and more places for brains, not muscles. . . . [They] used to be perceived as gigantic pieces of engineering, with largely interchangeable parts. We talked of their structures and their systems, of inputs and outputs, of control devices and of managing them, as if the whole was one large factory. Today the language is not of engineering but politics, with talk of cultures and networks, of teams and coalitions, of influence or power rather than control, of leadership not management."[42]

The emphasis on open and public communication, and the importance placed on one's participation in the market for new ideas, shadows Athenian ideology that public life is not only the responsibility of the citizen but also for his/her individual benefit (Principle 10). In other words, participation in the life of the organization improves the members and brings out the best in them. The ideology of the traditional "command and control" organization had it that knowledge was power; that is, the more you knew, the higher up in the hierarchy you could rise; hoarding and secrecy was therefore desirable. By contrast, in the new organization, those who hoard knowledge do not partake in the ongoing dialectic of innovation—the forums that continually build new knowledge. Members who are not active in the market of new ideas thus can neither advance the overall enterprise nor their own individual success within the organization. In the knowledge-based organization, one gains power by giving knowledge away, not hoarding it; the more you help your colleagues, the more you are helped yourself, because you accelerate the organizational learning in which you are an active shareholder. To paraphrase from the Periclean speech, "one who keeps only to his own business has no business here at all."

There is one final and complementary point to be made about the democratic ideology of the new knowledge-based organization. Today leaders and managers of these "communities" are discovering what Cleisthenes, Pericles, and their successors clearly understood: that giving people a say in their own futures, and allowing them to make decisions for themselves through the process of debate, free speech, and consensus building, liberates the human spirit (Principles 2, 3, 7, 10). The new flatter organizations that encourage and require active and deliberate participation of all members in reaching common goals increase productivity because people get excited about what they're doing. In the old "command and control" organization, managers told subordinates what to do and fired them if they disobeyed. In the new organization, empowered workers are given the authority to apply their knowledge, as they know best, toward the common goals—and are held accountable by their peers as well as leaders for the success of their actions. The results of this more democratic approach of new organizations have reflected often-dramatic increases in productivity and other measurements of performance. As M. M. Stuckey, a former IBM manager now working with companies to redefine their organizational structures, said very simply, "The mess of democracy is what motivates people to do their best."[43] Alan Webber, again from his article in the *Harvard Business Review,* expounded more fully on the benefits of democratic thinking in the emerging knowledge society: "In the new economy, individuals at all levels of the company and in all kinds of companies are challenged to develop new knowledge and to create new value, to take responsibility for their ideas and pursue them as far as they can go. . . . People who manage in the new economy . . . tap into the emotional energy that comes from wrestling with their own destiny. In the end, that's a job description that most people would welcome."[44]

LIMITS OF THE ANCIENT AND MODERN COMPARISON

Critics of an earlier draft of this paper (and its original form as an oral presentation) naturally stressed contrasts more than comparisons between the ancient democracy and modern organizations, knowledge-based or otherwise. Ellen Wood, echoing other Marxist-inclined voices, was "deeply skeptical" that any enterprise in the commercial sphere could be democratic.[45] On this view, all profit-making enterprises are fundamentally coercive and admit of no possibility of genuine worker empowerment. The new "democratic organization" is thus seen as a manipulative hoax, designed to give employees some spurious sense of responsibility but ultimately only making them more responsive to the entrenched needs of the managing elite.

Wood's arguments seem to me misguided or exaggerated in many places, but her critique does bring us back to the more general question—raised at the beginning of this paper—whether two organizational forms with very different missions, one economic, one not, ought to be compared at all (put aside for the moment that many of the new knowledge-based organizations are also not-for-profit). If one sees the world through a Marxist lens, the answer is a resounding "no"; if one uses a different lens, the answer is "maybe"—and the degree to which commonalities are instructive can tip the balance. On the other side of the balance, however, are the differences between our ancient and modern cases and it is to those that we might now turn. Doing so will lead us further into the question of economic versus noneconomic, "democratic" organizations.

Working through the key points of the ancient democratic ideology, one sees many obvious differences between the classical Athenian polis and the new modern organization. In the latter the "citizens" are often not the "polis," since employees may not own the company in which they work. Though many organizations are made up of employee shareholders, as often as not an outside group of owners or shareholders are the owners of the enterprise. And because of that the community will not be, in the Aristotelian sense of the word, autonomous. Second, even in the new, "flatter" organizations, not all hiring and firing—i.e., "membership"—decisions are made by employees. Further, most new organizations are not purely democratic with regard to leadership. Typically they still retain some kind of management structure, and many of the leadership positions are not open to election, much less to selection by lot. "Ruling and being ruled" does happen in some circumstances in some organizations but is not all-pervasive. And then finally we return to a very basic objection we have referenced many times before: the ancient democratic polis aimed at a noneconomic moral purpose, whereas modern organizations are usually formed to provide products or services to a market, and usually to create material benefits for their owners.

In reflecting on these objections to our ancient-modern comparisons, three general arguments need to be addressed. First, how can one claim that two organizational forms share a democratic ideology when one typically includes many more distinctions of status and hierarchical relationships than the other? Second, since it is assumed by many scholars—following in the tradition of Hasebroek and M. I. Finley—that ancient Greece had no real concepts of commercialism and markets in the modern sense of those words, doesn't that a fortiori suggest an even greater gulf between an ancient political organization and a contemporary economic one—to the point that any comparison is an unacceptable distortion?[46] Third (and related to both other objections), how can one ever compare the personal fulfillment of the individual derived from life in the democratic polis to fulfillment in a modern economic organization, when, since antiquity, philosophers have taught us that the "good life"—the goal of the membership in the polis—is necessarily divorced from all commercial, "banausic" activity?[47] Let us take each of these challenges in turn.

First, it is certainly true that most modern organizations still have some kinds of hierarchy and status distinctions, but then again so did ancient Athenian society. As Raaflaub, Cartledge, and others have noted in this volume, Athenian democratic society was a bundle of contradictions when it came to the status and freedom of the individual and loyalty among citizens.[48] Citizens were generally equal in political terms, but differences in economic power and class clearly persisted throughout the democratic period (cf. Principle 9). And even in the political dimension, some citizens "were more equal than others," both in terms of legal prerogatives for certain *telē* (orders) versus others, and in terms of de facto hierarchies based on political power and success ("under Pericles, the Athenian government was in name a democracy but in actual fact was really the rule of one man": Thuc. 2.31).[49] Democracy in practice is never completely pure, and one of the interesting aspects of the Athenian case was the ability of the citizens to manage the contradictions of different kinds and degrees of equality at the same time. Raaflaub suggests that the co-existence of both equalities and inequalities perhaps heightened the desire among citizens—especially poorer ones—to participate more vigorously in the political realm, where equality was more certain.[50]

I would suggest that a similar phenomenon can be observed even within a single realm and even if it is economic. A "democratic" community can exist as a niche in a larger and complex commercial environment. Similarly, employees can work "democratically" within a framework of some hierarchy and may even participate vigorously because they understand that in some other regards their decision making will be limited by management structures.

To believe this doctrine of democratic empowerment within a broader economic sphere, one has to believe that people can be energized, and the human spirit excited, as much, and in at least some similar way, in a commercial setting as in a political one—for example, the town meeting of employees deciding on a make-or-break project for their business can be as dynamic, exciting, and engaging as the Athenian demos deciding on a new law. Or, stated more generally, one must believe that human behavior may show some consistency across different activities that may nonetheless be organized around similar processes.

This, however, brings us to our second main objection. Those historians who insist that ancient culture was devoid of any sensibilities of modern economic life will deny that any such commonality of behavior could be possible. This challenge, however, rests on a controversial assumption, and one that has been hotly debated over the last hundred years, i.e., that classical Greece was innocent of market thinking, and that ancient democratic citizens did not engage in modern commercial behavior.[51] In fact, the opposite case is increasingly and forcefully being made by critics of the Finley school. There is considerable evidence to support the view that ancient Athenians indeed understood markets and commercialism much as we do today, though obviously in a less sophisticated and less comprehensive way.[52]

This challenge to nonmarket orthodoxy allows us to take seriously the views of those scholars who have argued that the rise of democracy was closely linked to economic change, specifically to the growing commercial power of "new men" who challenged the traditional hierarchies of society based on birth and broke down "old ways of thinking."[53] If this is true, it is not a huge leap to posit some continuity between the mind-set of the market, with its equalities of opportunity, based on the merit of providers serving customers, and the mind-set characteristic of the democratic system, with its equalities of political functions, based on the merit of individuals serving the polis.

Faced with this assertion, the critic might still insist that political and economic kinds of excellence are qualitatively different; even if there is some "continuity of thinking," excellence in the polis and excellence in markets should never, in any formal way, be compared. This naturally leads to our third objection: that the moral goal of the polis and the commercial goal of the modern organization are fundamentally incompatible and that this incompatibility invalidates any kind of historical analogy.

I am happy to concede the point that the "good life" that ancient philosophers linked to the classical polis may be of a higher spiritual order than the more mundane happiness that can accrue from engagement in the best kind of modern organization.[54] I leave further pursuit of this argument to the ongoing tradition of philosophical inquiry. At the same time, however, I don't think we need to concede that just because the goals of one organization are more "spiritually refined" than those of another organization, the comparison of their processes and ethos is fundamentally flawed; surely a democratic ideology need not be restricted only to criteria developed by Plato and Aristotle (especially since both were basically critical of democracy!). Furthermore, those theorists who endeavor to keep the experience of antiquity hermetically sealed from any modern reflections risk abandoning the greatest legacy of the historical past— its status as a source of instruction for thinking about the future.

Indeed, for all its imperfections and necessary caveats, a comparative perspective based on ancient democratic ideology can be very useful in helping members of modern organizations understand the dynamics of the new, more "democratic" workplace. It has, in fact, helped me as a manager of such an organization, and been a source of useful reference and discussion with members of my 130-person department in a contemporary professional services firm. Let me conclude this paper with a few reflections on democracy in this particular business setting.[55]

At McKinsey & Company, my department's function is to provide information and technology services to our management consulting firm. The department is made up of people with various kinds of technical specialties, and because of that, is very knowledge-intensive. The rapid changes in technology that our department must manage, plus the fast-paced and high demands of our internal customers call for an organization that is flexible and responsive. The nature of the work also requires that individual members of the department, because of their different expertises, be able to complement each other's skills in solving complex problems. Further, each must be able to exercise much individual judgment, since managers don't have the knowledge to supervise each of the multiple technical (and other) decisions that must be made in the course of completing what are usually very complicated projects.

Given these requirements, my colleagues and I came to realize that this knowledge-based organization—like many others in business today—needed to become "self-managing," that the traditional hierarchies of management should be considerably flattened, and that a culture among members ought to be encouraged that allowed for more democratic thinking, behavior, and decision making. Over the course of the last four years, we have been working to develop such a culture, and put in place various organizational mechanisms to support it. The members of the department play a major role in recruiting and finding new members for the organization, and they evaluate each other for performance reviews. Decisions about priorities and allocation of resources are made in councils, and open debate and communication about all issues facing our department is encouraged and even expected—both face-to-face and in the multiple computer-based conferences we all participate in. The entire department meets in plenum periodically (three to four times per year), and issues are debated and discussed in the course of the daylong meetings. Members of the department are evaluated for their contribution to the development of the organization in addition to their service to our customers. In addition to problem-solving and organizational skills, the ability to speak persuasively in meetings and show "thought leadership" among the group is highly rewarded. Project teams meet regularly to debate solutions to the business problems they are confronting, in the widely held belief that better answers come from multiple perspectives and from vigorously challenging ideas put forward.

Reflecting back on the evolution of this organization, I can identify some key turning points in its democratic development. In the earliest days after the "revolution," the members, used to traditional hierarchical management structures, were confused by the newfound freedom they were given. Many people floundered about in their jobs and came to me or other senior members in the department and asked "just to be told what to do." Many people left or were asked to leave because they couldn't handle the responsibility implied in their roles and didn't understand that because of the knowledge intensity of what they were doing, they had to take more accountability for contributing to the work at hand. The organization overall suffered some low morale, and many people reported a general feeling of ambiguity and confusion.

The situation improved when a few people began to take leadership in developing a sense of mission and an overall strategy for the organization and began building an understanding of that strategy among their colleagues. As this evolving process was discussed and debated, and structural mechanisms were instituted to provide more focused decision-making, morale improved and efficiency increased.

The next phase in our history, however, raised some new democratic problems. As leadership started to consolidate around certain people who led key decision-making committees and/or took lead responsibility for some of our most important projects, jealousy arose, and hallway gossip turned against "the self-appointed elite." Eventually we addressed the problem, and our solution was purely Athenian—leadership roles were more consciously rotated, and our governing council deliberately gave, in turns, important responsibilities for various departmental functions to newer and more junior members. The spirit of "rule and being ruled" helped rebalance the overall spirit of our group.

One of the most vital aspects of the "democratic" behavior of the department is the way membership is managed. When new people are needed (or want to join, for many now apply to us), candidates are screened and interviewed by multiple people before any decision is made. Decisions are made in a broadly representative council, and discussion centers as much on "cultural fit" and mind-set as skills needed for our business. The firing of people is also handled in a democratic manner: essentially it is the reverse of the hiring process. Over time, if, because of attitude or abilities, a person is not performing well or generally "fitting in," he/she becomes increasingly isolated—people do not want to have her/him on their teams, and his/her contributions to various organizational activities are not sought out. The performance evaluation process—which seeks opinions of co-workers and customers—surfaces the problems. If it is felt that the problems cannot be addressed by training, coaching, or other forms of help, the governing council recommends that the person be asked to leave. And he/she does, because it has become clear to the unlucky individual, as to everybody else, that he/she does not belong in this organization. Through such experiences we have all come to realize that democracy is not all ideals and fond feelings; it can also be harsh, unpleasant, and sometimes disappointing.

In the truest sense of the word, this organization is not a pure democracy. Not all decisions are open to plenary discussion, and various dimensions of (mostly budgetary) control are exercised by some management hierarchy. But its "ideology" is certainly more democratic than old-style technology organizations, and certainly more democratic than most other departments in our area of the company. Most of our current people, and just about all of the people who have left us for the right reasons (to return to school, or accept better opportunities

elsewhere that we can't provide) tell me that they are having/have had a fulfilling experience in their employment with us. Typically they report how they
have grown professionally from the kind of organizational setting we have provided, and their comments call to mind some of the spirit of ancient democracy.

What's been best of all, they say, is having lots of individual responsibility
and accountability, especially as judged by one's peers; participating in open
meetings and lively intellectual debates, and learning the value of getting one's
ideas across; playing an active role in devising the values of the organization
and reinforcing them through the process of recruiting and decision making.
They are motivated and fulfilled in their jobs by, in some small way (to quote
again from Alan Webber) having had the chance to "wrestle with their own destiny"—and not just as individuals, but as members of a community with whom
they have come to feel a kindred spirit.

For all its benefits, democracy in our workplace has had some of the same disadvantages cited by political theorists through the ages. It has been discourag-
ing to some employees who believe they are more "naturally born" to certain
privileges; it is messy and complicated, and considerably less efficient in achieving certain short-term tasks. The point is often made that benevolent dictatorship is sometimes the best way to get something done. Finally, as many of our
members have come to understand, our work sometimes depends on a group of
less skilled people (plus various outside contractors) who don't have the abilities or franchise to participate fully in our departmental activities. Like Athenians, we must accept our own versions of "metics" and "alien" in the community.

Despite such disadvantages, however, it is hard to imagine our workplace or
others like ours elsewhere becoming *less* democratic in the coming years, i.e.,
returning to traditional, hierarchical management. As the knowledge revolution
continues, and the intelligence, experience, and judgment of the individual becomes more and more important, organizations must continue to find ways to
enable and direct those skills to agreed-on ends. Organizations will increasingly
be defined by the people themselves, and the people themselves will increasingly need to devise the mechanisms to manage what they agree must get done.
It will not be the first time that the question will be faced of how the "power of
the people" can be actualized. Those who have reflected on the classical society that offered one solution—the practice of *dēmokratia*—may be better
equipped to reinvent the future.

ACKNOWLEDGMENTS

This paper is a considerably revised version of that which I read at the conference, "Democracy Ancient and Modern" in April 1993. The final draft of this
paper has benefited from the advice and suggestions of many people since then,
including several fellow conference participants, the anonymous reader of this
volume, and business colleagues at McKinsey & Co. and elsewhere. Special

thanks to Tom Peters; Michael Schrage; Doug Smith; Barry Strauss of Cornell University; Partha Bose, Stuart Flack, Jennifer Futernick, Nathaniel Foote, Leif Knutsen, Ellen Nenner, Christy Rector, Nancy Taubenslag, all of McKinsey; Alan Kantrow, formerly of McKinsey and now with the Monitor Company; Allan Webber of *Fast Company* magazine. I would particularly like to offer my gratitude to Josh Ober of Princeton for his encouragement, inspiration, and editorial advice along the way.

NOTES

1. My definition of *ideology* differs somewhat from that provided by Ober, *Mass and Elite,* 38–40, but is obviously indebted to his thinking and that of the other scholars whom he cites.

2. On the different traditions and forms of "democracy," see Dahl, *Democracy.*

In fairness to the diverse audiences whom I am potentially addressing in this paper, I have not assumed any significant a priori expertise about either the ancient or modern case in the argument that follows. Those knowledgeable about one or the other will excuse, I hope, the simplifications and generalizations I found necessary to describe both in some equivalent context.

Handy, "Federalist," makes good use of a political model in explaining new organizational forms for multinational corporations. He does, however, align his case more with some concepts of a nation-state than those of a direct democracy. But his focus is on the centralized versus decentralized split of responsibilities, not "representational government."

3. For the controversy about the true beginning of classical democracy see, for example, the essay by Raaflaub in this volume, and the several works he cites. Stockton, *Athenian Democracy,* 52 and Sinclair, *Democracy and Participation,* xi and 1–23 are mainline cases espousing the view I follow.

4. Ober, "Athenian Revolution" and "Revolution Matters" are recent and very helpful articulations of this point of view.

5. On the evolution of democratic institutions, see Ostwald, *Nomos* and *Popular Sovereignty;* Ober, *Mass and Elite,* 53 ff.; Stockton, *Athenian Democracy,* 19ff., and others cited in their references.

6. Quotation is from typescript of Ober, "Revolution Matters."

7. See discussion and references in Manville, *Citizenship,* 38ff. and "New Paradigm," 23–24; Hansen, "The *Polis* as a Citizen-State."

8. Manville, *Citizenship,* 4ff.

9. On freedom and equality, see essays in this volume by Cartlege, Hansen, Ostwald, Raaflaub, Strauss, Wallace, Wolin, Wood.

10. Manville, *Citizenship,* 20–23, plus references; also Ober, *Mass and Elite,* passim, especially 266ff.

11. On *ho boulomenos* in this sense, see Harrison, *Law,* 77; Hansen, *Athenian Assembly,* 216 (summarizing lots of his other work related to the topic) notes that the term could more generally refer to "a citizen who took political initiative, proposing a decree or a law, acting as prosecutor or *synēgoros* in a public action, or volunteering in election or sortition of magistrates, ambassadors, or other officials."

12. On the procedure for approving citizens and enfranchising new ones, see Manville, *Citizenship,* 3ff. On ostracism, Sinclair, *Democracy and Participation,* 169–70, with references; for *atimia,* see Manville, *Citizenship,* 147–48 and references.

13. On the trial of Socrates and its context in the workings of democracy, see Kraut, *Socrates,* especially 194ff. For the limits on freedom and equality, see also the several papers in this volume referenced above, n. 9.

14. Discussion and references in Manville, *Citizenship,* 17–20.

15. Scrutiny of officials: Sinclair, *Democracy,* 77–79; *eisangeleia:* Hansen, "Eisangelia"; *graphē paranomōn,* Sinclair, *Democracy,* 68.

16. See Ober, *Mass and Elite,* 163–65. Closely related to the point of the "wisdom of the demos" is the underlying assumption of democratic ideology of what Dahl (*Democracy,* 30–31) called the "Strong Principle of Equality"; i.e., the emergence and persistence of a democratic system depends on the shared belief of a group of people that they are all equally qualified to participate in decision-making. See also the paper by Morris in this volume.

17. The relative authority of the demos sitting in assembly as the *ekklesia* versus that of some other institutional bodies (e.g., the Council of 500), the date by which it gained its authority, and the question of whether that authority was diminished by the reforms after 403 B.C. are all controversial. My assertions follow scholars such as Ober (*Mass and Elite,* 71–98) and Sinclair (*Democracy,* 19, 67); Hansen in various works (e.g., *Assembly,* 101ff.) battles for a different view.

18. For the legal distinctions between citizens and noncitizens (including Athenian women, resident aliens, slaves, etc.), see Manville, *Citizenship,* 11–13; for their various roles in supporting the democracy of adult Athenian male citizens, and their separation from the political but not social life of the polis, see Finley "Slave Labor"; Ste. Croix, *Class Struggle,* 283ff.; Wood, *Peasant-Citizen;* Ober, *Mass and Elite,* 22–27, and references therein. See also the papers of Wood and Raaflaub in this volume.

19. Ober, *Mass and Elite,* 293ff.; for the question of equality in Athenian democracy in general, see papers by Wood, Raaflaub, Roberts, Cartledge in this volume.

20. On Pericles' oration, Manville, *Citizenship,* 14–17; Loraux, *Invention,* passim. For discussion of civic ideology in tragedy, Goldhill, *Tragedy,* 57ff.; in art, Pollitt, *Art and Experience,* 64ff.

21. Manville, *Citizenship,* 43ff., with references. General discussion of the philosophers and the polis's role in "the good life": Sinclair, *Greek Political Thought;* Farrar, *Origins,* passim.

22. See, for example, Forrest, *Emergence;* Connor, *New Politicians.*

23. Snodgrass, "Hoplite Reform Revisited," with references; cf. paper by Hanson in this volume.

24. See paper by Connor in this volume.

25. Drucker, *Post-Capitalist,* 1–16.

26. Ibid., 19–47

27. Ibid., 48–67.

28. Stewart, "Organization."

29. Personal conversation with several Microsoft employees. See also Seabrook, "E-Mail," 48–61.

30. Welch and Hood, *Annual Report,* 2;5.

31. Drucker, "New Organization."

32. Quoted in Walters, "Leader." For another not-for-profit going through similar organizational changes, see Stewart, "Organization," 98—on the San Diego zoo.

33. Wheatley, *Leadership,* 94.

34. Quoted in Webber, "New Economy," 30.

35. Drucker, *Post-Capitalist,* 57.

36. Haspeslagh and Jemison, *Acquisition,* 142ff.

37. Personal conversation with the management consultant and author, Tom Peters.

38. One well known example is Ben & Jerry's Ice Cream Company. See Sonenclar, "Ben & Jerry's," 26. "Cultural fit" is critical in the recruiting of many other firms, including McKinsey & Company, EDS, Coopers & Lybrand, Nordstrom, and others. See generally discussion in Peters, *Liberation,* passim, for various examples.

39. Lewis, "Small."

40. Quoted in Peters, *Liberation,* 472.

41. Webber, "New Economy," 28–29.

42. Charles Handy, quoted in Peters, *Liberation,* 150.

43. Quoted in *Information Week,* April 5, 1993: 26.

44. Webber, "New Economy," 42.

45. Essay in this volume, 136n. 8.

46. References and discussion in Manville, *Citizenship* 84n.52.

47. On the antibanausic tradition, see Wood, *Peasant-Citizen,* 137ff.

48. See essays of Raaflaub, Cartledge, Wood in this volume.

49. For some differential privileges accorded different *telē,* see Sinclair, *Democracy and Participation,* 66, with references.

50. Essay in this volume.

51. References in Manville, *Citizenship,* 84–86.

52. Cohen, *Athenian Economy.*

53. Forrest, *Emergence,* 148ff., is a representative example of this view.

54. It is worth noting that the ancient philosophers themselves did not even agree about the final definition of the "good life." Contrast, for example, Aristotle's different view in the *Ethics* (contemplation) and the *Politics* (political activity). See generally Sinclair, *Political Thought.*

55. Josh Ober reminds me that 130 citizens was probably about the size of a typical Attic deme, each of which had their own democratic processes within the larger whole of the Athenian polis. In fact, many other parts of McKinsey & Company reflect comparable "horizontal communities" within the firm's overall organizational structure.

BIBLIOGRAPHY

Abercrombie, Nicholas, Stephen Hill, and Bryan Turner. *The Dominant Ideology Thesis.* London: George, Allen, and Unwin, 1980.

———, eds. *Dominant Ideologies.* London: Unwin Hyman, 1990.

Ackerman, Bruce. *We the People: Foundations.* Cambridge: Harvard University Press, 1991.

Adams, John. *The Works of John Adams, Second President of the United States.* Charles Francis Adams, ed. Boston: Little Brown, 1850–56.

Adcock, F. E. *The Greek and Macedonian Art of War.* Sather Classical Lectures no. 30. Berkeley: University of California Press, 1957; 2d ed. 1974.

Adkins, A.W.H. *Moral Values and Political Behaviour in Ancient Greece.* New York: Norton, 1972.

Alty, John. "Dorians and Ionians." *Journal of Hellenic Studies* 102 (1982): 1–14.

Amit, M. *Athens and the Sea. A Study in Athenian Sea Power.* Collection Latomus 74. Brussels: Latomus, 1965.

Amouretti, M. C. *Le Pain et l'huile dans la Grèce. Annales Littéraires de l'Université de Besançon* 67.328. Paris: Université de Besançon, 1986.

Anderson, Benedict. *Imagined Communities. Reflections on the Origins and Spread of Nationalism.* 2d ed. London: Verso, 1992.

Anderson, J. K. *Ancient Greek Horsemanship.* Berkeley: University of California Press, 1961.

Andrewes, Antony. "The Hoplite *Katalogos.*" In *Classical Contributions: Studies in Honour of Malcolm Francis McGregor.* Gordon Spencer Shrimpton and David Joseph McCargar, eds. Locust Valley, N.J.: J. J. Austin, 1981, 1–3.

———. "The Growth of the Athenian State." *Cambridge Ancient History.* 2d ed. Vol. 3.3. Cambridge: Cambridge University Press, 1982, 360–91.

Andreyev, V. N. "Some Aspects of Agrarian Conditions in Attica in the Third Century." *Eirene* 12 (1974): 5–46.

Antonaccio, Carla. *An Archaeology of Ancestors.* Lanham, Md.: Rowman and Little-field, 1995.

Apffel, Helmut. *Die Verfassungsdebatte bei Herodot 3.80–82.* Dissertation Erlangen. 1957. Rept. New York: Arno Press, 1979.

Appadurai, Arjun. "Introduction: Commodities and the Politics of Value." In *The Social Life of Things.* Arjun Appadurai, ed. Cambridge: Cambridge University Press, 1986, 3–63.

Archives Parlementaires de 1787 à 1860; recueil complet des débats législatifs et politiques des chambres françaises. First series, 1787–1799. Paris, 1862–93.

Arendt, Hannah. *The Human Condition.* Chicago: University of Chicago Press, 1958.

———. *Eichmann in Jerusalem: A Report on the Banality of Evil.* New York: Viking Press, 1964.

———. *On Revolution.* New York: Viking Press, 1965.

————. *Between Past and Future: Eight Exercises in Political Thought.* New York: Penguin Books, 1968.

————.*The Life of the Mind.* New York: Harcourt Brace Jovanovich, 1978.

Arnheim, M.T.W. *Aristocracy in Greek Society.* London: Thames and Hudson, 1977.

Arnold, Matthew. "Equality." In his *Mixed Essays, Irish Essays and Others.* New York: Macmillan, 1883.

Aron, Raymond. *Progress and Disillusion. The Dialectics of Modern Society.* Harmondsworth: Penguin, 1972.

Arthur, Marylin. "Early Greece: The Origins of the Western Attitude to Women." In *Women in the Ancient World: The Arethusa Papers.* John Peradotto and John Sullivan, eds. Albany: State University of Albany Press, 1984, 7–58.

Asheri, David. *Distribuzione di terre nell'antica Grecia.* Memorie dell'Accademia delle Scienze di Torino, classe di scienze morali, storiche e filologiche. Series 4ª X. Turin, 1966.

————. "Osservazioni sulle origini dell'urbanistica ippodamea." *Rivista Storica Italiana* 87 (1975): 5–16.

Aubenque, Pierre. "Aristote et la démocratie." In *Aristote politique. Etudes sur la Politique d'Aristote.* Pierre Aubenque and Alonso Tordesillas, eds. Paris: Presses Universitaires de France, 1993, 255–64.

Auger, Danièle, Michèle Rosellini, and Suzanne Saïd. *Aristophane, les femmes et la cité.* Les cahiers de Fontenay 17. Fontenay aux Roses: Ecole Normale Supérieure, 1979.

Austin, Colin, ed. *Nova Fragmenta Euripidea.* Berlin: De Gruyter, 1968.

Aylmer, G. E. *The Levellers in the English Revolution.* Ithaca: Cornell, 1975.

Aymard, André. "Hiérarchie du travail et autarchie individuelle dans la Grèce archaïque." In *Etudes d'histoire ancienne.* Paris: Presses Universitaires de France, 1967, 316–33.

Bailyn, Bernard, ed. *Pamphlets of the American Revolution, 1750–1776.* Cambridge, Mass.: Harvard University Press, 1965–.

Baker, John. *Arguing for Equality.* London: Verso, 1987.

Bakhtin, Mikhail. *The Dialogical Imagination.* Austin: University of Texas Press, 1981.

Baldry, H. C. *The Unity of Mankind in Greek Thought.* Cambridge: Cambridge University Press, 1965.

Ball, Terence, James Farr, and Russell L. Hanson, eds., *Political Innovation and Conceptual Change.* Cambridge: Cambridge University Press, 1988.

Barber, Benjamin R. *Strong Democracy: Participatory Politics for a New Age.* Berkeley and Los Angeles: University of California Press, 1984.

————. *The Conquest of Politics.* Princeton: Princeton University Press, 1988.

————. "The Reconstruction of Rights." *The American Prospect* (Spring 1991): 36–46.

————. "Democracy without Foundations." In *Democracy and Difference: Contesting Boundaries of the Political.* S. Benhabib, ed. Princeton: Princeton University Press, 1996.

Barbieri, Gabriela, and Jean-Louis Durand. "Con il bue a spalla." *Bolletino d'arte* 29 (1985): 1–16.

Barker, Ernest. *Greek Political Theory: Plato and His Predecessors.* London: Methuen, 1918.

Barnes, Jonathan. "Aristotle and the Methods of Ethics." *Revue Internationale de Philosophie* 34 (1980): 490–511.

Barr, Stringfellow. *The Will of Zeus*. Philadelphia and New York: Lippincott, 1961.

Barrett, Michèle. "Marxist-Feminism and the Work of Karl Marx." in *Feminism and Equality,* Phillips, ed., 44–61.

Barron, John P. "Milesian Politics and Athenian Propaganda." *Journal of Hellenic Studies* 82 (1962): 1–6.

———. "Religious Propaganda of the Delian League." *Journal of Hellenic Studies* 84 (1964): 35–48.

Bartlett, Katharine, and Rosanne Kennedy, eds. *Feminist Legal Theory: Readings in Law and Gender.* Boulder, Colorado, and Oxford: Westview Press, 1991.

Basch, Lucien. *Le Musée imaginaire de la marine antique.* Athens: Institut Hellénique pour la Préservation de la Tradition Nautique, 1987.

Baslez, M.-F. *L'Etranger dans la Grèce antique.* Paris: Les Belles Lettres, 1984.

Becker, Carl. *The Declaration of Independence: A Study in the History of Political Ideas.* New York: Harcourt, Brace, 1922.

Bedau, Hans A., ed. *Justice and Equality.* Englewood Cliffs: Prentice Hall, 1971.

Beitz, Charles R. *Political Equality: An Essay in Democratic Theory.* Princeton: Princeton University Press, 1991.

Beloch, Julius. *Die Bevölkerung der griechisch-römischen Welt.* 1886. Rept. Rome: "L'Erma" di Bretschneider, 1968.

———. *Griechische Geschichte.* Vol. I (3 vols.). Strassburg: Trubner, 1893–1904.

Benedetto, V. di. "Il *Filottete* e l'efebia secondo P. Vidal-Naquet." *Belfagor* 33 (1978): 191–207.

Bengl, Hans. *Staatstheoretische Probleme im Rahmen der attischen, vornehmlich euripideischen Tragödie.* Dissertation Munich, 1929.

Bengtson, Hermann. *Die Staatsverträge des Altertums.* Vol. II. Munich: C. H. Beck, 1962.

Bennett, William J. *The Devaluing of America: The Fight for Our Country and Our Culture.* New York: Summit Books, 1992.

Bérard, Claude, et al. *A City of Images: Iconography and Society in Ancient Greece.* Tr. Deborah Lyons. Princeton: Princeton University Press, 1989.

Berger, Harry, Jr. "Facing Sophists: Socrates' Charismatic Bondage in *Protagoras.*" *Representations* (Winter 1984): 66–89.

———. "Levels of Discourse in Plato's Dialogues." In *Literature and the Question of Philosophy.* Anthony J. Cascardi, ed. Baltimore: Johns Hopkins University Press, 1987, 75–100.

Berger, Shlomo. *Revolution and Society in Greek Sicily and Southern Italy. Historia* Einzelschrift 71. Stuttgart: Franz Steiner, 1992.

Berlin, I. "Equality." [1956]. In his *Concepts and Categories.* Oxford: Oxford University Press, 1978, 81–102.

———. *Four Essays on Liberty.* London and New York: Oxford University Press, 1969.

Berubé, Michael. "Public Image Limited: Political Correctness and the Media's Big Lie." In *Debating P C.* Paul Berman, ed. New York: Dell, 1992, 124–49.

Beschi, L. "Rilievi votivi attici composti." *Annuario della Scuola Archeologica di Atene e delle Missioni Italiane in Oriente* 47–48 n.s. 31–32 (1969–70): 85–132.

Bickerman, E. J. "Autonomia. Sur un passage de Thucydides (1.144.2)." *Revue internationale des droits de l'antiquité* 5 (1958): 313–44.

Bisinger, J. *Der Agrarstaat in Platons Gesetzen. Klio* Beiheft 17. 1925. Rept. Aalen: Scientia Verlag, 1963.

Bisset, Robert. *Sketch of Democracy.* London, 1796.

Bledstein, Burton J. *The Culture of Professionalism.* New York: W. W. Norton, 1978.

Bleicken, Jochen. *Die athenische Demokratie.* 2d ed. Paderborn: Schöningh, 1994.

Bloom, Allan. *The Closing of the American Mind.* New York: Simon and Schuster, 1987.

Boardman, John. *The Greeks Overseas.* 3d ed. London: Thames and Hudson, 1980.

———. "Sex Differentiation in Grave Vases." *Annali di Istituto Universitario Orientale, sezione di archeologia e storia antica* 10 (1988): 171–79.

———. "Symposion Furniture." In *Sympotica.* Oswyn Murray, ed. Oxford: Clarendon Press, 1990, 122–31.

Boas, George. *Vox Populi. Essays in the History of an Idea.* Baltimore: Johns Hopkins University Press, 1968.

Bobbio, Norberto. *Democracy and Dictatorship: The Nature and Limits of State Power.* Oxford: Polity Press, 1989.

Boedeker, Deborah. "Euripides' Medea and the Vanity of *Logoi.*" *Classical Philology* 86 (1991): 95–112.

Boegehold, Alan L. "Perikles' Citizenship Law of 451/0 B.C." In *Athenian Identity and Civic Ideology.* Boegehold and Scafuro, eds., 57–66.

Boegehold, Alan, and Adele Scafuro, eds. *Athenian Identity and Civic Ideology.* Baltimore: Johns Hopkins University Press, 1994.

Boer, Willem Den. *Private Morality in Greece and Rome: Some Historical Aspects.* Mnemosyne Supplement 57. Leiden: Brill, 1979.

Bolton, J.D.P. *Aristeas of Proconnesus.* Oxford: Clarendon Press, 1962.

Bonner, Robert J., and Gertrude Smith. *The Administration of Justice from Homer to Aristotle.* Vol. I. Chicago: University of Chicago Press, 1930.

Borecký, Borivoj. "The Primitive Origin of the Greek Conception of Equality." In *GERAS. Studies Presented to George Thomson on the Occasion of his 60th Birthday.* V. Varcl and R. F. Willetts, eds. Prague: Charles University Press, 1963, 41–60.

———. "Die politische Isonomie." *Eirene* 9 (1971): 5–24.

Borell, Brigitte. *Attische geometrische Schalen. Eine spätgeometrische Keramikgattung und ihre Beziehung zum Orient.* Mainz: von Zabern, 1978.

Borthwick, E. K. "P. Oxy. 2738: Athena and the Pyrrhic Dance." *Hermes* 98 (1970): 318–31.

Bourdieu, Pierre, *Outline of a Theory of Practice.* Tr. Richard Nice. Cambridge: Cambridge University Press, 1977.

———. *Distinction: A Social Critique of the Judgement of Taste.* Tr. Richard Nice. Cambridge: Harvard University Press, 1984.

Boutros, L. *Phoenician Sport: Its Influence on the Origin of the Olympic Games.* Uithoorn: Poitlarow, 1981.

Bowden, Hugh. "Hoplites and Homer: Warfare, Hero Cult, and the Ideology of the Polis." In *War and Society in the Greek World,* Rich and Shipley, eds., 45–63.

Bowersock, Glen Warren. "Pseudo-Xenophon." *Harvard Studies in Classical Philology* 71 (1966): 33–55.

Bradeen, Donald. "Athenian Casualty Lists." *Hesperia* 33 (1964): 16–62.

———. "The Athenian Casualty Lists." *Classical Quarterly* 19 (1969): 149–59.

Braun, E. "Die Summierungstheorie des Aristoteles." *Jahreshefte des Österreichischen Archäologischen Institutes in Wien* 44 (1959): 157–84.

Brickhouse, Thomas C., and Nicholas D. Smith. *Socrates on Trial.* Princeton: Princeton University Press, 1989.

Brown, Henry Phelps. *Egalitarianism and the Generation of Inequality.* Oxford and New York: Oxford University Press, 1988.

Brown, Wendy. *Manhood and Politics: A Feminist Reading in Political Theory.* Totowa, N.J.: Rowman and Littlefield, 1988.

Bruit-Zaidman, Louise, and Pauline Schmitt-Pantel. *Religion in the Ancient Greek City.* Paul Cartledge, ed. and tr. Cambridge: Cambridge University Press, 1992.

Brunt, P. "Spartan Policy and Strategy in the Archidamian War." *Phoenix* 9 (1965): 255–80 (= Brunt, *Studies in Greek History and Thought.* Oxford and New York: Clarendon Press, 1993, 84–111).

Bryant, J. M. "Military Technology and Socio-Cultural Change in the Ancient Greek City." *The Sociological Review* 38 (1990): 484–516.

Bugh, Glenn Richard. *The Horsemen of Athens.* Princeton: Princeton University Press, 1988.

Burckhardt, Jacob. *Griechische Kulturgeschichte.* R. Marx, ed. Leipzig: A. Kroner, 1929.

———. *History of Greek Culture.* Tr. R. Hilty. New York: Ungar, 1963.

Burdeau, G. *La Démocratie.* Paris: Editions de Seuil, 1956.

Burford, A. (Cooper). "The Family Farm in Ancient Greece." *Classical Journal* 73 (1977–78): 162–75.

Burford, A. *Land and Labor in the Greek World.* Baltimore: Johns Hopkins University Press, 1993.

Burkert, Walter. *Greek Religion.* Cambridge, Mass.: Harvard University Press, 1985.

———. *The Orientalizing Revolution.* Tr. Margaret Pinder and Walter Burkert. Cambridge, Mass.: Harvard University Press, 1992.

Burnett, Anne P. "Medea and the Tragedy of Revenge." *Classical Philology* 68 (1973): 1–24.

———. *Three Archaic Poets: Archilochus, Alcaeus, Sappho.* Cambridge, Mass.: Harvard University Press, 1983.

———. *The Art of Bacchylides.* Cambridge, Mass.: Harvard University Press, 1985.

Callaway, Cathy. "Perjury and the Unsworn Oath." *Transactions of the American Philological Association* 123 (1993): 15–25.

Cancik, Hubert. "'Herrschaft' in historiographischen und juridischen Texten der Hethiter." In *Anfänge politischen Denkens in der Antike,* Raaflaub and Müller-Luckner, eds., 115–34.

Canfora, Luciano. *Ideologie del Classicismo.* Turin: G. Einaudi, 1980.

Canovan, Margaret. *Hannah Arendt: A Reinterpretation of Her Political Thought.* Cambridge: Cambridge University Press, 1992.

Carey, C., and R. A. Reid. *Demosthenes: Selected Private Speeches.* Cambridge: Cambridge University Press, 1985.

Cargill, Jack. *The Second Athenian League.* Berkeley, Los Angeles, and London: University of California Press, 1981.

Carlier, Pierre. *La Royauté en Grèce avant Alexandre.* Strasbourg: Association pour L'Etude de la Civilisation Romaine, 1984.

Carrithers, Michael. *Why Humans Have Cultures.* Oxford: Oxford University Press, 1993.

Carroll, M. D. "The Erotics of Absolutism: Rubens and the Mystification of Sexual Violence." *Representations* 25 (1989): 3–30.

Carson, Anne. "The Burners: A Reading of Bacchylides' Third Epinician Ode." *Phoenix* 38 (1984): 111–19.

———. "How Not to Read a Poem: Unmixing Simonides from *Protagoras.*" *Classical Philology* 87 (1992): 110–30.

Carter, Jane. "Masks and Poetry in Early Sparta." In *Early Greek Cult Practice.* Robin Hägg and Nanno Marinatos, eds. Stockholm: Skrifter Utgivna i Svenska Institutet i Athen, 1988, 89–98.

Carter, L. B. *The Quiet Athenian.* Oxford: Clarendon Press, 1986.

Cartledge, Paul A. "Hoplites and Heroes: Sparta's Contribution to the Technique of Ancient Warfare," *Journal of Hellenic Studies* 97 (1977): 11–28.

———. *Sparta and Lakonia: A Regional History, 1300–362 B.C.* London and Boston: Routledge and Kegan Paul, 1979.

———. "The Peculiar Position of Sparta in the Development of the Greek City-State." *Proceedings of the Royal Irish Academy* 80C (1980): 91–108.

———. "Rebels and *Sambos* in Classical Greece: A Comparative View". In *CRUX: Essays in Greek History Presented to G.E.M. de Ste. Croix on His 75th Birthday.* Paul Cartledge and F. David Harvey, eds. Exeter: Imprint Academic; and London: Duckworth, 1985, 16–46.

———. *Agesilaos and the Crisis of Sparta.* London: Duckworth; and Baltimore: Johns Hopkins University Press, 1987.

———. *The Greeks: A Portrait of Self and Others.* Oxford: Oxford University Press, 1993.

———. "La nascita degli opliti e l'organizzazione militare." In *I Greci.* Salvatore Settis et al., eds. Turin: Einaudi, forthcoming, vol. 2, chap. 23.

———. *Political Thought in Ancient Greece: Elite and Mass from Homer to Plutarch.* Key Themes in Ancient History. Cambridge: Cambridge University Press, forthcoming.

Cartledge, Paul, and Antony J. S. Spawforth. *Hellenic and Roman Sparta.* New York: Routledge, 1989.

Cary, Max. "Athenian Democracy." *History,* n.s. 12 (1928): 206–14.

Casabona, J. *Recherches sur le vocabulaire des sacrifices en Grec.* Aix-en-Provence: Annales de la Faculté des Lettres, 1966.

Casson, Lionel. *Ships and Seamanship in the Ancient World.* Princeton: Princeton University Press, 1971.

Castoriadis, Cornelius. *The Imaginary Institution of Society.* Tr. Kathleen Blamey. Cambridge, Mass.: MIT Press, 1987.

Catling, Hector. "Workshop and Heirloom: Prehistoric Bronze Stands in the East Mediterranean." *Report of the Department of Antiquities, Cyprus* (1984): 69–91.

Catling, Richard W. V., and Irene S. Lemos. *Lefkandi* II. *The Protogeometric Building at Toumba.* Part 1: *The Pottery.* British School at Athens Supplementary Volume 22. London: Thames and Hudson, 1990.

Ceaser, James W. *Liberal Democracy and Political Science.* Baltimore: Johns Hopkins University Press, 1990.

Ceccarelli, Paola. "Sans thalassocratie, pas de démocratie? Le rapport entre thalassocratie et démocratie à Athènes dans la discussion du Ve et IVe siècle av. J.-C." *Historia* 42 (1993): 444–70.

———. "La Pirrica di Frinico e le *pyrrhichai* attribuite a Frinico figlio di Melanthas." In *Historie. Studi offerti . . . a Giuseppe Nenci.* Salvatore Alessandrì, ed. Lecce: Congedo, 1994, 77–93.

———. *Intorno alla danza armata nell'antichità greca: la pirrica.* Forthcoming.

Cerri, G. "*Isos dasmos* come equivalente di *isonomia* nella silloge teognidea." *Quaderni Urbinati di cultura classica* 8 (1969): 97–104.

Chambers, Mortimer H. *Aristoteles. Der Staat der Athener.* Berlin: Akademie-Verlag, 1990.

Chartier, Roger. *The Cultural Origins of the French Revolution.* Tr. Lydia G. Cochrane. Durham, N.C.: Duke University Press, 1993.

Chroust, Anton-Hermann. *Aristotle: New Light on His Life and on Some of His Lost Works.* 2 vols. London: Routledge and Kegan Paul, 1973.

Clay, Diskin. "Reading the Republic." In *Platonic Writings, Platonic Readings.* Charles Griswold, ed. New York and London: Routledge, 1988, 19–32.

Cobb, Thomas. *An Historical Sketch of Slavery from the Earliest Periods* (1858). Detroit:Negro History Press, 1858.

Cochrane, C. N. *Christianity and Classical Culture: A Study of Thought and Action from Augustus to Augustine.* Rev. ed. London, New York, and Toronto: Oxford University Press, 1944.

Cohen, David. *Law, Sexuality, and Society: The Enforcement of Morals in Classical Athens.* Cambridge: Cambridge University Press, 1991.

Cohen, E. E. *Athenian Economy and Society. A Banking Perspective.* Princeton: Princeton University Press, 1992.

Colbourn, H. Trevor. *The Lamp of Experience: Whig History and the Origins of the American Revolution.* Chapel Hill: University of North Carolina Press, 1965.

Coldstream, J. Nicolas. *Geometric Greece.* London: Methuen, 1977.

———. "Gift Exchange in the Eighth Century B.C." In *The Greek Renaissance of the Eighth Century B.C.* Robin Hägg, ed. Stockholm: Skrifter Utgivna i Svenska Institutet i Athen, 1983, 201–7.

Connor, W. Robert. *The New Politicians of Fifth-Century Athens.* Princeton: Princeton University Press, 1971.

———. "Lycomedes against Themistocles?" *Historia* 22 (1972): 569–74.

———. *Thucydides.* Princeton: Princeton University Press, 1984.

———. "The Razing of the House." *Transactions of the American Philological Association* 115 (1985): 79–102.

———. "Tribes, Festivals and Processions." *Journal of Hellenic Studies* 107 (1987): 40–50.

———. "'Sacred' and 'Secular.'" *Ancient Society* 19 (1988): 161–87.

———. "City Dionysia and Athenian Democracy." *Classica et Mediaevalia* 40 (1989): 7–32.

———. "The Ionian Era of Athenian Identity." *Proceedings of the American Philosophical Society* 137, no. 2 (1993): 194–206.

Constant de Rebecque, Henri Benjamin. *De la Liberté des anciens comparée à celle des modernes* (1819). In *Cours de politique constitutionelle ou Collection des ouvrages publiés sur le gouvernement représentatif.* Edouard Laboulaye, ed. Paris, 1861.

Cook, J. M. "Ionia and Greece in the Eighth and Seventh Centuries B.C." *Journal of Hellenic Studies* 66 (1946): 67–98.

Cooper, John M. "Political Animals and Civic Friendship." In *Aristoteles' "Politik": Akten des XI. Symposium Aristotelicum, 1987.* G. Patzig, ed., 220–41; with Julia Annas, "Comments on J. Cooper," 242–48.

Cornell, Timothy J. "Rome and Latium to 390 B.C." In *Cambridge Ancient History,* 2d ed. Vol. 7.2. Cambridge: Cambridge University Press, 1989, 243–308.

———. "Rome: The History of an Anachronism." In *Athens and Rome, Florence and Venice: City-States in Classical Antiquity and Medieval Italy.* Anthony Molho, Kurt Raaflaub, and Julia Emlen, eds. Stuttgart: Steiner; and Ann Arbor: University of Michigan Press, 1991, 53–69.

Cornford, Francis Macdonald. *Thucydides Mythistoricus.* 1907. Rept. London: Routledge and Kegan Paul, 1965.

Crawford, Harriet. *Sumer and the Sumerians.* Cambridge: Cambridge University Press, 1991.

Crombie, I. M. *An Examination of Plato's Doctrines.* 2 vols. London: Routledge, 1962.

Crotty, Kevin. *Song and Action: The Victory Odes of Pindar.* Baltimore: Johns Hopkins University Press, 1982.

Crüsemann, Frank. "'Theokratie' als 'Demokratie': Zur politischen Konzeption des Deuteronomiums." In *Anfänge politischen Denkens in der Antike: Die nahöstlichen Kulturen und die Griechen.* Kurt Raaflaub and Elisabeth Müller-Luckner, eds. Munich: Oldenbourg, 1993, 199–214.

Curtin, Philip. *Cross-Cultural Trade in World History.* Cambridge: Cambridge University Press, 1984.

Dagger, Richard. "Rights." In *Political Innovation and Conceptual Change.* Terence Ball, James Farr, and Russell L. Hanson, eds. Cambridge: Cambridge University Press, 1988, 292–308.

Dahl, Robert A. *Democracy and Its Critics.* New Haven: Yale University Press, 1989.

Daux, Georges. "Le Calendrier de Thorikos au Musée J. Paul Getty." *Antiquité Classique* 52 (1983): 150–74.

Davies, John K. "Athenian Citizenship: The Descent Group and the Alternatives." *Classical Journal* 73 (1977–78): 105–21.

———. *Wealth and the Power of Wealth in Classical Athens.* New York: Arno Press, 1981.

———. "Society and Economy." In *Cambridge Ancient History,* 2d ed. Vol. 5. Cambridge: Cambridge University Press, 1992, 287–305.

———. *Democracy and Classical Greece.* 2d ed. Cambridge, Mass.: Harvard University Press, 1993.

Davies, Malcolm. "Monody, Choral Lyric, and the Tyranny of the Handbook." *Classical Quarterly* 38 (1988): 180–95.

Degler, Carl. "Starr on Slavery." *Journal of Economic History* 19 (1959): 271–77.

de Jong, Irene. "The Voice of Anonymity: Tis-Speeches in the *Iliad.*" *Eranos* 85 (1987): 69–84.

Delbrück, Hans. *History of the Art of War.* Vol. I: *Antiquity.* Tr. Walter J. Renfroe, Jr. Westport, Conn.: Greenwood Press, 1975.

Dentzer, J.-M. *Le Motif du banquet couché dans le Proche-Orient et le monde grec du VIIème au IVème siècle avant J-C.* Paris: Mélanges de l'école française à Rome, 1982.

Depew, David J. "Politics, Music, and Contemplation in Aristotle's Ideal State." In *A Companion to Aristotle's Politics.* D. Keyt and F. Miller, eds., 346–80.

Descat, Raymond. *L'Acte et l'effort: Une Idéologie du travail en Grèce ancienne.* Paris: Belles Lettres, 1986.

Desmoulins, Camille. *Le Vieux Cordelier.* Henri Calvet, ed. Paris: A. Colin, 1936.

Detienne, Marcel. "En Grèce archaïque: Géométrie, politique et société." *Annales ESC* 20 (1965): 425–41.

———. *Les Maîtres de vérité dans la Grèce archaïque.* 2d ed. Paris: Maspero, 1967.

———. *Dionysus Slain.* Baltimore: Johns Hopkins University Press, 1979.

Dew, Thomas. *Review of the Debate in the Virginia Legislature of 1831 and 1821.* Richmond: T. W. White, 1832.

Dewey, John. *The Quest for Certainty.* New York: Capricorn Books edition, n.d.

———. *The Public and Its Problems.* New York: Holt, 1927.

———. *Liberalism and Social Action.* New York: Capricorn Books, 1963.

Diakov, V., and S. Kovalev, eds. *Histoire de l'antiquité.* Moscow, n.d. (probably 1959).

Diaz-Plaja, F. *Griegos y Romanos en la revolución francesa.* Madrid: Revista de Occidente, 1960.

Dickinson, H. T. *Liberty and Property: Political Ideology in Eighteenth-Century Britain.* London: Weidenfeld and Nicolson, 1977.

Diels, Hermann, and Walther Kranz. *Die Fragmente der Vorsokratiker.* 8th ed. Berlin: Weidmann, 1956.

Dodds, Eric Robertson. *Plato, Gorgias. A Revised Text with Introduction and Commentary.* Oxford: Clarendon Press, 1959.

Dolezal, Joseph Paul. *Aristoteles und die Demokratie.* Frankfurt am Main: Akademische Verlagsgesellschaft, 1974.

Donlan, Walter. "Changes and Shifts in the Meaning of Demos in the Literature of the Archaic Period." *Parola del passato* 25 (1970): 381–95.

———. *The Aristocratic Ideal in Ancient Greece: Attitudes of Superiority from Homer to the End of the Fifth Century B.C.* Lawrence, Kansas: Coronado Press, 1980.

———. "The Pre-State Community in Greece." *Symbolae Osloenses* 64 (1989): 5–29.

Dougherty, Carol. *The Poetics of Colonization: From City to Text in Archaic Greece.* New York: Oxford University Press, 1993.

Dover, Kenneth J. "Anapsephisis in Fifth-Century Athens" *Journal of Hellenic Studies* 75 (1955): 17–20. Rept. in his *The Greeks and Their Legacy: Collected Papers.* Vol. 2. Oxford and New York: Blackwell, 1988, 187–93.

———. "The Poetry of Archilochus." In *Archiloque:* Entretiens Hardt 10 (1964): 183–222.

———. *Greek Popular Morality in the Time of Plato and Aristotle.* Oxford: Blackwell, 1974.

———. *Greek Homosexuality.* New York: Vintage Books, 1978.

———. *Aristophanes, Frogs.* Edited with introduction and commentary. Oxford: Clarendon Press, 1993.

Dow, F. D. *Radicalism in the English Revolutions 1640–1660.* Oxford: Blackwell, 1985.

Drucker, Peter. "The Coming of the New Organization." *Harvard Business Review* (January–February 1988): 45–53.

———. *Post-Capitalist Society.* New York: Harper Collins, 1993.

Drummond, Anthony. "Rome in the Fifth Century II: The Citizen Community." In *Cambridge Ancient History,* 2d ed. Vol. 7.2. Cambridge: Cambridge University Press, 1989, 172–242.

duBois, Page. *Centaurs and Amazons: Women and the Pre-History of the Great Chain of Being.* Ann Arbor: University of Michigan Press, 1982.

———. *Sowing the Body: Psychoanalysis and Ancient Representations of Women.* Chicago: University of Chicago Press, 1988.

Duncan, Graeme., ed. *Democratic Theory and Practice.* Cambridge: Cambridge University Press, 1983.

Dunn, John. *Western Political Theory in the Face of the Future.* Cambridge: Cambridge University Press, 1979.

———, ed. *Democracy: The Unfinished Journey 508 BC to AD 1993.* Oxford: Oxford University Press, 1993.

Durand, Jean-Louis. "Le Boeuf à la ficelle." In *Images et société en Grèce ancienne: L'Iconographie comme méthode d'analyse. Coll. Lausanne 1984.* Claude Bérard, Christianne Bron, Alessandra Pomari, eds. Lausanne: Institut d'archéologie et d'histoire ancienne de l'Université, 1987, 227–41.

Durand, Jean-Louis, and Alain Schnapp. "Sacrificial Slaughter and Initiatory Hunt." In *A City of Images: Iconography and Society in Ancient Greece.* Claude Bérard et al., eds. and Deborah Lyons, tr. Princeton: Princeton University Press, 1989, 53–70.

Eder, Walter. "The Political Significance of the Codification of Law in Archaic Societies." In *Social Struggles in Archaic Rome: New Perspectives on the Conflict of the Orders.* Kurt A. Raaflaub, ed. Berkeley and Los Angeles: University of California Press, 1986, 262–300.

———. "Self-Confidence and Resistance: The Role of *demos* and *plebs* after the Expulsion of the Tyrants in Athens and the King in Rome." In *Forms of Control and Subordination in Antiquity.* T. Yuge and M. Doi, eds. Tokyo: Society for Studies on Resistance Movements in Antiquity; Leiden and New York: Brill, 1988, 465–75.

———. "Who Rules? Power and Participation in Athens and Rome." In *Athens and Rome, Florence and Venice: City-States in Classical Antiquity and Medieval Italy.* Anthony Molho, Kurt Raaflaub, and Julia Emlen, eds. Stuttgart: Steiner; Ann Arbor: University of Michigan Press, 1991, 169–96.

———. "Polis und Politai. Die Auflösung des Adelsstaates und die Entwicklung des Polisbürgers." In *Euphronios und seine Zeit.* I. Wehgartner, ed. Berlin: Staatliche Museen zu Berlin, 1992, 24–38.

Edmunds, Lowell. *Chance and Intelligence in Thucydides.* Cambridge, Mass.: Harvard University Press, 1975.

Effenterre, Henri van. "Clisthène et les mesures de mobilisation." *Revue des Etudes Grecques* 89 (1976): 1–17.

Ehrenberg, Victor. "Der Damos im archaischen Sparta." *Hermes* 68 (1933): 288–305 (=Ehrenberg, *Polis und Imperium,* 202–20).

———. "When Did the Polis Rise?" *Journal of Hellenic Studies* 57 (1937): 147–59 (=Ehrenberg, *Polis und Imperium,* 83–97).

————. "An Early Source of Polis-Constitution." *Class. Quarterly* 37 (1943): 14–18 (=Ehrenberg, *Polis und Imperium,* 98–104).

————. "The Foundation of Thurii." *American Journal of Philology* 69 (1948): 149–70 (=Ehrenberg, *Polis und Imperium,* 298–315).

————. "Das Harmodioslied." *Wiener Studien* 69 (1956): 57–69 (=Ehrenberg, *Polis und Imperium,* 253–64).

————. "Von den Grundformen griechischer Staatsordnung." *Sitzungsberichte der Akademie Heidelberg* 1961, no.3 (=Ehrenberg, *Polis und Imperium,* 105–38).

————. *The People of Aristophanes: A Sociology of Old Attic Comedy.* 3d rev. ed. New York: Schocken Books, 1962.

————. *Der Staat der Griechen.* 2d ed. Zurich/Munich: Artemis, 1965.

————. *Polis und Imperium: Beiträge zur Alten Geschichte.* Zurich/Stuttgart: Artemis, 1965.

————. *The Greek State.* 2d ed. London: Methuen, 1969.

Ehrenreich, Barbara, and Deirdre English. *For Her Own Good.* Garden City: Anchor Books, 1979.

Elliott, E. N., ed. *Cotton Is King, and Pro-Slavery Arguments: Comprising the Writings of Hammond, Harper, Christy, Stringfellow, Hodge, Bledsoe, and Cartwright, on This Important Subject.* Augusta, Georgia: Pritchard, Abbott, and Loomis, 1860.

Elwes, R.H.M. *Aristotle, Ethics.* New York: Dover, 1883; rept. 1955.

Emlyn Jones, C. M. *The Ionians and Hellenism.* London and Boston: Routledge and Kegan Paul, 1980.

Engels, Friedrich. *The Origin of the Family, Private Property and the State, in the Light of the Researches of Lewis H. Morgan.* 1884. Rept. New York: International Publishers, 1942.

Euben, J. Peter. "Political Equality and the Greek Polis." In *Liberalism and the Modern Polity: Essays in Contemporary Political Theory.* M.J.G. McGrath, ed. New York: Books Demand UMI, 1978, 207–28.

————. "The Battle of Salamis and the Origins of Political Theory." *Political Theory* 14 no. 3 (August 1986): 359-90.

————, ed. *Greek Tragedy and Political Theory.* Berkeley: University of California Press, 1986.

————. *The Tragedy of Political Theory: The Road Not Taken.* Princeton: Princeton University Press, 1990.

————. "The Debate of the Canon." *The Civic Arts Review* 7, no. 1 (Winter 1994): 3–15.

————. *Corrupting Youth: Political Education, Democratic Culture, and Political Theory.* Princeton: Princeton University Press, forthcoming.

Euben, J. Peter, John R. Wallach, and Josiah Ober, eds. *Athenian Political Thought and the Reconstruction of American Democracy.* Ithaca N.Y.: Cornell University Press, 1994.

Eucken, Christoph. "Der aristotelische Demokratiebegriff und sein historisches Umfeld." In *Aristoteles' "Politik": Akten des XI. Symposion Aristotelicum, 1987.* G. Patzig, ed., 277–91.

Evans, G. "Ancient Mesopotamian Assemblies." *Journal of the American Oriental Society* 78 (1958): 1–11.

Ewen, Stuart. *All-Consuming Images: The Politics of Style in Contemporary Culture.* New York: Basic Books, 1988.

Fagles, Robert. *Sophocles' Three Theban Plays. Antigone, Oedipus the King, Oedipus at Colonus.* Harmondsworth: Penguin, 1984.

Fantham, Elaine, et al. *Women in the Classical World: Image and Text.* New York: Oxford University Press, 1994.

Faraone, Christopher A. "Molten Wax, Spilt Wine and Mutilated Animals: Sympathetic Magic in Near Eastern and Early Greek Oath Ceremonies." *Journal of Hellenic Studies* 113 (1993): 60–80.

Farrand, Max, ed. *The Records of the Federal Convention of 1787.* New Haven and London: Yale University Press, 1937.

Farrar, Cynthia. *The Origins of Democratic Thinking: The Invention of Politics in Classical Athens.* Cambridge: Cambridge University Press, 1988.

Fehr, Burkhard. *Orientalische und griechische Gelage.* Bonn: Bouvier, 1971.

Ferguson, William Scott. "The Attic Orgeones." *Harvard Theological Review* 37 (1944): 62–140.

Filippakis, S., E. Photou, C. Rolley, and G. Varoufakis. "Bronzes grecs et orientaux: Influences et apprentissages." *Bulletin de correspondance hellénique* 107 (1983): 111–32.

Fink, Zera. *The Classical Republicans: An Essay in the Recovery of a Pattern of Thought in Seventeenth Century England.* Evanston, Il.: Northwestern University Press, 1945.

Finley, John H. *Thucydides.* 1942. Rept. Ann Arbor: University of Michigan Press, 1963.

Finley, M. I. *Studies in Land and Credit in Ancient Athens 500–200 B.C.: The Horos Inscriptions.* 1952. Rept. with introduction by P. Millett, New Brunswick, N.J.: Rutgers University Press, 1985.

———. "Was Greek Civilisation Based on Slave Labour?" *Historia* 8 (1959) 53–72 (= Finley, *Economy and Society,* 97–115).

———. "The Freedom of the Citizen in the Greek World." *Talanta* 7 (1976): 1–23 (= Finley, *Economy and Society,* 77–94).

———. *The World of Odysseus.* 2d ed. London: Chatto and Windus, 1977.

———. *Ancient Slavery and Modern Ideology.* London: Chatto and Windus, 1980.

———. *Early Greece. The Bronze and Archaic Ages.* 2d ed. London: Chatto and Windus, 1981.

———. *Economy and Society in Ancient Greece.* Brent Shaw and Richard Saller, eds. New York: Viking, 1982.

———. *Politics in the Ancient World.* Cambridge: Cambridge University Press, 1983.

———. *The Ancient Economy.* 2d ed. Berkeley: University of California Press, 1985.

———. *Democracy Ancient and Modern.* 2d ed. New Brunswick: Rutgers University Press, 1985.

Fisher, N.R.E. *Hybris.* Warminster: Aris and Phillips, 1992.

Fitzhugh, George. "Black Republicanism in Athens." *De Bow's Review* 23 (1857): 20–26.

———. *Cannibals All! or Slaves without Masters.* 1857. Rept. with an introduction by C. Vann Woodward, Cambridge, Mass.: Belknap Press (Harvard), 1960.

———. *Sociology for the South.* 1854. Rept. in *Ante-Bellum Writings of George Fitzhugh and Hinton Rowan Helper on Slavery.* Harvey Wish, ed. New York: Capricorn, 1960.

Fontenrose, J. *The Delphic Oracle.* Berkeley: University of California Press, 1978.

Forbes, Clarence A. *Neoi: A Contribution to the Study of Greek Associations.* Middletown, Conn.: American Philological Association, 1933.

Ford, Andrew. *Homer: The Poetry of the Past.* Ithaca: Cornell University Press, 1992.

Fornara, Charles W. "The Hoplite Achievement at Psyttaleia." *Journal of Hellenic Studies* 86 (1966): 51–54.

———. *Archaic Times to the End of the Peloponnesian War.* 2d ed. Translated documents of Greece and Rome, I. Cambridge: Cambridge University Press, 1983.

Fornara, Charles W., and Loren J. Samons II. *Athens from Cleisthenes to Pericles.* Berkeley and Los Angeles: University of California Press, 1991.

Forrest, W. George. *The Emergence of Greek Democracy 800–400 B.C.* New York and Toronto: McGraw Hill, 1966.

———. *A History of Sparta, 950–192 B.C.* London: Hutchinson, 1968.

Foucault, Michel. *Language, Counter-Memory, Practice.* Tr. Donald F. Bouchard and Sherry Simon. Ithaca: Cornell University Press, 1977.

Frank, Richard. "Marxism and Ancient History." *Arethusa* 8 (1975): 43–58.

Fränkel, Hermann. *Early Greek Poetry and Philosophy.* Tr. Moses Hadas and James Willis. Oxford: Blackwell, 1973.

Fränkel, Max. "Der attische Heliasteneid." *Hermes* 13 (1878): 452–66.

Frankena, William K. *Three Historical Philosophies of Education: Aristotle, Kant, Dewey.* Chicago: Scott, Foresman, 1965.

Frede, Michael. "Plato's Arguments and the Dialogue Form." In *Oxford Studies in Ancient Philosophy.* Julia Annas, ed. Supplementary Volume, *Methods of Interpreting Plato and his Dialogues.* James C. Klagge and Nicholas D. Smith, eds. Oxford: Clarendon Press, 1992, 201–19.

Freese, J. H., tr. *Aristotle, Rhetoric.* Cambridge, Mass.: Harvard University Press, 1926.

Freire, Paolo. *Pedagogy of the Oppressed.* New York: Continuum Books, 1971.

Frisch, Hartvig. *The Constitution of the Athenians.* Copenhagen: Gyldendalske Boghandel/Nordisk Forlag, 1942.

Fritz, Kurt von. "Protagoras," *RE* 23.1 (1957): 908–21.

———. "Die griechische ELEUTHERIA bei Herodot." *Wiener Studien* 78 (1965): 5–31.

Fuks, Alexander. *The Ancestral Constitution. Four Studies in Athenian Party Politics at the End of the Fifth Century B.C.* London: Routledge and Kegan Paul, 1953.

———. "Patterns and Types of Social-Economic Revolution in Greece from the Fourth to the Second Century B.C." *Ancient Society* 5 (1974): 51–81 (= Fuks, *Social Conflict,* 9–39).

———. *Social Conflict in Ancient Greece.* Jerusalem: Magnes Press; Leiden: Brill, 1984.

Furet, F. *Marx et la Révolution Française.* Paris: Flammarion, 1986.

Fustel de Coulanges, Numa-Denis. *The Ancient City.* 4th ed. Tr. Willard Small. Boston: Lee and Shepard, 1882.

Gabrielsen, Vincent. *Financing the Athenian Fleet: Public Taxation and Social Relations.* Baltimore: Johns Hopkins University Press, 1994.

Gagarin, Michael. *Early Greek Law.* Berkeley and Los Angeles: University of California Press, 1986.

Gager, John G. *Curse Tablets and Binding Spells from the Ancient World.* Oxford: Oxford University Press, 1992.

Gallant, T. W. *Risk and Survival in Ancient Greece: Reconstructing the Rural Domestic Economy.* Stanford: Stanford University Press, 1991.

Garlan, Yvon. *Recherches de poliorcétique grecque.* Athens: Ecole française d'Athènes; Paris: Dépositaire, Diffusion de Boccard, 1974.

———. *War in the Ancient World: A Social History.* Tr. J. Lloyd. New York: Chatto and Windus, 1975.

———. *Slavery in Ancient Greece.* Tr. Janet Lloyd. Ithaca: Cornell University Press, 1988.

Garnsey, Peter. *Famine and Food Supply in the Graeco-Roman World: Responses to Risk and Crisis.* Cambridge: Cambridge University Press, 1988.

Gates, Henry Louis, Jr. "Whose Canon Is It Anyway?" *New York Times Book Review,* Februay 26, 1989. Rept. in *Debating P C.* Paul Berman, ed. New York: Dell, 1992, 190–200.

Gauthier, Philippe. *Un Commentaire historique des Poroi de Xénophon.* Geneva: Droz, 1976.

———. "La Citoyenneté en Grèce et à Rome; participation et intégration." *Ktema* 6 (1981): 167–79.

Gaventa, John. *Power and Powerlessness: Quiescence and Rebellion in an Appalachian Valley.* Urbana: University of Illinois Press, 1980.

Gawantka, Wilfried. *Isopolitie: Ein Beitrag zur Geschichte der zwischenstaatlichen Beziehungen in der griechischen Antike.* Munich: Beck, 1975.

———. *Die sogenannte Polis. Entstehung, Geschichte und Kritik der modernen alt-historischen Grundbegriffe der griechische Staat, die griechische Staatsidee, die Polis.* Stuttgart: Steiner Verlag, 1985.

Geddes, A. G. "Rags to Riches." *Classical Quarterly* 37, no. 2 (1987): 307–31.

Gehrke, Hans-Joachim. *Stasis. Untersuchungen zu den inneren Kriegen in den griechi-schen Staaten des 5. und 4. Jahrhunderts. vor Chr.* Vestigia 35. Munich: Beck, 1985.

———. *Jenseits von Athen und Sparta. Das Dritte Griechenland und seine Staatenwelt.* Munich: Beck, 1987.

———. "Gesetz und Konflikt. Überlegungen zur frühen Polis." In *Colloquium aus An-lass des 80. Geburtstages von Alfred Heuss.* Frankfurter Althistorische Studien 13. Jochen Bleicken, ed. Kallmünz, Opf.: Michael Lassleben, 1993, 49–67.

Gentili, Bruno. *Poetry and Its Public in Ancient Greece.* Tr. Thomas Cole. Baltimore: Johns Hopkins University Press, 1988.

Gentili, Bruno, and Carlo Prato, eds. *Poetarum Elegiacorum Testimonia et Fragmenta.* 2 vols. Leipzig: B. G. Teubner, 1979–85.

Giddens, Anthony. *Central Problems in Social Theory.* Berkeley: University of Califor-nia Press, 1979.

———. *The Class Structure of the Advanced Societies.* 2d ed. London: Hutchinson, 1980.

Golden, Mark. "The Uses of Cross-Cultural Comparison in Ancient Social History." *Echos du Monde Classique/Classical Views* 11 (1992): 309–31.

Goldhill, Simon. *Reading Greek Tragedy.* Cambridge: Cambridge University Press, 1986.

———. "The Great Dionysia and Civic Ideology." *Journal of Hellenic Studies* 107 (1987): 58–76 (revised in *Nothing to Do with Dionysos?* Winkler and Zeitlin, eds., 97–129).

———. *The Poet's Voice.* Cambridge: Cambridge University Press, 1991.

Gomme, A. W. *The Population of Athens in the Fifth and Fourth Centuries B.C.* Oxford: Basil Blackwell, 1933.

——— (with Antony Andrewes and Kenneth J. Dover). *A Historical Commentary on Thucydides.* 5 vols. Oxford: Clarendon Press, 1945–81.

———. "Concepts of Freedom." In *More Essays in Greek History and Literature.* David A. Campbell, ed. Oxford: Blackwell, 1962, 139–55.

———. "The Working of the Athenian Democracy." In *More Essays in Greek History and Literature.* David A. Campbell, ed. 1962. Rept. New York: Garland, 1987, 177–93.

Gouldner, Alvin W. *Enter Plato. Classical Greece and the Origins of Social Theory.* New York: Basic Books, 1965.

Graf, Fritz. "Apollon Delphinios." *Museum Helveticum* 36 (1979): 2–22.

Graham, A. J. "Abdera and Teos." *Journal of Hellenic Studies* 112 (1992): 44–73.

———. "Thucydides 7.13.2 and the Crews of Athenian Triremes." *Transactions of the American Philological Association* 122 (1992): 257–70.

Graham, A. J., and Gary Forsythe. "A New Slogan for Oligarchy in Thucydides III.82.6." *Harvard Studies in Classical Philology* 88 (1984): 25–45.

Graham, A. J., and R. Alden Smith. "An Ellipse in the Thasian Decree about Delation (*ML* 83)." *American Journal of Philology* 110 (1989): 405–12.

Gray, J. 1984. "On Negative and Positive Liberty." In *Conceptions of Liberty in Political Philosophy.* Z. Pelzcynski and J. Gray, eds. New York: St. Martin's Press, 1984, 321–48.

——— 1986: *Liberalism: Milton Keynes.* Minneapolis: University of Minnesota Press, 1986.

Gray, Paul. "Whose America? A Growing Emphasis on the Nation's Multicultural Heritage Exalts Racial and Ethnic Pride at the Expense of Social Cohesion." Cover story, *Time Magazine,* July 8, 1991, 12–17.

Green, Philip. *Retrieving Democracy. In Search of Civic Equality.* London: Methuen, 1985.

Greenhalgh, P.A.L. *Early Greek Warfare: Horsemen and Chariots in the Homeric and Archaic Ages.* Cambridge: Cambridge University Press, 1973.

Griffith, Mark. "Personality in Hesiod." *Classical Antiquity* 2 (1983): 37–65.

Griswold, Charles L., Jr. "Plato's Metaphilosophy: Why Plato Wrote Dialogues." In *Platonic Writings, Platonic Readings.* Charles L. Griswold, Jr., ed. New York: Routledge, 1988, 143–67.

Grossmann, Gustav. *Politische Schlagwörter aus der Zeit des Peloponnesischen Krieges.* Dissertation Basel. Zurich: Dissertationsdruckerei Leemann, 1950.

Grote, George. *A History of Greece: From the Earliest Period to the Close of the Generation Contemporary with Alexander the Great.* 12 vols. 1859–65. Rept. London: Dent; New York: Dutton, 1907.

Grube, G.M.A., tr. *Plato's Republic.* Indianapolis: Hackett, 1974.

Grundy, G. B. *Thucydides and the History of His Age.* 2d ed. Oxford: Blackwell, 1948.

Gschnitzer, Fritz. *Griechische Sozialgeschichte.* Wiesbaden: Steiner, 1981.

———. "Der Rat in der Volksversammlung." In *Festschrift Robert Muth.* Paul Händel and Wolfgang Meid, eds. Innsbruck: Verlag des Instituts für Sprachwissenschaft, 1983, 151–63.

Guerci, Luciano. *Libertà degli antichi e libertà dei moderni: Sparta, Atene e i "philosophes" nella Francia del Settecento.* Naples: Guida, 1979.

Guiraud, P. *La Propriété foncière en Grèce jusqu'à la conquête romaine.* Paris: Hachette, 1893.

Gummere, Richard. *The American Colonial Mind and the Classical Tradition: Essays in Comparative Culture.* Cambridge, Mass.: Harvard University Press, 1963.

Guthrie, W.K.C. *A History of Greek Philosophy.* Vol. 3. Cambridge: Cambridge University Press, 1971.

Gutmann, Amy. *Liberal Equality.* Cambridge: Cambridge University Press, 1980.

Habermas, Jürgen. *Legitimation Crisis.* Tr. Thomas McCarthy. Boston: Beacon Press, 1975.

———. *The Theory of Communicative Action.* Vol. 1. Tr. Thomas McCarthy. Boston: Beacon Press, 1981.

———. "Further Reflections on the Public Sphere." In *Habermas and the Public Sphere.* Craig Calhoun, ed. Cambridge, Mass.: MIT Press, 1992.

Habicht, Christian. "Falsche Urkunden zur Geschichte Athens im Zeitalter der Perserkriege." *Hermes* 89 (1961): 1–35.

Hägg, Robin, Nanno Marinatos, and Gullög Nordquist, eds. *Early Greek Cult Practice.* Stockholm: Skrifter Utgivna i Svenska Institutet i Athen, 1988.

Hall, Edith. *Inventing the Barbarian.* Oxford: Oxford University Press, 1989.

Halliwell, Stephen. *Aristotle's Poetics.* London: Duckworth, 1986.

Halperin, David. *One Hundred Years of Homosexuality and Other Essays on Greek Love.* New York and London: Routledge, 1990.

Hamilton, Alexander, James Madison, and John Jay. *The Federalist.* New York: New American Library, 1961.

Hamowy, R. "Jefferson and the Scottish Enlightenment: A Critique of Garry Wills's 'Inventing America; Jefferson's Declaration of Independence." *William and Mary Quarterly* 36 (1979): 503–23.

Hampshire, Stuart. *Thought and Action.* New York: Viking Press, 1959.

Handy, Charles. "Balancing Corporate Power: A New Federalist Paper." *Business Review* (Nov.–Dec. 1992): 59–72.

Hanfmann, George "Ionia, Leader or Follower?" *Harvard Studies in Classical Philology* 61 (1953): 1–27.

Hansen, Mogens Herman. "Misthos for Magistrates in Classical Athens." *Symbolae Osloenses* 54 (1979): 5–22.

———. "The Duration of a Meeting of the Athenian *Ecclesia.*" *Classical Philology* 74 (1979): 43–49.

———. "Eisangelia in Athens." *Journal of Hellenic Studies* 100 (1980): 59–72.

———. "The Number of Athenian Hoplites in 431 B.C." *Symbolae Osloenses* 56 (1981): 19–32.

———. "Demographic Reflections on the Number of Athenian Citizens 451–309." *American Journal of Ancient History* 7 (1982): 172–89.

———. "The Number of Rhetores in the Athenian Ekklesia, 355–322." *Greek, Roman and Byzantine Studies* 25 (1984): 123–55.

———. *Demography and Democracy: The Number of Athenian Citizens in the Fourth Century B.C.* Herning, Denmark: Forlaget Systime, 1985.

———. *The Athenian Assembly in the Age of Demosthenes.* Oxford: Blackwell, 1987.

————. "Solonian Democracy in Fourth-Century Athens." *Classica et Mediaevalia* 40 (1989): 71–99.

————. *Was Athens a Democracy? Popular Rule, Liberty and Equality in Ancient and Modern Political Thought.* Historisk-filosofiske Meddelelser 59. Copenhagen: The Royal Danish Academy of Sciences and Letters, 1989.

————. *The Athenian Democracy in the Age of Demosthenes.* Oxford: Blackwell, 1991.

————. "The Tradition of the Athenian Democracy A.D. 1750–1990." *Greece and Rome* 39 (1992): 14–30.

————. "The Polis as a Citizen-State." *The Ancient Greek City-State.* Mogens Herman Hansen, ed. Historisk-filosofiske Meddelelser 67. Copenhagen: Munksgaard, 1993, 7–29.

————. "The 2500th Anniversary of Cleisthenes' Reforms and the Tradition of Athenian Democracy." In *Ritual, Finance, Politics: Athenian Democratic Accounts Presented to David Lewis.* Robin Osborne and Simon Hornblower, eds. Oxford: Clarendon Press, 1994, 25–37.

Hanson, Russell L. "Democracy." In *Political Innovation and Conceptual Change,* Ball, Farr, and Hanson, eds., 68–89.

Hanson, Victor Davis. *Warfare and Agriculture in Classical Greece.* Pisa: Giardini, 1983.

————. *The Western Way of War: Infantry Battle in Classical Greece.* New York: Oxford University Press, 1989.

————, ed. *Hoplites: The Classical Greek Battle Experience.* London and New York: Routledge, 1991.

————. "Thucydides and the Desertion of Attic Slaves during the Decelean War." *Classical Antiquity* 11, no. 2 (1992): 210–28.

————. *The Other Greeks. The Family Farm and the Agrarian Roots of Western Civilization.* New York: Free Press, 1995.

Harper, Chancellor. *Slavery in the Light of Social Ethics.* In *Cotton Is King, and Pro-Slavery Arguments: Comprising the Writings of Hammond, Harper, Christy, Stringfellow, Hodge, Bledsoe, and Cartwright, on this Important Subject.* E. N. Elliott, ed. Augusta, Georgia: Pritchard, Abbott, and Loomis, 1860.

Harris, E. "Pericles' Praise of Athenian Democracy. Thucydides 2.37.1." *Harvard Studies in Classical Philology* 94 (1992): 157–67.

Harrison, A.R.W. *The Law of Athens.* Vol. 2, *Procedure.* Oxford: Clarendon Press, 1971.

Hart, Roderick P. *Seducing America: How Television Charms the Modern Voter.* New York: Oxford University Press, 1994.

Harvey, F. D. "Two Kinds of Equality." *Classica et Mediaevalia* 26 (1965): 101–46; 27 (1966): 99–100 (corrigenda).

Harvey, P. "New Harvests Reappear: The Impact of War on Agriculture." *Athenaeum* 64 (1986): 205–18.

Haspeslagh, Philippe C., and David. B Jemison. *Managing Acquisition: Creating Value through Corporate Renewal.* New York: Free Press, 1991.

Hättich, M. *Begriff und Formen der Demokratie.* Mainz: Hase and Koehler, 1966.

Havelock, E. A. *The Liberal Temper in Greek Politics.* New Haven: Yale University Press, 1957.

Headlam, James W. *Election by Lot at Athens.* 2d ed. Cambridge: Cambridge University Press, 1933.

Hedrick, Charles. "The Temple and Cult of Apollo Patroos in Athens." *American Journal of Archaeology* 92, no. 2 (1988): 185–210.

———. *The Decrees of the Demotionidai.* American Classical Studies 22. Atlanta: Scholars Press, 1990.

———. "The Zero Degree of Society: Aristotle and the Athenian Citizen." In *Athenian Political Thought and the Reconstruction of American Democracy,* Euben, Wallach, and Ober, eds., 289–318.

Hegel, Georg Wilhelm Friedrich. *Lectures on the Philosophy of History.* Tr. J. Sibree. 1899. Rept. New York: Dover, 1956.

Held, David. *Models of Democracy.* Stanford: Stanford University Press, 1987.

———, ed. *Political Theory Today.* Oxford: Polity Press, 1991.

Henderson, Jeffrey. "'Lysistrata': The Play and Its Themes." In *Aristophanes: Essays in Interpretation.* Jeffrey Henderson, ed. *Yale Classical Studies* 26 (1980): 153–218.

———. *Aristophanes' Lysistrata, Edited, with Introduction and Commentary.* Oxford: Clarendon Press, 1987.

Hennig, Dieter. "Besitzgleichheit und Demokratie." In *Demokratie und Architektur: Der hippodamische Städtebau und die Entstehung der Demokratie,* Schuller, Hoepfner, and Schwandner, eds., 25–35 (incl. discussion).

Herman, Gabriel. *Ritualised Friendship and the Greek City.* Cambridge: Cambridge University Press, 1987.

Herrmann, Peter. "Teos und Abdera im 5. Jahrhundert v. Chr." *Chiron* 11 (1981): 1–30.

Hervagault, M. P., and M. M. Mactoux. "Esclaves et société d'après Démosthène." *Actes du Colloque 1972 sur l'esclavage* (Annales littéraires de l'Université de Besançon: 163; Centre de recherche d'histoire ancienne, vol. 11). Paris: Belles Lettres, 1974, 57–102.

Herzfeld, Michael. *A Place in History. Social and Monumental Time in a Cretan Town.* Princeton: Princeton University Press, 1991.

———. "Pride and Perjury: Time and the Oath in the Mountain Villages of Crete." *Man* 25 (1990): 305–22.

Heuss, Alfred. "Die archaische Zeit Griechenlands als geschichtliche Epoche." *Antike und Abendland* 2 (1946): 26–62 (= *Zur griechischen Staatskunde.* Fritz Gschnitzer, ed. Darmstadt: Wissenschaftliche Buchgesellschaft, 1969, 39–96).

Hignett, C. *A History of the Athenian Constitution to the End of the Fifth Century B.C.* Oxford: Clarendon Press, 1952.

Hill, Christopher, and Edmund Dell. *The Good Old Cause. The English Revolution of 1640–1660.* New York: Kelly, 1969.

Hirzel, Rudolf. *Der Eid, Ein Beitrag zu seiner Geschichte.* Leipzig: S. Hirzel, 1902.

———. *Dike, Themis und Verwandtes. Ein Beitrag zur Geschichte der Rechtsidee bei den Griechen.* Leipzig: S. Hirzel, 1907.

Hobbs, Thomas. *Leviathan.* Michael Oakeshott, ed. Oxford: Blackwell, n.d.

Hobsbawm, Eric, and Terence Ranger, eds. *The Invention of Tradition.* Cambridge: Cambridge University Press, 1983.

Hodkinson, Stephen. "Social Order and the Conflict of Values in Classical Sparta." *Chiron* 13 (1983): 239–81.

Hoepfner, Wolfram. "Die frühen Demokratien und die Architekturforschung." In *Demokratie und Architektur,* Schuller et al., eds., 9–16.

Hoepfner, Wolfram, and Ernst Ludwig Schwandner. *Haus und Stadt im klassischen Griechenland.* Munich: Deutscher Kunstverlag, 1986.

Holden, B. *Understanding Liberal Democracy.* Oxford: Philip Allan, 1988.

Hölkeskamp, Karl-Joachim. "Written Law in Archaic Greece." *Proceedings of the Cambridge Philological Society* 38 (1992): 87–117.

———. "Demonax und die Neuordnung der Bürgerschaft von Kyrene." *Hermes* 121 (1993): 404–21.

———. "Arbitrators, Lawgivers, and the 'Codification of Law' in Archaic Greece." *Metis* 7 (1992 [1995]): 49–81.

———. *Schiedsrichter, Gesetzgeber und Gesetzgebung im archäischen Griechenland. Historia* Einzelschrift. Stuttgart: Steiner, forthcoming.

Holladay, A. J. "Hoplites and Heresies." *Journal of Hellenic Studies* 102 (1982): 94–104.

Holmes, Stephen. *Benjamin Constant and the Making of Modern Liberalism.* New Haven: Yale University Press, 1989.

Hornblower, Simon. *A Commentary on Thucydides.* Volume I: *Books I–III.* Oxford: Clarendon Press, 1991.

Horwitz, M. "Tocqueville and the Tyranny of the Majority." *Review of Politics* 28 (1966): 293–307.

Howe, Irving. "The Value of the Canon." In *Debating P C.* Paul Berman, ed. New York: Dell, 1992, 158–72.

Hubbard, Ruth, and Elijah Wald. *Exploding the Gene Myth.* Boston: Beacon Press, 1993.

Humphreys, S. C. "The Nothoi of Kynosarges." *Journal of Hellenic Studies* 94 (1974): 88–95.

———. *Anthropology and the Greeks.* London and Boston: Routledge and Kegan Paul, 1978.

———. "Kinship Patterns in the Athenian Courts." *Greek, Roman and Byzantine Studies* 27 (1986): 57–91.

Hunt, Lynn. *Politics, Culture and Class in the French Revolution.* Berkeley: University of California Press, 1984.

———. *The Family Romance of the French Revolution.* Berkeley and Los Angeles: University of California Press, 1992.

Hunter, Virginia. *Policing Athens: Social Control in the Attic Lawsuits, 420–320 B.C.* Princeton: Princeton University Press, 1994.

Huxley, George, *The Early Ionians.* New York: Humanities Press, 1966.

Institut Ferdinand-Courby, ed. *Nouveau choix d'inscriptions grecques: Textes, traductions, commentaires.* Paris: Belles Lettres, 1971.

Irwin, Terence. *Plato's Moral Theory.* Oxford: Clarendon Press, 1977.

Irwin, Terence, tr. *Plato, Gorgias.* Oxford: Clarendon Press, 1990.

Isager, S., and J. E. Skydsgaard. *Ancient Greek Agriculture. An Introduction.* London and New York: Routledge, 1992.

Izard, Michel, and Pierre Smith, eds. *Between Belief and Transgression. Essays in Religion, History and Myth.* Chicago: University of Chicago Press, 1979; rept. 1982.

Jackson, Alastar. "War and Raids for Booty in the World of Odysseus." In *War and Society in the Greek World,* Rich and Shipley, eds., 64–76.

Jacobsen, Thorkild. "Primitive Democracy in Ancient Mesopotamia." *Journal of Near Eastern Studies* 2 (1943): 159ff.

———. "Mesopotamia." In Henri Frankfort, H. A. Frankfort, John A. Wilson, Thorkild Jacobsen, and William A. Irwin, *The Intellectual Adventure of Ancient Man: An Essay on Speculative Thought in the Ancient Near East*. 1946. Rept. Chicago: University of Chicago Press, 1977, 125–219.

Jacoby, Felix. "Genesia." *Classical Quarterly* 38 (1944): 65–75.

Jaeger, Werner. *Paideia*. 3 vols. Tr. G. Highet. Oxford: Oxford University Press, 1944.

Jaher, F. C., ed. *The Rich, the Well-Born and the Powerful: Elites and Upper Classes in History*. Urbana, Il.: University of Illinois Press, 1973.

James, C.L.R. *The Black Jacobins*. New York: Vintage Books, 1963.

James, William. *Pragmatism and the Meaning of Truth*. Cambridge: Harvard University Press, 1978.

Jameson, Michael. "The Provisions for Mobilization in the Decree of Themistocles." *Historia* 12 (1963): 385–404.

———. "Agriculture and Slavery in Classical Athens." *Classical Journal* 73 (1977–78): 122–45.

———. "Apollo Lykeios in Athens." *Archaiognosia* 1, no. 2 (1980): 213–35.

———. "Sacrifice and Animal Husbandry in Classical Greece." In *Pastoral Economies in Classical Antiquity*. C. R. Whittaker, ed. *Proceedings of the Cambridge Philological Society*, Supplementary Vol. 14. Cambridge: Cambridge University Press, 1988, 87–119.

———. "Agricultural Labor in Ancient Greece." In *Agriculture in Ancient Greece*. B. Wells, ed. Stockholm: Svenska Institut i Athens, 1992, 135–46.

———. "Class in the Ancient Greek Countryside." In *Structures Rurales et Sociétés Antiques*. P. N. Doukellis and L. G. Mendoni, eds. Paris: Belles Lettres, 1994, 55–63.

Janko, Richard. *Homer, Hesiod and the Hymns*. Cambridge: Cambridge University Press, 1982.

Jardé, A. *Les Céréales dans l'antiquité grecque*, I. *La Production*. Paris: E. de Boccard, 1925.

Jenkins, Ian. "Is There Life after Marriage? A Study of the Abduction Motif in Vase Paintings of the Athenian Wedding Ceremony." *Bulletin of the Institute of Classical Studies* 30 (1983): 137–45.

———. *The Parthenon Frieze*. Austin: University of Texas Press, 1994.

Johnston, Kenneth R. "The NEH and the Battle of the Books." *Raritan* 12, no. 2 (Fall 1992): 118–32.

Johnston, Paul Forsythe. *Ships and Boat Models in Ancient Greece*. Annapolis, Md.: Naval Institute Press, 1985.

Jones, Arnold Hugh Martin. *Athenian Democracy*. 1957. Rept. Baltimore: Johns Hopkins University Press, 1986.

Jones, N. *Public Organization in Ancient Greece. A Documentary Study* (Memoirs of the American Philosophical Society, vol. 176). Philadelphia: American Philosophical Society, 1987.

Jordan, Borimir. *The Athenian Navy in the Classical Period*. University of California Publications, Classical Studies Vol. 13. Berkeley and Los Angeles: University of California Press, 1975.

Just, Roger. *Women in Athenian Law and Life.* London: Routledge, 1989.

Kagan, Donald, ed. *The Great Dialogue: History of Greek Political Thought from Homer to Polybius.* New York and London: Free Press, 1965.

———. *The Fall of the Athenian Empire.* Ithaca: Cornell University Press, 1987.

———. *Pericles of Athens and the Birth of Democracy.* New York: Touchstone, 1991.

Kahn, Victoria. *Rhetoric, Prudence, and Skepticism in the Renaissance.* Ithaca: Cornell University Press, 1985.

Kain, Philip. *Schiller, Hegel, and Marx: State, Society and the Aesthetic Ideal of Ancient Greece.* Kingston and Montreal: McGill-Queens University Press, 1982.

Kajanto, Iiro, ed. *Equality and Inequality of Man in Ancient Thought.* Commentationes Humanarum Litterarum, vol. 75. Helsinki: Societas Scientiarum Fennica, 1984.

Kann, Mark E. "Challenging Lockean Liberalism in America: The Case of Debs and Hillquit." *Political Theory* 8, no. 2: 214.

Karavites, Peter. *Promise-Giving and Treaty-Making. Homer and the Near East.* Mnemosyne Supplement 119. Leiden: E. J. Brill, 1992.

Kassel, Rudolf, and Colin Austin. *Poetae Comici Graeci,* V. Berlin: Walter de Gruyter, 1986.

Kastely, James L. "In Defense of Plato's Gorgias." *Publications of the Modern Language Association* (January 1991): 96ff.

Kelly, T. "Thucydides and Spartan Strategy in the Archidamian War." *American Historical Review* 87 (1982): 25–54.

Kelsen, H. *General Theory of Law and State.* Cambridge, Mass.: Harvard University Press, 1946.

Kerferd, G. B. "Protagoras' Doctrine of Justice and Virtue in the *Protagoras* of Plato." *Journal of Hellenic Studies* 73 (1953): 42–45.

———. *The Sophistic Movement.* Cambridge: Cambridge University Press, 1981.

———. "The Concept of Equality in the Thought of the Sophistic Movement." In *Equality and Inequality of Man in Ancient Thought,* Kajanto, ed., 7–15.

Kettner, James H. *The Development of American Citizenship, 1608–1870.* Chapel Hill: University of North Carolina Press, 1978.

Keuls, Eva C. *The Reign of the Phallus: Sexual Politics in Ancient Athens.* New York: Harper and Row, 1985.

Keyt, David. "Aristotle's Theory of Distributive Justice." In *A Companion to Aristotle's* Politics. Keyt and Miller, eds., 238–78.

Keyt, David, and Fred D. Miller, Jr., eds. *A Companion to Aristotle's* Politics. Oxford and Cambridge, Mass.: Blackwell, 1991.

Kiechle, Franz. *Lakonien und Sparta.* Munich: Beck, 1963.

Kilian-Dirlmeier, I. "Fremde Weihungen in griechischen Heiligtümern vom 8. bis zum Beginn des 7. Jhs. v. Chr." *Jahrbuch des römisch-germanischen Zentralmuseums Mainz* 32 (1985): 215–54.

Kimball, Bruce A. *Orators and Philosophers: A History of the Idea of Liberal Education.* New York: Columbia University Press, 1986.

Kinzl, Konrad. "Athens: between Tyranny and Democracy." In *Greece and the Eastern Mediterranean in Ancient History and Prehistory: Studies Fritz Schachermeyr.* Konrad Kinzl, ed. Berlin: De Gruyter, 1977, 199–223 (=Kinzl, *Demokratia,* 213–47).

———, ed. *Demokratia: Der Weg zur Demokratie bei den Griechen.* Wege der Forschung 657. Darmstadt: Wissenschaftliche Buchgesellschaft, 1995.

Kirkwood, Gordon. *Early Greek Monody.* Ithaca: Cornell University Press, 1974.

Kock, Theodor. *Comicorum Atticorum Fragmenta.* Leipzig: Teubner, 1880–88.

Kolodny, A. *The Lay of the Land: Metaphor as Experience and History in American Life and Letters.* Chapel Hill, N.C.: University of North Carolina Press, 1975.

Kosman, Aryeh. "Silence and Imitation in the Platonic Dialogues." In *Methods of Interpreting Plato and His Dialogues.* Oxford Studies in Ancient Philosophy, supplementary vol. James C. Klagge and Nicholas D. Smith, eds. Oxford and New York: Clarendon Press, 1992, 73–92.

Kratz, Corinne A. "Genres of Power: A Comparative Analysis of Okiek Blessings, Curses and Oaths." *Man* 24 (1989): 636–57.

Kraut, Richard. *Socrates and the State.* Princeton: Princeton University Press, 1984.

Krentz, Peter. *The Thirty at Athens.* Ithaca: Cornell University Press, 1982.

———. "The Nature of Hoplite Battle." *Classical Antiquity* 4 (1985): 13–20.

Kromayer, J., and G. Veith. *Heerwesen und Kriegführung der Griechen und Römer.* Handbuch der Altertumswissenscharft, part.3. 2 vols. Munich: Beck, 1928.

Krumeich, Ralf. "Zu den goldenen Dreifüssen der Deinomeniden in Delphi." *Jahrbuch des deutschen archäologischen Instituts in Athen* 106 (1991): 37–62.

Kullmann, Wolfgang. "Equality in Aristotle's Political Thought." In *Equality and Inequality of Man in Ancient Thought,* Kajanto, ed., 31–44.

Kurke, Leslie. "Pindar's Sixth *Pythian* and the Tradition of Advice Poetry." *Transactions of the American Philological Association* 120 (1990): 85–107.

———. *The Traffic in Praise.* Ithaca: Cornell University Press, 1991.

———. "The Politics of *Habrosynê* in Archaic Greece." *Classical Antiquity* 11 (1992): 91–120.

———. "Crisis and Decorum in Sixth-Century Lesbos: Reading Alkaios Otherwise." *Quaderni Urbinati di Cultura Classica* n.s. 47 (1994): 67–92.

Kymlicka, Will. *Contemporary Political Philosophy: An Introduction.* Oxford: Clarendon Press, 1990.

Kyrieleis, Helmut. "Babylonische Bronzen im Heraion von Samos." *Jahrbuch des deutschen archäologischen Instituts* 94 (1979): 32–48.

Lacey, W. K. *The Family in Classical Greece.* Ithaca, N.Y.: Cornell University Press, 1968.

Lamb, W.R.M., ed. *Plato. Dialogues.* Cambridge, Mass.: Harvard University Press, 1955.

Lamberton, Robert. *Hesiod.* New Haven: Yale University Press, 1988.

Larsen, Jakob A. O. "The Origin and Significance of the Counting of Votes." *Classical Philology* 44 (1949): 164–81.

———. "The Judgment of Antiquity on Democracy." *Classical Philology* 49 (1954): 1–14.

———. *Representative Government in Greek and Roman History.* Berkeley and Los Angeles: University of California Press, 1955.

Lasch, Christopher. *The Revolt of the Elites and the Betrayal of Democracy.* New York: W. W. Norton, 1995.

Latacz, Joachim. *Kampfparänese, Kampfdarstellung und Kampfwirklichkeit in der Ilias, bei Kallinos und Tyrtaios.* Munich: Beck, 1977.

Lavelle, Brian M. *The Sorrow and the Pity: A Prolegomenon to a History of Athens under the Peisistratids, c. 560–510 B.C. Historia* Einzelschrift 80. Stuttgart: Steiner, 1993.

Leduc-Fayette, D. *J. J. Rousseau et le mythe de l'antiquité.* Paris: J. Vrin, 1974.

Lee, Simon. *The Cost of Free Speech.* London: Faber, 1990.

Leigh, R. A. "Jean-Jacques Rousseau and the Myth of Antiquity in the Eighteenth Century." In *Classical Influences on Western Thought A. D. 1650–1870.* R. R. Bolgar, ed. Cambridge and New York: Cambridge University Press, 1979, 155–68.

Leisi, Ernst. *Der Zeuge im Attischen Recht.* Frauenfeld: Huber, 1908.

Lekas, Padelis. *Marx on Classical Antiquity: Problems of Historical Methodology.* Sussex and New York: St. Martin's Press, 1988.

Lengauer, Wlodzimierz. "Die politische Bedeutung der Gleichheitsidee im 5. und 4. Jh.v.Chr.: Einige Bemerkungen über *isonomia.*" In *Zu Alexander dem Grossen. Festschrift Gerhard Wirth.* Vol. 1. W. Will and J. Heinrichs, eds. Amsterdam: Hakkert, 1988, 53–87.

———. "Das griechische Gleichheitsdenken zwischen Aristokratie und Demokratie." In *Demokratie und Architektur: Der hippodamische Städtebau und die Entstehung der Demokratie,* Schuller, Hoepfner, and Schwandner, eds., 17–24 (incl. discussion).

Leslie, Margaret. "In Praise of Anachronism." *Political Studies* 18, no. 4 (1970): 433–47.

Lévêque, Pierre, and Pierre Vidal-Naquet. *Clisthène L'Athénien.* Besançon: Macula, 1964.

Levi, Primo. *If This Is a Man* and *The Truce.* London: Sphere Books, 1987 (Italian originals 1947 and 1963).

Levine, Lawrence W. "Slave Songs and Slave Consciousness: An Exploration in Neglected Sources." In *Anonymous Americans. Explorations in Nineteenth-Century Social History.* Tamara K. Hareven, ed. Englewood Cliffs, N.J.: Prentice-Hall, 1971, 99–130.

———. *Black Culture and Black Consciousness: Afro-American Folk Thought from Slavery to Freedom.* New York: Oxford University Press, 1977.

Lewis, Anthony. "Small Is Powerful." *New York Times,* March 15, 1993, A15.

Lewis, D. M. "The Athenian Rationes Centesimarum." In *Problèmes de la terre en Grèce ancienne.* Civilisations et sociétés, 33. M. I. Finley, ed. Paris: Mouton, 1973, 187–212.

———. "Public Property in the City." In *The Greek City from Homer to Alexander.* Oswyn Murray and Simon Price, eds. Oxford: Clarendon Press, 1990, 245–63.

Leyden, Wolfgang von. *Aristotle on Equality and Justice.* London: Macmillan, 1985.

Lichtheim, Miriam. *Ancient Egyptian Literature.* 3 vols. Berkeley: University of California Press, 1975–80.

Link, Stefan. *Landverteilung und sozialer Frieden im archäischen Griechenland.* Historia Einzelschrift 69. Stuttgart: Franz Steiner, 1991.

Lintott, Andrew. *Violence, Civil Strife, and Revolution in the Classical City.* London: Croom Helm, 1982.

Lipsius, J. H. *Das Attische Recht und Rechtsverfahren.* 3 vols. Leipzig: Reisland, 1905–15.

Littleton, Christine. "Reconstructing Sexual Equality." In *Feminist Legal Theory: Readings in Law and Gender,* Bartlett and Kennedy, eds., 35–56.

Litwack, Leon F. "Free at Last." In *Anonymous Americans. Explorations in Nineteenth-Century Social History.* Tamara K. Hareven, ed. Englewood Cliffs, N.J.: Prentice-Hall, 1971, 131–71.

Lobel, Edgar, and Denys Page. *Poetarum Lesbiorum Fragmenta.* Oxford: Clarendon Press, 1955.

Loenen, Dirk. *Vrijheid en Gelijkheid in Athene.* Amsterdam: Seyffardt, 1930.

Lonis, Raoul, ed. *L'Etranger dans le monde grec.* Nancy: Presses Universitaires, 1988.

Lonsdale, Stephen. *Dance and Ritual Play in Greek Religion.* Baltimore: Johns Hopkins University Press, 1993.

Loraux, Nicole. "'Marathon' ou l'histoire idéologique." *Revue des études anciennes* 75 (1973): 13–42.

———. "Solon au milieu de la lice." In *Aux origines de l'hellénisme, la Crète et la Grèce. Hommages à Henri van Effenterre.* Paris: Publications de la Sorbonne, 1984, 199–214.

———. *The Invention of Athens. The Funeral Oration in the Classical City.* Tr. Alan Sheridan. Cambridge, Mass., and London, England: Harvard University Press, 1986.

———. "Kreousa the Autochthon: A Study of Euripides' *Ion.*" In *Nothing to Do With Dionysos?* Winkler and Zeitlin, eds., 168 206.

———. "Reflections of the Greek City on Unity and Division." In *Athens and Rome, Florence and Venice: City-States in Classical Antiquity and Medieval Italy,* Molho, Raaflaub, and Emlen, eds., 33–51.

———. *The Children of Athena: Athenian Ideas about Citizenship and the Division between the Sexes.* Tr. Caroline Levine. Princeton: Princeton University Press, 1993.

Lord, Albert B. *The Singer of Tales.* Cambridge, Mass.: Harvard University Press, 1960.

Lord, Carnes. "Aristotle's History of Poetry." *Transactions of the American Philological Association* 107 (1977): 183–202.

———. "On the Intention of Aristotle's Rhetoric." *Hermes* 109 (1981): 326–39.

———. *Education and Culture in the Political Thought of Aristotle.* Ithaca: Cornell University Press, 1982.

———. *The Politics of Aristotle.* Tr. Carnes Lord. Chicago: University of Chicago Press, 1984.

———. "Politics and Education in Aristotle's Politics." In *Aristoteles' "Politik": Akten des XI,* Patzig, ed., 202–15.

———. "Aristotle's Anthropology." In *Essays on the Foundations of Aristotelian Political Science.* Carnes Lord and David K. O'Connor, eds. Berkeley: University of California Press, 1991, 49–73.

Lotze, Detlev. "Zum Begriff der Demokratie in Aischylos' 'Hiketiden.'" In *Aischylos und Pindar.* Ernst Günther Schmidt, ed. Berlin: Akademie-Verlag, 1981, 207–16.

———. "Entwicklungslinien der athenischen Demokratie im 5.Jh.v.Chr." *Oikumene* 4 (1983): 9–24.

———. "Die sogenannte Polis." *Acta Antiqua* 33 (1990–92): 237–42.

Lucas, J. R. *Democracy and Participation.* Harmondsworth and Baltimore: Penguin, 1976.

Lukacs, Georg. *Ästhetik.* 2 vols. Berlin: Luchterhand, 1963.

Lukes, Steven. *Power: A Radical View.* London: Macmillan, 1974.

———. "Equality and Liberty: Must They Conflict?" In *Political Theory Today.* David Held, ed. Oxford: Polity Press, 1991, 48–66.

Lynch, John P. *Aristotle's School.* Berkeley: University of California Press, 1972.

Macaulay, Thomas. "On the Athenian Orators." In the *Complete Works of Lord Macaulay.* 8 vols. G. M. Trevelyan, ed. New York and London, n.d.

MacCarthy, George. *Marx and the Ancients: Classical Ethics, Social Justice, and Nineteenth-Century Political Economy.* Savage, Md.: Rowman and Littlefield, 1990.

————. *Marx and Aristotle. Nineteenth-Century German Social Theory and Classical Antiquity.* Savage, Md.: Rowman and Littlefield, 1992.

MacDowell, Douglas M., ed. *Andocides. On the Mysteries.* Oxford: Clarendon Press, 1962.

————. *The Law in Classical Athens.* Ithaca, N.Y.: Cornell University Press, 1978.

MacLachlan, Bonnie. *The Age of Grace: Charis in Early Greek Poetry.* Princeton: Princeton University Press, 1993.

Macpherson, C. B. *The Life and Times of Liberal Democracy.* Oxford and New York: Oxford University Press, 1977.

Madison, James. *The Complete Madison.* Saul Padover, ed. New York: Harper, 1953.

Maehler, H., ed. *Pindari Carmina cum Fragmentis.* Vol. 2. Leipzig: Teubner, 1989.

Maier, Pauline. *From Resistance to Revolution: Colonial Radicals and the Development of American Oppposition to Britain, 1765–1776.* New York: Random House, 1972.

Mahaffy, John Pentland. *Social Life in Greece from Homer to Menander.* London: Macmillan, 1874.

Malkin, Irad. *Religion and Colonization in Ancient Greece.* Leiden: Brill, 1987.

Mansbridge, Jane J. *Why We Lost the ERA.* Chicago: University of Chicago Press, 1983.

Manville, Philip Brook. *The Origins of Citizenship in Ancient Athens.* Princeton: Princeton University Press, 1990.

————. "Towards a New Paradigm of Athenian Citizenship." In *Athenian Identity and Civic Ideology.* Boegehold and Scafuro, eds., 21–33.

Markle, Minor M. III. "Jury Pay and Assembly Pay at Athens." In *CRUX: Essays in Greek History Presented to G.E.M. de Ste. Croix.* Paul A. Cartledge and F. D. Harvey, eds. Exeter: Imprint Academic; London: Duckworth, 1985, 265–97.

————. "Participation of Farmers in Athenian Juries and Assemblies." *Ancient Society* 21 (1990): 149–65.

Markoe, Glenn. *Phoenician Bronze and Silver Bowls from Cyprus and the Mediterranean.* University of California Classical Studies 26. Berkeley: University of California Press, 1985.

Marrou, H. I. *History of Education in Antiquity.* Tr. George Lamb from the 3d ed. New York: Sheed and Ward, 1956.

Martin, Jochen. "Von Kleisthenes zu Ephialtes." *Chiron* 4 (1974): 5–42 (= *Demokratia*, K. Kinzl, ed., 160–212).

————. "Aspekte antiker Staatlichkeit." In *Staat und Staatlichkeit in der frühen römischen Republik.* Walter Eder, ed. Stuttgart: Steiner, 1990, 220–32.

Martin, R. *Recherches sur l'agora grecque.* Paris: E. de Boccard, 1951.

Martin, Richard P. "Hesiod, Odysseus, and the Instruction of Princes." *Transactions of the American Philological Association* 114 (1984): 29–48.

————. "Hesiod's Metanastic Poetics." *Ramus* 21 (1992): 11–31.

Matthäus, Hartmut. "Heirloom or Tradition? Bronze Stands of the Second and First Millennium B.C. in Cyprus, Greece and Italy." In *Problems in Greek Prehistory.* E. B. French and K. A. Wardle, eds. Bristol: Bristol Classical Press, 1988, 285–300.

Mattingly, Harold. "Athenian Imperialism and the Foundation of Brea." *Classical Quarterly* 16 (1966): 172–92.

Mazarakis-Aenian, Alexandros. *From Rulers' Dwellings to Temples. Studies in Mediterranean Archaeology.* Göteborg: Paul Äströms Förlag, forthcoming.

Mazzarino, S. *Fra oriente e occidente: Ricerche di storia greca arcaica.* Firenze: Nuova Italia, 1947.

McClelland, J. S. *The Crowd and the Mob: From Plato to Canetti.* London and Boston: Unwin Hyman, 1989.

McCulloch, H. Y., and D. O. Cameron. "*Septem* 12–13 and the Athenian *Ephebia.*" *Illinois Classical Studies* 5 (1981): 1–14.

McGlew, James. *Tyranny and Political Culture in Ancient Greece.* Ithaca: Cornell University Press, 1993.

McKechnie, P. *Outsiders in the Greek Cities in the Fourth Century B.C.* London and New York: Routledge, 1989.

McKim, Richard. "Shame and Truth in Plato's *Gorgias.*" In *Platonic Writings, Platonic Readings.* Charles L. Griswold, Jr., ed. New York and London: Routledge, 1988, 34–48.

Meder, Anton. *Der athenische Demos zur Zeit des Peloponnesischen Krieges im Lichte zeitgenössischer Quellen.* Dissertation Munich. Lengerich: Handelsdruckerei, 1938.

Meier, Christian. "Drei Bemerkungen zur Vor- und Frühgeschichte des Begriffs Demokratie." In *Discordia concors: Festgabe Edgar Bonjour.* Vol. 1. Basel and Stuttgart: Helbing and Lichtenhahn, 1968, 1–29.

———. Review of Ehrenberg, *Der Staat der Griechen. Gnomon* 41 (1969): 365–79.

———. *Die Entstehung des Begriffs 'Demokratie.'* Frankfurt am Main: Suhrkamp, 1970.

———. "Freiheit." In *Geschichtliche Grundbegriffe,* II. Otto Brunner et al., eds. Stuttgart: Klett, 1975, 426–29.

———. "Entstehung und Besonderheit der griechischen Demokratie." *Zeitschrift für Politik* 25 (1978): 1–31 (= *Demokratia,* Kinzl, ed., 248–301).

———. "Arbeit, Politik, Identität: Neue Fragen im alten Athen." *Chronik der Ludwig-Maximilians-Universität München* (1983–84): 69–95 (= *Der Mensch und seine Arbeit.* V. Schubert, ed. St. Ottilien: Eos-Verlag, 1986, 47–109).

———. "Der Umbruch zur Demokratie in Athen (462/61 v.Chr.)." In *Epochenschwelle und Epochenbewusstsein.* Reinhart Herzog and Reinhart Koselleck, eds. Poetik und Hermeneutik 12. Munich: Wilhelm Fink Verlag, 1987, 353–80.

———. "Bürgeridentität und Demokratie." In Christian Meier and Paul Veyne, *Kannten die Griechen die Demokratie?* Berlin: Wagenbach, 1988, 47–95.

———. *Die Welt der Geschichte und die Provinz des Historikers.* Berlin: Wagenbach, 1989.

———. "Die Entstehung einer autonomen Intelligenz bei den Griechen." In his *Welt der Geschichte,* 70–100.

———. *The Greek Discovery of Politics.* Tr. David McLintock. Cambridge, Mass.: Harvard University Press, 1990.

———. "The Political Identity of the Athenians and the Workings of Periclean Democracy." In his *Greek Discovery of Politics,* 140–54, 270–75.

———. "Die Rolle des Krieges im klassischen Athen." *Historische Zeitschrift* 251 (1990): 555–605.

————. *The Political Art of Greek Tragedy.* Tr. Andrew Webber. Baltimore: Johns Hopkins University Press, 1993.

Meiggs, Russell. *The Athenian Empire.* Oxford: Clarendon Press, 1972.

Meiggs, Russell, and David Lewis. *A Selection of Greek Historical Inscriptions to the End of the Fifth Century B.C.* 2d ed. Oxford: Clarendon Press, 1988.

Meijer, Fik. *A History of Seafaring in the Classical World.* London: Croom Helm, 1986.

Mendus, Susan. "Losing the Faith: Feminism and Democracy." In *Democracy: The Unfinished Journey 508 BC to AD 1993.* John Dunn, ed. Oxford: Oxford University Press, 1992, 7–20.

Meritt, Benjamin. "Greek Inscriptions." *Hesperia* 21 (1952): 340–80.

Merkelbach, Reinhold. "Der Theseus des Bakchylides (Gedicht für ein attisches Ephebenfest)." *Zeitschrift für Papyrologie und Epigraphik* 12 (1973): 56–62.

Merkelbach, Reinhold, and Martin West. *Fragmenta Hesiodea.* Oxford: Clarendon Press, 1967.

Michels, Robert. *Political Parties: A Sociological Study of the Oligarchical Tendencies of Modern Democracy.* Tr. Eden Paul and Cedar Paul. New York: Hearst's International Library Company, 1915.

Midgley, Mary. *Beast and Man.* Ithaca: Cornell University Press, 1978.

Mikalson, Jon D. *Athenian Popular Religion.* Chapel Hill and London: University of North Carolina Press, 1983.

————. *Honor Thy Gods.* Chapel Hill: University of North Carolina Press, 1991.

Mill, John Stuart. "Grote's History of Greece." In *Essays on Philosophy and the Classics* in vol. 11 of his *Collected Works.* Toronto: University of Toronto Press, 1978.

————. *On Liberty and Other Essays.* John Gray, ed. Oxford: Oxford University Press, 1991.

Miller, David. "The Resurgence of Political Theory." *Political Studies* 38 (1990): 421–37.

Miller, Margaret. "The Parasol: An Oriental Status-Symbol in Late Archaic and Classical Athens." *Journal of Hellenic Studies* 112 (1992): 91–105.

Millett, Paul. "Hesiod and His World." *Proceedings of the Cambridge Philological Society* n.s. 30 (1984): 84–115.

Mills, C. Wright. *The Sociological Imagination.* New York: Oxford University Press, 1959.

Miltner, F. "Seewesen," *RE* Suppl. 5 (1931): 946–52.

————. "Paralos." *RE* 18.3 (1949): 1209–11.

Miralles, Carles, and Jaume Pòrtulas. *Archilochus and the Iambic Poetry.* Rome: Ateneo, 1983.

Mirhady, David. "Non-Technical *Pisteis* in Aristotle and Anaximenes." *American Journal of Philology* 112 (1991): 5–28.

————. "Oath-Challenge in Athens." *Classical Quarterly* 41 (1991): 78–83.

Mitchel, Fordyce W. "The So-Called Earliest Ephebic Inscription." *Zeitschrift für Papyrologie und Epigraphik* 19 (1975): 233–43.

Molho, Anthony, Kurt Raaflaub, and Julia Emlen, eds. *Athens and Rome, Florence and Venice: City-States in Classical Antiquity and Medieval Italy.* Stuttgart: Steiner; Ann Arbor: University of Michigan Press, 1991.

Moore, J. M., ed. *Aristotle and Xenophon on Democracy and Oligarchy.* Berkeley and Los Angeles: University of California Press, 1975.

Morgan, Catherine. *Athletes and Oracles.* Cambridge: Cambridge University Press, 1990.

Morgan, Edmund S. *Inventing the People. The Rise of Popular Sovereignty in England and America.* New York and London: Norton, 1988.

Morgan, Kathryn. "Pindar the Professional and the Rhetoric of the *Komos.*" *Classical Philology* 88 (1993): 1–15.

Morgan, Lewis. *Ancient Society: or, Researches in the Lines of Human Progress from Savagery, Through Barbarism to Civilization.* New York: H. Holt, 1877.

Morris, Ian. "The Use and Abuse of Homer." *Classical Antiquity* 5 (1986): 81–138.

———. *Burial and Ancient Society: The Rise of the Greek City-State.* Cambridge: Cambridge University Press, 1987.

———. "Tomb Cult and the 'Greek Renaissance': The Past in the Present in the Eighth Century B.C." *Antiquity* 62 (1988): 750–61.

———. *Death-Ritual and Social Structure in Classical Antiquity.* Cambridge: Cambridge University Press, 1992.

———. *Darkness and Heroes: Manhood, Equality, and Democracy in Iron Age Greece.* Oxford: Blackwell, forthcoming in 1997.

———. *The Archaeology of Democracy.* In preparation.

Morris, Ian, and Kurt A. Raaflaub, eds. *Democracy 2500: Questions and Challenges.* Archaeological Institute of America Colloquium series, forthcoming.

Morrison, J. S. "Hyperesia in Naval Contexts in the Fifth and Fourth Centuries B.C." *Journal of Hellenic Studies* 104 (1984): 48–59.

Morrison, J. S., and J. F. Coates. *The Athenian Trireme.* Cambridge: Cambridge University Press, 1986.

Morrison, J. S., and R. T. Williams. *Greek Oared Ships, 900–322 B.C.* Cambridge: Cambridge University Press, 1968.

Mossé, Claude. *La Fin de la démocratie athénienne.* Paris: Presses Universitaires de France, 1962.

———. "Le Rôle de l'armée dans la révolution à Athènes." *Revue Historique* 231 (1964): 1–10.

———. "La Démocratie athénienne et la protection de la propriété." *Symposion* 4 (1981): 263–71.

———. *L'Antiquité dans la Révolution Française.* Paris: Albin Michel, 1989.

———. "Egalité démocratique et inégalités sociales: Le Débat à Athènes au IVème siècle." *Metis* 2 (1987): 165–76, 195–206.

Most, Glenn W. *The Measures of Praise.* Hypomnemata 83. Göttingen: Vandenhoeck and Ruprecht, 1985.

Mouffe, Chantal, ed. *Radical Democracy: Pluralism, Citizenship, Community.* New York: Verso, 1992.

Mueller-Goldingen, Christian. *Untersuchungen zu den Phoenissen des Euripides.* Stuttgart: Steiner, 1985.

Mulgan, R. G. *Aristotle's Political Theory.* Oxford: Clarendon Press, 1977.

———. "Liberty in Ancient Greece." In *Conceptions of Liberty in Political Philosophy.* Z. Pelczynski, ed. New York: St. Martin's Press, 1984, 7–26.

————. "Aristotle and the Value of Political Participation." *Political Theory* 18 (1990): 195–215.

————. "Aristotle's Analysis of Oligarchy and Democracy." In *A Companion to Aristotle's* Politics. David Keyt and Fred D. Miller, Jr., eds. Oxford and Cambridge, Mass.: Blackwell, 1991, 307–22.

Mulhall, Stephen, and Adam Swift. *Liberals and Communitarians.* Oxford: Blackwell, 1992.

Müller, Carl Werner. *Gleiches zu Gleichem: Ein Prinzip frühgriechischen Denkens.* Wiesbaden: Harrassowitz, 1965.

Munn, M. *The Defense of Attica. The Dema Wall and Boiotian War of 378–375 B.C.* Berkeley: University of California Press, 1993.

Murakawa, Kentarô. "Demiurgos." *Historia* 6 (1957): 385–415.

Murray, Oswyn. "The Symposion as Social Organisation." In *The Greek Renaissance of the Eighth Century B.C.* Robin Hägg, ed. Stockholm: Skrifter Utgivna i Svenska Institutet i Athen, 1983, 195–99.

————. "Cities of Reason." In *The Greek City from Homer to Alexander.* Oswyn Murray and Simon Price, eds. Oxford: Clarendon Press, 1990, 1–25.

————. "The Solonian Law of Hybris." In *Nomos. Essays in Athenian Law, Politics, and Society.* Paul Cartledge, Paul Millett, and Stephen Todd, eds. Cambridge: Cambridge University Press, 1990, 139–46.

————. "Sympotic History." In *Sympotica.* Oswyn Murray, ed. Oxford: Clarendon Press, 1990, 3–13.

————. *Early Greece.* 2d ed. Cambridge, Mass.: Harvard University Press, 1993.

Muscarella, Oscar. "Greek and Oriental Cauldron Attachments: A Review." In *Greece Between East and West, 10th-8th Centuries B.C.* Günter Kopcke and Isabelle Tokumaru, eds. Mainz: Philipp von Zabern, 1992, 16–45.

Myres, John L. *The Political Ideas of the Greeks.* Berkeley, Los Angeles, and London: University of California Press, 1927.

Naess, A., et al. *Democracy, Ideology and Objectivity: Studies in the Semantics and Cognitive Analysis of Ideological Controversies.* Oslo: Oslo University Press, 1956.

Nagel, Thomas. *Equality and Partiality.* Oxford: Oxford University Press, 1991.

Nagy, Gregory. *The Best of the Achaeans.* Baltimore: Johns Hopkins University Press, 1979.

————. "Theognis and Megara: A Poet's Vision of His City." In *Theognis of Megara.* Thomas J. Figueira and Gregory Nagy, eds. Baltimore: Johns Hopkins University Press, 1985, 22–81.

————. *Greek Mythology and Poetics.* Ithaca: Cornell University Press, 1990.

————. *Pindar's Homer.* Baltimore: Johns Hopkins University Press, 1990.

————. "Homeric Questions." *Transactions of the American Philological Association* 122 (1992): 15–60.

Nauck, A. *Euripidis Tragoediae.* 3 vols. Leipzig: Teubner, 1902–5.

————. *Tragicorum Graecorum Fragmenta.* 2d ed. Hildesheim: G. Olms, 1964.

Negbi, Ora. "Early Phoenician Presence in the Mediterranean Islands." *American Journal of Archaeology* 96 (1992): 599–616.

Nehamas, Alexander. "What Did Socrates Teach and to Whom Did He Teach It?" *Review of Metaphysics* 46 (December 1992): 279–306.

Newell, W. R. "Superlative Virtue: The Problem of Monarchy in Aristotle's Politics." In *Essays on the Foundations of Aristotelian Political Science.* Carnes Lord and David K. O'Connor, eds. Berkeley: University of California Press, 1991, 191–211.

Newman, William Lambert. *The Politics of Aristotle.* 4 vols. Oxford: Clarendon Press, 1887–1902.

Nichols, Mary P. *Citizens and Statesmen: A Study of Aristotle's "Politics."* Savage, Md.: Rowman and Littlefield, 1992.

Nicolai, Walter. "Gefolgschaftsverweigerung als politisches Druckmittel in der Ilias." In *Anfänge politischen Denkens in der Antike: Die nahöstlichen Kulturen und die Griechen.* Kurt Raaflaub and Elisabeth Müller-Luckner, eds. Munich: Oldenbourg, 1993, 317–41.

Nicolet, Claude. *Le Métier du citoyen dans la Rome républicaine.* Paris: Gallimard, 1976.

Nielsen, Kai. *Equality and Liberty.* Totowa, N.J.: Rowman and Allanheld, 1985.

Nietzsche, Friedrich. *Beyond Good and Evil.* Walter Kaufmann, ed. New York: Random House, 1966.

———. "The Twilight of the Idols." In *The Portable Nietzsche.* Walter Kaufmann, ed. New York: Viking Press, 1968.

———. *On the Genealogy of Morals.* Walter Kaufmann, ed. New York: Random House, 1969.

———. *The Gay Science.* Tr. Walter Kaufmann. New York: Random House, 1974.

Nilsson, Martin P. *Geschichte der griechischen Religion,* I. 3d ed. Munich: C. H. Beck, 1967.

Nisbet, Robert A. *The Quest for Community.* Oxford: Oxford University Press, 1953.

———. "The Contexts of Democracy." *The Kettering Review* (Summer 1992): 15–23 [excerpted from his *The Quest for Community,* 221–47].

Norman, Richard. *Free and Equal: A Philosophical Examination of Political Values.* Oxford: Oxford University Press, 1987.

North, Helen. *Sophrosyne.* Ithaca: Cornell University Press, 1966.

Nowag, Werner. *Raub und Beute in der archaischen Zeit der Griechen.* Frankfurt am Main: Haag and Herchen, 1983.

Nussbaum, Martha. *The Fragility of Goodness.* Cambridge: Cambridge University Press, 1986.

———. *Love's Knowledge.* New York: Oxford University Press, 1992.

Oakeshott, Michael. *Rationalism in Politics.* New York: Basic Books, 1962.

Oakley, John, and Rebecca Sinos. *The Athenian Wedding.* Madison: University of Wisconsin Press, 1993.

Ober, J. *Fortress Attica: Defense of the Athenian Land Frontier.* Leiden: E. J. Brill, 1985.

———. "Thucydides, Pericles, and the Strategy of Defense." In *The Craft of the Ancient Historian: Essays in Honor of Chester G. Starr.* J. W. Eadie and J. Ober, eds. Lanham, Md.: University Press of America, 1985, 171–88.

———. *Mass and Elite in Democratic Athens. Rhetoric, Ideology, and the Power of the People.* Princeton: Princeton University Press, 1989.

———. "Aristotle's Political Sociology: Class, Status, and Order in the Politics." In *Essays on the Foundations of Aristotelian Political Science.* Carnes Lord and David K. O'Connor, eds. Berkeley: University of California Press, 1991.

———. "The Athenian Revolution of 508/7 B.C.: Violence, Authority, and the Origins of Democracy." In *The Cultural Politics of Archaic Greece.* Leslie Kurke and Carol Dougherty, eds. Cambridge: Cambridge University Press, 1993, 215–32.

———. "The *Polis* as a Society. Aristotle, John Rawls and the Athenian Social Contract." In *The Ancient Greek City-State.* Mogens Herman Hansen, ed. Acts of the Copenhagen Polis Centre 1. Copenhagen: Munksgaard, 1993, 129–60.

———. "How to Criticize Democracy in Late Fifth- and Fourth-Century Athens." In *Athenian Political Thought and the Reconstruction of American Democracy,* Euben, Wallach, and Ober, eds., 149–71.

———. *Athenian Critics of Popular Rule.* Forthcoming.

———. "Revolution Matters: Democracy as Demotic Action, Response to Kurt Raaflaub." Forthcoming in *Democracy 2500,* Morris and Raaflaub, eds.

Okin, Susan Moller. *Women in Western Political Thought.* Princeton: Princeton University Press, 1979. (7th printing, 1992, has a new Afterword.)

———. *Justice, Gender and the Family.* New York: Basic Books, 1989.

———. "Gender, the Public and the Private". In *Political Theory Today.* David Held, ed. Oxford: Polity Press, 1991, 67–90.

O'Neil, James L. *The Origins and Development of Ancient Greek Democracy.* Lanham, Md.: Rowman and Littlefield, 1995.

Osborne, Michael J. *Naturalization in Athens.* 4 vols. Brussels: Academie voor Wetenschapen. Letteren en Schone Kunsten (WLSK), 1981–83.

Osborne, R. G. *Demos: The Discovery of Classical Attika.* Cambridge: Cambridge University Press, 1985.

———. *Classical Landscape with Figures: The Ancient Greek City and Its Countryside.* London: Philips, 1987.

———. "The Viewing and Obscuring of the Parthenon Frieze." *JHS* 107 (1987): 98–105.

Ostwald, Martin. *Nomos and the Beginnings of the Athenian Democracy.* Oxford: Clarendon Press, 1969.

———. "Isokratia as a Political Concept (Herodotus 5.92a.1)." In *Islamic Philosophy and the Classical Tradition. Essays Presented by His Friends and Pupils to Richard Walzer.* Oxford: Oxford University Press, 1972, 277–91.

———. *From Popular Sovereignty to the Sovereignty of Law: Law, Society and Politics in Fifth-Century Athens.* Berkeley and Los Angeles: University of California Press, 1986.

———. "The Reform of the Athenian State by Cleisthenes." In *Cambridge Ancient History,* 2d ed. Vol. 5. Cambridge: Cambridge University Press, 1988, 303–46.

———. "Public Expense: Whose Obligation? Athens 600–454 B.C.E." In *Proceedings of the American Philosophical Society* 139 (1995): 368–79.

Owen, A. S. *Euripides' Ion.* 1939. Rept. Bristol: Bristol Classical Press, 1987.

Owen, G.E.L. "*Tithenai ta phainomena.*" In *Logic, Science and Dialectic: Collected Papers in Greek Philosophy.* Martha Nussbaum, ed. London: Duckworth, 1985, 239–51.

Ozouf, Mona. "Equality." In *A Critical Dictionary of the French Revolution.* Tr. Arthur Goldhammer. François Furet and Mona Ozouf, eds. Cambridge, Mass.: Belknapp Press of Harvard University Press, 1989, 669–83. (French original, 1989)

Pachlatko, Paul. *Die Stellung der Griechen zum Problem der Verschiedenheit der Menschen.* Dissertation Zurich, 1940.

Padgug, Robert. "Classes and Society in Classical Greece." *Arethusa* 8 (1975): 201–25.

Page, Denys L. *Sappho and Alcaeus.* Oxford: Clarendon Press, 1955.

———. *Poetae Melici Graeci.* Oxford: Clarendon Press, 1962.

Palmer, R. R. "Notes on the Use of the Word 'Democracy' 1789–1799." *Political Science Quarterly* 68 (1953): 203–26.

Pangle, Thomas L. "Plato's *Gorgias* as a Vindication of Socratic Education." *Polis* 10, nos. 1, 2 (1991): 3–21.

———. *The Ennobling of Democracy: The Challenge of the Post-Modern Era.* Baltimore: Johns Hopkins University Press, 1992.

Parke, H. W., and D.E.W. Wormell. *The Delphic Oracle.* Oxford: Blackwell, 1956.

Parker, Harold. *The Cult of Antiquity and the French Revolutionaries: A Study in the Development of the Revolutionary Spirit.* Chicago, Il.: University of Chicago Press, 1937.

Parker, Robert. "Festivals of the Attic Demes." In *Gifts to the Gods: Proceedings of the Uppsala Symposium. Boreas* 15. T. Linders and G. Nordquist, eds. Uppsala: Academia Ubsliensis; Stockholm: Almqvist and Wiksell International, 1987, 137–47.

Pateman, Carole. "Feminism and Democracy." In *Democratic Theory and Practice.* Graeme Duncan, ed. Cambridge: Cambridge University Press, 1983, 204–17.

———. *The Sexual Contract.* Cambridge: Cambridge University Press, 1988.

———. *The Disorder of Women.* Cambridge, England: Polity Press (with Basil Blackwell); Stanford: Stanford University Press, 1989.

Patterson, Cynthia. *Pericles' Citizenship Law of 451/0 B.C.* New York: Arno Press, 1981.

———. "*Hai Attikai:* The Other Athenians." *Helios* 13.2 (1987): 49–67.

———. "Those Athenian Bastards." *Classical Antiquity* 9 (1990): 40–73.

———. "The Case Against Neaira." In *Athenian Identity and Civic Ideology,* Boegehold and Scafuro, eds., 199–216.

Patzig, Günther., ed. *Aristoteles' "Politik": Akten des XI. Symposium Aristotelicum, 1987.* Göttingen: Vandenhoeck and Ruprecht, 1990.

Pečírka, J. "The Crisis of the Athenian Polis in the Fourth Century B.C." *Eirene* 14 (1976): 5–29.

Pečírka, J., and M. Dufkova. "Excavations of Farms and Farmhouses in the Chora of the Chersonesos in the Crimea." *Eirene* 8 (1970): 123–74.

Pélékidis, Chrysis. *Histoire de l'éphébie attique des origines à 31 av. J.-C.* Paris: de Boccard, 1962.

Pennock, J. R. *Democratic Political Theory.* Princeton: Princeton University Press, 1979.

Pennock, J. R., and John W. Chapman, eds. *Equality: NOMOS IX.* New York: Atherton Press, 1967.

Peradotto, John. "Oedipus and Erichthonius: Some Observations on Paradigmatic and Syntagmatic Order." *Arethusa* 10, no. 1 (1977): 85–101.

Peremans, Willy. "Sur l'acquisition du droit de cité à Athènes au VIᵉ s. av. J.-C." In *Antike und Universalgeschichte: Festschrift Hans-Erich Stier.* Ruth Stiehl and Gustav Adolf Lehmann, eds. Münster: Aschendorff, 1972, 122–30.

Peters, Tom. *Liberation Management.* New York: Random House, 1995.

Peterson, Erik. "Zur Bedeutungsgeschichte von *parrhesia.*" In *Festschrift Reinhold Seeberg.* I. W. Koepp, ed. Leipzig: A. Deichertsche Verlagsbuchhandlung, 1929, 263–97.

Petropulos, J.C.B. *Heat and Lust: Hesiod's Midsummer Festival Scene Revisited.* Lanham, Md.: Rowman and Littlefield, 1994.

Pettinato, Giovanni. *The Archives of Ebla.* Garden City, New York: Doubleday, 1981.

Phelps Brown, Henry. *Egalitarianism and the Generation of Inequality.* Oxford: Oxford University Press, 1988.

Philipp, Hanna. "Archaische Gräber in Ostionien." *Istanbuler Mitteilungen* 31 (1981): 149–66.

Phillips, Anne, ed. *Feminism and Equality.* New York: New York University Press, 1987.

Pickard-Cambridge, Arthur Wallace. *The Dramatic Festivals at Athens.* 2d ed. Oxford: Oxford University Press, 1988.

Plamenatz, J. "Equality of Opportunity." In *Aspects of Human Equality.* L. Bryson et al., eds. New York: [distributed by] Harper, 1956.

———. "Diversity of Rights and Kinds of Equality." In *Equality: NOMOS IX,* Pennock and Chapman, eds., 79–98.

Pleket, Harry W. "Isonomia and Cleisthenes: A Note." *Talanta* 4 (1972): 63–81.

Plescia, Joseph. *The Oath and Perjury in Ancient Greece.* Tallahassee: Florida State University Press, 1970.

Poliakoff, Michael B. *Combat Sports in the Ancient World.* New Haven, London: Yale University Press, 1987.

Polignac, François de. *La Naissance de la cité grecque.* Paris: La Découverte, 1984.

———. "Influence extérieure ou évolution interne? L'Innovation culturelle en Grèce géométrique et archaïque." In *Greece Between East and West, 10th–8th Centuries B.C.* Günter Kopcke and Isabelle Tokumaru, eds. Mainz: Philipp von Zabern, 1992, 114–27.

Pollitt, Jerome J. *Art and Experience in Classical Greece.* Cambridge: Cambridge University Press, 1972.

Pollitt, Katha. "Why Do We Read?" In *Debating P C.* Paul Berman, ed. New York: Dell, 1992, 208–18.

Pomeroy, Sarah. *Goddesses, Whores, Wives and Slaves: Women in Antiquity.* New York: Schocken, 1975.

Postgate, Nicholas. *Early Mesopotamian Society and Economy at the Dawn of History.* London and New York: Routledge, 1992.

Postman, Neil. *Amusing Ourselves to Death: Public Discourse in the Age of Show Business.* New York: Viking Press, 1985.

Poursat, Jean-Claude. "Les Représentations de danse armée dans la céramique attique." *Bulletin de correspondance hellénique* 92 (1968): 550–615.

Prinz, F. *Gründungsmythen und Sagenchronologie.* Zetemeta 72. Munich: Beck, 1979.

Pritchard, James B. *Ancient Near Eastern Texts Relating to the Old Testament.* 2d ed. Princeton: Princeton University Press, 1955.

Pritchett, W. K. "The Attic Stelai, Part II." *Hesperia* 25 (1956): 178–328.

———. *The Greek State at War.* 5 vols. Berkeley: University of California Press, 1971–1991.

The Pro-Slavery Argument; as Maintained by the Most Distinguished Writers of the Southern States. Charleston: Walker, Richards, 1852.

Raaflaub, Kurt. "Des freien Bürgers Recht der freien Rede." In *Studien zur antiken Sozialgeschichte: Festschrift Friedrich Vittinghoff.* Werner Eck, Hartmut Galsterer, and Hartmut Wolff, eds. Cologne/Vienna: Böhlau, 1980, 7–57.

———. "Zum Freiheitsbegriff der Griechen." In *Soziale Typenbegriffe im alten Griechenland und ihr Fortleben in den Sprachen der Welt.* Vol. 4. Charlotte Elisabeth Welskopf, ed. Berlin: Akademie-Verlag, 1981, 180–405.

———. "Democracy, Oligarchy and the Concept of the 'Free Citizen' in Late Fifth-Century Athens." *Political Theory* 11 (1983): 517–44.

———. *Die Entdeckung der Freiheit. Zur historischen Semantik und Gesellschafts-geschichte eines politischen Grundbegriffes der Griechen.* Vestigia. Vol. 37. Munich: Beck, 1985.

———. "Politisches Denken im Zeitalter Athens." In *Pipers Handbuch der politischen Ideen* I: *Frühe Hochkulturen und europäische Antike.* Iring Fetscher and Herfried Münkler, eds. Munich: Piper, 1988, 273–368.

———. "Contemporary Perceptions of Democracy in Fifth-Century Athens." *Classica et Mediaevalia* 40 (1989): 33–70.

———. "Homer und die Geschichte des 8.Jh.s v.Chr." In *Zweihundert Jahre Homer-Forschung: Rückblick und Ausblick.* Joachim Latacz, ed. Stuttgart: Teubner, 1991, 205–56.

———. "Homer to Solon: The Rise of the Polis. The Written Sources." In *The Ancient Greek City-State.* M. H. Hansen, ed. Copenhagen: Royal Danish Academy of Sciences and Letters 1993, 41–105.

———. "Democracy, Power, and Imperialism in Fifth-Century Athens." In *Athenian Political Thought and the Reconstruction of American Democracy.* Euben, Wallach, and Ober, eds., 103–46.

———. "Kleisthenes, Ephialtes und die Begründung der Demokratie." In *Demokratia,* K. Kinzl, ed., 1–54, 451–52.

———. "Power in the Hands of the People: Foundations of Athenian Democracy." In *Democracy 2500.* Morris and Raaflaub, eds., forthcoming.

———. "The Thetes and Democracy: Response to J. Ober." In *Democracy 2500.* Morris and Raaflaub, eds., forthcoming.

———. "Citizens, Soldiers, and the Evolution of the Early Greek Polis." In *The Development of the Polis in Archaic Greece.* P. J. Rhodes and Lynette Mitchell, eds. London: Routledge, forthcoming.

Raaflaub, Kurt, and Elisabeth Müller-Luckner, eds. *Anfänge politischen Denkens in der Antike: Die nahöstlichen Kulturen und die Griechen.* Munich: Oldenbourg, 1993.

Radt, S. L., ed. *Tragicorum Graecorum Fragmenta.* Vol. 3. Göttingen, Vandenhoeck and Ruprecht, 1985.

Rae, Douglas. *Equalities.* Cambridge, Mass.: Harvard University Press, 1981.

Rahe, Paul. *Republics Ancient and Modern: Classical Republicanism and the American Revolution.* Chapel Hill: University of North Carolina Press, 1993.

Rankov, Boris. "Rowing *Olympias:* A Matter of Skill." In *Trireme Project.* Shaw, ed., 50–57.

———. "Reconstructing the Past: The Operation of the Trireme Reconstruction, *Olympias* in the Light of the Historical Sources." *Mariner's Mirror. The Journal of the Society for Nautical Research* 80, no. 2 (1994): 131–46.

Raubitschek, A. E. "Greek Inscriptions." *Hesperia* 12 (1943): 12–88.

———. *Dedications from the Athenian Acropolis: A Catalogue of the Inscriptions of the Sixth and Fifth Centuries B.C.* Edited in collaboration with Lilian H. Jeffery. Cambridge, Mass.: Archaeological Institute of America, 1949.

Rauh, N. K. *The Sacred Bonds of Commerce.* Amsterdam: J. C. Gieben, 1993.

Rawls, J. "The Basic Liberties and Their Priority." In *Liberty, Equality and Law: Selected Tanner Lectures on Moral Philosophy.* Sterling M. McMurrin, ed. Cambridge: Cambridge University Press, 1987, 1–87.

———. *Political Liberalism.* New York: Columbia University Press, 1993.

Rawson, Elizabeth. *The Spartan Tradition in European Thought.* Oxford: Oxford University Press, 1969.

Reinmuth, Oscar William. *The Ephebic Inscriptions of the Fourth Century B.C.* Leiden: Brill, 1971.

Rhodes, Peter J. "The Five Thousand in the Athenian Revolutions of 411 B.C." *Journal of Hellenic Studies* 92 (1972): 115–27.

———. *A Commentary on the Aristotelian Athēnaiōn Politeia.* Oxford: Clarendon Press, 1981.

———. "The Selection of Ephors at Sparta." *Historia* 30 (1981): 498–502.

———. *The Athenian Boule.* 1972. Rept. with corrections and additions. Oxford: Clarendon Press, 1985.

———. *Thucydides, History II, Edited with Translation and Commentary.* Warminster: Aris and Phillips, 1988.

———. "The Athenian Revolution." In *Cambridge Ancient History,* 2d ed. Vol. 5. Cambridge: Cambridge University Press, 1992, 62–95.

Rich, John, and Graham Shipley, eds. *War and Society in the Greek World.* London and New York: Routledge, 1993.

Rickert, Gail Ann. "*Akrasia* and Euripides' *Medea.*" *Harvard Studies in Classical Philology* 91 (1987): 91–117.

Ridley, Ronald T. "The Hoplite as Citizen: Athenian Military Institutions in Their Social Context." *L'Antiquité classique* 48 (1979): 508–48.

Rihll, T. "The Attic *naukrariai.*" *Liverpool Classical Monthly* 12 (January 1987): 10.

Robert, Jeanne, and Louis Robert. "Une Inscription grecque de Téos en Ionie. L'Union de Téos et de Kybarissos." *Journal des Savants* (1976): 153–235.

Robert, Louis. "Inscriptions du dème d'Acharnai." *Etudes épigraphiques et philologiques.* Paris: Boccard, 1938, 293–315.

Roberts, Jennifer T. "Aristocratic Democracy: The Perseverance of Timocratic Principles in Athenian Government." *Athenaeum* n. s. 74 (1986): 355–69.

———. "Thinking about Democracy: Ancient Greece and Modern America." *Prologue: Quarterly of the National Archives* 25 (1993): 137–47.

———. *Athens on Trial: The Antidemocratic Tradition in Western Thought.* Princeton: Princeton University Press, 1994.

Robertson, Noël. "False Documents at Athens: Fifth-Century History and Fourth-Century Publicists." *Historical Reflections* 3 (1976): 3–24.

Robinson, Eric. *Greek Democracies outside Athens. Historia* Einzelschrift. Stuttgart: Steiner, forthcoming.

Rodgers, Daniel T. *Contested Truths: Keywords in American Politics since Independence.* New York: Basic Books, 1987.

Roemer, John E. *Egalitarian Perspectives: Essays in Philosophical Economics.* Cambridge: Cambridge University Press, 1994.

Romilly, Jacqueline de. *Thucydides and Athenian Imperialism.* Tr. Philip Thody. Oxford: Blackwell, 1963.

────. "Les Phéniciennes d'Euripide ou l'actualité dans la tragédie grecque." *Revue de Philologie* 39 (1965): 28–47 (tr. in *Bucknell Review* 15 [1967]: 108–32).

────. *Problèmes de la démocratie grecque.* Paris: Hermann, 1975.

Roscam, Paule. "Remarque sur l'éphébie attique." *Platon* 21 (1969): 187–215.

Rose, Peter W. "Thersites and the Plural Voices of Homer." *Arethusa* 21 (1988): 5–25.

────. *Sons of the Gods, Children of the Earth: Ideology and Literary Form in Ancient Greece.* Ithaca: Cornell University Press, 1992.

Rose, V., ed. *Aristotle, Fragmenta.* Stuttgart: Teubner, 1967.

Rosen, Ralph M. "Hipponax, Boupalos, and the Conventions of the *Psogos.*" *Transactions of the American Philological Association* 118 (1988): 29–41.

Rosenmeyer, Patricia. *The Poetics of Imitation: Anacreon and the Anacreontic Tradition.* Cambridge: Cambridge University Press, 1992.

Rosivach, Vincent. "Autochthony and the Athenians." *Classical Quarterly* 37 (1987): 294–306.

────. "Manning the Athenian Fleet, 433–426 B.C." *American Journal of Ancient History* 10, no. 1 (1985 [1992]): 41–66.

────. "Redistribution of Land in Solon, fragment 34 West." *Journal of Hellenic Studies* 112 (1992): 153–57.

────. *The System of Public Sacrifice in Fourth-Century Athens.* American Classical Studies 34. Atlanta: Scholars Press, 1994.

Rothwell, Kenneth S., Jr. *Politics and Persuasion in Aristophanes' Ecclesiazusae.* Mnemosyne Supplement 111. Leiden: Brill, 1990.

Rousseau, Jean-Jacques. *The Social Contract.* New York: J. M. Dent, Everyman edition, n.d.

────. *Restoration of the Sciences and Arts.* In *The First and Second Discourses together with the Replies to Critics and Essay on the Origin of Languages.* V. Gourevitch, ed. New York: Harper and Row, 1986.

Rudhardt, Jean. *Notions fondamentales de la pensée religieuse et actes constitutifs du culte dans la Grèce classique.* Geneva: Librairie E. Droz, 1958.

Runciman, W. G. "Doomed to Extinction: The Polis as an Evolutionary Dead-End." In *The Greek City. From Homer to Alexander.* O. Murray and S. Price, eds. Oxford: Clarendon Press, 1990, 348–67.

Ruschenbusch, Eberhard. "ΠΡΩΤΟΝ ΔΙΚΑΣΤΗΡΙΟΝ." *Historia* 6 (1957): 257–74.

────. ΣΟΛΩΝΟΣ ΝΟΜΟΙ: *Die Fragmente des solonischen Gesetzeswerkes mit einer Text- und Überlieferungsgeschichte. Historia* Einzelschriften 9. Wiesbaden: Steiner, 1966.

────. *Untersuchungen zu Staat und Politik in Griechenland vom 7.-4.Jh.v.Chr.* Bamberg: aku-Fotodruck und Verlag, 1978.

────. *Athenische Innenpolitik im 5. Jahrhundert v. Chr.: Ideologie oder Pragmatismus?* Bamberg: aku-Fotodruck und Verlag, 1979.

────. "Zur Besatzung athenischer Trieren." *Historia* 28 (1979): 106–10.

────. "Die Polis und das Recht." In *Symposion 1979. Beiträge zur griechischen und hellenistischen Rechtsgeschichte.* Panayotis Dimakis, ed. Cologne-Vienna: Böhlau, 1983, 305–26.

────. "Zur griechischen Verfassungsgeschichte der archäischen Zeit." In *Demokratia,* K. Kinzl, ed., 432–45.

Russell, Bertrand. "The Study of Mathematics." In *Mysticism and Logic*. N.Y.: Longmans, Green, 1921, 58–73.

Rusten, Jeffrey S. *Thucydides, The Peloponnesian War, Book II*. Cambridge: Cambridge University Press, 1989.

Ruzé, Françoise. "Les Tribus et la décision politique dans les cités grecques archaïques et classiques." *Ktèma* 8 (1983): 299–306.

———. "*Plethos*. Aux origines de la majorité politique." In *Aux origines de l'hellénisme, la Crète et la Grèce. Hommage à Henri van Effenterre*. Paris: Publications de la Sorbonne, 1984, 247–63.

Ryan, A. "Freedom." In *The Blackwell Encyclopaedia of Political Thought*. David Miller, ed. Oxford and New York: Basil Blackwell, 1987, 163–66.

Ryan, Frank. "Thetes and the Archonship." *Historia* 43 (1994): 369–71.

Sahlins, Marshall. *Stone Age Economics*. Chicago: University of Chicago Press, 1972.

———. *Historical Metaphors and Mythical Realities: Structure in the Early History of the Sandwich Islands Kingdom*. Ann Arbor: University of Michigan Press, 1981.

Ste. Croix, G.E.M. de. "The Character of the Athenian Empire." *Historia* 3 (1954–55): 1–41.

———. "The Constitution of the Five Thousand." *Historia* 5 (1956): 1–13.

———. "The Estate of Phainippos (Ps. Demosthenes XLII)." In *Ancient Society and Institutions: Studies Presented to Victor Ehrenberg*, E. Badian, ed. Oxford: Blackwell, 1966, 109–14.

———. *The Origins of the Peloponnesian War*. Ithaca: Cornell University Press, 1972.

———. "Karl Marx and the History of Classical Antiquity." *Arethusa* 8 (1975): 7–41.

———. *The Class Struggle in the Ancient Greek World. From the Archaic Age to the Arab Conquests*. London: Duckworth; Ithaca: Cornell University Press (corrected impression), 1983.

Sakellariou, M. B. *La Migration grecque en Ionie*. Centre d'études d'Asie mineure [collection] 10 Ionie, 1. Athens: n.p., 1958.

———. *The Polis-State: Definition and Origin*. Athens: Research Centre for Greek and Roman Antiquity; National Hellenic Research Foundation. Paris: Diffusion de Boccard, 1989.

Salkever, Stephen G. *Finding the Mean: Theory and Practice in Aristotelian Political Philosophy*. Princeton: Princeton University Press, 1990.

———. "Aristotle's Social Science." In *Essays on the Foundations of Aristotelian Political Science*. Carnes Lord and David K. O'Connor, eds. Berkeley: University of California Press, 1991, 11–48.

Sallares, Robert. *The Ecology of the Ancient Greek World*. Ithaca N.Y.: Cornell University Press, 1991.

Salmon, John. *Wealthy Corinth*. Oxford: Clarendon Press, 1984.

Sandel, Michael. *Liberalism and the Limits of Justice*. Cambridge: Cambridge University Press, 1982.

Sargent, R. *The Size of the Slave Population at Athens during the Fifth and Fourth Centuries before Christ*. 1924. Rept. Westport, Conn.: Greenwood Press, 1973.

Sartori, Franco. "Verfassung und soziale Klassen in den Griechenstädten Unteritaliens seit der Vorherrschaft Krotons bis zur Mitte des 4. Jhs. v. u. Z." In *Hellenische Poleis*. Vol. 2. Elisabeth Welskopf, ed. Berlin: Akademie-Verlag, 1974, 700–773.

Sartori, G. *Democratic Theory*. Detroit: Wayne State University Press, 1962.

————. "Democracy." In *International Encyclopaedia of the Social Sciences,* 112–21.

————. *The Theory of Democracy Revisited.* Chatham, N.J.: Chatham House, 1987.

Saxenhouse, Arlene. "Myths and the Origins of Cities: Reflections on the Autochthony Theme in Euripides' *Ion.*" In *Greek Tragedy and Political Theory,* Euben, ed., 252–73.

Scafuro, Adele C. "Witnessing and False Witnessing: Proving Citizenship and Kin Identity in Fourth Century Athens." In *Athenian Identity and Civic Ideology,* Boegehold and Scafuro, eds., 156–98.

Scarpi, Paolo. "La Pyrrhiche o le armi della persuasione." *Dialoghi di archeologia* 1 (1979): 78–97.

Scheffler, I. *Four Pragmatists: A Critical Introduction to Peirce, James, Mead, and Dewey.* New York: Humanities Press, 1974.

Schilardi, Demetrius U. "Anaskaphi stin Paro." *Praktika tis en Athinis Arkhaiologikis Etaireias* (1979): 236–48.

Schlaifer, Robert. "Greek Theories of Slavery from Homer to Aristotle." *Harvard Studies in Classical Philology* 47 (1936): 165–204 (= *Slavery in Classical Antiquity.* M. I. Finley, ed. Cambridge: Cambridge University Press, 1960, 93–132).

————. "The Cult of Athena Pallenis." *Harvard Studies in Classical Philology* 54 (1943): 35–67.

Schmidt, G. "Fluch und Frevel als Elemente politischer Propaganda im Vor- und Umfeld des Peloponnesischen Krieges." *Rivista Storica dell' Antichità* 20 (1990): 8–30.

Schmitt, Hatto H. *Die Staatsverträge des Altertums,* III. Munich: C. H. Beck, 1969.

Schmitt Pantel, Pauline. *La Cité au banquet.* Collection de l'Ecole Française de Rome 157. Rome: Ecole Française de Rome, 1992.

Schmitz, Wilfried. *Wirtschaftliche Prosperität, soziale Integration und die Seebundpolitik Athens.* Munich: Tuduv-Verlag, 1988.

Schnapp, Alain. "Pratiche e immagini di caccia nella Grecia antica." *Dialoghi di archeologia* 1 (1979): 36–59.

Schofield, Malcolm. "Ideology and Philosophy in Aristotle's Theory of Slavery." In *Aristoteles' "Politik": Akten des XI. Symposium Aristotelicum, 1987.* G. Patzig, ed., 1–27.

Schuller, Wolfgang. *Die Herrschaft der Athener im Ersten Attischen Seebund.* Berlin: De Gruyter, 1974.

————. "Wirkungen des Ersten Attischen Seebunds auf die Herausbildung der athenischen Demokratie." In Jack Martin Balcer et al., *Studien zum Attischen Seebund.* Xenia. Konstanzer Althistorische Vorträge und Forschungen. Vol. 8. Konstanz: Universitätsverlag, 1984, 87–101.

————. "Zur Entstehung der griechischen Demokratie ausserhalb Athens." In *Auf den Weg gebracht: Festschrift Kurt Georg Kiesinger.* Horst Sund and Manfred Timmermann, eds. Konstanz: Universitätsverlag, 1979, 433–47 (= *Demokratia,* K. Kinzl, ed., 310–23).

Schuller, Wolfgang, Wolfram Hoepfner, and Ernst Ludwig Schwandner, eds. *Demokratie und Architektur: Der hippodamische Städtebau und die Entstehung der Demokratie.* Munich: Deutscher Kunstverlag, 1989.

Schütrumpf, Eckart. *Die Analyse der Polis durch Aristoteles.* Amsterdam: B. R. Grüner, 1980.

————. *Aristoteles, Politik Buch I*. Berlin: Akademieverlag, 1991.

Schutter, X. de. "La Culte d'Apollon Patrôos à Athènes." *Antiquité Classique* 56 (1987): 103–29.

Schwyzer, Eduard. *Dialectorum Graecarum Exempla Epigraphica Potiora*. 1923. Rept. Hildesheim: Georg Olms, 1960.

Seabrook, John. "E-Mail from Bill." *The New Yorker,* January 10, 1994, 48–61.

Seager, Robin. "Elitism and Democracy in Classical Athens." In *The Rich, the Well-Born and the Powerful: Elites and Upper Classes in History,* Jaher, ed., 7–26.

————. Review of Loraux, *L'Invention d'Athènes* (Paris and New York: Mouton, 1981). In *Journal of Hellenic Studies* 102 (1982): 267–68.

Sealey, Raphael. "The Origins of *Demokratia*." *California Studies in Classical Antiquity* 6 (1973): 253–95.

————. *A History of the Greek City-States 700–338 B.C.* Berkeley and Los Angeles: University of California Press, 1976.

————. "Ephialtes, *Eisangelia,* and the Council." In *Classical Contributions: Studies Malcolm Francis McGregor*. G. S. Shrimpton and D. J. McCargar, eds. Locust Valley, New York: J. J. Augustin, 1981, 125–34.

————. "How Citizenship and the City Began in Athens." *American Journal of Ancient History* 8 (1983): 97–129.

————. *The Athenian Republic: Democracy or the Rule of Law?* University Park, Pa., and London: Pennsylvania State University Press, 1987.

Sen, Amartya. "Equality of What?" In *The Tanner Lectures on Human Values*. Vol. 1. Sterling M. McMurrin, ed. Salt Lake City: University of Utah Press; Cambridge: Cambridge University Press, 1980, 195–220.

————. *Inequality Re-Examined*. Oxford: Oxford University Press, 1992.

Sen, Amartya, and Martha C. Nussbaum, eds. *The Quality of Life*. Oxford: Oxford University Press, 1993.

Shaw, Joseph W. "Phoenicians in Southern Crete." *American Journal of Archaeology* 93 (1989): 165–83.

Shaw, Timothy, ed. *The Trireme Project. Operational Experience 1987–90. Lessons Learnt*. Oxbow Monograph 31. Oxford: Oxbow, 1993.

Sherwin-White, A. N. *Roman Citizenship*. 2d ed. Oxford: Clarendon Press, 1973.

Siewert, Peter. *Der Eid von Plataiai*. Vestigia 16. Munich: Beck, 1972.

————. "The Ephebic Oath in Fifth-Century Athens." *Journal of Hellenic Studies* 97 (1977): 102–11.

————. *Die Trittyen Attikas und die Heeresreform des Kleisthenes*. Munich: Beck, 1982.

Simms, William Gilmore. *Morals of Slavery*. In *The Pro-Slavery Argument*. Charleston: Walker, Richards, 1852.

Simon, Christopher. "The Archaic Votive Offerings and Cults of Ionia." Unpublished dissertation, University of California-Berkeley, 1986.

Sinclair, R. K. *Democracy and Participation in Athens*. Cambridge: Cambridge University Press, 1988.

Sinclair, T. A. *A History of Greek Political Thought*. 2d ed. London: Routledge and Kegan Paul, 1967.

Sisti, F. "Le due Palinodie di Stesicoro." *Quaderni Urbinati di Cultura Classica* 39 (1965): 303–13.

Skinner, Quentin R. D. "Language and Political Change" and "The State." In *Political Innovation and Conceptual Change.* Terence Ball, James Farr, and Russell L. Hanson, eds. Cambridge: Cambridge University Press, 1988, 6–23, 90–131.

———. "A Reply to My Critics." In *Meaning and Context, Quentin Skinner and His Critics.* James Tully, ed. Cambridge: Cambridge University Press, 1988, 231–88.

Smith, G. "Athenian Casualty Lists." *Classical Philology* 14 (1919): 351–64.

Smyth, Herbert Weir. *Aeschylus.* Vol. 2. *Agamemnon, Libation-Bearers, Eumenides, Fragments.* Cambridge, Mass.: Harvard University Press, 1926; revised by Hugh Lloyd-Jones, 1957.

Snell, Bruno, and Herwig Maehler. *Bacchylidis Carmina cum Fragmentis.* Leipzig: Teubner, 1970.

Snodgrass, Anthony M. *Early Greek Armour and Weapons, from the End of the Bronze Age to 600 B.C.* Edinburgh: Edinburgh University Press, 1964.

———. "The Hoplite Reform and History." *Journal of Hellenic Studies* 85 (1965): 110–22.

———. *Arms and Armour of the Greeks.* Ithaca, N.Y.: Cornell University Press, 1967.

———. *The Dark Age of Greece.* Edinburgh: Edinburgh University Press, 1971.

———. *Archaic Greece: The Age of Experiment.* Berkeley and Los Angeles: University of California Press, 1980.

———. "The Economics of Dedication at Greek Sanctuaries." *Scienze dell' antichità* 3–4 (1989–90): 287–94.

———. "The 'Hoplite Reform' Revisited." *Dialogues d'histoire ancienne* 19 (1993): 47–61.

———. "The Rise of the *Polis.* The Archaeological Evidence." In *The Ancient Greek City-State.* Mogens H. Hansen, ed. Copenhagen: Munksgaard, 1993, 30–40.

Sokolowski, Franciszek, ed. *Lois sacrées des cités grecques, Supplement.* Paris: de Boccard, 1962.

Sonenclar, Robert J. "Ben & Jerry's: Management with a Human Flavor." *Hemisphere* (March 1993): 25–26.

Sourvinou-Inwood, Christiane. "A Series of Erotic Pursuits: Images and Meanings." *Journal of Hellenic Studies* 107 (1987): 131–53.

———. "Priestess in the Text: Theano Menonos Agrylethen." *Greece and Rome* 25 (1988): 29–39.

Spahn, Peter. *Mittelschicht und Polisbildung.* Frankfurt am Main, Bern, and Las Vegas: Peter Lang, 1977.

———. "Individualisierung und politisches Bewusstsein im archäischen Griechenland." In *Anfänge politischen Denkens in der Antike: Die nahöstlichen Kulturen und die Griechen,* Raaflaub and Müller-Luckner, eds., 343–63.

Spence, I. G. "Perikles and the Defence of Attika during the Peloponnesian War." *Journal of Hellenic Studies* 110 (1990): 91–109.

Stadter, Philip A. *A Commentary on Plutarch's Pericles.* Chapel Hill, N.C.: University of North Carolina Press, 1989.

Stahl, Michael. *Aristokraten und Tyrannen im klassischen Athen.* Stuttgart: Steiner, 1987.

Stanton, G. R., and P. J. Bicknell. "Voting in Tribal Groups in the Athenian Assembly." *Greek, Roman, and Byzantine Studies* 28 (1987): 51–92.

Starr, Chester. "An Overdose of Slavery." *Journal of Economic History* 18 (1958): 17–32.

———. *The Economic and Social Growth of Early Greece, 800–500 B.C.* New York and Oxford: Oxford University Press, 1977.

———. *The Influence of Sea Power on Ancient History.* New York and Oxford: Oxford University Press, 1989.

———. *The Birth of Athenian Democracy: The Assembly in the Fifth Century.* New York and Oxford: Oxford University Press, 1990.

Stein-Hölkeskamp, Elke. *Adelskultur und Polisgesellschaft.* Stuttgart: Steiner, 1989.

Stengel, Paul. *Opferbräuche der Griechen.* Leipzig and Berlin: B. G. Teubner, 1910.

———. "Zu den griechischen Schwuropfern." *Hermes* 49 (1914): 90–101.

Stewart, Thomas. A. "The Search for the Organization of Tomorrow." *Fortune,* May 18, 1992, 92–98.

Stobaeus. *Anthologium.* C. Wachsmuth and O. Hense, eds. Berlin: Weidmann, 1909.

Stockton, David. *The Classical Athenian Democracy.* Oxford: Oxford University Press, 1990.

Strauss, Barry S. "Ritual, Social Drama, and Politics in Classical Athens." *American Journal of Ancient History* 10, no. 1 (1985 [1992]): 67–83.

———. *Athens after the Peloponnesian War: Class, Faction, and Policy 403–386 B.C.* Ithaca, N.Y.: Cornell University Press, 1987; London: Croom Helm, 1986.

———. "On Aristotle's Critique of Athenian Democracy." In *Essays on the Foundations of Aristotelian Political Science.* Carnes Lord and David K. O'Connor, eds. Berkeley and Los Angeles: University of California Press, 1991, 212–33.

———. *Fathers and Sons in Athens. Ideology and Society in the Era of the Peloponnesian War.* Princeton: Princeton University Press; London: Routledge, 1993.

———. "Genealogy, Ideology, and Society in Democratic Athens." In *Democracy 2500,* Morris and Raaflaub, eds., forthcoming.

Strauss, Leo. *Natural Right and History.* Chicago: University of Chicago Press, 1953.

Strøm, Ingrid. "Evidence from the Sanctuaries." In *Greece Between East and West, 10th–8th Centuries B.C.* Günter Kopcke and Isabelle Tokumaru, eds. Mainz: Philipp von Zabern, 1992, 46–60.

Stroud, Ronald. *Drakon's Law on Homicide.* University of California Publications: Classical Studies, 3. Berkeley and Los Angeles: University of California Press, 1968.

———. "Greek Inscriptions: Theozotides and the Athenian Orphans." *Hesperia* 40 (1971): 280–301.

Strubbe, J.H.M. "'Cursed Be He That Moves My Bones.'" In *Magika Hiera.* Christopher A. Faraone and Dirk Obbink, eds. New York and Oxford: Oxford University Press, 1991, 33–59.

Svenbro, Jesper. *La Parole et le marbre.* Lund: Lund University Press, 1976.

Swanson, Judith A. *The Public and the Private in Aristotle's Political Philosophy.* Ithaca, N.Y.: Cornell University Press, 1992.

Szegedy-Maszak, Andrew. "Legends of the Greek Law-Givers." *Greek, Roman and Byzantine Studies* 19 (1978): 199–209.

Taaffe, Lauren K. *Aristophanes and Women.* London: Routledge, 1994.

Tarcov, Nathan. *Locke's Education for Liberty.* Chicago: University of Chicago Press, 1984.

Tarkiainen, Tuttu. *Die athenische Demokratie.* Zurich: Artemis, 1966; paperback ed. Munich: Deutscher Taschenbuch Verlag, 1972.

Tausend, Klaus. "Der Lelantische Krieg—ein Mythos?" *Klio* 69 (1987): 499–514.

Taylor, Charles. "What's Wrong with Negative Liberty?" In *The Idea of Freedom: Essays in Honour of Isaiah Berlin.* A. Ryan, ed. Oxford and New York: Oxford University Press, 1979.

Temkin, Larry S. *Inequality.* Oxford: Oxford University Press, 1994.

Terray, Emmanuel. *La Politique dans la Caverne.* Paris: Seuil, 1990.

Thalheim, Theodor, ed. *Antiphontis Orationes et Fragmenta.* Leipzig: B. G. Teubner, 1914.

Thalmann, William G. "Thersites: Comedy, Scapegoats, and Heroic Ideology in the *Iliad.*" *Transactions of the American Philological Association* 118 (1988): 1–28.

Thesaurus Linguae Graecae. CD ROM. Irvine: University of California, 1985–.

Thesleff, Holger. "Plato and Inequality." In *Equality and Inequality of Man in Ancient Thought,* Kajanto, ed., 17–29.

Thomas, Rosalind. *Oral Tradition and Written Record in Classical Athens.* Cambridge: Cambridge University Press, 1989.

Thompson, Edward Palmer. *The Making of the English Working Class.* New York: Vintage Books, 1963.

Thomsen, Rudi. *Eisphora: A Study of Direct Taxation in Ancient Athens.* Copenhagen: Gyldendal, 1964.

Thornton, Agathe. *Homer's "Iliad." Its Composition and the Motif of Supplication.* Hypomnemata 81. Göttingen: Vandenhoeck and Ruprecht, 1984.

Thraede, Karl. "Gleichheit." In *Reallexikon für Antike und Christentum.* Theodor Klauser et al., eds. Vol. 11. Stuttgart: Hiersemann, 1981, 122–64.

Thür, Gerhard. *Beweisführung vor den Schwurgerichtshöfen Athens, Die Proklesis zur Basanos.* Die österreichische Akademie der Wissenschaften, Philosophisch-Historische Klasse, Sitzungsberichte 317. Vienna: Die österreichische Akademie der Wissenschaften, 1977.

Tigerstedt, E. N. *The Legend of Sparta in Classical Antiquity.* 3 vols. Stockholm: Almqvist and Wiksell, 1965–78.

Timpe, Dieter. "Das Kriegsmonopol des römischen Staates." In *Staat und Staatlichkeit in der frühen römischen Republik.* Walter Eder, ed. Stuttgart: Steiner, 1990, 368–87.

Tocqueville, Alexis de. *Democracy in America.* 2 vols. Tr. Henry Reeve, rev. Francis Bowen, ed. Phillips Bradley. New York: Knopf, Vintage, 1945.

Tod, Marcus N. *A Selection of Greek Historical Inscriptions.* Vol. 2. Oxford: Clarendon Press, 1948.

Todd, Stephen. "*Lady Chatterley's Lover* and the Attic Orators: The Social Composition of the Athenian Jury." *Journal of Hellenic Studies* 110 (1990): 146–73.

———. "The Purpose of Evidence in Athenian Courts." In *Nomos. Essays in Athenian Law, Politics and Society.* Paul Cartledge et al., eds. Cambridge: Cambridge University Press, 1990, 19–39.

Torr, C. *Ancient Ships.* Cambridge: Cambridge University Press, 1895.

Tracy, Stephen V. "The Panathenaic Festival and Games: An Epigraphic Inquiry." *Nikephoros* 4 (1991): 133–53.

Treu, Max. "Pseudo-Xenophon." *RE* 9A 2 (1967): 1910–82.

Triebel-Schubert, Charlotte. "Der Begriff der Isonomie bei Alkmaion." *Klio* 6 (1984): 40–50.

Turner, Bryan. *Equality*. Chichester, England: Ellis Horwood, 1986.

Turner, Frank. *The Greek Heritage in Victorian Britain*. New Haven and London: Yale University Press, 1981.

Ulf, Christoph. *Die homerische Gesellschaft: Materialien zur analytischen Beschreibung und historischen Lokalisierung*. Vestigia 43. Munich: Beck, 1990.

Vallet, George. "La Cité et son territoire dans les colonies grecques d'occident." In *Atti del VII convegno di studi sulla Magna Grecia*. Taranto: L'Arte Tipografica, 1968, 67–142.

Van Loon, Hendrik W. *The Story of Mankind*. New York: Boni and Liveright, 1926.

Vatin, Claude. *Citoyens et non-citoyens dans le monde grec*. Paris: SEDES, 1984.

Vernant, Jean-Pierre. "Remarques sur la lutte de classe dans la Grèce ancienne." *Eirene* 4 (1965): 5–19.

———. "Travail et nature dans la Grèce ancienne." In his *Mythe et pensée chez les Grecs*. Vol. 2. Paris: Maspero, 1965, 16–36.

———. *The Origins of Greek Thought*. Ithaca, N.Y.: Cornell University Press, 1982.

———. "Speech and Mute Signs." In *Mortals and Immortals. Collected Essays*. Froma I. Zeitlin, ed. Princeton, N.J.: Princeton University Press, 1991, 303–17.

Vernant, Jean-Pierre, and Pierre Vidal-Naquet. *Myth and Tragedy in Ancient Greece*. New York: Zone, 1988.

Veysey, Laurence R. *The Emergence of the American University*. Chicago: University of Chicago Press, 1965.

Vickers, Brian. *In Defence of Rhetoric*. New York: Oxford University Press, 1988.

Vidal-Naquet, Pierre. "Tradition de la démocratie grecque." Introduction to Monique Alexander's translation of M. I. Finley, *Démocratie antique et démocratie moderne*. Paris: Petite Bibliothèque Payot, 1976.

———. *The Black Hunter: Forms of Thought and Forms of Society in the Greek World*. Tr. Andrew Szegedy-Maszak. Baltimore and London: Johns Hopkins University Press, 1986.

———. "The Black Hunter Revisited." *Proceedings of the Cambridge Philological Society* 212 (1986): 126–44.

———. *La Démocratie grecque vue d'ailleurs*. Paris: Flammarion, 1990.

———. "Sophocles' *Philoctetes* and the *Ephebeia*." In Vernant and Vidal-Naquet, *Myth and Tragedy in Ancient Greece,* 161–79.

Vinogradoff, P. *Outlines of Historical Jurisprudence*. Vol. 2, *The Jurisprudence of the Greek City*. Oxford: Clarendon Press, 1922.

Vlastos, Gregory. "Solonian Justice." *Classical Philology* 41 (1946): 65–83 (= Vlastos, *Studies in Greek Philosophy*. Vol. 1. Daniel W. Graham, ed. Princeton: Princeton University Press, 1995, 32–56).

———. "Equality and Justice in Early Greek Cosmologies." *Classical Philology* 42 (1947): 156–78 (= *Studies in Presocratic Philosophy*. David J. Furley and Reginald E. Allen, eds. New York: Humanities Press, 1970, 56–91).

———. "*Isonomia*." *American Journal of Philology* 74 (1953): 337–66.

———. "Justice and Equality." In *Social Justice*. Richard B. Brandt, ed. Englewood Cliffs: Prentice Hall, 1962, 31–62.

————. "*Isonomia politike.*" In *Isonomia: Studien zur Gleichheitsvorstellung im griechischen Denken.* Jürgen Mau and Ernst Günther Schmidt, eds. Berlin: Akademie-Verlag, 1964, 1–35 (=Vlastos, *Platonic Studies.* Princeton: Princeton University Press, 1981, 164–203).

————. "The Historical Socrates and Athenian Democracy." *Political Theory* 11, no. 4 (1983): 495–516.

————. "Socrates' Disavowal of Knowledge." *The Philosophical Quarterly* 35 (1985): 1–31.

————. *Socrates: Ironist and Moral Philosopher.* Ithaca: Cornell University Press, 1990.

Vogt, Josef. *Ancient Slavery and the Ideal of Man.* Tr. Thomas Wiedemann from the 2d German ed. (Wiesbaden: Steiner, 1972). Cambridge, Mass.: Harvard University Press, 1975.

Voigtländer, Hans-Dieter. *Der Philosoph und die Vielen.* Stuttgart: Steiner, 1980.

Walcot, Peter. "Hesiod and the Instructions of 'Onchsheshonqy.'" *Journal of Near Eastern Studies* 21 (1962): 215–19.

————. *Hesiod and the Near East.* Cardiff: Cardiff University Press, 1966.

Wallace, Robert W. *The Areopagos Council to 307 B.C.* Baltimore: Johns Hopkins University Press, 1989.

————. "Personal Conduct and Legal Sanction in the Democracy of Classical Athens." In *Questions de responsabilité, XLVème session de la Société Internationale "Fernand de Visscher" pour l'Histoire des Droits de l'Antiquité.* J. Zlinszky, ed. Miskolc, Hungary: n.p., 1993.

————. "Private Lives and Public Enemies. Freedom of Thought in Classical Athens." In *Athenian Identity and Civic Ideology,* Boegehold and Scafuro, eds., 127–55.

Wallinga, H. T. *Ships and Sea-Power before the Great Persian War: The Ancestry of the Ancient Trireme. Mnemosyne* Supplement 121. Leiden: Brill, 1993.

Walsh, George B. *The Varieties of Enchantment.* Chapel Hill: University of North Carolina Press, 1984.

————. "The Rhetoric of Birthright and Race in Euripides' Ion." *Hermes* 106, no. 2 (1986): 301–15.

Walter, Uwe. *An der Polis teilhaben: Bürgerstaat und Zugehörigkeit im Archaischen Griechenland. Historia* Einzelschrift 82. Stuttgart: Steiner, 1993.

Walters, Laurel Shapre. "A Leader Redefines Management." *Christian Science Monitor,* September 22, 1992, 14.

Walzer, Michael. *Spheres of Justice.* New York: Basic Books, 1983.

Wardman, A. E. "Tactics and Tradition of the Persian Wars." *Historia* 8 (1959): 49–60.

Wason, Margaret. *Class Struggles in Ancient Greece.* 1947. Rept. New York: H. Fertig, 1973.

Watson, Lindsay. *Arae: The Curse Poetry of Antiquity.* Melksham: Francis Cairns, 1991.

Webber, Alan. "What's So New about the New Economy?" *Harvard Business Review* (Jan.-Feb. 1993): 24–42.

Weber, Max. *Economy and Society.* Guenther Roth and Claus Wittich, eds. Tr. Ephraim Fischoff et al. 3 vols. New York: Bedminster, 1968.

————. "Parliament and Government in a Reconstructed Germany." In his *Economy and Society,* Roth and Wittich, eds., vol. 3, 1381–1469.

Wees, Hans van. *Status Warriors: War, Violence and Society in Homer and History.* Amsterdam: Gieben, 1992.

———. "The Homeric Way of War: The *Iliad* and the Hoplite Phalanx." *Greece and Rome* 41 (1994): 1–18, 131–55.

Welch, John F., and Edward J. Hood. "To Our Share Owners." *Annual Report of the General Electric Corporation,* February 14, 1992, 1–5.

Welskopf, Charlotte Elisabeth, ed. *Hellenische Poleis: Krise - Wandlung - Wirkung.* Vol. 1. Berlin: Akademie-Verlag, 1974.

Welwei, Karl-Wilhelm. *Unfreie im antiken Kriegsdienst,* I. *Athen und Sparta.* Wiesbaden: Franz Steiner Verlag, 1974.

———. "Adel und Demos in der frühen Polis." *Gymnasium* 88 (1981): 1–23.

———. *Die griechische Polis.* Stuttgart: Kohlhammer, 1983.

West, Martin L. *Hesiod. Theogony.* Oxford: Oxford University Press, 1966.

———. *Studies in Greek Elegy and Iambus.* Berlin: de Gruyter, 1974.

———. *Hesiod. Works and Days.* Oxford: Oxford University Press, 1978.

———. *Greek Metre.* Oxford: Oxford University Press, 1982.

———. *Iambi et Elegi Graeci.* 2d ed. 2 vols. Oxford: Clarendon Press, 1991–1992.

Westen, Peter. *Speaking of Equality: An Analysis of the Rhetorical Force of "Equality" in Moral and Legal Discourse.* Princeton: Princeton University Press, 1990.

Wheatley, Margaret. *Leadership and the New Science.* San Francisco: Gerrett-Koehler, 1992.

Wheeler, Everett L. "*Hoplomachia* and Greek Dances in Arms." *Greek, Roman and Byzantine Studies* 23 (1982): 223–33.

Whibley, Leonard. *Greek Oligarchies. Their Character and Organization.* 1896. Rept. Chicago: Ares, 1975.

Whitehead, David. *The Ideology of the Athenian Metic.* The Cambridge Philological Society, Supplementary Vol. 4. Cambridge: Cambridge University Press, 1977.

———. "Immigrant Communities in the Classical Polis." *L'Antiquité classique* 53 (1984): 47–59.

———. *The Demes of Attica 508/7–ca. 250 B.C.: A Political and Social Study.* Princeton: Princeton University Press, 1986.

———. "Norms of Citizenship in Ancient Greece." In *Athens and Rome, Florence and Venice: City-States in Classical Antiquity and Medieval Italy.* Anthony Molho, Kurt Raaflaub, and Julia Emlen, eds. Stuttgart: Steiner; Ann Arbor: University of Michigan Press, 1991, 135–54.

Whitley, James. "Social Diversity in Dark Age Greece." *Annual of the British School at Athens* 86 (1991): 341–65.

———. *Style and Society in Dark Age Greece.* Cambridge: Cambridge University Press, 1991.

Whitman, Walt. *Democratic Vistas.* 1871. Rept. in *The Portable Walt Whitman.* James van Doren, ed. New York: Viking, 1974, 317–82.

Will, Edouard, *Le Monde grec et l'orient.* Vol. 1. Paris: Presses Universitaires de France, 1972.

Williams, Bernard A. O. "The Idea of Equality." In *Politics, Philosophy and Society.* Peter Laslett and W. Garry Runciman, eds. 2d series. Oxford: Blackwell, 1962, 110–37 (= Bedau, ed., *Justice and Equality,* 116–37).

————. *Shame and Necessity.* Berkeley, Los Angeles, and London: University of California Press, 1993.

Williams, Wendy. "The Equality Crisis: Some Reflections on Culture, Courts, and Feminism." In *Feminist Legal Theory: Readings in Law and Gender,* Bartlett and Kennedy, eds., 15–34.

Wills, Garry. *Inventing America: Jefferson's Declaration of Independence.* Garden City, N.Y.: Doubleday, 1978.

————. *Lincoln at Gettysburg: The Words That Remade America.* New York: Simon and Schuster, 1992.

Wiltshire, Susan Ford. "Jefferson, Calhoun, and the Slavery Debate: The Classics and the Two Minds of the South." *Southern Humanities Review* 11 (Special Issue, 1977): 33–40.

————. *Greece, Rome, and the Bill of Rights.* Norman, Okla.: University of Oklahoma Press, 1992.

Wimmer, F. *Theophrasti Eresii Opera.* 1866. Rept. Frankfurt: Minerva, 1964.

Winkler, John J. "The Ephebes' Song: *Tragôidia* and *Polis.*" *Representations* 11 (1985): 26–62 (=*Nothing to Do with Dionysos?* Winkler and Zeitlin, eds., 20–62).

————. *The Constraints of Desire.* London: Routledge, 1990.

Winkler, J., and Froma I. Zeitlin, eds., *Nothing to Do with Dionysos? Athenian Drama in Its Social Context.* Princeton, N. J.: Princeton University Press, 1990.

Wolgast, Elizabeth. *Equality and the Rights of Women.* Ithaca: Cornell University Press, 1980.

Wolin, Sheldon S. *Politics and Vision: Continuity and Innovation in Western Political Thought.* Boston: Little, Brown, 1960.

————. *The Presence of the Past.* Baltimore: Johns Hopkins University Press, 1989.

————. "Democracy, Electoral and Athenian." *PS: Political Science and Politics* 26, no. 3 (Sept. 1993): 475–77.

————. "Norm and Form: The Constitutionalizing of Democracy." In *Athenian Political Thought and the Reconstruction of American Democracy.* Euben, Wallach, and Ober, eds., 29–58.

Wollheim, Richard. "Democracy." *Journal of the History of Ideas* 19 (1958): 225–42.

Wood, Ellen Meiksins. *Peasant-Citizen and Slave: The Foundations of Athenian Democracy.* London: Routledge; New York: Verso, 1988.

————. "Democracy: An Idea of Ambiguous Ancestry." In *Athenian Political Thought and the Reconstruction of American Democracy.* Euben, Wallach, and Ober, eds., 59–80.

————. *Democracy against Capitalism: Renewing Historical Materialism.* Cambridge: Cambridge University Press, 1995

Wood, Ellen Meiksins, and Neal Wood. *Class Ideology and Ancient Political Theory.* New York: Oxford University Press, 1978.

————. "Socrates and Democracy: A Reply to Gregory Vlastos." *Political Theory* 14, no. 1 (February 1986): 55–82.

Wood, Gordon S. *The Creation of the American Republic, 1776–1787.* New York: Norton, 1972.

————. *The Radicalism of the American Revolution.* New York: Alfred A. Knopf, 1992.

Woodhead, Arthur Geoffrey. "Isegoria and the Council of 500." *Historia* 16 (1967): 129–40.

Woodhouse, A.S.P., ed. *Puritanism and Liberty.* London: Dent, 1938.

Woodruff, Paul. "Plato's Early Theory of Knowledge." In *Epistemology.* Stephen Everson, ed. New York: Cambridge University Press, 1990, 60–84.

Woozley, A. D. *Law and Obedience. The Arguments of Plato's Crito.* Chapel Hill, N.C.: University of North Carolina Press, 1979.

Wycherley, R. E. *The Athenian Agora,* III. *Literary and Epigraphical Testimonia.* Princeton: Princeton University Press, 1957.

Wyse, W. *The Speeches of Isaeus.* Cambridge: Cambridge University Press, 1904.

Yack, Bernard. "Community and Conflict in Aristotle's Political Philosophy." *Review of Politics* 47 (1985): 92–112.

————. "A Reinterpretation of Aristotle's Political Teleology." *History of Political Thought* 12 (1991): 15–33.

Young, David C. *The Olympic Myth of Greek Amateur Athletics.* Chicago: Ares Press, 1984.

Young, William. *The History of Athens Politically and Philosophically Considered with the View to an Investigation of the Immediate Causes of Elevation and Decline, Operative in a Free and Commercial State.* 2d ed. London: J. Robson, 1786.

————. *The British Constitution of Government Compared with That of a Democratic Republic.* London: J. Stockdale, 1793.

Yovel, Yirmiyahu. *Spinoza and Other Heretics.* 2 vols. Princeton: Princeton University Press, 1989.

Zeitlin, Froma I. "Mysteries of Identity and Designs of the Self in Euripides' *Ion.*" *Proceedings of the Cambridge Philological Society* 35 (1989): 144–97 (= Zeitlin, *Playing the Other* [Chicago: University of Chicago Press, 1995], 285–338.)

————. "Thebes: Theater of Self and Society." In *Nothing to Do with Dionysos? Athenian Drama in Its Social Context,* Winkler and Zeitlin, eds., 130–67.

Ziebarth, Erich. *De iureiurando in iure graeco quaestiones.* Göttingen: Vandenhoeck and Ruprecht, 1892.

————. "Der Fluch im griechischen Recht." *Hermes* 30 (1895): 57–70.

Ziehen, Ludwig. "Eid." *RE* 5.2 (1905): 2076–83.

Zimmermann, Hans-Dieter. "Frühe Ansätze der Demokratie in den griechischen Poleis." *Klio* 57 (1975): 293–99.

Zimmern, Alfred. *The Greek Commonwealth: Politics and Economics in Fifth Century Athens.* 1911. 5th ed. 1931. Rept. Oxford and New York: Oxford University Press (Galaxy), 1961.

INDEX

oligarchy, 124. *See also* aristocracy; elitism; ideology
openness: and political education, 353; in the text of Plato, 15, 351–53. *See also* polyphony
oracles, and civic identity, 263–64, 269n72
oral poetry, and heroism, 25–26
orgēones, and decision making, 221
Orientalism, ideology of, 33–36, 38
origins: of democracy (*see under* democracy); of equality, 9; of *isonomia,* 143–45; of laws, 29; of tragedy, 39; of tyranny, 36
Osborne, R. G., 310n14
ostracism, 108, 112–13, 116, 302; of Damon, 8, 114
Ostwald, M., 7, 144, 165n62, 356n30; **cited by Cartledge on freedom, 182n12; cited by Connor on rights, 223; cited by Hansen on rights, 96; cited by Manville on freedom and equality, 397n9; cited by Morris on shares in the polis, 43n16; cited by Raaflaub on Aristotle, 160n5, 163nn40 and 41; cited by Raaflaub on the extension of citizenship in the United States, 169n117; cited by Wallace on positive rights, 118n6; cited by Wallace on rights, 107; cited by Wood on rights, 125**
Ostwald, M. E., 60n35
Ozouf, M., 182

Padgug, R., 196
Page, D., 45n59
paideia, 13; definition of, 273–74. *See also* education
Paine, Tom, 126
Pangle, T. L., 286n1, 357n47
parrhēsia, 105, 114, 223. *See also* free speech; *isegoria*
Parthenon frieze, and civic ideology, 14, 158, 174n158, 313–14, 321, 325n36
participation: and citizenship, 55–57, 107, 111, 116, 342, 380–81, 389–90; and equality, 140; limits on, 155. *See also* community; demos; lot; office holding; pay
Pateman, C., 11, 199
Patterson, C., 242n11, 311n36
Pausanias, on Athens and Ionia, 252
pay, for public service, 140, 142, 148, 154–55, 158, 204, 301–2, 318, 320, 381. *See also* citizenship; demos; participation

Peirce, C. S., 367
Peisistratus, 79
Peloponnesian War, 68–69
Pennock, J. R., 101n15
people (U.S.), contrasted with demos, 124–29
Peradotto, J., 269n72
Pericles, 80–82; as democratic actor, 67; and education, 336; military strategies of, 297, 298; as moderate democrat, 127; representations of, 336, 339, 341, 351. *See also* funeral oration
Persia, and democracy, 37. *See also* Herodotus
persuasion, and the laws, 211–12
Peters, T., 399nn37, 38
phalanx: in Homer, 151; as metaphor for citizenship, 22, 33, 35; in the polis, 151–52. *See also* farming; hoplites
Pherecydes, on Athens and Ionia, 252
philosophy: as antidemocratic, 76; and class, 334; and community, 329; contrasted with action, 347, 350, 373; contrasted with politics, 343, 366–72; constrasted with tragedy, 364; and democracy, 76, 337, 362–65, 383; and education 275, 282, 287–88n28, 344, 367–68; and exclusion, 338; and freedom, 106, 113; and politics, 343, 346, 366–72; and power, 338, 349; and rhetoric, 334; and self-interest, 346. *See also* knowledge; truth
Phocylides, "middling" ideology of, 27, 35
Pindar: ideology of, 37–38, 47n84; Lydia in, 89n47; *Pythian 9,* 258–59. *See also* Bacchylides; praise poetry
Plamenatz, J., 181, 184n44
Plato: on abrogation of laws, 210–12; *Apology,* 11, 212, 329–31; and authority, 345; on autochthony, 255; on class, 188; on class and *eleutheria,* 130; on constitutions, 369; *Crito,* 11, 210–12; and democratic context of the *Gorgias,* 334–35; as dramatist, 351, 364; on education, 271, 281–82; and education (U.S.), 328–32; *Gorgias,* 14, 141, 327–59, 361–66; inconsistencies in, 335–36, 343–47, 348–49, 350–51; interpretation of, 351–353; irony in, 347; on *isegoria,* 122; *Menexenus,* 255–56, 259–60, 266n29; on military service and social relations, 315; polyphony of, 335–36, 338–39 351–53, 363–64; *Protagoras,* 106, 122, 354n8; *Republic,* 75–76, 315, 329. *See also* Socrates
Plescia, J., 243n22, 244n49

Ranger, T., 26, 265n2

Rankov, B., 324n23

rape, in colonial narratives, 13, 257–59, 267n48

Raubitschek, A., 156

Rawls, J., 63, 87n1

Redfield, J., 268n64

reforms, of Solon, 56–57, 76–77, 85, 153, 203–5

Reinmuth, O., 173n149

religion: and citizenship, 57; and community, 222–24, 227–48; and equality, 24–25; and freedom, 113 and 119n26; and revolution, 223–24. *See also* Dionysus; oaths; ritual; sacrifice

representation, as curb on democracy, 123–24, 125–26

representations: of American democracy, 351; of the demos, 73–74; of Pericles, 336, 339, 341, 351. *See also* discourse; ideology; imaginary; interpretation; narrative

Republic (Plato), 75–76, 114, 315, 329

revolution: antidemocratic, 302–7; and corporate democracy, 384–90, 394–95; and democracy, 4, 7, 15, 146, 368–70, 374n10, 377–78, 383–84, 384–90; as essence of democracy, 368–70, 374n10; and religion, 223–24. *See also* Cleisthenes; Ephialtes; transgression

rhetoric: of Cleisthenes, 143–45; and corporate democracy, 394; and corruption, 337–38, 356–57n42; in democracy, 13, 14; of *eleutheria,* 92–95; of equality, 14, 65, 139, 143–45, 176, 188–89, 200; of freedom, 14, 139; and management, 389–90; and manufactured consent, 333; and philosophy, 334; and political education, 284–85; and power, 340–41; and truth, 333, 356–57n42. *See also* language; speech

Rhetoric (Aristotle), 84–85

Rhodes, P. J., 166n68, 174n157, 324n31

riddles, and civic identity, 263–64, 269n72

Ridley, R. T., 166n78, 171nn139 and 140, 172n149, 323n14

rights, 7, 8, 176, 182n11, 370, 372; absence of in Greek theory, 52–55; in Athens, 95–99, 105–19; conceptions of, 49–61; contrasted with shares, 55–57; limits of, 107–10; negative, 56, 107, 118n11; of minorities, 54; positive, 56, 107, 111–12; and power, 65; protection of, 8, 97–98; —(U.S.), 51, 52,

106–7; of Socrates, 109, 113–15. *See also* freedom, negative and positive

Rihll, T., 225n12

ritual: and community, 12, 227–48; and gender, 12, 231–33. *See also* oaths; religion; sacrifice

Roberts, J. T., 10, 14; **cited by Cole on limits of equality, 246n82; cited by Euben on equality, 355n21; cited by Manville on equality, 398n19; cited by Wood on history of democracy, 136n6**

Robertson, N., 173n149

Rodgers, D. T., 58n6

Rome, as model for Federalists (U.S.), 124, 132–33; —U.S. democracy, 133

Roscam, P., 172n149

Rose, P., 35, 45n55

Rosivach, V., 171n137, 244n36, 254, 255–56, 266n22, 324n24, 324–25n32

Rousseau, J.-J., 4, 15, 73, 88–89n27, 197, 368, 370, 373

Rudhardt, J., 233

Ruschenbusch, E., 166n69, 325n32

Rush, Benjamin, 369

Russell, B., 367

sacrifice, 12; and castration, 232–34; and equality, 24; and gender, 231–32; and oath ritual, 230–33; and self-directed curses, 231–32. *See also* religion; ritual

Sahlins, M., 22

Ste. Croix, G.E.M. de, 79, 88n20, 167n84, 182n13, 195, 305, 398n18

Salkever, S. G., 288n38

Samons, L. J., 144

Sartori, G., 102n46, 286n2

Savage, C., 388–89

Scafuro, A. C., 245n53

Schlaifer, R., 225n11

Schuller, W., 323nn8, 9, 13

sea, metaphors of, 367

Seaford, R., 226n16

Second Athenian Confederacy, laws of, 208–9

self-awareness, of the demos, 64, 76–77, 146

self-control, 94. *See also* prudence; *sōphrosunē*

self-interest, and philosophy, 346

Sen, A., 23

shares: contrasted with rights, 55–57; and citizenship, 93, 96, 98, 128, 141–42, 148; in the polis, 23–24, 49–61, 107